READING AND UNDERSTANDING THE OLD TESTAMENT

The Foundation of Judaism, Christianity, and Islam

READING AND UNDERSTANDING THE OLD TESTAMENT

The Foundation of Judaism, Christianity, and Islam

DR. THOMAS B. LANE

Outskirts Press, Inc.
Denver, Colorado

The opinions expressed in this manuscript are solely the opinions of the author and do not represent the opinions or thoughts of the publisher. The author has represented and warranted full ownership and/or legal right to publish all the materials in this book.

Reading and Understanding the Old Testament
The Foundation of Judaism, Christianity, and Islam

v3.0 r1.1

Outskirts Press, Inc.
http://www.outskirtspress.com

ISBN: 978-1-4327-4989-7

Outskirts Press and the "OP" logo are trademarks belonging to Outskirts Press, Inc.

PRINTED IN THE UNITED STATES OF AMERICA

Reading and Understanding the Old Testament: The foundation of Judaism, Christianity, and Islam will be followed by a series on the New Testament to continue to help people read and understand the Bible. I am dedicating these writings to Andrea my wife, Lee Anne, and Lana my two daughters who for many years kept encouraging me to write, and to my best buddy, my first grandson, my little guy Samuel Lane Durkee who was born three months early at two pounds five ounces. My hope is that when he is old enough he will read this humble attempt that begins to reveal the one God and will develop a relationship with that one God. A special thanks goes to my wife Andrea for the many hours she spent going through the manuscript to help me proofread and correct my writing. Also to Carl DeCaspers, a life long friend who attempted to answer many of my writing questions. Do not hold any of these responsible for my writing shortcomings. A final tribute to the one who originally inspired me to learn more about the Scriptures: Roy Ruckman from whom I took my initial courses in the Old and New Testaments at the University of Texas-El Paso.

Table of Contents

INTRODUCTION

This book is written for anyone who is interested in acquiring basic knowledge and understanding of the content of the books of the Old Testament (OT), or what Judaism calls the Bible, the Tanakh, and Torah, and what Muslims call the Torah. It is written to help those who have never read through these books, and for those who have previously tried, but became overwhelmed by the 1600 plus double columned pages with no explanations and never tried again.

The book is also written to enable one to begin to understand the religious and theological foundation of Judaism, Christianity, and Islam, for all three religions root themselves in the history and stories of these OT Scriptures. It is also important to understand that all three of these religions believe the OT is the word of God. Even though this writer's approach is basically religious and theological, it is still rooted in the scholarship of historical and literary criticism.

This is a basic, introductory study of the OT; it is not an advanced scholarly study. It is designed to supply a foundation that will enable one to eventually read the books themselves. It is hoped that some of the readers will possibly be motivated to continue to a more advanced scholarly study, as well as enter into a deeper study of any or each of the religions who use the OT as their foundation.

Overall, the purpose and goal of this book is to help one gain a basic literacy of the OT content and to help one better understand the book which historically has been the foundation of Judaism, Christianity, and Islam as well as Western and Middle Eastern civilization. It is foundational in the sense that all three religions define the basic nature and character of the one God from these OT books.

This book is a canonical-synchronic study that takes into account modern scholarship. Canonical-synthetic means that the books of the Bible as they are completed contain all of God's inspired word, and that all parts need to be understood according to their structure and meaning and in unity with the whole of all of the books.

Taking into account modern scholarship means that this writer attempts to utilize in a practical and applied way the principles of modern scholarship. But this book is not about modern scholarship. In a beginning study of the content of the Bible this writer does not want to overwhelm the reader with the methodology and intricacies of scholarship. It is preferable that beginning students see scholarship applied in a practical way before they are faced with its intricacies and challenges.

In order to study modern scholarship's approach to the Bible such as historical and literary criticism, archeological research and methodology, Hebrew and Greek word studies, who wrote the books, when, why, and to whom they wrote them, how they were originally put together, and such debates, as well as other scholarly concerns, one will have to consult other works, and this writer encourages that endeavor.

This writer is a Christian who respects Judaism and Islam but who is basically writing to other Christians. The writer attempts to present fairly the point of view of each of the different religions discussed in this book, but even though the writer taught World Religions in a major university, he does not pretend to be a scholar of Judaism or Islam. One will also notice that even though an honest attempt is made to better understand the three religions, there will be a noticeable leaning toward the presentation of a Christian approach.

At times there will be an attempt to interpret and apply to our lives in a practical way some of these writings. This writer will do so in an attempt to clarify some underlying meanings and themes in order to challenge and enable the readers to begin to make some of their own responsible applications. Even so, one will notice a notable bias toward a Christian understanding of the OT.

Until modern times the Bible was basically studied in order to better understand and serve God. Soon scholars allowed the historical critical method to dominate that approach to the point that the Bible was broken into small pieces, dissected and left there. The primary purpose of these early scholars was to discover how the Bible came about and what was historically real and what was not.

This served a purpose, but it is now time to put the Scriptures back together again into a unified whole to enable its readers to, once again, use it to better understand and serve God; thus the reason for a canonical-synchronic approach. Again, it will be obvious that the writer is a Christian living in twenty-first century America, who respects the historical critical method but sees the need to build upon that approach in a practical way.

For Christians the Bible consists of an Old Testament and a New Testament where the word *testament* is also translated as law or covenant. The Tanakh is what Jews call the OT, although they will use the term the Bible and even Old Testament. Torah means the Law or the Teachings, and Tanakh means Bible, but it is the Hebrew Bible.

For Christians the New Testament is based upon and rooted in the Old Testament but is also a reinterpretation of some of it which is one reason why it is called the NT. Jews reject the NT since they do not believe Jesus was the Messiah, the Son of God who rose from the dead. For Jews Jesus was simply a prophet.

Muslims use both the OT and the NT, believing that the history of the world is divided into periods in which prophets are the dominant figures. Beginning with Genesis and through the OT and the NT the emphasis is on the prophets who exemplify for them God's call and God's morality. Muslims do believe Jesus was born of a virgin and rose from the dead, and will come back again, but they do not believe he was crucified or is divine. He is only a prophet.

Above all Muslims believe in the Qur'an which is God's (Allah) inspiration to Mohammad. The Qur'an takes up many themes, ideas, and narratives contained in the OT and the NT. They believe God sent different prophets to different peoples at different times. But as Christians say the NT supersedes the OT, and Jews say the Talmud interprets the Tanak, Muslims say the Qur'an supersedes the OT, and the NT, and at times even corrects both testaments. According to Muslims the Qur'an is God's final word to humankind, and Mohammad is God's final prophet. He is called the seal of the prophets.

The methodology used is from the perspective of Catholicism, the Orthodox, mainline Protestantism, the more moderate Evangelicals, as well as from the perspective of Reformed and some Conservative Judaism. The point in stating this is to be upfront in saying that this approach is not from the perspective of any Fundamentalist group whether they be Jewish, Christian or Muslim. Fundamentalists who are open to better understanding other viewpoints will appreciate this book, but it is not written to present a fundamentalist perspective.

Most Muslim groups are basically fundamentalist in their approach when they understand the Qur'an. They believe the Qur'an is God's uncreated word directly given in Arabic and written with no human influence; therefore, it has no textual errors and there is nothing to interpret. It is to be memorized and recited.

It is important to note that the Qur'an is not written as a primary historical document, but it presents information from both the Old and New Testaments in a meditative, spiritual way, and as a type of commentary, but when it interprets the Scriptures, it does so in the manner of fundamentalism.

This writer does believe the Bible to be inspired of God, and does take the Bible seriously but not always literally as defined by all fundamentalists groups. Literal does not mean, "The Bible says what it means and means what it says," implying there is nothing to interpret.

Literal means the author's original sense, or as Calvin said the "plain sense" as an attempt to understand the underlying meaning of what the biblical writers intended, and then applying it in today's world in order to better understand and serve God. This includes understanding and applying the different literary forms in the manner the writers used them in order to express their intention and purpose. Consequently, the Bible is seen as a living book not a dead historical document. Its purpose is to tell us the truth about God and the truth about ourselves.

In approaching the Bible it is important to understand the writings are more concerned with why things happened not how things happened; whereas we moderns are more concerned with the how and the details of what happened. We are scientific while they were more pictorial and symbolic. We are concerned with now and the immediate cause and effect while they were concerned with ultimate purposes.

The ancient writers did not write history as we moderns write it. To understand the ancient writers, we must understand their methodology and not try to force our modern day historiography, methodologies, and ideologies onto their writings.

The Bible was not designed to be an exact history or science book. Exact historical and scientific facts, based on our modern day method of analysis and thinking, was not the way of thinking, methodology, or purpose of ancient writers. Those early writers lived in an oral society where the majority of people could not read or write. These early writers were simply responding by faith to God working in their every day lives, and then expressing it in a manner appropriate with their culture not our modern day culture.

This writer believes that the main themes of the Bible are to tell us who God is, who we are, and how God wants us to relate to him, to ourselves, to other humans he created, and how to relate to his created order. The main thrust of the Bible is about relationships. The key to understanding the Bible, especially in relating it to those areas, is to look for the underlying meaning and themes within the different literary forms in order to learn the truth about God and the truth about ourselves.

We must also keep in mind that the Bible is not a book to tell us everything we would like to know but to give us the basics of what we need to know. For many Christians, Jews, and Muslims the Bible is primarily a book of faith, a type of catechism, a book of theological truths embedded in the context of the lives of real historic people.

Therefore, look more for the essential truths, the message, the theological and moral themes, the virtues, values, vices, and God's vision for his people rather than detailed exact historical descriptions, ideologies, and moralisms. For Jews in addition to being a book of faith and love, it is also a book of law. In fact the Jews are known for extracting 613 laws from it. For Christians the NT is understood through the words and acts of Jesus with an emphasis on the spirit of the law and not the letter of the law. We will see that for Christians many of the OT teachings will adapt and develop, then later be fulfilled and reinterpreted through Christ. In order to understand these fulfilled teachings, as well as apply them to our lives today, we need to see and understand their development but in the process not get stuck in any of the developing stages.

In order to better understand the three religions we must understand that for Christians Christ is the fulfillment and final interpreter of the OT, and that Christians understand the OT in the light of the NT. For Jews the Talmud sheds more light on the OT and develops it more fully. For Muslims the Qur'an explains the OT and is its explanation. But the starting point for all three religions is the OT.

As this writer takes the reader through the books, chapters, and verses of the OT, he will most often use the exact verses that contain the information he is discussing. The hope is that the reader will experience and get a sense of the Scriptures themselves, and at times, open the Bible, turn to the chapter, and read the account, or at least some of the account in more detail.

In this writer's opinion there is no better way to learn about the Bible and be confronted by God's word than by actually reading it. Even though the purpose is to acquaint the reader with the Bible's content and to better understand three major religions of the world, the goal is also to have readers eventually get into the books and read them for themselves.

There will be an introduction to each of the OT books that will give a summary and the essence of each book. Therefore in addition to reading through the book there are other options. The introductions to all the books can be read first in order to get a sense of what each OT book is about. Then, at a later time, one can go back to a more in-depth reading and explanation of the books to learn more about their details. Finally, one can then go to the Bible itself and read it in an in depth manner. None of this needs to be done all at once, but accomplished at one's level of readiness, as one builds upon portions of knowledge gained. This work can also be a handy reference book.

This book is also designed to enable the professor of the OT and NT in a college or university, or the leader of Bible study in the church, to take all of the students through a single book or books of the Bible while the students follow using their Bibles. In that way the student gets more familiar with and experiences the biblical text. For a Bible study it is possible to begin with any of the OT books. It is not necessary to begin at Genesis and follow all in order, even though that may be the logical approach in an OT survey. This text book can also be a secondary resource while the Bible is the primary resource. Of course the student can also simply follow the main verses in this book as one listens to the instructor.

Depending on the level of the students, the instructor may also want to use the text as a reading assignment to discuss during class. This writer has used both of these methods at many different levels including adult church studies, as well as at the college and university level where he has taught over a twenty year period.

The way this book is structured is basically the way this writer has taught his Biblical Studies courses, always insisting the students open and follow along with a Bible. This writer is convinced that there is a basic lack of understanding in Scripture because people have no experience in using a Bible and have not experienced the Scripture verses themselves. They may have read books about the Bible but have never experienced the Bible for themselves. It is important to go to and experience the Bible by itself. This book is written to enable the reader to experience the actual biblical verses.

The major purpose of the bibliography is to list the sources used by this writer and is an attempt to give credit for much of the information used in this book. Much of the information has been gathered together from teaching notes used down through the years as this writer taught courses in university, college, and adult church education classes. The purpose of the bibliography of sources is to give credit for information learned and used even when this writer no longer remembers exactly where some of the information used came from.

It must be said that there are two books in particular whose authors have been excellent in summarizing much of my learning down through the years. Both are listed in the bibliography. One of the books is written by Protestants: *A Theological Introduction to the Old Testament* by Bruce Birch, Walter Bruggemann, Terence Freitheim, and David Peterson, and the other book is written by a Roman Catholic: *Reading the Old Testament: An Introduction* by Lawrence Boadt. My desire would be to be able to put things in writing for beginning students as well as they can.

At some places within the text, instead of long and numerous footnotes and endnotes, parentheses will be used to refer one to the author listed in the bibliography of sources. This is done in order to produce an easier reading of the text for beginning students. It is important to say that this writer has also benefited from numerous outstanding professors he has studied under, and he does not take credit for too much original thinking other than the way this text is put together.

When this writer uses Scripture in this book, it is from the New Revised Standard Version. This version is acceptable to Roman Catholic, the Orthodox, numerous Protestant groups, and some Jewish groups. The notes from the New Oxford Annotated NRSV Bible have also been used at times in the commentary. Other than the biblical text, capitalization and spelling will be from the Society of Biblical Literature (SBL) Handbook of Style for Ancient Near Eastern, Biblical, and Early Christian Studies.

Capitalization and punctuation found in the Bible sometimes are quite different from contemporary American usage. Also the Handbook of Style this writer is using, as noted above, has spelling and capitalization rules that are different from both the Bible and contemporary American usage. For example in the Handbook of Style used by this writer, Sabbath is capitalized, but in the Bible it is not capitalized. Some styles capitalize Scripture, but others do not. Another example is the word temple.

Contemporary style is to capitalize Temple. But neither the Handbook of Style used or the Bible capitalize temple. The Handbook and contemporary usage capitalize Passover, but the OT does not. To summarize, when this writer quotes from Scripture he will use the style the Bible uses, but when he discusses what the Bible is about he will use the Handbook of Style for Ancient Near Eastern, Biblical and Early Christian Studies.

Another concern is the following. Sometimes the Bible uses LORD and other times Lord. Sometimes it is LORD GOD and other times Lord God, and still others Lord GOD or LORD God. In general the words LORD and GOD translate the Hebrew Yahweh (YHWH). The regular lowercase form Lord and God translate Adonai and other words denoting deity. Adonai is used in speaking and writing when one, out of respect, fears to even say the word God.

Because much of what is written in this book is to highlight what the Bible says, quotation marks will not be used except when there are quotation marks in the biblical text. It is realized this is rare, but according to the Chicago Manual of Style (14th Edition) under certain alternatives to quotation marks, it is acceptable. The reader will be able to tell what is written from Scripture. Most often Scripture will follow the words *say* or *said* followed by a *comma*. It will be quite obvious. The chapter and verse or verses will always be noted in order for the reader to examine. Also when the reader sees a parenthesis ( ) with a number inside that will indicate the verse or verses referenced.

This approach is being taken in the belief that constantly looking at pages filled with quotation marks would be too cumbersome for the reader as well as the writer. The notation of the verse(s) involved is better, for it enables the reader to go right to the specific area. Again, the Sources at the end of the book attempts to give credit to those who have enabled this writer to assemble this book but also serves as a bibliography.

THE PENTATEUCH

Pentateuch is a Greek term meaning five which refers to the first five books of the Old Testament. According to the Jews they were the books of Moses; this is the heart of the Torah. The five books are Genesis, Exodus, Leviticus, Numbers, and Deuteronomy. Torah is a Hebrew word that means the teaching or instruction, and the revelation that God gives his people. The Torah is eventually expanded to include all Jewish religious teachings.

Even though there is history in these books, the form that prevails is narrative history which expresses a type of history through story telling. The purpose of the books in their oral culture is not to present an exact detailed historical account but to confess faith in God in a form that helps them better remember the thrust of what happened. Thus the Pentateuch is mainly a confession, a type of catechism but set in the context of their historical roots, their basic historical setting. Literary forms such as story telling and poetry that circulated orally before being put into writing are indispensible for these people of God as they confess their inspired faith.

The heart of this confession of faith centers on God's call of Abraham in Genesis and God's call of Moses found in the book of Exodus. All Jewish tradition returns to these root experiences. God promises Abraham a nation from his descendants, a land for this nation, and a blessing from him and his descendants that will benefit all nations. Then, many years later, after God's people had become enslaved in Egypt,

God called Moses to liberate his people from their slavery and oppression. He will be their God, and they will be his people. This God named Yahweh, who Scripture claims is the only real God, will be their God, and they will be his people.

Many scholars have detected primarily four different written documents that comprise these books. Source Criticism is used by scholars to trace the written documents that comprise the Bible. Form Criticism attempts to trace the oral history before the documents became written. The word *criticism* basically means analysis. We must always remember ancient cultures were basically oral, and few could read and write.

The four written documents are labeled J, E, D, and P by scholars. They are thought to be put together by numerous writers and editors by at least four different groups from at least four different places over a period of possibly five hundred to a thousand years. This has been the most prevalent theory about the origin of the Torah, but the theory has recently been challenged by numerous scholars.

The Pentateuch is a great work of art. It tells a vital story of God's beginning relationship to the world and its people with power and beauty. It proposes stories that teach us by sharing experiences to be compared with our experiences. The Pentateuch proposes history but does not allow us to question too closely exact descriptions. It proposes religious and theological themes, lessons, and laws in order to help us see who God is and what he is about, and it enables us to understand how God's relationship with his people developed and continues to develop.

Christianity as a whole warns not to treat the Pentateuch and the whole OT like a textbook full of dogma and moralisms that are static, even though some do that very thing. Overall, Christians, Jews, and Muslims look at the law differently. For the Jew it is the law of Moses; the Jews found 613 laws from the Pentateuch that became the source of their life. For Jews the Pentateuch is the foundation from which all Judaism is based. It is the Torah. Muslims use the OT also but not as thoroughly as the Christians, and even though they base some of their laws on the OT it is not their primary law book as it is for the Jews.

To learn more about how the Pentateuch and the OT were finally put together this writer will refer you to the many scholarly books that are available. A few of those books are listed in the sources also serving as a bibliography at the end of this book.

GENESIS

As one begins the reading of the OT, this writer would suggest that if the reader encounters sections that have no interest for you, simply skip them for the moment, and then move on to another section or to another part of the book. Even though it is best to move through the books in order, there is no rule that says the reader must proceed in that way. Read the books you think may interest you, and then go back later to ones you missed. Feel free to even begin with the Prophets, if that is your current interest. It is very possible to cover the OT in that manner. Since most people do begin with Genesis, let us begin there with that fascinating book of origins.

Genesis is a literary narrative, a collection of God inspired events and stories. The title means beginning, the beginning of the world, the beginning of a nation of God's people, the beginning of nations. In Genesis there are two creation accounts, each with its own purpose; the first account is covered in Genesis chapter 1 through chapter 2:4a, and the second account is found in chapter 2:4b-23.

Most scholars agree that the first creation account is not a scientific treatise on the exact detail of creation but a hymn in praise of the God who created everything. The first account expresses a transcendent God who leads us to rest and worship on the Sabbath. The second expresses an immanent God who works among us and leads male and female to marriage and developing a family in order to populate and take care of the earth as God's stewards. The two accounts support and complement each other and are written to inform us as to why God created.

When it is stated that the first two chapters are not written as a scientific treatise, it must also be said that they are not written to discuss the concept of evolution, a topic that never entered the ancient mind. Making that statement does not mean that this writer believes religion and science are in conflict. Most scholars do not believe there is a conflict. Most simply believe the Bible is not written or meant to be a science book; consequently, it is not meant to discuss or debate the concept of evolution. Actually, the writer is attacking Babylonian paganism in defense of the one God stating that God is the creator.

One of the first lessons in any historical and literary analysis of Scripture is to understand that the Bible is not meant to be interpreted in a total literal manner, even though it is meant to be taken seriously, especially theologically, morally, and spiritually. In attempting to understand the Bible for our times; we have to attempt to understand why the ancients wrote what they did, what they are attempting to say, what the underlying meaning is, and what type of literary methods they are using.

Some of the many different types of literature discovered by scholars are the following: historical narratives, myths, legends, short stories, sermons, genealogies, chronicles, songs, meditations, letters, blessings and curses, legal sayings and codes of law, prophetic sayings, proverbial sayings, poetry and poetic dialogue, gospels, letters, epistles, parables, allegories, and more. Each form of literature contains God's inspired truths. In religious literature literary forms such as myths and legends do not rule out the fact that actual history may be involved.

For certain, we must look at the historical context, and then attempt to analyze the different types of literature authors used in the historical context to establish their purposes. It is especially important to analyze as far as possible what the particular biblical author is attempting to do, and how he is doing it. Even though the Bible is God inspired, it was still written by human authors, using different styles and different forms of literature in order to express God's inspired theological and religious truths.

Genesis is the first book of the Pentateuch. The first creation account tells us that it is the one and only God who created everything, and it tells us what God is doing with creation. The second account tells us what God is doing with and for humans that he created and put on his created earth. The latter emphasizes in more detail what took place on earth with the creation of humans. The creation accounts are considered to be myths, but as stated myths in religious literature are not considered untrue. They are foundational narratives that establish basic values, goals, and religious truths.

After the creation accounts the first act of disobedience toward God enters the picture. This is called original sin by some Christians but not by Jews and Muslims. For Christians the loss of original sanctification (perfected holiness) becomes the problem because humankind is now tainted by sin, and it has spread to all. How that happens and how it affects humans is not agreed upon by everyone. In fact there are some Christian groups that do not even call the first act of disobedience original sin. The issue integrated into the concept of original sin is basically over inheritance. Is sin inherited or not?

God's created humans become increasingly evil until God sends a flood to destroy his creation, but he saves Noah in an ark. From Noah and his three sons the world becomes repopulated. In chapter 12 God chooses to work through Abraham. Abraham, Sarah, Isaac and Jacob will produce the 12 tribes of Israel who eventually become the Israelites and the Jews. Abraham and Sarah's maid Hagar will produce Ishmael and the Arab tribes who later become Muslims.

It is interesting that the setting is Mesopotamia which is modern day Iraq. As the reader compares the faith of Abraham with the faith of Jacob, it will be seen that Abraham's faith will be strong, and Jacob's faith will be weak until Jacob struggles with God and is transformed. From chapter 37 on we have the narrative story of Joseph, and how God's providence led his people to Egypt in order to preserve his people. Let us return to the first verses of chapter 1.

The Bible begins in Genesis chapter 1:1-2 by saying, In the beginning when God created the heavens and the earth, the earth was a formless void and darkness covered the face of the deep, while a wind (spirit) from God swept over the face of the waters.

In the opening verses the writer is making a statement. He is asserting that it is the one God who created not the gods of the surrounding countries. This is the beginning of God's creation. Now he will order this apparent mass called chaos. It will be interesting to note that everything will be differentiated including humans from this original created mass.

Verses 3-5 say, Then God said, "Let there be light; and there was light." And God saw that the light was good; and God separated the light from the darkness. God called the light Day, and the darkness he called Night. And there was evening and there was morning, the first day.

We learn that in this first creation account the day begins with the evening. The Jewish day begins in the evening even in our times. Therefore the Jewish Sabbath begins after sunset on Friday for the Jews. In reading the two accounts it is interesting to note what he created on different days. A basic outline with differences is as follows (Hauer and Young 1994).

1st day - creation of light	4th day- creation of heavenly bodies of light
2nd day - creation of heavens and waters	5th day - creation of creatures that fly and swim
3rd day - creation of land and vegetation	6th day – creation of land life and humans

Some differences between chapter 1 and chapter 2 are as follows.

Chapter 1	Chapter 2
1. God is transcendent.	1. God is immanent.
2. Creation begins by overcoming water.	2. Creation overcomes the desert.
3. Emphasis of creation is an ordered universe.	3. Emphasis is an ordered humanity.
4. Story is one of order and peace.	4. Story is one of tension, no peace.
5. Humans are created after animals/ vegetables.	5. Humans are created before animals.
6. Humans are created one, then differentiated.	6. Male and female are created separately.
7. Elohim is the word for God.	7. YHWH is the word for God.
8. Worship and order are the concern.	8. Marriage and birthing are the concern.
9. Creation takes place in seven days.	9. Creation takes place in one day.

The two creation accounts do not contradict each other because historical and scientific accuracy are not the concern in this pre-scientific age. The two accounts are different forms of literature that balance and complement each other as they present major concepts concerning God and his creation. Right from the beginning we are confronted and challenged with how to read and understand the biblical literature in a way that the ancients intended.

The purpose of these accounts is to teach us that God, not the gods, created everything, and everything he created was good, including nature and human nature. God's created world is not a place of chaos; it is a product of the plan of the one true God. God speaks, and the world responds. In reading the accounts we learn that of all that God created, humans are special because both man and woman are made in his image, and they are able to be in a relationship with God and take responsibility.

Humans are also given charge over creation as God's stewards in order to take care of the earth as God would. Relationships are central to the story. Humankind is not really human apart from relationships. This involves a relationship to God, self, humans, animals, and all of nature.

Another purpose of the first account is to show people that because God created the world, the sabbath worship is built into the cosmos. Another purpose of the second account is to show that because God created man and woman for marriage and having children, the family is built into the cosmos.

In the first creation the Hebrew people are writing against the Babylonians and their gods, to show that the God of Israel was the one God, and all other gods are attempts by people to deny the one God and to create their own gods. Who is God, and preserving the one God concept is one of the main purposes and themes throughout the OT. We will see that there are numerous times in the history of God's people that the one God concept is in danger of being lost.

For Islam the Qur'an only refers to creation as a whole; it does not mention the different works created according to the different days. Allah (God) also created seven heavens and many earths which are not mentioned in Genesis. But all creation praises God as in the Bible, and humankind must join in those praises. Muslims must give thanks to God for creation and all that God does just like Jews and Christians.

Overall, Muslims give the one God the same basic characteristics and praise as Jews and Christians simply because they are also rooted in the OT. Part of the Muslim Basmala is an invocation formula, found in all surahs (chapters) of the Qur'an; it is a text repeated often in prayer like the Christian Our Father and the Jewish Shema (Deut 6:4-9).

The following is the complete Basmala. In the name of God, Compassionate and Merciful. Praise to Allah, Lord of the worlds, Compassionate and Merciful, Master of the Day of Judgment. Thee we worship; Thee we beseech for help. Guide us on the right path, The path of those Thou hast favored, not of those against whom Thou art angry, not of those who go astray.

In Genesis chapter 1:26-28 God said, " Let us make humankind in our own image, according to our likeness; and let them have dominion over the fish of the sea, and over the birds of the air, and over the cattle, and over all the wild animals of the earth, and over every creeping thing that creeps upon the earth." So God created humankind in his image, in the image of God he created them; male and female he created them. God blessed them, and God said to them, "Be fruitful and multiply, and fill the earth and subdue it; and have dominion over the fish of the sea and over the birds of the air and over every living thing that moves upon the earth." God said, "See I have given you every plant yielding seed that is upon the face of the earth, and every tree with seed in its fruit; you shall have for food." (Notice that no meat is permitted.)

Being created in God's image is open to debate, but basically it refers to those characteristics of humans that makes communication with God possible and enables them to be responsible for the choices God gives them. Islam does not really talk about humans being created in the image of God, and humans do not really have a personal immanent relationship with God; God is more transcendent than immanent in Islam. He does not really live in and through individuals. He is nearer to us than our own carotid artery as the Shia Muslim emphasizes, but the emphasis is not immanence even though Muslims believe God does take part in history. All that humans need is knowledge to obey God. His grace is not really working in and through individuals even though his grace, mercy and compassion are great toward us.

The command in Genesis to have dominion over every living thing is God delegating responsibility to humans in a power sharing relationship that is to be understood in terms of stewardship and care for their use. It is not to be understood that humans can do anything they want for their selfish interests where the earth is exploited and raped solely for profits and the greed of humans. Humans are to love as God would, and this includes the earth that God created.

The idea is that we are in a sense co-creators with God. He is the creator, but he uses his people to continue creating for his purposes. As we go on we will see that among other acts of creating, cosmological and ecological themes will continue to be significant. Verse 31 says, God saw everything that he made, and indeed, it was very good. And there was evening and there was morning, the sixth day.

In chapter 2 God creates Adam from the ground. Adam means ground, and in the Hebrew language it is both a personal name and a word for humankind. Verse 7 says, then the LORD God formed man from the dust of the ground, and breathed into his nostrils the breath of life; and the man became a living being. (Humans are created from the same source as the animals and the earth itself. The difference is that God breathed into man creating the human being as human.)

The Qur'an, the sacred Scriptures of Islam, says that after creating Adam from dust, then from a life germ, then from clotted blood, then from a lump of flesh partly formed and unformed. Then God breathed his spirit in him, and made Adam his vice-regal representative on earth. It also says that he is made higher than the angels, which is in contrast to the OT which says humans are created lower than the angels (see Psalm 8). Islam says that God required the angels to bow down to Adam, and all did but Iblis who is banned and becomes Satan.

The Qur'an is structured differently than the OT. Much of the OT reads as historical narratives whereas the Qur'an is more esoteric, poetic, and psalm like and structured more to be recited and meditated upon. One also finds in the Qur'an summaries and commentary type material. The characters of the OT are presented without flaw with much less detail assuming that the reader already knows the detail.

In the Qur'an and the Hadith (sayings of Muhammad developed by his friends) much is similar, but often information is added that is different, and sometimes even contradictory to the OT. Muslims believe God's revelation is found mainly in the Pentateuch, Psalms, Gospels and the Qur'an, but the Qur'an is God's final revelation that even corrects the former revelation. The real redemptive act of God is God's revelation to Muhammad not Jesus. The Qur'an also affirms the role of angels, predestination, and a final judgment by God.

In the Qur'an there are no narratives with the exact wording of the Bible because it is a different type of literature with a different purpose. There are numerous varying accounts but with many of the same themes. Also included are accounts from rabbinic literature, apocryphal literature, as well as others that are specific to the Qur'an. It must be stated that everything Muslims learn about the Bible is from the Qur'an only. They do not read the OT; it is assumed in the Qur'an that the reader knows the basics of the OT.

Genesis 2: 8-9 says, And the LORD God planted a garden in Eden, in the east; and there he put the man whom he had formed. Out of the ground the LORD God made to grow every tree that is pleasant to the sight and good for food, the tree of life also in the midst of the garden, and the tree of knowledge of good and evil. Verse 18 says, Then the LORD God said, "It is not good that man should be alone; I will make him a helper as his partner." (That the word helper does not mean subordination is likely since that is its common use for God, see Psalms 10:14, 54:4, 121:1-2.)

In verses 19-20 God forms animals and birds out of the ground and brings them to the man to name, and so he names them, but there was not found a helper as a partner for him, so from Adam's side he creates Eve which means mother of all living. Verses 21-25 say, So the LORD God caused a deep sleep to fall upon the man, and he slept; then he took one of his ribs and closed up its place with flesh. And the rib that the LORD God had taken from the man he made into a woman and brought her to the man. Then the man said, This at last is bone of my bones and flesh of my flesh; this one shall be called Woman, for out of Man this one was taken. Therefore a man leaves his father and his mother and clings to his wife, and they become one flesh. And the man and his wife were both naked and not ashamed.

From these two chapters we learn that God created everything, and man and woman are created as partners. Eve is not created from Adam's head to be over him or his feet to be under him but from his side to be his partner and helper. Being created from a part of the man does not entail subordination for the woman any more than man being created from the ground puts him in subordination to the ground. Later the NT book of Ephesians tells us they are to submit to each other and serve each other as Christ served the Church (see Eph 5:21-33).

This will be the goal of a perfected relationship between man and woman, but it will be quite some time before man and woman come to that understanding. We will see that the way Scripture is interpreted as well as the type of culture that will surround Jews, Christians, and Muslims, it will be a long time before God's perfected goals for man and woman even begin to occur.

In chapter 3 the Christian concept of original sin (humankinds first act of disobedience), and the loss of original sanctification (perfected holiness) become the problem. Often this is used as an explanation as to why everyone will die. Some Christians believe human nature becomes totally depraved at conception, and one can do nothing good on their own. Because of this, humans can not do anything to save themselves.

Others believe human nature is just broken, but individuals can still do good on their own, even though they are not able to save themselves. Other Christians do not believe in original sin at all with respect to human nature being affected and sin being inherited. Whether they believe in original sin or not, Christians believe that only the mercy and grace of Christ can save them. Christians do not believe they can save themselves. Only Christ can save them eternally because only he can eliminate sin.

Judaism and Islam have no teaching on original sin or a change in nature with sin being inherited. Jews believe that after eating the fruit of the tree of knowledge of good and evil, humankind is now in the image of God. Now humans have the freedom to serve God or deny him; humanity has exchanged a perfect existence for knowledge. Islam also emphasizes knowledge and choice even though some may emphasize predestination.

The unfolding history of Israel is the story of the covenant offered to them and the consequences that follow when they choose to follow or reject God. Because people can know good and evil, they can enter into a relationship with God. Jews believe in the mercy and grace of God but do not emphasize the concept of salvation after death. Some do not believe in a literal salvation after death; others do; others leave it in God's hands.

Islam does believe at birth Satan touches everyone, but there is no change in nature. It is interesting to note that Islam believes the only two Satan did not touch were Jesus and Mary, and they believe she remained a virgin (Jomier 2002). Islam believes each person has a nature that instinctively knows God. The natural state of humans is to live in submission to God. Islam does not believe humans have the power to sin on their own; they are simply distracted by Iblis (the devil) and the Jinn who are evil spirits.

On the other hand they believe humans choose to follow or reject Allah (God). Even before creation God made a covenant that Muslims believe humanity as a whole recognized God as Lord. Muslims also believe in angels who are regarded as perfect beings incapable of rebellion, and they are created lower than humans, which is in contradiction to the OT.

It is this covenant relationship to which all are called. Islam does not put much emphasis on God establishing a covenant between himself and a particular people; the first primordial covenant basically remains firm and all-inclusive. The potential for all to recognize God was fixed long before the creation of Adam. Each human has a nature that instinctively knows God, even though one may be distracted by the world and choose to ignore it. Islam stresses life after death much more than Judaism, mainly by its emphasis on escaping hell.

Islam does not accept any mediator between individuals and God, and no sacrifice for sin is necessary. No one can vicariously atone for another's sin. Islam does not emphasize a personal relationship with God; therefore, sin does not break it; no savior is needed. All one needs is knowledge to obey God. It is by knowledge that God guides humans. There is no spiritual indwelling. God is more transcendent than near.

Much time has been taken on these first three chapters, for in attempting to understand the three major religions of western civilization it is important to have this basic analysis. Keeping this background in mind will be important as we continue through this book and will help to categorize the different meanings the three religions take from the OT.

In the first two chapters of Genesis the theme is harmony. Now, and in the rest of the story, we see alienation and separation from God resulting from humans refusing to accept their God given limitations. Now, limited humanity through Adam and Eve want to be co-equal with God in order to do things their way. Human pride enters the picture.

In chapter 3 a talking serpent challenges them by speaking half truths. Serpents are associated with pagan goddesses. The serpent is a symbol for anything that presents options to humans which can seduce them away from God. Verses 1-5 say, Now the serpent was more crafty than any other wild animal that the LORD God had made. He said to the woman, "Did you say, 'You shall not eat from any other tree in the garden'?" The woman said to the serpent, "We may eat of the fruit of the trees in the garden; but God said, 'You shall not eat of the fruit of the tree that is in the middle of the garden, nor shall you touch it, or you shall die.' " But the serpent said to the woman, "You will not die; for God knows that when you eat of it your eyes will be opened, and you will be like God, knowing good and evil."

Verses 6-7 say, So when the woman saw that the tree was good for food, and that it was a delight to the eyes, and that the tree was to be desired to make one wise, she took of its fruit and ate; and she also gave some to her husband, who was with her, and he ate. Then the eyes of both were opened, and they knew they were naked; and they sewed fig leaves together and made loin cloths for themselves.

Thus we have what Christians call the *fall*, the consequence of the first act of disobedience. For most Christians it is a fall from grace, the perfected way in which humankind was originally created. It brings a world filled with sin and corruption, and it brings death.

For Christians the first sin is not a sexual sin as many believe, nor does it have anything to do with apples. Islamic teaching tends to disagree with that statement as do some Jews, and neither call it a fall. This first act of disobedience does have to do with pride and a lack of trust in God and what God said. It also has to do with rejecting God's love. The first sin, beginning with the age old problem of human pride and a lack of trust, leads to rebellion against what God said to them.

In verses 11-13 when God asked what happened, instead of taking responsibility, the man blames the woman, and the woman blames the snake. Because of this original sin, or first act of disobedience, verses 14-19 tell us that something happens that affects males, females, animals, and the earth in a way that mars the original perfection. Verses 17-18 inform us that the earth is now cursed bringing forth thorns and thistles.

In other words life and the earth patterns will no longer bring perfect joy. In Christianity humans can never enter a perfect relationship with God until a perfect offering is made. This is the reason for Christ. Neither Jews nor Muslims accept this analysis.

With this first act of disobedience humankind's relationship with God, with other people, with themselves, and with the environment is broken as portrayed in verses 13-24. Man, woman, animals, and the earth will suffer. Man will suffer in labor; woman will suffer in childbirth, and the ground will be cursed bringing forth thorns and thistles; thus, sin has a cosmic affect. Verse 24 says, He (God) drove out the man;

and at the east of the garden of Eden he placed the Cherubim, and a sword flaming and turning to guard the way to the tree of life.

Christians interpret this to mean that humankind is barred from eternal life, and there can no longer be a perfect relationship with God or offer of eternal life until the perfect offering is made. Cherubim guard holy areas. Later they guard the holiest section of the temple. With this first act of disobedience life now goes from perfect harmony to separation, alienation, competition, and domination where sin affects every aspect of life. Martin Luther will say humankind sins even in the good they do. Everyone may not agree with his statement, but it does make us think about our motives, something that Christ was greatly concerned with as he taught during his time on earth.

In chapter 4 Cain, the son of Adam and Eve, murders his brother Abel. In (9) the LORD God asks Cain, "Where is your brother Abel?" He said, "I do not know; am I my brother's keeper?" His unashamed response is saying what makes you think I am supposed to care for my brother? (This question is raised every day even in our world. This begins humankind's violence and strife against each other and their lack of compassion and care for each other.)

Cain becomes a fugitive from the settled rural life of farming. His descendants become the founders of cities and makers of tools. It does not get any better as cities begin and civilization grows. Sin, which is disobedience to God's ways, becomes rampant. Four generations later in (23-24) Lamech sings a boast to his wives that he is more vengeful than Cain.

In verse 25 Seth is born to Adam and Eve. Seth means anointed. Eventually, from his descendants will be Abraham, Isaac, Jacob, Aaron, Moses, and the Jewish people, and then eventually Christians. Also from Seth comes Ishmael, Abraham's son through Hagar, whose descendants will be many of the Arabs and Muslims. Verse 26 says, To Seth also a son is born, and he named him Enosh. At that time people began to invoke the name of the LORD. (Is this the beginning of organized religion?)

Chapter 5 shows the ten generations of descendants of Adam and Eve through Noah. In (21-29) Enoch becomes the father of Methuselah, and Enoch walks with God; then he was no more because God took him. This is traditionally interpreted that he did not die. Methuselah lived nine hundred sixty-nine years before he died. Methuselah's son Lamech has a son who he names Noah, and (32) tells us that Noah at the age of five hundred became the father of Shem, Ham, and Japheth.

Chapter 6:1-4 says, When people began to multiply on the face of the ground, and daughters were born to them, the sons of God saw that they were fair; and they took wives for themselves of all that they choose. Then the LORD said, "My spirit shall not abide in mortals forever, for they are flesh; their days shall be one hundred twenty years." The Nephilim were on the earth in those days--and also afterward--when the sons of God went in to the daughters of humans, who bore children to them. These were the heroes that were of old, warriors of renown.

These are very difficult verses to understand. The corruption of the earth is now described in terms of cosmic catastrophe. Was this the time of dinosaurs and giant animals and humans? When Scripture talks of longer years of life for humans, some seem to think it may be the way time was calculated. This passage sounds mythical as it depicts the crossing of boundaries between heaven and earth representing the cosmic aspect of sin which is a natural lead into the story of the *flood.* Some scholars call this story an etiological myth used by the writer to explain how giants and larger than life animals came unto the earth. Others think the story is about the line of God's anointed through Seth, who begin to marry pagan women, which initiates a problem throughout the OT.

In the flood story the entire cosmos is caught up in the effects of violence. Heaven and earth interact in a negative way for humankind. As we move through the OT keeping within God's boundaries in all areas will be an issue for God's people. Throughout the Pentateuch the crossing of any type of boundary or the mixing of characteristics that do not normally belong together will not be acceptable. This will make the difference between some of the clean and unclean things that we will see in their purity laws and worship system. The book of Leviticus will explain this in more detail. Also as we move throughout the OT we will continually see that Scripture indicates sin has an effect on the cosmos which then affects the environment.

Verses 5-8 say, The LORD saw that the wickedness of humankind was great on the earth, and that every inclination of the thoughts of their hearts was only evil continually. And the LORD was sorry that he made humankind on the earth, and it grieved him to his heart. So the LORD said, "I will blot out from the earth the human beings I have created--people together with animals and creeping things and birds of the air, for I am sorry that I made them." But Noah found favor in the sight of the LORD.

In verses 11-14 the earth is described as corrupt in God's sight and filled with violence, for all flesh had corrupted its ways upon the earth. In (13-21) God said to Noah, "I have determined to make an end of all flesh, for the earth is filled with violence because of them; now I am going to destroy them along with the earth. Make yourself an ark . . ." In verses 14-21 God tells him exactly how to make it and what to put in it. Verse 22 says, Noah did this; he did all that God commanded him.

Chapters 6-9 tell the story of Noah and the flood which is God's judgment on a world that has become so sin filled that God is sorry he created them. We know that stories of a great flood have been handed down in many languages in most parts of the then known world. Even though some scholars reject the idea of a flood, apparently, around 3000 B.C. there was a severe flood in the Tigris Euphrates Valley that spread to such an extent that most of the nations in the known world recorded it.

The difference in the Genesis account of the flood compared to other ancient accounts, such as the Gilgamesh epic of Babylon, is primarily over theology. In reading the Genesis story it becomes apparent that at least two accounts of the story, first passed along orally, just like the two creation accounts, are fused together. There are different accounts such as different numbering systems for how long the water lasted, how many days they were in the ark, and the number of clean and unclean animals involved.

One account says all animals and birds went in two by two; another states the unclean animals march into the ark two by two while clean animals enter by sevens. Going in by sevens is done to allow for food and the sacrifice of animals. None of this is mentioned in the Qur'an in order to focus on their main interest which is the warning given by Noah. The Qur'an simplifies the story into a graphic presentation of the consequences of ignoring the warnings. This is typical of how the Qur'an uses the OT narratives.

In chapter 8 the flood subsides. Verses 3-4 say, At the end of one hundred fifty days the waters had abated; and in the seventh month, on the seventeenth day of the month, the ark came to rest on the mountains of Ararat (Armenia, Turkey). Verses 6-11 say, At the end of forty days Noah opened the window of the ark that he had made and sent out the raven; and it went to and fro until the waters were dried up from the earth. Then he sent out the dove from him, to see if the waters had subsided . . . and it returned to him to the ark, for the waters were still on the face of the whole earth . . . He waited another seven days, and again he sent out the dove from the ark; and the dove came back to him in the evening, and there in its beak was a freshly plucked olive leaf; so Noah knew that the waters had subsided from the earth. Verse 12 says, he waited another seven days, and sent out the dove; and it did not return to him anymore.

Verses 20-22 say, Then Noah built an altar to the LORD, and took of every clean animal and of every clean bird and offered burnt offerings on the altar. And when the LORD smelled the pleasing odor, the LORD said in his heart, "I will never again curse the ground because of humankind, for the inclination of the human heart is evil from its youth; nor will I ever again destroy every living creature as I have done. As long as the earth endures, seedtime and harvest, cold and heat, summer and winter, day and night, shall not cease."

Chapter 9:1-7 says, God blessed Noah and his sons, and said to them, "Be fruitful and multiply, and fill the earth . . . Every moving thing that lives shall be food for you; and just as I gave you the green plants, I give you everything. Only you shall not eat flesh with its life, that is, its blood . . . Whoever sheds the blood of a human, by a human shall that life be shed; for in his own image God made humankind. And you, be fruitful and multiply, abound on the earth and multiply in it." (They can now eat meat, but it must be drained of blood properly or made kosher. Blood represents life, and returning it to the ground acknowledges that life belongs to God. Capital punishment is also established.)

God then establishes his covenant with Noah and his descendants. Verses 11-13 say, I establish my covenant with you, that never again shall all flesh be cut off from the waters of a flood, and never again shall there be a flood to destroy the earth. God said, "This is the sign of the covenant that I make between me and you and every living creature that is with you, for all future generations: I have set my bow in the clouds, and it shall be a sign of the covenant between me and the earth . . ." (The sign of the covenant is the bow in the clouds (rainbow), a promise sign of grace and peace for both humans and nature that God will never again destroy the earth by water.)

Though the image of God remains in humans, there appears to be dysfunction in all of creation. Once again history will be seen as a process of going from bad to worse. In verses 18-28 the sons of Noah, Shem, Ham, and Japheth leave the ark with Noah. In verses 21-22 Noah, the Bible's first winemaker, became drunk, and Canaan, the son of Ham, is cursed because in some way Ham dishonored Noah.

Some say this may possibly have been a homosexual sin, but the Scripture does not relate what the real issue is. The Scripture simply says, he looked upon Noah's nakedness. Looking on one's father's nakedness was taboo. Later in the book of the law this is suggested as a possible sexual sin (See Lev 17:6). Others say the something done was castration which was sometimes done cross culturally to describe the transfer of power from father to sons. Later writers will use this incident to indicate that it is no wonder God cast the Canaanites out of the land, for they acted just like their ancestors.

Later the people of Israel go into the promised land, which is the land of Canaan inhabited by the Canaanites, and conquer it. The Canaanites, sometimes called the Amorites, will worship pagan gods in that land, and in the process use sexual rites in their worship. This makes them obnoxious to the one God which will be one of the reasons they will lose their land to the Israelites, but we will get to that later.

Islam denies Noah's drunkenness and anything negative about any of the OT characters including future characters like Abraham, Lot, Saul, David, and Solomon, who they hold in high esteem as examples of excellence in morality.

The writer in verses 28-29 says, After the flood Noah lived three hundred fifty years. All the days of Noah were nine hundred fifty years; and he died. (Brian Brown (2007) says that the family and generation of Noah are the last to measure time by cycles of the moon rather than the sun. This is why they lived to be six hundred or even nine hundred years, rather than fifty or even one hundred years as time spans are calculated later. If there is any truth to this idea, a different light would be thrown upon the old ages of these early people.)

The Qur'an does not give Noah's family tree, nor set a context for Noah, except to mention Noah is living in a time of great immorality. The Qur'an does add a story to emphasize the consequences of ignoring God's warnings. The Qur'an story says a son of Noah rejected Noah's plea to leave his immoral friends and get in the ark. The son said that he would climb a mountain and be saved from the water. Later he drowned. The Hadith, which is outside the Qur'an but is the literature by friends of Muhammad who recorded his sayings, says the son's name was Canaan. Noah then encourages his son Ham to name his grandson after him. According to Islam it is this Canaan who is cursed after the story of the flood.

The Qur'an is structured differently than the Bible. It begins with a short psalm, and then has 113 Surahs (chapters) arranged according to length from the largest to the shortest. They resemble psalms, and a major purpose of the Qur'an is to recite them and meditate upon them. When it speaks of the OT it becomes a type of commentary for meditation.

In chapters 10-11 the three sons of Noah, Shem, Ham, and Japheth repopulate the earth to fulfill the command to be fruitful and multiply. According to some scholars many of those descendants can be traced through their names. The families of Japheth move toward Europe and some toward Asia. Ham (an Egyptian word that means black) goes toward Africa and Egypt while Ham's son, Canaan, goes into the land which will later be called the promised land.

Shem stays in the area of Mesopotamia and the area known as the Middle East and from him will come the Jews and Arabs. The word Semite comes from his name. At this point in Genesis we are in what is known as the cradle of civilization which is today known as Iraq, Turkey, Syria, and Iran. The area of Iraq is central and is also known as Mesopotamia. The world is being populated, and Mesopotamia later becomes part of the great Babylonian and Assyrian civilizations. In 10:21 Eber is mentioned from which the word Hebrew is thought to come.

Chapter 11 is the story of the tower of Babel. The climax of the breakdown of relationships is the essence of the story. People no longer understand each other; races become segregated. This is another ancient story usually classified as etiological which attempts to account for the way things are, or how they became that way. In the incident with the tower of Babel the writer is explaining in his way why we are so divided and spread out in this world, why people do not understand each other, and why there are so many languages.

Civilization again is moving in the wrong direction. The people begin to build an urban culture all on their own without the one God who created. Again, the problem is their desire to be co-equal with God in order to be independent of his decrees. With their technology they are building a great tower that attempts to reach into heaven where on top of it they plan to worship their own man-made gods. It all sounds like a modern day story where modern gods are worshiped while trust in technology is the answer to all problems.

Ancient Babylon called these tower structures Ziggurats. Babel means gate of God. The summit of a ziggurat was believed to be the gateway to where the gods were located. The ziggurats are probably the first urban skyscrapers. Mesopotamian city culture was characterized by these ziggurats. As impressed as they are with their accomplishment of the tower of Babel, God in (5) has to come down to see it. It is as if it is so small, he can barely see it.

In verses 6-7 the LORD said, "Look, they are one people, and they have all one language; and this is only the beginning of what they will do; nothing that they propose to do will now be impossible for them. Come, let us go down, and confuse their language there, so that they will not understand one another's speech." Because God is not happy with their efforts, in (7-9) he confuses their language, and then divides and separates them. (The word *Babel* is now interpreted by the Hebrew word confuse.)

This appears to be the real beginning of the spread of the earth's population. The story may also be saying we humans can not reach God by our own efforts. It may also be saying that when we create and live for our own glory instead of living for the glory of the one God who created, we will bring destruction upon ourselves and the culture we have created.

In the Qur'an the theme is basically the same but the context and the story are different. The context seems to be a controversy in the time of King Solomon where leaders of the confusion are teaching blasphemy, division, and images of magic. Also, there is a man named Haman in Egypt (see book of Esther) whom Pharaoh asks to build him a tower into heaven. The OT Haman was in Persia and not Egypt, but often the Qur'an uses names in a symbolic way.

The rest of the chapter (10-31) continues the descendants of Shem showing how they lead to Abram. Re-creation with Noah is a failure; God will have to start all over again. This time he will call a nation. Abram and his father Terah then leave Ur of the Chaldeans (Babylon) and settle in Haran. Verse 31 says Terah took his son Abram and his grandson Lot son of Haran, and his daughter-in-law Sarai, his son Abram's wife, and they went out together from Ur of the Chaldeans to go to the land of Canaan; but when they came to Haran, they settled there. Terah died in Haran at two hundred five years. (Haran is also known as Nahor, a city in northern Mesopotamia.)

In the following chapters (12-36) Abram (Abraham), Sarai (Sarah), Isaac, Jacob and his sons, those who will become the twelve tribes of Israel, are highlighted. In chapter 12 God calls Abram and makes him a covenant of three promises. It is important to know that Islam does not understand this covenant like the Jews do. For Muslims the important covenant is the one God made with all people before creation.

Chapter 12:1-3 says, Now the LORD said to Abram, "Go from your country and your kindred and your Father's house to the land that I will show you. I will make of you a great nation, and I will bless you, and make your name great, so that you will be a blessing. I will bless those who bless you, and the one who curses you I will curse; and in you all the families of the earth shall be blessed."

Here Abram receives a promise of a nation, a promise of land for that nation, and a promise that all the nations would be blessed through him. Why does God want a covenant with a group of people? Apparently, the one God wants a people and a nation who will make him their God as they reject all the other false gods. He wants a people to whom he can reveal himself in order to teach and preserve the one God truth, and he wants a people through whom he can work and eventually reveal the Messiah. He will be their God, and they will be his people. God wants a people to love and wants a people to love him. All three religions, Judaism, Christianity, and Islam believe in a Messiah but in different ways.

God chooses Abram to be the one who will begin the process. Verse 4 says, So Abram went, as the LORD had told him; and Lot went with him. Abram was seventy-five years old when he departed from Haran. Verses 6-8 say, Abram passed through the land to the place at Shechem, to the oak of Moreh . . . So he built there an altar to the LORD, who had appeared to him. From there he moved on to the hill country on the east of Bethel, and pitched his tent, with Bethel on the west and Ai on the east; and there he built an altar to the LORD and invoked the name of the LORD.

This choice of Abram is totally by grace which means unmerited favor. Abram did nothing to earn or deserve this choice, for it was by grace alone. But Abram has the choice to respond to this grace to obey or not to obey, and he responds obediently to God's call. So at the age of seventy-five Abram leaves Mesopotamia to go toward the land God has chosen for him.

Abram will be characterized as one who freely and totally submits to God's will. From him the world will be exposed to monotheism, the belief that there is only one God. Muslims believe Islam is a religious attitude predestined and written by God in human nature, and it cites that the definition of a Muslim is one who submits to God and his will. Thus they claim Abram (Abraham) as their Father as do Jews and Christians.

At the end of chapter 12 Abram and Sarai go to Egypt because of famine. Abram gives Sarai to the Pharaoh for his wife in order to protect both of them from death. In verses 11-12 he said to Sarai, "I know well that you are a woman beautiful in appearance; and when the Egyptians see you, they will say, 'This is his wife'; then they will kill me, but they will let you live. Say that you are my sister, so that it may go well with me . . . that my life may be spared on your account." (Actually she was a half sister of Abram.)

It is a strange story that is basically repeated in chapter 20, even though there it will happen in Gerar of the Philistines with King Abimelech. Also, the theology of the story will be somewhat different. Islam will tell this story in another way, for Islam rejects anything negative about OT characters especially Abram and Lot. For Muslims Abram (Abraham) and Lot are models of God's morality.

The biblical story tells us in (12:17-20) that when the leader of Egypt is afflicted with great plagues from God, he is angry with Abram for lying to him saying she is his sister, and he sends both of them away. Then in chapter 26 Isaac does basically the same thing with his wife Rebekah and King Abimelech in Gerar of the Philistines.

Obviously, a number of different sources are being mixed together in the three stories which were first passed down orally through time until written. Notice that God protects the woman in all these incidents which is something unique in the ancient world. The purpose of the three stories is difficult to discern. It may be that the message is that God in order to realize his purposes has to constantly overcome the obstacles his people put before him.

An interesting passage in 26:8 tells us how King Abimelech learned that it is not the sister but his wife. Verse 8 says, Abimelech of the Philistines looked out of a window and saw him fondling his wife Rebekah. (This is how the half-truth is exposed.)

Chapter 13 says they returned to the promised land. In verses 2-4 we learn that Abram is wealthy in livestock, silver, and, gold, and he returns to the area between Bethel and Ai. Abram and his nephew Lot in (8-12) will split because there is not enough grazing land for both of them. Abram gives Lot a choice, and he chooses the land near Sodom. Verse 13 says, Now the people of Sodom were wicked, great sinners against the LORD.

In verses 14-18 the LORD says to Abram, after Lot had separated from him, "Raise your eyes now, and look from the place where you are, . . . for all the land that you see I will give to you and to your offspring forever. I will make your offspring like the dust of the earth . . ." So Abram moved his tent, and came and settled by the Oaks of Mamre, which are at Hebron; and there he built an altar to the LORD.

In chapter 14 Lot is taken captive by some of the local kings in the area, but Abram chases them down, defeats them, and rescues Lot. On his return the king of Salem, Melchizedek, a priest of the God Most High, meets him bringing him bread and wine. Melchizedek in (19-20) blesses him, and says, "Blessed be Abram by God Most High, maker of heaven and earth; and blessed be God Most High, who has delivered your enemies into your hands!" And Abram gave him one tenth of everything. (This is the first mention of the tithe. We learn more about the mysterious Melchizedek in the New Testament (Hebrews chapters 5, 6 and 7) as the NT writer considers him a type of Christ, but who he really is, we are not told.)

Chapter 15:1-3 says, After these things the word of the LORD came to Abram in a vision, "Do not be afraid, Abram, I am your shield; your reward shall be very great." But Abram said, "O Lord GOD, what will you give me, for I continue childless, and the heir of my house is Eliezer of Damascus?" And Abram said, "You have given me no offspring, and so a slave born in my house is to be my heir." (This seems to be the law of the times.) Verse 4 says, But the word of the LORD came to him, "This man shall not be your heir; no one but your very own issue shall be your heir." Verses 5-6 say, He brought him outside and said, "Look toward heaven and count the stars, if you are able to count them." Then he said to him, "So shall your descendants be." And he believed the LORD; and the LORD reckoned it to him as righteousness.

There are a number of meanings for the word righteousness in the Bible, but one main understanding centers on belief, disposition, or attitude. Another meaning of the word has to do with a relationship with God based on his grace and trust, while another meaning centers on moral responses in the social and family sphere that please God. At different times Scripture uses the word in all these ways.

In chapter 16 because Sarai was not able to bear Abram any children, she tells Abram to have relations with her Egyptian slave, who was her maid, named Hagar. In (2) Sarai said to Abram, "You see that the LORD has prevented me from bearing children; go into my slave-girl; it may be that I shall obtain children by her." And Abram listened to the voice of Sarai. Verse 4 says, He went into Hagar, and she conceived; and when she saw that she had conceived, she looked with contempt on her mistress.

In this culture of the ancients bearing children in this manner is acceptable. At least there is nowhere in the Old Testament where concubines, and even polygamy are prohibited. Islam says Hagar is one of his legitimate wives. Muslims allow four wives.

When Abram was 86 years old a son is born to Hagar, Sarai's maid. From this point on Sarai and Hagar are in strife with each other. Hagar runs away and while by a spring in the wilderness the angel of the LORD appears to her and in (9) says to her "Return to your mistress and submit to her." Verses 10-12 say, The angel of the LORD also said to her, "I will so greatly multiply your offspring that they can not be counted for multitude." And the angel of the LORD said to her, "Now you have conceived and shall bear a son; you shall call him Ishmael, for the LORD has given heed to your affliction. He shall be a wild ass of a man, with his hand against everyone, and everyone's hand against him; and he shall live at odds with all his kin."

Ishmael will be the father of the Arabs, which makes this an interesting prediction, at least from the Hebrew point of view. Naturally Muslims will take offense to this view. Muslims say the Jews are distorting Scripture. Islam sees Ishmael as the perfect representative of the one God's religion. They revere him as the lord of the desert and a prophet of God.

Chapter 17:1-8 says, When Abram was ninety-nine years old, the LORD appeared to Abram, and said to him, "I am God Almighty; walk before me, and be blameless. And I will make my covenant between me and you, and will make you exceedingly numerous." Then Abram fell on his face; and God said to him, "As for me, this is my covenant with you: you shall be the ancestor of a multitude of nations. No longer shall your name be Abram, but your name shall be Abraham; for I have made you the ancestor of a multitude of nations. I will make you exceedingly fruitful; and I will make nations of you, and kings shall come from you. I will establish my covenant between me and you, and your offspring after you throughout their generations, for an everlasting covenant, to be God to you and to your offspring after you. And I will give to you, and your offspring after you, . . . the land of Canaan for a perpetual holding; and I will be their God."

In verses 9-14 he tells him, "As for you, you shall keep my covenant, you and your offspring after you throughout their generations. This is my covenant, which you shall keep, between me and you and your offspring after you: Every male among you shall be circumcised . . . when he is eight days old . . . Any uncircumcised male . . . shall be cut off from the people; he has broken my covenant." Verses 15-16 say, God said to Abraham, "As for Sarai your wife, you shall not call her Sarai, but Sarah shall be her name. I will bless her, and moreover I will give you a son by her. I will bless her, and she shall give rise to nations; kings of peoples shall come from her." (New names signify a new status. Abraham means, the ancestor is exalted. Sarah means, princess.)

Verses 17-21 say, Then Abram fell on his face and laughed, and said to himself, "Can a son be born to a man who is one hundred years old? Can Sarah who is ninety years old bear a child?" And Abraham said to God, "O that Ishmael might live in your sight!" God said, "No, but your wife Sarah shall bear you a son, and you shall name him Isaac. I will establish my covenant with him as an everlasting covenant for his offspring after him. (The point of this is that God can and will do the impossible. He overcomes all obstacles for his people.) As for Ishmael, I have heard you; I will bless him, and make him fruitful and exceedingly numerous; he shall be the father of twelve princes, and l will make him a great nation. But my covenant I will establish with Isaac, whom Sarah shall bear to you at this season next year."

Ishmael, who at this point is thirteen years old, will become the father of many Arab nations that eventually become Muslims. Isaac the son that Abraham and Sarah have will become the father of the twelve tribes of Israel who become the Jews. Today, both Muslims and Jews will circumcise their males at eight days as a sign of the covenant that God has chosen them. Abraham is the father of Jews, Muslims, and Christians. Again, Muslims do not mention much about God having a special covenant with Israel; for Islam relates circumcision to the covenant made with humankind before the world was created.

Chapters 18 and 19 tell the story of Sodom and Gomorrah. In 18:1 The LORD appeared to Abraham by the oaks of Mamre, as he sat at the entrance of the tent in the heat of the day. Verse 2 states there were three men. In (10 and 13) the plurality becomes a single person, and verse 13 calls him the LORD. This is quite difficult to put together. Is God one with two others, or is the God being symbolized by all three? Christians ask if this a hint of the Trinity? Both Judaism and Islam deny the concept of a Trinity.

In chapter 19:1-11 the two angels come to Sodom, and Lot offers them the hospitality of his home. Soon the men of the city surround the house wanting to *know* the visitors. The men in verse 5 say, "Where are the men who came to you tonight?

Bring them out to us, so that we may know them." (Know in this sense means to have sex.)

Lot being concerned with the hospitality rules of the ancients offered his two daughters to the men of the city. But the men reject the offer and try to break down the door. The men are then struck with blindness, and God decides to destroy the area. (Lot seems to have more respect for the hospitality rules than he does for his daughters.)

The Qur'an tells the story in another way. It says when the intruders demanded sexual favors from the visitors, Lot tells them they should get married in order to abandon their immoral life style. When he offers his daughters, it is not for pleasure but for marriage with his neighbors. In the Qur'an Lot's goal is to warn the people of the area of the consequences of their immoral life and to call them to submit to the one God. For Muslims Lot is one of the great heroes of the faith.

In the meantime in 19:13 Lot is told Sodom and Gomorrah are about to be destroyed because of their sins. These sins include their failure to respect the hospitality laws including their attempted violent homosexual rape, pursued unnatural lust, sexual immorality, their injustice against the poor, their pride and arrogance, their excess food and prosperous ease. These are all listed as the sins of Sodom and Gomorrah in other biblical books such as Ezekiel 16:48-50, and Jude 7.

God decides to destroy Sodom and Gomorrah. Abraham in 18:23-25 says, "Will you indeed sweep away the righteous with the wicked? Suppose there are fifty righteous within the city; will you then sweep away the place and not forgive it for the fifty righteous who are in it? . . . Shall not the judge of all the earth do what is just?" In (24-32) Abraham attempts to bargain with the God until in (32) Abraham says, "Oh do not let the Lord be angry if I speak just once more, suppose ten are found there?" He (God) said "For the sake of ten I will not destroy it." Obviously there are not ten to be found. (Ten is the minimal number for communal organization in later Israelite life. For example, to have a synagogue there must be at least ten people.) Verse 33 says, And the LORD went his way, when he had finished speaking to Abraham; and Abraham returned to his place.

Chapter 19:1 says, The two angels came to Sodom in the evening, and Lot was sitting in the gateway of Sodom. They are apparently two of the same three who visited Abraham and Sarah. So, the question is: Do the angels represent God as they do at other times in the Pentateuch? Those who believe this is part of the Trinity believe so. Others including Jews and Muslims reject that theory. We do know Jacob will later wrestle with an angel of the LORD and Moses receiving the Ten Commandments are other examples of an angel that also seems to be God. (We will look at both of these in more detail later.)

In verses 13-14 we learn the area is going to be destroyed, so Lot is warned to get his family out. In (17) they are told, "Flee for your life; do not look back or stop anywhere in the plain; flee to the hills, or else you will be consumed." Verses 24-26 say, Then the LORD rained on Sodom and Gomorrah sulfur and fire from the LORD out of heaven; and he overthrew those cities, and all the Plain, and all the inhabitants of the cities, and what grew on the ground. But Lot's wife, behind him, looked back, and she became a pillar of salt.

This may possibly be a type of literary form to show that if one disobeys God, one will bring destruction upon oneself. It may also be saying if one lives life looking back one dies to a vibrant life. In that land today tourists are shown many salt formations, one is supposed to be Lot's wife. This could be another example of etiological literature that tends to be a type of legend which is a form of writing explaining how certain things came to be. In this case the issue is about all the salt pillars in the area. Being part legend does not necessarily deny that she died in the destruction.

Another example of etiological literature in (30-37) is the story of the origin of Moab and Ammon, who will eventually be enemies of Israel and Judah. As Lot was living in a cave with his two daughters the first born in (31-32) said to the younger, "Our father is old, and there is not a man on earth to come into us after the manner of all the world. Come, let us make our father drink wine, and we will lie with him, so that we may preserve offspring through our father." In Verses 33-35 they did this on successive nights. Both of the daughters of Lot in (36-38) became pregnant by their father. The firstborn bore a son and named him Moab. The younger bore a son and named him Ben-ammi; he is the ancestor of the Ammonites.

Later the Moabites and Ammonites become the constant enemies of Israel. Some believe that later Hebrew writers probably told the story this way to indicate, no wonder Moab and Ammon are such jerks, look how they originated. Islam denies this story and blames the Jews for corrupting the text because their offspring become Arab nations.

Again, the picture of Lot given in the OT by Jewish writers is not very positive since he is the ancestor of Israel's enemies. This picture is insulting to Muslim readers who give a different picture of Lot, one that is all positive. They say the Jews drew this picture of Lot because of his closeness to the Arabs. Also according to Muslims he was the first to make a pilgrimage (Hajj) to Mecca to worship at the sacred Ka'aba stone.

Chapter 21:1-5 says The LORD dealt with Sarah as he had said, and the LORD did for Sarah as he had promised. Sarah conceived and bore Abraham a son in his old age, . . . Abraham gave the name Isaac to his son whom Sarah bore him. And Abraham circumcised his son Isaac when he was eight days old, as God had commanded him. Abraham was a hundred years old when his son Isaac was born to him. (The message is that God can do the impossible.)

The birth of Isaac leads to more problems between Sarah and Hagar, which begin as a result of Sarah's jealousy of Hagar when she gives birth to Ishmael. After the birth of Isaac, Sarah in (10) says to Abraham, "Cast out this slave woman with her son; for the son of this slave woman shall not inherit along with my son Isaac." Abraham casts them out even though verses 11-13 say, The matter was very distressing to Abraham on account of his son. But God said to Abraham, "Do not be distressed because of the boy and because of your slave women; whatever Sarah says to you, do as she tells you, for it is through Isaac that offspring shall be named for you. As for the son of the slave woman, I will make a nation of him also, because he is your offspring."

Abraham in (14) gives Hagar some supplies along with the child and sends them away. She departs and wanders about in the wilderness of Beer-sheba. Islam says they finally settled in Mecca which is the Muslim holy city and where the Ka'aba stone, the Muslim most sacred place, is located today. Islam believes it is here that God first created humans and Adam worshiped. According to Muslims it is here that proper worship was eventually restored by Abraham as he visited Hagar and Ishmael.

As Hagar and Ishmael wander they are close to dying of thirst. Finally, an angel of the LORD appears in (17-19) and tells her a great nation will come from Ishmael. Then God opened her eyes and she saw a well of water. (Islam says this is the well of Zam Zam, which today is a very sacred place for Muslims.)

The story is telling us about God's concern for the homeless, the poor, the powerless, the outcast, women, and the mistreated. The inspired writer is telling us God has compassion on all who suffer and are in need.

Verse 20 says, God was with the boy, and he grew up; he lived in the wilderness, and became an expert with the bow. He lived in the wilderness of Paran; and his mother got a wife for him from the land of Egypt. (Hagar will become the matriarch of Islam. All through the biblical writings there is respect, compassion, and care given to women that is unlike any in the ancient world.)

Chapter 22:1-2 says, After these things God tested Abraham. He said to him, "Abraham!" And he said, "Here I am." He said, "Take your son, your only son, Isaac, whom you love, and go to the land of Moriah, and offer him there as a burnt offering on one of the mountains I shall show you." (Islam says that the son was Ishmael and not Isaac.)

On the way in (7-8) Isaac said to Abraham, "The fire and the wood are here, but where is the lamb for a burnt offering?" Abraham said, "God himself will provide the lamb for a burnt offering, my son." So the two of them walked on together. When it is time to offer the sacrifice, Isaac is laid upon the altar. Abraham in obedience to God's command lifts his knife, but God stops him. In verse 12 God says, "Do not lay your hand on the boy or do anything to him; for now I know that you fear God, since you have not withheld your son, your only son, from me." The writer tells us that God provided a ram to sacrifice instead. Abraham in (14) calls that place, "The LORD will provide"; as it is said to this day, "On the mount of the LORD it shall be provided."

This is a time when sacrificing a son to the pagan gods is the norm, and apparently, Abraham is not fazed when the one God who created everything called him to sacrifice his son. In the law of Moses sacrificing children as a burnt offering will not be permitted; it will only be associated with pagan gods.

Verses 15-17 say, The angel of the LORD called to Abraham a second time from heaven, and said, "By myself I have sworn, says the LORD: Because you have done this, and have not withheld your son, your only son, I will indeed bless you, and I will make your offspring as numerous as the stars of heaven and as the sand that is on the seashore. And your offspring shall possess the gate of your enemies, and by your offspring shall all the nations of the earth gain blessings for themselves, because you have obeyed my voice."

For Christians the incident of Abraham's willingness to sacrifice his only son is called typology which is a type of New Testament interpretation of the Old Testament. When in the Old Testament, a person, place, thing, or event is seen as having a counterpart in the New Testament, we have what theologians call type and anti type or typology. Abraham is willing to sacrifice his only son but is spared from doing so when God provides a ram.

Christians believe this is fulfilled later in Jesus Christ. He is the only son of God and is the lamb provided as the sacrifice for the world's sins including our personal sins. When the Old Testament narrative is said to have a hidden meaning that is later fulfilled or related to a New Testament theme, we have what scholars call typology. Naturally, Judaism and Islam reject this belief.

In chapter 23:1-2 Sarah, who is one hundred twenty-seven years old, dies at Kiriatharba (Hebron). Abraham purchases land, and then in (17-19) buries her in the land called the Cave of Macpelah facing Mamre (that is Hebron) in the land of Canaan. He buys this land from a Hittite named Ephron.

This is the first purchase of the land that will be called the Jew's promised land. Abraham, Isaac, Rebekah, Jacob, and Leah will also be buried here. This spot which is on the West Bank is now a very contentious area. Jews consider it the second-holiest place on earth, but Hebron is an Arab town. Hebron's few very religious Jewish settlers live here in conflict usually violently. In 1929 Arabs killed sixty-seven Jews in Hebron. In 1994 a Jew killed twenty-nine Palestinians at this cave.

In chapter 24 Abraham sends his servant to the city of Nahor in Mesopotamia where Abraham originated. The city is named after Nahor who was kin to Abraham. The purpose is to go back to his family to find a wife for his son, Isaac. Here we meet Laban who is to inherit the family property and possessions from Nahor.

It is here that we also meet Rebekah, the daughter of Betheul and Laban's sister, who will go with the servant that Abraham sent. She will become Isaac's wife. Verse 67 says, Then Isaac brought her into his mother Sarah's tent. He took Rebekah, and she became his wife; and he loved her. So Isaac was comforted after his mother's death. (To this day, a blessing at Jewish weddings is the wish that the couple's marriage might be like that of Isaac and Rebekah.)

In chapter 25:1-6 Abraham takes another wife whose name is Keturah. The children from the two are listed with Midian being one of them. Verses 5-6 say, Abraham gave all he had to Isaac. But to the sons of his concubines Abraham gave gifts, while he was still living, and he sent them away from his son Isaac, eastward to the east country.

These sons become tribal chiefs of Arabia, one of which is the Midianites who also seem to be called Ishmaelites or at least appear to culturally merge with them. Most of Abraham's children married into local Arab populations and from them will eventually come the Muslim population.

In verses 7-9 Abraham dies and is buried by Isaac and Ishmael to be with his wife Sarah in the cave of Macpelah. The rest of the chapter shows the descendents of Ishmael, the father of the Arab nations and later Muslims. One person mentioned in (13) is Kedar. (Many years ago this writer had a professor who stated that Kedar is the descendant of Muhammad. A reference for this could not be found.)

In verses 21-23 the first sons of Isaac and Rebekah the twins Jacob and Esau come into the story. The children struggle within her. Verse 23 says, the LORD said to her, "Two nations are in your womb, and two peoples born of you shall be divided; the one shall be stronger than the other, the elder shall serve the younger." The narrative says in (33-34) that Esau sells his birthright for a bowl of lentil stew. Therefore, Jacob becomes the heir of the covenant.

Jacob and Esau are twins. Because Esau came out first, he is the rightful inheritor of the covenant. The writer is saying that Esau really did not care about taking seriously God and his covenant. The NT book of Hebrews 12:16 adds that Esau was a godless and immoral man. (Muslims deny this.)

Chapter 26:34 also shows that Esau marries two women outside the people of the covenant. Because of a combination of these actions, and through the conspiracy of Jacob and his mother, Jacob will then receive the blessing of the covenant from Isaac. Chapter 27 describes how Jacob was dressed to smell and feel like Esau in order to get the blind Isaac to give Jacob the blessing. Esau then in 28:9 adds a daughter of Ishmael, the father of the Arabs, to his harem of two Hittite wives.

Esau eventually becomes the ancestor of the Edomites. In the time of Christ Herod the Great was an Edomite. Some scholars focus on what they term the deceit, manipulation, and conniving of Jacob and his mother in chapter 27 to get the blessing of the covenant. That is true to some extent, but this writer questions putting too much focus on this type of thinking. There does seem to be some deceit involved, but this writer thinks the Israelites tell this story to show how wise Jacob and his mother are in knowing that Esau is not the type of character needed to be the father of the twelve tribes that will make up the nation of Israel. Some even think Isaac also knew which is why he allows himself to be maneuvered. After all Esau basically eliminated himself by selling the birthright and marrying foreign wives.

This writer seriously doubts that the Israelites would be telling this story, which is saying the Israelite people coming from Jacob began by deceit and manipulation, if wisdom were not the main theme or reason for telling the story. This writer believes the oral Torah of Judaism would basically agree with him on the interpretation of this issue. From a Christian standpoint one could say that possibly the story is also indicating one of Luther's main themes which says there is always some sin even in the good we do.

Verse 41 says, Esau hated Jacob because of the blessing which his father had blessed him, and Esau said to himself, "The days of mourning for my father are approaching; then I will kill my brother Jacob." In (42-45) Rebekah tells Jacob to go back to her brother in Haran to escape from Esau, so in chapter 28, Jacob returns to his ancestral home.

On the way he receives a vision where God informs him that the promise given to Abraham will go through him. This occurs at Bethel where (12-14) say, he dreamed that there was a ladder set up on earth, the top of it reaching to heaven; and the angels of God were ascending and descending on it. And the LORD stood beside him and said, "I am the LORD, the God of Abraham your father and the God of Isaac; the land on which you lie I will give to you and your offspring; and your offspring shall be like the dust of the earth, . . . and all the families of the earth shall be blessed in you and your offspring."

Jacob awakes in verses16-17 and says, "Surely the LORD is in this place—and I did not know it!" And he was afraid, and said, "How awesome is this place! This is none other than the house of God, and this is the gate of heaven." In verses 18-22 he sets up the stone under his head, pours oil on it, and names the place Bethel, God's house.

According to the British tradition the stone was eventually brought to Scotland, and Scottish kings were crowned while sitting on it. It is now the stone that sits beneath the queen's throne in Westminster Abbey (Ramsay 1994).

Jacob makes a conditional vow. Verse 20 says, "If God will be with me, and will keep me in this way that I go, and will give me bread to eat and clothing to wear, so that I come again to my Father's house in peace, then the LORD shall be my God, and this stone, which I have set up for a pillar, shall be God's house; and of all that you give me I will surely give one-tenth to you."

This vow is different from Abraham who unconditionally always trusted God, but for Jacob it is a start in the right direction. At this point Jacob is a negotiator of his self interest. Twenty years later on his return he will encounter God again in this same place.

Chapter 29:1 says, Then Jacob went on his journey, and came to the land of the people of the east (his ancestors). Laban, Jacob's mother's brother, again, enters the picture. Verses 16-17 say, Laban had two daughters; the name of the elder one was Leah, and the name of the younger one was Rachel. Leah's eyes were lovely, and Rachel was graceful and beautiful.

In verses 18-23 the writer states that Jacob loved Rachel, so he said he would serve seven years for her. After seven years verse 21 says, Then Jacob said to Laban, "Give me my wife that I may go into her, for my time is completed." But in the evening we are informed that he took his daughter Leah, and Jacob went into her without knowing it was her. In the morning Jacob saw it was Leah and not Rachel and knew he was deceived.

Laban explained that in his country they do not give the younger one before the older, but he tells him in (27) to complete the week of this one, and then he will give the other also in return for serving him another seven years. Jacob did so, and completed her week; then Laban gave him his daughter Rachel as a wife. Verse 30 says, So Jacob went into Rachel also, and he loved Rachel more than Leah. He served Laban for another seven years.

Jacob the deceiver seems to have met his match in his uncle Laban; he is tricked into working twice the years. The idea may be those who uses trickery as Jacob did with Esau will also get tricked. But as we will see Jacob is not done yet.

Chapters 30 and 31 have deceit, struggle, and conflict as the major theme. Jacob has twelve sons through his two wives and their maids. Again, this is legitimate in those times. If it were not, this writer does not believe the Israelites would tell this story which would then be saying that the nation had developed illegitimately.

Jacob serves Laban six more years for the right to gain livestock to support his family. In the process through trickery by both Laban and Jacob 30:25-43 show how Jacob prospers and Laban loses. God greatly increases the livestock of Jacob. Jacob and his family eventually leave to return to the promised land, but there are more problems between the two. Finally, in 31:48-50 they make a treaty at Mizpah and are able to make accommodations to each other.

Chapter 32 explains the uneasy truce made between Jacob and Esau. Jacob is returning to his home when he sees Esau coming with four hundred of his men. Jacob prepares for a military confrontation. Jacob then continues onward to Peniel and prepares to sleep.

During the night verses 24-28 say, Jacob was left alone; and a man wrestled with him until daybreak. When the man saw that he did not prevail against Jacob, he struck him on the hip socket; and Jacob's hip socket was put out of joint as he wrestled with him. Then he said, "Let me go, for the day is breaking." But Jacob said, "I will not let you go, unless you bless me." So he said to him, "What is your name?" And he said, "Jacob." Then the man said, "You shall no longer be called Jacob, but Israel (means God rules), for you have striven with God and with humans and have prevailed."

Verses 29-32 say, Then Jacob asked him, "Please tell me your name." But he said, "Why is it that you ask my name?" And there he blessed him. So Jacob called the place Peniel, saying, For I have seen God face to face, and yet my life is preserved. The sun rose upon him as he passed Penuel, limping because of his hip. Therefore to this day the Israelites do not eat the thigh muscle that is on the hip socket, because he struck Jacob on the hip socket at the thigh muscle.

This is another example of a man, an angel, and God seemingly being one. The incident is the writer's way of describing Jacob's mystical, life changing experience. Now, he understands in a mature way God's purpose for him. Being tested by God in struggle and conflict, and apparently, disabled by God, Jacob stands successfully.

In chapter 33 Jacob and Esau make an uneasy truce and both continue on their way. The three groups of descendants that come from both men are Israel from Jacob, and the Edomites and the Amalekites from Esau (see 36:12). Israel and the other two will rarely get along with each other. Jacob then returns to Shechem and buys the land from Hamor, Shechem's father.

In chapter 34 the writer inserts the story of the rape of Dinah, Jacob's only daughter by Leah. After Shechem's rape of Dinah in (8-17) Hamor, Shechem's father, spoke with Jacob and they agreed that Dinah would become Shechem's wife, if the people of Shechem agreed to circumcision.

The people of Shechem agree, but verses 25-29 inform us that on the third day while the men were in pain, Dinah's brothers, Simeon and Levi, who were the full brothers of Dinah, took Dinah out from Shechem's house and with the other sons of Jacob kill and plunder the Shechemites. (This is the first violence between the Israelites and the Canaanites. Up to this point they were at peace.)

It is interesting to note that the writers do not usually wash over their stories; they tell them warts and all recognizing that all of us are sinners in need of God's mercy. Jacob said to Simeon and Levi in (30-31), "You have brought trouble on me by your actions making me odious to the inhabitants of the land, the Canaanites and the Perizzites; my numbers are few, and if they gather themselves against me and attack me, I shall be destroyed, both I and my household." But they said, "Should our sister be treated like a whore?"

In chapter 35 the story returns to Jacob. In verses 1-3 God said to Jacob, "Arise, go up to Bethel, and settle there. Make an altar there to the God who appeared to you when you fled your brother Esau." So Jacob said to his household and to all who were with him, "Put away the foreign gods that are among you, and purify yourselves, and change your clothes; then come, let us go to Bethel, that I may make an altar there to the God who answered me in the day of my distress and has been with me wherever I have gone."

Verse 4 says, So they gave to Jacob all the foreign gods that they had, and the rings that were in their ears, and Jacob hid them under the oak that was near Shechem. (The rings in their ears were worn as amulets connected with pagan gods.) Verses 6-7 say Jacob came to Luz (that is, Bethel), which is in the land of Canaan, he and all the people who were with him, and there he built an altar and called the place El-bethel because it was there that God had revealed himself to him when he fled from his brother.

Again, God reaffirms his covenant with Jacob. In verses 10-12 God said to him, "Your name is Jacob; no longer shall you be called Jacob, but Israel shall be your name." So he was called Israel. God said to him, "I am God almighty: be fruitful and multiply; a nation and a company of nations shall come from you, and kings shall spring from you. The land that I gave to Abraham and Isaac I will give to you, and I will give the land to your offspring after you."

Later, in verses 16-18 as they journey from Bethel toward Ephrath (Bethlehem),

Rachel is in childbirth with hard labor. As she gives birth to Benjamin, the last of Jacob's twelve sons, she names him, then her soul departs from her. Verse 19 informs us that Rachel dies, and she is buried on the way to Ephrath (that is Bethlehem), and Jacob sets up a pillar at her grave.

In the process verse 22 says, While Israel lived in that land Reuben went and lay with Bilhah his father's (Jacob) concubine; and Israel heard of it. (This is a grievous offense and the reason he will lose his first born status.) Also, in this chapter in (29) Isaac dies at Hebron, and Jacob and Esau lay their aged father to rest in the family burial ground.

In verses 22-26 the sons of Jacob are listed as twelve. The sons of Leah, the eldest daughter of Laban whom Laban tricked Jacob into marrying first, were Reuben (Jacob's first born), Simeon, Levi, Judah, Issachar, and Zebulun. The sons of Rachel, Laban's younger daughter and the one Jacob loved the most, were Joseph and Benjamin. The sons of Billah, Rachel's maid, who Reuben lay with were Dan and Naphtali. The sons of Zilpah, Leah's maid, were Gad and Asher.

All of these were born in the land of Abraham's ancestors in Haran which was situated on the road between Mesopotamia and Syria. It was in the area called Paddan-aram. From these twelve sons will be the nation of Israel and the people eventually called the Jews. It can not help to be noticed that the children of Israel originated from the multiple wives and concubines of Jacob whose name was changed to Israel.

Before we leave the first thirty six chapters of Genesis, we need to note that those who say Jacob was basically a manipulator and conniver believe that he had those characteristics until his personal encounter with the sacred at Bethel. After that encounter his life is changed, and he becomes a man of strong faith. Now he understands God at a deeper level and understands he was created by God for God's purposes.

As we compare the faith of Abraham with the faith of Jacob we see two different personalities. We see that Abraham has strong faith from the beginning always ready to trust God and be obedient. Jacob is different. At first he is not strong in the faith, and his character probably is not as pure as Abraham until he has his encounter with God and is transformed in a deeper way.

Some of us are like Abraham, who seem to be people of faith right from the beginning; others struggle for awhile as their faith goes through stages and eventually needs some kind of encounter with God to be more serious and more mature in the faith.

As we move to the last chapter (36) in this section there is a long list of the descendants of Esau (Edomites). Verse 12 tells us Timna was a concubine of Eliphaz, Esau's son, and she bore Amalek to Eliphaz. (The Amalekites as well as the Edomites will later be Arab tribes that become enemies of the Israelites even though they are of mixed descent. It has always been noted that the Jews and Arabs are close relatives.)

Chapters 37-50 consist basically of a short story showing how the children of Israel became located in Egypt. Even though the literary form is a short story, the story apparently has its basis in history, although Egyptian records tell us nothing about a prime minister of Egypt named Joseph. Even so, it is an inspired story of God's providence.

Once again, it is important to remember that the truth of the Bible lies in its affirmations about God and ourselves, not in whether it can be confirmed by historians.

Jacob, now Israel, is settled in the land of Canaan, the promised land. Joseph is the main character in the narrative. He is a seventeen year old son of Israel shepherding the flock with his brothers. In the Qur'an the story of Joseph is one of the few that is similar in narrative form, even though it is much shorter.

Chapter 37:1-4 says, Jacob settled in the land where his father had lived as an alien, the land of Canaan. This is the story of the family of Jacob (who becomes Israel). Joseph, being seventeen years old, was shepherding the flock with his brothers; he was a helper to the sons of Bilhah and Zilpah, his father's wives; and Joseph brought a bad report of them to their father. Now Israel loved Joseph more than any other of his children, because he was the son of his old age; and he had made him a long robe with sleeves. (Others translate it as a coat of many colors. Joseph and Benjamin were the only sons of Jacob and Rachel.) But when his brothers saw that their father loved him (Joseph) more than all his brothers, they hated him, and could not speak peaceably to him.

In verses 6-10 we are informed that Joseph had a dream, and when he tells it to his brothers, they hate him even more. In telling his dreams to his brothers, Joseph tells them that he will rise up, and they will have to bow down to him. He has another dream where his father and mother with his brothers bow down to him. Verse 11 says,

So his brothers were jealous of him, but the father kept the matter in mind.

Later as the brothers are guarding the livestock near Shechem verses 18-24 inform us that they see Joseph coming from a distance. Angry at him his brothers seek to kill him. Verses 19-20 say, They said to one another, "Here comes the dreamer. Come now, let us kill him and throw him into one of the pits; then we shall say that a wild animal has devoured him, and we shall see what will become of his dreams." But in (22-23) Reuben said, "Shed no blood; throw him into this pit here in the wilderness, but lay no hand on him"—that he might rescue him out of their hand and restore him to his father. So when Joseph came to his brothers, they stripped him of his robe, the long robe with sleeves that he wore; and they took him and threw him into a pit. The pit was empty; there was no water in it.

Verses 26-28 say, Then Judah said to his brothers, "What profit is it if we kill our brother and conceal his blood? Come, let us sell him to the Ishmaelites, and not lay our hands on him, for he is our brother, our own flesh." And his brothers agreed. When some Midianite traders passed by, they drew Joseph up, lifting him out of the pit, and sold him to the Ishmaelites for twenty pieces of silver. And they took Joseph to Egypt. (The Midianites had descended from a son born to Abraham's wife, Keturah, see 25:1-2. Eventually, they seem to merge as one with the Ishmaelites.)

Meanwhile, in (31-34) the brothers have to answer to their father, so they take Joseph's robe dip it in goat's blood and show it to their father who mourns him deeply thinking a wild animal has devoured him. Verse 36 informs us that the Midianites sell Joseph in Egypt to Potiphar, one of Pharaoh's officials, the captain of the guard.

For some reason in chapter 38 the story of Judah and Tamar is inserted. Judah's son is married to Tamar. In (7-8) the son, Er, who was wicked in the sight of the LORD, was put to death by God. (The Levirate law said, if a man dies childless, his brother is bound to raise heirs to him by his widow. Therefore, Onan is the son of Judah who is to marry Tamar.)

Since Onan knows the offspring will not be his, verses 9-10 say, he spilled his semen on the ground whenever he went into his brother's wife, so that he would not give offspring to his brother. What he did was displeasing in the sight of the LORD, and he puts him to death also. Later when a younger son is old enough to marry, (14) informs us that Judah ignores his responsibility toward Tamar. Then one day after Judah's wife dies he sees a woman on the road to Timnah dressed as a temple prostitute.

Verses 16-18 say, He went over to her at the roadside, and said, "Come, let me come into you," for he did not know she was his daughter-in-law. She said, "What will you give me, that you may come into me?" He answered, "I will send you a kid from the flock." And she said, "Only if you give me a pledge, until you send it." He said, "What pledge shall I give you?" She replied, "Your signet and your cord, and the staff that is in your hand." So he gave them to her and went into her, and she conceived by him.

The signet and cord was for business transactions, and the staff was a walking stick with a family emblem carved on it. Today these two items would be like a credit card and a license to drive.

About three months later (24-26) say, Judah was told, "Your daughter-in-law Tamar has played the whore; moreover she is pregnant because of her whoredom." Judah said, "Bring her out and let her be burned." As she was being brought out she sent word to her father-in-law, "It was the owner of these who made me pregnant." And she said, "Take note, please, whose these are, the signet and the cord and the staff." Then Judah acknowledged them and said, "She is more in the right than I, since I did not give her my son Shelah." Tamar conceived twins named Perez and Zerah.

Zerah comes first, but like Esau and Jacob the first will not be chosen. God works in mysterious ways; most often he does not do the expected. Again, we see an example in Hebrew literature of a female being protected. It is the line of Perez that will lead to David and then to Christ (see Ruth 4:18-22, Mt 1:3). After this chapter we return to Joseph.

Chapter 39:1-3 says, Now Joseph was taken down to Egypt, and Potiphar, an officer of Pharaoh, the captain of the guard, an Egyptian, bought him from the Ishmaelites who had brought him down there. The LORD was with Joseph, and he became a successful man; he was in the house of his Egyptian master. His master saw that the LORD was with him, and that the LORD caused all that he did to prosper in his hands. Verse 4 says, he made him overseer of his house and put him in charge of all that he had.

In verses 7-18 Potiphar's wife tries to seduce him day after day, but Joseph denies her. She then attempts to make it look like Joseph tried to seduce her. In (20) Joseph's master believes her instead of Joseph and has Joseph put in prison. While in prison (23) says, the LORD was with him; and whatever he did, the

LORD made it prosper.

In chapters 40 and 41 while Joseph is in prison he becomes proficient interpreting dreams. The word gets around, and when Pharaoh has a dream and wants it interpreted, Joseph is brought before him. As Joseph interprets the dream in 41:25-32 he tells Pharaoh that there will be seven years of plenty and seven years of famine. In verses 33-36 Joseph gives Pharaoh a plan to deal with those years. He is to store grain in the seven years of plenty so there will be grain in the seven years of famine.

Pharaoh is impressed, and because of this in (39-44), Pharaoh puts Joseph as second in command of all Egypt. Only Pharaoh is over him in the power structure. Because of Joseph's astute planning, when famine comes, Egypt is prepared and has plenty. The entire known world then becomes indebted to Egypt, for it is the only way to obtain grain and survive. Verse 45 says, Pharaoh gave Joseph the name of Zaphenath-paneah; and he gave him Asenath daughter of Potiphera, priest of On, as his wife. Thus Joseph gained authority over the land of Egypt. In the meantime in (50-52) Joseph has two sons, Manasseh, the first born, and Ephraim. (Obviously, they are born to a non-Israelite wife.)

In verses 53-57 famine comes and everyone comes to Joseph in Egypt to buy grain. Because of the famine, Jacob, in chapters 42 and 43, sends his sons to Egypt to buy grain, but 42:4 says, Jacob did not send Joseph's brother Benjamin with his brothers, for he feared that harm might come to him. When they arrived to buy the grain, verses 8-9 say, Although Joseph had recognized his brothers, they did not recognize him. Joseph also remembered the dreams that he had dreamed about them. He said to them, "You are spies; you have come to see the nakedness of the land!" They deny this saying they came for food.

In verses 10-17 Joseph decides to put them to several tests before he reveals himself to them. The first test is to accuse the brothers of spying. Joseph does not reveal himself to his brothers, but when he learns that Jacob and Benjamin are well, he demands the youngest brother's presence as proof of their innocence. Joseph and Benjamin are the sons of Rachael, Jacob's favorite wife, so Joseph especially wants to see him. Simeon agrees in (24) to be put in prison as a pledge of security while the others return to get Benjamin. When they return, they tell their father what had happened, but in (38) Jacob rejects the idea of sending Benjamin back to Egypt. (Did he not care that Simeon was in prison?)

Chapter 43:1-6 says, Now the famine was severe in the land. And when they had eaten up the grain they had brought from Egypt, their father said to them, "Go again buy us a little more food." But Judah said to him, "The man solemnly warned us, saying, 'You shall not see my face unless your brother is with you.' If you will send our brother with us, we will go down and buy you food; but if you will not send him, we will not go down, for the man said to us, 'You shall not see my face, unless your brother is with you.' "

In verses 8-9 Judah says to his father, Israel, "Send the boy with me, and let us be on our way, so that we may live and not die—you and we and also our little ones. I myself will be surety for him; you can hold me accountable for him. If I do not bring him back to you and set him before you, then let me bear the blame forever. If we had not delayed, we would now have returned twice." Jacob agrees, so the sons journey to Egypt.

When Benjamin arrives, Joseph in (29-30) secretly weeps. As they were being feasted verse 34 says, Portions were taken to them from Joseph's table, but Benjamin's portion was five times as much as any of theirs. So they drank and were merry with him.

In chapter 44:1-5 Joseph has one further move to make. The brothers are given grain and sent back home, but Joseph's personal silver cup and the money given for the grain is hidden in Benjamin's sack. Joseph tells his servants that when they leave and go toward Canaan pretend to discover it, and then bring them back, which they do.

At this point Judah explains the dilemma concerning their father, Jacob. In (32-34) Judah explains how he has become surety for Benjamin, and how he has said to his father, if I do not bring him back to you, then I will bear the blame all my life. He asks Joseph to let him remain as a slave in place of Benjamin, for he feared if Benjamin would not return to their father, the father would suffer.

In chapter 45:1-2 Joseph can no longer control himself . . . and he wept. In verses 3-9 Joseph said to his brothers, "I am Joseph. Is my father still alive?" But his brothers can not answer him, so dismayed are they at his presence. Then Joseph said to his brothers, "Come closer to me." And they came closer. He said, "I am your brother, Joseph, whom you sold into Egypt. And do not be distressed, or angry with yourselves, because you sold me here; for God sent me before you to preserve life.

For the famine has been in the land these two years; and there are five more years in which there will be neither plowing nor harvest. God sent me before you to preserve for you a remnant on earth, and to keep alive for you many survivors. So it was not you who sent me here, but God; he has made me a father to Pharaoh, and lord of all his house and ruler over all the land of Egypt . . ." (The writer is saying it is all God's providence. The theology of the writer is that God is in control and is working his plan.)

In verses 9-10 Joseph tells them to go to his father and bring him and your people here to settle in Goshen. Verse 14 says, Then he fell upon his brother Benjamin's neck and wept, while Benjamin wept upon his neck. And he kissed all his brothers and wept upon them; and after that his brothers talked with him. In 16-21 when Pharaoh heard, he loaded up wagons with plenty to take with them and invited them to settle on good land in Egypt. When they returned and told Jacob, he prepared to leave for Egypt.

Chapter 46 lists the names of those who headed the clans, and (26-27) say, All the persons belonging to Jacob who came into Egypt, who were his own offspring, not including the wives of his sons, were sixty-six persons in all. The children of Joseph, who were born to him in Egypt, were two; all the persons of the house of Jacob who came into Egypt were seventy.

After a period of time in chapter 47:10-11, Pharaoh agrees to let them stay in the best part of Egypt in the land of Rameses (Goshen). (Rameses II had been one of the great Pharaohs of Egypt.) Verse 27 says, Israel settled in the land of Egypt, in the region of Goshen; and they gained possessions in it, and were fruitful and multiplied exceedingly.

Jacob whose name was changed to Israel was an old man and about to die. Verse 28 says, Jacob lived in the land of Egypt seventeen years; so the days of Jacob, the years of his life, were one hundred forty-seven years. In (29-31) he requests Joseph to make sure that he will eventually be buried in the promised land in the cave in the field of Machpelah (also in 49:28-33). Jacob in 48:5 adopts Joseph's two sons, but at his blessing of the sons in (17-20) it is the younger son, Ephraim, who receives the blessing that was due the elder son, Manasseh.

In Genesis the pattern of God always standing with the underdog and not doing what is expected is set and will continue through the whole Bible. The younger son seems to be always chosen even though the law gives the elder son the inheritance rights, and older barren women beyond child bearing age are graced with children. All this is usually to show God is behind the incidents and at work.

In chapter 49 Jacob now blesses his twelve sons; they will make up the nation of Israel. Judah receives a special blessing instead of the older son, Reuben, because the older son went into his father's concubine. Simeon and Levi are overlooked also because of their violence at Shechem. Judah receives the first born blessing when Jacob in (10) says, The scepter shall not depart from Judah, nor the ruler's staff from between his feet, until tribute comes to him; and the obedience of the peoples is his.

Jews and Christians believe this blessing of Judah foretells that David will become king, and Christians continue it to show that Jesus the Messiah will come from Judah. It is also interesting to note that when the Jews enter the promised land, Judah and Ephraim (house of Joseph) will eventually divide into the kingdom of the north and the kingdom of the south and be in constant conflict

In chapter 50 the last chapter of Genesis, Jacob dies and is embalmed. Joseph in (20) tells his brothers, "Do not be afraid! Am I in the place of God. Even though you intended to do harm to me, God intended it for good, in order to preserve a numerous people, as he is doing today. So have no fear; I myself will provide for you and your little ones." In this way he reassured them, speaking kindly to them.

In verse 25 Joseph makes them swear that when they return to the promised land they will take his body with them so he can be buried with them. When Joseph dies in (26) he is embalmed. (This a technique mastered by the Egyptians.) This ends the book of Genesis.

Wisdom themes abound in the person of Joseph who fits the ideal of both Egyptian wisdom and the later book of Proverbs. He speaks only when appropriate, keeps his own counsel, accepts misunderstanding, shows great skills as an administrator of public affairs, is adept at translating dreams, is skillful in political intrigue games, and avoids entanglement with foreign women. Above all Joseph is attentive to God's plan.

Through Joseph God works the unexpected. By ironical twists of fate and reversal of roles a lowly Palestinian shepherd becomes the second most powerful official in Egypt. Through him, one of the youngest of brothers, God will work his plan, despite the ambitions or hopes of the older and supposedly more deserving brothers. God works in ways we do not expect. He also chooses Jacob who is younger than

Esau, and follows the advice of the mother, Rebekah, instead of Isaac the father of the promise. Then, it is blessing Ephraim over Manasseh. God doing the unexpected will be consistent throughout Scripture.

Two major themes in Genesis are the promise of the covenant and the journey. God is using history to work out his purpose. We learn that life is both promise and journey and the way is always lined with a wilderness of bumps and bruises. The journey is filled with ups and downs, conflicts and accommodations, alienation and reconciliation, but God is always working out his purpose through his people as imperfect as they may be. All of us also find our meaning and purpose as God's created persons living in God's created order as we journey toward the promise he gives us by being what we are created to be, and doing what he created us to do.

Again we need to remember the main purpose of Scripture is theology and learning the truth about God and ourselves. The Bible is a faith document, a type of catechism, to teach us who God is, who we are, and how we are to relate to the God who created us, how we are to relate to ourselves, to others he created, and how to relate to God's created order. In the process we are to catch God's vision for his people and the earth he created.

One more thing to note, Genesis is foundational for understanding the beginning of three great religions: Judaism, Christianity, and Islam, and all three trace themselves back to their father, Abraham.

EXODUS

In Exodus Moses becomes the main character called by God to lead his people back to the promised land. We learn that Yahweh (YHWH) is God's name. Translated this means I AM WHO I AM or I WILL BE WHO I WILL BE. God sets his people free from oppression and slavery in Egypt by miraculously showing that he is the one true God not Pharaoh. Pharaoh is thought to be a god by the Egyptians, so the battle is set for who is the real God.

In Exodus Passover is established. It is a very important holy day also for today's Jews. Passover will develop as a result of the tenth plague, the last of a series of plagues that God brings upon the Egyptians. The ten plagues result from God's interplay with Pharaoh because he refuses to acknowledge YHWH and set his people free from slavery.

In the book of Exodus the first promise to Abraham is fulfilled as a nation of God's people is formed. Exodus describes Moses receiving the Ten Commandments at Mt Sinai which is also called Mt Horeb. It is interesting to note that the word ten is never mentioned. The Qur'an holds Moses in the highest esteem and refers to him as the one to whom Allah (God) gave the Law in its codified form.

The Decalogue (Greek for ten), is another name given to the Ten Commandments. Both it and the book of the covenant are ratified by blood. In Exodus we begin to learn about the 613 laws that govern the OT people of God. Also, we learn that a calf made of gold, an idol of Egypt, is formed by the high priest Aaron. The people request this from Aaron while Moses is on the mountain top receiving the commandments of God.

The making of this idol portrays the age old problem of God's people wanting to give allegiance to both God and the gods of their own creation. Exodus also consists of instructions for the priests and the building of the tabernacle which will eventually become the temple in Jerusalem.

In chapter 1 there is a gap of approximately 400 years between Genesis and Exodus. The Israelites are no longer a favored group. The Egyptians in (11-12) set taskmasters over them and oppress them with forced labor, but the more they are oppressed, the more they multiply and spread so that the Egyptians dreaded the Israelites.

Verses 13-14 say, The Egyptians became ruthless in imposing tasks on the Israelites, and made their lives bitter with hard service in mortar and brick and in every kind of field labor. They were ruthless in all the tasks that they imposed on them. Then in (22) Pharaoh commands, "Every boy that is born to the Hebrews you shall throw into the Nile, but you shall let every girl live."

In chapter 2:1-6 Moses is born, and when he can no longer be hidden, he is put in a basket and floated down the river. But God is working. Pharaoh's daughter sees him and has pity on him. In verses (7-9) the sister of Moses says to Pharaoh's daughter, "Shall I go and get you a nurse from the Hebrew women to nurse the child for you?" Pharaoh's daughter said to her, "Yes." So the girl went and called the child's mother. Pharaoh's daughter said to her, "Take this child and nurse it for me, and I will give you your wages." So the woman took the child and nursed it. Verse 10 says, When the child grew up, she brought him to Pharaoh's daughter, and she took him as her son. She named him Moses, "because," she said, "I drew him out of the water." (In this way Moses' real mother was able to be involved with Moses, and we can be assured over the years she remained in contact with him teaching him the traditions of the Hebrew people.)

Who was the daughter of Pharaoh? We do not know for sure, but Brian Brown (2007) relates an interesting theory about a Pharaoh named Amenhotep IV who took the name Akhenaten and married Nefertiti, a princess from the desert of Syria. She believed in the one God and convinced him of the same. When he died, their eldest daughter was married to the son of a powerful general in order to bear a son for the throne. His name was Tutmose, known as King Tut, but he died young with no heir.

This daughter of Nefertiti may be the daughter of the Pharaoh. Some think the name Moses came from the name Tutmose.

By the time Moses was a young adult Akhenaten had died. Tut had ruled briefly and died, and Nefertiti briefly shared power through generals. Then a cruel new Pharaoh came to the throne and ruled. If this is correct it would be that Moses heard about the one God through his mother and grandmother Nefertiti. It is an interesting theory but difficult to verify.

Years later when Moses becomes a grown man, he gets into an incident in (11-15) which results in the death of an Egyptian. Fearing his own death, he leaves Egypt and goes to Midian where in (22) he eventually marries the daughter of the priest of Midian.

Moses and his new wife, Zipporah, have a son named Gershom. Later another son is named Eliezer. Verses 23-25 say, After a long time the king of Egypt died. The Israelites groaned under their slavery and cried out. Out of their slavery their cry for help rose up to God. God heard their groaning, and remembered his covenant with Abraham, Isaac and Jacob. God looked upon the Israelites, and God took notice of them.

Chapter 3:1-3 says, Moses was keeping the flock of his father-in-law Jethro, the priest of Midian; he led his flock beyond the wilderness, and came to Horeb, the mountain of God. There the angel of the LORD appeared to him in a flame of fire out of a bush; he looked, and the bush was blazing, yet it was not consumed. In verses 4-6 God called to him out of the bush, "Moses, Moses!" And he said, "Here I am." Then he said, "Come no closer! Remove the sandals from your feet, for the place on which you are standing is holy ground." He said further, "I am the God of your father, the God of Abraham, the God of Isaac, and the God of Jacob." And Moses hid his face, for he was afraid to look at God. (Israelites thought if they saw God face to face they would die.)

Verses 7-10 say, the LORD said, "I have observed the misery of my people who are in Egypt; I have heard their cry on account of their taskmasters. Indeed I know their sufferings, and I have come down to deliver them from the Egyptians, and to bring them up out of that land to a good and broad land, a land flowing with milk and honey, to the country of the Canaanites, the Hittites, the Amorites, the Perizzites, the Hivites, and the Jebusites. The cry of the Israelites has come to me; I have also seen how the Egyptians oppress them. So come, I will send you to Pharaoh to bring my people, the Israelites, out of Egypt."

Verses 11-14 say, But Moses said to God, "Who am I that I should go to Pharaoh, and bring the Israelites out of Egypt?" He said, "I will be with you; and this shall be the sign for you that it is I who sent you: when you have brought the people out of Egypt, you shall worship God on this mountain." But Moses said to God, "If I come to the Israelites and say to them, 'The God of your ancestors has sent me to you,' and they ask me, 'What is his name?' what shall I say to them?" God said to Moses, "I AM WHO I AM." He said further, "Thus you shall say to the Israelites, 'I AM has sent me to you.' " (In Hebrew that is spelled YHWH. Scholars call this the Tetragrammaton.)

In the rest of the chapter Yahweh tells Moses exactly what he is going to do for his people. When the vowels from Elohim, one of the names used for God by one of the four sources of the Pentateuch, and Adonai, which means Lord, are added, God's name becomes Yahweh meaning I AM WHO I AM or I WILL BE WHAT I WILL BE, or HE CAUSES TO BE.

Out of reverence for God's name the Israelites when speaking will never pronounce God's name, for they believe they are not worthy to do so. Thus they will call him (Adoniah). In writing when LORD in small capital letters is seen in a Bible, it is the substitution for YHWH. When the lowercase form of Lord and God is written, the words are translating Adonai and other words denoting deity. In this book when this writer quotes exactly from the Scripture the word is capitalized if the word translated is Yahweh. And this writer because of convenience will use regular capital letters in place of small capital letters.

Moses said to God in Chapter 4:1 "But suppose they do not believe me or listen to me, but say, 'The LORD did not appear to you.' " God's answer in (2-5) was to give him a staff through which God would perform miracles. Moses in (10-12) still reluctant to be God's chosen, offers another excuse by saying, "O my LORD, I have never been eloquent, neither in the past nor even now that you have spoken to your servant; but I am slow of speech and slow of tongue." Then the LORD said to him, "Who gives speech to mortals? . . . Now go, and I will be with your mouth and teach you what you are to speak." But in (13) Moses said, "O my LORD, please send someone else."

Verses 14-17 say, Then the anger of the LORD was kindled against Moses and he said, "What of your brother Aaron the Levite? I know that he can speak fluently; even now he is coming out to meet you, and when he sees you his heart will be glad. You shall speak to him and put the words in his mouth; and I will be with your mouth and with his mouth, and will teach you what you shall do. He indeed shall speak for you to the people; he shall serve as a mouth for you, and you shall serve as God for him. Take in your hand this staff, with which you will perform the signs." Finally, Moses gives in and gets permission from his father-in-law to return to Egypt.

Verse 20 says, So Moses took his wife and his sons, put them on a donkey, and went back to the land of Egypt; and Moses carried the staff of God in his hand. Verses 24-25 say, On the way, at a place where they spent the night, the LORD met him and tried to kill him. But Zipporah took a flint and cut off her son's foreskin, and touched Moses' feet with it, and said, "Truly you are a bridegroom of blood to me!" So he let him alone. It was then she said, "A bridegroom of blood by circumcision."

There are some who think neither had been circumcised, for Zipporah did the circumcising when it was normally the male's responsibility. The writer by saying God tried to kill Moses is stressing how important circumcision is for the OT community. This is a difficult story because it appears some of the historical context is lost.

Chapter 5:1-2 says, Afterward Moses and Aaron went to Pharaoh and said, "Thus says the LORD, the God of Israel, 'Let my people go, so that they may celebrate a festival to me in the wilderness.' " But Pharaoh said, "Who is the LORD that I should heed him and let Israel go? I do not know the LORD, and I will not let Israel go." So Pharaoh makes it harder for the Israelites in (7) by not giving them any straw to make their bricks. Now they have to go find their own straw. This is a hardship for the people who are not able to meet their former requirements. As a result in (14) their supervisors are beaten by their taskmasters.

In verses 22-23 Moses turned again to the LORD and said, "O LORD, why have you mistreated this people? Why did you ever send me? Since I first came to Pharaoh to speak your name, he has mistreated this people, and you have done nothing at all to deliver your people."

Moses, like many of us, when things go wrong, we whine and complain to God. This sets the stage for the narrative known as the ten plagues of Egypt where God demonstrates who is the real God for both Moses and Pharaoh. The purpose of the ten plagues narrative is not only to set his people free from oppression but to highlight the issue of who God is.

In interpreting this narrative, historical and literary analysis, seek the underlying meaning of the writer not the exact historical details. Ancient writers did not write to preserve exact historical detail as modern historians do; they wrote to express their faith in ideas and concepts usually through narratives. Also, Hebrew writers, as Jesus will do later, used hyperbole. Hyperbole is a literary form where exaggeration is used to get a point across.

In the Exodus narrative Pharaoh represents the gods of Egypt, for Pharaoh himself was considered a god by the ancient Egyptians. Pharaoh also represents historical evil as well as power and wealth using political power in self serving and demeaning ways. The purpose is to crush hope and break the spirit of those under them. Moreover, Pharaoh is seen as a personification of the forces of chaos opposing the order of God's creation and the intended well being of God's people.

The story is about who God is, and God's liberating power verses the oppressive power of human empires. The plague narrative is written in a form that made sense to the ancient people for whom it was originally written. For us to understand this literary form, we must first attempt to understand it in the manner the ancient people living in an oral and agricultural society would understand it, and then how it was written.

The theology of the narrative attempts to show that Yahweh is God who overcomes obstacles to his intentions and who is ultimately in control even when at times it does not seem as though he is. After each incident the writer illustrates that rejecting God's word can have a cosmic effect, and it can have consequences for both the people who reject God and the environment in which they live (Birch, Brueggemann, et al. 1999).

Chapter 6 sets the narrative of the plagues in the backdrop of what will be one of Moses' major problems, the broken spirit of the Israelites. As we go through the next few books the writer wants his readers to understand the story of the ten plagues, as well as the wilderness wanderings, in that particular light. Moses tells the people that God is about to make due on his promise of land to Abraham, Isaac, and Jacob, but

6:9 says, they would not listen to Moses because of their broken spirit and their cruel slavery. (There is a point people can become so crushed, and so oppressed that they can not even respond to those helping them.)

The writer then proceeds with the story of the Exodus which the Israelites later will claim as the foundation of Jewish history. The story of the ten plagues is included in chapters 7-11. Moses goes to Pharaoh and tells him their God demands that he let his people go, so they can enter the land God promised them. Before each plague Pharaoh agrees and then changes his mind. Each time he changes his mind, God brings a plague upon Egypt. The writer seems to be indicating that sin can cause less than perfect things to occur in the cosmos upsetting the normal functioning of the earth.

This idea is illustrated in the following plague incidents. The first plague is water turned into blood (7:14-24), followed by frogs (8:1-15), then gnats (16-19), then flies (20-32), then pestilence of livestock (9;1-6), then boils (8-12), then hail (13-35), then locusts (10: 1-20), then darkness(21-29), and the tenth and last plague, death of the first born (11:1-12:30). It would be possible for each plague to produce the next one until the ninth plague which would not produce the tenth plague.

The water turning to blood could have been caused by the red clay of the region or from red algae which kills the fish causing the frogs to be driven from the river banks, causing the gnats, and flies. Then disease strikes the cattle, and then skin disease such as boils. Lightning and hail could destroy plants and crops. Wind bringing locusts would do more damage, then darkness to blot out the sun god. The plagues probably occur over a period of six months to a year.

Numerous scholars have documented natural disorders in Egypt that could be basically described as they are in these chapters. If that is what is experienced, then we could say, in each case, except the tenth plague, God chose to use natural disorders to confound Pharaoh and the gods of Egypt. The miracle would be the timing of the events as well as God using creation for his purposes.

This writer does not know the exact history or science of these incidents, but we need to remember this literature is about theology usually written in conjunction with some type of historical happenings. The incidents are not written to detail empirical history. On the other hand, could God have worked miracles as described in the ten plagues? It is God's creation, and he can do as he wills with his creation. This writer will let the reader form his own opinion as to how God worked.

The death of the first born, both human and animals is difficult to explain. Does it mean literally all first born in the land? Could it have possibly been the family of Pharaoh, his wives and relative's first born offspring and their animals, which would be to represent Egypt? Whatever it was we do know that God could announce the timing of each of these events and halt them when he wanted. We do know something incredible must have happened because Passover for the Jews that is rooted in this narrative becomes one of their most important feast days constantly stressed in Scripture and celebrated even today.

The plagues are brought on as Pharaoh, after each one, promises to let the people go, and then changes his mind. When he changes his mind in disobedience to God, another plague is sent. The time span involved is anyone's guess. There are those who believe a ten year period is possible which could mean a plague a year so that it took ten years for the people to exit Egypt. No one really knows.

Before we continue the reader should know that some scholars believe there is also a tradition of only seven plagues instead of ten (see Psalm 78 and 105). This may be to indicate that one or more oral and written traditions of the plagues were circulating. On the other hand, the Psalms are poetry and not overly concerned with historical details.

Chapter 6:2-9 sets the pace for the story of the ten plagues. In verse 2 God spoke to Moses and said, "I am the LORD . . . I have also heard the groaning of the Israelites, whom the Egyptians are holding as slaves, and I have remembered my covenant. Say therefore to the Israelites, 'I am the LORD, and I will free you from the burdens of the Egyptians and deliver you from slavery to them. I will redeem you with an outstretched arm and with mighty acts of judgment. I will take you as my people, and I will be your God. You shall know that I am the LORD your God, who has freed you from the burdens of the Egyptians. I will bring you into the land that I swore to give to Abraham, Isaac, and Jacob; I will give it to you as a possession. I am the LORD.' " Moses told this to the Israelites; but they would not listen to Moses, because of their broken spirit and cruel slavery.

Verses 10-12 say, The LORD spoke to Moses, "Go tell Pharaoh king of Egypt to let the Israelites go out of his land." But Moses spoke to the LORD, "The Israelites have not listened to me; how then shall Pharaoh listen to me, poor speaker that I am?"

Again in verse 30, Moses said in the LORD's presence, "Since I am a poor speaker, why would Pharaoh listen to me?" (The writer is setting his readers up to see what is accomplished will be done mainly by the one God and not Moses. Moses will simply be God's instrument.)

In 7:1-3 The LORD said to Moses, "See, I have made you like God to Pharaoh, and your brother Aaron shall be your prophet. You shall speak all that I command you, and your brother Aaron shall tell Pharaoh to let the Israelites go out of his land. But I will harden Pharaoh's heart, and I will multiply my signs and wonders in the land of Egypt . . . The Egyptians shall know that I am the LORD, when I stretch out my hand against Egypt and bring the Israelites out from among them." Moses and Aaron did so; they did just as the LORD commanded them. Moses was eighty years old and Aaron eighty three when they spoke to Pharaoh.

Then in verses 8-25 each time Moses uses the staff God gave him to perform a miracle, Pharaoh's magicians, representing the demons of false gods, are able to perform what appear to be miracles that equal what Moses performed. Finally, Pharaoh's people with their magical arts can no longer duplicate the miracles of Moses and Aaron. In 8:18-19 the magicians try to produce gnats by their secret arts, but they could not. There were gnats on both humans and animals. And the magicians said to Pharaoh, "This is the finger of God!" But Pharaoh's heart was hardened, and he would not listen to them, just as the LORD had said.

These incidents are to teach us that magicians and pagan spirits can fool us, but their magical powers are not the real thing. The magical powers that are in use both in the past and the present have their limitations. We will later learn in the New Testament that demons have some powers that appear to be miraculous, so God's people need to be careful when they depend on miracles to discover what is true and what is false.

In chapters 7-11 we learn that God is sovereign and can use evil and the choices people make to turn the choices made to his purposes. Our human choices of evil are permitted by God even though God could stop us from making them. God is in control. That is why the writer says God hardened Pharaoh's heart. In the next few chapters we will see that the writer says, God hardened the heart of Pharaoh, but it is also described as Pharaoh hardening his own heart. Ten times Pharaoh hardens his own heart, and ten times it says God hardened his heart (Birch et al. 1999).

The narrative plainly describes Pharaoh beginning with his own heart hardened against God; then God allows it to be hardened even more. God is sovereign; he is in control. He could have stopped it, but he did not. In Scripture when God allows something, God is given the credit for doing it, for God is sovereign. The idea is that God is ultimately in charge even though he allows our human choices of evil that cause people harm. But God can and often does turn evil choices to his advantage.

In the following narrative we will see the liberating power of Yahweh as opposed to the oppressive power of evil represented by Pharaoh. We will also see how God uses evil to bring about his purposes. Some ask why he does not stop evil in the first place. This writer's answer is heaven is not yet on earth, so people need to learn by instruction, by doing, or from their experience, and the consequences of their actions.

In chapter 7 verses 5 and 17 Yahweh tells Pharaoh that he is going to send plagues upon him and his people so they will know that, I am the LORD. Also, in 9:16 he tells Pharaoh, this is why I have let you live: to show you my power, and to make my name resound through all the earth.

In the rest of chapter 7 and through 11 we read of the ten plagues. As described above the plagues are brought about because Pharaoh said he would let God's people go but each time changed his mind in disobedience to the will of God. Chapter 11 includes the last plague. Yahweh warns that if Pharaoh does not let his people go, all of the first born in Egypt will die. (The continuing theology is that evil choices bring negative consequences, but God will prevail.)

In chapter 12:3-7 Yahweh tells Moses that to protect themselves from the death of the first born each family is to take a lamb on the tenth day of the first month. A small household may join a larger one in obtaining a lamb. It is to be one year old and without blemish taken from the sheep or goats. They are not to break any of its bones, and on the fourteenth day of the month slaughter it, then put its blood on the two doorposts and the lintel of the houses in which they eat it. Verses 8-11 say, They shall eat the lamb that same night; they shall eat it roasted over the fire with unleavened bread and bitter herbs. Do not eat any of it raw or boiled in water, but roasted over the fire, with its head, legs, and inner organs. You shall let none of it remain until the morning; anything that remains until the morning you shall burn. This is how you shall eat it: your loins girded, your sandals on your feet, and your staff in your hand; and you shall eat it hurriedly. It is the passover of the LORD.

Verses 12-14 say, I will pass through the land of Egypt that night, and I will strike down every firstborn in the land of Egypt, both human beings and animals; on all the gods of Egypt I will execute judgments: I am the LORD. The blood shall be a sign for you on the houses where you live: when I see the blood, I will pass over you, and no plague shall destroy you when I strike the land of Egypt. This day shall be a day of remembrance for you. You shall celebrate it as a festival to the LORD; throughout your generations you shall observe it as a perpetual observance. (This becomes known as the Jewish Passover; it becomes a sacred meal. Passover becomes a very sacred holy day for the Jews even today.)

Verses 21-27 say, Then Moses called all the elders of Israel and said to them, "Go, select lambs for your families and slaughter the passover lamb. Take a bunch of hyssop, dip it in the blood . . . touch the lintel and the two doorposts with the blood in the basin . . . For the LORD will pass through to strike down the Egyptians; when he sees the blood on the lintel and on the two doorsteps, the LORD will pass over that door and will not allow the destroyer to enter your houses to strike you down. You shall observe this rite as a perpetual ordinance for you and your children . . . When your children ask you, 'What do you mean by this observance?' you shall say, 'It is the passover sacrifice to the LORD, for he passed over the houses of the Israelites in Egypt, when he struck down the Egyptians but spared our houses.' " And the people bowed down and worshiped.

Christians will later read typology into this Passover and see Jesus as the lamb of God whose blood saves by passing over the sins of humankind. It is also interesting that in the New Testament the Gospel writers note that as Jesus died on the cross none of his bones are broken. The Eucharist (Holy Communion) will be what the Christians celebrate in place of the Passover. In the days before Jesus' resurrection, Christians believe Christ became the Passover lamb as he was crucified upon the wood of the cross.

Chapter 13:1-3 says, The LORD said to Moses: Consecrate to me the firstborn; whatever is the first to open the womb among the Israelites, of both humans and animals, is mine. Moses said to the people, "Remember this day on which you came out of Egypt, out of the house of slavery, because the LORD brought you out from there by strength of hand; no leavened bread shall be eaten. Today in the month of Abib, you are going out . . ." They are then told that they shall make this event a remembrance.

In (14-16) God's people are told, "When in the future your child asks you, 'What does this mean?' you shall answer, 'By strength of hand the LORD brought us out of Egypt, from the house of slavery. When Pharaoh stubbornly refused to let us go, the LORD killed all the firstborn in the land of Egypt, from human firstborn to the firstborn of animals. Therefore I sacrifice to the LORD every male that first opens the womb, but every firstborn of my sons I redeem.' It shall serve as a sign on your hand and as an emblem on your forehead that by strength of hand the LORD brought us out of Egypt."

Verses 19-21 say, Moses took with him the bones of Joseph who had required a solemn oath of the Israelites, saying, "God will surely take notice of you, and you must carry my bones with you from here." They set out from Succoth, and camped at Etham, on the edge of the wilderness. The LORD went in front of them in a pillar of cloud by day, to lead them along the way, and in a pillar of fire by night, to give them light, so that they might travel by day and by night.

The writer uses this symbolism to show that God was with his people. The question people have asked is, was this really miraculous? The same question can be asked in reference to the ten plagues as well as some of the other miracles which we will read about. Did miracles really occur? The answer is that we can not prove any of it one way or another. It depends on faith or one's point of view.

Some people say even if the plagues, the pillars, and the Exodus as a whole were not totally miraculous, there had to be some miracles involved. Others say they were all miracles; still others say there were no real miracles. It is simply the writer's faith statement and way of saying God was with them. Others believe the real miracle was in the timing of everything, while others say it is a form of symbolic history to show that God was working his purpose with his people which in itself can be labeled miraculous. Again, this writer will leave the answer to the reader and one's church tradition.

When it dawns upon the Egyptians that their free slave labor is leaving for good, Pharaoh once again changes his mind and orders his army to bring them back. As the army comes behind them, God orders Moses to lift his staff upon the water, and 14:21-23 says, Moses stretched out his hand over the sea. The LORD drove the sea back by a strong east wind all night, and turned the sea into dry land; and the waters were divided. The Israelites went into the sea on dry ground, the waters forming a wall for them on their right and on their left.

The Egyptians pursued, and went into the sea after them, all of Pharaoh's horses, chariots, and chariot drivers. In verses 26-31 the LORD said to Moses, "Stretch out your hand over the sea, so that the water may come back upon the Egyptians upon their chariots and chariot drivers." So Moses stretches out his hand over the sea, and at dawn the sea returned to its normal depth. As the Egyptians fled before it, the LORD tossed the Egyptians into the sea. The waters returned and covered the chariots and the chariot drivers, the entire army of Pharaoh that had followed them into the sea; not one of them returned. But the Israelites walked on dry ground through the sea, the waters forming a wall for them on the right and on the left. Thus the LORD saved Israel that day from the Egyptians; and Israel saw the Egyptians dead on the seashore. Israel saw the great work the LORD did against the Egyptians. So the people feared the LORD, and believed in the LORD, and in his servant Moses.

All this is used by the writer to symbolize, using the literary form of hyperbole to emphasize that God was with Moses and his chosen people, and the one God is God. That we can call it a symbol does not mean there is no truth to it. Again, did things happen exactly as described, or is the writer writing theology based upon a basic history to show God was working with them and for them as he set his people free from slavery and oppression? The reader can decide, but for sure we do know the writer is indicating that God is sovereign and in the end will defeat the forces of evil.

Chapter 15 includes both the Song of Moses and the Song of Miriam, the sister of Moses and Aaron. In the song of Moses in verses 1- 3 they sang, "I will sing to the LORD, for he has triumphed gloriously; horse and rider he has thrown into the sea. The LORD is my strength and my might, and he has become my salvation; this is my God, and I will praise him, my Father's God, and I will exalt him. The LORD is a warrior; the LORD is his name . . ."

This last statement seems harsh to modern ears, but this was normal thinking and literary style in those days when each nation had their own god who fought for them and protected them in a time when war was not only normal politics but also seemed to be a leading sport for males. The writer is showing that Yahweh is all powerful and fights oppression, evil, and whoever opposes him. God is a warrior, and he will prevail. The song continues through verse 18. Some scholars believe that the history in the OT is symbolic history where the purpose is still inspired theology, but the history contained is primarily developed to symbolize the real meaning of what the theology is expressing: Yahweh is God.

To those victimized by oppressive powers it is important to know there is a power capable of defeating those arrogant and oppressive powers. That is what God symbolized as a warrior means. The text is not for those who want to yield their own violent power, but it is for those who are being oppressed and taken advantage of by the wealthy and powerful. Evil and corruption and the powerful who are evil and corrupt will be defeated. The one God and those who side with him will prevail.

In verses 20-21 the prophet Miriam, the sister of Moses and Aaron, took a tambourine in her hand; and all the women go out after her with tambourines and dancing. And Miriam sang to them: "Sing to the LORD, for he has triumphed gloriously; horse and rider he has thrown into the sea."

Verses 22-25 say, Then Moses ordered Israel to set out from the Red Sea, and they went into the wilderness of Shur. They went three days into the wilderness and found no water. When they came to Marah, they could not drink the water because it was bitter (impure). That was why it was called Marah. And the people complained against Moses, saying, "What shall we drink?" He (Moses) cried out to the LORD, and the LORD showed him a piece of wood; he threw it into the water, and the water became sweet (fresh). (Again, the writer is showing that God has power over everything even nature.)

Verses 26-27 say, "If you will listen carefully to the voice of the LORD your God, and do what is right in his sight, and give heed to his commandments and keep all his statutes, I will not bring upon you any of the diseases that I brought upon the Egyptians, for I am the LORD who heals you." (Again, it is interesting to note that the command is conditional based upon the word, *if.* God is putting them to a test.) Then they came to Elim, where there were twelve springs of water and seventy palm trees; and they camped there by the water.

Chapter 16:1-3 says, The whole congregation of the Israelites set out from Elim; and Israel came to the wilderness of Sin, which is between Elim and Sinai, on the fifteenth day of the second month after they had departed from the land of Egypt. The whole congregation of the Israelites complained against Moses and Aaron in the wilderness. The Israelites said to them, "If only we had died by the hand of the LORD in the land of Egypt when we sat by the fleshpots and ate our fill of bread; for you have brought us out into this wilderness to kill this whole assembly with hunger."

In verses 4-5 The LORD said to Moses, "I am going to rain bread from heaven for you, and each day the people shall go out and gather enough for that day. In that way I will test them, whether they will follow my instructions or not. On the sixth day, when they prepare what they bring in, it will be twice as much as they gather on other days."

In verses 13-16 God causes quail to come to them, and he supplies them with a flakey substance on the ground caused by dew on the ground that was to be their bread. In (16-30) God commands that they gather only as much as they need, but they do not obey him, and worms destroy their excess. The bread is described in (31) as manna. It was like coriander seed, white, and the taste of it was like wafers made with honey.

Allen Vehey (2002) among others has developed a manna theology. The idea is that God has given the earth enough natural resources for everyone. If those who are fortunate to live where there are many natural resources and use only what they need, then others would be able to have what they need. God provides the world what it needs. It is up to others to work out a just system to share it. The Apostle Paul carries this manna thinking over into the NT (see II Corinthians 8:8-16 and Luke in Acts 2:44-45).

Chapter 17:1-4 says, From the wilderness of Sin the whole congregation of the Israelites journey by stages, as the LORD commanded. They camped at Rephidim, but there was no water for the people to drink. The people quarreled with Moses and said, "Give us water to drink." Moses said to them, "Why do you quarrel with me? Why do you test the LORD?" But the people thirsted there for water; and the people complained against Moses and said, "Why did you bring us out of Egypt, to kill us and our children and livestock with thirst?" So Moses cried out to the LORD, "What shall I do with this people? They are almost ready to stone me." (The writer is portraying broken human nature and how difficult it is to have complete faith in God and his word.)

In verses 5-7 the LORD said to Moses. "Go on ahead of the people . . . I will be standing there in front of you on the rock of Horeb. Strike the rock, and water will come out of it, so the people may drink." Moses did so, in the sight of the elders of Israel. He called the place Massah and Meribah, because the Israelites quarreled and tested the LORD, saying, "Is the LORD among us or not?"

At Rephidim in (8-13) the Amalekites, one of the descendant peoples of Esau, attack them. Moses climbs a hill with Aaron and Hur, and as long as they hold up the arms of Moses the Israelites prevail, but when he lets his arms rest, Amalek has the better of the fight. Finally, because of fatigue, Moses sits on a rock. Aaron and Hur hold up his arms and Joshua and the Israelites prevail over the Amalekites.

This writer thinks it is legitimate to interpret this lifting up of arms as a symbol of prayer, meaning as long as Moses prayed, the Israelites prevailed. The miracle is in the prayer. God miraculously defeats them as Moses prays. The writer of Exodus is showing that it is God who provides, and God who protects. It is not the people's doing; it is God, and this is the greatest miracle. All anyone has is what God permits, and God can take it away if he chooses. We will begin to notice that prayer from the leaders, Moses and Aaron always has an effect upon God.

In chapter 18 as Moses and God's people are camped in the wilderness his father-in-law brings his two sons, Gershom and Eliezar to be with him. In the meantime he watches Moses as he daily serves as judge for his people. After awhile in (14-23) he suggests to Moses that because he is trying to do everything by himself, he will soon suffer burnout. Moses listens and begins to delegate responsibility so that others will handle the minor cases while he handles the major ones.

This organizational change contributes to a smoother function of operations and will be an aid to Moses' mental and physical health. The theologian is saying no one can do everything by himself even if God is with him. To be more efficient God's leaders need to delegate responsibility. God is in control and helps his people, but his people need to use the help God has given them.

In chapter 19 as the people continue on their journey, they camp in front of the mountain called Sinai. Since Exodus is composed from more than one oral and written tradition, another key tradition calls Sinai, Horeb. The people will remain encamped in this area until Numbers 10:11-12. Verses 3-6 say, Then Moses went up to God; The LORD called to him from the mountain, saying, "Thus you shall say to the house of Jacob, and tell the Israelites: You have seen what I did to the Egyptians, and how I bore you on eagle's wings and brought you to my self. Now therefore, if you obey my voice and keep my covenant, you shall be my treasured possession out of all the peoples. Indeed the whole earth is mine, but you shall be for me a priestly kingdom and holy nation. These are the words that you shall speak to the Israelites."

Again, we see that the covenant is based upon the *if* clause. God is true to his promise, but the people can opt out by ignoring him and being disobedient. This principle is consistent throughout Scripture. God does not normally take away anyone's free will but allows people to reject him and bear the consequences. On the other hand he is always there to welcome them back if they have a change of mind.

Verses 7-9a say, So Moses came, summoned the elders of the people, and set before them all these words that the LORD commanded him. The people all answered as one: "Everything that the LORD has spoken we will do." Moses reported the words of the people to the LORD. Then the LORD said to Moses, "I am going to come to you in a dense cloud, in order that the people will hear when I speak with you and so trust you ever after."

Verses 9b-12 say, When Moses had told the words of the people to the LORD, the LORD said to Moses: "Go to the people and consecrate them today and tomorrow. Have them wash their clothes and prepare for the third day, because on the third day the LORD will come down upon Mt Sinai in the sight of all the people. You shall set limits for the people all around, saying, 'Be careful not to go up the mountain or to touch the edge of it. Anyone who touches the mountain shall be put to death . . . they shall not live.' When the trumpet sounds a long blast, they may go up on the mountain."

Verses 14-19 say, So Moses went down the mountain to the people. He consecrated the people, and they washed their clothes. And he said to the people, "Prepare for the third day; do not go near a woman." (If the people were ritually unclean in the presence of the holy God, they would die.) On the morning of the third day there was thunder and lightning, as well as a thick cloud on the mountain, and a blast of trumpet so loud that all the people who were in the camp trembled. Moses brought the people out of the camp to meet God. They took their stand at the foot of the mountain. Now Mount Sinai was wrapped in smoke, because the LORD had descended upon it in fire . . . the whole mountain shook violently. As the blast of the trumpet grew louder and louder, Moses would speak and God would answer him in thunder.

In verse 20 the LORD summons Moses to the top of the mountain. After Moses goes to the top of the mountain in (24-25) the LORD said to him, "Go down and come up bringing Aaron with you; but do not let either the priests or the people come up to the LORD; otherwise he will break out against them." So Moses goes down to the people and tells them.

In chapter 20:1-17 God gives Moses the Ten Commandments. These are the core values that protect order, life, and the well-being of the community. Verses 1-3 say, Then spoke God all these words: I am the LORD your God, who brought you out of the land of Egypt, out of the house of slavery; you shall have no other gods before me. Verses 4-5 say, You shall not make for yourself an idol, . . . You shall not bow down to them or worship them; Verse 7 says, You shall not make wrongful use of the name of the LORD your God, . . . Verse 8 says, Remember the sabbath day, and keep it holy . . . Verses 12-17 say, Honor your father and your mother . . . You shall not murder. You shall not commit adultery. You shall not steal. You shall not bear false witness against your neighbor. You shall not covet your neighbor's house; you shall not covet your neighbor's wife, or male or female slave, or ox, or donkey, or anything that belongs to your neighbor.

The Roman Catholic and the Lutheran Churches have the first commandment as, I am the LORD your God . . . You shall have no other gods before me, and the second commandment as, You shall not take the name of the LORD your God in vain. The Reformed, Anglicans (Episcopalians), and Orthodox make their first commandment as having no other gods before me, and the second commandment as not making any graven image. The Jews make the first commandment, I am the LORD your God; you shall have no other gods besides me. They have the second commandment as no graven image. The Jews make the ninth as no false witness and ten as no coveting as do the Reformed, Anglicans, and Orthodox. Lutherans and Roman Catholics both make the ninth commandment as not coveting your neighbor's wife and the tenth as not coveting his house or things.

The point is there is a difference on how the ten are numbered, and what is very interesting is that the word ten is never mentioned here although 34:28 calls them the Ten Commandments. Marc Zvi Brettler (2007) says there are thirteen statements. Exodus 34 and Deuteronomy 5 also lists the commandments which are similar but a little different. In fact it has been said there are over thirty minor variations. In the issue of posting the so-called Ten Commandments which group gets theirs posted?

One of the problems in posting teachings from the different world religions in public places in a multicultural society, which the United States is rapidly becoming, is whose teachings or whose version of the teachings (in reference to Christianity) will we place and why? Is the answer whoever is in the majority? If that is the answer for those who call themselves Christian, what will happen in areas or neighborhoods of the country that are not Christian? Or what will happen if this country continues its trend down through the years, and we have more Muslims or Hindus in an area where Christians are a minority, or even have a majority of those who do not believe in God? Another issue is: Does posting anyone's religious rules violate the Constitution of this country? The same problem presents itself with the issue of prayer in the schools.

Another name for the so-called Ten Commandments is the Decalogue. They are also called natural law by some, for they are reasonable. At least they are reasonable for how most of Western Civilization has historically defined reasonable, which is another issue in the discussion of natural law. The Ten Commandments are also called apodictic law, for they are considered to be basic, unconditional law. In the New Testament the Commandments are summed up by saying we are to love the Lord our God with all our heart, power, and might and our neighbor as ourselves.

In chapters 21-23 we see how from these basic laws, other laws were developed and expanded to meet the particular times and settings of the Israelite cultural situation. When they are applied culturally, they can become conditional and are called casuistic law or case law. The principle values remain permanent but how they are applied will change as situations change. Basically it is the type of situational law that is structured as follows, "if . . . then . . ." In these chapters of casuistic law we have what is called the book of the covenant or the Covenant Code.

For example, in Exodus 21:12-14 the difference in murder and manslaughter is distinguished. Those verses say, Whoever strikes a person mortally shall be put to death. If it was not premeditated, but came about by an act of God, then I will appoint for you a place to which the killer may flee. But if someone willfully attacks and kills another by treachery, you shall take the killer from my altar for execution. Verses 22-25 are an example. When people who are fighting injure a pregnant woman so that there is a miscarriage, and yet no further harm follows, the one responsible shall be fined what the woman's husband demands, paying as much as the judges determine. If any harm follows, then you shall give life for life, eye for eye, tooth for tooth, hand for hand, foot for foot, burn for burn, wound for wound, stripe for stripe.

In the first five books of the Bible the Israelites and later the Jewish Rabbis found 613 laws. An example of one of the laws is Ex 21:15-17, whoever strikes father or mother shall be put to death, and whoever curses father or mother shall be put to death. This is quite a challenge to those who pull different scriptures out of the OT as proof texts for modern day issues. As we move on this writer will give more examples of these 613 laws.

As law developed in the Old Testament (Torah) there is no real difference between civil, moral, religious, and ritual law, for Israel developed a type of theocracy. In a theocracy all law has a religious connotation as the government is controlled or greatly influenced by the religious leaders. In a theocracy there is no separation of church and state. Today in the Middle East this is called Sharia, and an example of what the Muslim fundamentalists are hoping to revive. There are some fundamentalist Christians in this country who also want to make their brand of Christianity the law as the OT did even though this is a violation of the Constitution.

In thinking about these issues we must deal with the fact that as there are different forms of Judaism, Islam, Hinduism and Buddhism so there are also many different forms of Christianity all using the Bible as their foundation. The issue is not if we would all use the Bible. The issue is how the different groups interpret and understand the Bible.

The book of the covenant or the Covenant Code begins at 20:22 and goes to 23:33. This writer will list a number of these laws in an interpretation of Bible exercise that will follow at the end of the Pentateuch found at the end of Deuteronomy. You may want to turn to them now to get a better idea what those laws entail.

It is important to understand that some of the laws are adjusted through time as the Israelites move through different rural cultures then become an urban society and eventually the strongest power in the world and then a conquered nation. To some extent the list of laws is expanded and adjusted through the years in view of the changing community needs and their moral development.

Again, this writer emphasizes, this is why it is dangerous for biblical novices or even those who are more than novices to pull out verses from the OT to prove a point. For example, in the OT taking interest on loaned money from a fellow believer is a sin; violation of the Sabbath law, and for a child to speak wrongly to his parents are both punished by death; but slavery, concubines, and polygamy are accepted. God's people today no longer accept such laws. Biblical interpretation is both a science and an art, so to be true to Scripture, responsible people need to pay attention to both its science and art as well as to the different methodologies that go with it. Understanding this principle does not mean there are no eternal truths.

The issue is how to determine those truths.

For the Jews the law is considered to be God's gift of grace, and it is considered a joy to obey God's laws. It is their loving response and thankful response to God for him choosing them as his special people. It is not considered to be a burden. They understand that the law is given by God to his people for their well being and the way to enter into a joyful relationship with him. Their obedience to the law is how they confirmed their covenant with God. Unfortunately, in NT times, and according to Jesus, many of the Pharisees made it a burden, and this is what Jesus will challenge.

In chapter 23 three very important annual religious festivals of worship called pilgrimage festivals are given in their origin. They are called pilgrimage festivals, for they are later held in Jerusalem at the temple, and all Jewish males who can are required to be there.

The Feast of Unleavened Bread in (15) at the time of the barley harvest became known as the Passover. No one is to appear before the Lord empty handed. An offering must always be made with worship. The second feast in (16) is the Feast of the Harvest or the Feast of Weeks at the time of the wheat harvest; it becomes known as Pentecost (Shavuoth). This will later be the time that the Jews celebrate the giving of the law to Moses. Also in (17) is the Feast of the Ingathering, called Tabernacles, Booths or Sukkoth. This is the harvest of fruits and vegetables. All these major religious holy days were first agricultural celebrations.

Chapter 24:4 says, And Moses wrote down all the words of the LORD. In (5-8) Moses takes blood from the sacrifices, and then reads the book of the covenant to the people. In verse 8 Moses takes the blood and dashes it on the people, and says, See the blood of the covenant that the LORD has made with you in accordance with all these words.

In the OT we learn that one enters the presence of God only through shed blood. We as humans have sinned, and sin means separation from God with death as the consequence. Only when the death penalty is satisfied, can one be brought back into the presence of God. The blood shows a death has taken place, and the animal is the substitute for the sinful human. The Qur'an rejects this theology, for they do not believe that God needs a mediator. Also they do not believe their sin is against God; sin only affects themselves and other humans.

The OT system of worship sets up worship rooted primarily in the sacrifice of animals. Over hundreds of years the people learn and have imprinted upon them the necessity and importance of shed blood. For Christians the ultimate sacrifice and the meaning of Christ's shed blood as the ultimate and final sacrifice for sin and death will then be understood as the culmination of a system begun centuries ago.

In chapter 25:1 The LORD said to Moses: Tell the Israelites to take for me an offering; from all whose hearts prompt them to give you shall receive the offering for me. Then through verse 7 he lists what the offering shall be. Verses 8-9 say, And have them make me a sanctuary, so that I may dwell among them. In accordance with all that I show you concerning the pattern of the tabernacle and of all its furniture, so you shall make it. Then the rest of the chapter describes the sanctuary and what shall be in it. (Later it will be called the tent of the meeting, then the tabernacle, then the temple. In the most holy place there will be an ark with a mercy seat on top representing God who covers sin.)

Verses 19-40 tell us that there is to be one cherub at one end and another at the other end, and they are to spread out their wings above the mercy seat facing each other. Their faces are turned toward the mercy seat which is on top of the ark. The mercy seat is the throne of the presence of God. (The Ten Commandments and Moses' staff will be kept in the ark. In the Jewish synagogue today the scrolls containing God's word are kept there.)

Separating the holy place from the most holy place will be a veil or curtain. In the holy place of the tabernacle will be the table of the bread of the presence, a lampstand of pure gold, and a menorah symbolizing God's light and freedom. (The menorah is still a major symbol in Jewish religion.) In chapter 26 the plan for the tabernacle or tent of meeting continues. It is very precise in order to show that one enters God's presence by following God's pattern. God dwells alone in the ark of presence. This chapter also mentions the curtain that is made to separate the holy place from the most holy place. Chapter 27 shows how the altar of burnt offerings is to be made for the animal sacrifices as well as the oil for the lamp.

Chapter 28 describes the vestments for the priests. The priests will come from Moses' brother Aaron and his sons who are Nadab, Abihu, Eleazar, and Ithamar. Even these had to be set apart and purified in order for one to be in the presence of the holy God. God lays down the terms by which anyone, even the priests, would enter his presence. The Urim and the Thummim are mentioned in verse 30. The Urim and the Thummim are used as lots of some type, used by the priests to help them make decisions. Some compare it to the throwing of the dice, except when done by the priest, the people believed that God would guide them.

Chapter 29 describes the ordination procedure, and chapter 30 describes the altar of incense where prayers offered to God rise up to him in the smoke of the incense. The sacred oil that consecrates, dedicates, and makes sacred is mentioned. Sacred oils (25-26) incense (7-9) and vestments (chapter 28) used by some modern Christian religions have their roots in these verses. They are used as symbols by some Christian churches.

In chapter 31 the importance of the Sabbath is stressed. Verses 15-16 say, Six days shall work be done, but the seventh day is a sabbath of solemn rest, holy to the LORD; whoever does any work on the sabbath day shall be put to death. Therefore the Israelites shall keep the sabbath, observing the sabbath throughout their generations, as a perpetual covenant. (In contemporary usage Sabbath is capitalized, but in the Bible it is not capitalized. The reader will observe this in the following paragraph and throughout the book.) (This writer wonders if this law were followed today how many Christians or Jews would be left.) Verses 17-18 say, It is a sign forever between me and the people of Israel that in six days the LORD made heaven and earth, and on the seventh day he rested, and was refreshed. When God finished speaking with Moses on Mount Sinai, he gave him the two tablets of the covenant, tablets of stone, written with the finger of God.

The Sabbath law is not only about God's desire to have humankind worship him consistently but to keep laborers from being exploited seven days a week in order to give them rest. Keeping the Sabbath is a holy sign between God and his people. It confirms the covenant between them and their God that he is their God and they are his people.

Chapter 32:1 says, When the people saw that Moses delayed to come down from the mountain, the people gathered around Aaron, and said to him, "Come, make gods for us, who shall go before us; as for this Moses, the man who brought us up out of the land of Egypt, we do not know what has become of him." They persuaded Aaron to make them a golden calf from their gold rings. It was just like the one in Egypt. In verses 5-6 Aaron builds an altar before it and the people worship it. Verses 9-10 say, The LORD said to Moses, "I have seen this people, how stiff-necked they are. Now let me alone, so that my wrath may burn hot against them and I may consume them;

and of you I will make a great nation."

Moses begs for their mercy in verses 11-14 saying, "O LORD, why does your wrath burn hot against your people, whom you brought out of the land of Egypt with great power and a mighty hand? Why should the Egyptians say, 'It was with evil intent that he brought them out to kill them in the mountains, and to consume them from the face of the earth'? Turn from your fierce wrath; change your mind and do not bring disaster on your people. Remember Abraham, Isaac, and Israel, your servants how you swore to them by your own self, saying to them, 'I will multiply your descendants like the stars of heaven, and all this land I have promised I will give to your descendants, and they shall inherit it forever.' " Verse 14 says, And the LORD changed his mind about the disaster that he planned to bring on his people.

When Moses came down from the mountain with the two tablets of God's writings and saw the false god, (19) says, he threw the tablets from his hands and broke them at the foot of the mountain. (This symbolized that the people had broken the covenant with God.) In verse 21 Moses said to Aaron, "What did these people do to you that you have brought so great a sin upon them?" Aaron in (22) said, "Do not let the anger of my lord burn hot; you know the people, that they are bent on evil . . ." (Like Adam and Eve he does not take responsibility for his part but blames the people. Is this not still a pattern with humankind?)

Then in (26) Moses stood in the gate of the camp, and said, "Who is on the LORD's side? Come to me!" And all the sons of Levi gathered around him. Then Moses told them to take their swords and kill those who worshiped the golden calf, and three thousand were killed that day. Moses in (29) said, "Today you have ordained yourselves for the service of the LORD, each one at the cost of a son or a brother, and so have brought a blessing on yourselves this day." (Many are appalled at this violence, but is the writer expressing God's feeling toward idolatry?)

Did the Levites really kill three thousand of their own that day, or is this the writer's attempt to show why only the Levites are permitted to work in the temple? Was that number correct, or is it a symbolic number to simply represent that a huge number of people were involved in false worship? Or is the story based on history but greatly exaggerated like a hyperbole to get the point across that those who worship false gods will eventually be destroyed, or destroy themselves? The point is that a holy God will not tolerate his people worshiping other gods.

Is this message just for those times, or is it also a message for people today, for those who worship the idols of money, wealth, things, country, family, sex, pleasure, or whatever it is that is more important for people, than the one God? As far as the notion of numbers in the Bible, most scholars agree that it is difficult to interpret numbers simply because the Israelites, many times, used numbers as symbols. Scholars know for sure that each Hebrew letter had a numerical amount assigned to it.

Moses continues to pray for God's forgiveness, and God forgave. Even so in (35) he sends a plague upon the people. The theology seems to be that God forgives the group for its sin, but those responsible must pay the price and reap the consequences of their sin. In the process we learn that the consequence of sin has an effect upon the group and even on those not responsible. The idea is that sin has lasting consequences even upon the innocent. From the beginning of the Bible to its end we learn that God is a God of love and full of mercy and forgiveness, but God is also a God of wrath and will execute justice upon those who ignore him, or make other things more important to them than him and his teachings.

Chapter 33:1-3 says The LORD said to Moses, "Go leave this place, you and the people you have brought up out of the land of Egypt, and go to the land of which I swore to Abraham, Isaac, and Jacob saying, 'To your descendants I will give it.' I will send an angel before you, and I will drive out the Canaanites, the Amorites, the Hittites, the Perizzites, the Hivites, and the Jebusites. Go up to a land flowing with milk and honey; but I will not go up among you, or I would consume you along the way, for you are a stiff-necked people."

Moses asks God to go with him, and in (14) God says to Moses, "My presence will go with you, and I will give you rest." Moses in (15-16) asks, "If your presence will not go, do not carry us up from here. For how shall it be known that I have found favor in your sight, I and your people, unless you go with us? In this way, we shall be distinct, I and your people, from every people on the face of the earth." Verses 17-20 say, the LORD said to Moses, "I will do the very thing that you have asked; for you have found favor in my sight, and I know you by name." But in (20) he said, "you cannot see my face; for no one shall see me and live."

In chapter 34 God tells Moses to prepare two tablets so he can once again write his commandments. Then God renews the covenant with Moses revealing more of his character. Verses 6-8 say, The LORD passed before him and proclaimed, The LORD, the LORD, a God merciful and gracious, slow to anger, and abounding in steadfast love and faithfulness, keeping steadfast love for the thousandth generation, forgiving iniquity and transgression and sin, yet by no means clearing the guilty, but visiting the iniquity of the parents upon the children and the children's children, to the third and fourth generation. (This means the consequence of a sinful life has its influence for generations.) Verse 8 says, Moses quickly bowed his head toward the earth and worshiped. He said, " If now I have found favor in your sight, O Lord, I pray, let the Lord go with us. Although this is a stiff necked people, pardon our iniquity and our sin, and take us for your inheritance."

In verses 11-16 God says, Observe what I command you . . . Take care not to make a covenant with the inhabitants of the land to which they are going, or it will become a snare among you. You shall tear down their altars, break their pillars, and cut down their sacred poles (for you shall worship no other god, because the LORD whose name is jealous is a jealous God). You shall not make a covenant with the inhabitants of the land, for when they prostitute themselves to their gods and sacrifice to their gods, someone from among them will invite you, and you will eat of the sacrifice. And you will take wives from among their daughters for your sons, and their daughters will prostitute themselves to their gods will make your sons also prostitute themselves to their gods. Then in (17-27) some key laws are listed which will be dealt with in more detail in an exercise listed after the Pentateuch.

Verse 28 says, He (Moses) was there with the LORD forty days and forty nights; he neither ate bread nor drank water. And he wrote on the tablets the words of the covenant, the Ten Commandments. Then (29) says, Moses came down from Mount Sinai. As he came down from the mountain with the two tablets of the covenant in his hand, Moses did not know that the skin of his face shone because he had been talking with God.

In chapters 35-39 the tabernacle is made with all the furnishings as well as the vestments for the priests. All of this will eventually be part of the temple at the time of David and Solomon. Bezalel and his partner Oholiab are in charge. Chapter 40 is a good summary on the set up for the tabernacle as the writer attempts to show that God's glory and presence reside in the tabernacle and with his people even though they are a stiff-necked people. For the next 300 years the tent will be the focal point for worshiping God until it is replaced by the temple of Solomon.

EXODUS

In Exodus journey is still a major theme as it is in Genesis. In Exodus the movement from slavery to the giving of God's laws to his people, and worship is a major advancement. God is now intensely present with the people he has chosen. He is present personally, rationally, and miraculously as he intervenes for them in the earth he has created.

The basic idea of Abraham, Joseph, and Moses is in the Qur'an. Some things are altered, and it is in a different format. Again, the Qur'an is written to recite and meditate upon. Much of it is psalm like, and often the literature can have a tendency to look like Daniel and the book of Revelation. In the Qur'an there is very little historical narration. The same pattern will be seen with Samuel, Saul, David, and Solomon. The Qur'an uses these great men basically only as moral examples to follow.

One promise to Abraham is in the process of being fulfilled, that is, I will make of you a great nation. The next promise to be fulfilled is for his people to have the land he promised to them. We will see fulfilling that promise will take awhile. First, more teaching has to be done, and the people need to go through more testing and discipline in order to develop into a more mature nation of people. We will see that God's people will wander for forty years in the wilderness because of their lack of faith and continued disobedience.

For Christians the writer of the NT book of 1 Corinthians 10:6-7 says concerning the events that are written in the OT, Now these things occurred as examples for us, so that we might not desire evil as they did. Do not become idolaters as some of them did; as it is written, the people sat down to eat and drink, and they rose up to play.

Islam on the other hand says when God disciplines or punishes a people as he does the Jews, he is rejecting them. Islam is very strong in their writings about staying away from idols in any form.

LEVITICUS

The name is taken from the tribe of Levi which was the tribe of Moses and his brother Aaron. Aaron and his descendants become the priests while the rest of the Levites become the assistants to the priests. In charge of the activity in the tabernacle, they become the teachers, musicians, administrators, judges, and in charge of the general care of the tabernacle. The Levites are the tribe set apart for the work and worship of God. God had claimed the first born from men and the flocks but took the Levites in place of the first born men. The Levites are to be supported by tithes.

The theme of Leviticus is that you shall be holy, for I your God am holy. The book describes the laws for worship much of it containing various animal sacrifices and burnt offerings. Many in the modern world are confounded by all the animal sacrifices, but in the ancient world the majority of religions had animal sacrifices. It is the outward way of worship to show inward devotion. Many ancient cultures even had human sacrifices.

In Leviticus the Holiness Code, including purity laws, and kosher food laws, in addition to the animal sacrifices, are highlighted. For Christians all these laws and sacrifices are provisional, reinterpreted and fulfilled in Christ, who is the fulfillment toward what the animal sacrifices are pointing. Jesus becomes the final and ultimate sacrifice, the true lamb of God that takes away the sin of the world.

For Christians all these OT sacrifices are types (typology) foreshadowing or pointing toward Christ. Because Christ fulfills what the OT is pointing toward, he has the authority to reinterpret the OT law for a new time and an eventual new covenant. In the new covenant there will be the elimination of the food laws and animal sacrifices. This is one major reason we need to be careful pulling out Scripture verses from the OT in order to support our current, particular theology or ideology.

Leviticus will express in more detail key holy days for the Jews such as Passover, Pentecost, Rosh Hashanah, Yom Kippur, and the Feast of Tabernacles developed from their agricultural festivals. The book of Leviticus is the center of the five books of the Pentateuch. This placement conveys the importance of worship for the life and well being of the community. Thus the primary emphasis of Leviticus is worship.

The book is also considered a manual for priests. Chapters 1-16 give matters that are handled directly by the priests. Chapters 17-27 treat the larger social areas of community behavior and public worship that express the spiritual heart of living within the covenant. The major theme is that a holy God desires worship from a holy people, and this holiness is to embrace all of life.

The nature of the sacrificial system in the first nine chapters is basically meaningless to moderns, but it is important to understand the concept and where it leads, for it is the foundation for understanding the death of Christ. If the reader decides to skim those chapters it is important to understand the basic concepts contained within them.

Chapter 1:1-3 says, The LORD summoned Moses and spoke to him at the tent of meeting, saying: Speak to the people of Israel and say to them: When any of you bring an offering of livestock to the LORD, you shall bring your offering from the herd or the flock. If the offering is a burnt offering from the herd, you shall offer a male without blemish; you shall bring it to the entrance of the tent of meeting, for acceptance in your behalf before the LORD.

In OT religion sin brings death and separation from God. The blood offered from the slain animal shows a death is being offered to satisfy the death penalty. The animal is God's acceptance for the human who is the sinner.

Verses 4-5 say, You shall lay your hand on the head of the burnt offering, and it shall be accepted in your behalf as atonement for you. The bull shall be slaughtered before the LORD; and Aaron's sons the priests shall offer the blood, dashing the blood against all sides of the altar that is at the entrance at the tent of meeting (See

Ex 29:10-14). In the laying on of hands the one who worships, symbolically identifies with the sacrifice presented. The act of atonement puts a cover over the sins of the one who worships. (see Ex 29: 30-37, Ezek 43:18-27).

Verse 9 says, its entrails and its legs shall be washed with water. Then the priest shall turn the whole into smoke on the altar as a burnt offering, an offering by fire of pleasing odor to the LORD. Verses 10-13 describe the burnt offering from the flock, the sheep, or goats. It is basically the same except it is offered on the north side of the altar. Verses 14-17 describe the burnt offering from birds which are turtledoves or pigeons.

Because God accepts this as atonement on behalf of the person, one can now enter God's presence.(Islam will reject the atonement concept for they do not believe God needs any sacrifice or mediation in order to forgive.) A holocaust offering is wholly burned signifying self dedication to God. It is offered as an atonement for the sins of the one who worships. As offerings are made glory, praise, and adoration are rendered to God. Verse 17 says the priest shall turn it into smoke on the altar . . . an offering by fire of pleasing odor to the LORD.

Chapter 2 describes the meal or cereal offerings of grain. Three different kinds of grain offerings are discussed: choice flour with olive oil, and the spice frankincense, or cakes without leaven, mixed with oil and parched or baked grain with oil, and frankincense.

In Jewish life leaven is not looked upon favorably. It is considered ritually unclean. Like leaven or yeast, honey causes flour to ferment and change grain products rendering them ritually impure. During Passover the home is cleared of leaven. Unleavened bread is the only bread used because during the Exodus, the Hebrews had to leave quickly; thus, the dough bread did not have time to rise.

Grain is a substitute offering for the poor who can not afford animals. The grain offering usually is a thanksgiving to God for good crops or to celebrate joyful times. In reference to the sacrifices (9) says, The priest shall . . . turn this into smoke on the altar, an offering by fire of pleasing odor to the LORD. Verse 13 says, with all your offerings you shall offer salt. (Salt symbolizes the covenant relationship upon which the system is based, for salt preserves. So salt shows the covenant is being preserved.) The priest may eat part of the grain offering as God's provision for their support.

Chapter 3 describes offerings of well being, or peace offerings. The sacrifice of well-being is a shared meal, a fellowship meal, a kind of communion service. Sometimes it seems to be called a peace offering. The meat is eaten by those who worship after the kidney, liver, and fat is burned. Verse 16 says, All fat is the LORD's. It shall be a perpetual statute throughout your generations, in all your settlements: you must not eat any fat or any blood. (Fat is defined as tail, inner organs, and their fat. Was this also God's way of protecting the human body from unhealthy fat?)

The main difference from the holocaust offering is that this offering is not burned up but is saved and eaten by the one who makes the offering with his family. It can be taken from either cattle, sheep, or goats, but not birds. Since it is for a group, a bird is too small. Like the holocaust it is without blemish, but unlike the holocaust it can be either male or female.

Chapter 4:1-5:13 describes the different sin or guilt offerings which are symbols of confession and repentance. This sacrifice deals with the times when a sacred thing has been violated, often by accident or without knowing it (unintentional sin). The sacrifice is necessary in order to atone for the loss of holiness and proper purity of holy things by an act of cleansing. This requires a bull to be killed if the offender is the group or a priest, but a goat suffices for a lay offender. The key part of the ritual is the sprinkling of the blood. Sprinkling of blood or oil seven times purifies the place of worship.

Chapter 5 describes the guilt or reparation offering. It differs from the sin offering slightly in its focus. Where the sin offering cleanses the defiled sanctuary and persons, the guilt offering is to strictly give back a reparation or payment to God for failure in something that should have been given or done. Not only must the wrong be fixed, but payment is due God. For this offering a ram (male) sheep is specified, and the blood is sprinkled on the altar. It is clearly a ritual of atonement for sin to heal the sinner of guilt.

Verses 5-7 say, When you realize your guilt in any of these, you shall confess the sin that you have committed. And you shall bring to the LORD as your penalty for the sin that you have committed, a female from the flock, a sheep or a goat, as a sin offering; and the priest shall make atonement on your behalf for your sin. But if you cannot afford a sheep, you shall bring to the LORD, as your penalty for the sin that you have committed, two turtle doves or two pigeons, one for a sin offering and the other for a burnt offering. (God always makes a way for the poor.)

In chapters 6:1-7:38 the specific actions of the priests for each of the above types of sacrifices are spelled out in more detail. The previous laws have dealt mainly with sacrifices to God. These laws concern injury to neighbor. Restitution must be made to the neighbor before the offender can be reconciled to God by a guilt or purification offering. There are drink offerings, wave offerings, heave offerings and other types. These are usually pared with other offerings.

Some scholars do not believe that in the OT there is a provision for intentional sins. Others believe they are included, but unintentional sins are stressed for the many who may think because they are unintentional sins, they do not need to be confessed with restitution made. Others say that only unintentional sins are atoned for in the daily sacrificial system, but intentional sins are atoned for once a year at the annual Day of Atonement (Lev 16).

Chapter 6:1-7 says, The LORD spoke to Moses, saying: When any of you sin and commit a trespass against the LORD by deceiving a neighbor in a matter of a deposit or a pledge, or by robbery, or if you have defrauded a neighbor, or have found something lost and lied about it—if you swear falsely . . . when you have sinned and realize your guilt, . . . you shall repay the principal amount and add one fifth to it . . . you shall bring to the priest, as your guilt offering to the LORD, a ram without blemish from the flock, or its equivalent, for a guilt offering. The priest shall make atonement on your behalf before the LORD, and you shall be forgiven for any of the things that one may do and incur guilt thereby.

In chapter 7 the instructions seem to combine the thanksgiving offering and the well-being offering into one thanksgiving sacrifice of well-being. Elsewhere the offerings seem to be distinct. Verse 16 mentions a votive offering and free will offering. A votive offering is a sacrifice offered to God by one who has successfully fulfilled a vow made to God. A freewill offering is a sacrifice offered to God as a voluntary and spontaneous expression of happiness and gratitude. In 7:28-36 the elevation offering is transferred from the one who worships to the priest to signify that the sacrifice to God comes through a mediator.

Chapter 8 describes the priestly ordination rites for Aaron and his sons who become the priests, and chapter 9 is the inauguration of Aaron's priesthood. (Previous to this time sacrifices were offered by heads of families.) Aaron is the first high priest. After Aaron dies the high priest is to come from Aaron's sons and their descendants.

Chapter 8:30 says, Moses took some of the anointing oil and some of the blood that was on the altar and sprinkled them on Aaron and his vestments, and also on his sons and their vestments. Thus he consecrated Aaron and his vestments, and his sons and their vestments. In chapter 9:7 Aaron begins his duties. Moses said to Aaron, "Draw near to the altar and sacrifice your sin offering and your burnt offering, and make atonement for yourself and for the people; and sacrifice the offering of the people, and make atonement for them; as the LORD commanded."

From verses 8-18 the offerings listed are sin, burnt, grain or meal, and well being or peace. The sin offering denotes purification, the burnt offering indicates self-surrender to God, the grain or meal offering indicates consecration of labor, and the well-being or peace offering symbolizes fellowship with each other and God.

Chapter 10:1-3 says, Now Aaron's sons, Nadab and Abihu, each took his censer, put fire in it, laid incense on it; and they offered *unholy* fire before the LORD, such as he had not commanded him. And fire came out from the presence of the LORD and consumed them, and they died before the LORD. Then Moses said to Aaron, "This is what the LORD meant when he said, 'Through those who are near me I will show myself holy, and before all the people I will be glorified.' " And Aaron was silent.

This is a lesson about God's holiness. Even the sons of Aaron will be struck down when they fail to observe the proper awe and correct manner of approaching the divine presence. When procedures are violated, God becomes a consuming fire. The modern day reaction of many usually is, why are not they given another chance; it seems so unfair? The message to be learned is that things are to be done God's way not humans' way.

The NT in 1 Corinthians 10: 6, in reference to the OT illustrations, says, these things occurred as examples for us, so that we may not desire evil as they did. God is beginning to teach us through the inspired writings that when we do things in opposition to God's command, we sin, and the eventual result is death. A holy God is serious about his direct commands. Here we are taught that coming before God is a serious thing not to be done with nonchalance. Moses then in (6) tells Aaron and his sons, Eleazer and Ithamar that because of Nadab and Abihu's flagrant violation of God's command, they are not to mourn them.

In Chapters 11-15 clean and unclean is established. All God's people including lay people are called to holiness. The word holy occurs more than eighty times.

These are the purity laws. These teachings are basically dealing with ritual cleanness and uncleanness. That which is unclean is pronounced ritually unholy, but it is not considered sin in the sense that we moderns understand sin. They are not issues of morality opposed to immorality. It should be seen more as a worship or ritual sin. The purity laws functioned as part of a social symbol system that identified certain natural boundaries and separated them from the pagan world in which they lived. When the boundaries are violated, the result is uncleanness.

Other than the ritual aspect and the boundaries issue, some of the possible reasons for declaring something unclean had to do with sanitation and hygiene issues in times much different from our own. This also is to create a people different from other nations, particularly, in religious practices where the effort is to be separate from pagan practices. Many Jews, even today, believe the purpose for the food laws is to turn every meal into a religious experience.

With respect to fish, animals, and birds, only fish that swim, birds that fly, and animals that graze are declared clean; all others are not quite perfect, thus declared unclean. Some theologians believe their imperfection, if that is the case, is the result of original sin impacting nature. Examples are flightless birds, sea creatures that walk like animals, animals that crawl close to the ground like insects. Examples will be seen in the next few chapters. There are those who think that because they do not quite reach the exact standard of original perfection, they are considered somewhat imperfect, and ritually unclean. Who knows?

With other areas such as birth, death, loss of bodily fluids, some ask why purity laws in those areas? One answer is that many areas of human life touch the mystery of the divine, and in those areas there can be nothing impure. Thus, it is not just sacred space such as places like temples, but also sacred moments such as birth, death, marriage, and holy days. It is also those areas of everyday experience that involve life and death, including the mysterious power of sexual activity, infection, and the dangerous loss of blood and other bodily fluids. Purity laws are necessary in these areas also. Overall, these statutes may be put forth because, at this particular time in world history, it was necessary to teach the people about holiness and even health. These laws do have the best interest of the community at heart.

In chapter 11:1-47 the unclean animals are listed. Some of them are the camel, rabbit, pig, rock badgers, anything in water that does not have fins and scales such as shrimp, lobster, oyster, clam, crab, and scallop. Also unclean are the eagle, vulture, osprey, raven, ostrich, hawk, sea gull, owl, stork, heron, weasel, mouse, lizard, and the gecko. Winged insects are unclean, but the locust, cricket, and grasshopper are considered clean. Most things that crawl are forbidden. Any animals with paws are forbidden.

Why some are considered clean and others unclean is, other than what is stated above, somewhat of a mystery. But even today some of these are not considered good to eat, and others seem to easily spread bacteria and are conducive to allergies. Basically, in some of these areas, it is possible that God is using the system of clean and unclean to teach a form of health and sanitation until science catches up.

It is also, and probably most importantly, a means to begin to teach his people about the concept of holiness and that God is a holy God calling his people to be holy. God is also teaching his people that they are to be different from the people of the culture who are worshiping the pagan gods. In the NT Jesus will completely eliminate this clean and unclean system and focus on a clean or unclean heart. Again, this is another good reason not to pull verses out of the context of scripture to prove a point.

Chapter 12:1-8 discusses purification after childbirth and rules of worship. Verse 2 says, If a woman conceives and bears a male child she shall be ceremonially unclean seven days; as at the time of her menstruation, she shall be unclean.

Why this is so has confounded many, but it appears that blood represents life, and any loss of blood even in childbirth represents death, thus making one unclean. The mother's time of purification in (4) is thirty-three days. During this time she may not touch anything holy or enter the sanctuary. Again ritual uncleanness in this sense is not sin as we understand it today. Verses 5-6 inform us that if a woman bears a female child the time for everything doubles. Why this is so is also a mystery. After her purification for childbearing she is to bring a first year lamb for a burnt offering and a pigeon or turtle dove for a sin offering. If she can not afford a lamb, she may bring two pigeons and two turtle doves, and then she will be pronounced clean by the priests.

In the Gospels, Mary, the mother of Jesus, brings pigeons and turtle doves signifying her poverty. Jesus grew up understanding poverty which is apparently why he is so concerned with it, and why he has such compassion for those in poverty. Contrary to so many today, he never once blamed people for their poverty. Instead he constantly castigates the rich and powerful in their comfort and their general unconcern for those without power and wealth, and those who are suffering.

The next two chapters, 13 and 14, center on attempts to control disease. Disease also makes one ritually unclean possibly because disease is never intended by God. The laws put forth in these chapters are at a time when understanding disease and classification of disease are not well developed, so the people have to do the best they can to figure things out and preserve the community. But, again, it must be stated that the Bible also is not meant to be a primer on science. Each generation must determine what best serves the health and stability of the community and their relationship with God. Possibly, this chapter for us today would be on par with such things as our modern day laws of sanitation, the operation of the Food and Drug Administration, guidelines for the manipulation of blood, and the Center for Disease Control.

We must keep in mind that in the OT health issues are religious issues. The ancients integrate all these issues with their religion where modern day people tend to separate them. It is interesting to note that new scientific studies are showing moderns the positive relationship between religion, prayer, and health.

Chapter 15 centers on what to do about semen and female genital discharge of blood. Keep in mind many of these laws are about being made holy (clean) in order to come into God's presence to worship. The Hebrew people believed that semen was for the purpose of conceiving life, and when it does not it is wasting its holy purpose; therefore, it is classified as ritual sin. Notice it is ritual sin not immoral sin. When the female is not impregnated, and the monthly discharge of blood results, it, too, is ritual sin. Semen and blood represent the forces of life and their loss represents death. In fact anyone sitting where someone has been makes them also ritually unclean. Therefore, the process of being made ritually clean again is stated, so one can enter worship. Again, it has nothing to do with what we moderns understand about being clean and unclean or sin; it is establishing boundaries for worship rituals in another time era.

The writer is teaching about a holy God who will only accept holiness in his presence and the importance of being made clean through the methods given by God before coming into his presence. Holiness will be defined in a different way in the NT. Verse 31 says, Thus you shall keep the people of Israel separate from their uncleanness, so that they do not die in their uncleanness by defiling my tabernacle that is in their midst. (From the teachings in this book Islam will develop purification and food laws also, but their rules will not be exactly as the Jews.)

Chapter 16 describes the importance of the Day of Atonement. Once a year the high priest goes into the most holy place of the tabernacle, which is the innermost part of the sanctuary. There the ark of the covenant and God's presence is located. The priest is to offer the blood of a bull and a ram for his sin, the sin of his people, and as (16-19) say, for the sanctuary, because of the uncleanness of the people of Israel, and because of their transgressions, . . . No one shall be in the tent of meeting from the time he enters to make atonement in the sanctuary until he comes out and has made atonement for himself and for his house and for all the assembly of Israel. Then he shall go out to the altar that is before the LORD and make atonement on its behalf, and shall take some of the blood of the bull and of the blood of the goat, and put it on each of the horns of the altar. He shall sprinkle some blood on it with his finger seven times, and cleanse it and hallow it from the uncleanness of the people of Israel.

In the Bible sin is to be considered both individual and communal. Because of the emphasis on individualism, we in America, too often do not consider the importance of communal or institutional sin. In the OT individual sin contaminated the community and the community had to be atoned for also. Later as we read the prophets, we will see how they understood that institutional or corporate sin also contaminates and influences individuals.

As the high priest made the sacrifice for both individual and communal sins, two goats are involved in the expiation or atonement for sin. Verses 7-8 say, He shall take the two goats and set them before the LORD at the entrance of the tent of meeting; and Aaron shall cast lots on the two goats, one lot for the LORD and the other for Azazel. No one really knows who or what Azazel is. Some think it may have been a desert demon, so the idea is to symbolize evil being deposited with evil. Others think it may be somehow associated with the Hebrew word for depart.

Verses 9-10 say, Aaron shall present the goat on which the lot fell for the LORD, and offer it as a sin offering; but the goat on which the lot fell for Azazel shall be presented alive before the LORD to make atonement over it, that it may be sent away in the wilderness to Azazel. Verses 21-22 say, Then Aaron shall lay both his hands on the head of the live goat, and confess over it all the iniquities of the people of Israel, and all their transgressions, all their sins, putting them on the head of the goat, and sending it away into the wilderness by means of someone designated for the task. The goat shall bear on itself all the iniquities to a barren region; and the goat shall be set free in the wilderness.

This goat is called the scapegoat which gives us the etiology of its modern day use. On this day the people's sins are covered and reborn to new life, but the sins are only covered to the next Day of Atonement a year away. The concept of being reborn is never a one time thing but a process that is to be renewed. It may be added that today each Jew is still to be yearly born of God. Thus for the Jew the Day of Atonement is still a very important holy day in Judaism. It is also called Yom Kippur. Today, the New Year begins with the blowing of the ram's horn called the Shofar, and these days are called the Days of Awe. It ends after ten days of repentance and the day called Yom Kippur.

Chapters 17 through 25 contain the Holiness Code. Many of these laws are included in the special exercise of interpretation at the end of Deuteronomy. The reader may want to turn to that section to view some of those laws.

Chapter 17 lays out instructions for slaughtering animals. All meat must be first offered to God and then eaten after it is made kosher. Chapter 18 lays out prohibitions concerning sexual relations, and new marriage laws are established. Verse 6 says, None of you shall approach anyone near of kin to uncover nakedness: I am the LORD. It seems that to uncover nakedness may mean to have sex with. In (24-30) we are informed that the land becomes defiled by the improper use of sex. The Canaanites defiled the land in this way with their worship of the pagan gods which is why God is giving the Israelites their land. Verse 28 says, the land will vomit you out for defiling it, as it vomited out the nation that was before you.

Chapter 19 stresses the ethical areas of life that bind all socially in their communal life. Verse 18 says, you shall love your neighbor as yourself. This entails being faithful to God and each other in both life and worship. God is attempting to move his people toward a world that once again can be considered good. Verses 33-34 extend the same love to resident aliens (immigrants). Love in this context is not so much an emotion but an action of kindness, social justice, and fairness.

Chapter 20 repeats a number of laws adding specific penalties for violations. Chapters 21-24 concentrate on the sacred areas of priestly ministry and worship.

This code of law centers on behaviors and rituals that promote communal stability in the sphere of daily life and worship. The purpose is stated in 19:2, You shall be holy, for I the LORD your God am holy. The call to be holy is a call to be true to the relationship in which God's people are called.

This code revises some of the covenant code called the book of the covenant located in Exodus. Here we learn that the laws move forward in a progressive manner building on the past as they adapt to new surroundings. We will see more of this development of the law in Deuteronomy, and much more when Jews apply the Talmud, Muslims the Qur'an, and for Christians when Jesus reinterprets the Old Testament law as the new covenant.

Chapter 23 describes in detail the major holy days: the Sabbath (3), Passover (5-8), The Feast of First Fruits (9-14), Pentecost (15-22), the Festival of Trumpets, Rosh Hashanah which is the New Year beginning the Days of Awe (23-29), leading to Yom Kippur (26-32) also called the Day of Atonement. Sukkoth is mentioned (33-43) which is also called the Festival of Booths, Tabernacles, or Sukkoth linked to the 40 years of wilderness wandering that we will learn about in the book of Numbers. The origin of these feast days is briefly described in previous chapters. Today, immediately after Sukkoth is Shmini Atzeret, the Eighth Day of Solemn Assembly and then Simhath Torah called the days of Rejoicing in the Torah. This is when the annual Torah reading for today's Jews is concluded and begins all over again.

In Chapter 24 the lamp in the holy place which is right outside the most holy place is described as well as its light which can only be lit by the high priest and is to continually burn. Also, twelve loaves of bread placed in two rows of six called the showbread are there, and they must be renewed each Sabbath.

Verses 13-23 inform us that all blasphemers are to be put to death; the whole congregation is to stone them. Anyone killing a human shall be put to death. Anyone killing an animal shall make restitution for it. Anyone maiming another shall suffer the same injury. There is to be the same law for the citizen as for the alien (immigrant).

In chapter 25:1-4 the LORD spoke to Moses on Mt Sinai saying: When you enter the land that I am giving you, the land shall observe a sabbath for the LORD. Six years you shall sow your field, and six years you shall prune your vineyard, and gather in their yield; but in the seventh year there shall be a sabbath of complete rest for the land, a sabbath for the LORD: you shall not sow your field or prune your vineyard.

This becomes known as the Sabbath year. In addition to this being a holy year this will also be a way to conserve the environment and fertility of the land. Thus early in the Bible God teaches his people that they are only stewards of the land, for the land is his. They are to respect the land and take care of it, for the land is only on loan to us.

Also the year of Jubilee (8-14) is established where after 49 years, in the fiftieth year, the land is to revert back to its original owner. Again, this is to remind everyone that the land is God's, but it is also a way to diminish poverty and to keep people who come upon hard times from being stuck in poverty forever. It is a way of giving people a new start. The land is not our private property forever. This is God's way to level the playing field, so everyone can get a new opportunity. This principle has been forgotten in modern times. Actually, we do not know even if the Hebrew people ever actually obeyed this law.

A verse from this passage about Jubilee (25:10) is inscribed on the Liberty Bell in Philadelphia. It says, Proclaim liberty throughout all the land. Notice the liberty in this context is not the liberty meant by most Americans when they apply the liberty bell statement. The Bible has a history of people taking from the Bible what they want and twisting it to support their particular religious, political, and economic ideology.

In this year of Jubilee all debts are cancelled, Hebrew slaves are to be set free, and lands returned to the original owners. The idea is that inherited wealth that keeps building up and elevating those who have not earned it is not good, especially if it is at the expense of giving all an equal opportunity. This is not beneficial for each individual or the community. It is interesting to note that some say inherited wealth in the United States may be as high as over sixty per cent. We are learning by experience that this is not necessarily positive for those who inherit the wealth or the country.

The original book of Leviticus seems to have ended here. The rest is an appendix. It is interesting at this point to note the number 7. Every 7th day is a Sabbath. Every 7th year is a Sabbatical year. Every 7th Sabbatical year is followed by a Jubilee year. The 7th month of the year is especially holy having three major sacred feasts. There are 7 weeks between Passover and Pentecost. Passover Feast lasts 7 days. Tabernacles Feast lasts 7 days. There is something mysterious and symbolic with the number 7.

Chapter 26 concludes the laws of Leviticus with a list of blessings and curses. Chapter 26:1-2 says, You shall make for yourself no idols and erect no carved images or pillars, and you shall not place figured stones in your land, to worship them; for I am the LORD your God. You shall keep my sabbaths and reverence my sanctuary: I am the LORD.

The commands of God will have cosmic consequences with the environment, for God in (3-6) says, If you follow my statutes and keep my commandments and observe them faithfully, I will give you your rains in their season, and the land shall yield its produce, and the trees of the field shall yield their fruit . . . you shall eat your bread to the full, and live securely in your land. And I will grant peace in the land, and (12) adds, I will walk among you, and will be your God, and you will be my people. (The writer is saying obedience to God has an effect in the cosmos.)

The OT teaches that corporate or institutional obedience and disobedience will have a consequence. Verses 27-33 inform us that on disobedience their cities will be destroyed, and they will be scattered among the nations. Verses 40-42 say, But if they confess their iniquity and the iniquity of their ancestors . . . if then their uncircumcised hearts are humbled and they make amends for their iniquity, then I will remember my covenant with Jacob . . . (Again, there is the "if" factor.)

Theologically the writer is saying disobedience has an adverse effect on both nature and the institutional socio-political realm while positive obedience is a means by which the divine order in creation can be actualized. Chapter 27, the last chapter in Leviticus, concerns vows made with respect to persons, animals, houses, land, and how to redeem those vows.

The emerging pattern of the tent of the meeting, later to become the tabernacle, and then the temple, symbolizes God's immanence and involvement with his people. Unlike the pantheism of some Far Eastern religions, the God of the Bible is transcendent and separate from his creation, yet still working his will and dwelling among his people while working in them, through them, and with them.

The book of Leviticus also makes plain that his people are sinful and may not enter his presence without being purified. In the Old Testament his people can not enter his presence directly. There must be a mediator. God's blessings come through a mediated presence; only the priests may offer sacrifice and enter the holy place in the temple, and only high priests can enter the most holy place.

Leviticus may not be a stimulating book for many, but for Christians it is the foundation for understanding the cross of Christ. The ninth chapter of the NT book of Hebrews connects the sacrifices of Leviticus with the sacrifice of Christ. Christ is the mediator of a new covenant (Testament). Under the law everything is purified by blood, and without the shedding of blood there is no forgiveness of sin (Heb 9:15-22). But for Islam they do not accept any mediator between God and humans, for in their opinion, God does not need a mediator in order to forgive sin.

For Christians Christ appeared once to remove sin for all by his sacrifice. In the OT sin is covered, but in the NT Christ not only covers sins but eliminates a person's sins forever. That does not mean Christians can not and will not sin again, for they will and do, but through his blood they believe they can be continually cleansed and purified. Other Christians retain the OT idea that sins are only covered believing that in this world they can not be eliminated.

Judaism, Christianity, and Islam are all rooted in the OT. Jews read Leviticus in the light of the Talmud; Muslims read it in the light of the Qur'an; and Christians read it in light of Christ and the NT; thus the OT is understood in different ways. The more modern people understand these basic writings, the more they will understand the teachings of Judaism, Christianity, and Islam.

For Christians, the NT is read in light of the OT, and the OT must be read in the light of the NT, and especially Jesus, for Jesus fulfilled the OT Scriptures and reinterprets them. The dietary laws, the clean and unclean laws, and even some moral practices such as polygamy, slavery, divorce, taking interest, and holy wars are just some examples of how Christians now read the old in light of Jesus and the NT.

Most Christians would accept the statement from St Augustine that God, the inspired author of both testaments, wisely arranged that the New be hidden in the Old and the Old be made manifest in the New. The books of the OT with all their parts are caught up in the proclamation of the gospel acquiring and showing forth their full meaning in the NT. It goes without saying that Jews and Muslims do not accept that teaching.

NUMBERS

Numbers is the story of forty years of wandering in the wilderness. The people murmur and complain even though God freed them from oppression and slavery and is leading them to the promised land. Manna, a honey like substance used for bread, quail for meat, and water are miraculously supplied. Men are sent into the new land to determine what it looks like, but when they return only Joshua and Caleb have the faith to go into the land. The rest are afraid.

As the people journey, Balaam, a prophet from Mesopotamia, is hired to curse God's people, but he is not able to do it. Instead an angel of God blocks the donkey, and the donkey speaks. Balaam eventually predicts a star will appear that NT writers will see as a prophecy of the Messiah. A strange story about a Bronze Serpent appears in this book. Those who complain about the food and water were bitten by poisonous snakes sent by God. God tells Moses to make a bronze serpent and put it on a pole. Then those who look upon the bronze serpent are healed. It becomes a type of Christ for Christians, for all who look to Jesus will also be healed.

The book of Numbers which the Hebrew Bible calls, "In the Wilderness," just as easily could be called the grumbling and complaining of a nation. It is a history of God's grace, human complaint, lack of faith, and subsequent disaster. It is also a story of God's patient perseverance with his people. It is called Numbers by Christians because of the numbering or census of the people in chapters 1-4 and again in chapter 26.

A major message is that the journey from faith to promise involves the challenge and testing of the wilderness. This concept can be applied to people's lives today. Life is a journey while we are in this world where challenge and testing will take place. Much of the time the Israelites spend in the wilderness is in an oasis called Kadesh-barnea. It seems that the time spent in the wilderness is a testing in order to discipline God's people and to teach them to trust and depend on God.

In chapter 1 Moses is commanded to take a census for military purposes. Males from twenty years and older are to be numbered, but no Levites are to be included, for they are in charge of the tabernacle and religious activity. The twelve tribes are maintained by counting the house of Joseph as two tribes: Ephraim and Manasseh. In Genesis Jacob adopted Joseph's two sons.

Chapter 1:1-3 says, The LORD spoke to Moses in the wilderness of Sinai, in the tent of meeting, on the first day of the second month, in the second year after they had come out of the land of Egypt, saying, Take a census of the whole congregation of Israelites, in their clans, by ancestral houses, according to the number of names, every male individually; from twenty years old and upward, everyone in Israel able to go to war. You and Aaron shall enroll them, company by company.

Verses 4-5 say, A man from each tribe shall be with you, each man the head of his ancestral house. These are the names of the men who shall assist you: The twelve tribes are then listed according to their numbers in 5-15. The names listed are Reuben, Simeon, Judah, Issachar, Zebulun, Ephraim, Manasseh, Benjamin, Dan, Asher, Gad, Naphtali. Levi is not listed, for the tribe will not be in military service. Then in (20-47) the exact number from each of the above tribes of those twenty years old and upward are listed.

Verses 48-54 involve only the Levites. They are not to be enrolled and no census taken on them. They are put in charge of the tabernacle and all its furnishings. Verse 51 says, When the tabernacle is to set out, the Levites shall take it down; and when the tabernacle is to be pitched, the Levites shall set it up. And any outsider that comes near shall be put to death.

In chapter 2 the twelve tribes are arranged around the tabernacle expressing the idea that God's presence is among his people. When the people move onward, each group marches in an assigned manner with the tribe of Judah in the lead.

Chapter 3 gives the lineage of Aaron and Moses who are Levites. Aaron's two sons, Eleazar and Ithamar, are the anointed priests while Aaron is the high priest. The first two sons of Aaron, Nadab and Abihu died before God because they offered improper worship. Aaron's descendants are to be the chief priests while the other Levites are to be the priestly assistants.

Chapter 3:11-13 says, Then the LORD spoke to Moses, saying: I hereby accept the Levites from among the Israelites as substitutes for all the first born that opens the womb among the Israelites. The Levites shall be mine, for all the firstborn are mine; when I killed all the firstborn in the land of Egypt, I consecrated for my own all the firstborn in Israel, both human and animal; they shall be mine; I am the LORD. Eleazar, son of Aaron the priest in (32) was to be chief over the leaders of the Levites and to have oversight of those who had oversight of the sanctuary.

In chapter 4 the Kohathites are to carry the holy things but only after the priests have assembled them, for only the priests may touch the holy things. If the Kohathites touch the holy things (15) says, they will die. God seems to be teaching that humans in general are too sinful to be in contact with the holy God. Only his special mediators can touch the holy vessels. (Is it possible that the holiness of God is a theme modern people need once again to be exposed to and understand?)

The Gershonites are in charge of transporting the curtains and coverings of the tent under the priest Ithamar's supervision. The Merarites are to look after and transport the framework also under Ithamar's supervision. Kohath, Gershon, and Merari are children of Levi (Gen 46:11). Moses was of the tribe of Levi, of the family of Kohath and was born to Amram and Jochebed. His brother was Aaron, and his sister was Miriam.

Chapter 5:1-3 says, The LORD spoke to Moses, saying: Command the Israelites to put out of the camp everyone who is leprous, or has a discharge, and everyone who is unclean through contact with a corpse; you shall put out both male and female, putting them outside the camp; they must not defile their camp, where I dwell among them. (This is because the tabernacle where God dwells is within the camp. This writer's guess is that health reasons are also involved in this decision.)

An interesting section of this chapter, which covers most of the chapter (11-31), is called the trial by ordeal something that was practiced by numerous ancient cultures. The trial is over a woman suspected of adultery who, if proven guilty, is put to death. The priest uses what is called holy water and orders the woman to drink it. Meanwhile, she takes the oath of a curse which states that if she has committed adultery she will have a miscarriage. (This is still done in parts of the developing world such as Africa and India. This writer wonders if the effect is more psychological than anything.)

Chapter 6 discusses the Nazirite vow which is a vow to separate oneself to God in a special way. The vow can be taken for a limited time or for life. Verses 1-4 say, The LORD spoke to Moses saying: Speak to the Israelites and say to them: When either men or women make a special vow, the vow of a Nazirite, to separate themselves to the LORD, they shall separate themselves from wine and strong drink; they shall drink no wine vinegar or other vinegar, and shall not drink any grape juice or eat grapes, fresh or dried. All their days as Nazirites they shall eat nothing that is produced by the grapevine, not even the seeds or the skins.

Verses 5-8 say, All the days of their Nazirite vow no razor shall come upon their head; until the time is completed for which they separated themselves to the LORD, they shall be holy; they shall let the locks of the head grow long. All the days that they separate themselves to the LORD they shall not go near a corpse. Even if their father or mother, brother or sister, should die, they may not defile themselves; because their consecration to God is upon the head. All their days as Nazirites they are holy to the LORD. When the vow was completed, the chapter describes the offerings to be made in worship which includes the hair from their shaved heads.

Chapter 6:24-26 also includes a well known blessing especially for Protestant Christians where God tells the priests to bless the people by saying the following. The LORD bless you and keep you; the LORD make his face to shine upon you, and be gracious to you; the LORD lift up his countenance upon you, and give you peace. Verse 27 says, So they shall put my name on the Israelites, and I will bless them.

Chapters 7-10 shift back to Exodus 40:17 and expands upon the setting up of the tabernacle and the preparation for moving the tabernacle as the people continue their journey.

In chapter 11 again the people complain that they do not have the good meat, fish, and vegetables they had in Egypt. They say in (4-6), "If only we had meat to eat! We remember the fish we used to eat in Egypt for nothing, the cucumbers, the melons, the leeks, the onions, and the garlic; but now our strength is dried up, and there is nothing at all but this manna to look at." Verse 10 says, Moses heard the people weeping throughout their families, all at the entrance of their tents. Then the LORD became very angry, and Moses was displeased.

In verses 11-15 Moses said to the LORD, "Why have you treated your servant so badly? Why have I not found favor in your sight, that you lay the burden of all these people on me? . . . Where am I to get meat to give to all this people? For they come weeping to me and say, 'Give us meat to eat!' I am not able to carry all this people alone, for they are too heavy for me. If this is the way you are going to treat me, put me to death at once—if I have found favor in your sight—and do not let me see my misery." (Eijah, Jeremiah, and many of the prophets called by God will also struggle under the pressure of standing with him and for him in a broken world. We learn that being a serious witness to God is not something to take lightly, and it is something most of us do not do very well.)

Verses 16-17 say, the LORD said to Moses, "Gather for me seventy elders of Israel, whom you know to be the elders of the people and officers over them; bring them to the tent of meeting, and have them take their place there with you. I will come down and talk with you there; and I will take some of the spirit that is on you and put it on them; and they shall bear the burden of the people along with you so that you will not bear it all by yourself. Verses 24-25 say, So Moses went out and told the people the words of the LORD; and he gathered seventy elders of the people, and placed them all around the tent. Then the LORD came down in the cloud and spoke to him, and took some of the spirit that was on him and put it on the seventy elders; and when the spirit rested on them, they prophesied. But they did not do so again.

Possibly in some way it may be compared to the miraculous activity upon the inspired men at the beginning of the Christian church but subsequently waned. This also suggests that Moses remains the one authoritative prophet or mediator of God's words to the people as in the time of the NT it will be Jesus.

Verses 26-30 say, Two men remained in the camp, one named Edad, and the other named Medad, and the spirit rested on them; they were among those registered, but they had not gone out to the tent, and so they prophesied in the camp. And a young man ran and told Moses, Eldad and Medad are prophesying in the camp." Joshua, son of Nun, the assistant of Moses, one of the chosen men, said, "My lord Moses, stop them!" But Moses said to him, "Are you jealous for my sake? Would that all the LORD's people were prophets, and that the LORD would put his spirit on them!" And Moses and the elders of Israel returned to the camp.

Then in verses 31-32 a wind went out from the LORD, and it brought quails from the sea and they fell beside the camp, about a day's journey on this side and a day's journey on the other side, all around the camp, about two cubits deep on the ground. So the people work all that day and night and all the next day, gathering the quails. But verse 33 says, the anger of the LORD was kindled against the people, and the LORD struck the people with a very great plague. (Apparently, God is wearied by their grumbling and complaining.)

In chapter 12:1-2 the first of many power struggles occurs in the community. The issue will always be who speaks for God. Miriam and Aaron spoke against Moses because of the Cushite woman whom he had married, and they said, "Has the LORD only spoken through Moses? Has he not spoken through us also?" Verse 3 adds, Now the man Moses was very humble, more so than anyone on the face of the earth.

The God heard this and in (10) makes Miriam leprous. Apparently she is the leader of the rebellion. Aaron saw this and in (11) said, "Oh, my LORD do not punish us for a sin we have so foolishly committed. Do not let her be like one stillborn . . ." In (13-14) Moses cried to the LORD, "O God, please heal her." But the LORD said to Moses, "If her father had but spit in her face, would she not bear her shame for seven days? Let her be shut out of the camp for seven days and after that she may be brought in again." (The issue is over who is in charge, and who speaks for God. God shows that it is Moses. Throughout the Pentateuch we see how positively God responds to the mediation of Moses.)

Chapter 13:1-3 says, The LORD said to Moses, "Send men to spy out the land of Canaan which I am giving to the Israelites; from each of their ancestral tribes you shall send a man, every one a leader among them." So Moses sent them from the wilderness of Paran, according to the command of the LORD, all of them leading men among the Israelites. Verses 4-15 name the twelve men selected, one from each of the tribes, and verse 16 says, Moses changed the name of Hoshea son of Nun to Joshua. (Notice it does not say son of a nun but is son of a man named Nun.)

At the end of 40 days they return. In (27-29) they said, "We came to the land to which you sent us; it flows with milk and honey, and this is its fruit. (Milk and honey symbolizes the land as one with good raw materials.) Yet the people who live in the land are strong, and the towns are fortified and very large; and besides we saw the descendants of Anak (giants) living there."

Verses 30-33 say, Caleb quieted the people before Moses, and said, "Let us go up at once and occupy it, for we are well able to overcome it." Then the men who had gone up with him said, "We are not able to go up against this people, for they are stronger than we." So they brought to the Israelites an unfavorable report of the land they had spied out saying, "The land that we have gone through as spies is a land that devours its inhabitants; and all the people we saw in it are of great size. There we saw the Nephilim (the Anakites come from the Nephilim); and to ourselves we seemed like grasshoppers, and so we seemed to them."

These people were associated with the giants, the goliaths of ancient times, and were gigantic and very strong people. This happened at Kadesh-barnea, the desert location where the camp will remain much of their remaining years.

Chapter 14:1-4 says, Then all the congregation raised a loud cry, and the people wept that night. And all the Israelites complained against Moses and Aaron; the whole congregation said to them, "Would that we had died in the land of Egypt! Or would that we had died in this wilderness! Why is the LORD bringing us into this land to fall by the sword? Our wives and our little ones will become booty; would it not be better for us to go back to Egypt?" So they said to one another, "Let us choose a captain and go back to Egypt."

Joshua and Caleb in verses 7-10 said, "The land that we went through as spies is an exceedingly good land. If the LORD is pleased with us, he will bring us into this land and will give it to us, a land that flows with milk and honey. Only do not rebel against the LORD; and do not fear the people of the land; for they are no more than bread for us; their protection is removed from them, and the LORD is with us; do not fear them." But the whole congregation threatened to stone them.

God is unhappy with the lack of faith and trust of the people and in (12) threatens to strike them with pestilence and begin all over with a new generation. In (19) Moses prays to God to forgive them. Verses 20-25 say, Then the LORD said, "I do forgive, just as you have asked; nevertheless--as I live, and as all the earth shall be filled with the glory of the LORD--none of the people who have seen my glory and the signs I did in Egypt and in the wilderness, and yet have tested me these ten times and have not obeyed my voice, shall see the land that I swore to give to their ancestors; none of those who despised me shall see it. But my servant Caleb, because he has a different spirit and has followed me wholeheartedly, I will bring into the land into which he went, and his descendants shall possess it. Now since the Amalekites and the Canaanites live in the valleys, turn tomorrow and set out for the wilderness by the way of the Red Sea." (God forgives through the mediation of Moses, but the people will bear the consequences of their sin.)

Verses 26-34 say, the LORD spoke to Moses and Aaron saying, How long shall this wicked congregation complain against me? I have heard the complaints of the Israelites, which they complain against me. Say to them, "As I live" says the LORD, "I will do to you the very things I heard you say: your dead bodies shall fall in this very wilderness; and of all your number, included in the census, from twenty years old and upward, who have complained against me, not one of you shall come into the land in which I swore to settle you, except Caleb son of Jephunneh and Joshua son of Nun . . . According to the number of the days in which you spied out the land, forty days, for every day a year, you shall bear your iniquity, forty years, and you shall know my displeasure."

In verses 40-42 The people went to the hill country saying, "Here we are we will go up to the place that the LORD has promised, for we have sinned." But Moses said, "Why do you continue to transgress the command of the LORD? That will not succeed. Do not go, for the LORD is not with you; . . ." They went anyway, and verse 45 says, the Amalekites and the Canaanites who lived in that hill country came down and defeated them, pursuing them as far as Hormah.

Chapter 15 shifts back to various laws. A statement is made about unintentional sin and intentional sin. Sacrifices for unintentional sin are mentioned, but apparently there is no forgiveness for intentional sin that is defined as bold sin. (This writer believes this may have reference to those who sin with no intention of repenting.)

Verse 30 says, whoever acts high-handedly, whether a native or an alien, affronts the Lord, and shall be cut off from among the people. Because of having despised the word of the LORD and broken his commandment, such a person shall be utterly cut off and bear the guilt. Then in (32-36) a man sins against the Sabbath, and his penalty is death. The whole congregation stones him to death. Apparently God took seriously the command to honor the Sabbath.

In verses 37-40 The LORD says to Moses, Speak to the Israelites, and tell them to make fringes on the corners of their garments throughout their generations and to put a blue cord on the fringe at each corner. You have the fringe so that, when you see it, you will remember all the commandments of the LORD and do them, and not follow the lust of your own heart and your own eyes. So you shall remember and do all my commandments, and you shall be holy to your God. (These become prayer shawls for the Jews called a tallit. External symbols are important, for they are to remind the people of what God expects.)

In chapter 16 there is another revolt. Some Reubenites revolt against the fact that only Levites from Aaron could be priests. A confrontation is set with Korah, Dathan, and Abiram being the leaders and 250 of their followers. Moses tells them in (5) that the LORD would decide the next day when they appear before the LORD to worship.

The next day as they appeared before the LORD, Moses in (28-30) said, "This is how you shall know that the LORD has sent me to do all these works; it has not been of my own accord: If these people die a natural death, or if a natural fate comes on them, then the LORD has not sent me. But if the LORD creates something new, and the ground opens its mouth and swallows them up, with all that belongs to them, and they go down alive into Sheol, then you shall know that these men have despised the LORD." In verses 31-35 the ground opens and swallows them all. Verse 35 says, fire came out from the LORD and consumed the two hundred fifty men offering the incense.

The writer is saying that God does not appreciate those who rebel against his commands or from those who teach those commands; they will bear the consequences of their actions.

Verses 38-39 inform us that their censers are then hammered into plates as a covering for the altar by Eliezar the priest. Verse 40 says this is a reminder to the Israelites that no outsider, who is not of the descendants of Aaron, shall approach to offer incense before the LORD, so as not to become like Korah and his company--just as the LORD had said to him through Moses.

Verse 41 says, On the next day, however, the whole congregation of the Israelites rebelled against Moses and against Aaron, saying, "You have killed the people of the LORD." In verse 46 wrath goes out from God, and he sends a plague upon the people. Moses tells Aaron to offer worship for the people to make atonement. In (47-49) Aaron does as Moses said, and as he makes atonement for the people, the plague stops.

Those who died from the plague were 14,700. (Notice the number includes a 7, then 2 x 7 x 1000 and then 7 x 100.) Numbers are not always to be understood literally, for the Israelites assigned meaning to numbers, meanings that we do not always understand.

In chapter 17:1-5 The LORD spoke to Moses saying: Speak to the Israelites, and get twelve staffs from them, one from each ancestral house, from all the leaders of their ancestral houses. Write their names on each one. On Levi's staff the name Aaron is to be written. God said, whoever's staff blossoms will be who he is validating as priest. The next day (8-9) tells us that the staff of Aaron from the house of Levi sprouts and put forth buds, producing blossoms, and bearing ripe almonds. In verses 10-11 the LORD says to Moses, "Put back the staff of Aaron before the covenant, to be kept as a warning to rebels, so that you may make an end of complaints against me, or else they will die." Moses did so; just as the LORD commanded him.

Chapter 18 states that when Aaron dies, only his sons will be responsible for the priesthood, while the other Levites will be their assistants. They are to be supported from the offerings, for when the Levites enter the land of Canaan, they will have no land assigned to them. As God said in verse 20, I am your share and your possession among the Israelites. Verses 25-30 tell us that the people are to tithe to the Levites, and the Levites are to tithe to the Aaronic priests.

In chapter 19 the ceremonial cleansing rite for purifying a person who is defiled by a corpse is given. Why one is declared unclean when a corpse is contacted is a mystery. Possibly it is a reminder that death was never intended by God and did not happen until humans sinned. The process of cleansing begins as the ashes of a red heifer are mixed with water. The people then purify themselves with this water so that when they enter the tabernacle, they do not contaminate it. Some of the early church fathers saw in this a type of the waters of baptism. Today the Roman Catholic Church has holy water as one enters to worship to remind them of their baptism. The Orthodox Church also uses holy water.

There seems to be a gap of 38 years between the nineteenth and twentieth chapters. In chapter 20:1-5 Miriam dies and is buried in Kadesh. Again, there is no water, so the people quarrel with Moses. Verses 3-5 say, "Would that we had died when our kindred died before the LORD! Why have you brought the assembly of the LORD into this wilderness for us and our livestock to die here? Why have you brought us out of Egypt, to bring us to this wretched place? It is no place for grain, or figs, or vines, or pomegranates; and there is no water to drink."

In verses 7-8 The LORD spoke to Moses, saying: Take the staff, and assemble the congregation, you and your brother Aaron, and command the rock before their eyes to yield its water. Thus you shall bring water out of the rock for them; thus you shall provide drink for the congregation and their livestock.

After the people gather, Moses in (10-11) said to the people, "Listen you rebels, shall we bring water for you out of the rock?" Then Moses lifted his hand and struck the rock twice with the staff; water came out abundantly, and the congregation and their livestock drank. But in (12-13) the LORD said to Moses and Aaron, "Because you did not trust in me, to show my holiness before the eyes of the Israelites, therefore you shall not bring this assembly into the land that I have given them." These are the waters of Meribah, where the people of Israel quarreled with the LORD, and by which he showed his holiness.

At this point it is very difficult to know what Moses and Aaron did wrong. Possibly they forgot to give the credit to God making it appear as though they accomplished the miracle, or maybe they doubted God could show mercy to such a rebellious people. Maybe that is why the rock was struck twice. A later book will suggest that the problem was in striking the rock when Moses was told to just command the rock to give water. Psalm 106:32-33 tells us that Moses spoke words that were rash. We will also be told that Moses will not enter because he will suffer vicariously for the sins of the people. The writers seem to be searching for a credible explanation. The passage may also be saying that God does not have to depend on any one leader no matter how great. A single answer is difficult to pin point.

In verses 14-21 Moses sent a request from Kadesh to the king of Edom requesting that the congregation be permitted to go through the land of Edom, but he is refused, so they went to Mt Hor, and in (29) Aaron dies and is buried. He is mourned for thirty days. Thirty days of mourning for a death will become a Jewish tradition.

In chapter 21 the people again murmur and complain about food and water wishing that they had stayed in Egypt. Verses 6-9 say, Then the LORD sent poisonous serpents among the people, and they bit the people, so that many Israelites died. The people came to Moses and said, "We have sinned by speaking against the LORD and against you; pray to the LORD to take away the serpents from us." So Moses prayed for the people. And the LORD said to Moses, "Make a poisonous serpent, and set it on a pole; and everyone who is bitten shall look at it and live." So Moses made a serpent of bronze, and put it on a pole; and whenever a serpent bit someone, that person would look at the serpent of bronze and live.

This is difficult to understand since they were not to make anything that represents or could represent an idol, but at this point the serpent is not an idol, for it is not to be worshiped. They are simply following the instructions that God gave Moses. This later becomes a type of Christ who later on a cross will bring life to those who look to him.

In verses 21-26 as the Israelites move on they want to pass through the land of King Sihon of the Amorites, but he will not let them pass through his territory. So they defeat him and pass through. Next they desire to go through the land of Bashan but King Og attempts to stop them. In verses 34-35 the LORD said to Moses, "Do not be afraid of him; for I have given him into your hand, with all his people, and all his land. You shall do to him as you did to King Sihon of the Amorites, who ruled in Heshbon." So they kill him, his sons, and all his people, and they took possession of his land.

The message of the writer seems to be that if anyone attempts to interfere in God's plan, they will bring destruction upon themselves. An interesting note is that King Og is one of the ancient giants. He is of the Rephaim who like the Anakim are a gigantic people. Deut:3:11-12 describes his huge bed that becomes a museum piece in Rabbah, a city on the Ammonite border.

Chapters 22-25 involve another short story based on the history of God supernaturally leading Israel to the promised land. Some call this a fable, but if it is a fable, God can also reveal his inspired message through fables. In 22:1-3 the Israelites go into Moab. The Moabite king, Balak, and his people are overcome with fear, for they saw what Israel did to the Amorites. So he invites a Mesopotamian diviner named Balaam to put a curse on the Israelites. Balaam and a talking donkey are central to the story as Balaam ends up blessing the Israelites even though it was not his desire or purpose.

Balaam in chapter 23:8 says, How can I curse whom God has not cursed? In (25-26) Balak said to Balaam, "Do not curse them at all, and do not bless them at all." But Balaam answers Balak, "Did I not tell you, 'Whatever the LORD says, that is what I must do'?" Chapter 24:2 says, the spirit of God came upon him. His famous prophecy in 24:17-19 is that a star shall come out of Jacob, and a scepter shall rise out of Israel; It shall crush the borderlands of Moab, and the territory of all Shethites. Verse 19 says, One out of Jacob shall rule, and destroy the survivors of Ir.

This will be applied by Jews to King David and his later victories over Moab and Edom. Christians apply it to both David and Jesus (see Matt 2:1-2) as a double fulfillment of prophecy. The followers of Bar Kochba used this to claim that he was the Messiah. He led the Jewish nation in a second revolt against Rome in AD 132-35. An independent Jewish state was declared, but Rome again crushed and completely destroyed Jerusalem.

In chapter 25 the Midianites are linked with the Moabites in opposing Israel. Now we learn the negative aspect of Balaam, for the incident which follows will be blamed on him (see 31:16). Verses 1-5 say, While Israel was staying in Shittim, the people begin to have sexual relations with the women of Moab. These invited the people to the sacrifice of their gods, and the people ate and bowed down to their gods. Thus Israel yoked itself to the Baal of Peor, and the LORD's anger was kindled against Israel. The LORD said to Moses, "Take all the chiefs of the people, and impale them in the sun before the LORD, in order that the fierce anger of the LORD may turn away from Israel." And Moses said to the judges of Israel, "Each of you shall kill any of your people who have yoked themselves to the Baal of Peor."

This is the first mention of Baal which will be the main god in the promised land. Baal of Peor is the Baal that is worshiped at Peor. This action apparently is related to the Canaanite fertility gods. The pagan gods, at this time, made part of their worship a uniting with the sacred prostitutes. Especially significant was a man and woman uniting in front of the god. These actions are supposed to encourage the gods to unite sexually, and then this action will produce rain to fertilize the crops in an agricultural society.

When Israel submits to these rites of worship, God is angry and sends a plague. Meanwhile, in 25:6-9 one of the Israelites brings a Midianite woman into his family in the sight of Moses and the whole congregation while the people are weeping at the entrance of the tent of meeting. When Phinehas, son of Eleazar, son of Aaron, sees it, he pierces the two of them together with a spear. The plague stops, but 24,000 die from the plague. Twelve is another symbolic number for Israel, and here we have 2 x 12 x 1000.

Verses 10-13 say, The LORD spoke to Moses saying: "Phinehas son of Eleazar, son of Aaron the priest, has turned back my wrath from the Israelites by manifesting such zeal among them on my behalf that in my jealousy I did not consume the Israelites. Therefore say, 'I hearby grant him my covenant of peace. It shall be for him and his descendants after him a covenant of perpetual priesthood, because he was zealous for his God, and made atonement for the Israelites.' " (This is a confirmation of what was first given to Aaron and his sons.)

Though this incident is difficult from which to make sense, we must remember that the purpose of the OT for Christians is to illustrate plainly, principles that need to be understood (see I Corinthians 10:6-13). God will not tolerate what we do as we give preference to the gods we create. Sex is a noble thing given to humankind for one's benefit and pleasure; its use is not to be distorted. One has to wonder if even today the sex god is one of the major gods of our society.

In 25:16 The LORD says to Moses, "Harass the Midianites, and defeat them; for they have harassed you by the trickery with which they deceived you in the affair of Peor, and in the affair of Cozbi, the daughter of a leader of Midian, their sister; she was killed on the day of the plague that resulted from Peor."

Chapter 22 presents Balaam as doing what God wants. But later in Numbers 31:8, 16 Balaam is slaughtered by the Israelites when he is with the Midianites because he led people astray at Baal Peor. This must stem from a separate tradition than that of Numbers 22-24. The real Balaam we may never know, or he is a combination of two personalities.

The Bible presents God as both a God of love and a God of wrath. There is great mercy and grace for those who follow his ways but wrath for those who ignore him. One of the major purposes of the OT is to illustrate this concept through life events. In the NT we are told that Balaam, because of money, is behind all this and is put to death. In the NT books of 2 Peter 2:16, Jude 11, and Revelation 2:14 Balaam is seen as a false teacher who is greedy for money. (It seems that with the Balaam story we have at least two oral traditions being integrated into the written account.)

Chapter 26 again numbers the people in a second census. This involves the new generation of people going into the promised land. The land to which they are going is to be divided among them by lot even though the larger groups will be assigned a larger heritage. This will be a new census for those about to enter the new land.

Because of this census and the one at the beginning of the book, the book is called Numbers. From now on the people look forward to the promised land instead of backward to Egypt. There will be no murmurings, no rebellions against God, or his chosen leadership, and no deaths. It is time to prepare for entrance.

In chapter 27 the daughters of Zelophehad obtain the right to inherit the family's ancestral land when there is no son to inherit it. Chapter 36 states that they may inherit, but if or when they marry, they must marry within the tribe. (This is a first for women's rights and is an example of how the law could develop. It is important to note that women are paid attention to with concern and compassion in the story of the Israelites. This does not take place when the stories of other peoples in the ancient world are read.) Also, in this chapter (18-23) Joshua is commissioned by Eleazar the priest to succeed Moses.

Chapter 27:12-23 explains the succession of leadership from Moses to Joshua. Verses 18-21 say, the LORD said to Moses, "Take Joshua son of Nun, a man in whom is the spirit, and lay your hands on him; have him stand before Eleazar the priest and all the congregation, and commission him in their sight. You shall give him some of your authority, so that all the congregation of the Israelites may obey. But he shall stand before Eleazar the priest, who shall inquire for him by the decision of the Urim (Ex 28:30) before the LORD; at his word they shall go out, and at his word they shall come in, both he and all the Israelites with him, the whole congregation."

Moses authority will only transfer in part to Joshua. Moses' leadership will remain unique and unrepeatable. Joshua's leadership will be supplemented by the priest Eleazar, who will seek guidance from the LORD through the Urim.

In chapters 28-29 offerings for each day, the Sabbath, and the major feasts are listed to emphasize how important it is to worship God and bring offerings. Chapter 28:9 is the Sabbath day. Verse 16 is Passover. Verse 26 is Pentecost. Chapter 29:1 is Rosh Hashanah and the blowing of the ram's horn, the shofar. Verse 7 is Yom Kippur. Verse 12 is Succoth, and verse 35 will become Atzeret.

Chapter 30:3-9 states rules to follow when vows are made to God. It is interesting to note that in (8) if a woman makes a vow and the father or husband disapproves, it is nullified.

Chapter 31:1-18 is controversial to moderns because God commands that women and children are to be put to death. In those times the enemy was offered to God as a sacrifice. The writer says, God told the Israelites to make war on the Midianites and to kill all the males including the male children. Also women who have had relations with a male are to be killed. Only virgins are to be spared. These apparently are the women acting on Balaam's advice to engage the Israelites with the Baal of Peor.

The writer is stressing how serious God takes those who engage in pagan worship. When the Israelites go into the land of Canaan, worship of pagan Gods with their sexual rites will be everywhere, and it will be their downfall; so, God is showing them how offensive it is to him. Keep in mind one of the key OT themes is maintaining the one God concept. According to Scripture that is a priority.

Chapter 32 shows how the tribes of Reuben, Gad, and the half tribe of Manasseh settle on the East side of the Jordan River, the land which formerly was the land of King Sihon of the Amorites and King Og of Bashan. First, they must agree to fight for the rest of the tribes who will to eventually settle on the West side of the Jordan. Then, if they agree, the rest of the tribes will agree to them settling on the land now.

Chapter 33 reviews the stages by which the Israelites left Egypt in military formation under the leadership of Moses and Aaron and the places they stopped. God told Moses that the Israelites shall drive out all the inhabitants of the land of Canaan and destroy their pagan gods. In the book of Numbers the twelve tribes are listed seven times and found in chapters 1, 2, 7, 13, 26, and 34, but they do not always agree exactly on who the twelve are.

In Numbers 34 the two tribes that stay across the Jordan, Reuben and Gad, are omitted. None of these list Levi, although he is included in all the lists in Genesis and Exodus. In his place Numbers always gives Joseph's two sons, Ephraim and Manasseh, as two tribes that replace Joseph and Levi. Several lists begin with Reuben, but others list Judah. Moreover, the tribes occur in varied orders throughout the seven lists.

Chapter 34 defines the boundaries they will occupy, and chapter 35 lists the 48 cities including the 6 cities of refuge where one may flee if a person kills someone unintentionally. In the OT if someone is killed intentionally it is an eye for an eye and a tooth for a tooth. If someone is killed unintentionally, the relative of the one killed is designated as the avenger of blood. He has the right to put to death the killer, but if the killer can get to one of the six cities of refuge, he is not permitted to be put to death. This is an attempt to put restraints on the law of revenge in a day that lacked a modern court system. As noted previously the law distinguishes between premeditated an unpremeditated murder (manslaughter) Ex 2:12-14, 22:25, Num 5:22.

The book of Numbers stresses that the journey from faith to the promised land involves a testing and trial in the wilderness. Throughout the Bible the number 40 will symbolize a trial and testing period. The message in Numbers to Christians today is summarized by the writer of 1 Corinthians 10 from the NT. This writer has mentioned this more than once because it is an important concept for Christians as they attempt to interpret the OT.

The writer of 1 Cor 10 says, these things occurred as examples for us, so that we may not desire evil as they did. Do not become idolaters as some of them did; . . . We must not indulge in sexual immorality as some of them did, . . . We must not put Christ to the test, as some of them did, . . . and do not complain, as some of them did and were destroyed by the destroyer. These things happened to them to serve as an example, and they have been written down to instruct us on whom the end of the ages have come. So if you think you are standing, watch out that you do not fall.

The writer of Romans 15:4 also says, For whatever was written in former days was written for our instruction, so that by steadfastness and encouragement of the Scriptures we might have hope.

DEUTERONOMY

Deuteronomy means second law. The book is both a type of summary of the Pentateuch and a prologue to the historical books that follow. To some extent a few laws will be added, some will be bypassed, and some will be modified and reinterpreted as they reaffirm the covenant and prepare to enter into a new environment. The laws that can change and adapt are the casuistic laws (see Exodus chapters 21-23).

We will learn that teachings such as the Ten Commandments are absolutes in that they will last and be valid for all time. Other laws such as those found in the book of the covenant will change, but their essence will remain especially when they represent values, virtues and vices. Other teachings may be eliminated because of new circumstances.

Deuteronomy consists of Moses giving a series of speeches that center on the choice of obedience to God or disobedience. In order for God's people to be blessed they must be obedient to the Torah (the law, the teachings). If they are not, God tells them they will be cursed. This theme will then be prevalent throughout the rest of the OT.

Deuteronomy is basically Moses' farewell address to the people as he rehearses the mighty acts of God, warns of the temptations of the new land, and pleads for loyalty to God as the condition to a good life in the new land. A distinctive teaching in Deuteronomy is that the primary worship of God is to be in one place. This is to keep the people from integrating their worship with the shrines of the local pagan gods.

In Deuteronomy the new generation prepares to go into the land God promised them. Previously God spoke to Moses, but now Moses speaks to God's people. Jews will call this the summary of the law, while some Christians will call this book a catechism; others call it spiritual direction. It is also applied theology.

After Moses speaks to the people, he will die. His work is completed. It will be time for a new leader to lead a new generation into a new era. There is a time when even the greatest of humans is to be retired.

Chapter 1:1-3 says, These are the words that Moses spoke to all Israel in the wilderness beyond the Jordan—in the wilderness, on the plain opposite Suph . . . In the fortieth year, on the first day of the eleventh month, Moses spoke to the Israelites just as the LORD had commanded him to speak to them.

Chapter 1:5-8 says, Beyond the Jordan in the land of Moab, Moses undertook to expound the law as follows: The LORD our God spoke to us at Horeb (Deuteronomy's name for Sinai), saying, "You have stayed long enough at this mountain. Resume your journey, and go into the hill country of the Amorites as well as into the neighboring regions . . . See I have set the land before you; go in and take possession of the land that I swore to your ancestors . . . and to their descendants after them."

Then Moses proceeds in chapters 1-3 to give an historical review of how God has fulfilled his promise and guided his people, but despite this the people have not trusted God. Consequently, that generation of people will not enter the new land except for Joshua and Caleb. Even Moses and Aaron will not enter.

Moses in 3:23-26 says, "O Lord GOD, you have only begun to show your servant your greatness and your might; what god in heaven or on earth can perform deeds and mighty acts like yours! Let me cross over to see the good land beyond the Jordan, that good hill country and the Lebanon." But the LORD was angry with me on your account and would not heed me.

This is another reason given for Moses not entering the promised land; Chapter 4:21 states the same. So it seems that one of the major reasons Moses will not enter is because he is to vicariously bear divine wrath for the people because he is their leader. God puts great trust in his leaders but also calls them to accountability.

Back in chapter 2:4-6 readers are informed that Edom will be spared and not possessed by God's people because they descended from Esau, Jacob's brother, and verses 8 and 19 say, it was the same for Moab and Ammon who were related to Abraham's nephew Lot.

In chapter 4:2 at the conclusion of his first address, Moses says, You must neither add anything to what I command you nor take away anything from it, but keep the commandments of the LORD your God with which I am charging you. Then Moses warns the people to observe God's teachings diligently and to teach them to their children. He warns them in (15-18) saying, take care and watch yourselves closely, so that you do not act corruptly by making an idol for yourselves, . . . He reminds them in (37) that they and their ancestors were chosen because of God's grace and love. They were not chosen because of their great holiness.

In chapter 5:6-21 Moses begins a second address which includes the Ten Commandments. This version of the Decalogue differs slightly from that in Ex 20:2-17. A real difference is the commandment to observe the Sabbath. They are to set free for one day each week their family, slaves, aliens, livestock, and animals so that they may rest and not have to work.

Chapter 6:4-9 states the *Shema* which means hear. The Shema is to be said daily. It says, Hear, O Israel: The LORD is our God, the LORD alone. You shall love the LORD your God with all your heart, and with all your soul, and with all your might. Keep these words that I am commanding you today in your heart. Recite them to your children and talk about them when you are at home and when you are away, when you lie down and when you rise. Bind them as a sign on your hand, fix them as an emblem on your forehead, and write them on the doorposts of your house and on your gates.

These become Scriptures put in a small box and when wrapped around the arms; they are called phylacteries or tephilim. When put on the doorpost, they are called mezuzahs. They are reminders to follow God's commands, and today are still worn by some Jews, especially Rabbis.

In chapter 7 the Israelites are told in (2-6), that when God brings them into the land he promised, they are to make no covenant with the people and not to intermarry. They are told to smash and tear down the culture's idols. If they obey his commands, God will bless them and multiply them.

In chapter 8 he tells them he is bringing them into a good land that will supply them with all they need. Verses 7-11 say, the LORD your God is bringing you into a good land, a land with flowing streams, with springs and underground waters welling up in valleys and hills, a land of wheat and barley, of vines and fig trees and pomegranates, a land of olive trees and honey, a land where you may eat bread without scarcity, where you will lack nothing, a land whose stones are iron and from whose hills you may mine copper. You shall eat your fill and bless the LORD your God for the good land he has given you. Take care that you do not forget the LORD your God, by failing to keep his commandments, his ordinances, and his statutes, which I am commanding you today.

In verse 14 he says to them, do not exalt yourself, forgetting the LORD your God . . . In (17-19) Moses says, Do not say to yourself, My power and the might of my own hand have gotten me this wealth. But remember the LORD your God, for it is he who gives you power to get wealth, so that he may confirm his covenant that he swore to your ancestors, as he is doing today. If you do forget the LORD your God and follow other gods to serve and worship them, I solemnly warn you today that you shall surely perish. (There is that "if" again.)

In chapter 9:4-5 he tells them that when he destroys their enemy, they must remember it is not because of their righteousness but because of the wickedness of the nations that inhabit the land, and because of the promise he made to Abraham, Isaac, and Jacob.

The theology of the writer is that a nation's evil will always be punished whether it is Israel or the other nations. When Israel goes into the land and defeats the nation living there, it is because of their wickedness and evil. Moses in (6) says, Know, then, that the LORD your God is not giving you this good land to occupy because of your righteousness; for you are a stubborn people. (Hebrew style is constant repetition which is also an excellent method of teaching.)

Chapter 10 continues to remind the Israelites of their history of stubbornness, lack of faith, disobedience, creation of gods such as the Golden Calf, and their challenges to Moses and Aaron as God's appointed leaders. In verses 12-13 he says, So now, O Israel, what does the LORD your God require of you? Only to fear the LORD your God, to walk in all his ways, to love him, to serve the LORD your God with all your heart and with all your soul, and to keep the commandments of the LORD your God and his decrees that I am commanding you today, for your own well-being.

In verse 16 Moses says, Circumcise, then, the foreskin of your heart, and do not be stubborn any longer. He tells them in (17-18) that they are to be like their God who is not partial and takes no bribes, who executes justice for the orphan and widow, (which symbolize all the poor, the needy, and the powerless), and who loves strangers (which symbolizes the immigrant) providing them with food and clothing. In (19) he reminds them, to love strangers for they were such in a foreign land.

In chapter 11:13-17 Moses says, If you will only heed his every commandment that I am commanding you today—loving the LORD your God, and serving him with all your heart and with all your soul—then he will give you rain for your land in its season, . . . Take care, or you will be seduced into turning away, serving other gods and worshiping them, for then the anger of the LORD will be kindled against you and he will shut up the heavens, so that there will be no rain and the land will yield no fruit; then you will perish quickly off the good land that the LORD is giving you.

Moses is saying that the moral order affects the cosmic order. The people lived in an agricultural society and to not get the needed rain would be catastrophic. Here we learn that when the nation is in serious disobedience, the land will suffer. This goes back to Gen 3:18 and the thorns and thistles of a cursed ground.

Again, Moses in (18-21) reminds them, to teach their children God's commands and to bind them on their arms, foreheads, and doorposts as reminders to follow the ways of God. Moses tells them in (26-28) the LORD your God says, I am setting before you today a blessing and a curse: the blessing, if you obey the commandments of the LORD your God that I am commanding you today; and the curse, if you do not obey the commandments of the LORD your God, but turn from the way I am commanding you today, to follow other gods that you have not known.

In verse 29 he tells them, to set the blessings on Mt Gerizim, which was covered by vegetation, and the curse on Mt Ebal, which was bare and desolate. If they are obedient as a nation, God will bless them, but if they are disobedient, he will curse them.

Chapters 12-26 contain the Deuteronomic code of law. Chapter 12 stresses the centralization of worship at the sanctuary. This is intended to guard Israel from the paganism at the local pagan shrines. In (3-5) they are to abolish the pagan shrines. They are to break, smash, cut down, and burn them. In verse 16 they are reminded, never eat the blood, for blood is life. (No sacrificial blood is to be eaten and all meat is to be properly drained before eating which makes the meat kosher.)

Chapter 13:1-13 warns the people to be aware of false prophets. False prophets are those who divine through magic, omens and portents, and encourage you to run after other gods. Just because a prophet says he has a vision does not mean he had one, and if he had a vision, it does not necessarily mean it came from God. Also, God may allow some apparent wonders to be done by false prophets to test the people's faith. If the wonders do not point to the one God and his teachings, then the one performing the wonders is a false prophet.

In verses 15-16 Moses tells them that if a city turns to idolatry, it must be put under the sacrificial ban and consumed as a whole burnt offering. This means all the inhabitants are to be put to death as well as the livestock and everything in it, and the town is never to be rebuilt. They are to be made an offering and sacrifice to God. (This approach will be changed by Jesus, but here the theology is that worshiping other gods brings death.)

Chapter 14:1-21 again stresses clean and unclean foods as in Leviticus and are mentioned in order to eat only what is kosher. Chapter 15:1-6 mentions the sabbatical year and its importance for conservation and the benefit of the poor. Debts are to be forgiven in the sabbatical year. In an agricultural society many could not pay their taxes for various reasons, and others are not surviving for various reasons, thus they go deep into debt. By forgiving debts every seven years they get a new chance to escape long term poverty.

To the comfortable he says in verses 7-8, If there is among you anyone in need, a member of your community in any of your towns within the land that the LORD your God is giving you, do not be hard-hearted or tight-fisted toward your needy neighbor. You should rather open your hand, willingly lending enough to meet the need, whatever it may be.

In verses 10-11 Moses says, Give liberally and be ungrudging when you do so, for on this account the LORD your God will bless you in all your work and all that you undertake. Since there will never cease to be some in need on this earth, I therefore command you, Open your hand to the poor and needy neighbor in your land. In (12) God also commands that a fellow Hebrew slave is to be set free in the seventh year, and (13) says, you shall not send him out free empty-handed.

This is so he can get a decent start. It was because American slaves were sent away empty handed after the civil war that they have struggled for so long. This is a good example for help in understanding laws like Jubilee. Verse 17 informs us that if after seven years the Hebrew slave does not want to be set free, the owner is to put an ear ring in his ear as a sign that he is a slave forever. (It is interesting to note that in these times of males wearing earrings, in the OT it meant one was a slave.)

Chapter 16 emphasizes the importance of Passover, Pentecost, and Tabernacles which will become the three major feasts. On those holy days all men, who are able, are to come to worship in Jerusalem. Judges are to be appointed in all the towns, and verses 19-20 say, You must not distort justice; you must not show partiality; and you must not accept bribes, for a bribe blinds the eyes of the wise and subverts the cause of those who are in the right. Justice, and only justice, you shall pursue, so that you may live and occupy the land that the LORD your God is giving you.

Chapter 17:1-6 informs us that an ox or sheep with a defect shall not be sacrificed. Anyone who sacrifices to the gods shall be put to death, and no one is to be put to death on the evidence of only one witness; there must be two or three witnesses as evidence. If there is a king, verses 16-17 inform us that he is not to acquire many horses, many wives, or great quantities of gold. (In those times horses represented the desire and ability for war, and foreign wives will bring in their pagan gods.)

Verses 18-20 concerning the king say, When he has taken the throne of his kingdom, he shall have a copy of this law written for him in the presence of the levitical priests. It shall remain with him and he shall read in it all the days of his life, so that he may learn to fear the LORD his God, diligently observing all the words of this law and these statutes, neither exalting himself above other members of the community . . . (Even the king must obey the law. This was different from the kings of those times, for kings in the nations were considered to be above the law, but this was not to be in Israel.)

Chapter 18:1-2 says, The Levitical priests, the whole tribe of Levi, shall have no allotment or inheritance within Israel. They may eat the sacrifices that are the LORD's portion, but they shall have no inheritance among the other members of the community; the LORD is their inheritance, as he promised them. (Therefore, they are entitled to support from the sacrifices. They officiate at the central sanctuary and will function as teachers and judges in the towns.)

Again, in (10-11) he reminds them that any form of pagan superstition is prohibited. Examples are sorcery, and the black magic of casting spells, necromancy or contacting the dead and consulting ghosts, soothsaying for divination, augurs or fortune telling.

Moses in (15-22) says, The LORD your God will raise up for you a prophet like me from your own people; you shall heed such a prophet . . . Then the LORD replied to me: "They are right in what they have said, I will raise up for them a prophet like you from among their own people; I will put my words in the mouth of the prophet, who will speak to them everything I command. Anyone who does not heed the words that the prophet shall speak in my name, I myself will hold accountable. But any prophet who speaks in the name of other gods, or who presumes to speak in my name a word that I have not commanded the prophet to speak—that prophet shall die." You may say to yourself, "How can we recognize a word that the LORD has spoken?" If a prophet speaks in the name of the LORD but the thing does not take place or prove true, it is a word that the LORD has not spoken. The prophet has spoken presumptuously; do not be frightened by it.

This prophet who is to be raised up is understood to be Joshua by some Jews but also in a messianic sense by others. The translation of the word prophet by some is also translated prophets not prophet. But staying with the singular prophet the Apostles will claim that this is a reference to the Christ, who is the Messiah.

Islam will claim this as a reference to Muhammad who they claim is the final prophet, the seal of the prophets. Muslims believe that later when Jesus said in John's gospel that he would send the Advocate, which Christians believe is the Holy Spirit, it was really a reference to the prophet God told Moses he would send in the future. The Greek word is paraclete and that translates into English as Advocate, which in Arabic is spelled Ahmad.

Muhammad's first name was Ahmad, and his principal identity to Muslims is not as an advocate, but as the final prophet in the line of prophets identified in the Old and New Testaments. Muslims then believe his revelation from God includes a spiritual summary that completes and corrects the record of previous revelations and presents them at last to Arabs, and through them to the world not reached by Jews and Christians.

Chapter 19 establishes six cities as Cities of Refuge. Three of those cities are located on the west side of the Jordan river in Canaan, and three of those cities are located on the east side of the Jordan River in Transjordan. The purpose of the refuge cities is to limit the ancient tribal laws of blood revenge. The cities enable a person who has unintentionally put someone to death to escape to safety as previously stated. (The cities are listed in Deut 4:41-43, and Josh 20:7-9).

Chapter 20 gives the laws for war. In ancient cultures war was a way of life. There was no recreation overload as in modern society, so war was even thought to be a sport, a way to release energy (see 1 Chron 20:1). In (5-8) those who built a new house, planted a new vineyard, or were betrothed, were excused from war up to a year. In (8) those who were fainthearted were to be excused. (This writer wonders if this is not the beginning of a stipulation for the conscientious objector and not just the faint hearted. Fainthearted in those times may include those opposed to war.)

Verses 10-14 say, When you draw near a town to fight against it, offer it terms of peace. If it accepts your terms of peace and surrenders to you, then all the people in it shall serve you in forced labor. If it does not submit to you peacefully, but makes war against you, then you shall besiege it; and when the LORD your God gives it into your hand, you shall put all its males to the sword. You may, however, take as your booty the women, the children, the livestock, and everything else in the town, all its spoil.

Concerning the land God is giving them as an inheritance verses16-18 say, you must not let anything that breathes remain alive. You shall annihilate them . . . so that they may not teach you to do all the abhorrent things that they do for their gods, and you thus sin against the LORD your God. (This teaching will stay in force until the one God idea is established. At this point it is a battle to see who is God.) It is interesting to note in (19-20), that trees producing food are not to be destroyed in building siegeworks to use against the walls of a town being attacked. (The message seems to be it is acceptable to use the environment for one's goals but do not exploit it.)

In chapters 21-26 there are various laws for everyday living. This writer will mention some here, but at the end of Deuteronomy many more will be listed in a special exercise. There are rules for taking a wife from a captured town (10-14). There are rules in (15-17) for a man who has two wives and the children produced when he likes one wife and dislikes the other. An incorrigible son in (18-21) is to be stoned to death. Verses 22-23 inform us that if a criminal is put to death and hung on a tree, the corpse must not remain overnight; he is to be buried the same day. The Apostle Paul quotes this and applies it to the crucified Christ who he says, redeemed us from the curse of the law by becoming a curse for us (see Gal 3:13).

Chapter 22:1-4 tells them they are to care for lost animals. Some interesting laws are the following. Verse 5 informs that men and women are not to dress in each other's clothes. In verses 13-21 if a man marries and later wants to divorce the woman claiming she was not a virgin, he can do that, but if the parents of the girl bring the cloth of the wedding night proving she was a virgin, he may not divorce her. (It makes one wonder how they would know it belonged to the one in question.) In verse 22 adultery is punishable by death, and both the man and the woman are put to death. (That would cut down today's population.) In (28-29) if a man seizes a virgin and lies with her and is caught, he must give fifty shekels of silver to the father and marry her. Because he violated her, he shall not be permitted to ever divorce her.

Chapter 23:1-2 says, No one whose testicles are crushed or whose penis is cut off shall be admitted to the assembly of the LORD. (This is probably because he can not be fruitful and multiply.) Those born of an illicit union (incest) shall not be admitted to the assembly of the LORD. If one has a nocturnal emission verses 10-11 say, he must go outside the camp, and then in the evening he must wash himself with water. (Apparently the reason is a reminder that semen is to fertilize, and it did not happen.) When the sun sets, then he can enter the camp. In verses 12-14 latrines must be outside the camp of the community. In (19-20) the Israelites are not to demand interest from fellow countrymen, but they are permitted to charge interest to a foreigner.

In 24:1-4 a divorced couple may not remarry each other. In (5) a recently married man may not go to war for one year. In (14-15) a poor man's wages must be paid the same day he works. In chapter 25:1-3 a person in the wrong may be flogged but with no more than forty lashes. The directions of the levirate law in (5-10) are given. If a brother dies without a son, the widow of the deceased is to be married by the living brother. This is called a levirate marriage. Verses 11-12 say, If men get into a fight with one another, and the wife of one intervenes to rescue her husband from the grip of his opponent by reaching out and seizing his genitals, you shall cut off her hand; show no pity. In (13-16), there is to be no cheating on weights and measures. At the end of chapter 26 the covenant is renewed.

Beginning in chapter 27 are the final words of Moses. A cultic ceremony at Mt Ebal and Mt Gerizim, which overlooks Shechem, is inaugurated to dramatize Israel's covenant responsibilities. Twelve curses are listed for individual disobedience, and chapter 28 lists the blessings for obedience and the curses for disobedience for the nation. Verse 24 lists the cosmic effect for disobedience saying, The LORD will change the rain of your land to powder, and only dust shall come down upon you from the sky until you are destroyed.

The curse continues in (47-50) saying, Because you did not serve the LORD your God joyfully and with gladness of heart for the abundance of everything, therefore you shall serve your enemies, whom the LORD will send against you, in hunger and thirst, in nakedness and lack of everything. He will put an iron yoke on your neck until he has destroyed you. The LORD will bring a nation from far away, from the end of the earth, to swoop down upon you like an eagle, a nation whose language you do not understand, a grim-faced nation showing no respect to the old or favor to the young. (This is an incredible prophesy simply because it happened more than once.)

Chapter 29 continues with a warning against idolatry and what will happen as punishment for their infidelity. Verses 24-28 say, When people ask, "Why has the LORD done thus to this land? What caused this great display of anger?" They will conclude, "It is because they abandoned the covenant of the LORD, the God of their ancestors, which he made with them when he brought them out of the land of Egypt. They turned and served other gods . . . so the anger of the LORD was kindled against that land, bringing on it every curse written in this book. The LORD uprooted them from their land in anger, fury, and great wrath, and cast them into another land, as is now the case." Then verse 29 says, The secret things belong to the LORD our God, but the revealed things belong to us and our children forever, to observe all the words of this law. (The secret things are those things not revealed to humans. The revealed things are those in his word, the law.)

In chapter 30:11 Moses said, Surely, this commandment that I am commanding you today is not too hard for you, nor is it too far away, and in (14-18) he says, No, the word is very near to you; it is in your mouth and in your heart for you to observe. See, I have set before you today life and prosperity, death and adversity. If you obey the commandments of the LORD your God that I am commanding you today, by loving the LORD your God, walking in his ways, and observing his commandments, decrees, and ordinances, then you shall live and become numerous, and the LORD your God will bless you and the land you are entering to possess. But if your heart turns away and you do not hear, but are led astray to bow down to other gods and serve them, I declare to you today that you shall perish; you shall not live long in the land that you are crossing the Jordan to enter and possess. (The message is primarily to the nation as a whole.)

Verses 19-20 say, I call heaven and earth to witness against you today that I have set before you life and death, blessings and curses. Choose life so that you and your descendants may live, loving the LORD your God, obeying him, and holding fast to him; for that means life to you and length of days, so that you may live in the land that the LORD swore to give to your ancestors, to Abraham, to Isaac, and to Jacob.

Chapter 31:9-11 says, Moses wrote down this law, and gave it to the priests, the sons of Levi, who carried the ark of the covenant of the LORD, and to all the elders of Israel. Moses commanded them: Every seventh year, in the scheduled year of remission, during the Festival of Booths, when all Israel comes to appear before the LORD your God at the place that he will choose, you shall read this law before all Israel in their hearing.

Verse 14 says, The LORD said to Moses, "Your time to die is near; call Joshua and present yourselves in the tent of meeting, so that I may commission him." Verses 23-29 say, Then the LORD commissioned Joshua, son of Nun, and said, "Be strong and bold, for you shall bring the Israelites into the land that I promised them; I will be with you."

When Moses had finished writing down in a book the words of this law to the very end, Moses commanded the Levites who carried the ark of the covenant of the LORD saying, "Take this book of the law and put it beside the ark of the covenant of the LORD your God; let it remain there as a witness against you . . . Assemble to me all the elders of your tribes and your officials, so that I may recite these words in their hearing and call heaven and earth to witness against them. For I know that after my death you will surely act corruptly, turning aside from the way I have commanded you. In time to come, trouble will befall you, because you will do what is evil in the sight of the LORD, provoking him to anger through the work of your hands." (People today would call Moses a negative thinker, but Moses knew human nature, and so he dealt with history and reality.)

Chapter 32 is the Song of Moses, which is a psalm, contrasting God's faithfulness with Israel's unfaithfulness. Then the LORD addresses Moses telling him to ascend Mt Nebo in the land of Moab across from Jericho to view the land of Canaan, the land God is giving the Israelites.

Verse 48-52 say, On that day the LORD addressed Moses as follows: "Ascend this mountain of the Abarim, Mount Nebo, which is in the land of Moab, across from Jericho, and view the land of Canaan which I am giving to the Israelites for a possession; you shall die there on the mountain that you ascend and shall be gathered to your kin, as your brother Aaron died on Mount Hor and was gathered to his kin; because you both broke faith with me among the Israelites at the waters of Meribath-kadesh in the wilderness of Zin, by failing to maintain my holiness among the Israelites. Although you may view the land from a distance, you shall not enter it—the land that I am giving to the Israelites."

It seems as though the writers are struggling with understanding the real reason Moses is prohibited from entering. It is important to understand that God does not depend on any one leader now matter how great. Even Moses can be denied entry into the promised land. This is a pointed spiritual message for all people, especially religious and political leaders, to always stay humble and not to think too highly of themselves.

Chapter 33 includes Moses' blessings upon the twelve tribes in the form of a hymn. In chapter 34 Moses dies looking across at the promised land. Verse 6 says, He was buried in a valley in the land of Moab, opposite Beth-peor, but no one knows his burial place to this day. Verses 7-8 say, Moses was one hundred twenty years old when he died; his sight was unimpaired, and his vigor had not abated. The Israelites wept for Moses in the plains of Moab thirty days; then the period of mourning for Moses was ended.

Verses 9-12 say, Joshua son of Nun was full of the spirit of wisdom, because Moses had laid his hands on him; and the Israelites obeyed him, doing as the LORD commanded Moses. Never since has their arisen a prophet in Israel like Moses, whom the LORD knew face to face. He was unequaled for all the signs and wonders that the LORD sent him to perform in the land of Egypt, against Pharaoh and all his servants and his entire land, and for all the mighty deeds and all the terrifying displays of power that Moses performed in the sight of Israel. This ends the book of Deuteronomy and the Pentateuch.

As we see the development of Israel, the law is understood not in static form but as a part of a dynamic reality within a living community. The basic core always remains, but from the core the law is also adapted to new situations. Law intersects with life as it is filled with constancy and change, simplicity, complexity and ambiguity. Law takes experience into account while remaining constant in its objective of working for the common good. This means new teachings and new laws are added and subtracted as new situations develop. If one compares Exodus chapters 21-23 with Deuteronomy chapters 14-19, one can readily see the process.

From the OT we learn that God is concerned that his vision, his virtues, and his values are applied to all aspects of life. Ancient Israel was a theocracy where the religious leaders were also the political, economic, and social leaders, and there was no separation of church and state. With the coming of the new covenant, we will learn that a theocracy is not the only way to make God's virtues, values and vision felt in all aspects of life.

In the OT God chooses a nation, but in the NT God chooses a church in which all nations are called to participate no matter what their form of government may be. The American form of government and the American form of economics is just one form that is acceptable. Concern for the overall common good and making the virtues, values and vision of God infused into government is key.

When the form of government and economics are not representing the virtues, values, and vision of God for the common good, then the church is called, as the OT prophets were called, to challenge its form of government, its form of economics, its form of social policy, and even its form of religion. This writer believes this is an area that the church in America needs to improve on and take more seriously.

One last thought concerning Moses. This writer does not believe Moses would be accepted any better in these times than he was then. People today would call him a negative thinker. Talking about our sin and tendency toward evil is not acceptable. Most want only to hear positive things about themselves and this nation from both political and religious leaders. This leaves the church, this nation, or any nation uncorrected which eventually enables it to stray from God's will.

As we complete the first five books of the Bible (Pentateuch), we want to look at some of these interesting teachings and begin to challenge ourselves on how to interpret them as well as how to interpret the Bible as a whole. As the reader looks at some of these teachings one needs to ask oneself which ones do you take literally, and which ones do you interpret? What is the method of your interpretation, why, and how did you develop it? Let us look at some of the biblical laws from Genesis through Deuteronomy.

LOOKING AT SOME OF THE TEACHINGS & LAWS FROM THE PENTATEUCH

GENESIS

8:21	The inclination of the human heart is evil.
9:3-4	No blood is allowed to be eaten, and meat had to be properly drained.
9-6	One who sheds human blood shall also be killed (capital punishment).
16:1-15	Polygamy and concubines are accepted. 35:22-25 shows the nation of the Israelites is formed from Jacob's wives and concubines.
17:1-12	Males must be circumcised on the eighth day.
50:1-10	The dead are mourned seven days.

EXODUS

19:1-25	No one is permitted direct access to God without a priest.
21:2	Slavery is lawful.
21:15	If one hits father or mother, one will be put to death.
21:16	A kidnapper is put to death.
21:17	If one curses father or mother, one is put to death.
21:24	If one puts out an eye or a tooth, his shall be put out also.
22:18	A female sorcerer or one practicing witchcraft or magic is to be killed.
22:19	Bestiality or intercourse with an animal is punishable by death.
22:25	One can not lend money or take interest from fellow believers.
22:29	First born sons and first born animals must be offered to God.
23:15	One can not go to worship without an offering.
23:19	No meat or dairy product may be eaten at the same meal (no cheeseburgers).

25:31-40	The menorah as a symbol of liberation is to be displayed.
25: 10-23	Torah scrolls are to be displayed within an ark of the covenant.
28: 1-42	Sacred vestments are to be worn.
28:42-43	If a clergyman exposes himself, he is to be put to death.
29:37	The altar is holy and whoever touches it is holy.
30:78	Incense is to be offered.
30:19-21	Priests must wash their hands and feet in approaching the altar or they die.
30:22-38	Sacred vessels are to be anointed with oil and incense to make them holy.
31:15	Anyone who works on the Sabbath shall be put to death.
35:3	You shall kindle no fire on the Sabbath (no fire or today no electric).
40:14-15	Ordination of priests and clergy is a necessity.

LEVITICUS

1:3-5	A sacrifice of blood must be offered to God.
2:14	Bread offered to God must be without yeast (unleavened).
5:5, 6:7	Sins must be confessed and a goat or sheep brought to a priest for sacrifice.
11:4-7	One can not eat pork or rabbit.
11:9-12	One can not eat lobster, shrimp, or oysters.
17:10-13	No eating blood in meat or anything, or one will be cut off from the people.
19:32	You shall rise before the aged, and defer to the old.
20:13	One shall not lie with a male as a woman (homosexuality); the penalty is death.

21:16-23	The lame, blind, and disabled are excluded from the sanctuary.
23:10	Nocturnal emissions cause a man to be unclean.
24:15	Wages must be paid each day before sunset.
25:5-6	If a brother dies with no son, it is the duty of the dead man's brother to marry the widow.
25:11	If two men have a fight and the wife of one tries to help her husband by grabbing hold of the other man's genitals, her hand shall be cut off.

NUMBERS

5:2	If one touches a dead body, he is unclean and must be purified.
15:37	One must put fringes on a garment for a prayer shawl.
19:11-12	Use of holy water is shown.
30:13	If a woman makes an oath, the husband may nullify it

DEUTERONOMY

5:12	The Sabbath must be observed.
6:7-9	Must wear boxes of Scripture around the head and hand and on the door post.
13: 12-16	Put all women and children to death if their faith is different.
15:1	Every seventh year one must forgive the debts owed to you.
15:11	Give to the poor and needy.
16:1-17	Attending Passover, Pentecost, and the Feast of Booths is mandatory.
20:10-15	In war all males are to be put to death, but women may be kept as booty.

21:20-21	Stubborn sons are to be put to death.
22:11	One may not wear clothes of wool and linen mixed.
22:20-21	If a man's wife is found not to be a virgin, she shall be put to death.
22:22	If a man and woman commit adultery, both shall be put to death.
23:1	Anyone with crushed testicles will not be permitted in the assembly.
23:2	Anyone born outside of marriage will not be permitted in the assembly.
24:1	If a man finds something objectionable with his wife, he may divorce her.

There are many other laws. These are samples of what is found in the Pentateuch. Which ones do you follow, and which ones do you not follow and why? Which ones do you use to proof text your particular belief? Why do you use some verses and ignore others? What is your reasoning? As we move on hopefully there will be some answers for you. The following are some things to think about:

Christians are no longer under the OT; they are under the NT (the new covenant, testament, or law), but this does not mean there is no purpose and value in the OT for Christians. The old law was for the Hebrews, the Israelites, for they needed directions on how to be God's people, both in their relationship with God, and with each other in order to shed the ways and culture of Egypt and to challenge the ways and culture of the Canaanites whose land they were entering.

This is a major role of the law in Israel's history. It was a way to express their loyalty. It was a way to confirm their covenant with God. Of course, these laws must be understood within the narrative in which they are embedded. Most of these exact laws are no longer binding on Christians unless renewed in the new covenant. What is binding are the virtues, values and principles behind the exact laws.

Many of the exact OT civil and religious laws have not been renewed nor have many of the OT's moral laws although many of the moral laws are restated in the NT. The once for all sacrifice of Jesus has eliminated many of these laws, such as the animal sacrifices, food laws, clean and unclean laws, and ritual laws. Jesus reinterpreted much of the OT. The OT is still God's word for his church, but we are not bound to its commands unless restated or the virtues, values and principles reinterpreted.

Even though Christians are not bound to many of these laws, it is important to understand the OT, for we learn who God is and how he works. Underlying themes are important, as well as how God wants to relate to us and how he wants us to relate to ourselves, others of his creation, and his created order. We learn about his virtues, values, and ideals, and his standards of fairness, justice, love and his overall vision for his people. We learn about his mercy, steadfast love, and grace. In the OT the essence of all law, the Ten Commandments, is there as well as the principle of loving God and neighbor.

As we read the OT we see illustrated many examples of good behavior, but also many examples of bad behavior. The Bible does not hide the imperfections of its people and heroes. Through it all there is a grounding in theology that prepares for the Messiah and his kingdom. For Christians the Apostle Paul said the OT functions to lead Christians to Christ. Without the OT Christians can not really understand completely the NT. It is the necessary foundation book.

It is the foundation document for Jews, Christians and Muslims. For the Jews it is their basic Torah. It is the book of books. From it comes all their basic teachings and the Talmud. For Muslims they are directed to the Qur'an, for it tells them how and what they are to understand about the OT. From it comes their ideas about Allah. It tells them what they are to recite and meditate upon, and how they are to think about the OT. It is not relied on as heavily as it is for Judaism and Christianity, but it is still the foundation book.

THE BOOKS OF HISTORY/ THE FORMER PROPHETS

Christians call the following books of Joshua, Judges, Samuel, and Kings the Historical Books, but Jews in the Hebrew Bible call the same books the Former Prophets. The Hebrew Bible is divided into the Law (Torah), the Prophets (Nevi'im), and the Writings (Ketuvim). As we move into the book of Joshua we will look more at the genre called narrative which is one of the most common literary forms of Scripture.

JOSHUA

Joshua was the right hand man of Moses and is now in charge after the death of Moses. He is from the tribe of Ephraim. The Greek form of his name is Jesus. He had been an attendant of Moses from the beginning. He was one of the twelve spies Moses sent to scout out the promised land. After the Israelites forty years in the wilderness, Joshua is commissioned to lead Israel in a holy war to take the promised land from the pagan Canaanites, who are also sometimes called Amorites (see Gen 15:16, Josh 10:5).

Joshua is the first book guided by the Deuteronomic historians (editors) in which the theological principal of reward for keeping the covenant and punishment for abandoning it prevails. This theology is taken from the book of Deuteronomy and with the book of Joshua will continue through to the end of the book of II Kings. Actually, it goes further, but it is primarily set and developed in these books.

Many of the narratives in Joshua are classified as sagas which are defined as stories that bear some relationship to fact but whose main concern is universal truth. Many of the sagas in the first half of the book are etiologies which are narratives to explain the origin of something such as the name of a person, tribe, place, a particular custom, or the like.

In Joshua God promises the land to his people upon obedience, and here it is carried out. Because this is a new generation of Israelites, who had not experienced the parting of the waters and being set free from Egypt, God will perform the miracle of parting the waters at the Jordan River as they enter the promised land. So, again, the water is parted; and God's people go into the land that God promised Abraham, Isaac, and Jacob.

Chapter 1:1-9 says, After the death of Moses the servant of the LORD, the LORD spoke to Joshua son of Nun, Moses' assistant, saying, "My servant Moses is dead. Now proceed to cross the Jordan, you and all this people, into the land I am giving to them, to the Israelites . . . No one shall be able to stand against you all the days of your life. As I was with Moses, so I will be with you; I will not fail you or forsake you. Be strong and courageous; for you shall put this people in possession of the land that I swore to their ancestors to give them. Only be strong and very courageous, being careful to act in accordance with all the law that my servant Moses commanded you; . . . This book of the law shall not depart out of your mouth; you shall meditate on it day and night, so that you may be careful to act in accordance with all that is written in it. For then you will make your way prosperous, and then you shall be successful . . . for the LORD your God is with you wherever you go."

In chapter 2:1 Joshua sent two men secretly from Shittim as spies, saying, "Go, view the land, especially Jericho." So they went, and entered the house of a prostitute whose name was Rahab, and spent the night there.

It is possible that Rahab is one who works in a pagan temple. In this agricultural society rain and sun for the crops are absolutely necessary for survival. So part of their worship is uniting with the temple prostitutes both male and female. This, they think, will encourage the gods to have sexual relations which will bring the sun and the rain to fertilize the crops. This is the pagan religion that is an abomination to God.

Meanwhile, the king of Jericho in (2-5) comes after the spies, but Rahab hides them. She hides them because in (11) she says, The LORD your God is indeed God in heaven above and on earth below. When the king leaves, she asks the men to spare her and her family when they come back to take the land. The men agree in (14) saying, "Our life for yours! If you do not tell this business of ours, then we will deal kindly and faithfully with you when the LORD gives us the land."

Her house was on the outer side of the wall that surrounded the city, and she lived within the wall which was normal in those times. Then in (21) she lets them escape out the window by using a crimson cord (rope). (Is this the origin of the red light district?) An agreement is made that when the Israelites return to take the land; she and her family will be spared if the crimson cord is hanging out the window.

The men spent three days spying out the land, and then returned to Joshua. Verse 24 says, They said to Joshua, "Truly the LORD has given all the land into our hands; moreover all the inhabitants of the land melt in fear before us." (There are many who believe it is this Rahab who later marries an Israelite, Salmon, and through her son, Boaz, she will become an ancestor of King David and Jesus, see Ruth 2-4 and Mt 1:5.)

In chapter 3:1-6 Joshua prepares to leave Shittim to cross over the Jordan River. He tells the people in (5) "Sanctify yourselves; for tomorrow the LORD will do wonders among you." They are to follow the ark of the covenant which represents the presence of God. The priests will be in front carrying the ark, and the people are to follow. As the people came to the Jordan verses 15-16 inform us the priests stand in the water, and the waters flowing from above stand still, rising up in a single heap as the people cross over opposite Jericho.

It is interesting to note that in 1927 the water parted at the same spot when earth tremors caused the collapse of the high river banks (Zondervan 1999). If this is what happened in Joshua's time, then the miracle would be God bringing the pile up of the water at the proper time.

Chapter 4:1-3 says, When the entire nation had finished crossing over the Jordan, the LORD said to Joshua: "Select twelve men from the people, one from each tribe, and command them, 'Take twelve stones from here out of the middle of the Jordan, from the place where the priest's feet stood, carry them over with you, and lay them down in the place where you camp tonight.' " Verses 4-7 inform us that their purpose is to set up a memorial to remind their children what took place. In this way when the children ask what the stones represent, they can be told what happened to the river on the day the people entered the land. This memorial was set up at Gilgal.

Verses 21-24 give the reason for this: "When your children ask their parents in time to come, 'What do these stones mean?' then you shall let the children know, 'Israel crossed over the Jordan here on dry ground.' For the LORD your God dried up the waters of the Jordan for you until you crossed over, as the LORD your God did to the Red Sea, which he dried up for us until we crossed over, so that all the people of the earth may know that the hand of the LORD is mighty, and so that you may fear the LORD your God forever." (Much later Saul will be made king here, see 1 Samuel 11:15.)

Chapter 5:2-5 says, At that time the LORD said to Joshua, "Make flint knives and circumcise the Israelites a second time." So Joshua made flint knives, and circumcised the Israelites at Gibeath-haaraloth. This is the reason why Joshua circumcised them: all the males of the people who came out of Egypt, all the warriors, had died during the journey through the wilderness after they had come out of Egypt. Although all the people who came out had been circumcised, yet all the people born on the journey through the wilderness after they had come out of Egypt had not been circumcised.

Verses 6-7 say, the Israelites had traveled forty years in the wilderness, until all the nation, the warriors who came out of Egypt, perished, not having listened to the voice of the LORD. To them the LORD swore that he would not let them see the land that he had sworn to their ancestors to give us, a land flowing with milk and honey. So it was their children, whom he raised up in their place, that Joshua circumcised; for they were uncircumcised, because they had not been circumcised on the way.

When the circumcising was completed, verses 9-12 say, the LORD said to Joshua, "Today I have rolled away from you the disgrace of Egypt." And so that place is called Gilgal to this day. (Gilgal means rolling). While the Israelites were camped in Gilgal they kept the passover . . . On the day after the passover, on that very day, they ate the produce of the land, unleavened cakes and parched grain. The manna ceased on the day they ate the produce of the land, and the Israelites no longer had manna; they ate the crops of the land of Canaan that year. (This ended the need for the manna from heaven.)

Later near Jericho Joshua is granted a theophany (manifestation of the divine). In verses 13-15 Joshua is near Jericho and saw a man standing before him with a drawn sword in his hand. Joshua went to him and said to him, "Are you one of us or one of our adversaries?" He replied, "Neither; but as commander of the LORD I have now come." And Joshua fell on his face to the earth and worshiped, and he said to him, "What do you command your servant, my lord?" The commander of the army of the LORD said to Joshua, "Remove the sandals from your feet, for the place you stand is holy." And Joshua did so. (This is a sign from God that he will be with them as they enter to take the land, for it is the same thing God told Moses at the burning bush, see Ex 3:5. This is why today Muslims take off their sandals or shoes when they enter the mosque.)

Chapter 6:1-7 says, Now Jericho was shut up inside and out because of the Israelites;

no one came out and no one went in. The LORD said to Joshua, "See I have handed Jericho over to you, along with its king and soldiers. You shall march around the city, all the warriors circling the city once. Thus you shall do for six days, with seven priests bearing seven trumpets of rams' horns before the ark. On the seventh day you shall march around the city seven times, the priests blowing the trumpets. When they make a long blast with the rams' horn, as soon as you hear the sound of the trumpet, then all the people will shout with a great shout; and the walls of the city will fall down flat, and all the people shall charge straight ahead." So Joshua son of Nun summoned the priests and said to them, "Take up the ark of the covenant, and have seven priests carry seven trumpets of rams' horns in front of the ark of the LORD." To the people he said, "Go forward and march around the city; have the armed men pass on before the ark of the LORD."

For six days the people with seven priests and the ark of the covenant march around the city one time each day with the priests continually blowing their horns. On the seventh day they march around the city seven times with seven priests blowing seven rams' horns. On the seventh trip around, and at the sound of the trumpet, they shouted, and the walls fell down flat. (Some say that at that point God brought an earthquake while other scholars say archeology shows Jericho had been destroyed long before the Israelites got there.)

Verse 21 says, Then they devoted to destruction by the edge of the sword all in the city, both men and women, young and old, oxen, sheep, and donkeys. In verse 25 only Rahab, the prostitute, and her family are spared as the promise to her is granted. Verses 26-27 say, Joshua then pronounced this oath saying, "Cursed before the LORD be anyone who tries to build this city—this Jericho! At the cost of his first born he shall lay its foundation, and at the cost of his youngest he shall set up its gates!" (This will be fulfilled in I Kings 16:34.) So the LORD was with Joshua; and his fame was in all the land.

In chapter 7 the Israelites attempt to defeat the city of Ai but they are turned back, and (5) says, The hearts of the people melted and turned to water. Joshua is distressed and in (7) said, "Ah Lord GOD! Why have you brought this people across the Jordan at all, to hand us over to the Amorites so as to destroy us?" (It turns out the treasure that is to be put into the treasury of the LORD is violated by a man named Achan who is discovered.) Then in verses 25-26, Joshua said to Achan, "Why did you bring trouble on us? The LORD is bringing trouble on you today." And all Israel stoned him to death; they burned them (his family) with fire, cast stones on them, and raised over him a great heap of stones that remains to this day. Then the LORD turned from his burning anger.

The theology is that disobedience has its consequences, and those who are disobedient will experience God's wrath. God is a God of love, but he is also a God of wrath to the disobedient. God then leads the Israelites to victory through an ambush in chapter 8. Verse 25 says, The total of those who fell that day, both men and women, was twelve thousand—all the people of Ai. Verses 28-29 say, Joshua burned Ai and made it forever a heap of ruins . . . And he hanged the king of Ai on a tree until evening; and at sunset Joshua commanded, and they took his body down . . . and raised over it a great heap of stones, which stands there to this day.

In verses 30-35 Joshua builds an altar to the Lord at Mt Ebal and wrote the law on stones (probably the blessings and the curses). Then Joshua reads the words of the law to the assembled Israelites as half of them were on Mount Gerizem and the other half on Mount Ebal. Verse 35 says, There was not a word of all that Moses commanded that Joshua did not read before all the assembly of Israel, and the women, and the little ones, and the aliens who resided among them.

In chapter 9 the Gibeonites, who were the Hivites, want to save their lives, so in (3-15) they trick the Israelites into making a treaty with them, and (15) says, Joshua made peace with them guaranteeing their lives by a treaty; and the leaders of the congregation swore an oath to them. Later when the Israelites discover they were tricked they are unhappy, but they honor the treaty because of the oath they swore to them. The Gibeonites agree to be their slaves to save their lives.

This action angers the five kings of the Amorites, and in (10:5-6) they make war on the Gibeonites. And the Gibeonites sent to Joshua at the camp at Gilgal saying, "Do not abandon your servants; come up to us quickly, and save us, and help us; for all the kings of the Amorites who live in the hill country are gathered against us." Joshua comes to their rescue. In the battle (11) says, the LORD threw down huge stones from heaven on them as far as Azekah, and they died; there were more who died because of the hailstones than the Israelites had killed with the sword. (The idea is that God defeated their enemies; it was not because the Israelites were superior in fighting skills.)

Verses 12-15 say, On the day when the LORD gave the Amorites over to the Israelites, Joshua spoke to the LORD; and he said in the sight of Israel, "Sun, stand still at Gibeon; and moon, in the valley of Aijalon." And the sun stood still, and the moon stopped, until the nation took vengeance on their enemies. Is this not written in the Book of Jashar? (For proof of this the writer appeals to a secular writing that appears to have been a collection of poetry that extolled Israel's heroes and military victories.) The sun stopped in mid-heaven, and did not hurry to set for about a whole day. There has been no day like it before or since, when the LORD heeded a human voice; for the LORD fought for Israel. Then Joshua returned, and all Israel with him, to the camp at Gilgal. In verse 26 Joshua hung the five kings on five trees. And they hung on the trees until evening.

Eventually Joshua will conquer Makkedah, Libnah, Gezer, Lackish, Eglon, Hebron, and Debir. Verses 40-43 say, So Joshua defeated the whole land, the hill country and the Negeb and the lowland and the slopes, and all their kings; he left no one remaining, but utterly destroyed all that breathed, as the LORD God of Israel had commanded. And Joshua defeated them from Kadesh-barnea to Gaza, and all the country of Goshen, as far as Gibeon. Joshua takes all these kings and their land at one time, because the LORD God of Israel fought for Israel. Then Joshua returned, and all Israel with him, to the camp at Gilgal.

The one God (Yahweh) fought the battles and won the battles, for as God said, if the nation obeys my teachings it will be blessed. The point the author wants to stress is that the victory was not because of the fighting skills of the Israelites; it was because of God himself fulfilling his promise.

In chapter 11 the kings in the northern hill country gather together to fight Israel. In (6) the LORD says to Joshua, "Do not be afraid of them, for tomorrow at this time I will hand over all of them . . ." And (8) says, the LORD handed them over to Israel . . . Verse 23 says, Joshua took the whole land . . . And the land had rest from war.

We will see in Judges that they did not occupy the whole land, but it does seem that they occupied enough of it that the twelve tribes could go in and make a claim and stake out their different territories. The second promise to Abraham is being fulfilled. They are becoming a nation, and now they are being given the land. Chapter 12 lists the kings conquered by Moses (2 kings) and Joshua (13 kings).

Chapter 13:1-7 says, Now Joshua was old and advanced in years; and the LORD said to him, "You are old and advanced in years, and very much of the land still remains to be possessed . . . Now therefore divide this land for an inheritance to nine tribes and the half tribe of Manasseh." The chapter lists parts of the land yet unconquered such as Philistine territory and areas north in Phoenicia and Lebanon. The chapter also lists the territory on the east side of the Jordan allotted to the tribes of Reuben, Gad, and the half tribe of Manasseh.

Chapter 14 begins the distribution of the land west of the Jordan. Caleb was rewarded in (13) with Hebron, formerly Kiriath-arba and the surrounding hill country. Formerly, he and Joshua were the only ones to have the courage to suggest they go into the promised land and take the land because of God's promise.

Chapter 15 lists the territory and towns of Judah. Chapter 16 lists the territory of the Josephites which includes Ephraim as well as the other half tribe of Manasseh that is listed in chapter 17. Chapter 18 includes the territory of Benjamin. Chapter 19 allots the territory of Simeon, Zebulun, Issachar, Asher, Naphtali, and Dan. Joshua was allotted the town of Timnath-Serah in the hill country of Ephraim.

Chapter 20 lists the Cities of Refuge. On the west side of the Jordan were Kedesh in Galilee, and to the south Shechem, and Hebron. On the east side were Bezer, Ramoth, and Golan. Chapter 21 lists the 48 cities of the Levites as they were dispersed about the territory as teachers and judges.

Then, verses 43-45 say, Thus the LORD gave to Israel all the land that he swore to his ancestors that he would give them; and having taken possession of it, they settled there. And the LORD gave them rest on every side just as he had sworn to their ancestors; not one of their enemies had withstood them, for the LORD had given all their enemies into their hands. Not one of all the good promises that the LORD had made to the house of Israel had failed; all had come to pass. (As we will see this is a bit of exaggeration in order to express the idea that God was working out his purposes.)

In chapter 22 because the land is basically settled, and the heavy part of the war is over, the tribes of Reuben, Gad, and the half tribe of Manasseh return to their land on the east side of the Jordan. In (11-12) all the other tribes prepare for war against them for building an altar. Holding strictly to the Deuteronomic law that forbade the offering of sacrifice anywhere but the central sanctuary, the other tribes apparently interpret the building of the altar as an act of disloyalty to Israel and its God. War is adverted when they explain in (26-27) that the altar was not built for burnt offerings or sacrifices but as a witness to the children of Reuben, Gad, and the half tribe of Manasseh that they are God's children just as those on the other side of the river are God's children.

Joshua gives his farewell address in chapter 23. Verses 1-3 say, Joshua was old and advanced in years, Joshua summoned all Israel, their elders and heads, their judges and officers, and said to them, "I am now old and advanced in years; and you have seen all that the LORD your God has done to all these nations for your sake, for it is the LORD your God who has fought for you.

Verses 6-13 continue, Therefore be very steadfast to observe and do all that is written in the book of the law of Moses . . . so that you may not be mixed with these nations here among you, . . . but hold fast to the LORD your God, as you have done to this day . . . Be very careful, therefore, to love the LORD your God. For if you turn back, and join the survivors of these nations . . . and intermarry with them, so that you marry their women and they yours, know assuredly that the LORD your God will not continue to drive out these nations before you, but they shall be a snare and a trap for you, a scourge on your sides, and thorns in your eyes until you perish from this good land that the LORD your God has given you.

Verses 14-16 continue, "And now I am about to go the way of all the earth, and you know in your hearts and souls, all of you, that not one thing has failed of all the good things that the LORD your God promised concerning you; . . . But just as all the good things that the LORD your God promised concerning you have been fulfilled for you, so the LORD will bring upon you all the bad things, until he has destroyed you from this good land . . . If you transgress the covenant of the LORD your God, which he enjoined on you, and go and serve other gods . . . you shall perish quickly from the good land that he has given you." (This is the same choice he gives to religious institutions and people today.)

Then in chapter 24:1-13 Joshua gathers all the leaders of the tribes together at Shechem. He reminds them of their history. In (14-15) Joshua says, "Now therefore revere the LORD, and serve him in sincerity and in faithfulness; put away the gods that your ancestors served beyond the River and in Egypt, and serve the LORD. Now if you are unwilling to serve the LORD, choose this day whom you will serve, whether the gods your ancestors served in the region beyond the River or the gods of the Amorites in whose land you are living; but as for me and my household we will serve the LORD." In (16-18) the people answer, "Far be it from us that we should forsake the LORD to serve other gods; . . . we also will serve the LORD, for he is our God." (This is the same choice people have today.)

Verses 25-29 say, So Joshua made a covenant with the people that day, and made statutes and ordinances for them at Shechem (Nablus of today). Joshua wrote these words in the book of the law of God; and he took a large stone, and set it up there under the oak in the sanctuary of the LORD. Joshua said to all the people, "See this stone shall be a witness against us; for it has heard all the words of the LORD that he spoke to us; therefore it shall be a witness against you, if you deal falsely with God." So Joshua sent the people away to their inheritances. After these things Joshua son of Nun, the servant of the LORD, died being one hundred and ten years old. The writer in (31) says, Israel served the LORD all the days of Joshua, and all the days of the elders who outlived Joshua and had known all the work that the LORD did for Israel.

Verse 32 says, The bones of Joseph, which the Israelites had brought up from Egypt, were buried at Shechem, in the portion of ground that Jacob had bought from the children of Hamor . . . it became an inheritance of the descendants of Joseph. Eleazer the priest, son of Aaron, also died and in (33) is buried in Gibeah in Ephraim the town of his son Phinehas. This ends the book of Joshua.

A major concern of many readers is that God is the Warrior who advocates holy war. First, we must remember that a major concern of the whole OT is to preserve the one God concept. The battle throughout is over who is God, or how many gods are legitimate? Each nation had its own god, so to the ancient people whoever prevailed was the one true God.

In a culture where war was not only normal but a form of recreation, it was normal and acceptable to have a god that guides, leads, and fights for the nation. Remembering that those people were living in a culture where everyone believed in a god, the issue was, who is the real God? That is unlike our culture today where for many the issue is not who is God, but is there really such a thing as God?

The other issue is how could the one God who is a God of love take a people and tell them to exterminate another people who are already located in a territory.

Does that legitimize holy war today? First of all what God does, does not mean the people of his creation have the right to do also. God is sovereign not the people of his creation. The people of the one God have the right to a territory in the world the one God created.

The people already located in the territory were people who descended from and who had fallen away from the one God. Now, they worship many gods, the gods of their own creation, and worship through sexual orgies considered by God as being totally depraved. All of this is an abomination to the one God who wants those ways extinguished. Again, the issue is who is God and what is he calling the people of his creation to be and do. (As a note this writer adds that scholars are divided, some not accepting that people worshiped only one God at the beginning of creation. There are those who believe that from the worship of many gods came the worship of one God.)

Because of the situation in Canaan, the one God has to establish who he is as a way of eventually leading civilization to understand who God is, and what God desires. This all starts with Pharaoh in Egypt and will continue with his people as he takes them into the promised land. God has a right to create his people and give them land. Once this is established there will be no need to continue so-called holy wars. In the future there will be no more need for God to prove himself. He has already done that, so the one God is now accepted by faith or rejected.

For Christians as they read the NT, they will understand that without faith it is impossible to please God (see Heb 11:6). God no longer needs to prove himself; he has already done that repeatedly. Also, in the NT Christians believe they get the fullness of truth and righteousness in Christ, who rejects violence and says blessed are the peacekeepers who love their enemies. NT writers never think of military conquest as the way to further the cause of God. They think the only way is to spread the good news of Jesus Christ by teaching, preaching, and by their example of love. Unfortunately, throughout Christian history that has not always been the reality practiced by his followers.

Lastly, we need to understand that God is not only a God of love but a God of wrath. This is a plain teaching also of Jews and Muslims. From Genesis through Deuteronomy and now in the book of Joshua we are being taught that as a nation if God's ways are followed, it will be blessed, but if his ways are not followed, it will eventually be cursed. This is a theological theme that continues for nations today as well as the Church. The NT confirms this teaching (see Matt 25:31-46). God will put to death all evil. Thus in a sense this holy war in Joshua symbolizes what will happen in the end to all people who oppose the one God. God is sovereign, and only he and his purposes, whatever they may be, will prevail.

As we go through the books of Scripture we learn that narrative stories are a key way that theology expresses itself. Because writing was not the main way people expressed themselves in those times, people passed their thoughts on orally and stories were the best way to do so. Joshua is a prime example as will be Judges. In the process the Bible contains poetry, hymns, legends, myths, epics, folktales, short stories, gospels, parables, hyperboles, letters, and other literary forms, many with theological and moral themes that move toward their fulfillment for Christians in Jesus the Messiah, for Judaism in their rabbis and the Talmud, and for Muslims in Muhammad and the Qur'an.

The writings one has been reading so far are based on some history but the purpose is to express faith, which gives a people a theology, and to have a type of catechism that reminds and teaches them. The OT is a divinely inspired combination of facts and literary creativity to give God's people something to hold onto as they express and pass their faith to their children. This narrative creativity will be plain to see as we continue through the book of Judges, Samuel, Kings, and Chronicles.

In attempting to put all this together, we must understand that the inspired words of Scripture are both human and divine. There are human words with human thoughts as well as words from God. The challenge before us is to determine the difference. That is why the Scriptures should also be studied and discussed, and listened to with the people in a local church, and the local church needs to listen to what the different churches are saying. Individual interpretation in isolation can lead to understandings not intended by God or the biblical writer.

JUDGES

Judges covers the period between Joshua's death and the rise of Samuel approximately 1220-1050 B.C. The time is approximate, for the ancients did not consider exact time important like we moderns. After the death of Joshua the Israelites have no strong central government. They are a confederacy of twelve independent tribes with no unifying force except their God who is their king. Unfortunately, too often, the people do not take their God seriously and continually fall into idolatry, like some Christians, Jews, and Muslims today.

Being in an unstable condition, hurting themselves with civil war among themselves, and surrounded by enemies who make attempt after attempt to exterminate them, the Hebrew nation is slow in its national development. It does not become a strong nation until it is organized into a kingdom in the days of Samuel, then developed in the time of David, and Solomon.

The following narratives are about epic heroes called Judges who are primarily military heroes and most certainly not always moral heroes. Their stories are usually conveyed in the form of hyperboles where they are somewhat exaggerated to express their importance. Some scholars see legends in many of the incidents. Legends in religious literature are in some way like myths in that they contain God's truths. Legends are regarded in some way historical but not verifiable and usually are about different characters. The important point is that within them can be found God's inspired truths.

The theme of Judges is that of the Deuteronomic historians which states: when God's people as a group obey God, they are successful, but when they disobey, they are unsuccessful. God, however, is always merciful, and at the first sign of repentance, God raises up a leader to set them free. The setting is at a time when the real understanding of God, and what he desires in the way of morality, is at a low.

The pattern is as follows. The people fall into idolatry and deep sin; God punishes them by having an enemy defeat them; the people repent, and because they repent, God delivers them by raising up another judge. Judges 3:7-11 as shown in the following pages is a perfect example. In the OT, responsibility and punishment are more collective and community oriented than individually oriented. This contrasts greatly with the thinking of many Americans today who focus on individual responsibility.

Corporate sin or institutional sin, something we moderns in America deemphasize, is strongly emphasized in the OT. Here Scripture teaches that corporate or institutional sin influences the life of individuals as much as or more than individual sin influences the life of a group. The OT strongly stresses the importance of the group and the responsibility of the individual to the common good of the group.

Later the prophets will begin to balance the nature of overall sin by also stressing the importance of individual sin. This writer believes we moderns need to have a better balance understanding how corporate or institutional sin has a negative affect on culture and its people. Judges begins to help us see that aspect of sin. Later the prophets will emphasize the aspect of institutional sin on the people and the nation.

We will see in the book of Judges that most judges are basically weak and very imperfect, but the theology is that God uses weak and imperfect people for his purposes. As imperfect as they are, they still have some faith in a time when there is little faith.

Joshua indicates that the Israelites are successful because the people are faithful. Judges will indicate they are not as successful as they could have been because they are disobedient. Some people attempt to say the books contradict each other, but a better way to analyze it is that they support and balance each other.

Chapters 1 and 2 show how the Israelites obtain enough of the land to establish themselves, but they are not able to completely drive out the inhabitants. Usually they are able to get only parts of the land. Chapter 1:1-2 says, After the death of Joshua, the Israelites inquired of the LORD, "Who shall go up first for us against the

Canaanites, to fight against them?" The LORD said, "Judah shall go up. I hereby give the land into his hand."

Verses 3-7 say, Judah said to his brother Simeon, "Come up with me into the territory allotted to me, that we may fight against the Canaanites; then I too will go with you into the territory allotted to you." So Simeon went with him. Then Judah went up and the LORD gave the Canaanites and the Perizzites into their hand; and they defeated ten thousand of them at Bezek. They came upon Adoni-bezek at Bezek . . . and cut off the thumbs and big toes. Adoni-bezek said, "Seventy kings with their thumbs and big toes cut off used to pick up scraps under my table; as I have done, so God has paid me back." They brought him to Jerusalem, and he died there.

Then in verses 8-18 the people of Judah capture Jerusalem, Kiriath-arbor (Hebron), Debir, Hormah, Gaza, Ashkelon, Ekron, and Bethel (Luz). Verses 19-21 say, The LORD was with Judah, and he took possession of the hill country, but could not drive out the inhabitants of the plain, because they had chariots of iron. Hebron was given to Caleb, as Moses had said; and he drove out from it the three sons of Anak. But the Benjamites did not drive out the Jebusites who lived in Jerusalem; so the Jebusites have lived in Jerusalem among the Benjaminites to this day.

From verses 22-36 the only success was with the house of Joseph at Bethel. Manasseh, Ephraim, Zebulun, Asher, Naphtali, and Dan did not drive out the inhabitants. From verses 27-34 areas, mostly of the northern tribes, not conquered are listed. Verse 34 says, The Amorites pressed the Danites back into the hill country; they did not allow them to come down to the plain. (The northern tribes had many failures.)

In chapter 2 we learn the problem of the Israelites was disobedience. After Joshua dies, instead of tearing down the pagan altars, they begin worshiping the Baals and the Astartes. Baal is the Caananite storm god who is the divine warrior. He is the god of weather and fertility. His wife is Astarte, the goddess of love and war, the popular fertility goddess; El is the chief god. There are some who think El may have been the original one God that eventually is corrupted when people begin to add the gods of their own creation. Because Baal is considered a divine warrior, it is important for Yahweh to be considered the same, for the battle is about who is the real God.

The background is set for the pattern of the Deuteronomic historian's theology which is prevalent in this book and will continue through II Kings. Chapter 2:11-13 says, Then the Israelites did what was evil in the sight of the LORD and worshiped the Baals; and they abandoned the LORD, the God of their ancestors . . . they followed other gods, from among the gods of the people who were all around them . . . and they provoked the LORD to anger. They abandoned the LORD, and worshiped Baal and the Astartes.

In verses 16-23 the pattern continues as God allows them to be dominated, but when they are oppressed he has pity on them and raises up a judge who liberates them. But when the judge dies, they will chase after foreign gods again, and the pattern begins all over as the people worship the Baals and bow down to them.

A good example of the pattern is seen in 3:7-11. The Israelites did what was evil in the sight of the LORD, forgetting the LORD their God, and worshiping the Baals and Asherahs. Therefore the anger of the LORD was kindled against Israel, and he sold them into the hand of king Cushan-rishathaim of Aramnaharaim, and the Israelites served Cushan-rishathaim eight years. But when the Israelites cried out to the LORD, the LORD raised up a deliverer for the Israelites, who delivered them, Othniel son of Kenaz, Caleb's younger brother. The spirit of the LORD came upon him, and he judged Israel; he went out to war, and the LORD gave him King Cushan-rishathaim of Aram into his hand; and his hand prevailed . . . So the land had rest forty years. Then Othniel son of Kenaz died.

The deliverer was called a judge. He was a military leader but also judged major disputes among the people. The land would be at rest or peace for 40 years, then the judge would die, and the pattern would begin all over again. Forty years is important in the Bible. The judges Othniel, Deborah, Barak, Gideon, and Eli each judge 40 years. Ehud judges twice 40 years for eighty years. Saul, David, and Solomon each reign for 40 years. In Noah's flood one version has the rain lasting 40 days. Moses leaves Egypt at 40 years, is in Midian 40 years, and is on the mountain 40 days. Israel wanders in the wilderness 40 years, the spies are 40 days in Canaan, Elijah will fast 40 days, and Nineveh is given respite for 40 days. Jesus fasts 40 days and spends 40 days in the wilderness, and is on this earth 40 days after his resurrection. Apparently 40 is a symbolic number sometimes meaning a long time, and sometimes meaning a generation.

Verses 12-15 say, The Israelites again did what was evil in the sight of the LORD; and the LORD strengthened King Eglon of Moab against Israel, because they had done what was evil in the sight of the LORD. In alliance with the Ammonites and the Amalekites, he went and defeated Israel; and they took possession of the city of Palms (Jericho). So the Israelites served King Eglon of Moab eighteen years. But when the Israelites cried out to the LORD, the LORD raised up for them a deliverer, Ehud son of Gera, the Benjaminite, a left handed man. (The pattern then begins all over again.)

The story of Ehud (15-30) is an interesting story as a part of this cycle that the Israelites also found amusing. Ehud is left handed as many of the Benjaminites were. This tribe's left handed slingers had an excellent reputation in war. Ehud tricks the king of Moab who is very fat into a private meeting. At the meeting verses 21-23 say, Then Ehud reached with his left hand, took the sword from his right thigh, and thrust it into Eglon's belly; the hilt went in after the blade, and the fat closed over the blade, for he did not draw the sword out of his belly; and the dirt came out. Then Ehud went out into the vestibule, and closed the doors of the roof chamber on him, and locked them. When his servants came to get him, they thought he was relieving himself so they waited outside. This gives Ehud time to escape. Then in (28-30) he leads an attack against Moab killing ten thousand of their able bodied men; Moab is subdued.

The pattern continues as chapter 4:1-3 says, The Israelites again did what was evil in the sight of the LORD after Ehud died. So the LORD sold them into the hand of King Jabin of Canaan, who reigned in Hazor; the commander of his army was Sisera . . . Then the Israelites cried out to the LORD for help, for he had nine hundred chariots of iron, and had oppressed the Israelites cruelly twenty years.

In verses 4-16 God calls and leads Deborah, a prophetess, and her general, Barak, to defeat the Philistines who have chariots of iron. As Barak scatters the Philistines in defeat, their general, Sisera, escapes and is lured into the tent of a woman named Jael. Verse 17 says, Sisera had fled away on foot to the tent of Jael wife of Heber the Kenite; for there was peace between King Jabin and the clan of Heber. After Jael invites him in, he asks her to stand guard for him while he sleeps. As he sleeps verse 21 says, Jael wife of Heber took a tent peg, and took a hammer in her hand, and went softly to him and drove the peg into his temple, until it went down into the ground—he was lying fast asleep from weariness—and he died.

Chapter 5 includes Deborah's song of victory and praise to God. God uses the woman Jael to bring victory to the peasants of Israel. Verse 24 says, "Most blessed of women be Jael, the wife of Heber the Kenite, of tent-dwelling women most blessed . . ." (This story extolling the virtues of women in war is very rare in ancient history.)

Chapters 6-8 are about Gideon. Chapter 6:1 says, The Israelites did what was evil in the sight of the LORD, and the LORD gave them into the hand of Midian seven years. The Midianites were using a new military tactic, the use of a camel cavalry (5). In 7-10 when the Israelites called to God because of the Midianites, God sends a prophet to call the Israelites to repentance.

In verses 11-25 Gideon is called, but he is slow to respond which symbolizes Israelite's problem throughout their history. Gideon is afraid to go to battle, but an angel from God sets his offering on fire. Gideon then destroys the Baal altar. When the town's people learn it is Gideon, they change his name in (32) to Jerubbaal which means, let Baal contend against him. Then in (33-35) all the Midianites and the Amalekites, and the people of the East (tribes of Ishmael) come together, and crossing the Jordan they camp in the valley of Jezreel. But the spirit of the LORD took possession of Gideon; and he sounds the trumpet, and the Abiezrites are called out to follow him. He sent messengers throughout all Manasseh, and they too are called out to follow him. He also sent messengers to Asher, Zebulun, and Naphtali, and they go up to meet him.

Gideon in (36-40) asks for proof from God that if he goes to battle, he will prevail. In verses 36-38 Gideon says, "In order to see whether you will deliver Israel by my hand, as you have said, I am going to lay a fleece of wool on the threshing floor; if there is dew on the fleece alone, and it is dry on all the ground, then I shall know that you will deliver Israel by my hand, as you have said." And it was so. (This challenge to God happens twice.) But the second time he switches the challenge in (39) to say, "Do not let your anger burn against me, let me speak one more time; . . . let me, please make trial with the fleece just once more; let it be dry only on the fleece, and on the ground let there be dew." Verse 40 says, And God did so that night.

In 7:1 Gideon gathers his troops to go against the Midianites. God will save the people through Gideon even in his lack of trust. Again this is meant to represent Israel's history. Here God uses a weak-willed person whose faith is suspect to bring about victory. As stated previously a certain aspect of biblical history is symbolic history. Incidents are told to symbolize something, and most often Israel is the one symbolized.

In chapter 7: 2 The LORD said to Gideon, "The troops with you are too many for me to give the Midianites into their hand. Israel would only take the credit away from me saying, 'My own hand has delivered me.' Now therefore proclaim this in the hearing of the troops, 'whoever is fearful and trembling, let him return home.' " Then in (3) Gideon trims the troops from twenty-two thousand to ten thousand. Verse 4 says, Then the LORD said to Gideon, "The troops are still too many; take them down to the water and I will sift them out for you there. When I say, 'This one shall go with you,' he shall go with you; and when I say 'This one shall not go with you,' he shall not go."

Verses 5-7 say, So he brought the troops down to the water; and the LORD said to Gideon, "All those who lap the water with their tongues, as a dog laps, you shall put to one side; all those who kneel down to drink, putting their hands to their mouths, you shall put to the other side." The number of those who lapped was three hundred; but all the rest of the troops knelt down to drink water. Then the LORD said to Gideon, "With the three hundred that lapped I will deliver you, and give the Midianites into your hand. Let all the others go to their homes." So led by God Gideon gets down to 300 men and in (9-23) through a strange war strategy of a night attack with swords, trumpets, jars, and torches, he surprises the Midianites causing havoc in their camp and routes them.

In chapter 8 after more impressive victories and the killing of the kings of Midian, Zebeh and Zalmunna, the Israelites ask Gideon to rule over them. But Gideon in (23) said, "I will not rule over you, and my son will not rule over you; the LORD will rule over you."

Verses 29-32 inform us that Jerubbaal (Gideon) had many wives and concubines, and had seventy sons. One of the sons from a concubine in Shechem was the ambitious Abimelech. When Gideon dies (33-35) says, the Israelites relapsed and prostituted themselves with the Baals making Baal-berith their god. The Israelites did not remember the LORD their God, who had rescued them from the hand of all their enemies on every side; and they did not exhibit loyalty to the house of Jerubbaal (that is Gideon) in return for all the good he had done to Israel.

Abimelech is a brutal man who makes himself the leader. He is a disinherited son of Gideon who seizes the royal dignity that Gideon rejected. In 9:4-6 with the money from the temple of Baal in Shechem he hires worthless and reckless men to kill seventy of his brothers. Then the lords of Shechem and all Beth-millo make him king by the oak at Shechem. But Jotham, the youngest brother survives by hiding himself. Jotham's fable in 8-13 displays cynicism about kingship similar to I Samuel 8 and calls Abimelech a worthless bramble. He denounces Abimelech's monarchy built on theft and murder.

Later in (22-23) after three years of Abimelech's rule the town divides in their loyalty, and a man named Gaal in (26-40) leads some of the people against Abimelech, but he is defeated. In (42-44) Abimelech storms Shechem and kills many. Verse 46 says, When all the lords of the Tower of Shechem heard of it, they entered the stronghold of the temple of El-berith. Verse 49 tells us that Abimelech's men set the stronghold on fire over them, so that all the people of the Tower of Shechem also died, about a thousand men and women.

Verse 50 says, Then Abimelech went to Thebez, and encamped against Thebez, and took it. Abimilech is fatally wounded when a woman (53) threw an upper millstone on him and crushes his skull as he is about to kill the lords and people in the tower of Thebez. It is considered a disgrace to be killed by a woman, thus Abimelech in (54) asks his armor bearer to finish him with his sword. So the young man thrust him through, and he died.

The end of Abimelech is a judgment on his attempt to re-establish the discredited Canaanite socio-political system. Abimelech's interest was socio-economic political power and nothing else. It is interesting to note that Shechem, where Abraham first went when he entered the promised land and built an altar, and the place where the people made an oath to Joshua to always choose and follow the one God, had now become a center for Baal worship.

Next Tola and Jair judge and not much is mentioned about them. After them chapter 10:6 says, The Israelites again did what was evil in the sight of the LORD, worshiping the Baals and the Astartes, the gods of Aram, the gods of Sidon, the gods of Moab, the gods of the Ammonites, and the gods of the Philistines. Thus they abandoned the LORD and did not worship him.

Verses 7-10 say, So the anger of the LORD was kindled against Israel, and he sold them into the hands of the Philistines and into the hands of the Ammonites, and they crushed and oppressed the Israelites that year. For eighteen years they oppressed all the Israelites that were beyond the Jordan in the land of the Amorites, which is in Gilead. So the Israelites cried out to the LORD, saying, "We have sinned against you, because we have abandoned our God and worshiped the Baals." Verse 16 says, So they put away the foreign gods from among them and worshiped the LORD; and he could no longer bear to see Israel suffer. Verse 18 says, The commanders of the people of Gilead said to one another, "Who will begin the fight against the Ammonites? He shall be head over all the inhabitants of Gilead."

In chapter 11 Jephthah, the son of a prostitute, becomes a mighty warrior. He is an opportunist who gathers outlaws who go raiding with him. When the Ammonites make war against Israel, the elders of Gilead make him their commander. In the battle with the Ammonites he vows in verses 30-31 to offer in a burnt offering the first person who comes out of his house when he returns home. (This is an indication of his devotion to pagan gods who demand child sacrifices. It is also an indication of how low the people's understanding of the one God is at this time. But God will use this person for his purposes, and the Ammonites will be defeated.)

After inflicting a massive defeat on the Ammonites, he returns home, and his only child, a virgin daughter, comes out to greet him singing and dancing over his victory. When he saw her in (35-36) he tore his clothes in grief, for a vow was irrevocable. He said to his daughter, "Alas my daughter . . . I have opened my mouth to the LORD, and I can not take back my vow." Verse 36 says, She said to him, "My father if you have opened your mouth to the LORD, do to me according to what has gone out of your mouth, now that the LORD has given you vengeance against your enemies, the Ammonites."

Apparently Jephthah was also a synergist. A synergist is one who worships all the gods including the one God. This is a strange story to be added to Scripture. It must have originated in a circle that still believed in human sacrifice, or the author is including it to demonstrate how pagan things had become in those times. Jephthah's daughter in (37-40) requests two months to wander on the mountains to bewail her virginity with her companions. After two months she returns, and it is done to her according to the vow.

Chapter 12:1-7 war breaks out between Ephraim and Gilead. Verses 4-5 say, Jephthah gathered all the men of Gilead . . . and defeated Ephraim . . . the Gileadites took to the fords of the Jordan against the Ephraimites. Whenever one of the fugitives of Ephraim said, "Let me go over," the men of Gilead would say to him, "Are you an Ephraimite?" When he said "No," they said to him, "Then say Shibboleth, and he said Sibboleth," for he could not pronounce it right. Then they seized him and killed him at the fords of the Jordan. Forty-two thousand of the Ephraimites fell at that time. Verse 7 says, Jephthah judged Israel six years. Then Jephthah the Gileadite died, and was buried in his town in Gilead. After him Ibzan, Elon, and Abdon judged Israel. Not much is mentioned about them.

Chapter 13:1 says, The Israelites again did what was evil in the sight of the LORD, and the LORD gave them into the hand of the Philistines for forty years. The rest of chapters 13-16 tell the story of Samson from the tribe of Dan on the Philistine border. Samson is born after an angel appeared to the wife of Manoah, then to Manoah himself to tell them that a child, is to be born to his barren wife and that he is to be a Nazirite. A Nazirite dedicates himself to God, does not touch strong drink, does not cut his hair, and can not touch a dead body. When the boy is born he is named Samson. Verse 24 says, The boy grew, and the LORD blessed him.

Chapter 14 jumps to the time of Samson's wedding age. Samson marries a Philistine to the chagrin of his parents. In (3-4) his parents say, "Is there not a woman among your kin, or among all our people, that you must go take a wife from the uncircumcised Philistines?" But Samson said to his father, "Get her for me, because she pleases me." Verse 4 says, His father and mother did not know that this was from the LORD; for he was seeking a pretext to act against the Philistines. At that time the Philistines had dominion over Israel. (Would God need a pretext such as this to act against the Philistines, or is this the writer's thinking?)

Samson goes to Timnah. When he comes to the vineyards, a lion attacks him. Verses 6-9 say, The spirit of the LORD rushed on him, and he tore the lion apart barehanded as one might tear apart a kid. But he did not tell his father or mother what he had done. Then he went down and talked with the woman, and she pleased Samson. After awhile he returned to marry her, and he turned aside to see the carcass of the lion, and there was a swarm of bees in the body of the lion, and honey. He scraped it out with his hands, and went on, eating as he went.

This is another indication of Samson moving in the wrong direction, for as a Nazirite he is not to touch anything dead. He not only makes contact with a dead animal and eats food from it, but he will let his wife cut his hair and will host a drinking party, all in violation of his Nazirite vow. Even so, God will use him as an instrument to defeat the Philistines.

Later at a feast with his wife, Samson proposes a riddle in verse 14 and wagers a bet to the others that they can not solve it. Samson's wife coaxes the answer from him and tells the others, who then give Samson the correct answer to the riddle. Samson in (18) says, "If you had not plowed my heifer, you would not have found out my riddle." Hot with anger in (19) he goes to Ashkelon and kills thirty men taking from them what he needs to pay off his bet. Verse 20 says, Samson's wife is given to his companion who had been his best man.

Chapter 15:1 says, After awhile, at the time of the wheat harvest, Samson went to visit his wife, bringing along a kid. He said, "I want to go into my wife's room." (Can the reader guess why?) But her father would not allow him to go in. Her father said, "I was sure that you rejected her; so I gave her to your companion. Is not her younger sister prettier than she? Why not take her instead?"

Samson takes revenge by destroying the grain crop of the Philistines, and this begins a cycle of revenge. In (4-8) Samson caught three hundred foxes, took some torches, then turned the foxes tail to tail and put a torch between each pair of tails. When he set fire to the torches, he let the foxes go into the grain, which set the field of grain on fire destroying it as well as the vineyards and olive trees.

The people of Judah turn Samson over to the Philistines because of their fear of the Philistines. The Philistines go and burn his wife and her father, and Samson takes revenge on them with a great slaughter. In verses 9-13 three thousand men of Judah bind him with ropes to give him to the Philistines, but in (14-16) the spirit of the LORD rushes on him. He breaks the ropes and picks up a jaw bone of a donkey and kills a thousand Philistines with it.

Chapter 16:1 says, Samson went to Gaza where he saw a prostitute and went into her. (The weakness of this strong man apparently is women, and he is led too much by his emotions and his desires rather than his reason.) In (2-3) the Gazites gather and prepare to capture him, he gets away without them knowing, and he pulls out the doors of the city gate, puts them on his shoulders and carries them to the top of the hill near Hebron.

In verses 4-16 is the story of Samson who falls in love with Delilah. The Philistine leaders then go to Delilah and offer her money to find out the secret of his strength. She asks him three different times, and three different times he makes up a reason. Three different times she tells the Philistines, and three different times they learn it is not the correct reason for Samson's strength. Finally, she coaxes it out of him. (Obviously he was not the sharpest knife in the drawer.) In verse 17 he says, "A razor has never come upon my head; for I have been a Nazirite to God from my mother's womb. If my head were shaved, then my strength would leave me; I will become weak, and be like anyone else."

In verse 18 Delilah tells the Philistine lords. They pay her bribe money to let Samson fall asleep on her lap while a man shaves off his hair. At that point (19) says, his strength left him. Verse 21 says, the Philistines seized him and gouged out his eyes. They brought him down to Gaza and bound him with bronze shackles; and he ground at the mill in prison.

In the meantime his hair begins to grow. At a great sacrifice to their god, Dagon, verses 25-27 say, And when their hearts were merry, they said, "Call Samson, and let him entertain us." So they called Samson out of the prison, and he performed for them. They made him stand before the pillars; and Samson said to the attendant who held him by the hand, "Let me feel the pillars on which the house rests, so that I may lean against them." Now the house was full of men and women; all the lords of the Philistines were there, and on the roof were about three thousand men and women, who looked on while Samson performed.

When he has his hands in place, in verse 28 he prays, "Lord GOD, remember me and strengthen me only this once, O God, so that with this one act of revenge I may pay back the Philistines for my two eyes." Verses 29-31 say, And Samson grasped the two middle pillars on which the house rested, and he leaned his weight against them, his right hand on the one and his left hand on the other. Then Samson said, "Let me die with the Philistines." He strained with all his might; and the house fell on the lords and all the people in it. So those he killed at his death were more than he had killed during his life. Samson had judged Israel twenty years and was buried in the tomb of his father Manoah.

The morality of Samson as well as many of the other leaders we have read about is weak to say the least. But God used what he had in order to work out his purposes. That does not mean God approved of their low form of morality. Thus many of the so-called heroes of the faith are not very heroic as far as morality is concerned, but God uses what he has. God's promises and God's plan will not fail even if he has to work through morally weak people. Again, a major issue in the OT is preserving the one God idea, an idea that came very close to being extinguished numerous times, but the one God was not going to allow it to fail.

Chapters 17-18 mention the migration of the Danites. The tribe of Dan had been assigned territory that included the Philistine plain which they had difficulty taking. Being cramped for room, part of the tribe migrates to the far north along with an idol they take from a man named Micah. Micah from the tribe of Ephraim had confessed to his mother that he had stolen eleven hundred pieces of silver from her. When he returned the money, she made an idol from it.

When the Danites passed through they persuaded the Levite from Bethlehem to be their priest. Chapter 18:27 says, The Danites, having taken what Micah had made, and the priest who belonged to him, came to Laish, to a people quiet and unsuspecting, put them to the sword, and burned down the city. Eventually they rebuild the city, and (29-30) say, They named the city Dan, after their ancestor Dan . . . Then the Danites set up their idol for themselves. (The story is included here to show how Dan became one of the worst places for idol worship.)

Chapter 19 tells of a Levite who took a concubine from Bethlehem to Gibeah which is the territory of Benjamin. While there enjoying themselves, perverse men of the city in (22-28) pounded on their door wanting to have intercourse with the Levite. The master of the house said no, but by the rules of hospitality in those times he offered his virgin daughter and his concubine. (Sounds like the beginning of the story of Sodom and Gomorrah all over again.)

As in the story of Lot, the host tries to protect the guest, offering his own virgin daughter and also the concubine which they refuse. Verse 25 says, the man seized his concubine and put her out to them. They wantonly raped her and abused her all through the night until morning. In the process she dies. In (29-30) the Levite puts her on his donkey and goes to his house where he cut her body into twelve parts. He then sends one part to each of the twelve tribes suggesting a call to war on the Benjaminites.

In chapter 20 the tribes gather together at Mizpah and declare war on the Benjaminites. The town of Gibeah is destroyed, and only 600 men are left The tribe of Benjamin is almost extinguished, and we will not hear very much about them in the future. Even so, chapter 21 tells us they are saved from total extinction because the people have compassion on them even though the twelve tribes took a vow that none of their women would marry a Benjaminite.

Part of the solution will center on Jabesh Gilead who had refused to show up in the civil war with the Benjaminites. So the leaders in (11-12) go there and put to death every one who had intercourse both male and female. Four hundred young virgins are left and brought to Shiloh where a wine festival is taking place, and they give them to 400 Benjaminites. (They are still 200 short.) So in (19-21) they go to Shiloh where some captured women of war are slaves. They told the men that when the women come out to dance, grab one of the women and take her for your wife. This is how the Benjaminites get the other 200 and are saved from extinction. (We certainly do not see much respect for women in this strange story.)

The last verse (21:25) summarizes the problem when it says, In those days there was no king in Israel; all the people did what was right in their own eyes. Four times from chapters 17-21 it says, in those days there was no king in Israel.

This last sentence summarized the problem. They had rejected God as their king, so everyone did what they felt like doing creating their own morality. The people had become lawless and self serving because there was no moral leadership at the top. It was a time of compromise with pagan religion, violent crime, civil wars, and anarchy. The tribes were basically independent of each other. They did not cooperate very much with each other, and it did not seem any of the judges had consistent control over all twelve tribes. Could the one God and his teachings survive this low state of affairs? This is what no leadership or poor leadership can do to any nation at any time.

One lesson in Judges is that God can use very imperfect people to accomplish his purposes. Even though their faith was imperfect, and their understanding of faith was not great, at least they had some faith in a time of practically no faith or very weak faith overall.

The reader may ask why is such a book in the Bible? We must keep in mind that if it had not been for the Judges, even though their faith was weak and imperfect, Israel would not have been preserved, and the one God concept would have disappeared. From the Christian point of view, it is because Israel is preserved that God can move on and prepare for the coming of the one who will become the perfect witness to God's righteousness.

This might be a good time to talk about the literary genre called narratives. Narratives are stories. They are purposeful stories retelling historical events usually passed down orally intended to give universal truths, meaning and direction for a given people. All narratives have characters, a plot, and a plot resolution. Narratives are not allegories or stories filled with hidden meanings, for they had plain meaning for the original hearers.

Also, narratives are not necessarily written to teach moral lessons. They are simply to tell what God did in history, even how God works in history. One may see the just consequences of good morality and bad morality, or one may not see the justness of either. For example, God chose Jacob not Esau even though some conniving may have taken place; God chose Judah even when he violated Tamar, God chose the tribe of Levi to lead his people in worship, even though he acted wrongly with his brother Simeon, and God chose the Judges, even though many were of low character.

The issue is not always the morality involved, but God working his plan. In the process God often does the unexpected. From the human point of view God does not always seem just, but who are we to judge God? God is sovereign; it is his world and his creation. Someday we will better understand. Life in this broken world is very often not fair, but usually it is not God's fault.

In any biblical narrative God is the ultimate character, so in summary we can say the OT narratives are written primarily to show progress of God's history of redemption not primarily to illustrate moral principles, even though we learn much about moral relationships and their consequences. There are no systematic ethics or systematic morality in the Bible even though from it we can get a foundation and a way to think about morality. The reader needs to be careful not to read into the Bible what one wants to see. The reader needs to just make an attempt to take from the Bible the plain meaning and direction toward which the text is moving.

Narratives record to some extent what basically happened and not necessarily what should have happened or what ought to happen, so do not always look for the moral of the story even though one may be there. What people do in a narrative is not necessarily a good example for us. Often, it is just the opposite. Everything we would like to know is not always included. Narratives are not written to answer all our questions. Even though it is all God inspired, what the people say and do is not necessarily God speaking. Many times it is simply humans speaking and doing their thing which God may not approve. A good example is Jephthah who thought he could not change his mind on his vow to sacrifice to God the first human he saw, if he was successful in battle. God never approved of human sacrifices so he certainly could have ignored his vow.

God's word is in Scripture, but many times humans are left to figure exactly what that is in the context of their worshiping fellowship. God has his purpose in that also. As we move on the reader will understand more clearly what this writer is saying in attempting to aid the reader with a deeper approach and comprehension of these writings.

1 & 2 SAMUEL

The theme of 1 and 2 Samuel is the origin of the Davidic monarchy. Samuel a future judge and prophet is conceived by Hannah his long time sterile mother. Her song of praise and thanksgiving foreshadows Mary's Magnificat. Samuel will later anoint Saul as the first king, and then David, who becomes the Israelite's greatest king. Saul is disobedient to God and becomes very jealous of David whom he attempts to kill.

The second book of Samuel is about David, his rule over Israel, and his family problems. These are a result of his sin with Bathsheba. The son born to Bathsheba dies but the second son, Solomon, will reign after David's favorite son Absalom dies fighting his father in a civil war. After Solomon the united kingdom splits into the kingdom of the north (Israel) and the kingdom of the south (Judah). In 2 Samuel 7 the prophet Nathan pronounces that the descendants of David will rule forever.

As we read we must keep in mind that all history is interpreted history. Facts are not simply reported but are selected and organized according to the interpretive stance of the historian as led by God who has inspired these writings. The Deuteronomistic writers have their own theological perspective as it governs their selection and arrangement of the materials. For these writers Israel's history becomes the story of its success or failure depending upon obedience and worship of the one God.

1 SAMUEL

The first book of Samuel comprises the history of about a century. It describes the close of the age of Judges and the beginning of monarchy in Israel under Saul and David. Samuel is the connecting link, and the approximate date is 1100-1050 B.C. Shiloh is an important geographical location, for the sacred tabernacle is here. Shiloh is about twenty miles north of Jerusalem in the mountains of Ephraim, north of Bethel. The tabernacle was moved to Shiloh by Joshua after it was moved from Gilgal.

Samuel, who is a priest and the last of the judges, is introduced. He is the first great prophet to begin a school for prophets. Samuel's devotion to God and his good character are unquestionable. Samuel plays such a large role in the transformation of Israel that his name is given to two books in the Bible. Samuel is certainly one of the great men of the OT.

As the reader moves through the book, one will notice there are two stories about how Saul became a prophet, two stories about why Samuel rejected Saul, two stories about how David found a place in Saul's court, two stories about Saul throwing his spear at David, and two stories of David sparing Saul's life (Ramsay 1994). This tells us that those who gathered and put together this information had numerous sources both oral and written that had been handed down over the years. Rather than smoothing everything out they included all of them. Perhaps including everything is a sign that the events do rest on a basic, genuine history. Always keep in mind that God's inspiration is about theology not giving us the exact details of history as moderns define history.

In chapter 1 a man named Elkanah from Ephraim has two wives, Hannah and Peninnah. The latter has children but the former, Hannah, has no children. Peninnah provokes her severely and irritates Hannah because as (6) says, the LORD had closed her womb. (This seems to be a pattern for women in Scripture who eventually bear a great leader.)

Elkanah goes yearly to sacrifice at Shiloh where the two sons of Eli, Hophni and Phinehas, are priests of the LORD. One day after weeping, Hannah in (9-11) goes to Shiloh and presents herself to the LORD and in (11) she made this vow: "O LORD of hosts, if only you will look on the misery of your servant, and remember me, and not forget your servant, but will give to your servant a male child, then I will set him before you as a Nazirite until the day of his death . . ." (A Nazirite is to be set aside for God in a special way. To show this the Nazirite drinks no wine or strong drink, does not eat grapes, does not cut his hair or beard, nor make contact with a dead body.)

As Hannah in (12-13) is praying before the LORD, Eli the priest thinks she is drunk. So Eli in (14-16) said to her, "How long will you make a drunken spectacle of yourself? Put away your wine." But Hannah answered, "No, my lord, I am a woman deeply troubled; I have drunk neither wine nor strong drink, but I have been pouring out my soul before the LORD . . ." Then in (17-18) Eli answered, "Go in peace; the God of Israel grant the petition you have made to him." And she said, "Let your servant find favor in your sight."

She returns to her home and (20) says, In due time Hannah conceived and bore a son. She named him Samuel, for she said, "I have asked him of the LORD." Verse 24 says, When she had weaned him, she took him up with her . . . She brought him to the house of the LORD at Shiloh; and the child was young. She presented him to Eli and in (26-28) said, "Oh my lord! As you live, my lord, I am the woman who was standing here in your presence, praying to the LORD. For this child I prayed; and the LORD has granted me the petition that I made to him. Therefore I have lent him to the LORD; as long as he lives, he is given to the LORD."

The gift of a son to Hannah shows God's favor toward the disadvantaged, and indicates Samuel is chosen for a purpose. Often in Scripture a barren woman, who has a child in later years, has a child chosen by God for his special purpose.

Chapter 2 contains Hannah's song, a poem of thanksgiving, which is the precursor to Mary's Magnificat in the Gospel of Luke.1:46-55. Hannah's song in 2:1-10 is a song of thanksgiving. Her song celebrates the reversals of power made possible by God. Verses 4-8 say, The bows of the mighty are broken, but the feeble gird on strength. Those who are full have hired themselves out for bread, but those who were hungry are fat with spoil. The barren has borne seven, but she who has many children is forlorn. The LORD kills and brings to life; he brings down to Sheol and raises up. The LORD makes poor and makes rich; he brings low, he also exalts. He raises up the poor from the dust; he lifts up the needy from the ash heap, to make them sit with princes and inherit a seat of honor.

Verse 12 says, the sons of Eli were scoundrels; they had no regard for the LORD or for the duties of the priests to the people. We learn that they are greedy for the offerings, and verse 17 says, Thus the sin of the young men was very great in the sight of the LORD; for they treated the offerings of the LORD with contempt. (Here we learn that a few corrupt clergy is not a new thing.) Verse 22 says, they lay with the women who served at the entrance to the tent of the meeting. In (23-25) he (Eli) said to them, "Why do you do such things? For I hear of your evil doings from all these people . . ." Verse 25 says, they would not listen to the voice of their father; for it was the will of the LORD to kill them. (It sounds like they had no choice, but it is the same as Pharaoh in Egypt. The writer is saying God is sovereign; he could have changed their attitude and behavior, but he allows them to bear the consequences of their choices. God is in control.)

Meanwhile verse 26 says, Now the boy Samuel continued to grow both in stature and in favor with the LORD and with the people. Then in (27-36) a man of God came to Eli and said to him, "Thus the LORD has said, 'I revealed myself to the family of your ancestor in Egypt when they were slaves to the house of Pharaoh. I chose him out of all the tribes of Israel to be my priest, to go up to my altar . . . Why then look with greedy eye at my sacrifices and my offerings that I commanded, and honor your sons more than me by fattening yourselves on the choicest parts of every offering on my people Israel?'

In verse 30 the LORD the God of Israel declares: 'I promised that your family and the family of your ancestors should go in and out before me forever'; but now the LORD declares: 'Far be it from me; for those who honor me I will honor, and those who despise me shall be treated with contempt. (Apparently, a forever promise goes two ways. If one rejects God, God will let them bear the consequences of their choices. God never takes away one's free will. This concept of forever as a promise of God is important.)

Verses 31-36 continue, See a time is coming when I will cut off your strength and the strength of your ancestor's family, so that no one in your family will live to an old age . . . The fate of your two sons, Hophni and Phinehas, shall be a sign to you—both of them shall die the same day. I will raise up for myself a faithful priest, who shall do according to what is in my heart and in my mind. I will build him a sure house, and he shall go in and out before my appointed one forever . . .' "

God is telling him that in the future his family will lose the priesthood to another family. Eli was an ancestor of Abiathar, and later under Solomon his descendants will be excluded from the priesthood in favor of Zadok and his family (see 1 Kings 1).

Chapter 3:1 says, Now the boy Samuel was ministering to the LORD under Eli. The word of the LORD was rare in those days; visions were not widespread. In (2-7) Samuel is lying down in his room which is in the temple of the ark of the LORD, and he hears a call for his name. He goes to Eli, and presents himself to him, but Eli tells him that he has not called him. This happens three times. Verses 8-9 say, Then Eli perceived that the LORD was calling the boy. Therefore Eli said to Samuel, "Go lie down; and if he calls you, say, 'speak LORD for your servant is listening.' "

In verses 10-14 the message God gives to Samuel is a confirmation that the house of Eli is about to be punished because of the iniquity of Eli's sons and his failure to restrain them. Samuel is afraid to tell Eli, but Eli in (17-18) said, "What was it that he told you? Do not hide it from me . . ." So Samuel told him everything and hid nothing from him. Then he (Eli) said, "It is the LORD; let him do what seems good to him."

Verses 19-21 say, As Samuel grew up, the LORD was with him and let none of his words fall to the ground. And all Israel from Dan to Beer-Sheba knew that Samuel was a trustworthy prophet of the LORD. The LORD continued to appear at Shiloh, for the LORD revealed himself to Samuel at Shiloh by the word of the LORD. (Samuel will become a prophet, priest, and judge who will bridge the transition from the judges to the monarchy.)

Chapter 4:1 says, In those days the Philistines mustered for war against Israel, and Israel went out to battle against them; . . . The rest of the chapter informs us that Israel takes the ark of the covenant, which is the presence of God, into battle. As Israel is defeated the ark of the covenant is captured, and the two sons of Eli die. A man then runs to tell Eli at Shiloh, and in (18) Eli falls over and breaks his neck because he is heavy, and he dies. He has judged Israel for forty years.

Verses 19-21 inform us that Eli's daughter-in-law, the wife of Phinehas, is about to give birth. When she hears the news, her labor pains overwhelm her and she gives birth. She named her son Ichabod which means the glory has departed from Israel. Verse 22 says, The glory has departed from Israel, for the ark of God has been captured.

In chapter 5:1-3 the Philistines take the ark to Ashdod and placed it in their temple beside Dagon, one of their gods. Verse 3 says, When the people of Ashdod rose early the next day, there was Dagon, fallen on his face to the ground before the ark of the LORD. (The writer is telling us that there is only one God, for even the pagan god fell to the ground before the ark of God. This happens twice.)

Verse 6 says, The hand of the LORD was heavy upon the people of Ashdod, and he terrified and struck them with tumors, both in Ashdod and in its territory. The people in (7) said, "The ark of the God of Israel must not remain with us. For his hand is heavy on us and on our god Dagon." The ark was moved to Gath in (8-9), and tumors break out again. (Apparently, this is a type of bubonic plague, for mice are throughout the land, and the disease produces tumors.)

Chapter 6:1-2 says, The ark of the LORD was in the country of the Philistine for seven months. Then the Philistines called for the priests and the diviners and said, "What shall we do with the ark of the LORD? Tell us what we should send with it to its place?" In (3-18) They are told to return it with a guilt offering of five gold tumors and five gold mice, and then they will be healed and ransomed. The five lords of the Philistines gather together and agree to send the ark back to Israel with a guilt offering consisting of five golden tumors and five golden mice to be put on a new cart carried by two milch cows. It is taken to Beth-shemesh, and there is great rejoicing.

Verse 19 says, The descendants of Jeconiah did not rejoice with the people of Beth-shemesh when they greeted (looked into) the ark of the LORD; and he killed seventy men of them. The people mourned because the LORD had made a great slaughter among the people. Then, in (20-21) the people of Beth-shemesh said, "Who is able to stand before the LORD, this holy God? To whom shall he go that we may be rid of him?" So they sent messengers to the inhabitants of Kiriath-jearim, saying, "The Philistines have returned the ark of the LORD. Come down and take it up with you."

The writer tells this story to stress the holiness of God and that humans are able to be in his presence only because of his great grace and mercy, and for this they must praise him and be thankful. Unfortunately, this message is missed by many even today.

In chapter 7:1-2 the ark is taken to Kiriath-jearim, a Gibeonite city that allied with Joshua. It is taken to the house of Abinadab on the hill, and it stays here for twenty years. They consecrated his son, Eleazar, to have charge of the ark of the LORD. Then in (3-4) Samuel said to the house of Israel, "If you are returning to the LORD with all your heart, then put away the foreign gods and the Astartes from among you. Direct your heart to the LORD, and serve him only, and he will deliver you out of the hands of the Philistines." So Israel put away the Baals and the Astartes, and they served the LORD only. God fought for Israel as the Philistines attacked them, and they were defeated. Verse 13 says, So the Philistines were subdued and did not again enter the territory of Israel; the hand of the LORD was against the Philistines all the days of Samuel.

Chapters 8-16 describe how Israel got a king. The people want a king like the other nations, but Samuel warns them about having a king other than the one God. The Scriptures include the traditions of both those who are for a king and those against probably to prepare the readers for the negative actions that will happen when the kings come to power. Boadt (1984) sees this as both a pro Saul source and an anti Saul source being accepted into Scripture in order to present both sides of the issue as to whether or not to have a human king. The anti Saul source reminds the people that the negative things would not have occurred if they had kept the one God as their king. Even so, kings will never have absolute power in Israel. They remain subject to prophets and the law of God, and they will stand against the king to mediate God's judgment. This aspect will be unique in the history of the ancient world.

Chapter 8:1-3 says, When Samuel became old, he made his sons judges over Israel. The name of his firstborn son was Joel, and the name of his second, Abijah; they were judges in Beersheba. Yet his sons did not follow in his ways; but turned aside after gain; they took bribes, and perverted justice. Therefore the elders of Israel in (6) ask Samuel to give them a king to govern them. (Again the Bible is reminding us of the dangers of inherited power, and we could add inherited wealth.)

Samuel prays to God, and in (7-10) the LORD says to Samuel, "Listen to the voice of the people in all that they say to you; for they have not rejected you, but they rejected me from being king over them . . . You shall solemnly warn them, and show them the ways of the king who shall reign over them." Samuel then describes in (11-18) all the negative things that will happen to them if they choose a king. He tells them a king will take the kingdom to war, tax and take their land, force people into labor, among other things, but it is to no avail.

Verses 19-21 say, But the people refused to listen to the voice of Samuel; they said, "No! but we are determined to have a king over us, so that we also may be like other nations, and that our king may govern us and go out before us and fight our battles." Verse 22 says, The LORD said to Samuel, "Listen to their voice and set a king over them."

Up to this point God has fought and won their battles for them. God will let the people make their choice between him as king or another, but they will also bear the consequences of their choice.

In chapter 9 a boy of Benjamin named Saul was sent to look for lost donkeys. In the meantime God reveals to Samuel in (16) "Tomorrow about this time I will send to you a man from the land of Benjamin, and you shall anoint him to be ruler over my people, Israel. He shall save my people from the hand of the Philistines; for I have seen the suffering of my people, because their outcry has come to me." As Saul looks for his donkeys he comes upon Samuel who tells him where to locate them. When Samuel sees him he tells Saul he is God's choice. Saul in (21) answered, "I am only a Benjamite from the least of the tribes of Israel, and my family is the humblest of all the families in the tribe of Benjamin. Why then have you spoken to me this way?" In verse 27 Samuel prepares to make known to Saul the word of God.

Saul's objection is typical of those who receive a divine call in the Bible. Moses and Jeremiah among other prophets are examples. It also shows Saul's early humility, and God's preference for the small and weak.

In chapter 10:1 Samuel anoints him as king. Samuel tells him that on the way home he will meet a band of prophets, and when he does, verse 6 says, Then the spirit of the LORD will possess you, and you will be in a prophetic frenzy along with them and be turned into a different person. Verse 9 says, As he turned away to leave Samuel, God gave him another heart; and all these signs were fulfilled that day. Then the people of the land in (11) ask, "What has come over the son of Kish? Is Saul also among the prophets?" In verses 20-25 Samuel summons all the tribes of Israel, and Saul is officially anointed king. As Samuel gathered the people together he uses a lottery to identify Saul in order to show the people that Saul the son of Kish is the choice of God.

In chapter 11 Nahash, the leader of the Ammonites attacks Jabesh-gilead and agrees to let the people live, but everyone's right eye will be gouged out bringing disgrace on Israel. Enraged by the news, Saul chops his oxen into parts and sends pieces to all in Israel with the call to battle. The people rally to his call and save Jabesh-gilead. Because of this victory, the people gain confidence in Saul and celebrate by renewing the kingship at Gilgal.

In chapter 12 Samuel officially turns responsibility for leading Israel over to Saul. In his address to the people Samuel reminds them of the teaching that God will bless the nation if they are obedient to God, but they will be cursed if they are not obedient. In verse 23 Samuel says that he will pray for them and instruct them in the good and right way. In verses 24-25 he says, Only fear the LORD, and serve him faithfully with all your heart; for consider what great things he has done for you. (Samuel is reminding them if they do wickedly, they will be swept away, both them and their king. God gave Saul a new heart, but most important is, how will he use that new heart?)

In chapter 13 the Philistines attack the Israelites. Before going into battle, they wait for Samuel to come and make the priestly sacrifice, but he is late. Some of the fighters begin to leave, so Saul offers the sacrifice himself. (This is a violation of the law, for only the Levites are permitted to offer the sacrifice. This may also be signifying that Saul is making a power grab for priestly and religious powers.)

When Samuel finally gets there and sees what happened, Samuel in verses 13-14 says, "You have done foolishly; you have not kept the commandment of the LORD your God, which he commanded you. The LORD would have established your kingdom over Israel forever, but now your kingdom will not continue; The LORD has sought out a man after his own heart; and the LORD has appointed him to be ruler over his people, because you have not kept what the LORD commanded you." (It is almost like God changed his thinking about Saul and was looking for the first opportunity to get rid of him as king. Later David and his sons act as priests, and it is acceptable, see 2 Sam 8:18.)

In chapter 14 Jonathan, Saul's son, routs the Philistines, but in the process his army slaughters the sheep, oxen, and calves and eats the blood. This is a major violation of God's law. Even so, Saul has great military victories over the Moabites, Ammonites, Edomites, Amalelikites, and the Philistines. Saul's uncle, Abner is his military commander. (Even though God is not happy with Saul, it seems that for the sake of the people he allows victory.)

It is important to know that the Philistines control the iron industry. As a result Israel is not armed with many swords, and in reality they are no match for the Philistines. Therefore any victory achieved by the Israelites is not because of them but because of God.

In chapter 15:1-9 Samuel tells Saul that God is going to punish the Amaleikites for opposing the Israelites when they came up from Egypt. They are to attack the Amalekites and destroy all they have. In Verses 7-8 Saul defeats and destroys the Amalekites. He takes King Agag of the Amalekites alive, but utterly destroys all the people with the edge of the sword. Verse 9 says, Saul and the people spared Agag, and the best of the sheep and of the cattle and of the fatlings, and the lambs, and all that is valuable, and would not utterly destroy them; all that was despised and worthless they utterly destroyed. Not destroying all was in violation of God's command.

Verse 10 says, The word of the LORD came to Samuel: "I regret that I made Saul king, for he has turned back from following me and has not carried out my commands." Samuel was angry; and he cried out to the LORD all night. In (12-21) Samuel goes to Saul and asks him why he has not obeyed God in his defeat of the Amelikites? He is told that he was to destroy all the Amelikites and offer all the booty to the one God, but he allowed King Agag to live, and from the spoil kept the best sheep and cattle. In verse 15 Saul tells him the people did it in order to save the best to sacrifice to the LORD. (When caught doing wrong, Saul, like many of us always has his excuses.)

In verses 22-23 Samuel said, "Has the LORD as great delight in burnt offerings and sacrifices, as in obeying the voice of the LORD? Surely, to obey is better than sacrifice, and to heed than the fat of rams. (This is the main point the writer wants to make with his readers.) For rebellion is no less a sin than divination, and stubbornness is like iniquity and idolatry. Because you have rejected the word of the LORD, he has also rejected you from being king."

Here the writer of Samuel emphasizes the problem of God's people as a whole throughout history. They offered worship but did not obey God's teachings. The writer indicates that worship is important, but obedience is even more important. Worship without obedience never pleases God.

In verse 30 Saul confesses his sins, but apparently he only confesses his sins when he is caught as we will continue to see. Samuel is not fooled, and neither is God. In (33) Samuel then took King Agag and hacked him into pieces (yuk). Apparently, God wanted all signs of idolatry eliminated as well as those responsible. Verse 35 says, Samuel did not see Saul again until the day of his death, but Samuel grieved over Saul. And the LORD was sorry that he had made Saul king over Israel.

Chapter 16:1 says, The LORD said to Samuel, "How long will you grieve over Saul? I have rejected him from being king over Israel. Fill your horn with oil and set out; I will send you to Jesse the Bethlehemite, for I have provided for myself a king among his sons." He then sends Samuel to anoint a new king among the sons of Jesse the Bethlehemite. In (2) Samuel said, "How can I go? If Saul hears of it, he will kill me." But verse 4 says, Samuel did what the LORD commanded and came to Bethlehem. God sends him to Jesse the Bethlehemite, and Jesse shows Samuel seven of his sons from the eldest down.

In verse 6 Samuel looks upon Eliab one of Jesse's son, and Samuel thought he was the one to be anointed, but (7) says, The LORD said to Samuel, "Do not look on his appearance or on the height of his stature, because I have rejected him; for the LORD does not see as mortals see; they look on the outward appearance, but the LORD looks on the heart." After passing through seven sons, Samuel asks Jesse in (11), "Are all your sons here?" Jesse says, "There remains yet the youngest, but he is keeping the sheep." Samuel asks him to send for him. When he comes, it is David, so God in (12-13) says, "Rise and anoint him, for this is the one!" The writer notes in (12) that he was handsome. Then Samuel anointed David in the presence of his bothers, and the spirit of the LORD came mightily upon David from that day forward. (Again as usual the youngest one is chosen.)

The rest of the chapter takes us back to Saul where the spirit of GOD has departed from him, and an evil spirit from God torments him. (The good heart God initially gave Saul had become hardened.)So they begin to look for someone who can soothe him with music. One of the young men tells them about David and describes him in (18) as skillful in playing, a man of valor, a warrior, prudent in speech, a man of good presence, and the LORD is with him. They sent for him, and (21) says, David came to Saul and entered his service. Saul loved him greatly, and he became his armor-bearer. Verse 23 says, And whenever the evil spirit came upon Saul, David took the lyre and played it with his hand, and Saul would be relieved and feel better, and the evil spirit would depart from him.

In chapter 17:1-3 the Philistines gather for battle. The Philistines stand on one mountain, and the Israelites on the other. A giant covered with armor, named Goliath, issues a challenge. In (8-9) he tells the Israelites to choose one man to fight him, and if their man beats him the Philistines will be their servants, but if Goliath wins, then the Israelites will be the servants of the Philistines. The Israelites are greatly afraid.

Verses 12-39 tell us that David has been at home with his father tending the sheep, but Jesse sends him to take food and visit his brothers who are in the army at the mountain. David happens to get there when Goliath issues the challenge. David asks Saul to allow him to challenge Goliath, and because no one has stepped up to meet Goliath's challenge, Saul gives him permission.

In verse 40 David takes his staff, his sling, and five smooth stones. Goliath thunders trash talk at him, but David says in (45-47), "You come to me with sword and spear and javelin; but I come to you in the name of the LORD of hosts, the God of the armies of Israel, whom you have defied. This very day the LORD will deliver you into my hand, and I will strike you down and cut off your head; and I will give the dead bodies of the Philistine army this very day to the birds of the air and to the wild animals of the earth, so that all the earth may know there is a God in Israel and that all this assembly may know that the LORD does not save by sword and spear; for the battle is the LORD's and he will give you into our hand."

Verses 49-51 say, David put his hand in his bag, took out a stone, slung it, and struck the Philistine on his forehead; the stone sank into his forehead, and he fell face down on the ground. So David prevailed over the Philistine with a sling, striking down the Philistine and killing him; there was no sword in David's hand. Then David ran and stood over the Philistine; he grasped his sword, drew it out of its sheath, and killed him; then he cut off his head with it. When the Philistines saw their champion was dead, they fled. Verses 52-54 inform us that the troops chased the Philistines and plundered their camp, and David took Goliath's head to Jerusalem.

Saul in (55) asks his commander, "Abner, whose son is this young man?" Abner said, "As your soul lives, O king, I do not know." The king said, "Inquire whose son the stripling is." On David's return from killing the Philistine, Abner took him and brought him before Saul, with the head of the Philistine in his hand. Saul said to him, "Whose son are you young man?" And David answered, "I am the son of your servant Jesse, the Bethlehemite."

This is one indication that in the development of 1 Samuel there are different sources, not always consistent in every detail, being woven together. As the reader has seen the story had previously introduced David who played the lyre for Saul, so why does Saul not know him? Some answer Saul is not really asking that question, for he already knew him. So this is an idiomatic phrase, but that does not explain why Abner did not know who he was. The majority of scholarship simply believes it is a matter of sources. It is also interesting that according to 2 Samuel 21:19 and 1 Chronicles 20:5, Goliath of Gath was slain at a later time by Elhanan, one of David's warriors. Keep in mind the purpose of these inspired Scriptures is not an exact detailed history as we moderns understand history.

A deep friendship develops between Jonathan the son of Saul and David. Chapter 18:1-2 says, When David had finished speaking with Saul, the soul of Jonathan was bound to the soul of David, and Jonathan loved him as his own soul. Saul took him that day and would not let him return to his father's house. Verses 3-4 say, Then Jonathan made a covenant with David, because he loved him as his own soul. Jonathan stripped himself of the robe he was wearing, and gave it to David, and his armor, and even his sword and his bow and his belt. (All this was a sign of devotion, even submission.)

Verses 5-8 say, David went out and was successful wherever Saul sent him; as a result Saul set him over the army. And all the people, even the servants of Saul, approved. As they were coming home, when David returned from killing the Philistine, the women came out of all the towns of Israel singing and dancing, to meet King Saul, with tambourines, with songs of joy, and with musical instruments. And the women sang to one another as they made merry, "Saul has killed his thousands, and David his ten thousands." Saul was very angry, for this saying displeased him.

Verses 10-16 say, The next day an evil spirit from God rushed upon Saul, and he raved within his house, while David was playing the lyre, as he did day by day. Saul had his spear in his hand; and Saul threw the spear, for he thought, I will pin David to the wall. But David eluded him twice. Saul was afraid of David, because the LORD was with him and departed from Saul. So Saul removed him from his presence, and made him commander of a thousand; and David marched out and came in, leading the army. David had success in all his undertaking, for the LORD was with him. When Saul saw he had great success, he stood in awe of him. But all Israel and Judah loved David; for it was he who marched out and came in leading them.

Saul's daughter, Michal, was promised to whomever killed Goliath, and (20-21) says, Michal loved David. Saul was told, and the thing pleased him. Saul thought, "Let me give her to him that she may be a snare for him, and that the hand of the Philistines may be against him." Therefore Saul said to David a second time, "You shall now be my son-in-law." In verse 25 David was told that Saul said, "Thus you shall say to David, 'The king desires no marriage present except one hundred foreskins from the Philistines, that he may be avenged on the king's enemies.' " Saul planned to make David fall by the hand of the Philistines. But in (27) David got the hundred foreskins and married Michal.

Verses 28-30 say, But when Saul realized the LORD was with David, and that Saul's daughter Michal loved him, Saul was still more afraid of David. So Saul was David's enemy from that time forward. Then the commanders of the Philistines came out to battle; and as often as they came out, David had more success than all the servants of Saul, so that his fame became very great. (Later Saul will change his mind on the marriage and take Michal from David and give her in marriage to a man named Paltiel.)

In chapter 19:1 Saul spoke with his son, Jonathan, and all his servants about killing David. But Saul's son Jonathan took great delight in David. Jonathan told him he would help protect him. There are numerous attempts by Saul to kill David. In one attempt in (11-17) Saul sent messengers to David's house to watch over him, planning to kill him in the morning, but David escapes with the help of his wife, Saul's daughter Michal. She put an idol in bed covered with clothes with a net of goats hair on its head to make it look like he was sleeping.

In verses 18-24 Samuel hides David, and three times three different sets of Saul's messengers come to get David. Each time God interferes; and the spirit of God falls on them, and they fall into a prophetic frenzy. Then Saul himself goes, and he too falls into a prophetic frenzy. The people respond in (24) by asking, "Is Saul also among the prophets?"

In chapter 20:1 David fled from Naioth in Ramah. He came before Jonathan asking what his sin was against his father the king, and why he was trying to take his life. Jonathan does not give him an answer because, apparently at this time, he does not know the answer. He and David renew their covenant of protection and friendship. Verses 16-17 say, Thus Jonathan made a covenant with the house of David saying, "May the LORD seek out the enemies of David." Jonathan made David swear again by his love for him; for he loved him as he loved his own life. (Again, in ancient covenants this is not only a statement of personal affection but also of political loyalty.)

Saul soon discovers that his son is protecting David, and in (30) he is angry. He says, "You son of a perverse, rebellious woman!" Jonathan asks him why he is trying to kill David, but (33) says, Saul threw his spear at him to strike him; so Jonathan knew that it was the decision of his father to put David to death. (Saul was no longer a humble person with a new heart; he allowed his own power and interests to become more important than God's interests. He has now rejected God's grace. God's grace, in most cases, works only if we respond to it.)

In chapter 21 David is on the run and comes to the priest Ahimelech at Nob. Nob was called the city of priests. (It seems that after the fall of Shiloh, the seat of Eli is moved here. Ahimelech is a great grandson of Eli.) David tells him the king has sent him on a mission, and that he is hungry. Ahimelech in (4-6) tells him all he has is the holy bread, the bread of the Presence, kept in the most holy place of the tabernacle. (Only the priests are to eat this bread, but he gives it to David because he is so hungry and in great need. Need trumps the teaching of the law (see Mk 2:23-28.)

In verse 7 Doeg the Edomite, the chief of Saul's shepherds, is there that day and sees everything. Ahimelech in (8-9) gives Goliath's sword to David. David then goes to the land of the Philistines to King Achish of Gath. David is afraid King Achish will put him to death so he pretends he has become insane.

In chapter 22:1-2 David leaves Gath and escapes to the cave of Adullam. As a fugitive from Saul's justice he becomes the champion of the distressed, the discontented, and those in debt. They come to him and eventually number about four hundred. Then the prophet Gad in (5) comes to him and tells him to go into the forest of Judah.

Meanwhile in (9-10) Doeg, the Edomite, who is in charge of Saul's servants (in the last chapter it was said he is in charge of the shepherds) tells Saul about the priest Ahimelech feeding and giving David Goliath's sword. In verses 17-18 Saul orders Doeg to kill Ahimelech and the priests. That day eighty-five priests were killed which almost eliminates the priests in the line of Eli. But one of the sons of Ahimelech escapes. His name is Abiathar, and he goes to David.

In chapter 23:1-5 the Philistines attack the city of Keilah. David inquires of the LORD, "Shall I go and attack the Philistines?" The LORD in (2) said, "Go and attack the Philistines and save Keilah." He inflicts on the Philistines a heavy defeat that day. It was at Keilah that Abiathar becomes David's priest, and it is his oracles that guide David. Verse 14 says, David remained in the strongholds in the wilderness, in the hill country of the wilderness of Ziph. Saul sought him every day, but the LORD did not give him into his hands. Instead of attending to the affairs of State, Saul becomes consumed with getting David. Jonathan comes to David, and in (17) he said to him, "Do not be afraid; for the hand of my father Saul shall not find you; you shall be king over Israel, and I shall be second to you; my father Saul also knows this is so." (We must remember Jonathan was the son of Saul and the rightful heir to the throne.)

In chapter 24 after Saul returns from pursuing some Philistines, he takes three thousand men and goes to look for David who is in the wilderness of En-gedi. Meanwhile Saul has to relieve himself and enters a cave where David and his men are sitting in the innermost part of the cave. Saul in relieving himself takes off his cloak, and David cuts off a corner of his cloak. David's men want to kill Saul, but in (6) David says, "The LORD forbid that I should do this thing to my lord, the LORD's anointed, to raise my hand against him, for he is the LORD's anointed."

After Saul leaves David exits the cave and calls to Saul. He shows him the cloak as visible evidence that he could have killed him. Saul said to David in (16-22), "Is this your voice, my son David?" Saul lifted up his voice and wept. He said to David, "You are more righteous than I; for you have repaid me good whereas I have repaid you evil . . . I know that you shall surely be king, and that the kingdom of Israel shall be established in your hand. Swear to me therefore by the LORD that you will not cut off my descendants after me, and that you will not wipe my name from my father's house."

David swears this to Saul. Then Saul goes home; but David and his men go up to the stronghold. Again, Saul for the moment seems repentant, but we will see if he is, it is only for the moment. He has already promised David forgiveness at least three times and changed his mind. Then he has the audacity to ask David to make a promise to him.

Chapter 25:1 says, Now Samuel died; and all Israel assembled and mourned for him. They buried him at his home in Ramah. The rest of the chapter, forty one verses, is about how David got his wife Abigail. Her husband, Nabal, his name meant fool, is very rich but also ill-natured and would not give David and his men food, even after David had protected his shepherds. David marches his army toward Nabal's farm. His wife decides to head them off to help and get them some food.

When Abigail tells Nabal what she has done in (36-38) his heart dies, and he becomes like stone. About ten days later he dies. One verse in the chapter (43) mentions David marrying another wife. Her name is Ahinoam. Verse 44 says Saul had given his daughter, Michal, David's wife, to Palti, son of Laish, who was from Gallim.

In chapter 26:1 the Ziphites came to Saul at Gibeah saying, David is in hiding on the hill of Hachilah, which is opposite Jeshimon. Saul takes three thousand men and goes to the wilderness of Zinn. David learns where Saul is and in (7) goes to him as Saul and Abner are sleeping with the army which is surrounding them.

Abishai, Joab's brother, who went along with David, finds Saul and Abner sleeping. Saul's spear is stuck in the ground beside him. Abishai in (8) says, "God has given your enemy into your hand today; now therefore let me pin him to the ground with one stroke of the spear; I will not strike twice." Again David in (9) rejects his plea.

David takes his spear and water jar, and they go away. Verses 13-14 say, Then David went over to the other side, and stood on top of a hill far away, with a great distance between them. David called to the army and Abner son of Ner saying "Abner! Will you not answer?" Then Abner replied, "Who are you that calls to the king?" David proceeds to tell him he deserves to die for not protecting the king. In (16) he asks, "where is the king's spear, or the water jar that was at his head?"

Verse 17 says, Saul recognizes David's voice and said, "Is this your voice my son David?" David said, "It is my voice, my lord, O king." In verse 21 Saul says, "I have done wrong; come back, my son David, for I will never harm you again because my life was precious in your sight today; I have been a fool, and have made a great mistake." In verses 22-24 David replied, "Here is the spear, O king! Let one of the young men come over and get it. The LORD rewards everyone for his righteousness and his faithfulness; for the LORD gave you into my hand today, but I would not raise my hand against the LORD's anointed. As your life was precious today in my sight, so may my life be precious in the sight of the LORD, and may he rescue me from all tribulation." (David was wise to the ways of Saul and then simply leaves. One wonders how many traditions were involved in this repetitious incident?)

In chapter 27 David returns to King Achish of Gath in the land of the Philistines, for he thought if he did not, Saul would kill him. Six hundred men go with him. In return for David's military help Achish gives David a town in the country called Ziklag. He lives there one year and four months. From here David makes raids on Israel's enemies while Achish thinks he is making raids into Judah.

In chapter 28 the Philistines again prepare to attack Saul and Israel. When Saul inquires of God, he does not answer him. Then Saul in (7) says to his servants, "Seek out for me a woman who is a medium, so I may go to her and inquire of her." His servants said to him, "There is a medium at Endor." (Seeking mediums is against the law of God, and Saul had chased all mediums and wizards from the land.) So Saul disguises himself and with two men goes to the woman by night. In (11-12) the woman said, "Whom shall I bring up to you?" He answered, "Bring up Samuel for me." The woman recognizes Saul and is afraid, but he tells her not to fear. In (13-14) she said to Saul, "I see a divine being coming up out of the ground." He said to her, "What is his appearance?" She said, "An old man is coming up; he is wrapped up in a robe." So Saul knew it was Samuel, and he bowed with his face to the ground, and did obeisance.

Samuel in verses 15-19 says, "Why have you disturbed me by bringing me up?" Saul answered, "I am in great distress, for the Philistines are warring against me, and God has turned away from me and answers me no more, either by prophets or by dreams; so I have summoned you to tell me what to do." Samuel said, "Why then do you ask me, since the LORD has turned from you and become your enemy? The LORD has done to you just as he spoke by me; for the LORD has torn the kingdom out of your hand, and given it to your neighbor, David. Because you did not obey the voice of the LORD, and did not carry out his fierce wrath against Amalek, therefore the LORD has done this thing to you today. Moreover the LORD will give Israel along with you into the hands of the Philistines; and tomorrow you and your sons will be with me; the LORD will also give the army of Israel into the hands of the Philistines."

In chapter 29 the Philistines gather their forces. Achish in (6) tells David that the other Philistine leaders do not trust David, so he is to leave. In chapter 30:1-2 he returns to Ziklag to learn that the Amalekites burned down his town and took away his wives. In (7) Abiathar the priest through divination with the ephod (a priestly garment) tells him he could find the attackers and overtake them. He accomplishes this in (18-20) recovering all the Amalekites had taken and rescuing his two wives. David returns part of the spoil he has taken from the Amalekites to his friends who helped him in Judah.

In chapter 31:1-6 the Philistines fight Israel and defeat them. At Mt Gilboa they kill Jonathan and all the sons of Saul. Saul is badly wounded and tells his armor bearer to finish him off so the Philistines can not make sport of him. But his armor bearer is unwilling, so Saul falls on his own sword.

Verses 8-13 say, The next day, when the Philistines come to strip the dead, they find Saul and his three sons fallen on Mt Gilboa. They cut off his head, stripped off his armor, and send messengers throughout the land of the Philistines to carry the good news to the house of their idols and the people. They put his armor in the temple of Astarte; and they fasten his body to the wall of Beth-shan. But when the inhabitants of Jabesh-gilead heard what the Philistines had done to Saul, all the valiant men set out, traveled all night long, and took the body of Saul and the bodies of his sons from the wall of Beth-shan. They came to Jabesh and burned them there. Then they took their bones and buried them under the tamarisk tree in Jabesh, and fasted seven days.

Jabesh-gilead was Saul's first great military victory against the Amalekites that convinced the people that he could be their king. David will eventually return them to the family tomb in Benjamin in Zela in the tomb of his father, Kish.

Saul is probably portrayed negatively because the people wanted a king like the nations instead of trusting God. In the literary genre of symbolic history, Saul becomes a symbol of Israel, for numerous times he shows a lack of trust in God, and his repentance is usually insincere since he keeps falling back into sinful actions.

2 SAMUEL

Chapter 1:1-4 says, After the death of Saul, when David returned from defeating the Amalekites, . . . a man came from Saul's camp, with his clothes torn and dirt on his head. When he came to David, he fell to the ground and did obeisance. David said to him, "Where have you come from?" He said to him, "I have escaped from the camp of Israel. David said to him, How did things go? Tell me!" He answered, "The army fled from the battle, but also many of the army fell and died; and Saul and his son Jonathan also died."

Then in verse 5 David asked the young man who was reporting to him, "How do you know that Saul and his son died?" The man who was an Amalekite in (6-10) said, "I happened to be on Mount Gilboa; and there was Saul leaning on his spear, while the chariots and horsemen drew close to him . . . He said to me, 'Come stand over me and kill me; for convulsions have seized me and yet my life still lingers.' So I stood over him, and killed him, for I knew he could not live after he had fallen. I took the crown that was on his head and the armlet that was on his arm, and I have brought them here to my lord."

This Amalekite just happened to be there in the midst of a great battle where Saul would have been surrounded by his own people? And he was in battle fighting with a crown on his head? Many believe the man was lying in order to gain favor with David, but if he is lying, how did he get the crown and armlet? David had just come from fighting the Amalekites, and one of the reasons Saul was condemned centered on his failure to annihilate the Amalekites. It is interesting to note that if the man was telling the truth, Saul was finally killed by one of those he was to annihilate but did not in his disobedience to God's command.

Verses 14-16 say, David said to him, "Were you not afraid to lift your hand to destroy the LORD's anointed?" Then David called one of the young men and said, "Come here and strike him down." So he struck him down and he died. David said to him, "Your blood be on your head; for your own mouth has testified against you, saying, 'I have killed the LORD's anointed.' " (David does not want to be seen taking this crown, for it would open him to charges that he is involved and is usurping the throne. The man's falsifying the truth, if that is what he is doing, backfires.)

Then in verses 19-26 David intones a lamentation over Saul and his son, Jonathan. The poem ends in (26-27) by saying, I am distressed for you, my brother Jonathan; greatly beloved were you to me; your love to me was wonderful, passing the love of women. How the mighty have fallen, and the weapons of war perished!

Both sides of the homosexual issue use the passages of love that David and Jonathan express to each other more than once, to support their position on the issue. One side says the OT makes it plain that homosexual sex is disobedience to God's teachings; therefore, their expression of love to each other is just the way an ancient culture expresses friendship. Surely Israel's greatest hero-king, who will supply Jesus with his descendants, would not be indicating that David is homosexual.

Those on the other side of the issue say that this relationship between two men is a bona fide love relationship, therefore it is not illicit sex. This side says, nowhere in the Bible is a forever, true committed love relationship between members of the same sex, one that is not for sexual pleasure only, condemned. These people argue that the homosexuality condemned in the OT is sex for pleasure outside a forever, committed love relationship.

Their argument is that at that time in history it had yet to dawn on anyone that a time would come when two people of the same sex will want to live in a committed married relationship. Many of those taking this position do not believe the Bible condemns the latter relationship where two people want to commit to each other in a forever relationship of love. Their argument is that it simply was not a biblical issue. Most churches do not accept that line of thinking. Even if that would be true, the problem is that David has wives. This writer will let each reader decide the issue for themselves or send each back to one's church for discussion.

Some things to think about from an academic point of view are the following. We do know that there are sexual relationships in the OT permitted outside the marriage of one man and one woman. Examples are polygamy and concubines. Also, we know that there are things such as interest money not favored in Scripture, but because of new circumstances, culture has decided it is now acceptable. We also know slavery is permitted in Scripture but now is unacceptable. That being said, does that mean that sometimes culture does help determine what is permissible and what is not? And if so, does that or does it not shed light on the issue?

We do know that Scripture does not give definite answers to some of the different issues that emerge in different cultures even though Scripture does give principles, virtues, values, and the basics to help us develop answers. But it is also true that different churches as well as the different cultures develop different answers as they apply the Scriptures to new circumstances. Sometimes there are simply no easy answers.

Chapter 2:1-4 says, David inquired of the LORD, "Shall I go up into any of the cities of Judah?" The LORD said to him, "Go up." David said, "To which shall I go up?" He said, "To Hebron." So David went there, along with his two wives, Ahinoam of Jezreel and Abigail the widow of Nabel of Carmel. David brought up the men who were with him, everyone with his household; and they settled in the towns of Hebron. Then the people of Judah came, and there they anointed David king over the house of Judah.

In the meantime in (8-9) Abner, commander of Saul's army, takes Ishbaal, son of Saul, and makes him king at Gilead, thus making him king of the northern tribes. Soon a civil war begins, and in (17) Abner and the men of Israel are beaten by David's servants. Joab, the son of David's sister Zeruiah, is the commander of David's army. Verse 18 says, The three sons of Zeruiah were there, Joab, Abishai, and Asahel. They are David's military leaders. Now Asahel was as swift of foot as a wild gazelle.

Verses 19-24 inform us that as Abner is running away Asahel chases him to kill him but instead he is killed. Joab and Abishai continue to pursue him. Verses 25-26 say, the Benjaminites rallied around Abner and . . . they took their stand on the top of a hill. Then Abner called to Joab, "Is the sword to keep devouring forever? Do you not know that the end will be bitter? How long will it be before you order your people to turn from the pursuit of their kinsmen?" Verse 28 says, Joab sounded the trumpet and all people stopped; they no longer pursued Israel or engaged in battle any further.

Chapter 3:1 says, There was a long war between the house of Saul and the house of David; David grew stronger and stronger, while the house of Saul grew weaker and weaker. In verse 2 we learn that one of the sons born to David at Hebron was Absalom.

Because Abner saw the writing on the wall, in (12) he makes a covenant with David where Abner vows to bring the support of Israel to him. Abner has become the power while Ishbaal has become the puppet king.

David agrees to the covenant on the condition in (14) that he will have his wife, Michal, returned to him. Saul had annulled the marriage and had given her to Paltiel. So Ishbaal takes her from her husband Paltriel, and (16) says, her husband went with her, weeping as he walked behind her all the way to Bahurim. Then Abner said to him, "Go back home!" So he went back. (David requires the return of his wife Michal, who was Saul's daughter, because she is the basis of his claim to the throne.)

In the meantime, Joab, David's commander, is not pleased with the addition of Abner, for he is Joab's competition. Abner also killed Joab's brother Asahel. Joab waits for the opportune time, and then verses 27-30 say, When Abner returned to Hebron, Joab took him aside in the gateway to speak with him privately, and there he stabbed him in the stomach. So he died for shedding the blood of Ashael, Joab's brother.

Verses 28-29 say, Afterward, when David heard of it, he said, "I and my kingdom are forever guiltless before the LORD for the blood of Abner, son of Ner. May the guilt fall on the head of Joab, and all his father's house . . ." Verses 30-34 say, So Joab and his brother Abishai murdered Abner because he had killed their brother Ashael in the battle of Gibeon. Then David said to Joab and to all the people who were with him, "Tear your clothes, and put on sackcloth, and mourn over Abner." They buried Abner at Hebron. The king lifted up his voice and wept at the grave of Abner, and all the people wept. The king lamented for Abner, saying, "Should Abner die as a fool dies? . . . as one falls before the wicked you have fallen." And all the people wept over him again.

Verses 37-39 say, all Israel understood that day that the king had no part in the killing of Abner son of Ner. And the king said to his servants, "Do you not know that a prince and a great man has fallen this day in Israel? Today I am powerless, even though anointed king; these men, sons of Zeruiah, are too violent for me. The LORD pay back the one who does wickedly in accordance with his wickedness."

In chapter 4 Ishbaal, Saul's son, is assassinated, and his head cut off. Those who did it go to David, and tell him in hopes that he will reward them. Instead David in (12) puts them to death, cuts off their hands and feet, and hangs their bodies by the pool of Hebron (no mercy or thanks on this one). David then takes Ishbaal's head and buries it. Now, there is no other suitable candidate for king in Saul's line. (David's weeping, fasting, and grieving and what he does after the assassination of Ishbaal will be David's attempt to unify and heal the breach between the two nations instead of sparking more civil war.)

In chapter 5:1-5 all the tribes come to David at Hebron, and they anoint David king over Israel. David is thirty years old when he begins to reign and he reigns forty years. At Hebron he reigns over Judah seven years and six months; at Jerusalem he reigns over Israel and Judah thirty three years.

The king and his men march to Jerusalem against the Jebusites and take the stronghold of Zion, which will become the city of David. During the battle the Jebusites in (6-7) said, "You will not come in here, for even the blind and lame will turn you back"—thinking, "David can not come in here." Nevertheless David took the stronghold of Zion, which is now the city of David. Verses 8-10 say, David had said on that day, "Whoever would strike down the Jebusites, let him get up the water shaft to attack the lame and the blind, those whom David hates." Therefore it is said, "The blind and the lame shall not come into the house." David occupied the stronghold and named it the city of David. David built the city from the Millo inward. And David became greater and greater, for the LORD, the God of hosts, was with him.

The Millo is a mystery though some think it is some type of earthwork south of the temple area; it is thought the word means a filling, so it could have been a landfill. It is also thought that possibly the lame and the blind may have been a key in the Jebusites defense in a way not explained, or is somehow related to David's attack through the water shaft, which is how he eventually subdued the Jebusites. Jerusalem will be a good place for the new capitol of a united north and south, for it will be right between the two nations.

Another issue is not allowing the lame and disabled to enter the house (temple?). These verses are very confusing and I Chronicles 11:5-6 does not include them. Leviticus in 21:16-23 does have a law that does not permit the disabled priest to perform his duties, but there does not seem to be any real answer for David's decree against the lame and the blind.

Some of the things we read about in the OT are a challenge for moderns because our culture is so very different. We do know this, eventually Jews and Muslims will not discriminate against the disabled. For Christians Jesus will change this way of thinking about the lame and the blind, for he will come especially for the poor and broken and will heal them.

Verses 11-12 say, King Hiram of Tyre (Lebanon) sent messengers to David, along with cedar trees, and carpenters and masons who built David a house. David then perceived the LORD had established him king over Israel, and that he had exalted his kingdom for the sake of his people Israel. The writer in (13-16) adds, In Jerusalem, after he came from Hebron, David took more concubines and wives; and more sons and daughters were born to David. The names of the children are then listed.

Verses 22-25 say, Once again the Philistines came up, and were spread out in the valley of Rephaim. When David inquired of the LORD, he said, "You shall not go up, go around to their rear, and come upon them opposite the balsam trees. When you hear the sound of marching in the tops of the balsam trees, then be on the alert; for then the LORD has gone out before you to strike down the army of the Philistines." David did just as the LORD had commanded him; and he struck down the Philistines from Geba all the way to Gezer. (The author is saying that God is leading and defeating the enemy not David.)

In chapter 6 David brings the ark from Baale-judah, another name for Kiriath-jearim, (see Josh 15:9). He places it in Jerusalem. It is taken from the house of Abinadab and placed on a new cart. Uzzah and Ahio, the sons of Abinadad were driving the new cart. Verses 6-7 say, When they came to the threshing floor of Nacon, Uzzah reached out his hand to the ark of God and took hold of it, for the oxen shook it. The anger of the LORD was kindled against Uzzah; and God struck him there because he reached out his hand to the ark; and he died there beside the ark of God. (Was there an accident with the cart and Uzzah died, and this becomes the way it was explained, or did God really kill him for trying to save the ark from falling?)

Verses 8-10 say, David was angry because the LORD had burst forth with an outburst upon Uzzah; so that the place is called Perez-uzzah, to this day. David was afraid of the LORD that day; he said, "How can the ark of the LORD come into my care?" So David was unwilling to take the ark of the LORD into his care in the city of David; instead David took it to the house of Obed-edom the Gittite.

The law said only the Levites could touch the ark. For most of us living in today's culture, the death of Uzzah caused by God for attempting to save the ark is an outrage. Even so, some of the following is a feeble attempt to explain these difficult verses. The OT teaches and emphasizes over and over the absolute holiness of God and the ungodliness of humans. This is why the people need a mediator between them and God. In the OT the people who are not Levites are not to touch the holy things of God. Only the high priest can enter God's presence, and that is only one day of the year. Therefore the law is violated. The issue is obedience to God whether it makes sense or not to humans.

Christians believe these types of laws are eliminated under the new covenant because Jesus will become the permanent mediator that will enable humankind to enter God's presence, but for the time being the laws are for a teaching purpose. In the NT for Christians Galatians 2:16 says, the law was our disciplinarian until Christ came, so that we might be justified by faith in Jesus Christ. It is also correct to translate this as the faith of Jesus Christ. This writer believes the correct answer is the latter.

In the OT the law is interpreted and applied by the letter of the law. At least this is how many of the Pharisees in the time of Christ will interpret the law. Some Christians believe one of the reasons for incidents such as Uzzah is to help the people learn by experience the necessity for a new law that will be interpreted primarily by the spirit of the law. The old law for Christians according to the Apostle Paul in the NT is to be a schoolmaster to bring us to Christ and the new law, the new covenant. The spirit of the law will then actually drive people to a higher and deeper morality that was not possible through the letter of the law. Judaism and Islam will not agree with this explanation or this understanding of a new covenant.

For Christians the letter of the law is often times too rigid and not flexible, which will be the example of the Pharisees in the NT, while the spirit of the law will focus on what is behind the law, or the highest intention of the law, or the virtues and values expressed in the law. Many ask why did God not start with the highest form of the law? One answer is that learning theory states one really learns by going from one step to another; therefore the people were not ready to begin with the highest form of the law; they had to be led to it. It is a learn by doing type of action where one learns from experience. It is also true that many Christians do not understand the spirit of the law and are very rigid and inflexible, even as rigid and inflexible as the NT Pharisees.

Meanwhile, in (11-12) the ark at the house of Obed-edom the Gittite remains there for three months blessing him and his household. These blessings are relayed to David who finally sent for the ark and placed it in the city of David with great rejoicing.

Verses 16-19 say, As the ark of the LORD came into the city of David, Michal daughter of Saul looked out of the window, and saw King David leaping and dancing before the LORD; and she despised him in her heart. They brought in the ark of the LORD, and set it in its place, inside the tent David had pitched for it; . . . When David had finished offering the burnt offerings and offerings of well-being, he blessed the people, in the name of the LORD of hosts, and distributed food among all the people . . . Then all the people went back to their homes.

Verse 20 says, David returned to bless his household. But Michal the daughter of Saul came out to meet David and said, "How the king of Israel honored himself today, uncovering himself today before the eyes of his servants' maids, as any vulgar fellow might shamelessly uncover himself!" David explains in (21) that he was dancing before the LORD. The writer adds in (23) that Michal had no child to the day of her death.

Chapter 7:1-7 says, Now when the king was settled in his house, and the LORD had given him rest from all his enemies around him, the king said to the prophet Nathan, "See now, I am living in a house of cedar, but the ark of God stays in a tent." Nathan said to the king, "Go, do all that you have in mind; for the LORD is with you." But that same night the word of the LORD came to Nathan: "Go and tell my servant David: Thus says the LORD: Are you the one to build me a house to live in? . . . "Why have you not built me a house of cedar?"

Verses 9-17 say, I will make for you a great name . . . and I will appoint a place for my people Israel and will plant them, so that they may live in their own place, . . . and I will give you rest from all your enemies. Moreover the LORD declares to you that the LORD will make you a house. When your days are fulfilled and you lie down with your ancestors, I will raise up your offspring after you, who shall come forth from your body, and I will establish his kingdom. He shall build a house for my name, and I will establish the throne of his kingdom forever. I will be a father to him, and he shall be a son to me. When he commits iniquity, I will punish him with a rod such as mortals use, with blows inflicted by human beings. But I will not take my steadfast love from him, as I took it from Saul, whom I put away from before you. Your house and your kingdom shall be made sure forever before me; your throne shall be established forever. In accordance with all these words and with all this vision, Nathan spoke to David.

When God tells David his house and his kingdom will be established and made sure forever, Christians take this as a reference first to Solomon, and then to the Christ and his kingdom. This seems to be an eternal, unconditional promise, but it is conditional for particular earthly kings (Birch et al. 1999). Jews take this in reference to Solomon, and then to the Messiah, a human they still seek. Muslims will believe in Jesus as the Messiah, but he will be just a man who will be resurrected and will come again to initiate a golden age, but will again die a human death. This Messiah will not judge anyone, for only God can judge, but he will pray to God at the judgment. In the rest of the chapter David offers God his prayer of thanks.

Chapter 8 mentions David's wars. David makes this small insignificant nation into the most powerful kingdom on earth. He attacks and defeats the Philistines, Moabites, the Arameans of Damascus, Edomites, and Ammonites. Verses 14-15 say, the LORD gave victory wherever David went. So David reigned over all Israel; and David administers justice and equity to all his people. (David is the great king who builds the nation, expands the nation, and unites the nation.)

Verses 16-18 inform us that Joab his nephew will be over the army. (Abishai and Asahel also nephews will be involved.) Jehoshaphat was the recorder. Zadok and Ahimelech will be David's priests. Seraiah was secretary. Benaiah is over the Cherethites and the Pelethites (a special guard of Philistine mercenaries); and David's sons were priests. (Apparently in David's day the king and his sons could serve as priests even though one of the reasons Saul loses his kingship is because he acts as a priest. This is not explained.)

In chapter 9:1 David asked, "Is there still anyone left of the house of Saul to whom I may show kindness for Jonathan's sake?" A servant named Ziba from Saul's house was summoned who told David that Mephibosheth was a son of Jonathan who was lame in both feet. David brought him to eat at the king's table, and in (10) David declares that Mephibosheth would always eat at his table. (This incident is mentioned to illustrates David's compassion.)

In chapter 10 the Arameans (Syrians) and Ammonites are defeated. Chapter 11 contains the story of David and Bathsheba. The chapter begins in (1) by saying, In the spring of the year, the time when kings go out to battle, David sent Joab with his officers and all Israel with him; they ravaged the Ammonites, and besieged Rabbah (modern day Amman, Jordan). But David remained in Jerusalem. (It seems as though war was a type of recreation and sport.)

Verse 2 says, It happened, late one afternoon, when David rose from his couch and was walking about on the roof of the king's house, that he saw from the roof a woman bathing; the woman was very beautiful. In (3) David learns her name is Bathsheba the wife of Uriah the Hittite. Verses 4-5 say, So David sent messengers to get her, and she came to him, and he lay with her. (Now she was purifying herself after her period.) Then she returned to her house. The woman conceived; and she sent and told David, "I am pregnant."

Bathsheba's husband is Uriah the Hittite who is fighting the Ammonites with Joab. David sends word to Joab to send Uriah home. When Uriah comes to David, David asks him how the war is going, and then in (8) said to Uriah, "Go down to your house and wash your feet." (This means go enjoy sexual relations with your wife. David, being shrewd, does not want blamed for the pregnancy.) Instead of going to his wife verse 9 says, Uriah slept at the entrance of the king's house with all the servants of his lord, and did not go down to his house.

The next day when David in (10) said to him, "You have just come from a journey. Why did you not go down to your house?" Uriah basically tells David that it is not right for him to do that that while the others are on the battlefield. Verse 13 says, David invited him to eat and drink in his presence and made him drunk; and in the evening he went out to lie on his couch with the servants of his lord, but he did not go down to his house. So in verses 14-17 David sends him back to the battle with a letter to Joab telling him to put Uriah in the front lines so he will be killed. Uriah is killed in battle, and (27) says, When the mourning was over, David sent and brought her (Bathsheba) to his house, and she became his wife, and bore him a son. But the thing David had done displeased the LORD.

In chapter 12:1-4 the LORD sends Nathan to David who tells David a parable about a powerful, rich man who took advantage of his position. David is angry and says the man should die. Nathan in (7-12) said to David, "You are the man! . . . Why have you despised the word of the LORD, to do what is evil in his sight? You have struck down Uriah the Hittite with the sword, and have taken his wife, and have killed him with the sword of the Ammonites. Now therefore the sword shall never depart from your house, for you have despised me, and have taken the wife of Uriah the Hittite to be your wife. Thus says the LORD: I will raise up trouble against you from within your own house; and I will take your wives before your eyes and give them to your neighbor, and he shall lie with your wives in the sight of this very sun. For you did it secretly; but I will do this thing before all Israel, and before the sun."

In verses 13-15 David said to Nathan, "I have sinned against the LORD." Nathan said to David, "Now the LORD has put away your sin; you shall not die. Nevertheless, because by this deed you have utterly scorned the LORD, the child that is born to you shall die." Then David went to his house.

In verses 15-21 God strikes the child ill, and David pleads before the LORD, weeping, fasting, and praying, but the child dies. David, then, rises and eats. David is asked why he has gotten over his agony so quickly. David in (22) said, "While the child was still alive, I fasted and wept; for I said, 'Who knows? The LORD may be gracious to me, and the child may live.' But now he is dead; why should I fast? Can I bring him back again? I shall go to him, but he will not return to me." Verse 24 says, Then David consoled his wife Bathsheba, and went to her, and lay with her; and she bore a son, and he named him Solomon. (David here seems to indicate there is something after death where loved ones will be together. The idea of life after death develops slowly in the OT.)

In chapter 13 David's son Amnon rapes his beautiful half sister, Tamar. Tamar is devastated, for a woman not to be a virgin at marriage is life destroying in those times. She becomes a very despondent and desolate woman. David's weakness where his sons are concerned is clearly shown in the fact that he takes no action against Amnon. Absalom, also David's son, hates his half brother Amnon for what he has done and has him killed. Absalom in (37-38), flees to Geshur where he stays three years. Verse

39 says, And the heart of the king went out, yearning for Absalom; for he was now consoled over the death of Amnon.

In chapter 14:1-20 Joab perceiving the king's mind was on Absalom sent for a wise woman from Tekoa to confront David in order to encourage David to allow Absalom to return to Jerusalem. In verse 14 she says, We must all die; we are like water spilled on the ground, which can not be gathered up. But God will not take away a life; he will devise plans so as not to keep an outcast banished forever from his presence. David learns Joab put her up to this, and David permits Joab to bring Absalom back to the city.

But for two years he does not enter into the presence of the king. Absalom attempts to get Joab to intercede for him, but Joab does not answer his messages. Finally to get Joab's attention, he burns his field down. Joab gets the message then intercedes for Absalom, and finally the king and Absalom reconcile. Absalom is described in (25-26) as being praised for his beauty and having no blemish; no one was praised more for his beauty. He also had over five pounds of hair (200 shekels), for he only cut his hair once a year at the end of the year.

Chapter 15:1 says, After that Absalom got himself a chariot and horses, and fifty men to run ahead of him. He spends his time politicking, and Absalom steals the hearts of the people. Verses 2-6 say, Absalom used to rise early and stand beside the road into the gate; and when anyone brought a suit before the king for judgment, Absalom would call out and say, "See, your claims are good and right; but there is no one deputed by the king to hear you." Absalom said moreover, "If only I were judge in the land! Then all who had a suit or cause might come to me, and I would give them justice." Whenever people came near to do obeisance to him, he would put out his hand and take hold of them, and kiss them. Thus Absalom did to every Israelite who came to the king for judgment; so Absalom stole the hearts of the people of Israel.

After four years Absalom in (7-10) asks the king, his father, for permission to go to Hebron. He said that he had made a vow while at Geshur in Aram to worship God in Hebron, if he were brought back to Jerusalem. The king in (9-10) said to him, "Go in peace." So he got up, and went to Hebron. But Absalom sent secret messengers throughout all the tribes of Israel saying, "As soon as you hear the sound of the trumpet, then shout: Absalom has become king at Hebron!" In (12) David's counselor Ahithophel joins Absalom, and the conspiracy grows in strength, and the people with Absalom kept increasing. (Because of David's great palace, his harem, his newly acquired territories, and his bureaucracy, some Israelites apparently regard him as a tyrant.)

Verse 13 says, a messenger came to David saying, "The hearts of Israel have gone after Absalom." Absalom was in the process of making a power play for Jerusalem, so King David decides to evacuate Jerusalem, and (16) says, So the king left, followed by all his household, except ten concubines whom he left behind to look after the house.

In a pledge of loyalty a foreigner, Ittai, the Gittite in (19-24) asks and gets permission for him and his family to stay with David. His loyalty, as a foreigner, contrasts sharply with the disloyalty of Absalom, the king's own son. Verse 23 says, The whole country wept aloud as they passed by; the king passed the Wadi Kidron, and all the people moved on toward the wilderness. (This indicates David is still very popular with many of the people.)

In (24-37) the priests Abiathar and Zadok along with the Levites carrying the ark go with David, but David sends them back. He also develops a plan with Zadok and Abiathar to keep him informed. Verse 32 says Hushai the Archite came to meet him with his coat torn and earth on his head (a sign of mourning). David develops a plan that involves Hushai telling Absalom that he will serve him, and then Hushai will inform Abiathar and Zadok about what Absalom and Ahithophel are planning. They will then inform David. (Ahithopel is David's former counsel who is now with Absalom.)

In chapter 16:1-4 Ziba, the servant of Mephibosheth meets David with donkeys, bread, raisins, fruits, and wine. Verse 2 says, The king said to Ziba, "Why have you brought these?" Ziba answered, "The donkeys are for the king's household to ride, the bread and summer fruit for the young men to eat, and the wine is for those to drink who faint in the wilderness." The king said, "And where is your master's son?" Ziba said to the king, "He remains in Jerusalem, for he said, 'Today Israel will give me back my grandfather's kingdom.' " Then the king said to Ziba, "All that belonged to Mephibosheth is now yours."

As David moves forward a man from the house of Saul, Shimei, throws stones and curses David calling him a murderer and scoundrel. In (7-8) Shimei shouted while he cursed, "Out! Out! Murderer! Scoundrel! The LORD has avenged on all of you the blood of the house of Saul, in whose place you have reigned; and the LORD has given the kingdom into the hand of your son Absalom. See disaster has overtaken you; for you are a man of blood." Abishai wants to kill Shimei, but David does not allow it. (Most of the time, David is depicted as being kind and restrained with the house of Saul.) Verse 13 says, So David and his men went on the road, while Shimei went along on the hillside opposite him and cursed as he went, throwing stones and flinging dust at him.

The rest of the chapter (15-23) shows Absalom entering Jerusalem with Ahithophel, his adviser. Ahithophel advises Absalom to go into his father's concubines, and Absalom does this upon the roof in the sight of all Israel. This fulfilled Nathan's prophecy made to David after the incident with Bathsheba (see 2 Sam 12:11-12). (During the time of the ancients, going into the king's concubines accounted for a claim to the throne.)

In chapter 17 Absalom asks Ahithophel for his plan to defeat David. Then Absalom asks Hushai the Archite, what he thinks, and he takes his advice instead. Verse 14 says, the LORD had ordained to defeat the good counsel of Ahithophel, so that the LORD might bring ruin on Absalom. Then in (15) Hushai told Zadok and Abiathar who relayed the plans to David. Verse 23 says, When Ahithophel saw his counsel was not followed, he straddled his donkey and went off to his home to his own city. He set his house in order, and hanged himself; he died and was buried in the tomb of his father.

Meanwhile, in chapter 18, David divides his army into three commands under Joab, Abishai, and Ittai the Gittite. The king in (5) says, "Deal gently for my sake with the young man Absalom." Verses 6-8 say, the battle was fought in the forest of Ephraim. The men of Israel were defeated there by the servants of David, and the slaughter there was great on that day, twenty thousand men. The battle spread over the face of all the country; and the forest claimed more victims that day than the sword.

As Absalom in (9-10) is riding his mule under the thick branches of oak trees, the hair of his head gets caught in the branches, and he is left hanging. Verses 14-17 say, Joab said, "I will not waste time like this with you." He took three spears in his hand, and thrust them into the heart of Absalom, while he was still alive in the oak. And ten young men, Joab's armor-bearers, surrounded Abasolom and struck him, and killed him. Then Joab sounded the trumpet, and the troops came back from pursuing Israel, for Joab restrained the troops. They took Absalom threw him into a great pit in the forest, and raised over him a very great heap of stones. When David learns his son is dead, verse 33 says, The king was deeply moved, and went up to the chamber over the gate, and wept; and as he went, he said, "O my son Absalom, my son, my son Absalom! Would I had died instead of you, O Absalom, my son, my son."

Chapter 19:1-2 says, It was told to Joab, "The king is weeping and mourning for Absalom." So the victory that day was turned into mourning for all the troops; for the troops heard that day, "The king is grieving for his son." Verse 4 says, The king covered his face, and the king cries with a loud voice, "O my son Absalom, O Absalom, my son, my son."

Verses 5-8 says, Then Joab came into the house to the king, and said, "Today you have covered with shame the faces of all your officers who have saved your life today, and the lives of your sons and your daughters, and the lives of your wives and your concubines, for love of those who hate you and for hatred of those who love you. You have made it clear today that commanders and officers are nothing to you; for I perceive that if Absalom were alive, and all of us were dead today, then you would be pleased. So go out at once and speak kindly to your servants; for I swear by the LORD if you do not go, not a man will stay with you this night; and this will be worse for you than any disaster that has come upon you from your youth until now." Then the king got up and took his seat in the gate. The troops were all told, "See the king is sitting in the gate"; and all the troops came before the king.

In verses 13-14 David names Amasa, his nephew, as his commander of the army in place of his long time commander Joab who had killed his son. It is interesting that Amasa was Absalom's commander (see 17:25). David then in (18-23) pardons Shimei. Shimei wants to save his life, so he asks forgiveness for his throwing stones and cursing David. Mephibosheth greets David in (24-29) telling him that his servant Ziba deceived him when he told David that he (Mephibosheth) had said that God was returning the kingdom to Saul's family. Mephibosheth told David he had never made that statement. (Mephibosheth was of the family of Saul.)

David does not attempt to learn who is telling the truth; what he does is to divide the heritage between the two. Mephibosheth tells David because he is so happy to see him back in Jerusalem, let Ziba have it all. It seems Mephibosheth is attempting to save himself also. The twelve tribes are again united under David.

In verses 31-40 Barzillai greets him to escort him over the Jordan. Barzillai is very old at eighty years. He is very wealthy and had helped to provide for David in Mahanaim when he was in exile. David now invites him to live in his palace in Jerusalem, but he replies that he is too old to enjoy it. So he said take my son Chimham instead, and David agrees.

In chapter 20 a scoundrel named Sheba, a Benjaminite, leads a revolt against David. Verse 2 says all the people of Israel withdrew from David and followed Sheba son of Bichri; but the people of Judah followed their king steadfastly from the Jordan to Jerusalem. Again, we have civil war.

Joab goes after Sheba along with David's newly appointed commander, Amassa. Along the way Joab pretends to be friends with Amassa, but verses 9-10 inform us that Joab took Amassa by the beard with his right hand to kiss him. But Amassa did not notice the sword in Joab's hand; Joab struck him in the belly so that his entrails poured out on the ground, and he died. He did not strike a second blow. Joab and his brother Abishai then pursue Sheba who takes refuge behind a city wall. They are about to destroy the wall and the city, but in (20-22), a wise woman tells him if he halts the damage Sheba's head will be thrown over the wall. When the head comes over the wall, the revolt against David ends. Joab returns to Jerusalem and becomes the new commander of the army.

The last four chapters appear to be a loose collection of stories handed down about David. Chapter 21:1-2 says, Now there was a famine in the days of David for three years, year after year; and David inquired of the LORD. The LORD said, "There is blood guilt on Saul and on his house, because he put the Gibeonites to death." So the king called the Gibeonites and spoke to them. (The Gibeonites are not the people of Israel but are the remnant of the Amorites; although the people of Israel had sworn to spare them, Saul had tried to wipe them out in his zeal for the people of Israel and Judah.)

Verse 3 says, David said to the Gibeonites "What shall I do for you? . . ." In verses 4-6 the Gibeonites said to him, "It is not a matter of silver and gold . . . let seven of his sons be handed over to us, and we will impale them before the LORD at Gibeon on the mountain of the LORD." The king said, "I will hand them over." The seven sons are put to death and the famine ends, but the writer tells us that David spares Mephibosheth, the son of Saul's son Jonathan, because of the oath of the LORD that was between them. Later in (12-14) David takes the bones of Saul and Jonathan and buries them in Benjamin territory at Zela in the tomb of his father, Kish.

The rest of the chapter (15-22) is about the Philistines going to war with Israel. Especially mentioned are the four giants from Gath. One has six fingers on each hand, and six toes on each foot. It is also interesting to note that verse 19 says, Elhanan, not David, kills Goliath the Gittite at Gob. (In I Samuel 17:4 David kills Goliath at Socoh. This indicates different sources, probable oral sources passed down, that came together to form the editors final writing. Numerous times in Scripture the writers include the various sources even when they differ from each other.)

The Fundamentalist teaching that everything in the Bible including history is literally true is an impossibility as the careful reader is able to see all through these readings. This theory is built upon a philosophy developed in modern times. It is a philosophical theory that has no basis in Scripture and has nothing to do with the inspiration of these Scriptures.

Chapter 22 is Psalm 18 David's song of thanksgiving and praise on the day God delivered David from the hand of Saul and his enemies. In verses 21-25 he sings, The LORD rewarded me according to my righteousness. According to the cleanness of my hands he recompensed me. For I have kept the ways of the LORD and have not wickedly departed from my God. For all his ordinances were before me, and from his statutes I did not turn aside. I was blameless before him, and I kept myself from guilt. Therefore the LORD has recompensed me according to my righteousness, according to my cleanness in his sight.

Verses 26-30 say, With the loyal you show yourself loyal; with the blameless, you show yourself blameless; with the pure you show yourself pure, and with the crooked you show yourself perverse. You deliver a humble people, but your eyes are upon the haughty to bring them down. Indeed, you are my lamp, O LORD; the LORD lightens my darkness. By you I can crush a troop, and by my God I can leap over a wall. This God—his way is perfect; the promise of the LORD proves true; he is a shield for all who take refuge in him. The psalm continues through the rest of the chapter.

This psalm may be seen as a little exaggeration by David, but in those times, where it is the one God verses many gods, it is to emphasize that he is not an idolater and is open to the ways of the one God, and even though a sinner, he repents and receives forgiveness. This makes him righteous and keeps him from guilt.

Chapter 23 includes the last words of David. David says in (2), The spirit of the LORD speaks through me, his word is on my tongue. Verse 5 says, he has made with me an everlasting covenant, ordered in all things and secure. The chapter ends by listing some of David's warriors.

Chapter 24 along with 21:14 and numerous other verses in the OT reflect the belief that natural calamity is or can be caused by the wrath of God against human sin, and that this wrath is to be appeased before the calamity can be stopped. It should not be understood that all natural calamities are caused by the wrath of God, but when a calamity does occur, a nation or religious institution needs to ask if God might be saying something. Or is the natural disaster happening because nature is simply broken as humans are because of original sin? We do know that there will be instances in the NT where natural disasters have nothing to do with God's wrath (see Lk 13:1-5).

Chapter 24:1 says, Again the anger of the LORD was kindled against Israel, and he incited David against them saying, "Go count the people of Israel and Judah." 1 Chronicles 21:1 substitutes Satan for the LORD. Verse 10 says, But afterward, David was stricken to the heart because he had numbered the people. David said, "I have sinned greatly in what I have done. But now, O LORD, I pray you take away the guilt of your servant; for I have done very foolishly."

Ancient cultures thought it was dangerous to be counted and that evil forces would punish the group for doing so. On the other hand, if was done for military purposes it could have been thought that it was an act of trusting the military instead of God. It is strange that David says he has sinned by obeying God. First Chronicles may be right by substituting Satan as the one who ordered David to count.

Verse 15 informs us that the LORD sent a pestilence on Israel from that morning until the appointed time, and seventy thousand people died from Dan to Beersheba. But Jerusalem is spared. The angel of the LORD was then by the threshing floor of Araunah the Jebusite. Verse 17 says, When David saw the angel who was destroying the people, he said to the LORD, "I alone have sinned . . . Let your hand, I pray, be against me and against my father's house."

From verses 18-23 we are informed on that day the prophet Gad came to David and told him to erect an altar to the LORD on the threshing floor. Following Gad's instructions David went up as the LORD commanded. David told Araunah he needed to buy the threshing floor so that the plague can be averted from the people. Verses 24-25 say, David bought the threshing floor and the oxen for fifty shekels of silver. David built there an altar to the LORD, and offered burnt offerings and offerings of well-being. So the LORD answered his supplication for the land, and the plague was averted from Israel. (This area in the future will become the place for the altar of the temple of the one God in Jerusalem.) This ends 2 Samuel.

It is during the time of David that Israel is united as a nation and has its territory expanded to great lengths. David will always be considered Israel's greatest king, even though Solomon was greater politically since his land space went from Egypt to Iraq. Saul is the first king and David the second. Both Saul and David are great sinners just as Samuel said the kings would be. But there is a major difference between the two. David makes a real attempt to be a man of God where Saul's attempt is weak to say the least. Also, David's repentance is from the heart where Saul's repentance, when it is mentioned, appears to be superficial and used as an attempt to keep power.

The strong faith of David can be seen in many of the Psalms he wrote. He is a musician who expresses his beliefs and his heart in his songs. David is portrayed as being fully human. At times he is vain, manipulative, arrogant, a shrewd politician, one the Scriptures would call a sinner. But David is also humble, sensitive, loyal, repentant, forgiving, and fully devoted to God's teachings and concerns for justice. For a king at that time in a very brutal world, he is a great man and king. In a world filled with idolatry and violence, and a nation of God's people constantly falling into idolatry, David stands like a rock for the one God.

Over and over as we go through the OT books, we will see that keeping the one God idea alive is a real challenge, and often it almost becomes extinct. This is a major theme in the OT. More often than not the problem is idols. Islam in the Qur'an highlights this problem and emphasizes it over and over.

There are times when believing in the one God will seem to disappear, but God will cause things to happen to revive it. David is always remembered as a great king, not so much because he was great politically or economically, even though his accomplishments were many, but he is remembered as Israel's greatest king because he was a man of God who truly believed and trusted in the one God. He was a sinner but a repentant sinner who was truly a man of God. Because of this, he will constantly be mentioned as Israel's greatest throughout Scripture.

One last thought. The stories of Samuel, Saul, and David testify to the complexity of the human person, especially in relationship to God. On a personal level these stories will have meaning for us where we find the truth of our own lives reflected in the lives of these leaders. Also, we can affirm the presence and activity of God in our lives as individuals and in our lives as a nation. God is still listening, speaking, and acting.

1 & 2 KINGS

The theme of 1 and 2 Kings is the history of the monarchy from Solomon in 970 B.C. to the destruction of Jerusalem in 586 B.C. Kings was originally one book but then divided. There are some problems with dates and chronology throughout. First Kings opens with the Hebrew nation in glory, and Second Kings closes with it in ruin.

Solomon is first known for his trust in God and wisdom, but later he is known for foreign women, extravagance, heavy taxes, forced labor, and ignoring God's word, all of which destroys the United Kingdom. At Solomon's death there is civil war and the kingdom divides into the north (Israel) and the south (Judah). Each king will be known for whether or not they are obedient to the one God and for promoting proper worship. These are the Deuteronomic editors at work. The analysis by these editors of the kings has nothing to do with their political acumen; it all has to do with their obedience to God's word and worship. Remember the purpose of Scripture is religious and theological not exact history.

All the kings in the north fail following the sin of Jeroboam, who set up a pagan idol, while only Hezekiah and Josiah are labeled without reservation as great kings in the south. There are a few kings in the south labeled as good because their attitude is right, but they did not destroy the high places where some of the people worshiped. None of them measured up to Hezekiah or Josiah.

In 1 and 2 Kings we find two cycles of accounts of miracle stories surrounding the stories of Elijah and Elisha. Many of their miracles are almost exactly like the miracles Jesus will do. In 2 Kings the kingdom of the north will be destroyed by the Assyrians from upper Mesopotamia (Iraq) in 722 B.C., while the southern kingdom will be destroyed by the Babylonians from middle Mesopotamia in 586 B.C. The city of Jerusalem and the temple will be completely destroyed.

When reading these books, a suggestion for first time readers is not to get mired down in trying to remember all the names. Read to understand the message, themes, and theology. At the end of the book of 2 Kings is a list of all the northern kings in order and beside it all the southern kings in order. The list includes the dates and how many years they reigned. The reader may want to refer to this list from time to time.

The writers/editors of the books from Joshua through Kings are known as the Deuteronomic historians because of their analysis of why the people are in exile. The reason according to them is as Deuteronomy stated, if they obey, the nation will be blessed, but if they disobey, the nation will be cursed. The people of God disobey, so they are punished, but God still loves his people and offers them redemption, if they repent.

We must always remember the writer is not writing history as we understand it today. In addition to being called religious and theological history, Scripture is also called salvation history. For Christians it culminates in God's living word, his incarnated Son. The writers are writing theology based on a narrative form of history. The overall interest of the writers is religious rather than historiography. The concern is not exact historical detail even though exact historical detail is there at times. This writer has stated this numerous times because of its importance, and the fact that it is not a concept normally understood by beginning readers. The experience of this writer is that beginning readers and students struggle greatly with this concept.

In a sense the Bible is not word for word God's word, for men are permitted to express God's word in their human words. If one compares different accounts of the same narratives in Scripture, one usually discovers different words to describe the same thing. A number of examples have been pointed out as we have moved through the OT. Even so, the Bible does witness to God's inspired word. This is also a difficult concept for many readers. As we begin with chapter one, we come to the end of David's time on earth.

1 KINGS

In chapter 1 King David is about to die, so a beautiful girl named Abishag, the Shunammite, is brought in to keep him warm. She serves her purpose, but (4) says, the king did not know her sexually (no Viagra in those times). Meanwhile in (5-8), Adonijah, David's son next in line for David's crown, prepares to take the throne supported by Joab and the priest Abiathar. Those who do not support him are Zadok the priest, Benaiah who is in charge of David's special guard, the prophet Nathan, Shimei, and David's warriors.

In verses 11-14 Nathan advises Bathsheba to inform the king about what Adonijah is doing. He tells her he will support her. While Bathsheba is talking to the king, Nathan enters and in (24-27) informs David concerning what is happening and who is involved. Then the king in (28-30) said, "Summon Bathsheba to me." So she came into the king's presence, and stood before the king. (The movements of Bathsheba and Nathan are confusing. The reader must assume that each of them leaves the king's presence when he talks to the other.) The king swore saying, "As the LORD lives . . . 'Your son Solomon shall succeed me as king, and he shall sit on my throne in my place,' so will I do this day." In verses 32-34 David summons the priest, Zadok, and Nathan the prophet to anoint Solomon as king. In an act of mercy verse 52 informs us that Solomon will spare Adonijah's life as long as he refrains from any wickedness.

Chapter 2:1-3 says, When David's time to die drew near, he charged his son

Solomon saying: "I am about to go the way of all the earth. Be strong, be courageous, and keep the charge of the LORD your God, walking in his ways and keeping his statutes, his commandments, his ordinances, and his testimonies, as it is written in the law of Moses, so that you may prosper in all that you do and wherever you turn . . ." Then in (10-11) David dies and is buried in the city of David. He ruled forty years, seven years in Hebron and thirty-three years in Jerusalem.

Adonijah in (13-25) asks Bathsheba to get Abishag for his wife. This is interpreted as an attempt to get the throne or at least be a co-ruler. So in (24-25) Solomon announces that Adonijah shall be put to death. King Solomon then sends Benaiah son of Jehoida; he strikes him down, and he dies.

In verses 26-27 Solomon spares Abiathar, the priest but strips him from being a priest because he backed Adonijah. He is put in exile at Anathoth. His life is spared because he carried the ark of God for David and because he shared David's hardships. This fulfills the word of the LORD that he had spoken in Shiloh concerning the end of the line of priests through Eli (I Sam 2:27-36).

In verses 28-34 Solomon sends his enforcer Benaiah to kill Joab for his killing of Abner, Amassa, and Absalom. Joab runs to the temple grasping the horns of the altar, but Solomon says to kill him, which Benaiah does, and he dies the violent death that he had meted out to others. Verse 35 says, The king put Benaiah son of Jehoiada over the army in his place, and the king put the priest Zadok in the place of Abiathar.

In verses 36-46 Shimei, another potential trouble maker, is put on parole in Jerusalem to keep him away from his fellow Benjaminites, but when he breaks parole, he is put to death for cursing David. David said he would not put him to death, but back in (8-9) on his death bed he tells Solomon to put him to death. Verse 46 says, Then the king commanded Benaiah son of Jehoiada; and he went out and struck him down, and he died. So the kingdom is established in the hand of Solomon. (Violence never seems to cease.)

Chapter 3:2-5 says, The people were sacrificing at the high places, however, because no house had yet been built for the name of the LORD. Solomon loved the LORD, walking in the statutes of his father David; only, he sacrificed and offered incense at the high places. The king went to Gibeon to sacrifice there, for that was the principal high place; Solomon used to offer a thousand burnt offerings on that altar.

The high places are areas throughout the land where worship to the one God is offered. Because throughout their history the people also mixed in foreign gods with their worship at these high places a law was made that said the only place to worship God is the temple in Jerusalem. As we will see the only kings to follow that law will be Hezekiah and Joshua which is one of the reasons why the Deuteronomistic writers rated these two as the only excellent kings.

Chapter 3:5 says, At Gibeon the LORD appeared to Solomon in a dream by night; and God said, "Ask what I should give you." Solomon in verses 6-9 said, "You have shown great and steadfast love . . . Give your servant therefore an understanding mind to govern this your people, able to discern between good and evil; for who can govern this your great people?" Verse 10 says, It pleased the LORD that Solomon had asked this.

God said to him in verses 11-15 "Because you have asked this, and have not asked for yourself long life and riches, or for the life of your enemies, . . . I now do according to your word. Indeed I give you a wise and discerning mind; no one like you has been before you, and no one like you shall arise after you. I give you also what you have not asked, both riches and honor all your life; no other king shall compare with you. If you will walk in my ways, keeping my statutes and my commandments, as your father David walked, then I will lengthen your life." Then Solomon awoke; it had been a dream. The Scriptures make it plain that Solomon's wisdom and riches will be God's gift.

Later in (16-27) two prostitutes came to the king for a judgment. Both had delivered babies, but the one baby died because one of the women rolled over onto her baby while sleeping at night. The woman whose son died then took the other lady's baby while she was sleeping. Both the women appear before Solomon and claim the child was their child. Solomon takes a sword and in (25) said, "Divide the living boy in two, then give half to the one, and half to the other."

Verses 26-27 say, But the woman whose son was alive said to the king--because compassion for her son burned within her—"Please, my lord, give her the living boy; certainly do not kill him!" The other said, "It shall be neither mine nor yours; divide it." Then the king responded: "Give the first woman the living boy; do not kill him. She is the mother." Verse 28 says, All Israel heard of the judgment that the king had rendered; and stood in awe of the king, because they perceived that the wisdom of God was in him, to execute justice.

In chapter 4:1-34 Solomon now introduces a vast bureaucracy to administer the kingdom including twelve administrative units. One of its purposes is for taxation. Verses 20-21 say, Judah and Israel were as numerous as the sand by the sea; they ate and drank and were happy. Solomon was sovereign over all the kingdoms from the Euphrates to the land of the Philistines, even to the border of Egypt; they brought tribute and served Solomon all the days of his life. (This fulfills the promise made to Abraham.)

Verse 26 says, Solomon also had forty thousand stalls of horses for his chariots, and twelve thousand horsemen. (This is his military arsenal.) Verses 29-30 inform us that God gave Solomon very great wisdom, discernment, and breadth of understanding as vast as the sand on the seashore, so that Solomon's wisdom surpassed the wisdom of all the people of the east, and all the wisdom of Egypt. Verses 32-34 say, He composed three thousand proverbs, and his songs numbered a thousand and five. He would speak of trees, from the cedar that is in Lebanon to the hyssop that grows in the wall; animals, and birds, and reptiles, and fish. People came from all the nations to hear the wisdom of Solomon; they came from all the kings of the earth who had heard of his wisdom.

In chapter 5 because there is peace, Solomon can now build a house for God. Verses 1-12 inform us that Solomon requests Hiram of Tyre (Phoenicia) to supply the cedar and cypress wood. Hiram in (7) rejoices greatly, and says, Blessed be the LORD today, who has given to David a wise son to be over this great people. (He would not be saying that because he just made a good business deal, would he?) Solomon will supply Hiram with wheat and oil.

King Solomon in (13-17) then conscripts forced labor out of Israel; the levy numbers thirty thousand men. Adoniram is in charge of forced labor. Solomon also had seventy thousand laborers, and eighty thousand stonecutters in the hill country, besides Solomon's three thousand three hundred supervisors who are over the work . . . At the king's command, they quarried out great, costly stones in order to lay the foundation of the house with dressed stones.

In chapter 6 Solomon builds the temple. Verse 14 says, Solomon built the house and finished it. The rest of the chapter describes the temple and its furnishings. The temple itself is really more of a big chapel than a cathedral. It is more to house God than to hold people. The furnishings are beautiful, walls gleaming of gold, carved and decorated cedar panels, and creatures with great golden wings spanning the sanctuary.

Verses 37-38 say, In the fourth year the foundation of the LORD was laid in the month of Ziv. In the eleventh year, in the month of Bul, which is the eighth month, the house was finished in all its parts, and according to all its specifications. He was seven years in building it. Chapter 7:1 says, Solomon was building his own house thirteen years, and he finished his entire house. The rest of the chapter describes Solomon's new house, its furnishings and the temple furnishings.

Chapter 8 is the dedication of the temple. All the heads of the tribes are assembled as the ark is brought to the temple. The whole temple shone with God's presence. In verse 27 of Solomon's long prayer he says, "But will God indeed dwell on the earth? Even heaven and the highest heaven can not contain you, much less this house I have built! . . ." At this point Solomon is still humble and he offers his prayer.

Overall Solomon's prayer of dedication is an archetypical statement of Deuteronomistic theology. If the people follow the ways of God, the nation will be blessed, and if it does not, it will be cursed. Also mentioned in (35-40) is how sin can influence the cosmos. Rain will be withheld and plagues, sickness, and famine will come. After the prayer Solomon blesses the people and great sacrifices are offered. Then the Feast of Tabernacles or Booths (Sukkoth) is celebrated. Verse 66 says, On the eighth day he sent the people away; and they blessed the king, and went to their tents, joyful and in good spirits because of all the goodness that the LORD had shown to his servant David and to his people Israel.

In chapter 9:2-3 the LORD appeared to Solomon a second time, as he had appeared to him at Gibeon. The LORD said to him, "I have heard your prayer and your plea, which you have made before me; I have consecrated this house that you have built, and put my name there forever; my eyes and my heart will be there for all time . . ."

Then God warns Solomon and his descendants in verses 6-9 saying. "If you turn aside from following me, you or your children, and do not keep my commandments and my statutes that I have set before you, but go and serve other gods and worship them, then I will cut Israel off from the land that I have given them; and the house that I have consecrated for my name I will cast out of my sight; and Israel will become a proverb and a taunt among all people. This house will become a heap of ruins; everyone passing by it will be astonished, and will hiss; and they will say, Why has the LORD done such a thing to this land and to this house? Then they will say, 'Because they have forsaken the LORD their God, who brought their ancestors out of the land of Egypt, and embraced other gods, worshiping them and serving them; therefore the LORD has brought this disaster upon them.' "

At the end of twenty years, for all Solomon's wealth, he has a balance of trade problem, so verses 11-14 say, King Solomon gave to Hiram twenty cities in the land of Galilee. But when Hiram came from Tyre to see the cities . . . they did not please him. Therefore he said, "What kind of cities are these that you have given me, my brother?" So they are called the land of Cabul (meaning good for nothing) to this day. But Hiram had sent to the king one hundred twenty talents of gold.

Verses 15-24 give an account of some of the things accomplished with the forced labor. But verse 22 says of the Israelites Solomon made no slaves; they were the soldiers, they were his officials, his commanders, his captains, and the commanders of his chariotry and cavalry. At the end of the chapter in (26-28) Solomon builds a fleet of ships at Ezeon-geber to sail to Ophir where Solomon imports much gold.

Chapter 10:1-3 says, When the Queen of Sheba heard of the fame of Solomon, (fame due to the name of the LORD), she came to test him with hard questions. She came to Jerusalem with a very great retinue, with camels bearing spices, and very much gold, and precious stones; and when she came to Solomon, she told him all that was on her mind. Solomon answered all her questions . . .

It is thought that Sheba probably is modern day Yemen. Solomon welcomes her visit, for he is interested in establishing a trade relationship with Sheba and the area beyond. This is Solomon's attempt to expand his economic base. The location of Ezion-geber is at the Gulf of Aqaba. Solomon intends to use the Red Sea and the Persian Gulf for access to ports in east Africa, southern Arabia, and beyond.

When the Queen observes all of Solomon's wisdom, in (6-9) she says, "The report was true that I heard in my own land of your accomplishments and of your wisdom, but I did not believe the reports, until I came and my own eyes had seen it. Not even half had been told me; your wisdom and prosperity far surpass the report I had heard . . . Blessed be the LORD your God, who has delighted in you and set you on the throne of Israel! Because the LORD loved Israel forever, he has made you king to execute justice and righteousness."

Solomon is to become enriched with his trade ventures with the Queen of Sheba and his trade with Hiram of Tyre. Verses 22-25 say, Once every three years the fleet of ships of Tarshish used to come bringing gold, silver, ivory, apes, and peacocks. Thus King Solomon excels all the kings of the earth in riches and in wisdom. The whole earth sought the presence of Solomon to hear his wisdom, which God had put in his mind. Every one of them brought a present, objects of silver and gold, garments, weaponry, spices, horses, and mules, so much year by year.

Solomon's kingdom is one of splendor. He devotes himself to commerce and gigantic public works. He controls the trade routes of Arabia, India, and Africa. The era of David and especially Solomon is the golden era of Hebrew history. Israel is the most powerful kingdom in the world, Jerusalem is the most magnificent city, and the temple is the most splendid building on earth.

In chapter 11 we begin to learn of Solomon's failures. Verses 1-3 say, King Solomon loved many foreign women along with the daughter of Pharaoh: Moabite, Ammonite, Edomite, Sidonian, and Hittite women, from the nations concerning which the LORD had said to the Israelites, "You shall not enter into marriage with them, neither shall they with you; for they will surely incline your heart to follow their gods"; Solomon clung to these in love. Among his wives were seven hundred princesses and three hundred concubines; and his wives turned away his heart. (That number simply means he had a lot.) Verse 4 says, For when Solomon was old, his wives turned away his heart after other gods, and his heart was not true to the LORD his God, as was the heart of his father David.

Verses 5-9 say, Solomon followed Astarte the goddess of the Sidonians, and Milcom the abomination of the Ammonites. So Solomon did what was evil in the sight of the LORD, and did not completely follow the LORD, as his father David had done. Then Solomon built a high place for Chemosh the abomination of Moab, and for Moloch the abomination of the Ammonites, on the mountain east of Jerusalem. He did the same for all his foreign wives, who offered incense and sacrificed to their gods. Then the LORD was angry with Solomon, because his heart had turned away from the LORD, the God of Israel, who had appeared to him twice, and had commanded him concerning this matter, that he should not follow other gods; but he did not observe what the LORD commanded.

It is interesting to note that never does it say Solomon is anointed with the Holy Spirit or that the Spirit is with him. This remains true of all the kings that succeed him. The Spirit of God is found in the book of Kings but in association with the prophets. The prophets will speak the word of God.

Verses 11-13 say, the LORD said to Solomon, "Since this has been your mind and you have not kept my covenant and my statutes that I have commanded you, I will surely tear the kingdom from you and give it to your servant. Yet for the sake of your father David I will not do it in your lifetime; I will tear it out of the hand of your son. I will not, however, tear away the entire kingdom; I will give one tribe to your son, for the sake of my servant David and for the sake of Jerusalem, which I have chosen."

In verse 26 Jeroboam, who is in charge of the forced labor, rebels against Solomon. The prophet Ahijah from Shiloh in (29-36) tells Jeroboam that God is about to tear the kingdom from Solomon and give him ten tribes while one tribe will remain for Solomon. Verse 33 said, This is because he has forsaken me, worshiped Astarte the goddess of the Sidonians, Chemosh, the god of Moab, and Milcom the god of the Ammonites, and has not walked in my ways, doing what is right in my sight and keeping my statutes and ordinances, as his father David did.

In verses 37-38 Jeroboam receives the same promise of an enduring dynasty that was given to David if he is obedient to Yahweh. Solomon tries to kill Jeroboam in (40), so he escapes to Egypt to King Shishak. At the end of chapter 11 in verse 43 Solomon dies, and his son, Rehoboam, succeeds him. Solomon reigns for forty years as did Saul and David. Forty is more symbolic than literal, meaning a generation or a long time.

Solomon started out as a man of God following his commands and ways, but in his later years he no longer listened to God. Possibly, like many, he was overcome by his power and wealth, thinking it was his own doing. Looking back at Solomon's life there are many positive and negative aspects.

Some of the positives are the following. He solidifies David's political basis and geographical holdings. He builds the temple. He establishes enormous treasury reserves. He develops a positive international reputation. His court becomes known as a center of learning, such that much of Israelite literature (Song of Songs, Proverbs, Ecclesiastes) are attributed to him. God gave him wisdom, and for the most part, he used it until the end.

Some of the negatives of Solomon are the following. His rule is marked by forced labor. He creates an overextended economy, and heavily taxes the peasants. As usual the golden age is a golden age for the elite. His love for women, like Samson, ruins him, and he begins to worship the gods of his wives. He concentrates too much on the military (horses and chariots). Because of all this, he completes the fulfillment of Samuel's prophecy of the negatives that would happen when the people have a king other than the one God.

Chapter 12:1 says, Rehoboam (Solomon's son) went to Shechem, for all Israel had come to Shechem to make him king. All the assembly of Israel in (4) said to Rehoboam, "Your father made our yoke heavy. Now therefore lighten the hard service of your father and his heavy yoke that he placed on us, and we will serve you. Verses 8-11 say, But he disregarded the advice that the older men gave him, and consulted with the young men who had grown up with him and now attended him . . . The young men who had grown up with him said to him, "Thus you should say to this people who spoke to you 'Your father made our yoke heavy, but you must lighten it for us'; thus you should say to them, 'My little finger is thicker than my father's loins. Now whereas my father laid on you a heavy yoke, I will add to your yoke. My father disciplined you with whips, but I will discipline you with scorpions.' "

In verses 12-15 Rehoboam tells the people what his friends advised. The answer from the people in (18) is to stone to death Adoram who is in charge of the forced labor, and then to rebel against the house of David. Then Rehoboam hurriedly mounted his chariot to flee to Jerusalem where the houses of Judah and Benjamin remain loyal to him as he prepares to fight Israel to restore the united kingdom.

Meanwhile, in (20) since Solomon has died, Jeroboam returns from Egypt, and the ten northern tribes called Israel make him king at Shechem. In order to keep the people from going to Jerusalem to worship in (28-31), he makes two golden calves like the calves of Egypt and told the people that these would be their gods and the places where they would worship. He sets one in Bethel and the other one in Dan. This will be what is called the *Fatal Flaw* of the people of Israel. It is called the Fatal Flaw because every king that follows Jeroboam will be considered a failure by the editors, for they follow his example. Verse 31 says, He also made houses on high places, and appointed priests from among the people who were not Levites.

The politics of power becomes more important than true worship of the one

God, for he does not want the people to go to the temple in Jerusalem. At this point many priests from the north move to the south. The sacred poles the people worship on the high places are symbols of the Canaanite fertility goddess Asherah. Asherah is mentioned about forty times in the Hebrew Scriptures as a temptation to the Israelites. In an agricultural society the fertility goddess is always important because of the need for the produce from the plantings.

Chapter 13 continues the condemnation of Jeroboam begun in chapter 12. The chapter also emphasizes that a true prophet is one who listens, speaks, and obeys the word of God and his commands and never obeys another human even a prophet if there is a conflict in what is said.

In chapter 14:7-16 the prophet Ahijah at Shiloh announces, that Jeroboam, because he made for himself other gods, will lose the kingdom God gave him. The LORD will raise up for himself a king over Israel who shall cut off the house of Jeroboam. Jeroboam reigns twenty two years. In Judah, Rehoboam, the son of Solomon, rules seventeen years in Jerusalem.

After the death of Jeroboam the writer in (19) adds, the rest of the acts of Jeroboam, how he warred and how he reigned, are written in the books of the Annals of the Kings of Israel. After the death of Rehoboam the writer adds the same thing except in (29) he substituted Judah for Israel.

These were apparently government records or history kept in a government place. These statements are made by the writer after each king died. Also, with the kings of the south (Judah) the name of the king's mother is always listed, but the mothers are not listed in the northern kingdom (Israel).

Verses 22-24 say, Judah also did what was evil in the sight of the LORD; they provoked him to jealousy with their sins that they committed, more than all their ancestors had done. For they also built for themselves high places, pillars, and sacred poles (Asherah) on every high hill and under every green tree; there were also male temple prostitutes in the land. They committed all the abominations of the nations that the LORD drove out before the people of Israel.

In their agricultural society Canaanite worship is a fertility religion where worship involves intercourse with the sacred prostitutes in order to encourage the gods to have intercourse which they believe would bring rain to fertilize the crops of the land. God calls this an abomination. This is what took place in many of the high places.

In verses 25-28 during the fifth year of Rehoboam, King Shishak of Egypt raided the land of Judah and the temple treasury taking all the treasures. (Taking all is obviously a hyperbole, for as we go on all the treasures of the temple treasury will be taken numerous times.) Verse 30 says, There was war between Rehoboam and Jeroboam continually, and in (31) Rehoboam dies and his son Abijam succeeds him.

Chapter 15 informs us that Abijam commits all the sins his father did, but Abijam rules only three years. Abijam's son, Asa, follows. He reigns forty one years in Jerusalem. Verses 11-14 say, Asa did what was right in the sight of the LORD as his father David had done. He put away the male temple prostitutes out of the land and removed all idols that his ancestors had made. He also removed his mother Maacah from being queen mother because she made an abominable image for Asherah; Asa cut down her image and burned it at the Wadi Kidron. But the high places were not taken away. Nevertheless the heart of Asa was true to the LORD all his days. (The high places should have been completely destroyed.)

Verses 16-22 tell us that there was war between Asa and King Baasha of Israel all their days. He built Ramah, to prevent anyone from going out or coming in to King Asa of Judah. Baasha will reign in the north after Jeroboam and Nadab. Then King Asa and King Ben-hadad of Damascus joined together against Israel, but the requested help cost Asa silver and gold from the temple. Verses 23-24 inform us that in Asa's old age he was diseased in his feet, and then he dies. His son Jehoshaphat succeeds him. (Feet is usually an euphemism for penis indicating his death probably was because of a venereal disease.)

In verses 25-34 Nadab, son of Jeroboam, rules after Jeroboam in Israel but after two years is assassinated by Baasha an army general. Baasha also kills all the male heirs of the house of Jeroboam. This is customary practice. He rules twenty-four years. The writer in 34 says, He did what was evil in the sight of the LORD, walking in the way of Jeroboam and in the sin he caused Israel to commit.

Chapter 16:1-4 says, The word of the LORD came to Jehu son of Hanani against Baasha saying, "Since I exalted you out of the dust and made you leader over my people Israel, and you have walked in the way of Jeroboam, and have called my people to sin, provoking me to anger with their sins, therefore, I will consume Baasha and his house, and I will make your house like the house of Jeroboam son of Nebat. Anyone belonging to Baasha who dies in the city the dogs shall eat; and anyone of his who dies in the field the birds of the air shall eat." (The sin that Jeroboam caused other kings to follow was worship at the shrines of Dan and Bethel.)

Verses 8-10 inform us that Baasha's son Elah is the next king and only rules two years, for Zimri, his servant, kills him and succeeds him and kills all the male heirs. Zimri rules seven days. Israel in (16-18) makes Omri commander of the army and king; he besieges Zimri, and Zimri sets the king's house on fire and dies within it taking his life.

In verses 23-25 Omri reigned for twelve years. He bought the hill of Samaria from Shemer for two talents of silver; he fortified the hill, and called the city that he built, Samaria, after the name of Shemer, the owner of the hill. (After 722 B.C. the whole area will be known as Samaria, and the people will be called Samaritans.)

Historically Omri was very powerful, and he founded a dynasty that lasted through five kings. Even a long time after his death other countries called Israel the house of Omri. The fact that only a few verses are given to him shows that the purpose of the Deuteronomistic editors is theological and not historical.

Verses 25-26 say, Omri did what was evil in the sight of the LORD; he did more evil than all before him. For he walked in all the ways of Jeroboam, son of Nebat, and in the sins he caused Israel to commit, provoking the LORD, the God of Israel, to anger by their idols. (This is stated after most of the northern kings.)

Verses 29-33 tell us Omri's son Ahab follows him. He has learned well from his father. He reigns in Samaria twenty two years. Verse 30 says, Ahab son of Omri did evil in the sight of the LORD more than all who were before him. Ahab takes his wife Jezebel from the Sidonians and serves Baal, even erecting an altar for Baal and a sacred pole. Verses 33-34 say, Ahab also made a sacred pole. Ahab did more to provoke the anger of the LORD, the God of Israel, than had all the kings of Israel who were before him. In his days Hiel of Bethel built Jericho; he laid its foundation at the cost of Abirim his firstborn, and set up its gates at the cost of his youngest son Segub, according to the word of the LORD, which he spoke by Joshua son of Nun (see Josh 6:26).

Chapter 17 introduces Elijah the Tishbite from Gilead, and after Elijah we will be introduced to Elisha. Many scholars believe some of their stories are legends. But in religious literature God's truth can come through legends also. The fact that they are legends does not mean no history is involved. The modern reader is again advised to focus on the theology of the stories rather than debate their historical accuracy. It is theology that is inspired not historical accuracy. In the Gospel of Matthew 17:3-13 Elijah is called the greatest of prophets. Elijah is God's answer to Ahab and Jezebel.

In verse 1 Elijah tells Ahab that there was not going to be any rain for years except by his word. In verses 2-4 The word of the LORD came to him saying, "Go from here and turn eastward, and hide yourself by the Wadi Cherith, which is east of the Jordan. You shall drink from the wadi, and I have commanded the ravens to feed you there." Verses 7-10 say, But after awhile the wadi dried up, because there was no rain in the land. Then the word of the LORD came to him saying, "Go now to Zarephath, which belongs to Sidon, and live there; for I have commanded a widow there to feed you." So he set out and went to Zarephath.

When Elijah got there, Elijah asked for some water and bread. In (12) she told him that she just had a handful of meal in a jar and a little oil in a jug and was preparing it for herself and her son that they may eat it and die. Elijah told her in (13-14) "Do not be afraid; go and do as you have said; but first make me a little cake from it and bring it to me, and afterwards make something for yourself and your son. For thus says the LORD the God of Israel: the jar of meal will not be emptied and the jug of oil will not fail until the day that the LORD sends rain on the earth."

Verses 15-16 say, She went and did as Elijah said, so that she as well as he and her whole household ate for many days. The jar of meal was not emptied, neither did the jug of oil fail, according to the word of the LORD that he spoke by Elijah. (The teaching is that God will take care of those who obey his prophets.)

One day the son became ill and died. The woman in (18) said to Elijah, "What have you against me, O man of God? You have come to me to bring my sin to remembrance, and to cause the death of my son!" Elijah got the son and took him to the upper chamber. In verses 21-24 Elijah went to his bedroom, prays to the LORD for the child's life, and stretches himself over him three times, and life returns to the child. Verses 23-25 say, Elijah took the child, brought him down from the upper chamber into the house, and gave him to his mother; then Elijah said, "See, your son is alive." So the woman said to Elijah, "Now I know that you are a man of God and that the word of the LORD in your mouth is truth."

Chapter 18:1-4 says, After many days the word of the LORD came to Elijah, in the third year of the drought, saying, "Go present yourself to Ahab; I will send rain on the earth." So Elijah went to present himself to Ahab. The famine was severe in Samaria. Ahab summoned Obadiah, who was in charge of the palace. (Now Obadiah revered the LORD greatly; when Jezebel was killing off the prophets of the LORD, Obadiah took a hundred prophets, hid them fifty to a cave, and provided them with bread and water.)

Obadiah in (7) meets Elijah on the road, and Elijah asks Obadiah to set up a meeting between him and Ahab, which he does. When Ahab sees Elijah in (17-18) he says, "Is it you, you troubler of Israel?" He answered, "I have not troubled Israel; but you have, and your father's house, because you have forsaken the commandments of the LORD and followed the Baals. Now therefore have all Israel assemble for me at Mt Carmel, with four hundred fifty prophets of Baal and four hundred prophets of Asherah, who eat at Jezebel's table."

So Ahab sent to all the Israelites, and assembled the prophets at Mt Carmel. When the people assemble in (21-22) Elijah says, "How long will you go limping with two different opinions? If the LORD is God, follow him; but if Baal, then follow him." The people did not answer him a word. Then Elijah said to the people, "I, even I only, am left a prophet of the LORD; but Baal's prophets number four hundred fifty . . ."

In verses 23-26 Elijah tells them to choose one bull for sacrifice, and he would choose the other. The prophets of Baal will go first in sacrifice and Elijah will go second. He tells them to call upon the name of their gods, and then he will call upon the name of his God. The god who answers by fire (lightning?) and burns up the sacrifice will be the God. From morning until noon the prophets of Baal wail, but nothing happens. In verse 27 Elijah mocked them saying, "Cry aloud! Surely he is a god; either he is meditating, or he has just wandered away, or he is on a journey, or perhaps he is asleep and must be awakened." (Elijah's point is that they are praying to man made gods that are not God. Again as in Egypt the issue is who is the real god?)

Verses 28-30 inform us that there was no response from the gods. Then in (31-35) Elijah takes twelve stones according to the twelve tribes of Israel, makes a trench around the altar, and puts water on the sacrificial bull pouring so much on it that the trench is filled with water. Then Elijah prays to God, and in (38) the fire of the LORD fell and consumed the burnt offering, the wood, the stones, and the dust, and even licked up the water that was in the trench. Verses 39-40 say, When all the people saw it, they fell on their faces and said, "The LORD indeed is God; the LORD indeed is God." Elijah said to them, "Seize the prophets of Baal; do not let one of them escape." Then they seized them; and Elijah brought them down to the Wadi Kishon, and killed them there. (This certainly is not a time of gentleness and mercy.)

Verses 41-46 then inform us that a small cloud began to develop, and in a little while the heavens grew black with clouds and wind, and there was a heavy rain. Three years of drought ended. (The message is clear: God is the LORD.)

In chapter 19:1-3 Jezebel vows to do to Elijah what he has done to the prophets of Baal, so he flees for his life in the wilderness. In verses 4-5 he sits under a broom tree. He asked that he might die: "It is enough; now, O LORD, take away my life, for I am no better than my ancestors." Then he lay down under the broom tree and fell asleep. Suddenly an angel touched him and said to him, "Get up and eat."

So verses 8-10 say, He got up, and ate and drank; then he went in the strength of that food forty days and forty nights to Horeb (Sinai) the mount of God. At that place he came to a cave, and spent the night there. Then the word of the LORD came to him, saying, "What are you doing here, Elijah?" He answered, "I have been very zealous for the LORD, the God of hosts; for the Israelites have forsaken your covenant, thrown down your altars, and killed your prophets with the sword. I alone am left, and they are seeking my life, to take it away."

Verses 11-12 say, "Go out and stand on the mountain before the LORD, for the LORD is about to pass by." Now there was a great wind, so strong that it was splitting mountains and breaking rocks in pieces before the LORD, but the LORD was not in the wind; and after the wind an earthquake, but the LORD was not in the earthquake; and after the earthquake a fire, but the LORD was not in the fire; and after the fire a sound of sheer silence. (All but the last are signs of Baal, the storm god.)

Verses 13-14 say, When Elijah heard it, he wrapped his face in his mantle and went out and stood at the entrance of the cave. Then there came a voice to him that said, "What are you doing here, Elijah?' He answered, "I have been very zealous for the LORD, the God of hosts; for the Israelites have forsaken your covenant, thrown down your altars, and killed your prophets with the sword. I alone am left, and they are seeking my life to take it away."

Verses 15-18 say, Then the LORD said to him, "Go return on your way to the wilderness of Damascus; when you arrive, you shall anoint Hazael as king over Aram.

Also you shall anoint Jehu son of Nimshi as king over Israel; and you shall anoint Elisha son of Shaphat of Abel-meholah as prophet in your place. Whoever escapes from the sword of Hazael, Jehu shall kill; and whoever escapes from the sword of Jehu, Elisha shall kill. Yet I will leave seven thousand in Israel, all the knees that have not bowed to Baal, and every mouth that has not kissed him." (Elijah was not alone as he thought.)

Meanwhile, in chapter 20 King Ben-hadad of the Arameans (Damascus, Syria) marches on Samaria, but Ahab defeats the Arameans. Instead of putting him to death Ahab in (34) makes a treaty with him and spares his life. A prophet of the LORD went to him and in (42-43) said, "Thus says the LORD, 'Because you have let the man go whom I had devoted to destruction, therefore your life shall be for his life, and your people for his people.' " The king of Israel set out toward home, resentful and sullen, and came to Samaria.

In chapter 21:1-4 a man named Naboth of Jezreel has a vineyard beside the palace of King Ahab in Samaria. Ahab wants it, so he offers Naboth money worth its value. Naboth in verse 3 says, "The LORD forbid that I should give you my ancestral inheritance." Ahab went home resentful and sullen. He lay down on his bed, turned away his face, and would not eat. In verse 7 his wife Jezebel said to him, "Do you now govern Israel? Get up, eat some food, and be cheerful; I will give you the vineyard of Naboth the Jezreelite." So in (8-12) she wrote letters to the elders to frame him by getting two scoundrels to say he had cursed God and the king. The sentence for Naboth was death, and (13) says, they took him outside the city, and stoned him to death. In that way Ahab took Naboth's land.

Verses 17-19 say, the word of the LORD came to Elijah the Tishbite, saying; Go down to meet King Ahab of Israel who rules in Samaria; he is now in the vineyard of Naboth, where he has gone to take possession. You shall say to him, "Thus says the LORD: Have you killed, and taken possession?" You shall say to him, "Thus says the LORD: In the place where dog's licked up the blood of Naboth, dogs will also lick up your blood."

In verses 20-24 Ahab said to Elijah, "Have you found me, O my enemy?" He answered "I have found you. Because you have sold yourself to do what is evil in the sight of the LORD, I will bring disaster on you; . . . Also concerning Jezebel the LORD said, 'The dogs shall eat Jezebel within the bounds of Jezreel.' Anyone belonging to Ahab who dies in the city the dogs shall eat; and anyone of his who dies in the open country the birds of the air shall eat." The writer in 25-26 adds (Indeed, there was no one like Ahab, who sold himself to do what was evil in the sight of the LORD, urged on by his wife Jezebel. He acted most abominably in going after idols, as the Amorites had done, whom the LORD drove out before the Israelites.)

In verse 27 Ahab was deeply depressed and put on sackcloth which was a sign of mourning and repentance. Verses 28-29 say, Then the word of the LORD came to Elijah the Tishbite: "Have you seen how Ahab has humbled himself before me? Because he has humbled himself before me, I will not bring the disaster in his days; but in his son's days I will bring the disaster on his house." (The writer wants all to see the greatness of God's compassion, mercy, grace, and forgiveness. If Ahab can be offered forgiveness anyone can receive it.)

Chapter 22:1-2 says, For three years Aram and Israel continued without war. But in the third year King Jehoshaphat of Judah came down to the king of Israel. (Is this the person the term jumping Jehoshaphat came from?) In (3-4) they prepare to go to war against the king of Aram over the city of Ramoth-gilead, a Levitical city east of the Jordan. The Judean king is one of Ahab's vassals. Ahab sealed this relationship by marrying his daughter, Athaliah to Jehoshaphat's son Jehoram. (This will be one of the few times Israel and Judah are not fighting each other. But we will see that this marriage will be a disaster for Judah.)

The king of Israel in (6) gathers four hundred of his prophets and inquires about going to war, and they all agree it is good to do so. (Apparently, they are court prophets and not prophets of the one God.) In (7-8) Jehoshaphat said, "Is there no other prophet of the LORD here of whom we may inquire?" The king of Israel said to Jehoshaphat, "There is still one other by whom we may inquire of the LORD, Micaiah son of Imlah; but I hate him, for he never prophesies anything favorable about me, but only disaster."

The prophet Micaiah is summoned at Jehoshaphat's request, and in (19-23) Micaiah said, "Therefore hear the word of the LORD: . . . the LORD has put a lying spirit in the mouth of all these your prophets; the LORD has decreed disaster for you." Ahab is angry, and in (27) wants him put in prison, and fed on reduced rations of bread and water until the king returns from his victory in peace. In (28-29) Micaiah said to Ahab, "If you return in peace, the LORD has not spoken to me." So the king of Israel and

King Jehoshaphat of Judah went up to Ramoth-gilead.

During the battle verses 34-39 say a certain man drew his bow and unknowingly struck the king of Israel between the scale armor and the breastplate; so he said to the driver of his chariot, "Turn around and carry me out of the battle, for I am wounded." The battle grew hot that day, and the king was propped up in his chariot facing the Arameans, until at evening he died; the blood from the wound had flowed into the bottom of the chariot . . . So the king died, and was brought to Samaria; they buried the king in Samaria. They washed the chariot by the pool of Samaria; the dogs licked up his blood, and the prostitutes washed themselves in it, according to the word of the LORD that he had spoken (21:19). Verse 40 says, So Ahab slept with his ancestors; and his son Ahaziah succeeded him.

Verses 41-43 inform us that Jehoshaphat son of Asa reigned in Judah twenty five years. He walked in all the ways of his father Asa; he did not turn aside from it, doing what was right in the sight of the LORD; yet the high places were not taken away, and the people still sacrificed and offered incense on the high places. Jehoshaphat also made peace with the king of Israel (Ahab). Verse 46 says, The remnant of the male temple prostitutes who were still in the land in the days of his father Asa, he exterminated.

Ahaziah's son Jehoram succeeded him. Ahaziah, son of Ahab reigned two years over Israel. Verses 52-53 say, He did what was evil in the sight of the LORD, and walked in the way of his father and mother and in the way of Jeroboam son of Nebat who caused Israel to sin. He served Baal and worshiped him; he provoked the LORD, the God of Israel, to anger, just as his father had done.

At the end of 1 Kings the worst fears expressed in Deuteronomy have been fulfilled. Kings have amassed wealth, horses, chariots, wives. False prophets developed, and every commandment of God is broken including the worship of idols. The people have been oppressed and even made slave labor.

Before moving to 2 Kings a few words about Elijah: Elijah is cast as a new Moses. Lawrence Boadt (1984) compares the two. He says Moses is the great law giver while Elijah is the great prophet. Like Moses and Joshua we will see that he also parts the water (II Kings 2:7). Like Moses he experiences a theophany (I Kings 19:8). Elijah builds an altar with twelve stones (I Kings 18:30); Moses constructs an altar flanked by twelve pillars (Ex 24:4). Elijah performs a sacrifice consumed by the fire of God, and the people bow (I Kings 18:38). Moses offers a sacrifice after consecrating his altar, and the people bow (Lev 19:24). Like Moses Elijah has no tomb (Deut 34:6). Elijah is carried to heaven in a fiery chariot II Kings 2:11. Later in the transfiguration both Elijah and Moses appear with Christ. (Mk 9:2-12 Mt 17:1-13, Luke 9: 28-36).

It is also interesting that Elijah and his anointed follower, Elisha, who we will learn about next, performed the type of miracles that Jesus will perform, including raising the dead. There were only three times in the Bible where an abundance of miracles are the norm. Those times were during the time of Moses, during the time of Elijah and Elisha, and then in the NT during the time of Christ.

2 KINGS

Second Kings is simply a continuation of 1 Kings; originally they were one book. We call the books Kings, but the heroes are the prophets that God sends. About one-third of 2 Kings is about Elijah's successor Elisha. Again as a reminder when reading these books for the first time, do not to get mired down trying to remember all the names. Read them to understand the themes, the message, and theology.

Jehoshaphat's son Ahaziah succeeds him, and in his two year reign the kingdom of Moab seizes independence. In verses 2-6 Ahaziah falls through the lattice in his upper chamber in Samaria, and then sends messengers to inquire of Baalzebub, the god of Ekron (Philistia) to ask if he will survive. Elijah meets the messengers and sends them back. The king in (7-8) asks, "What sort of man was he who came to meet you and told you these things?" They answered, "A hairy man, with a leather belt around his waist." He said, "It is Elijah the Tishbite."

Then the king in (9-12) sends fifty men three different times to Elijah. The first two groups are consumed by the fire of heaven (lightning?), but the last group led by their captain pleads for mercy. Verses 15-17 say, Then the angel of the LORD said to Elijah, "Go down with him; do not be afraid of him." So he set out and went down with him to the king, and said to him, Thus says the LORD: "Because you have sent messengers to inquire of Baalzebub, the god of Ekron,--is it because there is no God in Israel to inquire of his word?--therefore you shall not leave this bed to which you have gone, but you shall surely die." So he died according to the word of the LORD that Elijah had spoken. His brother Jehoram succeeds him.

In chapter 2 Elijah and Elisha are traveling together and came to the Jordan. A company of fifty prophets in (7-8) watch as they walk. Elijah takes his mantle, strikes the water, and it parts as they cross on dry ground. Verses 9-12 say, When they had crossed, Elijah said to Elisha, "Tell me what I may do for you, before I am taken from you." Elisha said, "Please let me inherit a double share of your spirit." He responded, "You have asked a hard thing; yet, if you see me as I am being taken from you, it will be granted to you, if not, it will not."

As they continued walking and talking, a chariot of fire and horses of fire separated the two of them, and Elijah ascended in a whirlwind into heaven. Elisha kept watching and crying out, "Father, Father! The chariots of Israel and its horsemen!" But when he could no longer see him, he grasped his own clothes and tore them in two pieces. (This is a cultural expression for mourning a death.)

Verses 13-15 say, He picked up the mantle of Elijah that had fallen from him, and went back and stood on the bank of the Jordan. He took the mantle of Elijah that had fallen from him and struck the water saying, "Where is the LORD the God of Elijah?" When he had struck the water, the water was parted to the one side and to the other, and Elisha went over. When the company of prophets who were at Jericho saw him at a distance, they declared, "The spirit of Elijah rests on Elisha." They came to meet him and bowed to the ground before him.

The people of Jericho tell Elisha in (19-20) that the water is bad, so Elisha performs a miracle, and the water is made good. Then in (23) on the way to Bethel, some boys, probably young men who are troublemakers, call him baldhead, and they tell him to go away. Verse 24 says, When he turned around and saw them, he cursed them in the name of the LORD. Then two she-bears came out of the woods and mauled forty two of the boys.

Very few writers would tell a story like this to encourage respect for a prophet, or anyone as far as that goes, which gives us an indication how different ancient cultures are from ours today. First of all this is probably a legend passed down to teach a theological point. Forty two as a number is, as most numbers in Hebrew, used with a symbolic significance. Forty two is a negative significance in 10:14, Rev 11:2, 13:5. This writer guesses that this story is an ancient legend passed on orally to teach that anyone who rejects God's anointed will bring destruction upon themselves.

Chapter 3:1-3 says, In the eighteenth year of King Jehoshaphat of Judah, Jehoram son of Ahab became king over Israel in Samaria; he reigned twelve years. He did what was evil in the sight of the LORD, though not like his father and mother, for he removed the pillar of Baal that his father had made. Nevertheless, he clung to the sin of Jeroboam son of Nebat, which he caused Israel to commit; he did not depart from it. (Again this means he allows the worship at Dan and Bethel and the general worship of other gods.)

In verses 5-11 When Ahab dies, the king of Moab rebels against the king of Israel. King Jehoram of Israel got King Jehoshaphat of Judah and Edom to join him. But a drought is hindering them, so they inquired of Elisha. Elisha in (17-19) tells them God will bring water for the men and animals and hand Moab over to them. Afterward in (25-27) they battle Moab and defeat their cities. Only at Kirhareseth did a city remain. When the king of Moab sees the battle is going against him, he sacrifices his firstborn son who is to succeed him, and offers him as a burnt offering on the wall. Great wrath comes upon Israel, so they withdraw from him and they return to their own land.

Again, this is another surprising story found in Scripture where sacrificing one's son is successful. At least, it causes Israel to depart as great wrath falls upon them. This obviously must have happened, for it is difficult to understand why the story is even told.

In chapter 4:1-7 Elisha performs more miracles. Like Jesus his miracles show God's care of ordinary people. A widow whose husband was a prophet is so deep in debt that she is going to lose her two children as slaves to her creditor. All she has in her house is a jar of oil. Elisha overflows her jar of oil into all the jars she could find. In verse 7 Elisha tells her, "Go sell the oil and pay your debts, and you and your children can live on the rest.

Later when Elisha comes upon the childless Shunammite woman who had previously fed and housed him, Elisha tells her she will have a son. Soon she conceives and has a son. Later, when he is older the son has a headache and dies. The woman goes to Elisha, and in (32-34) he goes into her house and prays. Then verses 35-37 say, He got down, walked once to and fro in the room, then got up again and bent over him; the child sneezed seven times and the child opened his eyes. The mother came and fell at his feet, bowing to the ground; then she took her son and left.

Verse 38 says, When Elisha returned to Gilgal, there was famine in the land. As the company of the prophets was sitting before him, he said to his servants, "Put the large pot on, and make some stew for the company of prophets." In verses 39-41 we are told one of them went out into the field to gather herbs, and a poisonous vine got in by mistake, but Elisha threw some flour in the pot and made the stew acceptable to eat.

Then a man brings him twenty loaves of barley and fresh ears of grain in his sack. Elisha in (42-44) said, "Give it to the people and let them eat." But his servant said, "How can I set this before a hundred people?" So he repeated, "Give it to the people and let them eat, for thus says the LORD, 'They shall eat and have some left.' " He set it before them, they ate, and had some left, according to the word of the LORD. (Jesus will also feed the crowds miraculously in the gospels.)

In chapter 5:1-5 Syria is at war with Israel, and Naaman is the commander of the Syrian army and a leper. A young Israelite slave girl tells Naaman about Elisha's powers. When the king of Aram (Syria) sends Naaman to the King of Israel to be cured of his leprosy, the Israelite king thinks the king of Aram is asking the impossible, looking for an excuse to attack him, so he tears his clothes as an expression of grief. In (6-7) the commander came bringing a letter asking the king of Israel for a cure. The king of Israel was upset, but Elisha in (8) says to the king, "Why have you torn your clothes? Let him come to me that he may learn that there is a prophet in Israel."

In verses 9-11 Naaman comes with his horses and chariots and halts at the entrance of Elisha's house. Elisha sends a messenger to him saying, "Go wash in the Jordan seven times, and your flesh will be restored and you shall be clean." But Naaman becomes angry and went away saying, "I thought that for me he would surely come out, and stand and call on the name of the LORD his God, and would wave his hand over the spot and cure the leprosy!" (Naaman is upset with such a foolish remedy and is ready to return home.)

Verses 13-14 say, But his servants approached and said to him, "Father, if the prophet had commanded you to do something difficult, would you not have done it? How much more when all he said to you was, 'Wash, and be clean'?" So he went down and immersed himself seven times in the Jordan, according to the word of the man of God; his flesh was restored like the flesh of a young boy, and he was clean.

In verses 15-17 Naaman returns to the man of God and says to him, "Now I know that there is no God in all the earth except in Israel; please accept a present from your servant." But he said, "As the LORD lives, whom I serve, I will accept nothing!" He urged him to accept, but he refused. Then, Naaman said, "If not, please let two mule-loads of earth be given to your servant; for your servant will no longer offer burnt offering or sacrifice to any god except the LORD. (At that time the ancients did not think they were able to worship another nation's god if they did not worship on the god's soil.)

Verses 18-19 continue, But may the LORD pardon your servant on one account; when my master goes into the house of Rimmon to worship there, leaning on my arm, and when I bow down in the house of Rimmon, may the LORD pardon your servant on this one count." He said to him, "Go in peace." (Since the issue in the OT is worshiping the one God only, it is very strange that Elisha approved this request of bowing down, even though doing so saves Naaman's life and job and allows him to be a witness to the one God.)

When Gehazi, the servant of Elisha, sees that Elisha refuses the gift, and after Naaman leaves, he decides to go after him. In (22) he lies to Naaman telling him his master sent him to collect a talent of silver and two changes of clothing from him as a gift. Elisha through his extraordinary powers knew what he did, so when Gehazi returns Elisha asks him where he was, and he lies saying he was not anywhere. Elisha in (27) then tells him the leprosy of Naaman shall cling to him, and to his descendants forever. So he left his presence leprous, as white as snow. (Later in the NT book of Acts lying to the apostles brings death.)

In chapter 6 the company of prophets tells Elisha they need to go to the Jordan and build a bigger place to live. As they are building (5-6) tells us that an ax head fell into the water. Elisha threw a stick in the water and made the ax head float, and the man got it.

While they were in Dothan, the army of Aram surrounded them. Verses 15-17 say, When an attendant of the man of God rose early in the morning and went out, an army with horses and chariots were all around the city. His servant said, "Alas master! What shall we do?" He replied, "Do not be afraid, for there are more with us than there are with them." Then Elisha prayed: "O LORD, please open his eyes that he may see." So the LORD opened the eyes of the servant, and he saw; the mountain was full of horses and chariots of fire all around Elisha. (Obviously, they were given sight into the spiritual world of the angels.)

In verses 18-24 Elisha prays that the Arameans be struck with blindness, and as they are led to Samaria, instead of killing them they are fed by the Israelites. The Arameans were either so impressed by this act of hospitality, or they were in fear of the prophet's powers that (23) says, And the Arameans no longer came raiding into the land of Israel.

Some time later King Ben-hadad of Aram mustered his entire army; he marched against Samaria and laid siege to it. (Obviously their being impressed did not last long, or else the chronology is out of order.) As time went on the famine and war became so great that in (28-29) people cook their children and eat them.

In chapter 7 Elisha foretells the end of the famine and the defeat of Aram. As the Arameans are in their camp verses 6-7 inform us that the LORD causes the Aramean army to hear the sound of chariots and horses, the sound of a great army, so that they flee abandoning their tents and horses. (This happened as Elisha had foretold.)

In chapter 8 Elisha goes to Damascus while Ben-hadad is ill. Hazael who is Ben-hadad's assistant is told by Elisha in (7-15) that he will be the next king, for Ben-hadad is going to die. Elisha wept, for he knew what evil Hazael would do to Israel. Hazael then kills Ben-hadad while he is in bed, and he becomes the next king.

The rest of the chapter tells us that Jehoram, son of King Jehoshaphat of Judah, begins to reign, and he reigns eight years. Verses 18-19 say, He walked in the way of the kings of Israel, as the house of Ahab had done, for the daughter of Ahab was his wife. He did what was evil in the sight of the LORD. Yet the LORD would not destroy Judah for the sake of his servant David, since he had promised to give a lamp to him and to his descendants forever. (Disobedient kings will be rejected, but the promise will go on.)

During the time of Jehoram the kingdom Edom revolts against him and sets up its own king. Libnah also revolts. In (22-27) Ahaziah, son of King Jehoram of Judah, begins to reign. (He is not to be confused with his uncle with the same name who ruled in Israel.) This Ahaziah reigned one year in Jerusalem. His mother's name is Athaliah, a granddaughter of King Omri in Israel. As a son-in-law to the house of Ahab, he walks in Ahab's ways doing what is evil in the sight of the LORD, for he is son-in-law to the house of Ahab.

In chapter 9 Elisha tells one in the company of prophets to anoint Jehu, son of Jehoshaphat, as king of Israel. So the young prophet goes to Ramoth-gilead. Verses 5-10 say, He arrived while the commanders of the army were in council, and he announced, "I have a message for you, commander." "For which one of us?" asked Jehu. "For you commander." So Jehu got up and went inside; the young man poured oil on his head, saying to him, "Thus says the LORD the God of Israel: I anoint you king over the people of the LORD, over Israel. You shall strike down the house of your master Ahab, so that I may avenge on Jezebel the blood of my servants the prophets, and the blood of all the servants of the LORD. For the whole house of Ahab shall perish; I will cut off from Ahab every male, bond or free, in Israel. I will make the house of Ahab like the house of Jeroboam . . . The dogs shall eat Jezebel in the territory of Jezreel, and no one shall bury her." Then he opened the door and fled. (This was to fulfill the prophecy of Elijah.)

Later in verses 16-20 Jehu mounts his chariot and goes to Jezreel, where Joram (king of Israel) is lying ill. King Ahaziah of Judah had come down to visit Joram. In Jeezreel, the sentinel standing on the tower spied the company of Jehu arriving, and in (17) said, "I see a company." Joram said, "Take a horseman; send him to meet them, and let him say, 'Is it peace?' " Then he sends out a second horseman to meet him, but neither returns. In verse 20 the sentinel reported, "He reached him, but he is not coming back. It looks like the driving of Jehu son of Nimshi; for he drives like a maniac." Then in (21) King Joram and King Ahaziah, each in their own chariot, drive out to the property of Naboth, the Jezreelite.

Verse 22 says, When Joram saw Jehu, he said, "Is it peace, Jehu?" He answered, "What peace can there be, so long as the many whoredoms and sorceries of your mother Jezebel continue?" In (23-28) Joram tries to escape, but Jehu drew his bow and an arrow pierces the heart of Joram. Jehu tells his aid to throw him on the plot of ground of Naboth. Then as King Ahaziah flees, Jehu has him put to death also.

In verses 30-34 when Jehu comes to Jezreel, Jezebel paints her eyes and adorns her head and looks out the window. Jehu looks up and tells the two eunuchs to throw her down which they do. Her blood splatters on the wall and on the horses as the horses trample her. When they go to bury her (35-36) say, they found no more of her than the skull, the feet, and the palms of her hands. When they came back and told him, he said, "This is the word of the LORD, which he spoke through Elijah the Tishbite, 'In the territory of Jezreel the dogs shall eat the flesh of Jezebel; the corpse of Jezebel shall be like dung on the field in the territory of Jezreel, so that no one can say, This is Jezebel.' "

In chapter 10 Jehu's reign opens with the killing of Ahab's seventy sons in Samaria along with many of the prophets, priests, and worshipers in the temple of Baal. Verse 11 says, Jehu killed all who were left of the house of Ahab in Jezreel, all his leaders, close friends, and priests, until he left him no survivor. Then he got all the worshipers of Baal into the temple of Baal and (25) says, they put them to the sword. Verses 27-28 say, Then they demolished the pillar of Baal, and destroyed the temple of Baal, and made it a latrine to this day. Thus Jehu wiped out Baal from Israel.

But verse 29 says, Jehu did not turn aside from the sins of Jeroboam son of Nebat, which he caused Israel to commit—the golden calves which were in Bethel and Dan. Verse 31 says, Jehu was not careful to follow the law of the LORD the God of Israel with all his heart; he did not turn from the sins of Jeroboam, which he caused Israel to commit. Jehu reigned twenty eight years starting a new dynasty to last four generations. In his days Hazael of Syria took the territory east of the Jordan from Israel. Jehoahaz, Jehu's son, succeeded him.

Chapter 11:1 says, when Athaliah, Ahaziah's mother, saw that her son was dead, she set about to destroy all the royal family. (She had become the Jezebel of the southern kingdom.) Then we are informed in (2) that Ahaziah's sister (Jehosheba) hid Joash, Ahaziah's son. Athaliah, who was the daughter of Ahab and Jezebel, reigned six years. (These are some of the darkest years in the nation's history.)

The royal line of David is all but wiped out; only the baby Joash survives. But after six years the priest, Jehoida, husband of Jehosheba and sister of Ahaziah, who hid Joash, brought out the king's son in (12) and put the crown on him, and gave him the covenant; they proclaimed him king, and anointed him; they clapped their hands and shouted, "Long live the king." (The line of Judah is preserved.) Meanwhile, Athaliah in (16) is put to death. Verses 17-18 say, Jehoida made a covenant between the LORD, the king, and the people that they should be the LORD's people; also between the king and the people. Then all the people of the land went to the house of Baal and tore it down . . . Verse 21 says, Jehoash (Joash) was seven years old when he began to reign.

In chapter 12:1-3 In the seventh year of Jehu, Jehoash (also Joash) began to reign; he reigned forty years in Jerusalem. His mother's name was Zibiah of Beer-sheba. Verses 2-3 say, Jehoash did what was right in the sight of the LORD all his days, because the priest Jehoiada instructed him. Nevertheless the high places were not taken away; the people continued to sacrifice and make offerings on the high places.

In verses 4-8 money from the temple tax and freewill offerings going to the priests is to be set aside to repair the temple, but as years go by, the money gets no further than the priests. (There really is nothing new under the sun.) In verses 9-16 a new method of collection results in enough funds for repairs, but not enough to replace the valuable furnishings probably lost during Athaliah's reign. The rest of the chapter states that King Hazael attacked Jerusalem, and King Jehoash in (18) bought him off by giving him gold and the votive gifts from the temple treasury. Then Hazael withdrew from Jerusalem. Later Jehoash's servants assassinated him. (Siphoning off the top and bribes are a familiar theme throughout history for both clergy and non-clergy.)

Chapter 13:1-2 says, in the twenty-third year of King Joash son of Ahaziah of Judah, Jehoahaz son of Jehu began to reign over Israel in Samaria; he reigned seventeen years. He did what was evil in the sight of the LORD following the sins of Jeroboam which caused Israel to sin; he did not depart from them. Verses 3-4 say, The anger of the LORD is kindled against Israel, so that he gave them repeatedly into the hands of Hazael of Aram, then into the hand of Benhadad son of Hazael. (There were a number of Ben-hadads.) But Jehoida entreated the LORD and the LORD heeded him, for he saw the oppression of Israel, how the king of Aram oppressed them.

Verses 5-6 say, Therefore the LORD gave Israel a savior so that they escaped from the hand of the Arameans; and the people lived in their homes as formerly. Nevertheless they did not depart from the sins of the house of Jeroboam, which he caused Israel to sin, but walked in them; the sacred pole also remained in Samaria. At his death verse 9 says, his son, Joash succeeded him. He reigns sixteen years, and (11) says, He also did what was evil in the sight of the LORD; he did not depart from all the sins of Jeroboam son of Nebat, which he caused Israel to sin, but he walked in them.

Elisha is about to die after fifty years of prophetic activity. In (14-19) King Joash of Israel goes to see him, and Elisha using object lessons informs him that he will have three victories over Aram, and his prophecy comes true.

Verses 20-21 say, Elisha died, and they buried him. Now bands of Moabites used to invade the land in the spring of the year. As a man was being buried, a marauding band was seen and the man was thrown into the grave of Elisha; as soon as the man touched the bones of Elisha, he came to life and stood on his feet. (The writer is saying that even in death Elisha and his words bring life.)

In chapter 14 King Amaziah, son of Joash of Judah, reigns twenty nine years in Jerusalem. He does what is right in the sight of the LORD, but the high places are not removed. He has a great victory over Edom, but it goes to his head, and he challenges Israel. In verses 13-14 King Jehoash of Israel defeats him, and then breaks down the walls of Jerusalem and in (14) takes gold, silver, and the vessels from the house of the LORD as well as the treasures in the king's house.

In verses 23-24 King Amaziah's son Azariah succeeds him. Joash's son, Jeroboam II reigns in Israel for forty one years. (He is politically strong and defeats a weak Syria. He gives Israel its last moments of glory by re-establishing most of what had been Solomon's empire.) But the writer says, he did what was evil in the sight of the LORD; he did not depart from all the sins of Jeroboam son of Nebat, which he caused Israel to sin.

After his death the nation falls apart. We will see that the prophets Amos and Hosea will reveal the corruption within Israel which consists of extremes of wealth and poverty and the grinding down of the poor and weak. This will be one of God's main complaints against his people as we will learn when we read the prophets.

In chapter 15 Azariah, son of Amaziah, of Judah reigns fifty two years. Verses 3-5 say, He did what was right in the eyes of the LORD just as his father Amaziah had done. Nevertheless, the high places were not taken away; the people still sacrificed and made offerings on the high places. The LORD struck the king, so that he was leprous to the day of his death, and lived in a separate house. Jotham the king's son was in charge of the palace, governing the people of the land.

Verses 8-10 say, In the thirty-eighth year of King Azariah of Judah, Zechariah, son of Jeroboam reigned over Israel in Samaria six months. He did what was evil in the sight of the LORD, as his ancestors had done. He did not depart from the sins of Jeroboam son of Nebat, which he caused Israel to sin. Shallum son of Jabesh conspired against him, and struck him down in public and killed him, and reigned in place of him. Verse 12 says, This was the promise the LORD gave Jehu, "Your sons shall sit on the throne of Israel to the fourth generation."

Shallum ruled one month in Samaria, and in (14) Menahem killed him. Verses 17-18 say, he reigned ten years in Samaria. He did what was evil in the sight of the LORD; he did not depart all his days from any of the sins of Jeroboam son of Nebat, which he caused Israel to sin. He sacks Tiphsah in (16-19) and rips open all the pregnant women. Then he pays off King Pul (Tiglath-pilser III) of Assyria by taking silver from wealthy Israelites. This keeps the Assyrian king out of the land, at least for awhile.

In verses 23-31 Pekahiah, son of Menahem, rules two years, and then is overthrown by an army coup led by Pekah, who introduces a new dynasty and rules twenty years. Both kings do what is evil in the sight of the LORD following the ways of Jeroboam. Pekah's anti-Assyrian policy leads to a capture and mass deportation of the people by Tiglath-pilsner. Then Pekah is assassinated by Hoshea. (The time is 733-732 B.C. The New Oxford Annotated Bible states that in his records Tiglath-pileser says he had a hand in overthrowing Pekah by Hoshea.)

Verses 32-35 say, in the second year of King Pekah, son of Remaliah of Israel, King Jotham son of Uzziah of Judah began to reign . . . He did what was right in the eyes of the LORD just as his father Uzziah had done. Nevertheless the high places were not removed; the people still sacrificed and made offerings on the high places.

In chapter 16:1-2 King Ahaz son of Jotham of Judah began to reign for sixteen years. He did not do what was right in the sight of the LORD, but he walked in the way of the kings of Israel. Verses 3-4 say, He even made his son pass through the fire (child sacrifice), according to the abominable practices of the nations whom the LORD drove out before the people of Israel. He sacrificed and made offerings on the high places, on the hills, and under every green tree. Then in (5-9) Judah is under attack from King Rezin of Syria, King Pekah of Israel, and Edom. Ahaz takes silver and gold from the house of the LORD and gives it to King Tiglath-pileser of Assyria to protect him. When he dies in (20), his son Hezekiah succeeds him.

Some of the prophecies of Isaiah date to this time. One of note is that a virgin will conceive (Isa 7:14). The Gospel of Matthew will relate this prophecy to the Virgin Mary, and the one conceived will be Jesus (Matt 1:20-24). Jews will apply the prophecy to their time as they translate virgin as a young woman.

It is interesting to note that young woman is the proper translation, but it is also interesting to note that if a Jewish woman is not a virgin at marriage, she is to be put to death. Thus it would be easy for the Gospel of Matthew to translate the word from the Septuagint (the Greek translation of the Hebrew Scriptures used by the NT Christians) as virgin, especially for Mary who Christians believe bore God's son.

In chapter 17:1-6 Hoshea reigns over Israel for nine years. He did what was evil in the sight of the LORD, yet not like the kings of Israel who were before him. King Shalmanezar of Assyria attacks Samaria for three years and captures it in 722 B.C. Much of the population is deported. The writer in (7-8) says, This occurred because the people of Israel had sinned against the LORD their God, who had brought them up out of the land of Egypt . . . They had worshiped other gods and walked in the customs of the nations whom the LORD drove out before the people of Israel, and in the customs that the kings of Israel had introduced.

Verses 9-11 say, The people of Israel secretly did things that were not right against the LORD their God. They built for themselves high places at all their towns, from watchtower to fortified city; they set up for themselves pillars and sacred poles on every high hill and under every green tree; there they made offerings on all the high places, as the nations did whom the LORD carried away before them. (This is called syncretism where the people worship the one God but also the pagan gods of the land.)

Verses 16-18 say, They rejected all the commandments of the LORD their God and made for themselves cast images of two calves; they made a sacred pole, worshiped all the host of heaven, and served Baal. They made their sons and daughters pass through the fire; they used divination and augury; and they sold themselves to do evil in the sight of the LORD, provoking him to anger. Therefore the LORD was very angry with Israel and removed them out of his sight; none was left but the tribe of Judah alone.

As the reader goes through these books, it is important to remember that one of the main purposes of these writings is to notice all the obstacles God had to overcome to keep in civilization the one God concept and to pave the way for the Messiah.

Verses 22-23 say, The people of Israel continued in all the sins that Jeroboam committed; they did not depart from them until the LORD removed Israel out of his sight, as he had foretold through all his servants the prophets. So Israel was exiled from their own land to Assyria to this day. (Prophets are sent over and over to warn them to change their ways and follow the Lord and his commandments, but they are stubborn and do not listen. This will be especially seen when the reader gets to the Prophets.)

Verse 24 informs us that the king of Assyria took all the people who are competent away from Israel and then brought people from outlying lands and settled them in Samaria, but (25) says, When they first settled there, they did not worship the LORD;

therefore the LORD sent lions among them, which killed some of them.

Did God send the lions or is this the writer's human interpretation of the lions coming? We must remember the Bible is both human and divine including both God's thoughts and the thoughts of humans. Discerning the difference is not always easy. This writer's interpretation of the lions coming would be like those who said the earthquake that killed many was God's sending it. (Was it?)

In verses 26-29 the king of Assyria then commands one of the priests to go to the land to teach them how to worship their God. Verse 33 says, So they worshiped the LORD but also served their own gods, after the manner of the nations from among whom they had been carried away. Verse 41 says, So these nations worshiped the LORD, but also served their carved images; to this day and their children's children continue to do as their ancestor's did.

Chapter 18:1-2 informs us that Hezekiah is the son of King Ahaz. He reigns twenty nine years in Jerusalem. Verses 3-4 say, He did what was right in the sight of the LORD just as David had done. He removed the high places, broke down the pillars, and cut down the sacred poles. He broke in pieces the bronze serpent that Moses had made, for until those days the people of Israel had made offerings to it; it was called Nehushtan. (In the time of Moses it is used to heal the people of poisonous snakes. Later the people begin to make offerings to it and make it an idol.)

Verse 5-7 say, He trusted in the LORD the God of Israel; so that there was no one like him among all the kings of Judah after him, or among those who were before him. For he held fast to the LORD; he did not depart from following him but kept the commandments that the LORD commanded Moses. The LORD was with him; wherever he went, he prospered. He rebelled against the king of Assyria and would not serve him.

Verses 9-12 say, In the fourth year of King Hezekiah, which was the seventh year of King Hoshea son of Elah of Israel, King Shalmenezer of Assyria came up against Samaria, besieged it, and at the end of three years, took it . . . The King of Assyria carried the Israelites away to Assyria, . . . because they did not obey the voice of the LORD their God but transgressed his covenant—all that Moses the servant of the LORD had commanded; they neither listened nor obeyed.

Sennacherib of Assyria then in (13-36) attacks Hezekiah and Judah and captures the fortified cities. Hezekiah gives Sennacherib the treasures in the temple and the king's house, but Sennacherib comes again; he is upset that Hezekiah was looking for help from Egypt. Assyrian military officers (Rabshakeh) attempt to use scare tactics to get the people to defect and Hezekiah to surrender. (This is recorded also in Assyrian history and known as the siege of Lachish. Boadt (1984) says, The Assyrians left a record of their attack on Jerusalem in 701 that agrees almost completely with the account in 2 Kings 18:13-16. The only difference is the amount of tribute, and that may be due to either Assyrian exaggeration or a difference in weighing the talent. Sennacherib left a whole throne room in his palace covered with detailed scenes of his assault on Lachish. These can now be seen in a British museum.)

Chapter 19:1 says, When King Hezekiah heard it, he tore his clothes, covered himself with sackcloth, and went into the house of the LORD. Then he sends servants to Isaiah the prophet who in (6-7) said, "Say to your master, 'Thus says the LORD: Do not be afraid of the words you have heard, with which the servants of the king of Assyria have reviled me. I myself will put a spirit in him, so that he shall hear a rumor and return to his own land; I will cause him to fall by the sword in his own land.' "

In the meantime the Rabshakeh sent messengers and a letter threatening with the same scare tactics. Hezekiah in (14-19) received the letter; then goes to the house of the LORD and prays. He asks the LORD to save them, so that all the world's kingdoms will know that the LORD is God. Then verses 35-37 say, That very night the angel of the LORD set out and struck down one hundred eighty-five thousand in the camp of the Assyrians; when morning dawned, they were all dead bodies. (It is thought that God sent a plague. Ramsay (1994) suggests it was the bubonic plague.)

King Sennacherib went back to Assyria as Isaiah's prophecy was fulfilled. Then King Sennacherib of Assyria left, went home, and lived at Nineveh. As he was worshiping in the house of his god Nisroch, his sons Adrammelech and Sharezer killed him with the sword, and they escaped into the land of Ararat. His son Esar-haddon succeeded him.

In chapter 20:1-3 Hezekiah is sick and at the point of death. The prophet Isaiah comes to him and says, "Thus says the LORD, Set your house in order for you shall die; you shall not recover." Then Hezekiah turned his face to the wall and prayed to the LORD: "Remember now, O LORD, I implore you, how I have walked before you in faithfulness with a whole heart, and have done what is good in your sight." Hezekiah wept bitterly.

Verses 4-7 say, Before Isaiah had gone out of the middle court, the word of the LORD came to him: "Turn back, and say to Hezekiah prince of people, Thus says the LORD the God of your ancestor David: I have heard your prayer, I have seen your tears; indeed I will heal you; on the third day you shall go up to the house of the LORD. I will add fifteen years to your life. I will deliver you and this city out of the hand of the king of Assyria; I will defend this city for my own sake and for my servant David's sake." Then Isaiah said, "Bring a lump of figs. Let them take it and apply it to the boil, so that he may recover."

In verses 8-11 Hezekiah said to Isaiah, "What shall be the sign that the LORD will heal me, and that I shall go up to the house of the LORD on the third day?" Isaiah said, "This is the sign to you from the LORD, that the LORD will do the thing that he has promised: the shadow (on the sun dial) has now advanced ten intervals; shall it retreat ten intervals?" Hezekiah answered, "It is normal for the shadow to lengthen ten intervals; rather let the shadow retreat ten intervals." The prophet Isaiah cried to the LORD; and he brought the shadow back ten intervals, by which the sun had declined on the dial of Ahaz.

At that time in (12-15) King Merodach-baladen of Babylon sends envoys with presents and letters, for he heard Hezekiah was sick. Hezekiah welcomed them; he showed them all his treasure house . . . Then the prophet Isaiah came to King Hezekiah and said to him, "What did these men say? From where did they come to you?" Hezekiah answered, "They have come from a far country, from Babylon." He said, "What have they seen in your house?" Hezekiah answered, "They have seen all that is in my house; there is nothing in my storehouse that I did not show them."

Isaiah in (16-19) said to Hezekiah, "Hear the word of the LORD: Days are coming when all that is in your house and that which your ancestors have stored up until this day, shall be carried to Babylon; nothing shall be left, says the LORD. Some of your own sons who are born to you shall be taken away; they shall be eunuchs in the palace of the king of Babylon." Then Hezekiah said to Isaiah, "The word of the LORD that you have spoken is good." For he thought, "Why not, if there will be peace and security in my days?"

Sounds like many of our politicians today who only care about what benefits them at the moment. One of Hezekiah's great accomplishments is briefly mentioned: the construction of the Siloam tunnel which supplied Jerusalem with a secure water supply. The king cut a passage through 1,749 feet of solid rock to bring water from the Gihon spring outside the city to the pool of Siloam inside the city walls. (This tunnel can be seen and entered today in Israel.)

Verse 20 refers to this when it says, The rest of the deeds of Hezekiah, all his power, how he made the pool and the conduit and brought water into the city, are they not written in the book of the Annals of the Kings of Judah? Then (21) says, Hezekiah slept with his ancestors, and his son Manasseh succeeded him.

Chapter 21:1-2 says, Manasseh was twelve years old when he began to reign; he reigned fifty five years in Jerusalem. His mother's name was Hephizibah. He did what was evil in the sight of the LORD, following the abominable practices of the nations that the LORD drove out of the land now occupied by his people. (He seems to have adopted Assyrian culture and religion.)

Verses 3-7 inform us that he rebuilt the high places, erected altars for Baal, made a sacred pole, and worshiped and served the host of heaven, and built altars for the host of heaven in the house of the LORD and its courts. He even made his son pass through the fire as a child sacrifice, and he shed much innocent blood. He rebuilt the high places his father had destroyed. He practiced soothsaying, augury, and dealt with mediums and wizards. Manasseh is to Judah what Ahab was to Israel. Verse 9 says, Manasseh mislead them to do more evil than the nations had done that the LORD destroyed before the people of Israel.

The prophets declare the same fate for Judah as for Israel. In (11-15) the LORD says, "Because King Manasseh of Judah has committed these abominations, . . . I am bringing upon Jerusalem and Judah such evil that the ears of everyone who hears of it will tingle . . . I will wipe Jerusalem as one wipes a dish, wiping it and turning it upside down. I will cast off the remnant of my heritage and give them into the hands of their enemies; they shall become a prey and a spoil to all their enemies, because they have done what is evil in my sight and have provoked me to anger, since the day their ancestors came out of Egypt, even to this day."

Verse 16 says, Moreover Manasseh shed very much innocent blood, until he had filled Jerusalem from one end to another, besides the sin that he caused Judah to sin so that they did what was evil in the sight of the LORD. The writer in (17) informs us that all these things are written in the book of the Annals of the Kings of Judah. In (18-19) Manasseh dies and is buried. (Manasseh shed the innocent blood of those who belonged to the one God, and he drove the others into hiding.)

At this point there was no turning back the judgment of God. In (18-19) Amon his son becomes the next ruler and reigns two years. He does what is evil in the sight of the LORD just as his father had done. In (23-24) his servants assassinate him, and then the people of the land kill those who put him to death. The people of the land then make Amon's son, Josiah, the king.

Chapter 22:1-2 says, Josiah was eight years old when he began to reign. He reigned thirty one years in Jerusalem. His mother's name was Jedidah daughter of Adaiah of Bozkath. He did what was right in the sight of the LORD and walked in all the way of his father David; he did not turn aside to the right or to the left. (The writer portrays him as the best of Judah's kings. He is loyal to God's laws and carries out religious reform.)

Verses 3-7 inform us that in the eighteenth year of Josiah he initiates the repairing of the temple. Meanwhile, in the process, the high priest Hilkiah in verses 8-10 say, "I have found the book of the law in the house of the LORD." When Hilkiah gave the book to Shaphan, he read it. Then Shaphan the secretary came to the king, and reported to the king, "Your servants have emptied out the money that was found in the house, and have delivered it into the hands of the workers who have oversight of the house of the LORD." Shaphan the secretary informed the king, "The priest Hilkiah has given me a book." Shaphan then read it aloud to the king.

Some scholars believe the book he found was probably the book of Deuteronomy. The fact that the book had to be found certainly says something about the people of those times and their lack of concern for the covenant and God's teachings. Other scholars do not believe there was a book of Deuteronomy before this, so it was created at this time.

Verse 11 says, When the king heard the words of the book of the law, he tore his clothes (a sign of mourning and distress). In (13) the king commands, "Go inquire of the LORD for me, for the people, and for all Judah, concerning the words of this book that has been found; for great is the wrath of the LORD that is kindled against us because our ancestors did not obey the words of this book, . . ."

Huldah, a female prophet in (14-18), confirms the future disaster upon Judah, but because Josiah humbled himself before the LORD in repentance, verses 19-20 inform that he would not see the disaster of Judah and would be gathered to his grave in peace. (Unfortunately, her prophecy is wrong, for Josiah will not go to his grave in peace. Chapter 23:29 tells us Pharaoh Neco of Egypt kills him in battle.)

In chapter 23:1-3 Josiah gathers all the people together, and he reads in their hearing all the words of the book of the covenant found in the house of the LORD. Then the king and all the people make a covenant with the LORD. Josiah in (4-20), orders the temple and all of Judah and Israel to be cleansed of idolatry. Those verses include an excellent description of what was cleansed much of which has already been mentioned.

In verses 21-23 the king commands passover to be kept. No such passover had been kept since the days of the Judges. Verse 25 says, Before him there was no king like him, who turned to the LORD with all his heart, with all his soul, and with all his might, according to all the law of Moses; nor did any like him arise after him.

Verses 29-30 say, In his days Pharaoh Neco king of Egypt went up to the king of Assyria to the river Euphrates. King Josiah went to meet him; but when Pharaoh Neco met him at Megiddo, he killed him. (Babylon is in the process of becoming the world's power. Josiah is in revolt against Assyria and siding with Babylon, and Pharaoh Neco is protecting Assyria. Compare the fuller account of Josiah's death in 2 Chron 35:20-24.)

In verses 31-35 Josiah's son, Jehoahaz (Shallum) takes over and reigns three months. He does what is evil in the sight of the LORD as his ancestors did. Pharaoh Neco deposes Jehoahaz, also known as Shallum, who only rules three months and takes him to Egypt where he dies. He makes his brother Eliakim, the son of Josiah, the new king. He changes his name to Jehoiakim. Jehoiakim then taxes the land heavily by taking silver and gold from the people to pay Pharaoh Neco. Jehoiakim is to reign eleven years in Jerusalem as a vassal of Egypt. Verse 37 says, He did what was evil in the sight of the LORD, just as his ancestors had done.

Chapter 24:1 informs us that in the days of Jehoiakim King Nebuchadnezzar of Babylon comes up and makes Jehoiakim his servant for three years, then Jehoiakim rebels. The Babylonians who had defeated Assyria and Egypt at Carchemish (605 B.C.) along with the Arameans, Moabites, and Ammonites go against Judah. Verses 3-4 say, Surely this came upon Judah at the command of the LORD, to remove them out of sight, for the sins of Manasseh, all that he had committed, and also for the innocent blood that he had shed; for he had filled Jerusalem with innocent blood, and the LORD was not willing to pardon. In verses 8-9 Jehoakim's son, Jehoiachin, succeeds him and reigns three months. He did what was evil in the sight of the LORD, just like his father.

Verses 10-12 say, At that time the servants of King Nebuchadnezzar of Babylon came up to Jerusalem and the city was besieged. King Nebuchadnezzar of Babylon came to Jerusalem while the city was besieged . . . King Jehoiachin of Judah gave himself up to the king of Babylon, himself, his mother, his servants, his officers, and his palace officials. The king of Babylon took him prisoner in the eighth year of his reign.

Verses 13-15 say, He carried off all the treasures of the house of the LORD, and the treasures of the king's house; he cut in pieces all the vessels of gold in the temple of the LORD, which King Solomon of Israel had made, all this as the LORD had foretold. He carried away all Jerusalem, all the officials, all the warriors, ten thousand captives, all the artisans and the smiths; no one remained, except the poorest people in the land. He carried away Jehoiachin to Babylon; the king's mother, the king's wives, his officials, and the elite of the land, he took into captivity from Jerusalem to Babylon.

The statement that all Jerusalem was carried away is an obvious hyperbole, even though many of the upper class people were taken away. Ezekiel was included in this group. The fact that Jehoiachin, also called Jeconiah and Coniah, surrendered may be the reason that at this time (597 B.C.) the Babylonians did not destroy the city.

In verses 17-20 the Babylonian king makes Jehoiachin's uncle, Mattaniah, king and changes his name to Zedekiah. Zedekiah reigns eleven years. Verses 19-20 say, He did what was evil in the sight of the LORD just as Jehoiakim had done. Indeed Jerusalem and Judah so angered the LORD that he expelled them from his presence. Zedekiah rebelled against the king of Babylon.

In chapter 25:1-6 King Nebuchadnezzar comes with all his army against Jerusalem and lays siege to it. Jerusalem suffers a terrible eighteen month siege. Zedekiah attempts to escape to the south but is captured. Verse 7 says, They slaughtered the sons of Zedekiah before his eyes, then put out the eyes of Zedekiah; they bound him in fetters and took him to Babylon.

In verses 8-11 Jerusalem is looted and totally destroyed; the house of the LORD is burned down, the king's house, and all the houses of Jerusalem; every great house he burned down. The people were carried into exile; only the poorest of the poor were left. (This took place in 586 B.C. The book of Jeremiah will contain a wealth of additional information about the last days of Judah.)

Gedaliah son of Shaphan in (22-24) is made Governor of Judah. Gedaliah tells the people do not be afraid of the Chaldeans (Babylonians). Live in the land; serve the king, and it shall be well with you, but in (25) Ishmael of the royal family comes with ten men and strikes down Gedaliah, and he dies.

Verses 27-30 say, King Evil-merodach of Babylon, in the year that he began to reign, released King Jehoiachin of Judah from prison; he spoke kindly to him, and gave him a seat above the other seats of the kings who were with him in Babylon. So Jehoiachin put aside his prison clothes. Every day of his life he dined regularly in the king's presence. For his allowance, a regular allowance was given him by the king, a portion every day, as long as he lived. This ends the book of II Kings.

It is rather difficult to keep all the kings straight in the two books of Kings. The following summary chart developed by (Boadt 1984) should make it easier to see the chronology of the kings.

Kings of Israel		Kings of Judah	
Jeroboam	(922-901)	Rehoboam	(922-915)
Nadab	(901-90)	Abijah	(915-913)
Baasha	(900-877)	Asa	(913-873)
Elah	(877-876)	Jehoshphat	(873-849)
Zimri	(876)	Jehoram	(849-842)
Omri	(86-869)	Ahaziah	(842)
Ahab	(869-850)	Athaliah	(842-837)
Ahaziah	(850-849)	Joash	(837-800)
Jehoram	(849-842	Amaziah	(800-783)
Jehu	(842-815)	Uzziah (Azariah)	(783-742)
Jehoahaz	(815-801)	Jotham	(742-732)
Jehoash	(801-786)	Ahaz	(732-715)

Jeroboam II	(786-746)	Hezekiah	(715-686)
Zechariah	(746-745)	Manasseh	(686-642)
Shallum	(745)	Amon	(642-640)
Menahem	(745-738)	Josiah	(640-609)
Pekah	(744-732)	Jehoahaz	(609)
Pekahiah	(738-732)	Jehoiakim	(609-598)
Hoshea	(732-722)	Jehoiachin	(598-562(?))
Zedekiah	(597-586)		

In 721 B.C. the Assyrians destroyed Israel.

In 586 the Babylonians destroyed Judah.

In both conquests the people were taken into exile. In the Assyrian exile the ten northern tribes were never heard from again. Those of the very poor class who were allowed to stay married some of the Assyrians in their land, and they became known as Samaritans. In the Babylonian exile after approximately seventy years, many of the people of Judah, the southern tribe, will be allowed to return. From Judah will come the word Jew.

All the kings in Israel serve the golden calves, and the worst kings serve Baal. Most of the kings of Judah serve idols, although a few serve the one God. A good king is one that serves God. There are none in Israel, and in Judah only Hezekiah and Josiah are considered excellent and just a few more are considered good.

Remember this is a theological history not a political history. The fact is, politically, there were some good kings, but that is not the issue for the Deuteronimic writer/editors. The issue is, did they obey God or did they not. That is how the kings are rated.

This writer has stated numerous times that a major issue in the OT centers on the survival of the one God concept. That is one of the major issues the books called Kings desires to highlight. At times it appears as if the people are going to eliminate the one God who created and maintains all. But the one God is working, and elimination will not happen. One wonders today, with the creation of our modern gods and the syncretism that goes with it, if we are really any different from the ancients. Later in the Gospel of Matthew 6:24 Jesus says, no one can serve two masters. Are we in today's world attempting to imitate those people of the ancient world?

HISTORY AND THE WRITINGS AFTER THE EXILE

This section includes 1 and 2 Chronicles, Ezra, and Nehemiah which are a form of history, but are called Writings in the Hebrew Bible. Included in the Writings are Ruth, Esther, Job, Ecclesiastes, and Song of Solomon.

1 & 2 CHRONICLES

The books of 1 and 2 Chronicles follow Kings and cover much of the same information but from a different point of view. It is a different world after the exile so the leaders sense the need for an updated version of Israel's history.

The Greek title for Chronicles is Prolegomena which means things omitted or passed over in Samuel and Kings. Though that is true to some extent, it is not always true. What is omitted is anything negative concerning David and Solomon; only their virtues are mentioned, for it was the time of the nation's greatest power and influence. The Roman Catholics for hundreds of years in their Douay-Rheims version of the Bible called Chronicles the book of Paraleipomenon which also means things left out. Their modern versions use the name of Chronicles.

After experiencing seventy plus years of negativity for the nation, the writers only want to emphasize the positive. Also, the writer/editors virtually ignore material on the northern kingdom even though the northerners are invited to worship at the Jerusalem temple. The books record from the reign of Saul (covered sparsely), to David and Solomon and the kings of the south (covered in detail), to the return from the exile.

There is a strong note of divine retribution in these books. Only those kings who promote the worship of the one God are called good kings in all they do (Hezekiah and Josiah of Judah); a few kings were considered almost good, the rest are considered bad kings. From a secular point of view that is not accurate, but from a theological point of view it is.

While reading these two books, it is important to remember that the writer is not offering us scientific modern history but a theology of history based on a few theological convictions centering on David as the ideal king and the promotion of temple worship only in Jerusalem. Here David gets more of the credit for the temple than Solomon. The history is interpretive looking for what God approves rather than being like history today that attempts to emphasize factual accuracy, and to some extent, impartiality of judgment. Most scholars today say all history is interpretive, for all writers have their biases even though they may not be aware of them.

Because of the Chronicler's emphasis on the temple, genealogies, and temple music, they probably were priests and/or Levite cantors. These editors give prominence to the Levites as musicians and servers in the temple and attempt to clear up the confusion as far as who can be a priest and what the Levite duties entail. These writers or editors are especially interested in the centralization of worship at the temple in Jerusalem. A major theme is the messianic promise made to David by Nathan in 2 Samuel 7. He goes into much detail about the reigns of David and Solomon when the nation became a world power, but, again, he idealizes them and does not mention their sins or David's adultery.

The first nine chapters are basically genealogies connecting the people returning from the Babylonian exile with God at work from the beginning of history. Chronicles, Nehemiah, and Ezra usually go together as post exilic writings probably assembled around 400 B.C. These are the people who will rebuild Jerusalem and the temple after the complete destruction of both city and temple. The focus is on the southern tribes of Judah and Benjamin, and the priestly tribe of Levi which is dedicated to temple service.

The people need to be linked with their past. They need reassurance that God is still with them working out his purposes through them. They need to know how best to re-establish worship. They need to be reminded why God judged his people and that their future well-being depends on their faithfulness to God.

As in the other OT books the numbers quoted seem much too high, but the numbers given in Chronicles are much higher than the ones in Samuel and Kings. Some scholars think there is basically only one editor and that is Ezra. They think he is the editor, not only of these books, but he may be the editor of the whole OT. How accurate that is remains very difficult to know, and scholars do disagree.

Even though the Jewish Bible contains the same books as the Catholic and Protestant Bibles except for the Deuterocanonicals/Apocrypha, they are arranged differently. The Hebrew Bible ends with Chronicles.

1 CHRONICLES

In chapter 1 there is a general genealogy going from Adam to Abraham, and then from Abraham to Jacob. Then in chapter 2 the genealogy goes from the twelve sons of Israel to the descendants of Judah. Chapter 3 includes the descendants of David and Solomon.

Chapter 4 includes descendents of Judah and Simeon. A man from the line of Judah named Jabez is mentioned in verses 9-10. He is the subject of a popular book with those preaching a fundamentalist prosperity gospel. The verses say, Jabez was honored more than his brothers; and his mother named him Jabez, saying, "Because I bore him in pain." Jabez called on the God of Israel saying, "Oh that you would bless me and enlarge my border, and that your hand might be with me, and that you would keep me from hurt and harm!" And God granted what he asked. Those who promote the prosperity gospel say that all one has to do is make this prayer and believe it, and God will make whomever asks prosperous. Needless to say this writer does not know of any scholars who accept this thinking.

Chapter 5 includes the descendants of Reuben, Gad, and the half tribe of Manasseh. Chapter 6 lists the descendants of Levi, the musicians appointed by David and the settlements of the Levites. Chapter 7 includes the descendants of Issachar, Benjamin, Naphtali, the rest of Manasseh, Ephraim, and Asher. Chapter 8 includes more descendants of Benjamin. Chapter 9 lists some of the people of all the tribes who were in Jerusalem after the exile as well as the priestly families, Levitical families, the gatekeepers, those in charge of the utensils and stores, and the musicians.

Although the Chronicler does not tell the story of the northern kingdom, he wants to show the whole nation as being one in his representation. When the northern kingdom fell, the southern kingdom appropriated the name Israel, and because the southern kingdom was mainly Judah, the people are called Jews.

In chapter 9 Saul's family line is repeated from chapter 8 to introduce in chapter 10 the story of the death of Saul and his sons as told in 1 Samuel 31 and 2 Samuel 1. For the Chronicler the history of the monarchy begins with David, so it is sufficient to just show Saul's death and state the fact that God took his life because he was unfaithful to God and did not keep his commandments. Verses 13-14 say, Saul died for his unfaithfulness; he was unfaithful to the LORD in that he did not keep the command of the LORD; moreover, he consulted a medium, seeking guidance, and did not seek guidance from the LORD. Therefore, the LORD put him to death and turned the kingdom over to David son of Jesse.

The story of David's reign goes through to the end of Chronicles. It is a selective history omitting David's adultery with Bathsheba, the rape of Tamar, and the family dissension which ended in Absalom's rebellion.

In chapters 11 and 12 David is made king and captures Jerusalem. Chapter 11:4 says, David and all Israel marched to Jerusalem, that is Jebus, where the Jebusites were, the inhabitants of the land. Verses 5-9 inform us that David took the stronghold of Zion, now the city of David. David had said, "Whoever attacks the Jebusites first shall be chief and commander." Joab son of Zeruiah went up first, so he became the chief. David resided in the stronghold; therefore it was called the city of David. He built the city all around, from the Millo in complete circuit; and Joab repaired the rest of the city. And David became greater and greater, for the LORD of hosts was with him. (Benjamin and Judah are often linked in Chronicles, but the rest of the chapter and chapter 12 shows the support for David from all the tribes.)

In chapter 13:9-14 the ark of the covenant is moved from Kiriath-jearim to Jerusalem, and Uzzah attempts to save the ark from falling off the ox cart and is struck down. David is angry and does not take the ark to Jerusalem. The Levites are the only ones to carry the ark, and they are to do it with poles. Apparently, because they did not do that, they caused Uzzah's death and are responsible for the ark not going directly to Jerusalem (see 2 Sam 6). Keep in mind the OT is often used to teach by example how serious God is about keeping his teachings.

In chapter 14 when David and his men defeat the Philistines, he destroys the idols as required by the law instead of keeping them as booty as he did in II Samuel 5:21. Verses 16-17 say, David did as God had commanded him, and they struck down the Philistine army from Gibeon to Gezar. The fame of David went out into all lands, and the LORD brought the fear of him on all nations.

In chapters 15 and 16 David brings the ark of the covenant to Jerusalem and installs it in a tent. The tabernacle had been in Gibeon where the sacrifices were offered (16:39). Then the work of the Levites in Jerusalem with the ark is detailed, but all Israel participates as David establishes and oversees temple worship.

Chapter 15:1-2 says, David built houses for himself in the city of David, and he prepared a place for the ark of God and pitched a tent for it. Then David commanded that no one but the Levites were to carry the ark of God, for the LORD had chosen them to carry the ark and to minister to him forever. Verse 28 says, all Israel brought up the ark of the covenant of the LORD with shouting, to the sound of the horn, trumpets, and cymbals, and made loud music on harps and lyres.

In 16:1-3 They brought in the ark of God, and set it inside the tent that David had pitched for it; and they offered burnt offerings and offerings of well-being before God.

Verse 4 says, He appointed certain of the Levites as ministers before the ark of the LORD, to invoke, to thank, and to praise the LORD, the God of Israel. Verse 7 says, Then on that day David first appointed the singing of praises to the LORD by Asaph and his kindred.

They will then lead the praise using Psalms 105, 95, and 106. As part of that praise verses 29-31 say, Ascribe to the LORD the glory due his name; bring an offering and come before him. Worship the LORD in holy splendor; tremble before him, all the earth. The world is firmly established; it shall never be moved. Let the heavens be glad, and let the earth rejoice, and let them say among the nations, The LORD is king!

Chapter 17 repeats II Samuel 7 where David wants to build a house for the LORD. But in (10-15) Nathan the prophet says, I declare to you that the LORD will build you a house. When your days are fulfilled to go to be with your ancestors, I will raise up your offspring after you, one of your own sons, and I will establish his kingdom. He shall build a house for me, and I will establish his throne forever. I will be a father to him and he shall be a son to me . . . David then offers his prayer saying, there is no God other than the LORD. This offers great hope to the exiles returning to Jerusalem to once again establish themselves and rebuild the city and the temple.

In reference to the offspring to be raised up, Christians say this applies to Jesus; it is God's promise that through David's ancestors will come a son whose kingdom will last forever. Jews say this is a promise to Solomon then the messiah (anointed) who will establish a political kingdom on this earth. For Muslims Jesus is one of two messiahs. Jesus was resurrected and will come into the earth again to defeat the anti-Christ. He will bring a reign of righteousness over the earth for roughly eighty years. At the judgment he will pray at the Dome of the Rock, dying and returning to God. There he will pray for those facing judgment (B. Brown 2007).

In chapters 18, 19, and 20 much of the content from Samuel is repeated where David defeats the Philistines, Ammonites, and Arameans (Syrians) to solidify and expand his territory. Chapter 20:4-5 states Elhannan, not David, killed Goliath which is in conflict with 1 Samuel 17:51. (This writer believes this is significant because Chronicles usually idolizes everything David does.)

Of course, the next incident does not necessarily idolize David when in chapter 21:1-4 the census David took caused the LORD to bring a plague. But the writer said that Satan caused David to do this. Possibly he is saying it was not really David but Satan which would be the writer's attempt to release David from responsibility. Why did a plague come? Possibly the answer is because David was relying on his numbers for success instead of relying on God. By purchasing Ornan's threshing floor in (24-27) the plague is stopped. This will be the future site of the temple and worship.

In chapter 22:1 David said, "Here shall be the house of the LORD God and here the altar of burnt offering for Israel." David then gives orders to prepare for the building of the temple. He never stopped wanting to build a house for God, but God told him Solomon would build it. So verse 6 says, Then he called for his son Solomon and charged him to build a house for the LORD, the God of Israel.

Verses 7-16 say, David said to Solomon, "My son, I had planned to build a house to the name of the LORD my God. But the word of the LORD came to me, saying, 'You have shed much blood and have waged great wars; you shall not build a house to my name, because you have shed so much blood in my sight on the earth. See a son shall be born to you; he shall be a man of peace. I will give him peace from all his enemies on every side; for his name shall be Solomon, and I will give peace and quiet to Israel in his days. He shall build a house for my name. He shall be a son to me, and I will be a father to him, and I will establish his royal throne in Israel forever' . . . Now begin work, and the LORD be with you."

David spent so much time in war solidifying the nation and protecting himself that the time was not right. Solomon will build the house for God during his time of peace. Therefore, David prepares for its building by selecting the site, making plans, and gathering materials.

The next five chapters describe the organization of the nation's religious and civil organization. In chapter 23:3-5 the new duties of the Levites are described. No longer is the tent on the move; it is now permanent. The Levites no longer will have to carry the tabernacle or the things for its service, but the Levites will be in charge of taking care of and maintaining the temple at Jerusalem. They will be the judges, musicians, and singers in the choir, gatekeepers, and assistants to the priests. The three sons of Levi, Gershon, Kohath, and Merari provided the names for the Levitical divisions.

Verses 28-31 say, "but their duty shall be to assist the descendants of Aaron (priests) for the service of the house of the LORD, having the care of the courts and the chambers, the cleansing of all that is holy, and any work for the service of the house of God; to assist also with the rows of bread (the twelve loaves of the bread of the Presence), the choice flour for the grain offering, the wafers of unleavened bread, the baked offering, the offering mixed with oil, and all measures of quantity or size. And they shall stand every morning, thanking and praising the LORD, and likewise at evening, and whenever burnt offerings are offered to the LORD on sabbaths, new moons, and appointed festivals, according to the number required of them, regularly before the LORD. Thus they shall keep charge of the tent of meeting and the sanctuary, and shall attend the descendants of Aaron, their kindred, for the service of the house of the LORD."

Chapter 24:1-3 says, The divisions of the descendants of Aaron were these. The sons of Aaron: Nadab, Abihu, Eleazar, and Ithamar. But Nadab and Abihu died before their father, and had no sons; so Eleazar and Ithamar became the priests. Along with Zadok of the sons of Eleazar, and Ahimilech (Abiathar?, see vv. 6, 31, 18:16) of the sons of Ithamar, David organized them according to the appointed duties in their service.

The priests are only those who can trace their lineage back to Aaron. They are divided into twenty four groups each serving two weeks per year. The order is decided by lot. The priests are in charge of the sacrifices. Abijah (10) is the priestly course to which Zechariah, the Father of John the Baptist belonged (see Lk 1:5).

Chapter 25 lists the temple musicians who are also leaders in prophecy, proclaiming God's message. Asaph, Heman, and Jeduthun are among the most well known and are listed in the Psalms.

Chapter 26 includes the temple guards who are Levites in charge of guarding the temple and the storehouse. Treasurers, clerks, and magistrates are appointed to look after finances, legal affairs, and to keep records. The temple treasuries, gifts and taxes from the people and the spoils of war are vast. Chapter 27 lists the military commanders, the officers in charge of the tribes, those in charge of the king's property, and his personal advisers.

In chapter 28 the prophecy of Nathan (17:1-15) is fulfilled first of all in Solomon. Chronicles makes the point that David is much greater than Solomon and that all is done according to the divine will. The book of Kings emphasized political intrigue, but that is completely omitted in Chronicles.

David presents his son to the people and gives him a solemn charge after reminding the people that God gave David's lineage a kingdom that would last forever, but reminds Solomon the promise depends on loyalty to God and his commands. Then David gives Solomon in (11-19) the plan he developed for the temple with all its riches, and reminded Solomon it is all from God.

Chapter 29 lists all the riches David contributed toward the temple, and in (5-6) he invites the people to contribute. Then the people's contributions pour in to demonstrate all Israel's dedication to the temple. David then praises God in joy and humility. David reminds all in (14-19) that it is really God's kingdom, and all their gifts are really God's gift to them. David says, "But who am I, and what is my people, that we should be able to make this free will offering? For all things come from you, and of your own have we given you. For we are aliens and transients before you, as were all our ancestors; our days on earth are like a shadow, and there is no hope. O LORD our God, all this abundance that we have provided for building you a house for your holy name comes from your hand and is all your own . . . Grant to my son Solomon that with single mind he may keep your commandments, your decrees, and your statutes, performing all of them, and that he may build the temple for which I have made provision." Then in (20) David blesses the people, and all worship.

The last statement in I Chronicles 29:29-30 says, Now the acts of King David, from first to last, are written in the records of the seer Samuel, and in the records of the prophet Nathan, and in the records of the seer Gad, with accounts of all his rule and his might and of the events that befell him and Israel and all the kingdoms of the earth. (It is obvious that David's acts are cleansed and purified, and he is idealized by the editor of 1 Chronicles. The same will happen to Solomon in 2 Chronicles.)

2 CHRONICLES

The book begins with nine chapters devoted to Solomon, and seven of the nine chapters are devoted to Solomon's relationship with the temple. Chapter 1:1 says, Solomon son of David established himself in his kingdom; the LORD his God was with him and made him exceedingly great.

The Chronicler follows his source in 1 Kings 1-11 by selective editing and rearranging; he creates his own edition. The reference to Solomon's marriage to Pharaoh's daughter (1 Kings 3) of Egypt is omitted. The promise made to Jacob (Gen 28:14) is now fulfilled. Solomon asks for wisdom in (7-12), and God gives it plus power, wealth, and fame.

In chapter 2 Hiram of Tyre, who supplied David with building materials, is requested by Solomon in a letter to supply him with materials to build God's house. Hiram, now spelled by the Chronicler as Huram, responds to Solomon's letter in (11-12) saying, "Because the LORD loves his people, he has made you king over them." (Huram will supply the materials for the building of the temple.)

Solomon in (17-19) took a census of all the aliens in the land, and there were found one hundred fifty three thousand six hundred. Verse 18 says, Seventy thousand of them he assigned as laborers, eighty thousand as stonecutters in the hill country, and three thousand six hundred as overseers to make the people work. (But it says nothing of forced labor. In the idealized world of the Chronicler only aliens are forced labor. This contradicts 1 Kings 5:13-18, and 1 Kings 9:22, 12:4 which states that Solomon conscripted forced labor.)

Chapter 3:1 says, Solomon began to build the house of the LORD in Jerusalem on Mount Moriah, where the LORD had appeared to his father David, at the place that David had designated, on the threshing floor of Ornan the Jebusite. (The site is where Abraham attempted to sacrifice Isaac, and where David bought the threshing floor from Ornan. The building begins on the four hundred eightieth anniversary of the Exodus.)

Chapter 4 describes the furnishings of the temple. In chapter 5 the ark of the covenant is brought to the temple, and they praise God in song. In verses 13-14 it was the duty of the trumpeters and singers to make themselves heard in unison in praise and thanksgiving to the LORD, and when the song was raised, with trumpets and cymbals and other musical instruments, in praise to the LORD, "For he is good, for his steadfast love endures forever," the house, the house of the LORD, was filled with a cloud, so that the priests could not stand to minister because of the cloud; for the glory of the LORD filled the house of God.

Chapter 6:1-6 says, Then Solomon said, "The LORD has said that he would reside in thick darkness. I have built you an exalted house, a place for you to reside in forever." Then the king turned around and blessed all the assembly of Israel, while all the assembly of Israel stood. And he said, "Blessed be the LORD, the God of Israel, who with his hand has fulfilled what he promised with his mouth to my father David, saying, 'Since the day that I brought my people out of Egypt . . . I have chosen Jerusalem in order that my name may be there, and I have chosen David to be over my people Israel.' Verses 8-11 say, The LORD said to my father David, 'You did well to consider building a house for my name; nevertheless you shall not build the house, but your son . . . shall build the house for my name'. Now the LORD has fulfilled his promise . . . There I have set the ark, in which is the covenant of the LORD that he made with the people of Israel."

The rest of the chapter describes the dedication of the temple with Solomon's prayer of dedication. This was a prayer based on the fact in (10-11) that God and his promises are always dependable, that God loves his people, and is always ready to hear and forgive his people. A humble statement from Solomon in verse 18 says, "But will God indeed reside with mortals on earth? Even heaven and the highest heaven can not contain you, how much less this house I have built . . ."

As the Chronicler continues and closes the prayer he departs significantly from the source in 1 Kings 8. The reader can compare. In this writer's opinion the fundamentalist idea that every word in the Bible is exactly inspired of God needs to be put to rest.

Chapter 7:1-3 says, when Solomon had ended his prayer, fire (lightning?) came down from heaven and consumed the burnt offering and the sacrifices; and the glory of the LORD filled the temple. The priests could not enter the house of the LORD, because the glory of the LORD filled the LORD's house. When all the people of Israel saw the fire come down and the glory of the LORD on the temple, they bowed down on the pavement with their faces to the ground, and worshiped and gave thanks to the LORD, saying, "For he is good, for his steadfast love endures forever."

Then the king and all the people offered sacrifice before the LORD. King Solomon offered as a sacrifice twenty two thousand oxen and one hundred twenty thousand sheep. (Much of this is probably a hyperbole to emphasize the greatness of the occasion.) The celebration lasts a week, and then runs into the week long Feast of Tabernacles.

In a second appearing of God to Solomon in (12-22) God said, "I have heard your prayer, and have chosen this place for myself as a house of sacrifice. When I shut up the heavens so that there is no rain, or command the locusts to devour the land, or send pestilence among my people (cosmic disturbances), if my people who are called by my name humble themselves, pray, seek my face, and turn from their wicked ways, then I will hear from heaven, and will forgive their sin and heal their land . . . As for you, if you walk before me, as your father David walked, doing according to all that I have commanded you and keeping my statutes and my ordinances, then I will establish your royal throne, as I made covenant with your father David saying, 'You shall never lack a successor to rule over Israel.'

But if you turn aside and forsake my statutes and my commandments that I have set before you, and go and serve other gods and worship them, then I will pluck you up from the land that I have given you; and . . . I will cast you out of my sight . . . And regarding this house now exalted, everyone passing by will be astonished, and say, 'Why has the LORD done such a thing to this land and this house?' Then they will say, 'Because they abandoned the LORD . . . Therefore he has brought all this calamity upon them.' " (The Chronicler's readers would look back to the exile and see this as a warning. Others think this may have been added after the exile in order to explain why God sent them into exile.)

Chapter 8 lists some of the building projects mentioned in Kings but the writer changes some of them. Instead of Solomon giving away land to Huram of Tyre in payment for building materials as Kings stated (1 Kings 9), Chronicles in (2) states Solomon rebuilt the cities that Huram had given him, and settled the people of Israel in them. (Possibly the Chronicler was embarrassed that Solomon would give away any land of Israel.)

Whereas the book of Kings said that Solomon conscripted forced labor from God's people, in (8-9) the Chronicler mentions that he only forced people from other nations into forced labor. Kings said Solomon had many foreign wives, but the Chronicler ignores that and only mentions in (11) that Solomon had Pharaoh's daughter as a wife and moved her out of the city away from the temple because the ark of the covenant was there.

In chapter 9 the Chronicler includes the visit of the Queen of Sheba who admires his wisdom and wealth. From this they probably worked out their commercial interests, for Solomon established a fleet of ships neat Sheba (modern Yemen) on the Gulf of Aqaba in the Persian Gulf. The chapter gives an idealized picture of wealth in the United Monarchy in (13-28) probably to motivate the people to a goal that a united monarchy could do it again. Also, the extent of Solomon's kingdom fulfills God's promise to Abraham (Gen 15:18).

Verses 26-29 say, He ruled over all the kings from the Euphrates to the land of the Philistines, and to the border of Egypt. The king made silver as common in Jerusalem as stone, and cedar as plentiful as the sycamore of the Shephelah. Horses were imported for Solomon from Egypt and from all lands. Verses 30-31 say, Solomon reigned in Jerusalem over all Israel forty years. Solomon slept with his ancestors and was buried in the city of his father David; and his son Rehoboam succeeded him. (It is interesting that the writer does not mention anything about the civil strife that developed, and nothing is mentioned about how in later years Solomon disobeyed God's commands.)

From chapter 10 through 36 we see only the kings of Judah of the southern kingdom. The dates and length of each king are also given in 1 and 2 Kings. Much of the same information is included in Chronicles with the above mentioned nuances. The Chronicler does not recognize the kings of the north (Israel). Only David's descendants are the nation's true kings. He even frequently refers to Judah as Israel.

Even so, the ten tribes of the north are considered part of Israel. After the conquest of the north by the Assyrians in 722, the ten tribes are scattered and except for a remnant of the tribes they are never heard from again.

Chapter 10 reproduces almost exactly 1 Kings 12:1-19. Rehoboam inherits from Solomon a wealthy kingdom but the following is omitted: the kingdom was showing deep signs of decay and weakness, and by the time of his death only a fraction of that land and income are left to be handed down to his successor.

In chapter 11 the prophet Shemaiah successfully warns Rehoboam not to war against the north which results in a temporary truce. Many priests and Levites from the northern kingdom in (13-19) come to the southern kingdom because Jeroboam had appointed his own priests for the high places and for the goat-demons. Verse 16 says, Those who had set their hearts to seek the LORD God of Israel came after them from all the tribes of Israel to sacrifice to the LORD, the God of their ancestors.

It is thought that at this time they brought their writings and eventually merged them with the writings in Judah to begin to form the OT. Verse 21 informs us that Rehoboam took Maacah the daughter of Absolom as one of his wives and bore Abijah. He loved her more than all his wives and concubines. He had eighteen wives and sixty concubines.

Chapter 12:1 says, When the rule of Rehoboam was established and he grew strong, he abandoned the law of the LORD, he and all Israel with him. In verses 2-14 King Shishak of Egypt invaded and conquered much of the land, but because of repentance, Jerusalem was spared, but only after Shishak took all the treasures from both the king's house and the temple. Rehoboam reigned fourteen years, and verse 14 says, He did evil, for he did not set his heart to seek the LORD. The writer said there were continual wars between Rehoboam and Jeroboam. Verse 15 says, Now all the acts of Rehoboam from first to last, are they not written in the records of the prophet Shemaiah and of the seer Iddo, recorded by genealogy?

In chapter 13 Abijah is the next ruler of Judah. He engages in war with Jeroboam. Verses 4-5 say, Abijah stood on the slope of Mount Zemaraim that is in the hill country of Ephraim, and said, "Listen to me Jeroboam and all Israel! Do you not know that the LORD God of Israel gave the kingship over Israel forever to David and his sons by a covenant of salt?" In verses 8-9 he said, "And now you think you can withstand the kingdom of the LORD in the hand of the sons of David, because you are a great multitude and have with you golden calves that Jeroboam made as gods for you. Have you not driven out the priests of the LORD . . . and made priests for yourselves like the peoples of other lands? . . ."

Jeroboam is not impressed and in (14-20) tries to ambush him. But the priests of Judah blow the trumpets and raise the battle cry, and when the people shout, God defeats Jeroboam and all Israel before Abijah. Judah prevails because they rely on the LORD. Verses 20-22 say, Jeroboam did not recover his power in the days of Abijah; the LORD struck him down, and he died. But Abijah grew strong. He took fourteen wives, and became the father of twenty-two sons and sixteen daughters. The rest of the acts of Abijah, his behavior and his deeds, are written in the story of the prophet Iddo.

In chapter 14:1-8 Abijah's son Asa succeeds him. He does what is right in the sight of the LORD. He takes away the foreign altars and high places, breaks down the pillars, hews down the sacred poles, builds fortified cities, and a strong army and commands Judah to seek the LORD and obey his commandments. In verses 6-7 he fortifies the cities in Judah while the land is at rest. He had no war in those years, for the LORD gave him peace. He said to Judah, Let us build these cities, and surround them with walls and towers, gates, and bars; the land is still ours because we have sought the LORD our God; we have sought him and he has given us peace on every side. So they built and prospered.

In verses 9-10 Zerah the Ethiopian (Ethiopia/Cush is modern day Sudan) with a million men and three hundred chariots attack Asa. (Looks like those statistics might be a bit exaggerated to get a point across.) In verses 11-12 Asa cried to the LORD his God, "O LORD, there is no difference for you between helping the mighty and the weak. Help us, O LORD our God, for we rely on you, and in your name we have come against this multitude. O LORD, you are our God; let no mortal prevail against you." So the LORD defeated the Ethiopians before Asa and before Judah, and the Ethiopians fled. (The message is that the divine army completely destroys the million man army of the Ethiopians because Asa shows complete reliance on God.)

In chapter 15:1-7 the prophet Azariah (only mentioned here in the OT) goes to Asa. He encourages him to continue his reform. He tells him the LORD will be with him if he follows him. In (12-13) the people entered into a covenant to seek the LORD with all their heart, mind, and soul. Those who would not join the covenant were to be put to death (nice choice). All Judah rejoiced over the oath. Asa in verse 16 even removed his mother, the queen mother, Maacah because she made an image of Asherah. But the writer adds in (17) that the high places were not taken out of Israel. Nevertheless the heart of Asa was true all his days.

Then in chapter 16:1-6 in the thirty-sixth year of King Asa's reign he bribed King Ben-hadad of Aram (Damascus) with silver and gold from the temple to break his alliance with King Baasha of Israel. Baasha was causing Asa problems, but this stops it. In (7-9) the seer Hanani challenges him for bribing Ben-hadad and not relying on God as he had previously done. He says, "Because you have relied on the king of Aram, and did not rely on the LORD your God, the army of the king of Aram has escaped you . . . You have done foolishly in this; for from now on you will have wars." Verse 10 says, Asa was angry with the seer, and put him in stocks, in prison, for he was in a rage with him because of this. And Asa inflicted cruelties on some of the people at the same time.

The writer is indicating that Asa's faith weakened in his later years. The reader should notice how often this seems to happen. It seems that in a person's later years after success, humans tend to become too proud and self assured. Asa then had a foot disease that became severe (see 1 Kings 15). The writer in (12) said, he did not seek the LORD, but sought help from physicians.

This is the only time in the Bible where consulting a physician has a negative connotation. Therefore, he probably consulted a medium or pagan medicine man. He died in the forty-first year of his reign. As mentioned in the book of 1 Kings (15:23) the foot disease was probably a venereal disease.

Chapter 17:1-3 says, His son Jehoshaphat succeeded him, and strengthened himself against Israel. He placed forces in all the fortified cities of Judah . . . The LORD was with Jehoshaphat, because he walked in the earlier ways of his father; he did not seek the Baals, but sought the God of his father and walked in his commandments, and not according to the ways of Israel.

In verses 7-9 he sent out a sixteen person teaching commission of Levites throughout Judea to teach from the book of the law. Verse 10 says, The fear of the LORD fell on all the kingdoms of the lands around Judah, and they did not make war against Jehoshaphat. Verses 12-13 say, Jehoshaphat grew steadily greater. He built fortresses and storage cities in Judah. He carried out great works in the cities of Judah. He had soldiers, mighty warriors, in Jerusalem.

Chapter 18:1-3 says, Jehoshaphat had great riches and honor; and he made a marriage alliance with Ahab. After some years he went down to Ahab in Samaria. Ahab slaughtered an abundance of sheep and oxen for him and for the people who were with him, and induced him to go up against Ramoth-gilead. (His son, Jehoram, married Athaliah, the daughter of Ahab.) Virtually the rest of the chapter repeats the story of calling the prophet Micaiah and their defeat by the king of Aram because they did not listen to the prophet as told in I Kings 22.

Chapter 19:4-11 lists many of the reforms of King Jehoshaphat. He eliminates the sacred poles. He appoints civil judges, sets up local law courts, and a mixed court of appeal in Jerusalem. Many of the appointees are priests and Levites as well as heads of families of Israel. He tells them to let the fear of the LORD fall upon them, and he tells them not to pervert justice, take bribes, and to be impartial.

In chapter 20 the Moabites, Ammonites, and Edomites come against Jehoshaphat in battle. In (18-22) Jehoshaphat and all Judah prayed and worshiped. When the Levites begin to sing praise (not mentioned in Kings), verse 22 says, the LORD set an ambush against the Ammonites, Moab, and Mount Seir (the Edomites), who had come against Judah, so that they were routed. Verse 29 says, The fear of God came upon all the kingdoms of the countries when they heard that the LORD had fought against the enemies of Israel.

In chapter 21 Jehoshaphat's son Jehoram reigns next. He did what was evil in the sight of the LORD building high places in Judah which leads the people astray, and in (4) he put all his brothers to the sword, and also some of the officials of Israel. Verse 6 says, He walked in the way of the kings of Israel, as the house of Ahab had done; for the daughter of Ahab was his wife. He did what was evil in the sight of the LORD. (One would think that Jehoshaphat should have known something like this would happen when he made his alliance with Ahab.)

In verses 12-15 a letter came to him from the prophet Elijah informing him that because of his actions, the LORD would bring a plague on his people and a disease of the bowel would come upon him where his bowels would come out. In (18-19) he was struck with an incurable disease (cancer?), and after two years his bowels came out, and he died in great agony.

In chapter 22:1-4 his son Ahaziah reigns next. His mother was Athaliah, a granddaughter of Omri (daughter of Jezebel), who counseled him in doing wickedness.

He does what is evil and follows the ways of Ahab. This version is similar to 2 Kings 8-11. His friendship with Israel led to his death in Jehu's purge of the house of Ahab. At his death his mother Athaliah reigned and attempted to eliminate the Davidic line, but she was not successful because Joash in (11-12) was hidden from her.

In chapter 23:8-11 the priest Jehoida and the Levites brought Joash out of hiding and declare him king at the age of seven. Athaliah in (15) is put to the sword. The house of Baal is torn down, and then Jehoida in (18) assigns the care of the LORD's house to the Levites as David had organized.

In chapter 24 Joash repairs the temple and does what is right all the days the priest Johaida lived. But after Jehoida dies, in (17-19) he listens to bad advice from those who worship poles and idols that are dedicated to the goddess Asherah and refuses the warnings of the prophets.

Verses 20-22 say, Then the spirit of God took possession of Zechariah son of the priest Jehoiada; he stood above the people and said to them, "Thus says God: Why do you transgress the commandments of the LORD, so that you can not prosper? Because you have forsaken the LORD, he has forsaken you." But they conspired against him, and by command of the king they stoned him to death in the court of the house of the LORD. King Joash did not remember the kindness that Jehoiada, Zechariah's father, had shown him, but killed his son. As he was dying, he said, May the LORD see and avenge!

Verses 23-25 say, At the end of the year the army of Aram came up against Joash. They came to Judah and Jerusalem, and destroyed all the officials of the people from among them, and sent all the booty they took to the king of Damascus. Although the army of Aram had come with few men, the LORD delivered into their hands a very great army, because they had abandoned the LORD, the God of their ancestors. Thus they executed judgment on Joash. When they had withdrawn, leaving him (Joash) severely wounded, his servants conspired against him because of the blood of the son of the priest Jehoiada, and they killed him on his bed. So he died; and they buried him in the city of David, but they did not bury him in the tombs of the kings.

In chapter 25 Joash's son Amaziah reigns, and the first half of his rule is judged favorably, even though (2-3) says, He did what was right in the sight of the LORD, yet not with a true heart. As soon as the royal power was firmly in his hands he killed his servants who had murdered his father the king. But in (14) after defeating the Edomites he brings back their gods and worships them.

Verse 15 says, The LORD was angry with Amaziah and sent to him a prophet, who said to him, "Why have you resorted to a people's gods who could not deliver their own people from your hand?" King Joash of Israel then in (22-24) defeats King Amaziah of Judah and takes all the gold, silver, and vessels that were found in the house of God and the king's house as well as hostages and returns to Samaria.

In chapter 26 Uzziah succeeds his father Amaziah. As with Asa and Joash the Chronicler describes the good and the bad in Uzziah. Verses (4-5) say, He did what was right in the sight of the LORD, just as his father Amaziah had done. He set himself to seek God in the days of Zechariah, who instructed him in the fear of God; and as long as he sought the LORD, God made him prosper. In verses 6-15 he extended his control with great military and economic success. But (16) says, when he had became strong he grew proud, to his destruction.

Pride is always the downfall of the powerful. This was just as many in the past had done, and this was his downfall. In verses 17-21 he takes on the role of a priest and is struck as a leper and remained a leper to the day of his death. He even had to live in a separate house and could not enter the house of the LORD.

In chapter 27 Uzziah's son, Jotham, succeeds him. He does right in the sight of the LORD, but in (2) the people still follow corrupt practices. He builds strong cities in Judah, and he defeats the Ammonites. Verse 6 says, Jotham becomes strong because he ordered his ways before the LORD his God.

Chapter 28 is about Ahaz (2 Kings 16 and Isaiah7). Jerusalem nears destruction from Aram and Israel for his disobedience of God. Verses 1-4 say, Ahaz was twenty years old when he began to reign; he reigned sixteen years in Jerusalem. He did not do what was right in the sight of the LORD, as his ancestor David had done, but he walked in the ways of the kings of Israel. He even made cast images for the Baals; and he made offerings in the valley of the son of Hinnom, and made his sons pass through the fire (child sacrifice), according to the abominable practices of the nations whom the LORD drove out before the people of Israel. He sacrificed and made offerings on the high places, on the hills, and under every green tree. (We later learn that in every city of Judea he creates high places and makes images of the Baals.)

In verses 5-8 God gave him into the control of Aram and takes captive his people sending them to Damascus. Israel also defeats him with a great slaughter, and Pekah kills many in Judah. Verses 16-21 inform us that Ahaz sends to Assyria for help, for the Edomites, and Philistines are invading him, but Tilgath-pilsner of Assyria comes against him, and oppresses him instead of strengthening him. Ahaz plunders the house of the LORD and gives tribute to the king of Assyria, but it does not help him.

Verses 22-25 inform us that in the time of his distress when he is being invaded by the Edomites, Philistines, and Aram, he becomes more faithless and sacrifices to the gods of Damascus. He gathers the utensils of the house of God and cuts them in pieces. He shuts the doors of the house of the LORD. In every city of Judah he makes high places and makes offerings to other gods. (This is the Ahaz to whom Isaiah prophesies that a young woman will conceive; and then the gospel writer Matthew relates it to a virgin conceiving.) Verse 27 informs us that Ahaz dies and is buried in Jerusalem but not in the tombs of the kings. His son, Hezekiah, succeeds him.

Chapter 29 is about King Hezekiah (2 Kings 18-20). His first concern in (3-5) is to reopen and restore the temple. The detailed account of the cleansing and rededication of the desecrated temple is characteristic of the Chronicler. Verse 18 says, Then they went inside to Hezekiah and said, "We have cleansed all the house of the LORD . . ." Sacrifices are again offered. As is typical in Chronicles the Levites are featured, and in (25) the Levites lead the sacrifices and the singing. Chapter 30:1-5 is the celebration of the Passover. Hezekiah in (18-20) prays that God pardon all who seek him, and the LORD hears Hezekiah and heals the people.

Assyria had conquered the north in 722 B.C. and had taken the people into captivity, but with those remaining in the north Hezekiah in (18-22) invites them to come to the Passover. He encourages the priests and the Levites to return and take their rightful place in the temple. In (23-27) since there had been nothing like this since the time of Solomon, the feast is extended a week.

In chapter 31:1-2 we are informed that the idols in the cities are torn down, and the reforms are extended into the old northern kingdom. Laws governing worship and the support of the priests are reintroduced. Verses 20-21 say, Hezekiah did this throughout all Judah; he did what was good and right and faithful before the LORD his God. And every work he undertook in the service of the house of God, and in accordance with the law and the commandments, to seek his God, he did with all his heart, and he prospered. (The writer sees Hezekiah as a second Solomon who unites the people in sacrificial worship.)

Chapter 32 repeats II Kings 18-19. Having defeated Israel, the Assyrians and Sennacherib go into Judah but fail to take Jerusalem because Hezekiah trusted in the LORD. Hezekiah has a sickness and is about to die. He prays to the LORD and is given fifteen more years to live. The Chronicler said Hezekiah prospered in all he did. (He omits Isaiah's stern rebuke for showing off his riches to the Babylonians as noted in Kings, but it does note his pride gets him into trouble.) The Chronicler heaps praise unto Hezekiah. He does what is right, and he is faithful before the LORD his God.

Chapter 33:1-9 discusses the horrible reign of Hezekiah's son Manasseh, and how he rebuilds all the evil pagan shrines that his father eliminated. While he is as wicked as the book of Kings reports, in (10-17) the Chronicler states, when captured and taken to Babylon, he is repentant. The LORD even restores his kingdom to him where he cleanses Judah of idols.

None of this is mentioned in II Kings. This repentance is very questionable in the view of 2 Kings 21:10-17. Possibly the writer is teaching that since someone as evil as Manasseh can receive repentance and be reconciled to God, then anyone can receive the same. The Deuterocanonicals/Apocrypha contains his prayer. But for most of his life he desecrates the temple and sets up idols. He even practices child sacrifice, soothsaying, augury, sorcery, and deals with mediums and wizards. He does much evil in the sight of the one God.

Verses 20-23 say, Manasseh slept with his ancestors, and they buried him in his house. His son Amon succeeded him. Amon was twenty-two years old when he began to reign; he reigned two years in Jerusalem. He did what was evil in the sight of the LORD as his father Manasseh had done. Amon sacrificed to all the images that his father Manasseh had made, and served them. He did not humble himself before the LORD as his father Manasseh had humbled himself, but this Amon incurred more and more guilt.

Chapter 34 is the reign of Josiah who according to the Chronicler along with Hezekiah is one of the two greatest kings of Judah. Of course, all the kings of the north are bad because they follow the calf and idol worship of Jeroboam. In 2 Kings chapters 22-23 the same details for Josiah are given. He demolishes the pagan idols and their worship, and he repairs the temple. The book of the law is found which is probably Deuteronomy, and repentance and reform becomes the norm.

Chapter 35 is a greatly expanded report of Josiah's Passover Feast and the prominence given to the Levites. The Chronicler in (18-19) said, No passover like it had been kept in Israel since the days of the prophet Samuel; none of the kings of Israel had kept such a passover as was kept by Josiah, by the priests and the Levites, by all Judah and Israel who were present, and by the inhabitants of Jerusalem. In the eighteenth year of the reign of Josiah this passover was kept.

Unfortunately, Josiah is killed by Neco, the King of Egypt, who is on his way to prop up Assyria as a buffer against the rising power of Babylon. He desired safe passage through Judah. As Josiah attempts to stop him. Neco in (20-24) tells him that God will destroy him if he tries to stop him. Josiah ignores him and is killed. According to I Esdra (Apocrypha) Jeremiah had authenticated the message from Neco.

Verses 22-25 say, But Josiah would not turn away from him, but disguised himself in order to fight with him. He did not listen to the words of Neco from the mouth of God, but joined battle in the plain of Megiddo. (How would he know the words from the pagan Neco would be God's word?) The archers shot King Josiah; and the king said to his servants, "Take me away, for I am badly wounded." So his servants took him out of his chariot and carried him in his second chariot and brought him to Jerusalem. There he died and was buried in the tombs of his ancestors. All Judah and Jerusalem mourned for Josiah. Jeremiah also uttered lament for Josiah and all the singing men and women have spoken of Josiah in their laments to this day.

Chapter 36 needs to be read in its entirety basically as a review of II Kings 25 with some abridgement. It describes the destruction of Jerusalem and the beginning of the Babylonian exile. It begins with the people of the land taking Jehoahaz, the son of Josiah, and making him the next king. Verses 1-8 inform us that Josiah will be succeeded by three sons. They are Jehoahaz, Eliakim whose name was changed to Jehoiakim, Zedekiah, and one grandson, Jehoaichin. Jehoahaz reigns three months, and then is taken to Egypt by Neco. Then he makes Eliakim king and changes his name to Jehoiakim. He reigns eleven years and like his brother does evil in the eyes of the LORD. King Nebuchadnezzar comes to Jerusalem and carries back to Babylon some of the vessels of the temple.

In verse 9 Jehoiachin, Josiah's grandson reigns next for three months and ten days as an eight year old. King Nebuchadnezzar takes him to Babylon along with the rest of the temple vessels, and then makes his uncle Zedekiah the king. Verses 11-14 tell us, he reigns eleven years. He does evil in the sight of the LORD his God. He does not humble himself before the prophet Jeremiah who spoke from the mouth of the LORD. He also rebels against King Nebuchadnezzar.

Verses 14-16 say, All the leading priests and the people were exceedingly unfaithful, following all the abominations of the nations; and they polluted the house of the LORD that he had consecrated in Jerusalem. The LORD, the God of their ancestors, sent persistently to them by his messengers, because he had compassion on his people and on his dwelling place; but they kept mocking the messengers of God, despising his words, and scoffing at his prophets, until the wrath of the LORD against his people became so great that there was no remedy.

Verses 17-23 inform us that God allows Nebuchadnezzar and the Babylonians to burn down the temple and destroy Jerusalem and take the treasures of the king and the temple to Babylon. He took into exile in Babylon those who had escaped death. This was to fulfill the prophecy of Jeremiah, until the land had made up for its sabbaths. All the days that it lay desolate it kept sabbath, to fulfill seventy years.

Verses 22-23 say, In the first year of King Cyrus of Persia, in fulfillment of the word of the LORD spoken by Jeremiah, the LORD stirred up the spirit of King Cyrus of Persia so that he sent a herald throughout all his kingdom and also declared in a written edict: "Thus says King Cyrus of Persia: The LORD, the God of heaven, has given me all the kingdoms of the earth, and he has charged me to build him a house at Jerusalem, which is in Judah. Whoever is among you of all his people, may the LORD his God be with him! Let him go up." (Cyrus ruled Babylonia from 539-530 B.C.)

This ends II Chronicles. The Hebrew Bible has the books that follow, but in the way they arrange the Tanakh it ends with these books of Chronicles. As we have seen the major crisis of the OT is retaining the fact that there is only one God and his name is YHWH spoken by the people of God as Adonai or LORD. Over and over it looks as if the one God idea will not survive, but God is able to accomplish his will even when very often it looks like the one God of the Bible and his teachings and ways will be extinguished.

This writer believes one of the questions we moderns need to ask ourselves is: are things really much different today? Do people today really know the one God and his ways and teachings, or are we still creating gods in our own image? We read the OT and wonder how could those people create the same mistake over and over again? Can they not learn from history? This writer wonders if we moderns have learned from history?

EZRA & NEHEMIAH

In the Hebrew Bible these two books are one book called Ezra. The period covered by the books of Ezra and Nehemiah is approximately 538-410 B.C. The theme of the two books is the restoration of the Jewish religion based on the law of Moses and the worship of Yahweh in the Jerusalem temple. The temple is rebuilt and completed by 515 B.C., then the rebuilding of the walls of Jerusalem by Nehemiah from 445-433 B.C.

Although the temple is rebuilt and the city walls completed, the second temple is far less ornate than the one built by Solomon. Nehemiah's walls enclose only a fraction of the pre-exilic city. But most important a base is reestablished for preserving Jewish life and worship.

By 539 B.C. the Persians defeat the Babylonians and become the world's power. Cyrus, their leader frees the Jews, which they are now called because they are all from the southern kingdom of Judah. They begin to return to Jerusalem to eventually rebuild the city and temple. Nehemiah is the political leader while Ezra is the religious leader. The theme is a theological one for it tells us that the future of the Jews depends on worship and following the law (teachings).

Because the Jews had almost extinguished the one God concept by marrying foreign women and worshiping their gods, Ezra forbids them to marry foreign women. The goal is for Jew to marry Jew and to repopulate and keep their religion pure as God commanded. Because they did not do that in the past, they, their city, their temple, and their religion almost disintegrated.

Ezra and Nehemiah span the reign of six Persian kings. They are Cyrus 559-530, Cambyses 530-522, Darius 522-486, Xerxes (Ahasuerus) 486-465, Artaxerxes 464-423. In the story that follows it is difficult to place everything in exact order. Nearly fifty thousand Jews return from the exile. This is only a remnant of its former numbers. They will draw their nourishment from the law taught to them by Ezra. Ezra's work is so influential that some have called him the father of modern Judaism.

EZRA

Chapter 1:1-4 says, In the first year of King Cyrus of Persia, in order that the word of the LORD by the mouth of Jeremiah might be accomplished, the LORD stirred up the spirit of King Cyrus of Persia so that he sent a herald throughout all his kingdom, and also in a written edict declared: "Thus says King Cyrus of Persia: The LORD, the God of heaven, has given me all the kingdoms of the earth, and he has charged me to build him a house at Jerusalem in Judah. Any of those among you who are of his people—may their God be with them!—are now permitted to go to Jerusalem in Judah, and rebuild the house of the LORD, the God of Israel—he is the God who is in Jerusalem; and let all survivors, in whatever place they reside, be assisted by the people of their place with silver and gold, with goods and with animals, besides freewill offerings for the house of God in Jerusalem."

The heads of the families that returned in (5) are mainly of Judah and Benjamin along with the priests and Levites. Neighbors load them with goods, animals, silver, and gold for the trip. King Cyrus in (7) returns the vessels of the temple that Nebuchadnezzar had taken. Verse 8 says, King Cyrus of Persia had them released into the charge of Mithredath the treasurer, who counted them out to Sheshbazzar the prince of Judah. In 5:14 he is called the governor.

Chapter 2:2 informs us that they came with Zerubbabel, the grandson of the exiled king Jehoachin, Nehemiah, Jeshua the priest, and others. All twelve tribes are represented. The chapter lists the leaders of the twelve clans of Israel and the towns to which they returned.

In chapter 3:1-4 the people gather in Jerusalem. Then Jeshua with his fellow priests and Zerubbabel with his kin set out to build the altar of God. At the Festival of Booths they make sacrifice as prescribed in the law of Moses. (The writer is showing that they are reestablishing the tradition.)

Verse 8 says, In the second year after their arrival at the house of God at Jerusalem, in the second month, Zerubbabel son of Shealtiel and Jeshua son of Jozadak made a beginning, together with the rest of their people, the priests and the Levites and all who had come to Jerusalem from the captivity. They appointed the Levites, from twenty years old and upward, to have the oversight of the work on the house of the LORD.

Verses 10-11 say, When the builders lay the foundation of the temple of the LORD, the priests in their vestments were stationed to praise the LORD with trumpets, and the Levites, the sons of Asaph, with cymbals, according to the direction of King David of Israel; and they sang responsively, praising and giving thanks to the LORD, "For he is good, for his steadfast love endures forever toward Israel." And all the people responded with a great shout when they praised the LORD, because the foundation of the house of the LORD was laid.

Verse 12 says, But many of the priests, Levites, and heads of families, old people who had seen the first house on its foundation, wept with a loud voice when they saw this house, though many shouted aloud for joy, so that the people could not distinguish the sound of the joyful shout from the sound of the people's weeping, for the people shouted so loudly that the sound was heard far away. (Sixty-eight years have passed since the destruction of the first temple.)

In chapter 4:1-3 the people of Samaria go down to Jerusalem to offer help. They had been offering sacrifice to the one God in Samaria as well as offering sacrifice to other gods. Zerubbabel, Jeshua, and the heads of the families reject their help. Then the people of Samaria in (4) make the people of Judah afraid to build, and they bribed officials to frustrate their plan throughout the region of King Cyrus of Persia and until the reign of King Darius of Persia.

In the days of King Artaxerxes a letter (in the Aramaic language) was written to him about the Jews that returned to Jerusalem. Verses 11-20 say, "To King Artaxerxes: Your servants, the people of the province Beyond the River, send greeting . . . They are rebuilding that rebellious and wicked city; they are finishing the walls and repairing the foundations. Now may it be known to the king that, if this city is rebuilt and the walls finished, they will not pay tribute, custom, or toll, and the royal revenue will be reduced . . . You will discover in the annals that this is a rebellious city, hurtful to kings and provinces, and that sedition was stirred up in it from long ago. On that account this city was laid waste. We make known to the king that, if this city is rebuilt and its walls finished, you will then have no possession in the province Beyond the River." So in (21) the king issued a decree to stop the building, and in (24) it was stopped and discontinued until the second year of the reign of King Darius of Persia.

In chapter 5:1-2 the prophets Haggai and Zechariah son of Iddo urge the people to again begin building. Zerubbabel and Jeshua set out to rebuild the house of God in Jerusalem; and with them are the prophets of God helping them. This time, under their governor Tattenai, the people's attempt to make the new king stop building the temple does not work because in 6:1-7, Darius found the original authorization for the Jews to build. They found plans that even described the materials to be used and the designed dimensions, so permission is given to build.

Verses 14-16 say, So the elders of the Jews built and prospered, through the prophesying of the prophet Haggai and Zechariah son of Iddo. They finished their building by command of the God of Israel and by decree of Cyrus, Darius, and King Artaxerxes of Persia; and this house was finished on the third day of the month of Adar, in the sixth year of the reign of King Darius. The people of Israel, the priests and the Levites, and the rest of the returned exiles, celebrated the dedication of this house of God with joy. Then in (19) they kept the passover.

Beginning with chapter 7:1-6, the rest of the book focuses on Ezra, a scholar of the law who traces his priesthood back to Aaron the high priest. He is a scribe skilled in the law of Moses. Artaxerxes had become the king of Persia. In verses 25-28 the king gives him permission to teach the law and appoint magistrates and judges to offer sacrifices and beautify the temple. Ezra begins his journey back to Jerusalem with over seventeen hundred people. The heads of the families who return with him are listed. They fast and pray for protection on the journey taking gifts of silver and gold from the people.

Chapter 8 has a list of some of the remnant that returned. In chapter 9:1-4, the people as well as priests and Levites that had returned years ago with Zerubbabel had married the people of the land. This is forbidden in Deuteronomy 7:1-5 not because of racial prejudice but because of the danger of the idolatry it leads to. This very practice is what had led to the nation's downfall from the books of Joshua through Kings.

When Ezra sees this he is upset and in 9:2 he says, "The people of Israel, the priests, and the Levites have not separated themselves from the people of the lands with their abominations . . . For they have taken some of their daughters as wives for themselves and for their sons. Thus the holy seed has mixed itself with the peoples of the lands, and in their faithlessness the officials and leaders have led the way."

Most of chapter 9 is Ezra's prayer where he confesses the sin and guilt of the people for intermarrying which led them to worshiping other gods. Ezra fell on his knees and said to God in (6-15) "O my God I am too ashamed and embarrassed to lift my face to you . . . After all that has come upon us for our evil deeds and for our great guilt, seeing that you, our God, have punished us less than our iniquities deserved and have given us such a remnant as this, shall we break your commandments again and intermarry with the peoples who practice these abominations? Would you not be angry with us until you destroy us without remnant or survivor? O LORD, God of Israel, you are just, but we have escaped as a remnant, as is now the case. Here we are before you in our guilt, though no one can face you because of this."

Chapter 10:1-3 says, While Ezra prayed and made confession, weeping and throwing himself down before the house of God, a very great assembly of men, women, and children gathered to him out of Israel; the people also wept bitterly. Shecaniah son of Jehiel, of the descendants of Elam, addressed Ezra, saying, "We have broken faith with our God and have married foreign women from the peoples of the land, but even now there is hope for Israel in spite of this. So now let us make a covenant with our God to send away all these wives and their children, according to the counsel of my lord and of those who tremble at the commandment of our God; and let it be done according to the law. Take action, for it is your duty, and we are with you; be strong, and do it."

Ezra addressed the people in (10-12) saying, "You have trespassed and married foreign women, and so increased the guilt of Israel. Now make confession to the LORD the God of your ancestors, and do his will; separate yourselves from the peoples of the land and from foreign wives." The assembly of people agreed. From verse 18 until the end of the chapter appears a list of those who had married foreign wives.

This writer believes that the foreign wives who converted to the one God were safe. Only those who refused to put away their pagan Gods were the foreign wives that had to be sent away. This is based on other passages where foreigners who accepted the one God were permitted to convert. When a woman converted, she was no longer a foreigner. The issue is mixing God with gods called syncretism. If a woman has converted, there is no issue. This opinion is based on the fact that male and female converts were accepted through circumcision and water immersion (tevila).

Some in our modern times see the decree of putting away a foreign wife as drastic action and unacceptable. But for the Jews at that time the issue is preserving their identity which they are in danger of losing. As previously stated a major issue of the OT is the people chosen by God preserving the one God concept.

The other issue, one that is related to the first one, is preserving the one God's total message. Thus, this is not a racial purity or ethnic superiority issue; it is a survival issue for a group of people who are called to be holy as God is holy.

NEHEMIAH

In chapter 1:1-3 Nehemiah's brother brings the news that the wall in Jerusalem is badly broken. Nehemiah is in Susa, the capital of Persia (Iran). Verse 11 tells us that Nehemiah is the king's cupbearer. This means he drinks the first taste of wine and takes the first taste of food to make sure the king is not being poisoned by a subversive.

Nehemiah goes to King Artaxerxes taking his life in his hand because Artaxerxes was the one responsible for stopping the building in Jerusalem when those of Samaria accused the people of Jerusalem of being a rebellious people (Ezra 4:7-23). But Nehemiah's concern for his people is more important to him than his self interest.

Chapter 2:1-5 In the month of Nisan, in the twentieth year of King Artaxerxes, when wine was served him, I carried the wine and gave it to the king. Now, I had never been sad in his presence before. So the king said to me, "Why is your face sad, since you are not sick. This can only be sadness of heart." Then I was very much afraid. I said to the king, "May the king live forever! Why should my face not be sad, when the city, the place of my ancestors' graves, lies waste, and its gates have been destroyed by fire?" Then the king said to me, "What do you request?" So I prayed to the God of heaven. Then I said to the king, "If it pleases the king, and if your servant has found favor with you, I ask that you send me to Judah, to the city of my ancestors' graves so that I may rebuild it." Verse 8 says, the king granted me what I asked, for the gracious hand of my God was upon me.

Nehemiah returns and inspects the walls. He then speaks to the people and convinces them to start building. Verses 19-20 say, But when Sanballat, the Horonite and Tobiah, the Ammonite official, and Gershom the Arab heard of it, they mocked and ridiculed us saying, "What is this you are doing? Are you rebelling against the king?" Then I replied to them, "The God of heaven is the one who will give us success, and we his servants are going to start building; but you have no share or claim or historic right in Jerusalem."

Chapter 3:1 says, The high priest Eliashib set to work with his fellow priests and rebuilt the Sheep Gate. They consecrated it and set up its doors; . . . Those working are listed in the rest of the chapter. All the people participated.

In chapter 4:1 Sanballet, the governor of Samaria, and others on his side are angry and mock the Jews, and (8-9) says, all plotted together to come and fight against Jerusalem and to cause confusion in it. So we prayed to our God, and set a guard as a protection against them day and night.

Verses 16-20 say, From that day on, half of my servants worked on construction, and half held the spears, shields, bows, and body-armor; and the leaders posted themselves behind the whole house of Judah, who were building the wall. The burden bearers carried their loads in such a way that each labored on the work with one hand and with the other hand held a weapon. And each of the builders had his sword strapped on his side while he built. The man who sounded the trumpet was beside me. And I said to the nobles, the officials, and the rest of the people, "The work is great and widely spread out, and we are separated far from one another on the wall. Rally to us wherever you hear the sound of the trumpet. Our God will fight for us."

In chapter 5 while Nehemiah is buying back Hebrew slaves and loaning money and food to the poor, rich Jews are taking interest from their fellow countrymen. This is a violation of God's law. They are even selling them as slaves when they are not able to pay back the interest they owe. Nehemiah opposes this and sets it right, for he always acts out of respect for God and his laws.

In verses 14-18 Nehemiah requests God to remember the good work he did in his twelve years as governor. Verse 15 says, The former governors who were before me laid heavy burdens on the people, and took food and wine from them, besides forty shekels of silver. Even their servants lorded it over the people. But I did not do so, because of the fear of God. Indeed I devoted myself to the work on this wall, and acquired no land; and all my servants were gathered there for the work. Moreover there were at my table one hundred fifty people, Jews and officials, besides those who came to us from the nations around us . . . yet with all this I did not demand the food allowance of the governor, because of the heavy burden of labor on the people. Then in (19) he says, Remember for my good, O my God, all that I have done for this people. (Nehemiah refuses to collect the food tax, and feeds them from his own wealth.)

In chapter 6 Sanballet continues attempting to discredit and stop Nehemiah but it is to no avail. Verses 15-16 say, So the wall was finished on the twenty-fifth day of the month Elul, in fifty-two days. And when all our enemies heard of it, all the nations around us were afraid and fell greatly in their own esteem; for they perceived that this work had been accomplished with the help of our God.

Chapter 7:1-2 says, Now when the wall had been built and I had set up the doors, and the gatekeepers, the singers, and the Levites had been appointed, I gave my brother Hanani charge over Jerusalem, along with Hananiah the commander of the citadel—for he was a faithful man and feared God more than many. The rest of the chapter lists the returned exiles, which is the exact list of Ezra 2. So the people of Israel settle in their towns.

Chapters 8-10 take place only a few days after the wall around the city was finished. It is the seventh month which means it is time for the beginning of the new year and its important religious festivals. Ezra takes the lead in things religious. In chapter 8:1-2 the people gather together in the square before the Watergate. They tell Ezra to bring the book of the law of Moses, which the LORD had given to Israel. Ezra will read and explain the law to them with the help of the Levites.

To give the reader an example of how the Bible is often distorted the following actually happened. When the former President Richard Nixon was impeached because of dirty tricks called the Watergate incident, the name of the place where the dirty tricks took place was the Watergate. This writer remembers that certain fundamentalist Christians were telling their followers that the Watergate incident was foretold in the Bible. This is the verse they used as their proof text. If you open the Bible and read this chapter, you will see the chapter had nothing to do with the Nixon incident. Unfortunately, this type of distortion of Scripture continues.

As the people were gathered Ezra read the book of the law. Chapter 8:3 says, He read from it facing the square before the Water Gate from early morning until midday, in the presence of the men and women and those who could understand; and the ears of all the people were attentive to the book of the law. Ezra stands on a wooden platform, and the Levites help the people understand the law, while the people remain in their places. Verse 8 says, So they read from the book, from the law of God, with interpretation. They gave the sense, so that the people understood the reading.

Today's clergy need to be attentive to this principle, for this writer, along with many others, fear that the people of today have very little sense of the meaning of Scripture as a whole. Many have never been led to handle a Bible let alone been led through it while reading and having Scripture explained to them. Consequently we have a generation of people, including too many religious leaders, who do not really comprehend Scripture as a whole or know the methodology of interpretation. Thus they are not comfortable with or capable of explaining it to their people. Of course, the other problem is that in our modern society people do not take the time to come together to have the Scriptures read, explained and discussed.

Verse 9 says, Nehemiah, who was governor, and Ezra the priest and scribe, and the Levites who taught the people said to all the people, "This day is holy to the LORD your God; do not mourn or weep." For all the people wept when they heard the words of the law. In verses 10-12 they are encouraged to celebrate the day by eating the fat, drinking sweet wine, and sharing with others. And all the people go their way to eat and drink and to send portions to those who have nothing prepared and to make great rejoicing, because they understood the words that were declared to them.

As they came together the second day, verse 14 tells us they discover they are to celebrate the Festival of Booths. So for the first time since Jeshua son of Nun (17) tells us that they make booths as a reminder of the people wandering in the desert during the Exodus. Verse 18 says, And day by day, from the first day to the last day, he (Ezra) read from the book of the law of God. They kept the festival seven days; and on the eighth day there was a solemn assembly, according to the ordinance.

Chapter 9:1-38 continues the reading and explanation of the law. A national confession of sin takes place as the law is tied in with the rebellion of the people against God's teachings throughout their history. This produces a desire to affirm the covenant that was so often broken in the past which continues in chapter 10.

The people pledge to keep the law's requirements on marriage, the Sabbath, taxes, tithes and offerings to support temple services. They covenant to obey all that God demands. Chapter 10 lists all those who signed the covenant and a summary of their covenant.

Chapter 11 shows that the population of the city increases as did the villages outside Jerusalem. Chapter 12 lists the priests and Levites who returned with Zerubbabel, the descendants of the high priest Jeshua and records of the families of priests and Levites.

The point of the chapter is to show that the people are conscious of their roots and tradition of being God's people. Verse (27) says, Now at the dedication of the wall of Jerusalem they sought out the Levites in all their places, to bring them to Jerusalem to celebrate the dedication with rejoicing, with thanksgiving, and with singing, with cymbals, harps, and lyres. From verse 27 on, the celebration is described. In 31-43 the chapter shows that two processions each led by a choir make their way in opposite directions as they walk on top of the wall. They meet in the temple area for a thanksgiving and sacrifice service. It is a time of joy and celebration.

Chapter 13:1-3 informs us that they read in the law of Moses that no Ammonite or Moabite should ever enter the assembly of God because they had hired Balaam to curse God's people. When the people hear this from the law of Moses, the Ammonites and Moabites who are with them are separated out. (The law meant the assembly of worship, but here it is extended to the whole community.)

The rest of the chapter (4-31) includes some notes by the editor. He tells us that in 433 B.C. after twelve years as governor, Nehemiah spent some time back in Persia with King Artaxerxes. On his return to Jerusalem he discovers abuses that threaten the law of God, the nation's identity, and the priesthood. The people had already gone back on many of the promises they had made. The high priest allowed Nehemiah's old rival Tobiah to have a room in the temple. Levite income had not come in, sabbath laws were being broken, and they had begun marrying foreign women.

Nehemiah is angry and begins to teach once more. Again, there is reform. His last request is that God remembers the good he has done. In (30) he says, Thus I cleansed them from everything foreign, and I established the duties of the priests and Levites, each in his work; and I provided for the wood offering at appointed times, and for the first fruits. Remember me, O my God, for good.

Reading the books of Ezra and Nehemiah again point out how easy it is to fall away after individual rededication and reform. But it also points out how important good teachers are and the importance of constant teaching. God's people need to be constantly taking their learning deeper as well as to being constantly reminded of the basics of God's teachings. It also shows the importance of having the people open the Scriptures as a leader takes the people through them verse by verse explaining the meaning and sense of those Scriptures. When this does not happen, God's people revert back to ways that ignore the things and teachings of God, and soon culture has more influence on religion than God.

This writer strongly believes that a religious institution must place a high priority on the education of its people, for when that does not take place that church, synagogue or mosque is simply a generation or two away from insignificance.

RUTH

In most Bibles the book of Ruth is after Joshua and Judges and before the books of Samuel. This is because in the first verse of Ruth, the book is located in the context of the days of the Judges. This writer has chosen to include it with books that have more of a short story narrative. Thus, this writer has in this section Ruth, Esther, Job, Ecclesiastes, and the Song of Solomon.

Let us begin with Ruth. Ruth is a Moabite, a foreigner who embraces Yahweh as the only God. She marries Boaz through the land redemption and levirate marriage law and becomes the grandmother of the future King David making her an ancestor of Jesus.

The purpose of the book, even though the context is the time of the Judges, is probably an attempt to counter the teaching of Ezra who forbids marrying foreign women. In the book of Nehemiah the Moabites are not permitted in the worship assembly. The book of Ruth counteracts and balances the fear of marrying foreign women indicating that there should not be a hard and fast rule. This writer believes originally there was no problem marrying foreign women including Moabites, if they were converts.

Even though wars and hostile feelings often characterize the relationship between Israel and Moab, the great king David will have a Moabite ancestry as this story reveals. Also in 1 Sam 22:3 David brings his parents to Moab for safekeeping after Saul rejects him.

In the story Ruth, Boaz, and Naomi are presented as models living faithful to the spirit of the covenant even in difficult times. In the narrative Naomi blesses her two daughters-in-law; Boaz blesses Ruth for her loyalty to Naomi; Naomi blesses Boaz for his kindness to Ruth; and the blessings of fertility are bestowed upon Ruth by the citizens at the city gate. All these blessings are issued in God's name, but it is through the actions of the main characters that the blessings are fulfilled. God stands behind all as cause, but God's activity is mediated by those living faithful lives. God's providential guidance is at work.

The theology of the story is concerning God's universal love for all people not just God's particular people. Ruth is one of the five festival scrolls of the Jews called the Megilloth. This one is read at Pentecost (Feast of Weeks, Shavuoth).

In chapter 1:1-5 we are told that in the days when the judges ruled, there was a famine. Because of starvation, a family of refugees leaves their homeland in order to survive. Elimelech, his wife Naomi, and his two sons go to Moab. Elimelech dies and his two sons marry Moabite wives. Their names are Orpah and Ruth. Both their husbands die, and Naomi is left without her husband and two sons. It is now just Naomi, Orpah, and Ruth.

After living there ten years in (6-15) Naomi decides to return to Judah, but she encourages the daughters-in-law to remain in Moab and find security in their mothers' homes, for Naomi tells them she has nothing in Judah. Orpah agrees to stay in Moab, but Ruth desires to remain with Naomi.

In verses 16-17 Ruth responds by saying, "Do not press me to leave you or to turn back from following you! Where you go, I will go; where you lodge I will lodge; your people shall be my people, and your God my God. Where you die I will die--there will I be buried. May the LORD do thus and so to me, and more as well, if even death parts me from you!" In 19-22 the two then leave for Bethlehem arriving at the beginning of the barley harvest.

In chapter 2 Ruth goes to find food. The law said that when the harvest is reaped some must be left for the poor. Ruth finds herself gleaning in the field of Boaz. It just so happens that Naomi has a kinsman on her husband's side, a prominent rich man of Elimelech, whose name is Boaz. In verses 8-13 his kindness to Ruth goes far beyond what the law demands. Boaz in (11) has heard what Ruth has done for her mother-in-law and wants to help. When Ruth returns home, she tells Naomi, who informs her that he is a relative. Ruth continues to glean from the harvest through the barley and wheat harvests.

In chapter 3 Naomi has a plan based on the levirate law. When a man dies childless, his brother is bound to raise an heir to him by his widow. One of the main purposes of the law is to keep the property within the clan. The law extends to the next of kin so Naomi has a plan. She tells Ruth to watch where he lays down after he eats and drinks, and then go to him.

In verses 7-9 Boaz after eating and drinking and in a contented mood, goes to lie down at the end of a heap of grain. Ruth comes and uncovers his feet and lies down. At midnight the man is startled and turns over, and there lying at his feet is a woman. In verse 9 he says, "Who are you?" (Remember, there are no electric lights.) And she answers, "I am Ruth, your servant; spread your cloak over your servant, for I am next of kin." (In other words you have the responsibility of marrying me.)

In verses 10-13 Boaz said, "May you be blessed by the LORD, . . . do not be afraid, . . . though it is true that I am a near kinsman, there is another kinsman more closely related than I. Remain this night, and in the morning, if he will act as next-of-kin for you, good; let him do it. If he is not willing to act as next-of-kin for you, then, as the LORD lives, I will act as next-of-kin for you. Lie down until the morning."

In chapter 4 Boaz gathers with ten elders at the city gate which is where important business takes place. In addition to raising an heir to carry on the dead man's name the next of kin also has to buy his land to keep it in the family. The next of kinsman would have bought the land, but when he heard it would go to Ruth and her son and that he will have Ruth and her son to care for, he declares himself unable to purchase the land.

Verse 13 says, Boaz took Ruth, and she becomes his wife. When they come together, the LORD makes her conceive, and she bore a son. Verse 17 says, They named him Obed; he became the father of Jesse, the father of David. The genealogy of David is then listed starting with Perez one of the twins born to Judah by Tamar in Genesis 38.

The story of a family becomes the story of the royal family and finally the story of a nation. Ruth, the Moabite, a loyal daughter-in-law, becomes a descendant of both David and Christ (Ruth 4:17, Mt 1:4-6).

ESTHER

The main theme of the book of Esther is the providence of God. God will act to preserve his people. Through Esther God watches over his people and saves them from annihilation because of this Jewish queen, Esther, and her cousin and foster father, Mordecai. The purposes of the book are to show God's people how they can survive in a foreign country while still being loyal to God, how God uses his people for his purposes, and how the Jewish religious Feast of Purim developed.

When the book of Esther is read in today's synagogues during the Feast of Purim, the worshipers stomp their feet and hiss and boo when they hear the name of the villain who is Haman. They applaud when Esther and Mordecai are mentioned. Some may be wearing masks and funny costumes. The book is one of the five festival scrolls (Megilloth). It is the only book in the Hebrew Bible not found in the Dead Sea Scrolls.

Esther, a Jewess, rises from obscurity to become the queen of Persia. Ahasuerus (Xerxes), the king of Persia, has a Prime Minister, Haman, who hates Jews and tries to exterminate them. (The Qur'an has Haman in Egypt.) The plot fails because of Esther and Mordecai. This is the story of a plot to exterminate the entire Jewish nation (pogrom) in the days of the Persian king, Ahaseuras (Xerxes). He reigns from 486-465 B.C. He is the son of Darius I who leaves him much wealth and a huge kingdom.

The theme is that God watches over his people especially when they are faithful to him. There is a similarity of Esther rising in the Persian government, with Joseph rising in Egypt, and later the prophet Daniel rising in the Babylonian government. All is directed by God for his purposes. Divine providence is the theme when God is in control and works all things to his purposes.

Some see the book of Esther as an historical novel or a short story based on some basic history that contains theological truth. Others see this book as pure fiction but still inspired. For most fundamentalist Christians, if the book is inspired then its history can be relied upon. But for the rest of the Christian churches, factual history is not a criterion for inspiration. God can inspire what he wants in order to teach his people religious truth, his ways, and how he works. For most churches inspiration is not based on a philosophical theory rooted in modern times that requires exact historical detail as stated by those of fundamentalist persuasion.

In the book of Esther the Greek Septuagint text adds whole paragraphs and sometimes leaves out material in the Hebrew text. These passages will be included in the Protestant Apocrypha and Roman Catholic Deuterocanonicals.

In chapter 1 at the conclusion of a six month display of his great wealth in Susa, King Ahasuerus gives a seven day banquet for all his officials where eating and drinking is without restraint. On the last day while the king is merry with wine, verses 10-12 inform us that he commands Queen Vashti to come before him wearing the royal crown (only the royal crown?) in order to show the peoples and the officials her beauty; for she is fair to behold. But Queen Vashti refuses to come at the king's command.

At this the king is enraged, and his anger burns within him. The king is convinced by his officials that she should lose her position as queen; otherwise, she will be an example to all women to act in disobedience toward their husbands. The king did as proposed and in verse 22 declares, that every man should be master in his own house.

A feminist reading of the text makes Vashti the hero and not Esther, for Vashti refuses to become an object and insists on her dignity as a person even though she will lose her position as queen. But we must keep in mind this story is written for another reason in a time that has no concept of feminist issues.

In chapter 2 it is decreed that beautiful young virgins are being sought as the new queen. In the city of Susa is a Jew named Mordecai, who had been taken away when Nebuchadnezzar sacked Jerusalem and carried away the people. He has raised and adopted his cousin, a girl named Esther, who has neither father nor mother. She is entered into a twelve month contest for queen, but her identity as a Jew is not revealed.

After the twelve month contest is over verse 17 says, the king loved Esther more than all the other women; of all the virgins she wins his favor and devotion, so that he sets the royal crown on her head and made her queen instead of Vashti.

Because of his relationship to Esther, Mordecai is made an official of undetermined rank. One day in (21-23) while eating at the king's table, he learns of a plot to assassinate the king. He tells the queen who then tells the king what she learned from Mordecai. When the affair is investigated, the plotters are hanged.

Chapter 3:1-5 introduces Haman who is in charge of all the king's officials. All the king's servants at the king's gate are to bow down to Haman as commanded by the king. Verse 5 says, When Haman saw that Mordecai did not bow down or do obeisance to him, Haman is infuriated. Therefore in (6) he decides that he will do an ethnic cleansing (pogrom) to rid the empire of all Jews.

In verse 7 a Pur, which means a lot, is cast to decide what date the purge will begin. The lot falls on the thirteenth day of the twelfth month (Adar). Haman then in (8-11) goes to the king to make his case against all Jews. He tells the king the laws of the Jews are different, and they are not keeping the king's laws. The king agrees to Haman's purge against the Jews. A copy of the document is to be sent to all the provinces. Now Haman is an Agate which is an Amalekite. They are historical enemies of the Jews.

In chapter 4 Mordecai shares with Esther what Haman is doing, and how the king agreed. In (13-17) Mordecai relays to her that the fate of the Jews rests in her hands. She will have to initiate an audience with the king, and it may result in her death if her requests are rejected. She requests that Mordecai gather all the Jews in Susa to fast and pray for three days and nights. After that she will go to the king.

In chapter 5 she goes to the king, and he permits her an audience. In (4-8) she asks that Haman attend a dinner she will prepare for him and the king. Haman is pleased, for at this point he has no idea that Esther and Mordecai even know each other. After the dinner she requests another dinner for the next day, and then she will make her request known.

After the initial dinner verses 9-13 say, Haman went out that day happy and in good spirits. But when Haman saw Mordecai in the king's gate, and observed that he neither rose nor trembled before him, he was infuriated with Mordecai; nevertheless Haman restrained himself and went home. Then he sent for his friends and his wife Zeresh, and Haman recounted to them the splendor of his riches, the number of his sons, all the promotions with which the king had honored him, and how he had advanced him above the officials and ministers of the king. Haman added, "Even Queen Esther let no one but myself come with the king to the banquet that she prepared. Tomorrow also I am invited by her, together with the king. Yet all this does me no good so long as I see the Jew Mordecai sitting at the king's gate." In (14) His wife and friends tell him to have gallows built higher than the city wall to have Mordecai hanged upon. This advice pleases Haman, and he has the gallows built.

In chapter 6 the king learns that Mordecai has not been honored for his action that saved the king from an assassination attempt. At that very moment Haman enters the king's court in order to request that the king allow him to have Mordecai hanged on the gallows he has prepared. Before he makes the request the king in (6) asks Haman "What shall be done for a man whom the king wishes to honor?"

Haman thinks the man the king wants to honor is himself, so in (8-9) he says, "For the man whom the king wishes to honor, let royal robes be brought, which the king has worn, and a horse that the king has ridden, with a royal crown on its head. Let the robes and the horse be handed over to one of the kings most noble officials; let him robe the man whom the king wishes to honor, and let him conduct the man on horseback through the open square of the city, proclaiming before him: Thus shall it be done for the man whom the king wishes to honor."

Verses 10-12 say, Then The king said to Haman, "Quickly, take the robes and the horse, as you have said, and do so to the Jew Mordecai who sits at the king's gate. Leave out nothing that you have mentioned." So Haman took the robes and the horse and robed Mordecai and led him riding through the open square of the city, proclaiming, "Thus shall it be done for the man the king wishes to honor." Then Mordecai returns to the king's gate, but Haman hurries to his house mourning and with his head covered. Then verse 14 says, the king's eunuchs arrived and hurried Haman off to the banquet that Esther has prepared.

Chapter 7:1-2 says, So the king and Haman went in to feast with Queen Esther.

On the second day, as they were drinking wine the King again said to Esther, "What is your petition, Queen Esther? It shall be granted you. And what is your request? Even to the half of my kingdom, it shall be fulfilled." In verses 4-6 she tells him she wants her life and the lives of her people spared from the one demanding their lives. The king asked who is responsible, and she points to Haman. Haman is terrified. In (9-10) the king demands that Haman be hanged on the gallows he has prepared for Mordecai.

In chapter 8 there still remains the problem of Haman's edict. According to Persian law because it is issued in the king's name, it can not be revoked even by the king. So the king issues a second law in (11-12) permitting the Jews to fight back in order to protect themselves. When the time comes for the purge the Jews are prepared and defend themselves.

In chapter 9:5 the Jews strike down all their enemies with the sword slaughtering and destroying them, and doing as they pleased to those who hate them. Esther in (13) said, If it pleases the king, let the Jews who are in Susa be allowed tomorrow also to do according to this day's edict, and let the ten sons of Haman be hanged on the gallows, and (14) says, So the king commanded this to be done. In verses 18-19 a holiday of celebration is declared. In (26-32) a summary of the feast day called Purim is given.

In chapter 10 King Ahasuerus makes Mordecai second in rank to him in the kingdom. Verse 3 says, Mordecai the Jew is next in rank to King Ahasuerus, and he is powerful among the Jews and popular with his many kindred, for he sought the good of his people and interceded for the welfare of all his descendants.

In commemoration of the deliverance of the Jews the fourteenth and fifteenth of Adar becomes a feast day. To this day the Jews celebrate the Feast of Purim as they read the book of Esther out loud and remember recent times of deliverance. Once again the providence of God is displayed as God saves his people by working to have Esther made queen. Because of Esther, Haman's plot to extinguish the Jews fails, and God's people survive. God will always save his loyal people. In modern times a Jewish women's organization devoted to deeds of love and mercy has named itself Hadassah which is the Hebrew name for Esther.

DEUTEROCANONICAL (APOCRYPHAL) ESTHER

In the canonical book of Esther, God is not even mentioned. The Deuterocanonical or Apocryphal Esther begins with a dream where Mordecai sees two fighting dragons. They symbolize the struggle between the nations of the world and the righteous nation. When that nation cries out to God, a great river begins to flow, and the people are delivered. Also long prayers are given, prayed by both Mordecai and Esther, after they heard the decree against the Jews.

It is God not just Esther that changes the mind of the king. The king issues a decree that the Jews are the children of the living God. This most high and mighty God has directed the kingdom for them and their ancestors. The end of the book adds a meditation by Mordecai. He now understands the meaning of the dream that he had at the beginning of the chapter, and understands everything that happened was directed by God.

The text of Esther was originally written in Hebrew, then transmitted in two forms, a short Hebrew form and a longer Greek form. The Greek form consists of 107 additional verses inserted at appropriate places in the Hebrew form of the text.

If one reads a Roman Catholic version, such as the New American Bible, it is easy to see where the above differences from the Hebrew text are inserted. They are marked by chapter A-F inserted in the appropriate places. Roman Catholics and the Orthodox consider it all Scripture while Protestant and Jews do not consider these insertions Scripture.

Addition A writes of Mordecai's dream of impending conflict and Mordecai saves the king's life. It is clear that God controls the final destiny of Israel. God chooses Esther in answer to Jewish prayers.

Addition B is the King's letter ordering the massacre of the Jews.

Addition C includes Esther and Mordecai's prayers. The deliverance of the Jews is in response to those prayers.

Addition D is about Esther going to the king and being afraid, but God changes the spirit of the king to gentleness. The king's change of opinion toward the Jews results from God's response to the prayer of Esther.

Addition E is a copy of the letter denouncing Haman and directing his subjects to help the Jews.

Addition F is Mordecai's dream interpreted.

It is interesting to note that there is no mention of God in the Hebrew narrative, but in the Greek additions the words LORD or God appear more than fifty times.

JOB

The author is a profound poet, and most of the book is written in poetic form. The book offers the most profound treatment of the problem of evil that is to be found in world literature. The basic theme is the goodness and justice of God within the context of the suffering good person. Another theme is why good people seem to suffer while the wicked prosper. Theodicy is a word developed from the Greek word for "justifying God." It is the name given to the human attempt to explain the problem of evil.

Job is a prosperous and God fearing man. Satan tells God that Job is God fearing because things are so good and that he will curse God if things turn bad. So God allows Satan to test him. Eventually Job loses everything including his family. Job's friends tell him it is because he has sinned. Job does not accept that explanation and stays faithful. The climax is reached in Chapter 38 when God speaks.

God agrees with Job against his friends' arguments against Job, although he does not completely agree with Job. The answer to the problem of why good people suffer is not completely answered other than God is in control, and we do not have all the answers in this life. The author then begins to suspect ever so slightly that God's perfect justice will triumph in the next life.

Job comes to the conclusion that human reason does not have all the answers to the mysteries of God in this life. Job's experience is presented not as a way to understand evil as much as it is a way to live with it. The conclusion is that only faith and trust in God make evil tolerable.

Later in the NT we learn that good will be rewarded and evil punished but not necessarily in this life, for in this life good and bad fall both on the just and unjust. The new revelation in Jesus is that reward and punishment will not necessarily happen in this life but will happen in the next. Jews and Muslims agree to some extent but seem to lean more heavily on consequences in this life, although, the holocaust of Jews has had an influence on changing Jewish thinking.

A prose prologue introduces the debate between Job and his friends, which then is written in poetry. In chapter 1 the story is introduced by the style of once upon a time. The location of Job is Uz, a town in Edom (Lamentations 4:31). We are not told the time era, but an educated guess by many scholars is that the story was written in the late sixth or fifth century B.C.

Some think one of the reasons Job is written is to counter the idea of the Deuteronomic theologians and Proverbs that teach if one does right, good and blessings will come; and if one does evil, there will be punishment and curses. Although this thinking may be generally true, Job tells us that is not always true for individuals. It must be remembered that the Deuteronomic writers primarily applied this thinking to the nation.

Job is telling us that on the whole interpreting Scripture is about balance (on the one hand something is true but on the other hand something else is also true). One must be careful with extremist positions. God will not always fit into one's interpretive box.

One note in reading this book is the following. The book of Job is mainly poetry. Only chapters 1-2 and 42:1-17 are prose. Since most of the poetry is basically in quotation marks, out of convenience this writer is going to eliminate quotation marks from the poetry section since the emphasis by this writer is on expressing content. Quotation marks will be retained in the prose sections.

Chapter 1:1 begins as tales begin. It says, There was once a man in the land of Uz whose name was Job. The story proceeds to tell us that Job was very wealthy in servants and animals. The writer says he is blameless, upright, and one who fears God and turns away from evil. He has seven sons and three daughters. Seven and three are perfect numbers, so the writer is saying God blessed Job with a wonderful family.

Verses 6-8 say, One day the heavenly beings came to present themselves before the LORD, and Satan also came among them. The LORD said to Satan, "Where have you come from?" Satan answered the LORD, "From going to and fro on the earth, and from walking up and down on it." The LORD said to Satan, "Have you considered my servant Job? There is no one like him on earth, a blameless and upright man who fears God and turns away from evil."

Verses 8-12 say, Then Satan answered the LORD, "Does Job fear God for nothing? Have you not put a fence around him and his house and all that he has, on every side? You have blessed the work of his hands, and his possessions have increased in the land. But stretch out your hand now, and touch all that he has, and he will curse you to your face." The LORD said to Satan, "Very well, all that he has is in your power; only do not stretch out your hand against him!" So Satan went out from the presence of the LORD. (God gives Satan power to take away Job's blessings. All are under the authority of God and can only do what he allows.)

In verses 13-19 Job proceeds to lose all he has including his children. When all this happens Job mourns, but then worships God. Then Job in (21-22) says, "Naked I came from my mother's womb, and naked shall I return there; the LORD gave, and the LORD has taken away; blessed be the name of the LORD." In all this Job did not sin or charge God with any wrongdoing.

Chapter 2:1-3 says, One day the heavenly beings come to present themselves before the LORD, and Satan also came among them to present himself before the LORD. The LORD said to Satan, "Where have you come from?" Satan answered the LORD, "From going to and fro on the earth, and from walking up and down on it." The LORD said to Satan, "Have you considered my servant Job? There is no one like him on all the earth, a blameless and upright man who fears God and turns away from evil. He still persists in his integrity, although you incited me against him, to destroy him for no reason."

Verses 4-8 say, Then Satan answered the LORD, "Skin for skin! All that people have they will give to save their lives. But stretch out your hand now and touch his bone and his flesh, and he will curse you to your face." The LORD said to Satan, "Very well he is in your power; only spare his life." So Satan went out from the presence of the LORD and inflicted loathsome sores on Job from the sole of his foot to the crown of his head. Job took a potsherd with which to scrape himself, and sat among the ashes. (The teaching seems to suggest that God allows Satan to test his people during their temporary stay on this earth.)

In verses 9-10 his wife said to him, "Do you still persist in your integrity? Curse God and die." But he said to her, "You speak as any foolish woman would speak. Shall we receive the good at the hand of God and not receive the bad?" In all this Job did not sin or charge God with wrongdoing. When Job's three friends hear of all this, they come in (11-13) to comfort and console him. The friends are Eliphaz, Bildad, and Zophar. They sit with him for one week without saying anything, for his suffering is very great.

In chapter 3 the poetry section begins. Job curses the day he was born, cries out in agony, and wishes to find peace in death. Verse 11 says, Why did I not die at birth, come forth from the womb and expire? In 12-26 he asks a series of why questions asking God for an explanation of an unfair situation.

In chapter 4 he and his three friends begin an argument that covers almost the rest of the book. Eliphaz in verses 7-8 say, Think now, who that was innocent ever perished? Or where were the upright cut off? As I have seen those who plow iniquity and sow trouble reap the same. (He is saying that Job has to be guilty of wrongdoing because God does not hurt the innocent.) In verse 17 he says, Can mortals be righteous before God? Can human beings be pure before their Maker? Then in 5:17 he says, How happy is the one whom God reproves; therefore do not despise the discipline of the Almighty (He is telling him to repent and trust God who acts justly.)

In chapters 6 and 7 Job denies that he has offended God. In 6:24 he says, Teach me, and I will be silent; make me understand how I have gone wrong. (He does not think he did anything to deserve the suffering he is experiencing. His friends fail to show him empathy; all they do is blame him.)

In 7:1-7 Job says, Do not human beings have a hard service on earth, are not their days like the days of a laborer? I am allotted months of emptiness, and nights of misery are apportioned to me. When I lie down I say, When shall I rise? But the night is long, and I am full of tossing until dawn. My flesh is closed with worms and dirt; my skin hardens, then breaks out again. My days are swifter than a weaver's shuttle, and come to their end without hope. Remember that my life is a breath; my eye will never again see good. In (11-21) he says, Therefore I will not restrain my mouth; I will speak in the anguish of my spirit; I will complain in the bitterness of my soul, ... I loathe my life; I would not live forever. Let me alone for my days are a breath . . . Why do you not pardon my transgression and take away my iniquity? For now I shall lie in the earth; you will seek me, but I shall not be.

In chapter 8 Bildad continues the argument. In (2-6) he says, How long will you say these things, and the words of your mouth be a great wind? Does God pervert justice? Or does the Almighty pervert the right? If your children sinned against him, he delivered them into the power of their transgression. If you will seek God and make supplication to the Almighty, if you are pure and upright, surely then he will rouse himself for you and restore to you your rightful place. In (20-21) he says, See God will not reject a blameless person, nor take the hand of evil doers. He will yet fill your mouth with laughter, and your lips with shouts of joy. Those who hate you will be clothed with shame, and the tent of the wicked will be no more. (He wants Job to repent of his sins and get right with God.)

In chapters 9 and 10 Job replies that he believes in justice. Verses 9:1-2 say, Then Job answered: Indeed I know that this is so; but how can a mortal be just before God? He said in (15-20) that even though he is innocent he must appeal for mercy. But he still believes he has done nothing to deserve the suffering that has come to him. In verse 22 he states that he believes God destroys both the blameless and the wicked.

In chapter 10:18-22 Job asked God, Why did you bring me forth from the womb? Would that I had died before any eye had seen me . . . Are not the days of my life few? Let me alone, that I may find a little comfort before I go, never to return, to the land of gloom and chaos, where the light is like darkness. (This is how Job describes death.)

In chapter 11 Zophar speaks harsh words. He has no patience with Job's irreverent talk. He tells Job in (13-15) to put away his sin, and then God will restore him. (Zophar is a black and white legalist.) Job replies in chapter 12:4 by saying, I am a laughing stock to my friends; I, who called upon God and he answered me, a just and blameless man, I am a laughingstock.

In 13:7 Job attacks his friends as speaking falsely and deceitfully for God. In 13:18 before God he says, I have indeed prepared my case; I know that I shall be vindicated. In 13:23-24 he says, How many are my iniquities and my sins? Make me know my transgression and my sin. Why do you hide your face, and count me as your enemy? In 14:1-2 Job says, A mortal born of woman, few of days and full of trouble, comes up like a flower and withers, flees like a shadow and does not last. Then in (14) he asks, If mortals die, will they live again?

In chapter 15 Eliphaz speaks again. He continues in his attempt to force Job into their point of view. They completely ignore Job's position. In fact in (2) they say he is full of wind with his complaints against God, and in (6) that his attempts to justify himself just prove his guilt.

In chapter 16 Job reaffirms his innocence but says in (7) God has worn him out. In 17:1 Job says, My spirit is broken, my days are extinct, the grave is ready for me. In verse 10 he says, But you, come back now, all of you, and I shall not find a sensible person among you, and in (15) asks, where then is my hope? Who will see my hope? Will it go down to the bars of Sheol? Shall we descend together into the dust?

In chapter 18 Bildad enters again and is upset that Job does not accept his advice. He reminds Job of the fate of the wicked in (5-21). Verses 5-6 say, Surely the light of the wicked is put out, and the flame of their fire does not shine. The light is dark in their tent, and the lamp above them is put out.

In chapter 19:2 Job asks, How long will you torment me, and break me in pieces with words? (Job thinks everyone has turned against him.) In (13-19) he feels totally alone. He cries out to them in (21-25) saying, Have pity on me, have pity on me, O you my friends, for the hand of God has touched me! I know that my redeemer lives, and that at the last he will stand upon the earth; and after my skin has been thus destroyed, then in my flesh I shall see God.

In chapter 20 Zophar continues on Bildad's theme which is the punishment of the wicked. The idea is that wickedness receives just retribution. The problem is that they are not hearing Job, for their general rule did not fit Job's situation.

In chapter 21:7-18 Job sees that the wicked often go unpunished, live long, and become very prosperous. So to his friends in (34) he says, How then will you comfort me with empty nothings? There is nothing left of your answers but falsehood. In chapter 22 Eliphaz stays with the same line of thought. He even invents sins for Job in (5-9). In (21-23) he says to Job, Agree with God, and be at peace; in this way good will come to you. Receive instruction from his mouth, and lay up his words in your heart. If you return to the Almighty, you will be restored . . .

In chapter 23:1-7 Job feels that if only he could find God, and lay his case before him. Job feels that if he could reason with him, he would be acquitted, but in (8-9) he says, If I go forward, he is not there; I cannot perceive him; on the left he hides, and I cannot behold him; I turn to the right, but I can not see him.

In verses 12-17 he says, I have not departed from the commandment of his lips;

I have treasured in my bosom the words of his mouth. But he stands alone and who can dissuade him? What he desires, that he does. For he will complete what he appoints for me; and many such things are in his mind. Therefore I am terrified at his presence; when I consider, I am in dread of him. God has made my heart faint; the Almighty has terrified me; If only I could vanish in darkness, and thick darkness would cover my face!

In chapter 24 Job looks at the evil that goes on in the world, the violence on the earth. He basically says life is not fair. The wicked trample the poor and needy and get away with it. They even prosper. In (12) he says, From the city the dying groan, and the throat of the wounded cries for help; yet God pays no attention to their prayer. Verse 25 says, If it is not so, who will prove me a liar, and show that there is nothing in what I say. In chapter 25 with the arguments of Job's friends exhausted, Bildad in (4) simply says, How then can a mortal be righteous before God? How can one born of woman be pure? If even the moon is not bright and the stars are not pure in his sight, how much less a mortal, who is a maggot, and a human being, who is a worm!

His point to Job is no one is perfect which Job understands. Again, what he said and even what his friends said made sense, but it does not really apply to Job. This is the age old problem of applying words out of context. Job basically wanted to know why decent people suffer, and why do evil people seem to prosper?

Job continues in chapters 26 and 27. In 26 he insinuates that God's greatness, his power, and his majesty are beyond understanding. In chapter 27:5 Job tells his friends that he can not agree with them, for if he did, he would lose his integrity. (Job hopes for justice from the God who does not always seem to act justly.)

In chapter 28 Job's problem is understanding the ways of God. Verses 12-13 say, But where shall wisdom be found? And where is the place of understanding? Mortals do not know the way to it, and it is not found in the land of the living. Then in (23) he says, God understands the way to it, and he knows its place, and in (28) he says, Truly, the fear of the LORD, that is wisdom; and to depart from evil is understanding.

In chapters 29-31 Job finishes his case and challenges God. In chapter 29 Job looks back at the past and how things were good, and how he had been living. He had done right and good to others, and was respected by all. Because of this, he had expected all to go well during his lifetime. (Job is discovering this is not necessarily true.)

In chapter 30 he returns to his life now where everything is the opposite of his past. Nothing is going right. All respect for him is lost, and he is constantly being mocked. Verses 19-21 say, He has cast me into the mire, and I have become like dust and ashes. I cry to you, and you do not answer me. I stand and you merely look at me. You have turned cruel to me; with the might of your hand you persecute me.

In verses 26-28 he says, But when I looked for good, evil came; and when I waited for light, darkness came. My inward parts are in turmoil, and are never still; days of affliction come to meet me. I go about in sunless gloom; I stand up in the assembly and cry for help. (In his depressed state he can not understand why God is doing this to him and then will not explain it to him.)

In chapter 31 he lists all the good he has done and the wrong he has not done. In (1) and (9-13) he indicates that he has not lusted or committed adultery, and that he is fair to his slaves and his workers. He has kept his integrity. In verses 16-39 he states a number of his positives. Among them he states that he is fair to everyone, generous to all in need, shows hospitality to travelers, and is not obsessed with material things, is not an idolater, and has no secret sins. He even states in (35) that he is prepared to swear this before God. Then verse (40) says, The words of Job are ended.

In chapters 32-37 a man by the name of Elihu speaks. He must have been a silent bystander, but now he says he is full of words. He is a young man and his response is anger because he says Job justifies himself rather than God. He is also angry at Job's three friends because they have found no answer, though they declare Job to be in the wrong. He states that he has not spoken because he is letting the wisdom of the elderly three find the answer, but in 32:9 he says, It is not the old that are wise, nor the aged that understand what is right. Therefore I say, Listen to me; let me also declare my opinion.

In chapter 33:9-11 Elihu challenges Job's declaration of innocence and his belief that God will not answer. Then he summarizes in 33:14-25 that God speaks to people through dreams and visions in order to terrify them with warnings that may turn them aside from their deeds and keep them from pride. He also disciplines them with suffering and pain.

Then Elihu in (26) says, he prays to God and is accepted by him, he comes into his presence with joy, and God repays him for his righteousness. He does this as (28-30) say, to bring back their souls from the Pit. In (31-33) Elihu says, Pay heed, Job, listen to me; be silent, and I will speak. If you have anything to say, answer me; speak for I desire to justify you. If not, listen to me; be silent, and I will teach you wisdom.

In chapter 34 Elihu tells Job that God is just. If he has not done wrong, he will not be punished. In (35-37) he says, Job speaks without knowledge, his words are without insight . . . his answers are those of the wicked. For he adds rebellion to his sin; he claps his hands among us, and multiplies his words against God. In chapter 35:10-13 Elihu tells Job that God does not answer people because of the pride of evil doers; they care about themselves and not God, and in (16) he says, Job opens his mouth in empty talk, he multiplies words without knowledge.

In chapter 36 Elihu exalts God's goodness, defends God's justice, and proclaims God's greatness and majesty. He indicates that God opens eyes and ears when people do wrong, so Job should not be hoping for death but doing what God wants him to do. In chapter 37 Elihu symbolizes God's power with thunder, verse 5 says, he does great things that we cannot comprehend.

He goes on to state that we are nothing in his splendor. We can not find the Almighty. He is great in power and justice, and he will not violate his abundant righteousness. Verse 24 says, Therefore mortals fear him; he does not regard any who are wise in their own conceit. (When Elihu had finished, he really has not said anything different from the others. Again, much of what he said is true about God, but it did not really apply to Job.)

Just as Elihu had finished his reasons why God would not answer, he answered. God always seems to act in ways humankind does not expect. Chapter 38:1-3 says, Then the LORD answered Job out of the whirlwind: Who is this that darkens counsel by words without knowledge? Gird up your loins like a man, I will question you, and you shall declare to me.

It is as though God has had enough of everyone's lack of understanding, wisdom, compassion, empathy, and unthoughtful questions. The writer is telling his readers that God is both transcendent and immanent. God is other than us and beyond us, but he is also near and hears us.

Now, God will ask the questions. God throws at Job some forty plus questions. In verses 4-5 he asks, Job, Where were you when I laid the foundation of the earth? Tell me if you have understanding. Who determined its measurements—surely you know! Then by a series of examples he asks Job, what he knows about the creatures in the world. Did he make them and give them their abilities? He continues this way in chapters 38 and 39.

Chapter 40: 1-2 says, And the LORD said to Job: Shall a faultfinder contend with the Almighty? Anyone who argues with God must respond. Then in (4-9) Job answered the LORD: See I am of small account; what shall I answer you? I lay my hand on my mouth I have spoken once and will not answer; twice, but will proceed no further . . . then the LORD answered Job out of the whirlwind: Gird up your loins like a man; I will question you, and you will declare to me. Will you even put me in the wrong? Will you condemn me that you may be justified? Have you an arm like God, and can you thunder with a voice like his?

Then through a series of examples he questions if Job can even control the big animals he created? In the rest of this chapter and chapter 41 God informs him that only the Maker has complete control, and he asks how can anyone claim to be equal with God and attempt to put him on the spot and challenge him?

Job learns that God's ways are a mystery beyond the understanding of mere mortals. He learns we humans are not going to get all the answers we want when we want them. Much of life is incomprehensible, but he learns more about faith and trust as he experiences the grace and mercy of God.

In chapter 42 the prose section begins again. In verses 1-6 Job is humbled. Job answered the LORD: "I know that you can do all things, and that no purpose of yours can be thwarted. Who is this that hides counsel without knowledge? Therefore, I have uttered what I did not understand, things too wonderful for me, which I did not know. 'Hear, and I will speak; I will question you, and you declare to me.' I had heard of you by the hearing of the ear, but now my eye sees you; therefore I despise myself, and repent in dust and ashes."

Job now sees God and understands he has been treading on mystery. There is nothing to say. Job repents and accepts without understanding what happened to him. Job's response is not one of contrition, for sin is really not the issue as his friends believed. Job is overwhelmed by an actual encounter with the majesty and mystery of the creator. He confesses his humanness and that he has been presumptuous in challenging God.

The writer is telling his readers that God is not bound to what humans are bound, nor is he bound to the maxims of Job's friends, who had attempted to wrap God in the box they created for him. Job receives no real explanation for his predicament; it is enough that his creator has made himself known to him.

Verses 7-9 say, After the LORD had spoken these words to Job, the LORD said to Eliphaz the Temanite: "My wrath is kindled against you and against your two friends; for you have not spoken of me what is right, as my servant Job has. Now therefore take seven bulls and seven rams, and go to my servant Job, and offer up for yourselves a burnt offering; and my servant Job will pray for you . . . for you have not spoken of me what is right, as my servant Job has done." So Eliphaz the Temanite and Bildad the Shuite and Zophar the Naamathite went and did what the LORD had told them; and the LORD accepted Job's prayer.

Verse 10 says, And the LORD restored the fortunes of Job when he prayed for his friends; and the LORD gave Job twice as much as he had before. In (11-15) he gets sympathy and is comforted, and has seven more sons and three more daughters, and there was no one in the land more beautiful than his daughters. Verse 16 says, After this Job lived one hundred and forty years, and saw his children, and his children's children, four generations. And Job died, old and full of days.

When Job accepted his suffering and forgave his friends, God blessed him. So at the end everything works to Job's good fortune as all folk tales do. Yes, God can inspire stories, even folk tales, with important theological themes. Job's experience is an honest search for truth. The three friends were locked into dogma. They could not understand anything that would not fit into their narrow brand of thinking, so they were guilty of misrepresenting God.

There are religious people today who are not much different from Job's friends. If they do not understand something, or if it does not fit into their little box, then it can not be of God. This is an attempt by some people to conform God to their image and their way of thinking. This duplicates what has been a problem in the world since the beginning.

One of the messages of the story is that there are many things that we do not and will not understand on this side of the divide. We are finite while God is infinite. We can know God, but we can not know everything. God is sovereign.

Job was patient in that he struggled with God to understand. In the end he still does not know why good people sometimes suffer and evil people sometimes prosper. Humans must accept what is temporary injustice with the knowledge that in the end God's divine justice will prevail. Job being restored with plenty is a symbol of that concept.

Job learns to trust in a God he does not totally understand. Faith in God can not be a conditioned response of rewards and punishments. God is not a behaviorist practicing operant conditioning eliminating faith and trust. The universe does not revolve around humanity; it revolves around God. Job's suffering seems to be a test of disinterested piety. Do we have faith only to be rewarded on this earth or is there a deeper meaning for those of us he has created?

If God does not guarantee the moral order and retributive justice on this earth which he apparently does not, then the question of justice and mercy on this earth is thrown back to humanity. Will humans find ways to control evil and promote the good in a broken world? Will humans attempt to do things God's way or not?

It seems natural to assume that if God is in control of the world everything that happens must be his doing, according to his will. But Christians must remember that Scripture teaches that the world is fallen, corrupted by sin, and under the domination of Satan (John 12:31) and that human beings have choices. Job argues that life is unfair; the world is not as it should be. Even so, that still does not explain everything.

The real questions are, who is God, who are we, how are we to relate to God and his created humans, and his created earth as we live our short lives on this testing ground called earth. The issue is not primarily what God does or does not do, but what should we humans do to eliminate in greater depth this phenomenon called evil. The major problem of evil is basically a broken world caused by sin. We are never going to fully understand all the ramifications of evil.

If we return to the beginning we are reminded that God allowed Satan to put Job to the test, the test of trust and faith. God is still sovereign. We all must ask ourselves how have we responded, or how would we respond to a test of faith? Job's faithfulness can be an encouragement to us.

Here is a man not willing to accept unquestionably what he considers a grave injustice. He rejects the instruction of those regarded as wise or teachers of his religious tradition. Job is not blindly docile in his suffering; nor is he afraid to complain to God and question him in his frustration.

At this point we must be careful to understand Job's anger correctly. Job retains his faith even though he did not understand why God allowed him to suffer so much. He is like Teresa of Avila who complained to God by saying, No wonder you have so few friends. This is basically Job's feeling, even as he never loses faith. He seems to accept the NT concept in James that the rain does fall on the just and unjust.

Finally, an idea we need to give more thought to is that divine revelation does not tell us everything we want to know, only what we need to know. When it is all said and done our relationship to God still depends on faith and trust, and as NT Scripture says, without faith we can not please God (see Heb 11:6).

ECCLESIASTES

Ecclesiastes is one of the five festival scrolls called the Megilloth which is read during the Feast of Sukkoth (Booths, Tabernacles). The author identifies himself as Qoheleth which means the teacher/preacher, a son of David and king in Jerusalem. That person could be Solomon. The theme of the book is the value and purpose of life, and he writes from his lived experience.

He seems to think that much of life can be rather useless, if one lives only for the world's values. He says vanity of vanities. All is vanity. The author tries to find meaning in knowledge, various life styles, pleasure, wine, great projects, accumulating property, love, power, wealth, food, drink, sex, many wives, and children. Real meaning could not be found in any of those things, for all is vanity.

Nothing seems to fully satisfy the craving of the heart. St Augustine later summed up all these things in which humans attempt to find their reason for being. He said, "Our heart is restless, O God until it rests in you." The idea is that everything in this world has its own emptiness, for nothing seems to satisfy us permanently except God.

The writer says that even if something happens to satisfy, death may come at any time and deprive a person of everything, so what value is it? The writer believes life and history just go in circles. Life is unfair. Work is pointless. Pleasure fails to satisfy. Life as we live it without God is futile and meaningless.

At the time of this writing there is no real hope in a resurrection. The writer's advice is to work hard and enjoy life, for the present moment is all we have. So be present to the present, or what is present, as the way to satisfaction. Make each moment count. Then at the end of the book the writer seems to discover what life is about when he says, Fear God and keep his commandments; for this is the whole duty of everyone. God will bring into judgment every work, including every secret thing, whether good or evil.

In Deuteronomy the writer promises that if the nation is righteous, it will prosper but warns the opposite, if the nation is not righteous. The Deuteronomic theologians who wrote or edited Joshua, Judges, Samuel, and Kings demonstrated how true this was in the rise and fall of Israel. The book of Job, Proverbs, and some of the Psalms attempt to apply this lesson to individuals and their everyday lives. Ecclesiastes looks at things a bit differently.

Although we can say that, in general, if one follows the ways of God, things basically will go well, but that does not mean God always allows good to come to them or evil to those who do evil. Job and Ecclesiastes are written to balance and express the fact that there are exceptions to the general black and white teachings of Psalms and Proverbs. The ultimate example will be Christ on the cross.

The writer of Ecclesiastes seems to present much of the book from the point of view of secular wisdom in order to show how it will disappoint. From the lived experience and for many if one only lives for the world's values, much of life can seem rather useless. In the Gospels (Jn 18:38) Pilate struggles with the issue when he asks, "What is truth?" Ecclesiastes is a type of ancient wisdom literature even though, at times, the book presents a series of disconnected thoughts. Some interesting verses are as follows: 1:2, 12:8, 2:16, 3:20, 9:10, 5:7, 7:18, 12:12-15.

Chapter 1:1-5 says, The words of the Teacher, the son of David, king in Jerusalem. Vanity of vanities, says the Teacher, vanity of vanities! All is vanity. What do people gain from the toil at which they toil under the sun? A generation goes, and a generation comes, but the earth remains forever. The sun rises and the sun goes down, and hurries to the place it rises. (Some translate vanity to mean meaningless or futile. Therefore, everything is meaningless or futile.)

The writer in verses 8-9 says, All things are wearisome; more than one can express; the eye is not satisfied with seeing, or the ear filled with hearing. What has been is what will be, and what has been done is what will be done; there is nothing new under the sun.

In verse 14 he says, I saw all the deeds that are done under the sun; and see, all is vanity, and a chasing after the wind. In (16-18) he says, I said to myself, "I have acquired great wisdom, surpassing all who were over Jerusalem before me; and my mind has had great experience of wisdom and knowledge." And I applied my mind to know wisdom and to know madness and folly. I perceived that this also is but a chasing after the wind. For in much wisdom is much vexation, and those who increase knowledge increase sorrow.

Then in chapter 2 he lists some things he tried. He tried pleasure, but again this also is vanity. He tried wine, made great works, bought slaves, had great possessions, had much silver and gold, and he got singers and dancers, both men and women, had many delights of the flesh, and many concubines, but he says, it is all vanity. Verses 10-11 say, Whatever my eyes desired I did not keep from them; I kept my heart from no pleasure, for my heart found pleasure in all my toil, and this was my reward from all my toil. Then I considered all that my hands had done and the toil I had spent in doing it, and again, all was vanity and a chasing after the wind, and there was nothing to be gained under the sun.

In verses 12-14 he seeks wisdom and discovers the same thing. Verse 15 says, Then I said to myself, "What happens to the fool will happen to me also; why then have I been so very wise?" And I said to myself that this also is vanity. Verse 17 says, So I hated life, because what is done under the sun was grievous to me; for all is vanity and a chasing after the wind. (This is the experience of many even today. Eventually, things are so hopeless for some people that they end their lives in suicide.)

In verses 24-26 the writer says, There is nothing better for mortals than to eat and drink, and find enjoyment in their toil. This also, I saw, is from the hand of God; for apart from him who can eat or have enjoyment? For to the one who pleases him God gives wisdom and knowledge and joy; but to the sinner he gives the work of gathering and heaping, only to give to one who pleases God. This also is vanity and a chasing after the wind.

In chapter 3:1-8 he says, For everything there is a season, and a time for every matter under heaven: a time to be born, and a time to die; a time to plant, and a time to pluck up what is planted; a time to kill, and a time to heal; a time to break down, and a time to build up; a time to weep, and a time to laugh; a time to mourn, and a time to dance; a time to throw away stones, and a time to gather stones together; a time to embrace, and a time to refrain from embracing; a time to seek, and a time to lose; a time to keep, and to throw away; a time to tear, and a time to sew; a time to keep silence, and a time to speak; a time to love, and a time to hate; a time for war, and a time for peace. (He is saying that life seems to go from one end to the other, so one needs to keep a balance between the highs and lows.)

Verse 9 says, What gain have the workers from their toil? Verses 12-14 say, I know that there is nothing better for them than to be happy and enjoy themselves as long as they live; moreover it is God's gift that all should eat and drink and take pleasure in their toil. I know that whatever God does endures forever; nothing can be added to it, nor anything taken from it; God has done this, so that all should stand in awe before him.

In verses 16-22 he says, Moreover I saw under the sun that in the place of justice, wickedness was there, and in the place of righteousness, wickedness was there as well. I said in my heart, God will judge the righteous and the wicked, for he has appointed a time for every matter, and for every work. I said in my heart with regard to human beings that God is testing them to show that they are but animals. For the fate of humans and the fate of animals is the same; as one dies, so dies the other. They all have the same breath, and humans have no advantage over the animals; for all is vanity. All go to one place; all are from the dust, and all turn to dust again. Who knows whether the human spirit goes upward and the spirit of animals goes downward to the earth? So I saw that there is nothing better than that all should enjoy their work, for that is their lot; who can bring them to see what will be after them?

In chapter 4:1-3 he says, I saw all the oppressions that are practiced under the sun. Look, the tears of those oppressed--with no one to comfort them! On the side of their oppressors there was power--with no one to comfort them. And I thought the dead, who have already died, more fortunate than the living, who are still alive; but better than both is the one who has not yet been, and has not seen the evil deeds that are done under the sun. Verse 4 says, Then I saw that all toil and all skill in work come from one person's envy of another. This also is vanity and a chasing after wind. Verse 7 says, their eyes are never satisfied with riches. "For whom am I toiling," they ask, "and depriving myself of pleasure?" This also is vanity.

In chapter 5:1 he says, Guard your steps when you go to the house of God; to draw near to listen is better than the sacrifices offered by fools; for they do not know how to keep from doing evil. Verse 8 says, If you see in a province the oppression of the poor and the violation of justice and right, do not be amazed at the matter; for the high official is watched by a higher, and there are yet higher ones over them. Verse 10 says, The lover of money will not be satisfied with money; nor the lover of wealth, with gain. This also is vanity. Then in (18) he says, This is what I have seen to be good: it is fitting to eat and drink and find enjoyment in all the toil with which one toils under the sun the few days of the life God gives us; for this is our lot.

In chapter 6:1-2 he says, There is an evil that I have seen under the sun, and it lies heavy upon humankind: those to whom God gives wealth, possessions, and honor, so that they lack nothing of all that they desire, yet God does not enable them to enjoy these things, but a stranger enjoys them. This is vanity; it is a grievous ill. (His point is what value is long life if one can not enjoy that for which they have worked.) In verse 9 he says, Better is the sight of the eyes than the wandering of desire; this is also vanity, a chasing after the wind.

Chapter 7: 1 says, A good name is better than precious ointment, and the day of death, than the day of birth. Verse 5 says, It is better to hear the rebuke of the wise than to hear the song of fools. In verse 14 the writer says, In the days of prosperity be joyful, and in the day of adversity consider; God has made the one as well as the other, so that mortals may not find out anything that will come after them.

Verses 15-18 say, In my vain life I have seen everything; there are righteous people who perish in their righteousness, and there are wicked people who prolong their life in their evil-doing. Do not be too righteous, and do not act too wise; why should you destroy yourself? Do not be too wicked, and do not be a fool; why should you die before your time? It is good that you should take hold of one, without letting go of the other; for the one who fears God shall succeed with both. (He is saying to live life, one needs to balance the different perspectives of the different extremes. Be in moderation, enjoy life, and do all through God.) In verses 21-23 he says, Do not give heed to everything that people say, or you may hear your servant cursing you; your heart knows that many times you have yourself cursed others. All this I have tested by wisdom; I said, "I will be wise," but it was far from me.

In chapter 8 he teaches that human power is limited. In (14) he says, There is a vanity that takes place on earth, that there are righteous people who are treated according to the conduct of the wicked, and there are wicked people who are treated according to the conduct of the righteous. I said that this also is vanity. In reference to what God is doing verse 17 says, even though those who are wise claim to know, they cannot find out.

Chapter 9:5-6 says, The living know that they will die, but the dead know nothing; they have no more reward, and even the memory of them is lost. Their love and their hate and their envy have already perished; never again will they have any share in all that happens under the sun. (This is an another example of why taking a verse out of the Bible is dangerous.) Verse 7 says, Go, eat your bread with enjoyment, and drink your wine with a merry heart; for God has long ago approved what you do.

Verses 9-10 say, Enjoy life with the wife whom you love, all the days of your vain life that are given you under the sun, because that is your portion in life and in your toil at which you toil under the sun. Whatever your hand finds to do, do with your might; for there is no work or thought or knowledge or wisdom in Sheol, to which you are going. (Life can feel hopeless without the hope of life after death.) Then in (18) he says, Wisdom is better than weapons of war, but one bungler destroys much good.

In chapter 10 there is a collection of proverbs over to chapter 11. Then in 11:5 the writer says, Just as you do not know how breath comes to the bones in the mother's womb, so you do not know the work of God, who makes everything. In (9) he says, Follow the inclination of your heart and the desire of your eyes, but know that for all these things God will bring you into judgment.

In chapter 12:7-8 he says, the dust returns to the earth as it was, and the breath returns to God who gave it. Vanities of vanities, says the Teacher; all is vanity. In (11) he tells all to listen to the sayings of the wise, then in (12) he says, Of anything beyond these, my child, beware. Of making many books there is no end, and much study is a weariness of the flesh.

Most important in (13-14) he says, The end of the matter; all has been heard. Fear God, and keep his commandments; for that is the whole duty of everyone. For God will bring every deed into judgment, including every secret thing, whether good or evil. This ends the book of Ecclesiastes.

A few things the writer suggests everyone needs to give thought to are the following. God is the creator of all. God's ways are not always understandable. What is done in life does not always add up. Life is not always fair in this broken world, and life is not always as we think it should be. The great equalizer is death, so fear God, and do his commandments. What other hope is there?

Finally, Ecclesiastes (Qoheleth) is a personal account of the authors experience in living. He insists that one's goal is to live life in the fullest and to make the most of one's situation, for the primary goal of life is not the gods of modern society whether they be success, prosperity, wealth, knowledge, or pleasure, but living life as life comes to you. His message is: Be alive to the present. The greatest gift of God is life itself, so live it in the presence of God and enjoy it in a way that God desires. When one does so, the meaning of one's particular life is discovered.

SONG OF SOLOMON

The Song of Solomon is part of the Megilloth, the five festival scrolls. Jews read the Song as part of the Feast of Passover probably because it celebrates spring time and probably because the Song is understood as representing how the loving God chose Israel as his divine bride. Jewish Rabbis interpret the book as an allegory of God's beloved bride who is Israel. Christian interpreters understand the book as describing the love of Christ for his bride, the Church. Both could be right as a double fulfillment.

Others see the book simply as a series of lyric poems expressing a male and female's love for each other that includes sexual love. The poetry is filled with images of a rural landscape, and the five senses are given full play. It is possible that these songs were originally oral compositions used in weddings to express the newly married couple's deep love for each other.

The OT prophets repeatedly compare the covenant relationship between God and Israel to that of a husband and wife. The Apostle Paul compares the love of Christ for the church as married love, and John speaks of the new Jerusalem as a bride adorned for her husband.

Writers during the Middle Ages saw that the human love expressed in this book is a reflection of divine love. Perhaps the book is to remind us that the most intense lover's passion is just a shadow of the passion with which God loves us. A particular form of literature in the Song of Songs (Song of Solomon) is called a WASF. This is poetry that describes parts of the human body through a series of metaphors.

Chapter 1:1-4 begins by saying, The Song of Songs which is Solomon's. The woman says, Let him kiss me with the kisses of his mouth! For your love is better than wine, your anointing oils are fragrant, your name is perfume poured out; therefore the maidens love you. Draw me after you, Let us make haste. The king has brought me into his chambers. We will exult and rejoice in you; we will extol your love more than wine; rightly do they love you.

Verse 5 says, I am black and beautiful, O daughters of Jerusalem, like the tents of Kedar, like the curtains of Solomon. Do not gaze on me because I am dark, because the sun has gazed on me. The man in (9) says, I compare you, my love, to a mare among Pharaoh's chariots. In (12-13) she says, While the king was on the couch, my nard gave forth its fragrance. My beloved is to me a bag of myrrh that lies between my breasts. Then in (15) he tells her, Ah, you are beautiful, my love; your eyes are like doves.

In chapter 2 the woman in (3-4) says, his fruit is sweet to my taste. He brought me to the banqueting house, and his intention toward me was love. In verses 5-7 she says, Sustain me with raisins, refresh me with apples; for I am faint with love. O that his left hand were under my head, and that his right hand embraced me! I adjure you, O daughters of Jerusalem, by the gazelles, or the wild does: do not stir up or awaken love until it is ready! In (16-17) she says, My beloved is mine and I am his; he pastures his flock among the lilies . . . turn, my beloved, be like a gazelle or a young stag on the cleft of the mountains.

In chapter 3:1-5 the woman has a dream seeking the one her soul loved. She says that she has brought him into her mother's house, into the chamber of which her mother had conceived her. Then she told the daughters of Zion, do not stir up or awaken love until it is ready.

In chapter 4:1-5 the man says, How beautiful you are, my love, how beautiful! Your eyes are doves behind your veil. Your hair is like a flock of goats, moving down the slopes of Gilead. Your teeth are like a flock of shorn ewes that have come up from the washing, all of which bear twins, and not one among them is bereaved. Your lips are like a crimson thread, and your mouth is lovely. Your cheeks are like halves of a pomegranate behind your veil. Your neck is like the tower of David, built in courses; on it hang a thousand bucklers, all of them shields of warriors. Your two breasts are like two fawns, twins of a gazelle, that feed among the lilies. In (6) he says, I will hasten to the mountain of myrrh and the hill of incense. Again, in (7) he says, You are altogether beautiful, my love; there is no flaw in you. In (10-11) he says, How sweet is your love, my sister, my bride! how much better is your love than wine, and the fragrance of your oils than any spice! Your lips distill nectar, my bride; honey and milk are under your tongue. The scent of your garment is like the scent of Lebanon.

Verse 12 says, A garden locked is my sister, my bride, a garden locked, a fountain sealed. (The image of a garden is used which symbolizes the female sexual organ which at the moment is locked.) But in (13) he says, Your channel is an orchard of pomegranates with all choicest fruits . . . a garden fountain, a well of living water, and flowing streams from Lebanon. The woman then in (16) says, Blow upon my garden that its fragrance may be wafted abroad. Let my beloved come to his garden, and eat its choicest fruits.

In chapter 5 the man replies to her invitation. In (1) he says, I come to my garden, my sister, my bride; I gather my myrrh with my spice, I eat my honeycomb with my honey, I drink my wine with my milk. Eat friends, drink, and be drunk with love. In verses 2-3 she has a dream that her beloved was knocking, and he says to her,

"Open to me, my sister, my love, my dove, my perfect one; for my head is wet with dew, my locks with the drops of the night." She says, I had put off my garment; how could I put it on again? I had bathed my feet how could I soil them? Verses 4-6 say, My beloved thrust his hand into the opening, and my inmost being yearned for him. I arose to open to my beloved, and my hands dripped with myrrh, my fingers with liquid myrrh, upon the handles of the bolt. I opened to my beloved, but my beloved had turned and was gone . . . I called to him, but he gave no answer.

In verses 10-16 the woman praises him in a WASF. My beloved is all radiant and ruddy, distinguished among ten thousand. His head is of the finest gold; his locks are wavy black as a raven. His eyes are like doves . . . His cheeks are like beds of spices, yielding fragrance. His lips are like lilies, distilling liquid myrrh. His arms are rounded gold, set with jewels. His body is ivory work, encrusted with sapphires. His legs are alabaster columns set upon bases of gold. His appearance is like Lebanon, choice as the cedars. His speech is most sweet, and he is altogether desirable. This is my beloved and this is my friend, O daughters of Jerusalem.

In chapter 6 the man praises the woman in a WASF. In (5-7) he says, Your hair is like a flock of goats, moving down the slopes of Gilead. Your teeth are like a flock of ewes, that have come from the washing; all of them bear twins, and not one among them is bereaved. Your cheeks are like halves of a pomegranate behind your veil. In chapter 7:1-5 he says, Your rounded thighs are like jewels, the work of a master hand. Your navel is like a rounded bowl that never lacks mixed wine. Your belly is a heap of wheat, encircled with lilies. Your two breasts are like two twin fawns, twins of a gazelle. Your neck is like an ivory tower. Your eyes are pools in Heshbon, . . . Your nose is like a tower of Lebanon, overlooking Damascus. Your head crowns you like Carmel, and your flowing locks like purple; a king is held captive in the tresses.

He calls her his delectable maiden and in (7-9) says, You are stately as a palm tree, and your breasts are like its clusters. I say I will climb the palm tree and lay hold of its branches. Oh may your breasts be like clusters of the vine, and the scent of your breath like apples, and your kisses like the best wine that goes down smoothly, gliding over lips and teeth. In verses 10-13 the woman says, I am my beloved's, and his desire is for me. Come my beloved, let us go forth into the fields and lodge in the villages; let us go out early into the vineyards, . . . There I will give you my love. The mandrakes give forth fragrance . . . (Mandrakes were said to give sexual desire.)

In chapter 8:1-5 the bride longs to take the initiative and display her affection openly. In her mind her lover's arms are already about her in tender and passionate love. Then the two are together at last and love finds its fulfillment. In verses 6-7 she says, Set me as a seal upon your heart, as a seal upon your arm; for love is strong as death, passion fierce as the grave. Its flashes are flashes of fire, a raging flame. Many waters can not quench love, neither can floods drown it . . .

In verses 8-10 the woman says, we have a little sister, and she has no breasts. What shall we do for our sister, on the day when she is spoken for? If she is a wall, we will build upon her a battlement of silver; but if she is a door, we will enclose her with boards of cedar. I was a wall, and my breasts were like towers, then I was in his eyes as one who brings peace. In (14) she says, Make haste, my beloved, and be like a gazelle or a young stag on the mountain of spices! (Wow, is all this in the Bible?)

This ends the Song of Solomon, an expression of human love and sexuality in its purest form. The literal interpretation in reference to its plain meaning makes no apology for erotic imagery. It affirms that sexuality is one of the gifts that God gives for our inborn passion and enjoyment. The sexual pleasure, however is not sought promiscuously. It is pursued only within the context of faithful and exclusive commitment.

The portrait of the female is not the image of a sexually naïve and passive woman, dependent on a man for protection and sustenance but is the woman who takes the initiative in this romantic pursuit. She utters almost twice as much of the erotic poetry as the man. Her language is quite explicit and shattering any stereotypes suggesting women may be romantic but not sexually inclined. The song is devoid of male dominance and female subordination. The song teaches that human passion is both vital, noble and ennobling.

PSALMS AND PROVERBS

These two are considered together because they are a special form of literature. Psalms are considered the center of the people's spiritual life, and Proverbs are a set of basic guidelines on living life.

THE BOOK OF PSALMS

The book of Psalms is the hymn book of the Hebrews, their songs to God sung with instruments in the temple. The list of musical instruments in Psalm 150:3-5 gives us an idea how their use of the psalms sounded. It says, Praise him with trumpet sound; praise him with lute and harp. Praise him with tambourine and dance; praise him with strings and pipe! Praise him with clanging cymbals; praise him with loud clashing cymbals! Let everything that breathes praise the LORD! With the playing of the instruments there was dancing. Dancing was a big part of Hebrew celebrations.

The book of Psalms is God's word, but it is also the words of the people to God. Everyone does not classify the different psalms in the same way even though classifications are similar. There is much repetition in Psalms as there is in Proverbs, for that was the style of worship and learning in an oral culture.

The word *psalm* comes from a stringed instrument called the psaltry. The lyrics of the different psalms inform us that Hebrew poets do not rhyme sounds; they rhyme ideas. They delight in poetry with pairs of lines with matched meanings. Such couplets lend themselves to antiphonal singing. Usually the pairs express the same idea. For example, enter his gates with thanksgiving and his courts with praise (100:4). Also, the earth is the LORD's and all that is in it, the world and all who live in it (24:1). This is called synonymous parallelism.

Other times the opposite truth is expressed. For example, the LORD watches over the way of the righteous, but the way of the wicked will perish (1:6). This is called antithetical parallelism. Synthetic parallelism is when the second line adds to the first providing further information. For example, Deliverers will go up on Mt Zion to govern the mountains of Esau. And the kingdom will be the LORD's. Also, the kings of the earth set themselves, and the rulers take counsel together against the LORD and his anointed (2:2). Sometimes the second line makes the meaning of the first more specific.

Another characteristic of Hebrew poetry is figurative language. God is compared to a cup (16:5), a sheep farmer (23:1), a rock (28:1), a king (47:6), a judge (67:4), a loving father (103:13). God's people are compared to sheep that God protects, trees that stand firm, and grass that God sweeps away.

The nation of Israel is mentioned often. God chose a nation to be his people while he would be their God. When Christians read the Psalms as prayer, they can substitute church for nation. In the OT God called a nation, but in the NT God calls a church that is found in all nations and to which all nations are invited.

Psalms are thought of as the work of David. Muslims say God sent 104 psalms, and Seth wrote fifty of them. Most Jews and Christians count 150 psalms, and seventy-three psalms are said to be the work of David while another fourteen are linked with his life. Most scholars have basically given up on exactly who composed the different psalms and when they were composed, but there are some good educated guesses. There are numerous classification forms for the book of Psalms. The following is the classification by Lawrence Boadt (1984).

Hymns of Praise: Pss 8, 19, 33, 66, 100, 103, 104, 111, 113, 114, 117, 145-150.

Hymns of Thanksgiving: Pss 18, 30, 32, 34, 40, 65, 66, 67, 75, 92, 107, 116 118, 124, 136, 138.

Individual laments: Pss 3, 4, 5, 6, 7, 9, 10, 13, 14, 17, 22, 25, 26, 27, 28, 31, 35, 38, 39, 40, 41, 42, 43, 51, 52, 53, 54, 55, 56, 57, 59, 61, 64, 69, 70, 71, 77, 86, 88, 89, 109, 120, 130, 139, 140, 141, 142, 143.

Community laments: Pss 12, 44, 58, 60, 74, 79, 80, 83, 85, 90, 94, 123, 126, 129, 137.

Liturgical Psalms: Pss 15, 24, 50, 68, 81, 82, 115, 134.

Wisdom Psalms: Pss 1, 19, 36, 37, 49, 73, 78, 112, 119, 127, 128.

Trust Psalms: Pss 11, 16, 23, 27, 62, 63, 91, 121, 125, 131.

Royal Psalms: Pss 2, 18, 20, 21, 45, 72, 78, 89, 101, 110, 132, 144.

Zion hymns: Pss 46, 48, 76, 84, 87, 122.

Royal Psalms as Yahweh as king: Pss 29, 47, 93, 95, 96, 97, 98, and 99.

This writer adds the Imprecatory Psalms: God invites us to be angry but sin not. Expressions of anger are acceptable: 12, 35, 58, 59, 69, 70, 83, 109, 137, 140.

Psalms generally are lyrical or poetical hymns of praise to the God of Israel that cover the whole range of human experience. The one hundred fifty psalms are the hymnbook of the Hebrew people used at the temple but also in private prayer. The basic structure is simple (1) the theme is stated which is praise, thanks, or lament (2) the reason is given for the invocation (3) what God has or has not done is given for the one invoking him (4) the theme is repeated with the assurance that God will respond.

Psalms are primarily written to be sung with musical instruments. They are prayers directed to God in the sense of adoration, confession, thanksgiving, supplication or petition. The most important theme is God's steadfast love for his people. Of the OT books the book of Psalms and Isaiah are quoted most often in the NT.

As this writer goes through each individual psalm, there will be an attempt to state the heart of the content of each psalm without maintaining the sentence structure or the literary beauty of the poetry. This writer will stay with his original goal which is to give the reader a sense of the content. A basic description of each psalm will be stated, and then a paragraph exhibiting the content will follow. In most of the previous biblical books there is an attempt to get the reader to follow some key verses, but that will not be done in Psalms. Most of the psalms are short enough that after the description is read the reader can open the Bible to the psalm and read it quite easily. The reader is encouraged to read each psalm to appreciate the beauty of the poetry.

Psalm 1 is a wisdom psalm expressing the two paths of life. The life of the faithful person is contrasted with the life of the faithless.

Happy are those who do not follow the advice of the wicked or take the path that sinners tread, or sit in the seat of scoffers; but their delight is in the law of the LORD, and on his law they meditate day and night. They are like trees planted by streams of water which yield their fruit in its season, and their leaves do not wither. In all that they do, they prosper. The wicked are not so, but are like chaff that the wind drives away. Therefore the wicked will not stand in the judgment, nor sinners in the congregation of the righteous; for the LORD watches over the way of the righteous, but the way of the wicked will perish.

Psalm 2 is a royal psalm of God's ultimate rule. God's ruler, his anointed, the Messiah is established as ruler of the nations.

Why do the nations conspire and the peoples plot in vain? The kings of the earth set themselves, and the rulers take counsel together against the LORD and his anointed. Then he will speak to them in his wrath, and terrify them in his fury, saying, I have set my king on Zion, my holy hill. I will tell of the decree of the LORD: He said to me, "You are my son; today I have begotten you. Ask of me, and I will make the nations your heritage, and the ends of the earth your possession. You shall break them with a rod of iron, and dash them in pieces like a potter's vessel." Happy are those who take refuge in him. (Both the Jews and Christians take this as messianic.)

Psalm 3 is about trust in God for protection and peace especially during adversity.

Many are saying to me, there is no help for you in God. But you, O LORD, are a shield around me, my glory, and the one who lifts up my head. I cry aloud to the LORD, and he answers me from his holy hill. The LORD sustains me. Deliverance belongs to the LORD; may your blessing be on your people!

Psalm 4 is a prayer of faith and rejoicing in God's protection and peace. We can place our confidence in God because he will listen when we call on him.

Answer me when I call, O God of my right! You gave me room when I was in distress. Be gracious to me and hear my prayer. How long, you people, shall my honor suffer shame? How long will you love vain words and seek after lies? But know that the LORD has set apart the faithful for himself; the LORD hears when I call to him. When you are disturbed do not sin; put your trust in the LORD. I will both lie down and sleep in peace; for you alone, O LORD, make me lie down in safety.

Psalm 5 is a prayer for help from the lies of our enemies. God hears our prayers.

The boastful will not stand before your eyes; you hate all evil doers. You destroy those who speak lies; the LORD abhors the bloodthirsty and deceitful. Lead me, O LORD in your righteousness because of my enemies; make your way straight before me. For there is no truth in their mouths; their hearts are destruction; their throats are open graves; they flatter with their tongues. Make them bear their guilt, O God; let them fall by their own counsels; because of their many transgressions, cast them out, for they have rebelled against you. But let all who take refuge in you rejoice. For you bless the righteous, O LORD; you cover them with favor as with a shield.

Psalm 6 is a prayer of recovery from illness. God is able to rescue us in times of trouble.

O LORD, do not rebuke me in your anger, or discipline me in your wrath. Be gracious to me, O LORD, for I am languishing; O LORD, heal me, for my bones are shaking with terror. Turn, O LORD, save my life; deliver me for the sake of your steadfast love. For in death there is no remembrance of you. I am weary with my moaning; every night I flood my bed with tears. My eyes waste away because of grief; they grow weak because of all my foes. Depart from me, all you workers of evil, for the LORD has heard the sound of my weeping. All my enemies shall be ashamed and struck with terror; then they shall turn back, and in a moment be put to shame.

Psalm 7 is the prayer of an innocent man who prays for justice from his enemies. God is the judge who will punish those who persecute the innocent.

O LORD my God, in you I take refuge; save me from my pursuers, and deliver me, or like a lion they will tear me apart; they will drag me away, with no one to rescue. Rise up, O LORD, in your anger; awake, O my God, you have appointed a judgment. Judge me, O LORD, according to my righteousness and according to the integrity that is in me. God is my shield who saves the upright in heart. God is a righteous judge. If one does not repent, God will whet his sword. Their mischief returns upon their own heads, and on their own heads their violence descends. I will give to the LORD the thanks due to his righteousness, and sing praise to the name of the LORD, the Most High.

Psalm 8 praises God for his magnificent creation. God cares for the people he created.

O LORD, our sovereign, how majestic is your name in all the earth! You have set your glory above the heavens. When I look at your heavens, the work of your fingers, the moon and the stars that you have established; what are human beings that you are mindful of them, mortals that you care for them? You have made them a little lower than God (also translated angels) and crowned them with glory and honor. You have given them dominion over the works of your hands; you have put all things under their feet. O LORD our Sovereign, how majestic is your name in all the earth!

Psalm 9 is about God's power and justice. He never ignores our cries for help.

I will give thanks to the LORD with my whole heart; I will tell of your wonderful deeds. The LORD sits enthroned forever; he has established his throne for judgment.

He judges the world with righteousness; he judges the people with equity. The LORD is a stronghold for the oppressed, a stronghold in times of trouble. And those who know your name put their trust in you, for you, O LORD, have not forsaken those who seek you. He who avenges blood is mindful of them; he does not forget the cry of the afflicted. Be gracious to me, O LORD. See what I suffer from those who hate me. The LORD has made himself known, he has executed judgment; the wicked are snared in the work of their own hands. The wicked shall depart to Sheol, all the nations that forget God. For the needy shall not always be forgotten, nor the hope of the poor perish forever. Rise up, O LORD! Do not let mortals prevail; let the nations be judged before you. Put them in fear, O LORD; let the nations know that they are only human.

Psalm 10 petitions God on behalf of the poor. Although he may seem to be hidden at times, we can be assured that he is aware of all injustices.

Why, O LORD, do you stand far off? Why do you hide yourself in times of trouble. In arrogance the wicked persecute the poor--let them be caught in the schemes they have devised. For the wicked boast of the desires of their heart, those greedy for gain curse and renounce the LORD; all their thoughts are, "There is no God." Their eyes stealthily watch for the helpless; they lurk that they may seize the poor. Their ways prosper at all times. Their mouths are filled with cursing and deceit and oppression; under their tongues are mischief and iniquity. They lurk that they may seize the poor and drag them off in their net. They think in their heart, "God has forgotten, he has hidden his face, he will never see it." Rise up O LORD; O God lift up your hand; do not forget the oppressed. Why do the wicked renounce God, and say in their hearts, You will not call us to account? Do justice for the orphan and oppressed, so that those from earth may strike terror no more.

Psalm 11 is a song of trust. God will judge the people he created.

If the foundations are destroyed, what can the righteous do? The LORD is in his holy temple; the LORD's throne is in heaven. His eyes behold, his gaze examines humankind. The LORD tests the righteous and the wicked, and his soul hates the lover of violence. On the wicked he will rain coals of fire and sulfer; a scorching wind shall be the portion of their cup. For the LORD is righteousness; he loves righteous deeds; the upright shall behold his face.

Psalm 12 is a prayer for help for the poor and needy from those who attempt to take advantage of them in evil times.

Help, O LORD, for there is no longer anyone who is godly; the faithful have disappeared from humankind. They utter lies to each other; with flattering lips and a double heart they speak. May the LORD cut off all flattering lips, the tongue that makes great boasts, those who say, " With our tongues we will prevail; our lips are our own—who is our master?" "Because the poor are despoiled, because the needy groan, I will rise up said the LORD; I will place them in the safety for which they belong." You, O LORD, will protect us; you will guard us from this generation forever. On every side the wicked prowl, as vileness is exalted among humankind.

Psalm 13 is the cry of a sad, desperate soul who trusts God as he waits his help.

How long, O LORD? Will you forget me forever? How long will you hide your face from me? How long must I bear pain in my soul and have sorrow in my heart all day long? How long shall my enemy be exalted over me? Consider and answer me, O LORD my God! But I trusted in your steadfast love; my heart shall rejoice in your salvation I will sing to the LORD.

Psalm 14 is a denunciation of Godlessness in a wicked world and for those who deceive themselves about God.

The psalmist says, Fools say in their hearts, "There is no God." They are corrupt, they do abominable deeds; there is no one who does good. The LORD looks down from heaven on humankind to see if there are any who are wise, who seek after God. They have all gone astray, they are all alike perverse; there is no one who does good, no, not one. Have they no knowledge, all the evil doers who eat up people as they eat bread, and do not call upon the LORD? There they shall be in great terror, for God is with the company of the righteous. You would confound the plans of the poor, but the LORD is their refuge.

Psalm 15 is about who will abide with God and live a life pleasing to him.

Who may dwell on your holy hill? Those who walk blamelessly, and do what is right, and speak the truth from their heart; who do not slander with the tongue, who do no evil to their friends, who honor those who fear the LORD, who stand by their oath even to their hurt; who do not lend money at interest, and who do not take bribes against the innocent.

Psalm 16 is a psalm of trust because we know we are nothing without God.

Protect me, O God, for in you I take refuge. I say to the LORD, "You are my Lord; I have no good apart from you." I bless the LORD who gives me counsel; in the night also my heart instructs me. I keep the LORD always before me. Therefore my heart is glad and my soul rejoices. You show me the path of life. In your presence there is fullness of joy.

Psalm 17 is a prayer for deliverance from those who oppress.

Hear a just cause, O LORD; attend to my cry; give ear to my prayer from lips free of deceit. If you test me, you will find no wickedness in me; and my mouth does not transgress. I have avoided the ways of the violent. My steps have held fast to your paths. I will call upon you, for you will answer me, O my God; incline your ear to me, hear my words. Guide me as the apple of the eye; hide me in the shadow of your wings, from the wicked who despoil me, my deadly enemies who surround me. They close their hearts to pity; with their mouths they speak arrogantly. They track me down; now they surround me. Rise up, O LORD, confront them, overthrow them!

Psalm 18 is a thanksgiving for victory for those who remain humble and do what is right.

The LORD is my rock, my fortress, and my deliverer, my God, my rock in whom I take refuge, my shield, and the horn of my salvation, my stronghold. In my distress I called upon the LORD; to my God I cried for help. From his temple he heard my voice. The LORD rewarded me according to my righteousness; according to the cleanness of my hands he recompensed me. For I have kept the ways of the LORD, and have not wickedly departed from my God. You deliver a humble people, but haughty eyes you bring down. It is you who light my lamp; the LORD, my God, lights up my darkness. The LORD lives! Blessed be my rock and exalted be the God of my salvation.

Psalm 19 is about God's glory in creation and his word. We know God through his word and his created order.

The heavens are telling the glory of God, and the firmament proclaims his handiwork. Day to day pours forth speech, and night to night declares knowledge. The law of the LORD is perfect reviving the soul; the decrees of the LORD are sure, making wise the simple; the commandment of the LORD is clear enlightening the eyes; the fear of the LORD is pure, enduring forever; the ordinances of the LORD are true and righteous altogether. Moreover by them is your servant warned; in keeping them there is great reward. Let the words of my mouth and the meditation of my heart be acceptable to you, O LORD, my rock and my redeemer.

Psalm 20 is a prayer for victory. God will help his people through their challenges.

The LORD answers you in the day of trouble! The name of the God of Jacob protect you! Now I know that the LORD will help his anointed; he will answer him from his holy heaven with mighty victories by his right hand. Some take pride in chariots and some in horses, but our pride is in the name of the LORD our God. Give victory to the king, O LORD; answer us when we call.

Psalm 21 is a thanksgiving for saving the king's life and for victory. God's people must praise him and thank him in all circumstances especially when he allows them to live.

In your strength the king rejoices, O LORD, and in your help how greatly he exults! You have given him his heart's desire, and have not withheld the request of his lips. He asked you for life, and you gave it to him--length of days forever and ever. His glory is great through your help; splendor and majesty you bestow on him. Be exalted, O LORD, in your strength! We will sing and praise your power.

Psalm 22 is called a messianic psalm. Even in suffering one lives for God.

My God, my God why have you forsaken me? Why are you so far from helping me, from the words of my groaning? O my God, I cry by day, but you do not answer; and by night, but I find no rest. I am a worm, and not human; scorned by others, and despised by the people. All who see me mock me; they make mouths at me, they shake their heads; "Commit your cause to the LORD; let him deliver—let him rescue the one in whom he delights!" I am poured out like water, and all my bones are out of joint; my heart is like wax; my mouth is dried up like a potsherd, and my tongue sticks to my jaws; you lay me in the dust of death. For dogs are all around me; a company of evil doers encircles me. My hands and feet have shriveled; I can count all my bones. They stare and gloat over me; they divide my clothes among themselves, and for my clothing they cast lots. Deliver my soul from the sword, my life from the power of the dog! Save me from the mouth of the lion! All the ends of the earth shall remember and turn to the LORD. Dominion belongs to the LORD, and he rules over the nations. To him, indeed, shall all who sleep in the earth bow down; and I shall live for him. (Christians see Christ on the cross in this psalm.)

Psalm 23 is the shepherd psalm. God is faithful and will always care for his people.

The LORD is my shepherd. I shall not want. He makes me lie down in green pastures; he leads me besides still waters; he restores my soul. He leads me in right paths for his namesake. Even though I walk through the darkest valley, I fear no evil, for you are with me; your rod and staff comfort me. You prepare a table before me in the presence of my enemies; you anoint my head with oil; my cup overflows. Surely goodness and mercy shall follow me all the days of my life, and I shall dwell in the house of the LORD my whole life long.

Psalm 24 is a processional psalm entering into the temple. God accepts the worship of the pure in heart. Let us worship him always with a pure heart.

The earth is the LORD's and all that is in it, the world, and those who live in it; for he has founded it on the seas, and established it on the rivers. Who shall ascend the hill of the LORD? Who shall stand in his holy place? Those who have clean hands and pure hearts, who do not lift their souls to what is false, and do not swear deceitfully. They will receive blessing from the LORD, and vindication from the God of their salvation. Such is the company of those who seek him. Lift up your heads, O gates! and be lifted up, O ancient doors! that the king of glory can come in. Who is the king of glory? The LORD strong and mighty, the LORD mighty in battle. Who is the king of glory? The LORD of hosts, he is the king of glory.

Psalm 25 is a prayer asking God for guidance, and forgiveness.

To you, O LORD, I lift up my soul. In you I trust. Make me know your ways, O LORD; teach me your paths. Lead me in your truth and teach me, for you are the God of my salvation; for you I wait all day long. Do not remember the sins of my youth or my transgressions. Good and upright is the LORD; therefore he instructs sinners in the way. He leads the humble in what is right, and teaches the humble his way. All the paths of the LORD are steadfast love and faithfulness, for those who keep his covenant and his decrees. For your namesake, O LORD, pardon my guilt, for it is great. Relieve the troubles of my heart and bring me out of my distress.

Psalm 26 is a plea for justice and a vindication of righteousness. We must constantly let God test our hearts as we examine them daily.

Vindicate me, O LORD, for I have walked with integrity, and I have trusted in the LORD without wavering. Prove me, O LORD, and try me; test my heart and mind. For your steadfast love is before my eyes, and I walk in faithfulness to you. I do not sit with the worthless nor do I consult with hypocrites; I hate the company of evildoers, and will not sit with the wicked. I wash my hands in innocence, and go around your altar, O LORD, singing aloud a song of thanksgiving, and telling of your wondrous deeds. O LORD, I love the house in which you dwell. Do not sweep me away with sinners, nor my life with the bloodthirsty, those in whose hands are evil devices and whose right hands are full of bribes. I walk in my integrity; redeem me, and be gracious to me.

Psalm 27 is a song of confidence. God constantly offers us help and hope.

The LORD is my light and my salvation whom should I fear? The LORD is the stronghold of my life; of whom shall I be afraid? One thing I ask of the LORD, that will I seek after: to live in the house of the LORD all the days of my life, to behold the beauty of the LORD, and to inquire in his temple. Teach me your way, O LORD, and lead me on a level path because of my enemies. I believe that I will see the goodness of the LORD in the land of the living. Wait for the LORD; be strong, and let your heart take courage; wait for the LORD!

Psalm 28 is prayer of protection from enemies.

To you, O LORD, I call; my rock, do not refuse to hear me, for if you are silent to me, I shall be like those who go down to the Pit. Do not drag me away with the wicked, with those who are workers of evil, who speak peace with their neighbors, while mischief is in their hearts. Repay them according to the work of their hands; render them their due reward. Because they do not regard the works of the LORD, he will break them down, and build them up no more. Blessed be the LORD, for he has heard the sound of my pleadings. The LORD is my strength and my shield; in him my heart trusts; so I am helped, and my heart exults, and with my song I give thanks to him.

Psalm 29 is about God who reveals himself through his created order and controls nature.

Ascribe to the LORD the glory of his name; worship the LORD in holy splendor. The voice of the LORD is over the waters; the God of glory thunders, the LORD over mighty waters. The voice of the LORD is powerful; the voice of the LORD is full of majesty. The voice of the LORD breaks the cedars. The voice of the LORD flashes forth flames of fire. The voice of the LORD causes the oaks to swirl, and strips the forest bare; and in his temple all say, "Glory." The LORD sits enthroned over the flood; the LORD sits as king forever. May the LORD give strength to his people! May the LORD bless his people with peace.

Psalm 30 is a thanksgiving for life restored after a grave illness. God can bring us through our deepest crises so trust him and thank him.

O LORD, my God, I cried to you for help, and you have healed me. You brought up my soul up from Sheol, restored me to life from among those gone down to the Pit. Sing praises to the LORD, O you his faithful ones, and give thanks to his holy name. You have turned my mourning into dancing, so that my soul may praise you. O LORD my God I will give thanks to you forever.

Psalm 31 is a prayer of trust in God. Even in deep despair, we can trust God to make things right.

Into your hand I commit my spirit; you have redeemed me, O LORD, faithful God. I trust in the LORD. Be gracious to me, for I am in distress; my eyes waste away from grief, my soul and body also. For my life is spent with sorrow, and my years with sighing; my strength falls because of my misery, and my bones waste away. I am the scorn of all my adversaries, a horror to my neighbors, an object of dread to my acquaintances; those who see me in the street flee from me. I hear the whispering of many—terror all around!--as they scheme together against me, as they plot to take my life. But I trust in you, O LORD; I say, "You are my God." My times are in your hand; deliver me from the hand of my enemies and persecutors. Let the wicked be put to shame. Let the lying lips be stilled that speak insolently against the righteous with pride and contempt. Love the LORD all you his saints. The LORD preserves the faithful, but abundantly repays the one who acts haughtily. Be strong let your heart take courage, all you who wait for the LORD.

Psalm 32 is about the joy of forgiveness. Both physical and psychological relief comes through God's forgiveness when guilt is released.

Happy are those whose transgression is forgiven, whose sin is covered. Happy are those to whom the LORD imputes no iniquity and in whose spirit there is no deceit. While I kept silence my body wasted away through my groaning all day long. Then I acknowledged my sin to you, and I did not hide my iniquity. I said, "I will confess my transgressions to the LORD," and you forgave the guilt of my sin. (Suppressed guilt had become an intolerable burden. Relief came only when sins were confessed.)

Psalm 33 is about the greatness and goodness of God. War will never bring ultimate victory only God can do such.

Rejoice in the LORD, O you righteous. Sing to him a new song. For the word of the LORD is upright, and all his work is done in faithfulness. He loves righteousness and justice; the earth is full of the steadfast love of the LORD. Let all the earth fear the LORD; let all the inhabitants of the world stand in awe of him. For he spoke, and it came to be; he commanded, and it stood firm. The LORD brings the counsel of the nations to nothing; he frustrates the plans of the people. The counsel of the LORD stands forever, the thoughts of his heart to all generations. Happy is the nation whose God is the LORD, the people whom he has chosen as his heritage. The warhorse is a vain hope for victory, and by its great might cannot save. The eye of the LORD is on those who fear him. Our soul waits for the LORD. Our heart is glad in him because we trust in his holy name.

Psalm 34 is praising God's goodness. God listens to those who call upon him and rescues them from trouble, so praise him.

I will bless the LORD at all times; his praise shall continually be in my mouth. The angel of the LORD encamps around those who fear him and delivers him. O taste and see that the LORD is good; happy are those who take refuge in him. O fear the LORD, you his holy ones, for those who fear him have no want. Depart from evil and do good; seek peace and pursue it. When the righteous cry to the LORD, the LORD hears, and rescues them from all their troubles. The LORD is near the brokenhearted and saves the crushed in spirit. The LORD redeems the life of his servants; none of those who take refuge in him will be condemned.

Psalm 35 is an imprecatory psalm. God can handle our negative emotions.

Contend, O LORD, with those who contend with me; fight against those who fight against me! Draw the spear and javelin against my pursuers; say to my soul, "I am your salvation. Let them be put to shame and dishonor who seek my life. Let ruin come on them unawares. How long, O LORD, will you look on? Rescue me from their ravages, my life from the lions! Then I will thank you in the great congregation; in the mighty throng I will praise you. Let all who rejoice in my calamity be put to shame and confusion; let those who exalt themselves against me be clothed with shame and dishonor. Then my tongue shall tell of your righteousness and of your praise all day long.

Psalm 36 is about sin. It contrasts human wickedness with the character of God.

Transgression speaks to the wicked deep in their hearts; there is no fear of God before their eyes. For they flatter themselves in their own eyes that their iniquity can not be found out and hated. The words of their mouth are mischief and deceit;

they have ceased to act wisely and do good. Your steadfast love, O LORD extends to the heavens, your faithfulness to the clouds. Your righteousness is like the mighty mountains, your judgments are like the great deep; you save humans and animals alike, O LORD. (Here we learn of God's care for animals.)

Psalm 37 is a psalm of hope. Do not be discouraged by those who reject God and seem to prevail. God and his ways will prevail.

Do not fret because of the wicked; do not be envious of evil doers, for they will soon fade like the grass. Trust in the LORD, and do good; so you will live in the land, and enjoy security. Take delight in the LORD, and he will give you the desires of your heart. Commit your way to the LORD; trust in him, and he will act. Be still before the LORD and wait patiently for him; do not fret over those who prosper in their way, over those who carry out evil devises. The righteous shall be kept safe forever, but the children of the wicked shall be cut off. The righteous shall inherit the land and live in it forever. Wait for the LORD, and keep his way, and he will exalt you to inherit the land; you will look on the destruction of the wicked. Transgressors shall be altogether destroyed; the posterity of the wicked shall be cut off.

Psalm 38 is a plea for health as a result of sin that destroys us. Only God can set us free.

O LORD, do not rebuke me in your anger or discipline me in your wrath. There is no health in my bones because of my sin. For my iniquities have gone over my head; they weigh like a burden too heavy for me. My wounds grow foul and fester because of my foolishness; I am utterly bowed down and prostrate; all day long I go around mourning. I am ready to fall, and my pain is ever with me. I confess my iniquity. I am sorry for my sin. Do not forsake me, O LORD; O my God, do not be far from me; make haste to help me, O LORD, my salvation.

Psalm 39 is a prayer for wisdom and forgiveness. We can only know who we are in light of God.

"I will guard my ways that I may not sin with my tongue. I will keep a muzzle on my mouth as long as the wicked were in my presence." I was silent and still; I held my peace to no avail; my distress grew worse, my heart became hot within me. While I mused the fire burned; then I spoke with my tongue: "LORD, let me know my end, and what is the measure of my days; let me know how fleeting life is. You have made my days a few handbreadths, and my lifetime is nothing in your sight. Surely every one stands as a mere breath. My hope is in you. Deliver me from my transgressions. You chastise mortals in punishment for sin, consuming like a moth what is dear to them; surely everyone is a mere breath."

Psalm 40 gives thanks. As we wait patiently for God to act, we can be his person in the situation in which he has placed us.

I waited patiently for the LORD; he inclined to me and heard my cry. He drew me from the desolate pit, out of the miry bog, and set my feet upon a rock. He put a new song in my mouth. Happy are those who make the LORD their trust. You have given me an open ear. Then I said, "Here I am; in the scroll of the book it is written of me. I delight to do your will, O my God; your law is written within my heart." (Hebrews 10:7,16 has Christ saying this.) I have not concealed your steadfast love and your faithfulness from the congregation. Be pleased, O LORD, to deliver me; O LORD make haste to help me. Let all those be put to shame and confusion who seek to snatch away my life; let those be turned back and brought to dishonor who desire my hurt. You are my help and my deliverer; do not delay, O my God.

Psalm 41 is a prayer for healing from sickness and those who are oppressed. God is always there for his people.

Happy are those who consider the poor. The LORD delivers them in the day of trouble. The LORD protects them and keeps them alive; they are called happy in the land. You do not give them up to the will of their enemies. The LORD sustains them on their sickbed; heal me for I have sinned against you. My enemies wonder in malice when will I die, and my name perish. Even my bosom friend in whom I trusted, who ate of my bread, has lifted the heel against me. But you, O LORD, be gracious to me, and raise me up, that I may repay them. But this I know that you are pleased with me; because my enemy has not triumphed over me. But you have upheld me because of my integrity, and set me in your presence forever. Blessed be the God of Israel, from everlasting to everlasting.

BOOK II

Psalm 42 is about a soul seeking God. When you are alone and depressed think about God and meditate upon his word.

As a deer longs for flowing streams, so my soul longs for you, O God. My soul thirsts for God, for the living God. My tears have been my food day and night, while people say continually, "Where is your God?" My soul is cast down within me. I say to God, my rock, "Why have you forgotten me? Why must I walk about mournfully because the enemy oppresses me?" As with a deadly wound in my body, my adversaries taunt me, while they say to me continually, "Where is your God?" Why are you cast down O my soul, and why are you disquieted within me? Hope in God, for I shall again praise him, my help and my God.

Psalm 43 is a prayer for vindication. Hope in God is only found in God and his word.

Vindicate me, O God, and defend my cause against an ungodly people; from those who are deceitful and unjust deliver me! Why must I walk about mournfully because of the oppression of the enemy? O send out your light and truth; let them lead me; let them bring me to your holy hill and to your dwelling. Why are you cast down, O my soul, and why are you disquieted within me? Hope in God; for I shall again praise him, my help and my God. (Psalms 42 and 43 were probably originally one psalm.)

Psalm 44 is a cry to God who seems to be in hiding and not listening.

You have made us a byword among the nations, a laughingstock among the peoples. All of this has come upon us, yet we have not forgotten you, or been false to your covenant. Because of you, we are being killed all day long, and accounted as sheep for the slaughter. Rouse yourself! Why do you sleep O LORD? Awake, do not cast us off forever! Why do you hide your face? Why do you forget our affliction and oppression? Rise up, come to our help. Redeem us for the sake of your steadfast love.

Psalm 45 is about the king's marriage.

The king's majesty and his godly rule is expressed. The throne of God is said to endure forever. His royal scepter is a scepter of equity; he loves righteousness and hates wickedness. The king is anointed by God. The bride is told since he is your Lord bow to him. His name to be celebrated in all generations, and the people will praise him forever.

Psalm 46 is God defending the city and people. God is always there to help his people.

God is our refuge and strength, a very present help in trouble. Therefore we will not fear. There is a river whose streams make glad the city of God. God is in the midst of the city; it shall not be moved. Come, behold the works of the LORD; see what desolations he has brought on earth. He makes wars cease to the end of the earth. "Be still and know that I am God! I am exalted among the nations, I am exalted in the earth." The LORD of hosts is with us; the God of Jacob is our refuge.

Psalm 47 is about giving worship due to the one God; he will prevail.

Clap your hands, all you peoples; shout to God with loud songs of joy. For the LORD, the Most High, is awesome, a great king over all the earth. He subdued peoples under us, and nations under our feet. God is king over the nations; God sits on his holy throne.

Psalm 48 is about the glory and strength of Zion, the city of God. God is always present to his people, and he will guide us as we worship. (When Christians meditate, they substitute heaven for zion.)

Great is the LORD and greatly to be praised in the city of our God. His holy mountain, beautiful in elevation, is the joy of all the earth, Mt Zion, in the far north, the city of the great king. We ponder your steadfast love, O God, in the midst of your temple. Your name, O God, like your praise, reaches to the ends of the earth. He will be our guide forever.

Psalm 49 is about the foolishness of trusting in riches which can not bring salvation.

Truly, no ransom avails for one's life, there is no price one can give to God for it. For the ransom of life is costly, and can never suffice, that one should live on forever and never see the grave. Do not be afraid when some become rich, when the wealth of their houses increases. For when they die, they will carry nothing away; their wealth will not go after them. Mortals can not abide in their pomp; they are like the animals that perish.

Psalm 50 is a contrast between true faith that comes from the heart and a false faith.

Offer to God a sacrifice of thanksgiving, and pay your vows to the Most High. Call to me in the day of trouble; I will deliver you, and you shall glorify me. But to the wicked God says: What right have you to recite my statutes, or take my covenant on your lips? For you hate discipline, and you cast my words behind you. You make friends with a thief when you see one, and you keep company with adulterers. "Mark this, then, you who forget God, or I will tear you apart, and there will be no one to deliver. Those who bring thanksgiving as their sacrifice honor me; to those who go the right way I will show the salvation of God."

Psalm 51 is a prayer for cleansing. Sin is humankind's problem, and only God has the answer. The question is: are we humble enough for God to take care of it for us?

Have mercy on me, O God, according to your steadfast love; according to your abundant mercy blot out my transgressions. Wash me thoroughly from my iniquity, and cleanse me from my sin. For I know my transgressions and my sin is ever before me. Against you, you alone, have I sinned and done what is evil in your sight so that you are justified in your sentence and blameless when you pass judgment. Indeed I was born guilty, a sinner when my mother conceived me. You desire truth in the inward being; therefore teach me wisdom in my secret heart. Purge me with hyssop, and I shall be clean; wash me and I shall be whiter than snow. Create in me a clean heart, O God, and put a new and right spirit within me. The sacrifice acceptable to God is a broken spirit, and a broken and contrite heart, O God you will not despise. (Muslims do not believe their sin has any effect on God; it only effects people.)

Psalm 52 is a psalm confirming that God will prevail over all evil.

Why do you boast, O mighty one, of mischief done against the godly? All day long you are plotting destruction. Your tongue is like a sharp razor, you worker of treachery. You love evil more than good, and lying more than speaking the truth. You love all words that devour, O deceitful tongue. But God will break you down forever; he will uproot you from the land of the living. The righteous will see, and fear, and will laugh at the evil doer saying, "See the one who would not take refuge in God, but trusted in abundant riches, and sought refuge in wealth!"

Psalm 53 is exactly like Psalm 14.

Fools say in their hearts that there is no God. They live corrupt lives. God has rejected them and will put them to shame.

Psalm 54 is a prayer for vindication; it is another imprecatory psalm. It is acceptable to express one's negative feelings to God. He knows them anyway and can handle them.

Save me, O God, by your name, and vindicate me by your might. Hear my prayer, O God; give ear to the words of my mouth. For the insolent have risen against me, the ruthless seek my life; they do not set God before them. But surely, God is my helper; the Lord is the upholder of my life. He will repay my enemies for their evil.

In your faithfulness put an end to them.

Psalm 55 is an imprecatory psalm for those who have been betrayed by friends. God will deal even with the evil of those who claim God and attend worship.

I am distraught by the noise of the enemy, because of the clamor of the wicked. My heart is in anguish within me, the terrors of death have fallen upon me. Fear and trembling come upon me, and horror overwhelms me. Confuse, O LORD, confound their speech; for I see violence and strife in the city. It is not enemies who taunt me—I could bear that. But it is you, my equal, my companions, my familiar friend, with whom I kept pleasant company; we walked in the house of God with the throng. Let death come upon them, for evil is in their homes and in their hearts. God who is enthroned from of old will hear, and will humble them--because they do not change, and do not fear God. But you, O God, will cast them down into the lowest pit; the bloodthirsty and treacherous shall not live out half their days. But I will trust you.

Psalm 56 is a prayer of trust. When one is attacked and afraid, God is there.

Be gracious to me, O God, for people trample on me; all day long foes oppress me; many fight against me. O Most High, when I am afraid, I put my trust in you. In God whose word I praise, in God I trust; I am not afraid; what can flesh do to me?

Psalm 57 is about praise and assurance under persecution. Standing for the things of God will always bring out the opposition. Because of your witness, God will prevail.

Be merciful to me, O God, be merciful to me, for in you my soul takes refuge; in the shadow of your wings I will take refuge, until the destroying storms pass by. He will send from heaven and save me, he will put to shame those who trample me. God will send forth his steadfast love and faithfulness. I lie down among lions that greedily devour human prey. They dug a pit in my path, but they have fallen into it themselves. My heart is steadfast, O God, my heart is steadfast. I will sing and make melody. Awake, my soul! I will give thanks to you, O LORD, among the peoples; I will sing praises to you among the nations. For your steadfast love is as high as the heavens; your faithfulness extends to the clouds. Let your glory be over all the earth.

Psalm 58 is an imprecatory psalm. It is acceptable to express negative emotions to God.

Do you decree what is right, you gods? Do you judge people fairly? No, in your hearts you devise wrong; your hands deal out violence on the earth. The wicked go astray from the womb; they err from their birth, speaking lies. They have venom like the venom of a serpent. Let them vanish like water that runs away; like grass let them be trodden down and wither. Let them be like the snail that dissolves into slime. The righteous will rejoice when they see vengeance done; they will bathe their feet in the blood of the wicked. People will say, surely there is a reward for the righteous; surely there is a God who judges the earth.

Psalm 59 is an imprecatory psalm. In an evil world continue to worship God as you wait for him to eventually right all the wrongs.

Deliver me from those who work evil; from the bloodthirsty save me. Even now they lie in wait for my life; the mighty stir up strife against me. Each evening they come howling like dogs and prowling about the city. For the sin of their mouths, the words of their lips, let them be trapped in their pride. For the cursing and lies they utter, consume them in wrath; consume them until they are no more. Then it will be known to the ends of the earth that God rules over Jacob. I will sing aloud of your steadfast love in the morning. For you have been a fortress for me and a refuge in the day of my distress..

Psalm 60 is a prayer for the deliverance of God's people. Only God can reverse the impossible, but first we must examine ourselves to see if we are right with God.

O God you have rejected us; broken our defenses; you have been angry; now restore us! You have made your people suffer hard things. Give victory with your right hand, and answer us so that those whom you love may be rescued. O grant us hope against the foe, for human help is worthless.

Psalm 61 is a prayer of faith. God is always there to hear and respond to our prayers.

Hear my cry, O God; listen to my prayer. Lead me to the rock that is higher than I; for you are my refuge, a strong tower against the enemy. Let me abide in your tent forever, find refuge under the shelter of your wings. I will always sing praises to your name, as I pay my vows day after day.

Psalm 62 is a psalm of trust. God is in control so wait for him and trust him.

For God alone my soul waits in silence; from him comes my salvation. He alone is my rock and my salvation, my fortress; I shall never be shaken. Trust in him at all times, O people; pour out your heart before him; God is a refuge for us. Power belongs to God and steadfast love belongs to you, O LORD. For you repay all according to their work.

Psalm 63 is about comfort and assurance in God's presence. God is always there for you.

O God, you are my God, I seek you, my soul thirsts for you. Because your steadfast love is better than life; my lips will praise you. My soul is satisfied as with a rich feast, and my mouth praises you with joyful lips when I think of you on my bed and meditate on you in the watches of the night; for you have been my help, and in the shadow of your wings I sing for joy. My soul clings to you; your right hand upholds me.

Psalm 64 is a prayer for protection expressing the power of God's word over human words.

Hear my voice, O God, in my complaint; preserve my life from the dread enemy. Hide me from the secret plots of the wicked, from the scheming of evil doers, who whet their tongues like swords, who aim bitter words like arrows. They hold fast to their evil purpose. But God will shoot his arrow at them; they will be wounded suddenly. Because of their tongues, he will bring them to ruin; all who see them will shake with horror. Let the righteous rejoice in the LORD and take refuge in him.

Psalm 65 is a prayer of thankfulness. God is the world's only hope.

Praise is due to you, O God, in Zion; and to you shall vows be performed, O, you who answer prayer. To you all flesh shall come. When deeds of iniquity overwhelm us, you forgive our transgressions. By awesome deeds you answer us with deliverance. O God of our salvation; you are the hope of all the ends of the earth.

Psalm 66 is a psalm of thanksgiving. Remain faithful in worship, for God is faithful.

Make a joyful noise to God; sing to the glory of his name; give to him glorious praise. Say to God, "How awesome are your deeds! Because of your great power, your enemies cringe before you. All the earth worships you; they sing praises to you, sing praises to your name." I will come into your house with burnt offerings; I will pay you my vows. Blessed be God, because he has not rejected my prayer or removed his steadfast love from me.

Psalm 67 is a missionary psalm. We are God's presence to the world.

May God be gracious to us and bless us and make his face shine upon us that your way may be known upon the earth, your saving power among all nations. Let the nations be glad and sing for joy, for you judge the peoples with equity and guide the nations upon earth. Let the peoples praise you, O God; let all the peoples praise you.

The earth has yielded its increase; God, our God, has blessed us. May God continue to bless us; let all the ends of the earth revere him.

Psalm 68 is a liturgy for a festival celebration in the temple. Worship brings us the blessings of God's presence, and it is that which we take into the world as we serve him.

Let the righteous be joyful. Sing to God, sing praises to his name. Father of orphans and protector of widows is God in his holy habitation. God gives the desolate a home to live in; he leads out the prisoners to prosperity, but the rebellious live in a parched land. O God you provided for the needy. Summon your might, O God, show your strength, O God, as you have done for us before. Scatter the peoples who delight in war. Sing to God, O kingdoms of the earth; sing praises to the LORD. Awesome is God in his sanctuary, the God of Israel; he gives power and strength to his people. Blessed be God!

Psalm 69 is a prayer for deliverance. Some say it is a messianic psalm. It is often quoted in the NT. We may have to suffer injustice for a while, but God's justice will prevail.

Save me, O God, for the waters have come up to my neck. My eyes grow dim with waiting for my God. O God, you know my folly; the wrongs I have done are not hidden from you. Do not let those who hope in you be put to shame because of me. It is for your sake that I have borne reproach, that shame has covered my face. I have become a stranger to my kindred, an alien to my mother's children. It is zeal for your house that has consumed me; the insults of those who insult you have fallen on me. I am the subject of gossip. Answer me. Do not hide your face from your servant. They gave me poison for food, and for my thirst they gave me vinegar to drink. Let them be blotted out of the book of the living. I will praise the name of God with a song. This will please the LORD more than an ox or a bull. Let the oppressed see it and be glad; you who seek God, let your hearts revive. For the LORD hears the needy.

Psalm 70 is a plea for deliverance. In your most difficult times continue to trust God.

Be pleased, O God, to deliver me. O LORD, make haste to help me! Let those be put to shame and confusion who seek my life. Let all who seek you rejoice and be glad in you. Let those who love your salvation say evermore, "God is great!"

But I am poor and needy; hasten to me, O God. You are my help and deliverer. O LORD, do not delay!

Psalm 71 is a plea for deliverance by an elderly person.

In you, O LORD, I take refuge; let me never be put to shame. You are my rock and my fortress. Rescue me, O my God from the hand of the wicked. For you, O LORD, are my hope, my trust, O LORD, from my youth. Upon you I have leaned from my birth; it was you who took me from my mother's womb. My praise is continually to you. Do not cast me off in the time of old age; do not forsake me when my strength is spent. O God, do not be far from me; O my God, make haste to help me! So even to old age and gray hairs, O God, do not forsake me, until I proclaim your might to all generations to come. All day long my tongue will talk of your righteous help.

Psalm 72 is a prayer to God for the king to be just. May God bring those to power who will be concerned with justice and peace and who will make the needs of others holy.

Give the king your justice, O God, and your righteousness to a king's son. May he judge your people with righteousness and your poor with justice. May he defend the cause of the poor of the people, give deliverance to the needy, and crush the oppressor. In his days may righteousness flourish and peace abound, until the moon is no more. May all kings fall down before him, all nations give him service. For he delivers the needy when they call, the poor and those who have no helper. He has pity on the weak and needy and saves the lives of the needy. From oppression and violence he redeems their life; and precious is their blood in his sight. Long may he live! May all nations be blessed in him. Blessed be the LORD, the God of Israel, who alone does wondrous things. Blessed be his glorious name forever; may his glory fill the earth.

BOOK III

Psalm 73 is a meditation on the justice of God. How we need to act when we feel envy as the wicked seem to prosper.

Truly God is good to the upright, to those who are pure in heart. But as for me my feet had almost stumbled. For I was envious of the arrogant; I saw the prosperity of the wicked. They are not in trouble as others are. Pride is their necklace; violence covers them like a garment. They scoff and speak with malice; loftily they threaten oppression. They set their mouths against heaven. Therefore the people turn and praise them, and find no fault in them. But when I thought how to understand this, it seemed to me a wearisome task until I went into the sanctuary of God; then I perceived their end. When my soul was embittered, I was stupid and ignorant. Nevertheless I am continually with you; you guide me with your counsel, and afterward you will receive me with honor. Whom have I in heaven but you? And there is nothing on earth that I desire other than you. Indeed those that are far from you will perish; you put an end to those who are false to you. I have made the LORD God my refuge to tell of all your works.

Psalm 74 is a prayer for the deliverance of God's people after the destruction of Jerusalem. When things go wrong, we need to make sure we are standing with God in his causes and not our own personal or national causes.

O God, why do you cast us off forever? How long, O God, is the foe to scoff? Is the enemy to revile your name forever? Why do you hold back your hand? Do not let the downtrodden be put to shame; let the poor and needy praise your name. Rise up, O God, plead your cause; remember how the impious scoff at you all day long.

Psalm 75 is thanksgiving for God's mighty acts. When God decides to judge he will defeat the arrogant and lift up the humble.

We give thanks to you, O God; we give thanks; your name is near. At the set time that I appoint, I will judge with equity. When the earth totters with all its people, it is I who keep its pillars steady. I say to the boastful, "Do not boast," and to the wicked, "Do not lift up your horn (power); do not lift up your horn on high, or speak with insolent neck." It is God who executes judgment, putting down one and lifting up another. All the horns of the wicked I will cut off, but the horns of the righteous shall be exalted.

Psalm 76 is a song of God's people celebrating ultimate victory. The hope of God's people will be finalized on the last day.

You indeed are awesome! Who can stand before you when once your anger is roused? From the heavens you uttered judgment; the earth feared and was still when God rose up to establish judgment, to save all the oppressed of the earth. Make vows to the LORD your God and perform them; let all who are around him bring gifts to the one who is awesome, who cuts off the spirit of princes, who inspires fear in the kings of the earth.

Psalm 77 is a prayer for deliverance. When faith weakens remember what God has done.

In the day of my trouble I seek the LORD; my soul refuses to be comforted. I think of God, and I moan; I meditate, and my spirit faints. "Will the LORD spurn forever and never be favorable? Has his steadfast love ceased forever? Are his promises at an end for all time? Has God forgotten to be gracious? Has he in anger shut up his compassion." I will call to mind the deeds of the LORD. I will meditate on all your work, and muse on your mighty deeds. Your way, O God is holy. You are the God who works wonders, you have displayed your might among the peoples. With your strong arm you redeemed your people, the descendants of Jacob and Joseph.

Psalm 78 is about the guidance of God despite his people's unfaithfulness. We need to learn from the lessons of history.

Give ear, O my people, to my teaching; incline your ear to the words of my mouth. I will open my mouth in a parable; I will utter dark sayings from of old. We will not hide them from their children; we will tell to the coming generation the glorious deeds of the LORD and his might, and the wonders he has done so that they should set their hope in God, and not forget the works of God, but keep his commandments; and that they should not be like their ancestors, a stubborn and rebellious generation whose heart was not steadfast, whose spirit was not faithful to God. They did not keep God's covenant but refused to walk according to his law. They tested God in their heart by demanding food they craved. The anger of God rose against them and he killed the strongest of them. They remembered that God was their rock. Yet he being compassionate, forgave their iniquity. Yet they tested the Most High God, and rebelled against him. (The psalm goes on in this manner.) Then he chose Judah. He chose his servant David. With upright heart he tended them, and guided them with skillful hand.

Psalm 79 is a plea for mercy. When faced with injustice, it is important to remain faithful.

O God, the nations have come into your inheritance; they have defiled your holy temple; they have laid Jerusalem in ruins. We have become a taunt to our neighbors, mocked and derided by those around us. How long, O LORD? Will you be angry forever? Will your jealous wrath burn like fire? Do not remember against us the iniquities of our ancestors; let your compassion come speedily to meet us, for we are brought very low. Help us, O God of our salvation, for the glory of your name; deliver us, and forgive our sins, for your name's sake. Then we your people, the flock of your pasture, will give thanks to you forever; from generation to generation we will recount your praise.

Psalm 80 is a prayer for deliverance. There is no hope other than God.

Restore us, O God; let your face shine that we may be saved. How long will you be angry with your people's prayers? Turn again, O God of hosts; look down from heaven, and see; have regard for this vine, the stock that your right hand planted. Give us life, and we will call on your name. Restore us, O LORD God of hosts; let your face shine, that we may be saved.

Psalm 81 is a call to worship. When we attend the assembly, we worship God and hear the instructions he has for his people.

Sing aloud to God our strength; shout for joy to the God of Jacob. There shall be no strange god among you; you shall not bow down to a foreign god. O that my people would listen to me, that Israel would walk in my ways! Then I would quickly subdue their enemies, and turn my hand against their foes.

Psalm 82 is mythological poetry making use of a conception common to the ancient Near East that the world is ruled by a council of gods. God is on the side of those who are oppressed and taken advantage of by those of power and wealth.

God has taken his place in the divine council; in the midst of the gods he holds judgment: "How long will you judge unjustly and show partiality to the wicked? Give justice to the weak and the orphan; maintain the right and the lowly and the destitute. Rescue the weak and the needy; deliver them from the hand of the wicked." They have neither knowledge nor understanding, they walk around in darkness; all the foundations of the earth are shaken. I say, "You are gods, children of the Most High, all of you; nevertheless you shall die like mortals, and fall like any prince." Rise up, O God, judge the earth; for the nations belong to you!

Psalm 83 is a prayer for deliverance. God's people ask God to judge their enemies.

O God do not keep silence; those who hate you have raised their heads. They lay crafty plans against your people; they consult together against those you protect. They say, "Come, let us wipe them out as a nation; let the name of Israel be remembered no more." O, my God, make them like whirling dust, like chaff before the wind; let them perish in disgrace. Let them know that you alone, whose name is the LORD, are the Most High over all the earth.

Psalm 84 a psalm of one longing to be in the sanctuary. There is no greater place to be than in the presence of God.

How lovely is your dwelling place O LORD of hosts. My soul longs, indeed it faints for the courts of the LORD; my heart and my flesh sing for joy to the living God. Happy are those who live in your house, ever singing your praise. For a day in your court is better than a thousand elsewhere. I would rather be a doorkeeper in the house of my God than live in the tents of wickedness. No good thing does the LORD withhold from those who walk uprightly. O LORD of hosts, happy is everyone who trusts in you.

Psalm 85 is a prayer for mercy to Israel. Mercy comes with repentance.

Restore us again, O God of our salvation, and put away your indignation toward us. Will you be angry with us forever? Will you not revive us again, so that your people may rejoice in you? Surely his salvation is at hand for those who fear him that his glory may dwell in our land. Steadfast love and faithfulness will meet; righteousness and peace will kiss each other. Righteousness will go before him, and will make a path for his steps.

Psalm 86 is an appeal for help in trouble. When requesting God's help, we must make sure we are following his instructions.

Incline your ear, O LORD, and answer me, for I am poor and needy. Preserve my life for I am devoted to you; save your servant who trusts in you. You are great and do wondrous things; you alone are God. Teach me your way, O LORD, that I may walk in your truth; give me an undivided heart to revere your name. You, O LORD, are a God merciful and gracious, slow to anger and abounding in steadfast love and faithfulness. Show me a sign of your favor, so that those who hate me may see it and be put to shame, because you, LORD, have helped me and comforted me.

Psalm 87 is a song praising Zion as the mother of believers everywhere. God has established his foundation on earth.

On the holy mount stands the city he founded; the LORD loves the gates of Zion more than all the dwellings of Jacob. Glorious things are spoken of you, O city of God. And of Zion it shall be said, "This one and that one were born in it"; for the Most High himself will establish it. Singers and dancers alike say "All my springs (sources of welfare) are in you."

Psalm 88 is a desperate prayer for healing in sickness. There are times when we feel God is not there.

O LORD God of my salvation, when at night, I cry out in your presence, let my prayer come before you; incline your ear to my cry. For my soul is full of troubles, and my life draws near to Sheol (the place of the dead in the OT). I am like those who have no help, like those forsaken among the dead. Do you work wonders for the dead? Do the shades rise up to praise you? Is your steadfast love declared in the grave, or your faithfulness in Abaddon? (Abaddon was a poetic name for the realm of the dead.)Why do you hide your face from me? Your wrath has swept over me; your dread assaults destroy me. You have caused friend and neighbor to shun me; my companions are in darkness.

Psalm 89 is a king praying for deliverance. The Messiah, who is righteous and just is promised.

I will sing of your steadfast love, O LORD, forever; with my mouth I will proclaim your faithfulness to all generations. Let the heavens praise your wonders, O LORD, your faithfulness in the assembly of the holy ones. Righteousness and justice are the foundation of your throne; steadfast love and faithfulness go before you. I have found my servant David; with my holy oil I have anointed him; my hand shall always remain with him. I will make him the firstborn, the highest of the kings of the earth. I will establish his line forever, and his throne as long as the heavens endure.

BOOK IV

Psalm 90 is a reflection on mortality. Our time on this earth is temporary and short.

Lord, you have been our dwelling place in all generations. You turn us back to dust. You sweep them away; they are like a dream, like grass that is renewed in the morning and fades in the evening. You have set our iniquities before you, our secret sins in the light of your countenance. The days of our life are seventy years or perhaps eighty, if we are strong; even then their span is only toil and trouble; they are soon gone, and we fly away. So teach us to count our days that we may gain a wise heart. Have compassion on your servants! Let your work be manifest in your servants, and your glorious power to their children. Let the favor of our LORD be upon us and prosper for us the work of our hands—O prosper the work of our hands.

Psalm 91 is a psalm of trust. This is a meditation on God as the protector of the faithful.

You who live in the shelter of the Most High, who abide in the shadow of the Almighty, will say to the LORD, "My refuge and my fortress; my God in whom I trust." Under his wings you will find refuge. You will not fear the terror of the night or the arrow that flies by day, or the pestilence that stalks in the darkness, or the destruction that wastes at noonday. He will command the angels concerning you to guard you in all your ways. Those who love me I will deliver; I will protect those who know my name.

Psalm 92 is a psalm of thanksgiving. We need to express our thanks to God all day.

It is good to give thanks to the LORD, to sing praises to your name, O Most High; to declare your steadfast love in the morning and your faithfulness by night. How great are your works, O LORD! Your thoughts are very deep! The dullard can not know. My eyes have seen the downfall of my enemies. The righteous flourish like the palm tree. They are planted in the house of the LORD; they flourish in the courts of our God. In old age they still produce fruit; they are always green and full of sap, showing that the LORD is upright; he is my rock; and there is no unrighteousness in him.

Psalm 93 is a hymn extolling God as king. Because God is creator, his creation must listen and act upon his instructions.

The LORD is king. He is robed in majesty. He has established the world; it shall never be moved; your throne is established from of old; you are from everlasting. Your decrees are very sure; holiness befits your house, O LORD, forevermore.

Psalm 94 is an imprecatory psalm and a prayer of deliverance from evil people. God will not forsake his people.

O LORD, you God of vengeance, shine forth! Rise up, O judge of the earth; give to the proud what they deserve! O LORD, how long shall the wicked exalt? They pour out their arrogant words; all the evildoers boast. They crush your people, O LORD, and afflict your heritage. They kill the widow and the stranger, they murder the orphan, they say, "The LORD does not see; the God of Jacob does not perceive." The LORD knows our thoughts, that they are but an empty breath. Happy are those whom you discipline, O LORD, and whom you teach out of your law. The LORD will not forsake his people; for justice will return to the righteous. Can wicked rulers be allied with you, those who contrive mischief by statute? They band together against the life of the righteous, and condemn the innocent to death. He will repay them for their iniquity and wipe them out for their wickedness; the LORD our God will wipe them out.

Psalm 95 is a liturgy of God's kingship and an invitation to worship God.

O come, let us sing to the LORD; let us make a joyful noise to the rock of our salvation! Let us come into his presence with thanksgiving; let us make a joyful noise to him with songs of praise! For the LORD is a great God and a great King above all the gods. O come, let us worship and bow down; let us kneel before the LORD our maker! For he is our God, and we are the people of his pasture and the sheep of his hand. O that today you would listen to his voice! Do not harden your hearts, as at Meribah in the wilderness, when your ancestors tested me, and put me to the proof, though they had seen my work. Therefore in my anger I swore that they would not enter my rest.

Psalm 96 is a hymn praising God who comes in judgment.

O sing to the LORD a new song. Sing to the LORD all the earth. Sing to the LORD bless his name; tell of his salvation from day to day. Declare his glory among the nations, his marvelous works among all the peoples. For great is the LORD and greatly to be praised; he is to be revered above all gods. For all the gods of the peoples are idols, but the LORD made the heavens. Ascribe to the LORD the glory due his name; bring an offering and come into his courts. Worship the LORD in holy splendor; tremble before him all the earth. Say among the nations, "The LORD is king! The world is firmly established; it shall never be moved. He will judge the peoples with equity." Let the heavens be glad, and let the earth rejoice.

Psalm 97 is a hymn celebrating God's kingship. God is righteous and just.

The LORD is king! Let the earth rejoice; righteousness and justice are the foundation of his throne. The heavens proclaim his righteousness; and all the peoples behold his glory. For you, O LORD, are the most high over all the earth; you are exalted far above all gods. The LORD loves those who hate evil; he guards the lives of the faithful; he rescues them from the hand of the wicked. Rejoice in the LORD, O you righteous, and give thanks to his holy name!

Psalm 98 is a hymn proclaiming the joy of the establishment of God's kingdom on the earth. The victory of God has begun on this earth.

O sing to the LORD a new song, for he has done marvelous things. His right hand and his holy arm have gotten him victory. The LORD has made known his victory; he has revealed his vindication in the sight of the nations. All the ends of the earth have seen the victory of our God. With trumpets and the sound of the horn make a joyful noise to the LORD, all the earth; break forth into joyous song and sing praises. Make a joyful noise before the King, the LORD. He will judge the world with righteousness and the people with equity.

Psalm 99 is a hymn celebrating God's kingship. God is holy and just. Let us worship him.

The LORD is king; let the peoples tremble! Let them praise your great and awesome name. Holy is he! Mighty King, lover of justice, you have established equity; you have executed justice, and righteousness in Jacob. You were a forgiving God to them, but an avenger of their wrongdoing. The LORD our God is holy.

Psalm 100 is a hymn calling all nations to praise the Lord.

Make a joyful noise to the LORD, all the earth. Worship the LORD with gladness; come into his presence with singing. Know that the LORD is God. It is he that made us, and we are his; we are his people and the sheep of his pasture. Enter his gates with thanksgiving and his courts with praise. Give thanks to him, bless his name. For the LORD is good; his steadfast love endures forever, and his faithfulness to all generations.

Psalm 101 is the king pledging himself to rule justly. It is a prayer to walk a blameless path, to live with integrity.

I will sing of loyalty and justice; to you O LORD I will sing. I will study the way that is blameless. I will walk with integrity of heart within my house; I will not set before my eyes anything that is base. I hate the work of those who fall away; it shall not cling to me. Perverseness of heart shall be far from me; I will know nothing of evil. One who secretly slanders a neighbor I will destroy. A haughty look and an arrogant heart I will not tolerate. I will look with favor on the faithful in the land, so that they may live with me; whoever walks in the way that is blameless shall minister to me. No one who practices deceit shall remain in my house; no one who utters lies shall continue in my presence. I will destroy all the wicked in the land, cutting off all evil doers from the city of the LORD.

Psalm 102 is a prayer for healing in sickness. This prayer requests a longer life.

Incline your ear to me; answer me speedily in the day I call. For my days pass away like smoke, and my bones burn like a furnace. My heart is stricken and withered like grass; I am too wasted to eat my bread. My days are like an evening shadow; I wither away like grass. He (God) has broken my strength in midcourse; he has shortened my days. "O my God," I say, "do not take me away at the mid point of my life, you whose years endure throughout all generations."

Psalm 103 is a psalm of thanksgiving for God's compassion and his spiritual and physical healing.

Bless the LORD, O my soul and all that is within me, bless his holy name. Bless the LORD, O my soul, and do not forget all his benefits--who forgives all your iniquity, who heals all your diseases, who redeems your life from the Pit (Sheol), who crowns you with steadfast love and mercy, who satisfies you with good as long as you live so that your youth is renewed like an eagle's. The LORD works vindication and justice for all who are oppressed. The LORD is merciful and gracious slow to anger and abounding in steadfast love. As a father has compassion for his children, so the LORD has compassion on those who fear him. For he knows how we were made; he remembers that we are dust. As for mortals their days are like grass; they flourish like a flower of the field; for as the wind passes over it, and it is gone, and its place knows it no more. But the steadfast love of the LORD is from everlasting to everlasting on those who fear him and his righteousness to children's children, to those who keep his covenant, and remember to do his commandments. Bless the LORD, O my soul.

Psalm 104 is a hymn to God the creator. The creator calls his creation to praise him.

(The psalmist lists the things of creation.) Then the writer said, O LORD how manifold are all your works! In wisdom you have made them all; the earth is full of your creatures. When you send forth your spirit, they are created; and you renew the face of the ground. May the glory of the LORD endure forever; may the LORD rejoice in his works—who looks on the earth and it trembles, who touches the mountains and they smoke. I will sing to the LORD as long as I live; I will sing praise to my God while I have being. May my meditation be pleasing to him, for I rejoice in the LORD. Let sinners be consumed from the earth and let the wicked be no more.

Psalm 105 is the story of God's great deeds on behalf of his people. God saves his people in order for them to worship him, witness to him and to observe his laws.

Seek the LORD and his strength; seek his presence continually. Remember the wonderful works he has done, his miracles and the judgments he uttered. (A brief history of God setting his people free from Egypt is reviewed as well as their apostasies in the wilderness and the days of the Judges.) So he brought his people out with joy, his chosen ones with singing. He gave them the lands of the nations, and took possession of the wealth of the peoples, that they might keep his statutes and observe his laws. Praise the LORD!

Psalm 106 gives the reason for salvation.

Praise the LORD! O give thanks to the LORD, for he is good; for his steadfast love endures forever. (The people were in captivity to the nations because of their sins. Many of Israel's apostasies are mentioned.) The writer says, Save us, O LORD, and gather us from among the nations, that we may give thanks to your holy name and glory in your praise.

BOOK V

Psalm 107 is a liturgy of thanksgiving for escape from various dangers such as traveling across the desert or sea, being freed from prison, and being healed from sickness.

O give thanks to the LORD, for he is good; for his steadfast love endures forever. Let the redeemed of the LORD say so, those he redeemed from trouble and gathered in from the lands, from the east and from the west, from the north and from the south. Let them thank the LORD for his steadfast love, for his wonderful works to humankind. For he satisfies the thirsty, and the hungry he fills with good things. Let them extol him in the congregation of the people, and praise him in the assembly of the elders. Let those who are wise give heed to these things, and consider the steadfast love of the LORD.

Psalm 108 is a liturgical prayer for victory over enemies.

I will sing and make melody. Awake my soul! I will sing praises to you among the nations. Be exalted, O God, above the heavens, and let your glory be over all the earth. Give victory with your right hand, and answer me, so that those whom you love may be rescued. Have you rejected us, O God? You do not go out, O God, with our armies. O Grant us help against the foe, for human help is worthless. With God we shall do valiantly; it is he who will tread down our foes.

Psalm 109 is an imprecatory psalm. We can tell God our true feelings.

Do not be silent, O God of my praise. For wicked and deceitful mouths are opened against me, speaking against me with hate and lying tongues. In return for my love they accuse me, even while I make prayer for them. They reward me evil for good, and hatred for my love. (As a counter to the black magic curses of his enemy, he includes his curse such as, may his children be orphans and his wife a widow.) May the creditor seize all he has; may strangers plunder the fruits of his toil. May his memory be cut off from the earth. For he did not remember to show kindness, but pursued the poor and needy and the brokenhearted to their death. He loved to curse; let curses fall on him. With my mouth I will give great thanks to the LORD, I will praise him in the midst of the throng. For he stands at the right hand of the needy to save them from those who would condemn them to death.

Psalm 110 promises victory to the king. This is a messianic psalm.

The LORD said to my Lord, "Sit at my right hand until I make your enemies my footstool." (This verse is quoted frequently in the NT. Christian belief is that it was composed by David in honor of the Messiah.) The LORD sends out from Zion your mighty scepter. Rule in the midst of your foes. Your people will offer themselves willingly on the day you lead your forces on the holy mountains. The LORD has sworn he will not change his mind, "You are a priest forever after the order of Melchizedek." The LORD is at your right hand; he will shatter kings on the day of his wrath. He will execute judgment among the nations filling them with corpses; he will shatter heads over the wide earth.

Psalm 111 is a hymn of praise to God for his great deeds. Wisdom begins and ends with the fear of God.

I will give thanks to the LORD with my whole heart, in the company of the upright in the congregation. Great are the works of the LORD studied by all who delight in them. He provides food for those who fear him; he is ever mindful of his covenant. The fear of the LORD is the beginning of wisdom; all those who practice it have a good understanding.

Psalm 112 contrasts the fate of the righteous and the wicked.

Happy are those who fear the LORD, who greatly delight in his commandments. They are gracious, merciful, and righteous. For the righteous will never be moved;

they will be remembered forever. They have distributed freely; they have given to the poor; their righteousness endures forever; their horn is exalted in honor. The wicked see it and are angry; they gnash their teeth and melt away. The desire of the wicked comes to nothing.

Psalm 113 is a psalm of praise celebrating God as helper of the humble.

Blessed be the name of the LORD from this time on and forevermore. From the rising of the sun to its setting the name of the LORD is to be praised. The LORD is high above all nations, and his glory above the heavens. Who is like the LORD our God, who is seated on high. He raises the poor from the dust, and lifts the needy from the ash heap. Praise the LORD!

Psalm 114 is a hymn of praise of God's great work in creating a nation. Judah became God's sanctuary, Israel his domination.

Judah became God's sanctuary, Israel his dominion. Tremble, O earth, at the presence of the LORD, at the presence of the God of Jacob.

Psalm 115 is a liturgy contrasting God's power with the impotence of the gods.

Why should the nations say, "Where is your God?" Our God is in the heavens; he does whatever he pleases. Their idols are silver and gold, the work of human hands. They have mouths but do not speak; eyes, but do not see. They have ears, but do not hear; noses, but do not smell. O, Israel, trust in the LORD! He is their help and their shield. You who fear the LORD, trust in the LORD! The LORD has been mindful of us; he will bless us; he will bless those who fear the LORD, both small and great. The heavens are the LORD's heavens, but the earth he has given to human beings. Praise the LORD!

Psalm 116 is a thanksgiving for healing. Praise for being saved from death.

I love the LORD because he has heard my voice and my supplications. The snares of death encompassed me; the pangs of Sheol laid hold on me; I suffered distress and anguish. Then I called on the name of the LORD: "O LORD, I pray save my life!" Gracious is the LORD and righteous; our God is merciful. The LORD protects the simple; when I was brought low, he saved me. You have delivered my soul from death. O LORD I am your servant. I will offer you thanksgiving sacrifice and call on the name of the LORD.

Psalm 117 is the shortest psalm in the Bible. All nations need to praise God.

Praise the LORD all ye nations, for great is his steadfast love. The faithfulness of the LORD endures forever. Praise the LORD!

Psalm 118 is thanksgiving for deliverance in battle. Trust in God and his teachings instead of humans and their teachings that oppose God's ways.

O give thanks to the LORD, for he is good; his steadfast love endures forever! With the LORD on my side I do not fear. What can mortals do to me? It is better to take refuge in the LORD than to put confidence in mortals. The LORD is my strength and my might; he has become my salvation. I shall not die, but I shall live, and recount the deeds of the LORD. Open to me the gates of righteousness that I may enter through them and give thanks to the LORD. The stone that the builders rejected has become the chief cornerstone. (This is frequently quoted in the NT as a reference to Jesus.) This is the LORD's doing. This is the day the LORD has made; let us rejoice and be glad in it.

Psalm 119 has 176 verses which is a meditation on the law of God. It is the longest psalm in the Bible. Meditating on God's teachings puts us into God's presence. This writer encourages the reader to read and meditate on every verse.

Teach me, O LORD, the way of your statutes, and I will observe them until the end. My soul is consumed with longing for your ordinances. I will meditate upon your precepts. Oh how I love your law. It is my meditation all day long. (The psalm continues this way through all 176 verses.)

Psalm 120 is a prayer of help and deliverance from those who love war.

In my distress I cry to the LORD that he may answer me: "Deliver me, O LORD, from lying lips and from a deceitful tongue." Too long have I had my dwelling among those who hate peace. I am for peace; but when I speak, they are for war.

Psalm 121 is a liturgy of blessing. We can depend on God for help.

I lift up my eyes to the hills--from where will my help come? My help comes from the LORD who made heaven and earth. The LORD will keep you from all evil; he will keep your life. The LORD will keep your going out and your coming in from this time on and forevermore.

Psalm 122 is a prayer for peace and prosperity. For Christians often the Church takes the place of Jerusalem and sometimes Zion. Christians believe that in the OT God created a nation for his purposes, but in the NT he has created the church which is for all nations and all people.

I was glad when they said to me, "Let us go to the house of the LORD!" Pray for the peace of Jerusalem: "May they prosper who love you. Peace be within your walls, and security within your towers." For the sake of the house of the LORD God, I will seek your good.

Psalm 123 is a prayer for deliverance from enemies. Look to God for mercy and help.

To you I lift up my eyes, O you who are enthroned in the heavens. Our eyes look to the LORD our God until he has mercy upon us. We have had more than enough contempt. Our soul has had more than its fill of the scorn of those who are at ease, of the contempt of the proud.

Psalm 124 is a thanksgiving for deliverance. God is on the side of those who seek him.

If it had not been for the LORD who was on our side when our enemies attacked us, then they would have swallowed us up alive. Blessed be the LORD who has not given us up as prey for their teeth. We have escaped like a bird from the snare of the fowlers; the snare is broken, and we have escaped. Our help is in the name of the LORD who made heaven and earth.

Psalm 125 is about trust. As the mountains protect Jerusalem, God protects his people.

Those who trust in the LORD are like Mt Zion, which can not be moved, but abides forever. As the mountain surrounds Jerusalem, the LORD surrounds his people. Do good, O LORD, to those who are good, and to those who are upright in their hearts. But to those who turn aside to their own crooked ways, the LORD will lead away with evil doers. Peace be upon Israel!

Psalm 126 is a prayer of joy. God does great things for his people.

When the LORD restored the fortunes of Zion, we were like those who dream. Then our mouths were filled with laughter, and our tongues with shouts of joy; then it was said among the nations, "The LORD has done great things for them." May those who sow in tears reap with shouts of joy. Those who go out weeping, bearing the seed for sowing, shall come home with shouts of joy, carrying their sheaves.

Psalm 127 is about building a family on a sound foundation. Life without God is senseless. God needs to be first in our lives, and then the rest will fall into place.

Unless the LORD builds the house, those who built it labor in vain. Unless the LORD guards the city, the guard keeps watch in vain. Sons are indeed a heritage from the LORD, the fruit of the womb a reward. Like arrows in the hand of a warrior are the sons of one's youth. Happy is the man who has his quiver full of them.

Psalm 128 is about the sound foundation. This is called the marriage and family prayer.

Happy is everyone who fears the LORD, who walks in his ways. You shall eat the fruit of the labor of your hands; you shall be happy, and it shall go well with you. Your wife will be like a fruitful vine within your house; your children will be like olive shoots around your table. Then shall the man be blessed who fears the LORD. May you see your children's children.

Psalm 129 is a prayer for deliverance from enemies. God will get us through out trials.

The LORD is righteous; he has cut the cords of the wicked. May all who hate Zion be put to shame and turned backward. Let them be like the grass on the housetops that withers before it grows up. The blessing of the LORD be upon you!

Psalm 130 is about the assurance of the Lord's forgiveness. God is our hope.

LORD, hear my voice! Let your ears be attentive to the voice of my supplications. If you, O LORD, should mark iniquities, LORD, who could stand? But there is forgiveness with you, so that you may be revered. I wait for the LORD, my soul waits, and in his word I hope. O Israel, hope in the LORD! For with the LORD there is steadfast love, and with him a great power to redeem. It is he who will redeem Israel from all its iniquities.

Psalm 131 is a psalm of humble trust. Quiet trust in God is our hope.

I do not occupy myself with things too great and too marvelous for me. But I have calmed and quieted my soul like a weaned child with its mother; my soul is like the weaned child that is with me. O Israel, hope in the LORD from this time on and forever more.

Psalm 132 is a liturgy honoring God's choice. Out of Israel will come the world's hope, the Messiah from the line of David.

The LORD swore to David a sure oath from which he will not turn back: "One of the sons of your body I will set on your throne. If your sons keep my covenant and my decrees that I shall teach them, their sons also, forevermore shall sit on your throne." For the LORD has chosen Zion; he has desired it for his habitation: "This is my resting place forever; here I will reside, for I have desired it. I will abundantly bless its provisions; I will satisfy its poor with bread. Its priests I will clothe with salvation, and its faithful will shout for joy. There I will cause a horn to sprout up for David; I have prepared a lamp for my anointed one. His enemies I will clothe with disgrace, but on him his crown will gleam."

Psalm 133 is about unity. God wants us at peace not war.

How very good and pleasant it is when kindred live together in unity. It is like the precious oil on the head, running down upon the beard, on the beard of Aaron running down on the collar of the robes. It is like the dew of Hermon which falls on the mountains of Zion. For there the LORD ordained his blessing, life forevermore.

Psalm 134 is a liturgy of blessing. Our blessings come from worship.

Come, bless the LORD all you servants of the LORD, who stand by night in the house of the LORD. Lift up you hands to the holy place, and bless the LORD. May the LORD, maker of heaven and earth, bless you from Zion.

Psalm 135 is a hymn praising the Lord for his mighty deeds such as creation, delivering his people from Egypt, giving them a land.

Praise the LORD, for the LORD is good; sing to his name, for he is gracious. I know that the LORD is great; our LORD is above all gods. The LORD will vindicate his people and have compassion on his servants. O house of Israel, bless the LORD!

Psalm 136 is a thanksgiving. It follows closely the previous psalm, but is a congregational response. The writer lists some things throughout Israel's history to give thanks for which is followed by the response: For his steadfast love endures forever.

O give thanks to the Lord of lords, for his steadfast love endures forever; who alone does great wonders, who by understanding made the heavens, who spread out the earth on the waters, who made the great lights, the sun to rule over the day, the moon and stars to rule over the night, who struck Egypt through their first born and brought Israel out from among them and divided the Red Sea in two, who led Israel through the wilderness, who struck down great kings and gave their land to his servant Israel, who remembered us in our low estate and rescued us from our foes, who gives food to all flesh. (After each statement the psalmist says, for his steadfast love endures forever.)

Psalm 137 is an imprecatory psalm. It is prayer for vengeance on Israel's enemies. Our anger or sorrow sometimes makes it difficult to sing songs of joy to our God, but not for the Israelites. They included their anger and sorrow in their songs.

By the rivers of Babylon--there we sat down, and there we wept when we remembered Zion. For there our captors asked us for songs, and our tormentors asked for mirth saying, "Sing us one of the songs of Zion!" How could we sing the LORD's song in a foreign land? Remember, O LORD, against the Edomites the day of Jerusalem's fall, how they said, "Tear it down! Tear it down! Down to its foundations!" O daughter Babylon, you devastator! Happy shall they be who pay you back what you have done to us! Happy shall they be who take your little ones and dash them against the rock! (It is good to express anger in a controlled way; God can handle it.)

Psalm 138 is thanksgiving for deliverance from trouble. God is our help at all times.

I give thanks, O LORD with my whole heart; before the gods I sing your praise. I bow down to your holy temple for you have exalted your name and your word above everything. On the day I called, you answered me; you increased my sense of soul. All the kings of the earth shall praise you, O LORD, for they have heard the words of your mouth. They shall sing of the ways of the LORD, for great is the glory of the LORD. For though the LORD is high he regards the lowly, but the haughty he perceives from far away. The LORD will fulfill his purpose for me; your steadfast love, O LORD endures forever. Do not forsake the work of your hands.

Psalm 139 is about God's omnipotence, omnipresence, and omniscient. God knows all that we do and think.

O LORD you have searched me and known me. You know when I sit down and when I rise up; you discern my thoughts from far away. You search out my path and my lying down and are acquainted with all my ways. Even before a word is on my tongue, O LORD, you know it completely. It was you who formed my inward parts; you knit me together in my mother's womb. My frame was not hidden from you, when I was being made in secret, intricately woven in the depths of the earth. Your eyes beheld my unformed substance. In your book were written all the days that were formed for me, when none of them as yet existed. Search me, O God, and know my heart; test me and know my thoughts. See if there is any wicked way in me and lead me in the way everlasting. (This is a good anti-abortion psalm.)

Psalm 140 is a prayer for deliverance from those who desire war.

Deliver me, O LORD, from the evildoers; protect me from those who are violent who plan evil things in their minds and stir up wars continually. Guard me, O LORD, from the hands of the wicked; protect me against the violent who have planned my downfall. The arrogant have hidden a trap for me. Do not let the slanderers be established in the land. I know that the LORD maintains the cause of the needy and executes justice for the poor. Surely the righteous shall give thanks to your name; the upright shall live in your presence.

Psalm 141 is a prayer for help in controlling the tongue and accepting correction.

I call upon you, O LORD; come quickly to me. Let my prayer be counted as incense before you, and the lifting up of my hands as an evening sacrifice. Set a guard over my mouth, O LORD; keep watch over the door of my lips. Do not turn my heart to any evil, to busy myself with wicked deeds in company with those who work iniquity; do not let me eat of their delicacies. Let the righteous strike me; let the faithful correct me. Never let the oil of the wicked anoint my head, for my prayer is continually against their wicked deeds. My eyes are turned toward you, O God, my LORD; keep me from the trap that they have laid for me. Let the wicked fall into their own nets, while I alone escape.

Psalm 142 is a prisoner's prayer for deliverance.

I cry to the LORD; with my voice I make supplication to the LORD. I pour out my complaint before him; I tell my trouble before him. When my spirit is faint, you know my way. Save me from my persecutors, for they are too strong for me. Bring me out of prison, so that I may give thanks to your name. The righteous will surround me, for you will deal bountifully with me.

Psalm 143 is a prayer for help with feelings of hopelessness and depression.

Do not enter into judgment with your servant, for no one living is righteous before you. I meditate on the works of your hands. I stretch out my hands to you; my soul thirsts for you like a parched land. Answer me quickly, O LORD; my spirit fails me. Teach me the way I should go, for to you I lift up my soul. Teach me to do your will, for you are my God. Let your good spirit lead me on a level path.

Psalm 144 is a warrior's prayer.

Blessed be the LORD, my rock, who trains my hands for war, and my fingers for battle. O LORD, what are human beings that you regard them, or mortals that you think of them? They are like a breath; their days are like a passing shadow. Stretch out your hand from on high; set me free and rescue me from the mighty waters, from the hand of aliens, whose mouths speak lies, and whose right hands are false. Rescue me from the cruel sword, and deliver me from the hands of aliens, whose mouths speak lies, and whose right hands are false. May there be no breach in the walls, no exile, and no cry of distress in the streets.

Psalm 145 is a hymn epitomizing the character of the God of Israel.

I will extol you, my God and my king and bless your name forever. On the glorious splendor of your majesty, and on your glorious works, I will meditate. I will declare your greatness. The LORD is gracious, and merciful, slow to anger, and abounding in steadfast love. The LORD is good to all, and his compassion is over all that he has made. Your kingdom is an everlasting kingdom, and your dominion endures throughout all generations. The LORD is faithful in all his words and gracious in all his deeds. The LORD is just in all his ways; and kind in all his doings. The LORD is near to all who call him, to all who call on him in truth. My mouth will speak the praise of the LORD, and all flesh will bless his holy name forever.

Psalm 146 is an exhortation to trust God instead of humans.

Praise the LORD! Praise the LORD, O my soul! Do not put your trust in princes, in mortals, in whom there is no help. Happy are those whose help is the God of Jacob, whose hope is in the LORD their God who made heaven and earth, the sea and all that is in them; who keeps faith forever; who executes justice for the oppressed, who gives food to the hungry. The LORD sets the prisoners free; the LORD opens the eyes of the blind. The LORD lifts up those who are bowed down; the LORD loves the righteous. The LORD watches over strangers; he upholds the orphan and the widow, but the way of the wicked he brings to ruin. The LORD will reign forever.

Psalm 147 is a hymn praising God for his universal power and providential care.

Praise the LORD! How great it is to sing praises to our God; for he is gracious, and a song of praise is fitting. Great is our LORD and abundant in power; his understanding is beyond measure. The LORD lifts up the downtrodden; he casts the wicked to the ground. His delight is not in the strength of the horse (war), nor his pleasure in the speed of the runner, but the LORD takes pleasure in those who fear him, in those who hope in his steadfast love. He grants peace within your borders; he fills you with the finest wheat. He gives snow like wool; he scatters frost like ashes. He declares his word to Jacob, his statutes and ordinances to Israel. He has not dealt thus with any other nation; they do not know his ordinances. Praise the LORD!

Psalm 148 is a hymn calling all created things to praise God.

Praise the LORD! (Angels, sun, moon, stars, sea monsters, fire, hail, snow, frost, wind, mountains, hills, trees, kings, all peoples, princes, all rulers, men, women, old, young, are all called to praise the LORD.)

Psalm 149 is a praise song. We must never forgot that God created us to be in his presence.

Sing to the LORD a new song, his praise in the assembly of the faithful. Let Israel be glad in its maker; let the children of Zion rejoice in their King. Let them praise his name with dancing, making melody to him with tambourine and lyre. For the LORD takes pleasure in his people; he adorns the humble with victory. Let the faithful exult in glory; let them sing for joy in their couches. Praise the LORD!

Psalm 150 is a doxology marking the end of the Psalter.

Praise the LORD! Praise God in the sanctuary; praise him in his mighty firmament! Praise him for his mighty deeds; praise him according to his surpassing greatness! Praise him with trumpet sound; praise him with lute and harp! Praise him with tambourine and dance; praise him with strings and pipe! Praise him with clanging cymbals; praise him with loud clashing cymbals! Let everyone that breathes praise the LORD! Praise the LORD!

This ends the Psalms for Protestants and Roman Catholics.

Psalm 151. Greek manuscripts add this psalm about David. This Psalm has seven verses. The Orthodox includes it in their canon. They do not capitalize the word Lord.

It says, I was small among my brothers and was the youngest in my father's house. I tended my father's sheep. My hands made a harp; my fingers fashioned a lyre. And who will tell my Lord? The Lord himself; it is he who hears. It was he who sent his messenger and took me from my father's sheep, and anointed me with his anointing oil. My brothers were handsome and tall, but the Lord was not pleased with them. I went out to meet the Philistine, and he cursed me with his idols. But I drew his own sword; I beheaded him and took away disgrace from the people of Israel.

A VIEW OF GOD FROM SOME OF THE PSALMS

From the Psalms we can learn what the people of the one God thought about their God. This writer took some time one day and skimmed through the psalms and wrote down some characteristics that stood out. The reader might want to try it also to see how alike or different your list is from mine.

Judaism, Christianity, and Islam would agree on the following characteristics of the one God. The psalm and verse will follow each statement.

The LORD watches over the way of the righteous, but the way of the wicked will perish (1:6).

Those who take refuge in God are happy, but those who do not perish (2:11).

He is your glory who lifts you up and delivers you (3:3, 8).

He sets apart the faithful for himself and hears you when you call on him. God has put gladness in hearts (4:3, 7).

God does not delight in wickedness. He destroys those who speak lies, the bloodthirsty and the deceitful. God blesses the righteous (5:6, 12).

God rebukes, disciplines, and heals (6:1-2).

God is a righteous God who saves but punishes those who do not repent (7:10-12).

God has made humans responsible for all he created (8:6).

God is a stronghold for the troubled and oppressed (9:9-10) even though he sometimes hides himself in times of trouble (10:1).

God is your rock and redeemer (19:4).

God helps his anointed (20:6).

God's wrath and fire consumes his enemies (21:9).

Sometimes he makes one feel he has forsaken you, but he will rescue you. He is the hope of the poor. He does not hide from you (22:1, 19-26).

God is the shepherd that guides through the rough times (23:1, 4).

All the earth is the LORD's, for he has created everything (24:1-2).

He is the King of glory (24:10).

The LORD is the friend of those who fear him (25:14).

Because God is your light and your salvation you have nothing to fear (27:1).

God repays according to deeds (28:4-5).

God gives strength and peace to his people. He is to be worshiped (29:1, 11).

God's goodness is in abundance for those who fear him and take refuge in him (31:19). God brings happiness by forgiving sin (32:1, 4-5).

God instructs, teaches, and counsels. God frustrates human plans (32:8).

God delivers the righteous and condemns the wicked (34:16-17) even though at times the wicked seem to prevail (35:11-12).

God is a God of steadfast love (36:5) even though God rebukes and disciplines in his anger and wrath (38:1).

God comes to those who patiently wait for him (40:1-2).

God is your strength and refuge, a very present help in times of trouble (46:1).

God ransoms souls from the power of Sheol, the Pit, and he receives souls (49:15).

God is abundant in mercy, cleanses from sin, and teaches wisdom, creating clean hearts (51:1-10).

Only fools say there is no God (53:1).

He is a God of trust (56:11).

God is a mighty fortress, a rock (62:6-7).

He is a forgiving God, a God of awesome deeds, and a God of hope (65:3-5).

He is a God of great power (66:3).

He is a God who tests (66:10).

He is a gracious God who judges with equity (67:1-4).

He is a God of orphans and a protector of widows, a God who leads prisoners to prosperity. He is a God of presence who will shatter all his enemies and give his power and strength to his people (68:5-9, 21, 35).

He is a God who makes us wait. He is a God of the needy and oppressed who revives the hearts of those who seek him (69:3, 32-33).

He is a God of justice and righteousness who defends the cause of the needy and the poor (72:1-4).

He is a good God to the upright and pure in heart (73:1).

God liberates and redeems his people (77:15).

He is an unseen God (77:18).

He is both a compassionate God and a God of wrath (78:38).

He is a jealous God (79:5).

He is the God who set his people free from Egypt (81:10).

He is an everlasting God (90:2).

He is a God of vengeance judging the proud, arrogant, and wicked (94:1-3).

God is the rock of your salvation. He is a great God (95:1-3).

He is a God who hates evil and loves those who hate evil (97:10).

He is a holy God who establishes equity, justice, and righteousness. He is a forgiving God but also an avenger of those who do wrong (99:3-8).

He is a loyal God (100:1).

He is a God of wisdom. He is a God who renews his people (104:24, 30).

He is a God of miracles and wonderful works, and a God who keeps in mind his covenant with his people (105:1-8).

He is a good God whose steadfast love lasts forever (106:1).

God is a teacher (119:33).

God is righteous, and his judgments are right (119:137).

He is an understanding God (136:5).

He is a God who formed us and numbered our days, is omniscient (all knowing), omnipresent (everywhere), and omnipotent (all powerful) (139).

God is king and is gracious, merciful, slow to anger, and abounding in steadfast love (145:1, 8).

He is a God who asks his people to not put their trust in princes who are mortals but to put their trust only in him (146:3).

He is a God who takes pleasure in those who fear him (147:11).

He is a God who made heaven and earth, who keeps faith forever, who executes justice for the oppressed, who gives food to the hungry, who sets the prisoners free, who opens the eyes of the blind, who lifts up the broken, who loves the righteous, who watches over immigrants, who upholds the orphan and the widow, and brings to ruin the wicked (146:5-10).

All through the Psalms he is a God that is to be praised. Praise the LORD!

PROVERBS

The Bible says, The proverbs of Solomon son of David, king of Israel. It is supposedly preserved by the men of Hezekiah (25:1). The precise part Solomon plays in all this is not known. The book of Proverbs consists of sayings, commands, admonitions, and long poems. The sayings are usually two lines in parallel thought based on the idea that the fear of the Lord is the beginning of all wisdom.

With proverbs as in many other parts of the Bible, it is important to appreciate the prominence of poetry in the Bible. The modern world of science and technology does not always grasp or appreciate the aesthetic and non-scientific perspective of the ancient world. Moderns insist on the language of the exact sciences because we tend to perceive reality scientifically. Ancient Israel does not fit that pattern. Its encounter with reality was aesthetic expressing itself in artistic thought patterns and literary forms. Both are valid but different ways of looking at reality.

As in the psalms there are three major types of poetic parallelism. In synonymous parallelism the second half of the line repeats the first half. Antithetic parallelism contrasts ideas. The third type of parallelism called synthetic neither repeats or contrasts the initial idea. It advances it and moves it toward a new thought.

Many of the proverbs are generalizations. They state what is generally true, not what is invariably true or true without exception. Proverbs aims to develop many of the virtues and values that are taught throughout the Bible. It is that which has eternal and lasting value. These virtues and values have developed as a result of lived experience as being in the image of God. They are tried and tested as a result of life experiences.

Proverbs are not legal guarantees from God. They are basic ways to maturity. They must be balanced with others and understood in context and comparison with the rest of Scripture. Many proverbs are poetic, figurative and hyperbolic. It is important to use common sense in interpreting and applying them. Of course, that is what the proverbs are to be, good common sense. Wrongly used they justify a crass, materialistic and legalistic lifestyle. Rightly used they provide good, practical advice.

Wisdom rises from experience, observation, study, and reflection. Wisdom must be learned, thought through, reflected upon, and then applied. Proverbs is a type of text book attempting to teach the wisdom of some basic morality. There are some who think proverbs is an attempt to teach young men who are preparing for government service.

The theme of Proverbs is, the fear of the Lord is the beginning of wisdom. The book begins with a nine chapter poem on the value of wisdom. The book closes with a portrait of the ideal wife that indicates the woman's place is in the home. The only difficulty with the portrait in our times is that for the middle class and below both parents have to work because many of the decent paying jobs have been outsourced, and at minimum wage both parents must work to survive. If you doubt this, do the math on minimum wage and see what it buys for you, and then compare it to your costs. Some also believe that last proverb is somewhat sexist in our times.

On the other hand this writer is not convinced that it is saying the only place for a woman is in the home, for even then women worked in the fields and in the market place as they do today in developing nations. It can be read with the idea that the qualities mentioned are good qualities to have.

Another thought is that when different proverbs say something about a woman, it could also be said about the man and vice versa. For example, when it says, like a gold ring in a pig's snout is a woman without common sense, we could also substitute man for woman. When Proverbs mentions the evils of a loose woman, or an adulteress, it can also apply the same to a man, an adulterer.

Proverbs are wise sayings communicating practical knowledge or insight on right living. The book of Proverbs applies the principles of God's teachings to different aspects of life. The principles correspond to what we today call morality or ethics, both natural and divine revelation. All true morality comes from God whether found in the laws of nature or in divine revelation.

Certain themes keep reoccurring such as respecting parents and teachers, keeping the tongue under control, using words wisely, not being lax in trusting others, being careful about one's friends, avoiding women with loose morals, avoiding excessive wine drinking, keeping company with fools, practicing all the virtues especially humility, prudence, justice, temperance, courage, and obedience. A high point is the personification of wisdom. Wisdom is described as a companion with God from the beginning which will prepare Christians for the revelation of Jesus that he is the wisdom of God in person.

This writer will use the same format for Proverbs that was used in Psalms. A description of each chapter along with certain proverbs chosen by this writer will be given basically in the form given in Scripture. This is so the reader can see what the Scripture says. Also, the following will be used (. . .) to separate some of the proverbs.

As in the psalms hopefully the few brought to the reader's attention will interest one in reading and meditating on all of them. There are so many different proverbs, it is best for the reader to read through them to see which ones stand out. Let us look at some that stand out to this writer.

Chapter 1:1 says, The proverbs of Solomon, son of David, king of Israel: For learning about wisdom and instruction, for understanding words of insight, for gaining instruction in wise dealing, righteousness, justice, and equity; to teach shrewdness to the simple, knowledge and prudence to the young--Let the wise also hear and gain learning, and the discerning acquire skill to understand a proverb and a figure (i.e., a metaphor, parable, or allegory), the words of the wise and their riddles . . . The fear of the LORD is the beginning of knowledge; fools despise wisdom and instruction . . . Hear, my child, your father's instruction, and do not reject your mother's teaching . . . If sinners entice you, do not consent. If they say, Come with us, let us lie in wait for blood; let us wantonly ambush the innocent; we shall find all kinds of costly things; we shall fill our houses with booty; throw in your lot among us; we will all have one purse—my child do not walk in their way. They lie in wait--to kill themselves! And set an ambush—for their own lives! Such is the end for all greedy for gain; It takes away the life of its possessors . . . Wisdom cries out in the street. "How long, O simple ones will you love being simple?" How long will scoffers delight in their scoffing and fools hate knowledge? Give heed to my reproof; I will pour out my thoughts to you. I will make my words made known to you . . . Because they hated knowledge and did not choose the fear of the LORD, would have none of my counsel, and despised all my reproof, therefore they shall eat the fruit of their way and be sated with their own devices. For waywardness kills the simple, and the complacency of fools destroys them; but those who listen to me will be secure and will live at ease, without dread of disaster."

In chapter 2 the writer said on behalf of wisdom, If you accept my words and treasure up my commandments within you making your ear attentive to wisdom, and inclining your heart to understanding; if you indeed cry out for insight and raise your voice for understanding; if you seek it like silver, and search for it as for hidden treasures--then you will understand the fear of the LORD and find the knowledge of God. For the LORD gives wisdom; from his mouth comes knowledge and understanding; he stores up sound wisdom for the upright. He is a shield to those who walk blamelessly, guarding the paths of justice and preserving the way of his faithful ones. Then you will understand righteousness and justice and equity, every good path; for wisdom will come into your heart; and knowledge will be pleasant to your soul. It will save you from the way of evil. You will be saved from the loose woman, from the adulteress with her smooth words, who forsakes the partner of her youth and forgets her sacred covenant; for her way leads down to death. Those who go to her never come back, nor do they regain the paths of life. Therefore walk in the way of the good, and keep to the paths of the just. The wicked will be cut off from the land, and the treacherous will be rooted out of it.

Chapter 3 says, My child, do not forget my teaching, but let your heart keep my commandments . . . Do not let loyalty and faithfulness forsake you; bind them around your neck, write them on the tablet of your heart. So you will find favor and good repute in the sight of God and people . . . Trust in the LORD with all your heart; and do not rely on your own insight . . . Do not be wise in your own eyes; fear the LORD and turn away from evil. It will be a healing for your flesh and refreshment for your body . . . Honor the LORD with your substance and with the first fruits of all your produce, then your barns will be filled . . . Happy are those who find wisdom. Long life is in her right hand; in her left hand are riches and honor. Her ways are the ways of pleasantness, and all her paths are peace. The LORD by wisdom founded the earth, by understanding he established the heavens. Keep sound wisdom and prudence; and they will be life for your soul . . . Do not withhold good from those to whom it is due . . . Do not plan harm against your neighbor . . . Do not quarrel with anyone without cause . . . Do not envy the violent and do not choose any of their ways; for the perverse are an abomination to the LORD . . . To the humble he (God) shows favor . . . The wise will inherit honor, but stubborn fools will inherit disgrace.

In chapter 4 the teacher gives an urgent appeal to acquire wisdom after the example of the teacher who describes life in terms of the two ways: The way of wisdom or the way of the wicked. The beginning of wisdom is this: Get wisdom and whatever else you get, get insight . . . Do not enter the path of the wicked, and do not walk in the way of evil doers. They eat the bread of wickedness and drink the wine of violence . . . Put away from you crooked speech, and put devious talk far from you. Let your eyes look directly forward, and your gaze be straight before you . . . Keep straight the path of your feet, and all your ways will be sure.

Chapter 5 says, Hold on to prudence . . . The lips of a loose woman drip honey, and her speech is smoother than oil; but in the end she is more bitter than wormwood, sharp as a two-edged sword. Do not go near the door of her house, or you will give your honor to others, and your years to the merciless, and strangers will take their fill of your wealth . . . Rejoice in the wife of your youth. May her breasts satisfy you at all times; may you always be intoxicated by her love. Why should you be intoxicated, my son, by another woman and embrace the bosom of an adulteress? For human ways are under the eyes of the LORD, and he examines all their paths . . . The iniquities of the wicked ensnare them, and they are caught in the toils of their sin. They die for lack of discipline, and because of their great folly, they are lost.

In chapter 6 there is a warning about laziness. The writer said, Go to the ant you lazybones. Consider its ways, and be wise. Without having any chief or officer or ruler it prepares its food in summer and gathers its sustenance in harvest. How long will you lie there lazybones. A little sleep, a little slumber, a little folding of the hands to rest, and poverty will come upon you like a robber, and want like an armed warrior . . . A scoundrel and a villain goes around with crooked speech, winking the eyes, shuffling the feet, pointing the fingers, with perverted minds devising evil, continually sowing discord . . . There are six things the LORD hates, seven that are an abomination to him: haughty eyes, a lying tongue, and hands that shed innocent blood, a heart that devises wicked plans, feet that hurry to run to evil, a lying witness who testifies falsely, and one who sows discord in a family . . . Keep your father's commandments and do not forsake your mother's teaching . . . The commandment is a lamp and the teaching a light, and the reproofs of discipline are the way of life, to preserve you from the wife of another, from the smooth tongue of an adulteress . . . He who commits adultery has no sense; but he who does it destroys himself. He will get wounds and dishonor, and his disgrace will not be wiped away. For jealousy arouses a husband's fury, and he shows no restraint when he takes revenge.

In chapter 7 the writer said, Say to wisdom you are my sister, and call insight your intimate friend, that they may keep you from the loose woman. I observed among the youths a young man without sense. A woman comes toward him, decked out like a prostitute, wily of heart. She is loud and wayward; her feet do not stay at home. She seizes him and kisses him. She perfumes her bed and says to him, "Come, let us take our fill of love until morning, for my husband is not at home." With much seductive speech she persuades him; with her smooth talk she compels him. Right away he follows her like an ox going to slaughter. My children, listen to me; do not let your heart turn aside to her ways; do not stray into her paths. Many are those she has laid low, and numerous are her victims. Her house is the way to Sheol, going down to the chambers of death.

In chapter 8 Lady Wisdom pronounces a public address. "To you, O people, I call, and my cry is to all that live. Learn prudence; acquire intelligence, you who lack it. My mouth will utter truth; wickedness is an abomination to my lips. All the words of my mouth are righteous; there is nothing twisted or crooked in them. I, wisdom, live with prudence, and I attain knowledge and discretion. The fear of the LORD is hatred of evil. Pride and arrogance, the way of evil and perverted speech, I hate. I have good advice and sound wisdom. I have insight, I have strength. By me kings reign, and rulers decree what is just; by me rulers rule, and nobles, all who govern rightly. I love those who love me, and those who seek me diligently find me. Riches and honor are with me, enduring wealth and prosperity. The LORD created me at the beginning of his work, the first of his acts of long ago. Ages ago I was set up, at the first, before the beginning of the earth. When there was no depth, I was brought forth. When he established the heavens, I was there. When he marked out the foundation of the earth, then I was beside him, like a master worker; and I was daily his delight, rejoicing before him always, rejoicing in his inhabited world and delighting in the human race. Whoever finds me finds life and obtains favors from the LORD; all who hate me love death." (Christians apply this to the word made flesh who is Jesus. They will say in the NT that Christ is the wisdom of God.)

In chapter 9 Lady Wisdom invites the unwise (called the *simple* in Proverbs) to the banquet of wisdom. She calls the immature to the house of wisdom. "You that are simple, turn in here!" To those without sense she says, "Come, eat of my bread, and drink of the wine I have mixed. Lay aside immaturity, live, and walk in the way of insight." Give instruction to the wise, and they become wiser; teach the righteous and they will gain in learning. The fear of the LORD is the beginning of wisdom, and the knowledge of the Holy One is insight . . . The foolish woman is loud; she is ignorant and knows nothing. Calling to those who pass by, who are going straight on their way, "You who are simple, turn in here!" But they do not know that the dead are there, that her depths are in the depths of Sheol.

Chapter 10 says, the proverbs of Solomon. The following are a few of them: a wise child makes a glad father, but a foolish child is a mother's grief . . . The memory of the righteous is a blessing, but the name of the wicked will rot . . . The wise of heart will heed commandments, but a babbling fool will come to ruin . . . Whoever walks in integrity walks securely, but whoever follows perverse ways will be found out . . . Whoever winks the eye causes trouble, but whoever rebukes boldly makes peace . . . Hatred stirs up strife, but love covers all offenses . . . On the lips of one who has understanding wisdom is found . . . The wage of the righteous leads to life, the gain of the wicked leads to sin . . . Whoever heeds instruction is on the path to life, but one who rejects a rebuke goes astray . . . When words are many, transgression is not lacking, but the prudent are restrained in speech . . . The fear of the LORD prolongs life, but the years of the wicked will be short . . . The way of the LORD is a stronghold for the upright, but destruction for evil doers . . . The mouth of the righteous brings forth wisdom, but the perverse tongue will be cut off.

Chapter 11 says, a false balance is an abomination to the LORD, but an accurate weight is his delight . . . When pride comes, then comes disgrace; but wisdom is with the humble . . . The integrity of the upright guides them, but the crookedness of the treacherous destroys them . . . Riches do not profit in the day of wrath, but righteousness delivers from death . . . When the wicked die their hope perishes, and the expectation of the godless comes to nothing . . . Whoever belittles another lacks sense, but an intelligent person remains silent . . . A gossip goes about telling secrets, but one who is trustworthy in spirit keeps confidence . . . Where there is no guidance, a nation falls, but in an abundance of counselors there is safety . . . Crooked minds are an abomination to the LORD, but those of blameless ways are a delight . . . Like a gold ring in a pig's snout is a beautiful woman without good sense . . . Some give freely, yet grow all the richer; others withhold what is due, and only suffer want . . . Those who trust in riches will wither, but the righteous will flourish like green leaves.

Chapter 12 says, Whoever loves discipline loves knowledge, but those who have to be rebuked are stupid . . . A good wife is the crown of her husband, but she who brings shame is like rottenness in his bones . . . The righteous know the needs of their animals, but the mercy of the wicked is cruel. Fools think their own way is right, but the wise listen to advice . . . Fools show their anger at once, but the prudent ignore an insult . . . Rash words are like sword thrusts, but the tongue of the wise brings healing . . . Deceit is in the mind of those who plan evil, but those who counsel peace have joy . . . The righteous give good advice to friends, but the way of wicked leads astray.

Chapter 13 says, A wise child loves discipline, but a scoffer does not listen to a rebuke . . . Some pretend to be rich but have nothing; others pretend to be poor but have great wealth . . . Wealth hastily gotten will dwindle, but those who gather little by little will increase it . . . Those who despise the word bring destruction on themselves, but those who respect the commandment will be rewarded . . . The clever do all things intelligently, but the fool displays folly . . . Poverty and disgrace are for the one who ignores destruction, but one who heeds reproof is honored . . . Whoever walks with the wise becomes wise, but the companion of fools suffers harm . . . The field of the poor may yield much food, but it is swept away through injustice . . . Those who spare the rod hate their children, but those who love them are diligent to discipline them.Chapter 14 says, A faithful witness does not lie, but a false witness breathes out lies . . . Fools mock at the guilt offering (for sin), but the upright enjoy God's favor . . . There is a way that seems right to a person, but its end is the way of death . . . The simple believe everything, but the clever consider their steps . . . The wise are cautious and turn away from evil, but the fool throws off restraint and is careless . . . The poor are disliked even by their neighbors, but the rich have many friends . . . Those who despise their neighbors are sinners, but happy are those who are kind to the poor . . . In all toil there is profit, but mere talk leads only to poverty . . . Whoever is slow to anger has great understanding, but one who has a hasty temper exalts folly . . . Those who oppress the poor insult their Maker, but those who are kind to the needy honor him . . . Righteousness exalts a nation, but sin is a reproach.

Chapter 15 continues the proverbial sayings. A soft answer turns away wrath, but a harsh word stirs up anger . . . The eyes of the LORD are in every place, keeping watch on the evil and the good . . . The sacrifice (worship) of the wicked is an abomination to the LORD, but the prayer of the upright is his delight . . . Better is a dinner of vegetables where love is than a fatted ox and hatred with it . . . Those who are hot tempered stir up strife, but those who are slow to anger calm contention . . . The LORD tears down the house of the proud, but maintains the widow's boundaries . . . Those who are greedy for unjust gain make trouble for their households, but those who hate bribes will live . . . The fear of the LORD is instruction in wisdom, and humility goes before honor.

Chapter 16 says, The plans of the mind belong to mortals, but the answer of the tongue is from the LORD . . . All one's ways may be pure in one's own eyes, but the LORD weighs the spirit . . . Commit your work to the LORD, and your plans will be established . . . All those who are arrogant are an abomination to the LORD . . . When the ways of people please the LORD, he causes even their enemies to be at peace with them . . . The human mind plans the way, but the LORD directs the steps . . . How much better it is to get wisdom than gold . . . Pride goes before destruction, and a haughty spirit before a fall . . . Sometimes there seems to be a way that is right, but in the end it is the way of death . . . A perverse person spreads strife, and a whisperer separates close friends . . . The violent entice their neighbors and lead them in a way that is not good . . . One who winks the eyes plans perverse things . . . Grey hair is a crown of glory; it is gained in a righteous life.

Chapter 17 says, Better is a dry morsel with quiet than a house full of feasting with strife . . . Those who mock the poor insult their maker . . . Grandchildren are the crown of the aged, and the glory of children is their parents . . . One who forgives an affront fosters friendship, but one who dwells on disputes will alienate a friend . . . Evil will not depart from the house of one who returns evil for good . . . A friend loves at all times, and kinsfolk are born to share adversity . . . The one who begets a fool gets trouble; the parent of a fool has no joy . . . A cheerful heart is good medicine, but a downcast spirit dries up the bones . . . The wicked accept a concealed bribe to pervert the way of justice . . . Foolish children are a grief to their father and bitterness to her who bore them.

Chapter 18 says, A fool takes no pleasure in understanding but only in expressing personal opinion . . . Before destruction one's heart is haughty, but humility goes before honor . . . If one gives answer before hearing, it is folly and shame . . . A gift opens doors; it gives access to the great . . . The one who first states a case seems right until the other comes and cross examines . . . He who finds a wife finds a good thing and obtains favor from the LORD . . . Some friends play at friendship, but a true friend sticks closer than one's nearest kin.

Chapter 19 says, Better the poor walking in poverty than one perverse of speech who is a fool . . . Desire without knowledge is not good, and one who moves too hurriedly misses the way . . . To get wisdom is to love oneself; to get understanding is to prosper . . . A stupid child is ruin to a father, and a wife's quarreling is a continual dripping of rain . . . House and wealth are inherited from parents, but a prudent wife is from the LORD . . . Whoever is kind to the poor lends to the LORD and will be paid in full . . . Discipline your children while there is hope; do not set your heart on their destruction . . . A violent tempered person will pay the penalty . . . What is desirable in a person is loyalty . . . Those who do violence to their father and chase away their mother are children who cause shame and bring reproach.

Chapter 20 says, Wine is a mocker, strong drink a brawler, and whoever is led astray by it is not wise . . . It is honorable to refrain from strife, but every fool is quick to quarrel . . . The purposes in the human mind are like deep water, but the intelligent will draw them out . . . Many proclaim themselves loyal, but who can find one trustworthy . . . The righteous walk in integrity--happy are the children who follow them . . . who can say I have made my heart clean that I am pure from sin . . . Do not love sleep; or else you will come to poverty . . . A gossip reveals secrets; therefore do not associate with a babbler . . . Do not say, I will repay evil; wait for the LORD, and he will help you . . . All our steps are ordered by the LORD; how then can we understand our own ways . . . The human spirit is the lamp of the LORD, searching every innermost part . . . The glory of youth is their strength, but the beauty of the aged is their gray hair.

Chapter 21 says, All deeds are right in the sight of the doer, but the LORD weighs the heart . . . To do righteousness and justice is more acceptable to the LORD than sacrifice . . . Haughty eyes and a proud heart, the lamp of the wicked--are sin . . . The violence of the wicked will sweep them away because they refuse to do what is just . . . It is better live in a corner of the housetop than in a house shared by a contentious wife . . . If you close your ear to the cry of the poor, you will cry out and not be heard . . . When justice is done, it is a joy to the righteous but dismay to evil doers. Whoever pursues righteousness and kindness will find life and honor . . . To watch over mouth and tongue is to keep out of trouble . . . All day long the wicked covet but the righteous give and do not hold back . . . The horse is made ready for the day of battle, but victory belongs to the LORD.

Chapter 22 says, A good name is to be chosen rather than riches . . . Train children in the right way, and when they are old, they will not stray . . . The rich rules over the poor, and the borrower is the slave to the lender . . . Those who have a poor heart and are gracious in speech will have the king as a friend . . . Those who are generous are blessed, for they share their bread with the poor . . . Oppressing the poor in order to enrich oneself, and giving to the rich will lead only to loss . . . Do not rob the poor because they are poor, or crush the afflicted, for the LORD pleads their cause . . . Do not associate with hotheads, or you may learn their ways and entangle yourself in a snare . . . Do you see those who are skillful at work? They will serve kings; they will not serve common people.

Chapter 23 says, When you sit down to eat with a ruler, observe carefully what is before you, and put a knife to your throat if you have a big appetite . . . Do not desire the ruler's delicacies, for they are deceptive food . . . Do not wear yourself out to get rich; be wise enough to desist . . . Do not eat the bread of the stingy; do not desire their delicacies; for like a hair in the throat, so are they. Eat and drink they say to you; but they do not mean it . . . Do not speak in the hearing of a fool, who will only despise the wisdom of your words . . . Do not let your heart envy sinners, but always continue in the fear of the LORD . . . Let your father and mother be glad; let her who bore you rejoice . . . My child, give me your heart, and let your heart observe my ways . . . Do not look at wine when it is red, when it sparkles and goes down smoothly. At the last it bites like a serpent. Your eyes will see strange things, and your mind utter perverse things.

Chapter 24 says, By wisdom a house is built, and by understanding it is established; by knowledge the rooms are filled with all precious and pleasant riches . . . Know that wisdom is such to your soul; if you find it, you will find a future . . . Do not rejoice when your enemies fall, or else the LORD will see it and be displeased, and turn away his anger from them . . . Partiality in judging is not good . . . Whoever says to the wicked, "You are innocent," will be cursed by peoples, abhorred by nations; but those who rebuke the wicked will have delight, and a good blessing will come upon them . . . Do not say, "I will do to others as they have done to me; I will pay them back for what they have done."

Chapter 25 says, These are other proverbs of Solomon that the officials of King Hezekiah of Judah copied. With patience a ruler may be persuaded, and a soft tongue can break bones . . . If you have found honey, eat only enough for you, or else having too much, you will vomit it . . . Let your foot be seldom in your neighbor's house, otherwise the neighbor will become weary of you and hate you . . . Like a war club, a sword, or a sharp arrow is one who bears false witness against a neighbor . . . Like a bad tooth is trust in a faithless person in time of trouble . . . If your enemies are hungry, give them bread to eat; and if they are thirsty, give them water to drink; for you will heap coals of fire on their heads, and the LORD will reward you . . . It is not good to eat much honey or seek honor on top of honor . . . Like a city breached without walls is one who lacks self-control.

Chapter 26 says, Do not answer fools according to their folly, or you will be a fool yourself. Answer fools according to their folly, or they will be wise in their own eyes . . . Like somebody who takes a passing dog by the ears is one who meddles in the quarrel of another . . . Like a maniac who shoots deadly arrows, so is one who deceives a neighbor and says, I was only joking . . . The words of a whisperer are like delicious morsels; they go down into the inner parts of the body . . . A lying tongue hates its victims, and a flattering mouth works ruin . . . Like the glaze covering an earthen vessel are smooth lips with an evil heart . . . Whoever digs a pit will fall into it, and a stone will come back on the one who starts it rolling.

Chapter 27 says, Do not boast about tomorrow, for you do not know what a day may bring . . . Let another praise you, and not your own mouth—a stranger, and not your own lips . . . Wrath is cruel, anger is overwhelming, but who is able to stand before jealousy . . . The clever see danger and hide, but the simple go on, and suffer for it . . . A continual dripping on a rainy day and a contentious wife are alike . . . Riches do not last forever, nor a crown for all generations . . . Sheol and Abaddon are never satisfied, and human eyes are never satisfied . . . The crucible is for silver and the furnace is for gold, so a person is tested by being praised.

Chapter 28 says, A ruler who oppresses the poor is a beating rain who leaves no food . . . The evil do not understand justice, but those who seek the LORD understand it completely . . . Better to be poor and walk in integrity than to be crooked in one's ways even though rich . . . When the righteous triumph, there is great glory, but when the wicked prevail, people go into hiding . . . Like a roaring lion or a charging bear is a wicked ruler over a poor people. A ruler who lacks understanding is a cruel oppressor, but one who hates unjust gain will enjoy a long life . . . The greedy person stirs up strife, but whoever trusts in the LORD will be enriched . . . Those who trust in their own wits are fools, but those who walk in wisdom come through safely . . . Whoever gives to the poor will lack nothing.

Chapter 29 says, One who is often reproved, yet remains stubborn, will suddenly be broken beyond healing . . . By justice a king gives stability to the land, but one who makes heavy exactions ruins it . . . The righteous know the rights of the poor; the wicked have no such understanding . . . The bloodthirsty hate the blameless, and they seek the life of the upright . . . A fool gives full vent to anger, but the wise quietly hold it back . . . If a ruler listens to falsehood, all his officials will be wicked. If a king judges the poor with equity, his throne will be established forever . . . When the wicked are in authority transgressions increase, but the righteous will look upon their downfall . . . Where there is no prophecy, the people cast off restraint, but happy are those who keep the law . . . Do you see someone who is hasty in speech? There is more hope for a fool than for anyone like that . . . Many seek the favor of a ruler, but it is from the LORD that one gets justice.

Chapter 30 relays the words of Agur, son of Jakeh. I am weary, O God, how can I prevail. Surely I am too stupid to be human. I do not have human understanding. I have not learned wisdom, nor have I knowledge of the holy ones . . . Every word of God proves true; he is a shield to those who take refuge in him. Do not add to his words or else he will rebuke you, and you will be found a liar . . . Give me neither poverty nor riches; feed me with the food that I need . . . This is the way of the adulteress: she eats, and wipes her mouth, and says, I have done no wrong . . . Four things on earth are small, yet they are exceedingly wise: the ants are a people without strength, yet they provide their own food in the summer; the badgers are a people without power, yet they make their home in the rocks; the locusts have no king, yet all of them march in rank; the lizard can be grasped by the hand, yet it is found in king's palaces.

Chapter 31 says these are the words of King Lemuel. An oracle that his mother taught him: Do not let the ways of women and strong drink destroy you . . . Speak out for those who can not speak, for the rights of all the destitute . . . Speak out, judge righteously, and defend the right of the poor and needy . . . A capable wife who can find? She is far more precious than jewels. The heart of her husband trusts her, and he will have no lack of gain. She does him good, and not harm, all the days of her life. She rises while it is still night and provides food for her household. She seeks wool and flax and works with willing hands. She puts her hands to the distaff, and her hands hold the spindle. She opens her hands to the poor, and reaches out her hands to the needy. She makes linen garments and sells them. Strength and dignity are her clothing. She opens her mouth with wisdom and the teaching of kindness is on her tongue. Her children rise up and call her happy; her husband too, and he praises her. "Many women have done excellently, but you surpass them all." Charm is deceitful, and beauty is vain, but a woman who fears the LORD is to be praised. Give her a share in the fruit of her hands, and let her works praise her.

This ends the book of Proverbs. A meaningful exercise is for the reader to go through the different proverbs and write down the ones that stand out personally. This writer believes that modern people would do well to read through Proverbs along with the Ten Commandments, Sirach (Ecclesiasticus), and the Wisdom of Solomon as a beginning foundation for morality/ethics. They certainly do not touch all there is to deal with, but they do give one a good foundation from which to develop further thinking. Second, the process that produces the proverbs may be more significant than the content, for it teaches us the importance of serious reflection on experience, the use of reason, and the need to be pragmatic. Third, instead of making the different proverbs absolute laws, look for the virtues, values and vision contained within the proverbs. This is their lasting value.

THE LATTER PROPHETS

This section includes both the four major prophets of Isaiah, Jeremiah and Lamentations, Ezekiel, and Daniel. Lamentations is usually included with Jeremiah. In the Hebrew Bible Daniel is not considered one of the prophets but is included in the Writings as is Lamentations. Included also are the Minor Prophets that the Hebrew Bible calls the Book of the Twelve. They include Hosea, Joel, Amos, Obadiah, Jonah, Micah, Nahum, Habakkuk, Zephaniah, Haggai, and Malachi.

As the reader goes through the Prophets, it is important to understand that the idols of modern day people are more than wood and stone which were the major idols in the time of the Prophets. Modern day idols are things like profits, wealth, power, pleasure, leisure, sex, sports, technology, our nation, our ego, our special interests or anything that hinders us from making God and his priorities first in our lives.

THE MAJOR PROPHETS

Jewish scholarship uses the term Former Prophets for Joshua through 2 Kings and Latter Prophets for Isaiah through Malachi. Christian scholarship uses the term History for what the Jews call the Former Prophets. Christian scholarship uses the term Major and Minor for the Prophets. Christians have four major prophets and twelve minor prophets. They are Isaiah, Jeremiah, Ezekiel, and Daniel. Jewish scholarship includes Isaiah, Jeremiah, and Ezekiel but Daniel is placed in what they call their Writings. What Christian scholarship calls the minor prophets where each is listed separately, Jewish scholarship unites them into The Book of the Twelve. Christians use the terms major and minor only because of the length of the books; major and minor have nothing to do with the importance of the book.

Islam has basically the same message of the prophets as Judaism and Christianity, but all the prophets are not mentioned in the Qur'an. Their primary purpose is condemning idols. They never discuss any sacrifice or atonement for sin, for to them it is not necessary, and they rarely mention the exile. The fact that the Jews and Christians have to suffer is a sign of divine rejection. The Qur'an does not have the long development found in the Bible explaining that suffering may be a temporal chastisement sent by God to bring his people back to the right way. For Muslims God offers knowledge and guidance through the prophets; he does not offer atonement or even an imminent indwelling relationship.

The Qur'an deals with the prophets basically as it deals with most of the biblical characters. There is very little historical narration. For Muslims the Qur'an is an inspired book used for meditation and recitation and used as a type of commentary. Much of the time the material is out of context as far as the pure OT is concerned, but for Muslims that is no problem; the Qur'an assumes knowledge of the basic OT background.

In the OT Scriptures a prophet basically is one who speaks for God. Prophets are more forth tellers than they are foretellers, and contrary to popular Christian fundamentalism, they do not tell us everything we want to know about the end times. God calls the prophets primarily to speak to their current religious, political, economic, social, and cultural situation, and most of their foretelling is to the near future in the times in which they lived. The basic message to God's people is, if they do not repent and change their ways as a nation, God will punish the nation in order to bring it back to him. It is also important to understand that when the prophets use the word justice, it is primarily in reference to what we moderns call social justice.

The major exceptions are the times some of the prophets spoke of the coming of a future anointed which is translated as the Messiah in Hebrew or the Christ in Greek, and the few times a final end is mentioned. When one does not understand the primary purpose of the biblical prophets, the original purpose of the books is distorted. This is the issue with a number of current works such as the popular Left Behind series.

Much of modern scholarship in Jewish, Protestant, Roman Catholic, and Eastern Orthodox is in agreement that only a very small percentage of the OT is messianic, and even though a little more is referenced to the new covenant age, it is still a small percentage. Very little is in reference to things to come at the end times. It is also interesting to note that much of the writings of the prophets is written in poetry. Because of that, one must be careful of what is interpreted as literal.

The main role of a biblical prophet is to proclaim God's word, and call the people back from sin and rebellion to the obedience of God's teachings. Because there is much idolatry, the prophets are trying to make sure the nation preserves the one God idea. Their effort is to save monotheism which is the worship of the one God, who is called Yahweh, and bring the people back to him. The prophets are covenant enforcers reminding the people of God's covenant where God said he would bless the nation's obedience and curse their disobedience.

The blessings and curses pronounced by the prophets are not original, for they go back to the Deuteronomic historians and the book of Deuteronomy which contains the original Mosaic covenant warnings and promises. Most importantly the blessings and curses are meant primarily for the nation. They are not primarily used to tell individuals that if they follow God he will individually bless them with riches, as some Christians of the so called prosperity gospel, constantly use the blessings. It is indicated in a few verses that if one follows the ways of God, things will generally go well, but good interpretive principles do not make even that as a hard and fast rule.

It is important to understand that the message of the prophets is not their own; it is from God. The prophets are God's direct representatives who then put his message in their words using their own creative literary skills. Since these prophecies are spoken within a certain context of history, the more we understand that history, the more we will understand the prophecies. It is when authors do not really understand the historical context, that the prophecies are misunderstood and transposed into the wrong time era.

For each prophet there will be an introduction. In that introduction there will be an attempt to highlight the main characteristics of each prophet in order to illustrate what makes each prophet standout from the others. If the reader does not plan to read the whole book at this time, it would be a good idea to look up the verses listed in the introduction of each book. The verses listed will give the reader a good feel for the book.

It must also be remembered that much of the prophets is written in poetry. This writer will stay with the original goal of helping the reader understand basic content but encourages all readers to read the prophets and experience the poetry of the prophets.

ISAIAH

Isaiah spans a period of time from 740 - 420 B.C. or later. Isaiah himself prophesied between 740-701 B.C. The rest of his book is written by his disciples. The call of Isaiah (6:1-9) stresses the holiness of God where Isaiah realizes how unclean or unholy he is. God touches him and cleanses him and asks who he should send? Isaiah answered, "Here am I, send me."

Then in chapter 9 Isaiah talks about the coming of one from David's throne who will be the Prince of Peace, a Wonderful Counselor, who is given the kingdom. He will establish and uphold it with justice and with righteousness, and there will be endless peace.

Isaiah tells us in (40:1-11) that one will be called from the desert to prepare the way. Christians will say this is John the Baptizer. In chapters 40-66 a suffering servant is presented who the Jews believe stands for them as a nation, but who Christians believe represents the Messiah to come (42:1-4; 49:1-17; 50:4-9; 52:13-53:12). For Christians Christ is the suffering servant, but the Jews believe it represents them as a people.

In Isaiah 31:1 as in most of the prophets, God will say he opposes those who put their trust in the materials that make for war. Isaiah tells the kings to stay out of military alliances. They do not pay attention and will pay the price when the Babylonians destroy Jerusalem and the temple in 586-87 B.C. and take the people into exile in Babylon.

Their fundamental sin is a failure to trust in God and his teachings, and this leads to the vices that Isaiah sees both in individuals and the nation. We learn that because God is holy and just, he punishes his people with the goal of correcting and returning them to him as his holy people. Only a few will respond. A remnant of loyal people will be saved and brought back to Jerusalem to rebuild the temple in the *Day of the LORD*.

God's people will return from Babylon as a new creation. The term Day of the LORD is not used for only one time span but is used for different times and events even though there will be a final Day of the LORD. The Day of the LORD usually means a time of judgment and new creation at different times in history.

In 7:14 Isaiah informs King Ahaz that a child will be born of a young woman. The Hebrew language translates it as young woman, but the gospel writer Matthew translates it from the Geek Septuagint as a virgin. The child will be named Immanuel, meaning God with us. These verses are used to fulfill a prophecy in the time of Isaiah and Ahaz. The NT writers will use it as a prophecy for the birth of Christ. Scholars call this the full sense of Scripture or the *sensus plenoir*. It means that for a passage of Scripture there is more than one use or fulfillment of prophecy.

The book of Isaiah also has numerous passages pointing to a Messiah. Many are found in chapters 6-12. Also, the following point to a new and glorious age (3:13-26, 5:8-9, 9:1-6, 10:1-4, 11:1-6, 25:7-8, 55:6-11). It is important to remember that in Isaiah, as well as some of the other prophets the writings are not necessarily sequenced which sometimes can be confusing.

The name Isaiah means the salvation of Yahweh. He prophesies approximately seven hundred years before Christ at a time when religion is popular but not pleasing to God. Worship at the temple has become a mere formality. The nation as a whole has become corrupt. Those with power and wealth are oppressing the peasants, so Isaiah challenges the powers of society both religious and political.

Tradition says Isaiah died by being sawed in half by King Manasseh; Hebrews 11:37 hints at that possibility. Isaiah lives in Jerusalem and is called by God in the year of King Uzziah's death in 740 B.C. He prophesies at least forty years through the reigns of Jothan, Ahaz, one of Judah's worst kings, and Hezekiah who brought religious reform.

It is very possible that he prophesies to the early reign of King Manasseh who is Judah's most evil king. Most of the time Isaiah concentrates on prophesying in Jerusalem while the prophet Micah begins his prophesy about the same time concentrating on the villages and small towns. In the meantime Amos and Hosea are prophesying in the northern kingdom.

Most scholars see three books or at least three different eras in Isaiah. Only chapters 1-39 can be assigned to Isaiah's time. Chapters 40-66 come from the time of Cyrus of Persia (539 B.C. and later), and they are usually divided from 40-56, then 56-66 where the setting is Judah, and work on rebuilding the temple begins.

Chapter 1 begins with Isaiah's vision concerning Judah and Jerusalem in the days of Uzziah, Jotham, Ahaz, and Hezkiah, kings of Judah. God looks within the nation and sees a broken covenant. In verse 2 God says, I reared children and brought them up, but they have rebelled against me. In (4-5) he says, Ah, sinful nation, people laden with iniquity, offspring who do evil, children who deal corruptly, who have forsaken the LORD, who have despised the Holy One of Israel, who are utterly estranged! Why do you seek further beatings? Why do you continue to rebel? The whole head is sick, and the whole heart faint.

Verses 10-14 say, Hear the word of the LORD, you rulers of Sodom! Listen to the teachings of our God, you people of Gomorrah! What to me is the multitude of your sacrifices? Says the LORD; I have had enough of burnt offerings of rams and the fat of fed beasts; I do not delight in the blood of bulls, or of lambs, or of goats . . . Trample my courts no more; bringing offerings is futile; . . . I can not endure solemn assemblies with iniquity. Your new moons and your appointed festivals my soul hates; they have become a burden to me, I am weary of bearing them.

Verses 15-20 say, I will not listen; your hands are full of blood. Wash yourselves; make yourself clean; remove the evil of your doings from before my eyes; cease to do evil, learn to do good, seek justice, rescue the oppressed, defend the orphan, plead for the widow. (As usual the orphan and the widow represent the suffering and those in need.)

Come now, let us argue it out, says the LORD: though your sins are like scarlet, they shall be like snow; though they are red like crimson, they shall become like wool. If you are willing and obedient, you shall eat the good of the land; but if you refuse and rebel, you shall be devoured by the sword; for the mouth of the LORD has spoken.

In verse 21 Isaiah says, the faithful city has become a whore! She that was full of justice, righteousness lodged in her--but now murderers! In (23-24) he says, Your princes are rebels and companions of thieves. Everyone loves a bribe and runs after gifts. They do not defend the orphan, and the widow's cause does not come before them.

Therefore says the Sovereign, the LORD of hosts, the Mighty One of Israel: Ah, I will pour out my wrath on my enemies, and avenge myself on my foes! Verses 27-28 say, Zion shall be redeemed by justice and those in her who repent, by righteousness. But rebels and sinners shall be destroyed together, and those who forsake the LORD shall be consumed.

The theme of the prophets is Covenant-Judgment-Redemption. God made a covenant with his people. When they break the covenant, God judges them, then after judgment, God offers the hope of redemption.

In chapter 2 he offers hope. Verses 2-3 say, In the days to come the mountain of the LORD's house shall be established as the highest of the mountains, and shall be raised above the hills; all the nations shall stream to it. Many peoples shall come and say, "Come, let us go up to the mountain of the LORD, to the house of the God of Jacob; that he may teach us his ways and that we may walk in his paths." For out of Zion will go forth instruction, and the word of the LORD from Jerusalem.

Verses 4-6 say, He shall judge between the nations, and shall arbitrate for many peoples; They shall beat their swords into plowshares, and their spears into pruning hooks; nation shall not lift up sword against nation; neither shall they learn war anymore. O house of Jacob, come, let us walk in the light of the LORD! For you have forsaken the ways of your people, O house of Jacob. Indeed they are full of diviners from the east and of soothsayers like the Philistines, and they clasp hands with foreigners.

Verses 7-8 say, Their land is filled with silver and gold, and there is no end to their treasures; their land is filled with horses, and there is no end to their chariots. (Horses and chariots were the means to war.) Their land is filled with idols; they bow down to the work of their hands, to what their own fingers have made. (Arrogance is the root of idolatry.)

In verses 11-17 he says, The haughty eyes of people shall be brought low, and the pride of everyone shall be humbled; and the LORD alone shall be exalted in that day. For the LORD of hosts has a day against all that is proud and lofty, against all that is lifted up and high . . . The haughtiness of people shall be humbled, and the pride of everyone shall be brought low; and the LORD alone will be exalted on that day. (In Scripture the Day of the LORD is a day of judgment and retribution and a day where justice is established.)

In 3:8-9 Isaiah says, Jerusalem has stumbled and Judah has fallen because their speech and their deeds are against the LORD, defying his glorious presence. The look on their faces bears witness against them; they proclaim their sin like Sodom; they do not hide it. Woe to them! For they have brought evil on themselves. Verses 12 -15 say, your leaders mislead you, and confuse the course of your paths. The LORD rises to argue his case; he stands to judge the peoples. The LORD enters into judgment with the elders of the people: it is you who have devoured the vineyard; the spoil of the poor is in your houses. What do you mean by crushing my people, by grinding the face of the poor? says the Lord GOD of hosts. (This is God's case against his people.)

In verses 18-26 he tells them in that day the haughty, arrogant women and their riches will amount to nothing. Instead of perfume there will be stench; . . . instead of well-set hair, baldness; . . . instead of beauty, shame. Your men shall fall by the sword and your warriors in battle.

But in chapter 4 hope is given. Chapter 4:2-4 says, On that day the branch of the LORD shall be beautiful and glorious, and the fruit of the land shall be the pride and glory of the survivors of Israel. (The word branch usually is a messianic term.) Whoever is left in Zion and remains in Jerusalem will be called holy, everyone who has been recorded for life in Jerusalem, once the LORD has washed away the filth of the daughters of Zion and cleansed the bloodstains of Jerusalem from its midst by a spirit of judgment and by a spirit of burning.

Chapter 5:1-7 is the song of the unfruitful vineyard representing the nation of Israel for whom God did so much. The people's sin is ingratitude, taking their blessings for granted and using them selfishly. Instead of serving God and each other, they serve themselves, and the result is a corrupted nation. Verses 6-7 say, I will make it a waste; it shall not be pruned or hoed, and it shall be overgrown with briars and thorns; I will also command the clouds that they rain no rain upon it. For the vineyard of the LORD of hosts is the house of Israel, and the people of Judah are his pleasant planting; he (God) expected justice, but saw bloodshed; righteousness but heard a cry!

In verse 9 Isaiah says, The LORD of hosts has sworn in my hearing: surely many houses shall be desolate, large and beautiful houses without inhabitant. Verses 11-13 say, Ah, you who rise early in the morning in pursuit of strong drink, who linger in the evening to be inflamed by wine, whose feasts consist of lyre and harp, tambourine and flute and wine, but who do not regard the deeds of the LORD, or see the work of his hands! Therefore my people go into exile without knowledge; their nobles are dying of hunger, and their multitude is parched with thirst. (God's people are not acting with God's righteousness and justice; therefore they will be punished.)

Verses 20-25 say, Ah, you who call evil good and good evil, who put darkness for light and light for darkness, who put bitter for sweet and sweet for bitter! Ah, you who are wise in your own eyes, and shrewd in your own sight! Ah, you who are heroes in drinking wine, and valiant at mixing drink, who acquit the guilty for a bribe and deprive the innocent of their rights! . . . they have rejected the instruction of the LORD of hosts, and despised the word of the Holy One of Israel. Therefore the anger of the LORD is kindled against his people, . . . Verse 26 says, He will raise a signal for a nation far away, and whistle for a people at the ends of the earth; Here they come, swiftly, speedily!

Chapter 6:1-3 says, In the year that King Uzziah died, I saw the LORD sitting on the throne, high and lofty; and the hem of his robe filled the temple. Seraphs were in attendance above him; . . . And one called to another and said, "Holy, holy, holy is the LORD of hosts; the whole earth is full of his glory."

In verses 5-10 Isaiah says, "Woe is me! I am lost, for I am a man of unclean lips, and I live among people of unclean lips; yet my eyes have seen the King, the LORD of hosts!" Then one of the seraphs flew to me, holding a live coal that had been taken from the altar with a pair of tongs. The seraph touched my mouth with it and said: "Now that this has touched your lips, your guilt has departed and your sin is blotted out." Then I heard the voice of the LORD saying, "Whom shall I send, and who will go for us?" And I said, "Here am I, send me!" and he said, "Go and say to this people: 'Keep listening, but do not comprehend; keep looking, but do not understand.' Make the mind of this people dull, and stop their ears, and shut their eyes, so that they may not look with their eyes, and listen with their ears, and comprehend with their minds, and turn and be healed." Then I said, "How long, O LORD?" And he said: "Until cities lie waste without inhabitant, and houses without people, and the land is utterly desolate . . ."

Isaiah is being told to take God's message to the people, and keep repeating it. He is also being told that the people will be tired of hearing it and will not respond, but he is to keep repeating it.

Chapter 7 takes the reader to the days of Ahaz, king of Judah. King Rezin of Aram (Syria) along with King Pekah of Israel joined to attack King Ahaz. Verses 3-4 say, Then the LORD said to Isaiah, Go out to meet Ahaz, . . . and say to him, Take heed, be quiet, do not fear, and do not let your heart be faint . . . Verses 10-13 say, Again the LORD spoke to Ahaz, saying, Ask a sign of the LORD your God; let it be deep as Sheol or high as heaven. But Ahaz said, I will not ask, and I will not put the LORD to the test. (His desire was to trust Assyria to help him instead of God.)

Isaiah in (13-17) says, "Hear then, O house of David! Is it too little for you to weary mortals, that you weary my God also? Therefore the LORD himself will give you a sign. Look, the young woman is with child and shall bear a son, and shall name him Immanuel. He shall eat curds and honey by the time he knows how to refuse evil and choose the good. For before the child knows how to refuse the evil and choose the good, the land before whose two kings you are in dread will be deserted. The LORD will bring on you and on your people . . . the king of Assyria."

The immediate fulfillment of this verse is probably a reference to Hezekiah, a son that will soon be born to him. God will bring unto them the king of Assyria. Soon what Isaiah foretold will come to pass as the first fulfillment of prophecy. Matthew in his gospel will use this passage to also be a foretelling of the virgin, Mary, bringing forth the Christ and his kingdom as a double fulfillment of this verse according to Christians.

In chapter 8 the prophet has another child who becomes a living sign that the Assyrians will plunder Syria and Israel. Unlike Immanuel, this child is explicitly to be the prophet's son, even though the prophet's prediction is similar. In (3) Isaiah's wife is called a prophetess. (There are those who believe this son of Isaiah and his wife was the son Isaiah was referring to in 7:13-17, but it is a small minority group.) Verses 16-18 say, Bind up the testimony, seal the teaching among my disciples. I will wait for the LORD, who is hiding his face from the house of Jacob, and I will hope in him. See I and the children whom the LORD has given me are signs and portents in Israel from the LORD of hosts, who dwells on Mount Zion.

In chapter 9:1 another Messianic prophecy is made saying, But there will be no gloom for those who were in anguish. In the former time he brought into contempt the land of Zebulun and the land of Naphtali, but in the latter time he will make glorious the way of the sea, the land beyond the Jordan, Galilee of the nations. Isaiah gives hope in (2) by saying, The people who walked in darkness have seen a great light; those who lived in a land of deep darkness--on them light has shined.

The two cities of Galilee in the time of Ahaz will be the first to be destroyed by Assyria, and then later be the first to see the light of the Messiah. The NT writer Matthew has Jesus beginning his ministry in this area (see Matt 4:12-17).

Verses 6-7 say, For a child has been born for us, a son given us; authority rests on his shoulders; and he is named Wonderful Counselor, Mighty God, Everlasting Father and Prince of Peace. His authority shall grow continually, and there shall be endless peace for the throne of David and his kingdom. He will establish and uphold it with justice and with righteousness from this time onward and forever more. The zeal of the LORD of hosts will do this. (These verses will be used by Christians to refer to Christ.)

Then in the rest of chapters 9 and 10 beginning with 9:8, The LORD sends a word against Jacob, and it falls on Israel. But because of pride and arrogance they ignore his word, so (11) says, the LORD raised adversaries against them, and stirred up their enemies, the Arameans on the east and the Philistines on the west, and they devoured Israel with open mouth. Verses 15-17 say, elders and dignitaries are the head, and prophets who teach lies are the tail; for those who led this people led them astray, and those who were led by them were left in confusion . . . for everyone was godless and an evil doer, and every mouth spoke folly.

Chapter 10:1-4 says, Ah, you who make iniquitous decrees, who write oppressive statutes, to turn aside the needy from justice and to rob the poor of my people their right, that widows may be your spoil, and that you may make the orphans your prey! (Keep in mind in Scripture orphans and widows always stand for the powerless and the have-nots.)

What will you do on the day of punishment, in the calamity that will come from far away? To whom will you flee for help, and where will you leave your wealth, so as not to crouch among the prisoners or fall among the slain? For all this his anger has not turned away; his hand is stretched out still. In verse 5 he tells them, that he will send Assyria against this godless nation, and in (18) Isaiah said, the LORD will destroy both soul and body, and it will be as an invalid wastes away. But again hope is offered. Verse 21 says, A remnant will return, the remnant of Jacob, to the mighty God.

The Scriptures always lay out hope after judgment. It is not God's desire that punishment comes, but God is holy love and will not and can not let sin go as though it never happened. That would not be justice. He simply allows people to experience the consequences of their actions. Even so, hope is always held out in the form of repentance and change and the coming of the Messiah.

In chapter 11:1-6 hope is again offered through a messianic prophecy. Isaiah says, A shoot shall come out from the stump of Jesse (King David's father), and a branch shall grow out of his roots. The spirit of the LORD shall rest on him, the spirit of wisdom and understanding, the spirit of counsel and might, the spirit of knowledge and the fear of the LORD. His delight shall be in the fear of the LORD. He shall not judge by what his eyes see, or decide by what his ears hear; but with righteousness he shall judge the poor, and with equity for the meek of the earth; he shall strike the earth with the rod of his mouth, and with the breath of his lips he shall kill the wicked. Righteousness shall be the belt around his waist and faithfulness the belt around his loins. The wolf shall live with the lamb; the leopard shall be down with the kid, the calf and the lion and the fatling together, and a little child shall lead them.

Verses 10-12 say, On that day the root of Jesse shall stand as a signal to the peoples; the nations shall inquire of him, and his dwelling shall be glorious. On that day the LORD will extend his hand yet a second time to recover the remnant that is left from his people . . . He will raise a signal for the nations, and will assemble the outcasts of Israel, and gather the dispersed of Judah from the four corners of the earth.

Chapter 12:1-6 a psalm of thanksgiving says, You will say in that day: I will give thanks to you, O LORD, for though you were angry with me, your anger turned away, and you comforted me. Surely God is my salvation; I will trust and not be afraid, for the LORD GOD is my strength and my might; he has become my salvation. With joy you will draw water from the wells of salvation. And you will say in that day: Give thanks to the LORD, call on his name; make known his deeds among the nations; proclaim that his name is exalted. Sing praises to the LORD, for he has done gloriously; let this be known in all the earth. Shout aloud and sing for joy, O royal Zion, for great in your midst is the Holy One of Israel.

In chapters 13-23 Isaiah announces God's judgment on ten Gentile nations as well as Judah and Israel. In chapter 13 The nations and Babylon, the glory of kingdoms, will be overthrown like Sodom and Gomorrah. The fall of Babylon is seen as a Day of the LORD. Verses 6-13 say, Wail, for the day of the LORD is near; it will come like destruction from the Almighty! . . . See, the day of the LORD comes, cruel, with wrath and fierce anger, to make the earth a desolation, and to destroy its sinners from it. For the stars and the heavens and their constellations will not give their light; the sun will be dark at its rising, and the moon will not shed its light. I will punish the world for its evil, and the wicked for their iniquity; I will put an end to the pride of the arrogant, and lay low the insolence of tyrants . . . Therefore I will make the heavens tremble, and the earth will be shaken out of its place, at the wrath of the LORD of hosts on the day of his fierce anger.

Verses 19-20 say, Babylon, the glory of kingdoms, the splendor and pride of the Chaldeans, will be like Sodom and Gomorrah when God overthrew them. It will never be inhabited or lived in for generations; Arabs will not pitch their tents there, shepherds will not make their flocks lie down there.

In chapter 14, Assyria, who God uses to judge Israel, will be judged as will the Philistines of Tyre and Sidon. (This area today is Lebanon.) In chapters 15-16 God says that he will destroy the proud and arrogant Moabites. In chapter 17 it is Damascus (Syria). Her towns will be deserted forever. (Again, statements such as this are not literal but hyperbolic statements to get the point across.). In chapter 18 it is Ethiopia (Nubia/Cush) and the Sudan located east of the Nile. In chapter 19 Egypt will be judged. Chapter 19:23-25 indicates that Israel in the future will become the mediator and blessing for the nations.

Chapter 20 tells us that Isaiah was commanded by God to walk naked for three years as a sign against Egypt and Ethiopia showing that they will be led naked into captivity by King Sargon of Assyria. This was also a sign to warn Judah not to join the Philistines in their rebellion.

That probably did not mean that he did not wear any clothes for three years. It means he went naked at different times throughout this three year time period as a reminder of what God was going to do. When this writer lived in Senegal (Africa) in early 1960s, it was common to see older persons occasionally walking naked through the village while people did not seem to be concerned. Different times and different contexts bring different reactions. Remember David even danced naked before the LORD.

In chapters 21-23 the message is loud and clear. The nations of the world including Israel and Judah have become evil, unjust, living unrighteously in arrogance and pride as they worship their idols. The religious, political, business, and social leaders are taking advantage of anyone they can for their own selfish interests. The message is that there needs to be repentance from these ungodly actions, for when individuals and nations act in ungodly ways there will be judgment.

In chapter 22:8-14 Israel is told their military planning is a waste of time. Instead they should have placed their faith in God and repented of their sins. But as (13) says, instead there was joy and festivity . . . eating meat and drinking wine. "Let us eat and drink, for tomorrow we die." The LORD of host has revealed himself in my ears: Surely this iniquity will not be forgiven you until you die, says the Lord GOD of hosts.

In chapter 23:17-18 At the end of seventy years, the LORD will visit Tyre (Phoenician colony), and she will return to her trade, and will prostitute herself with all the kingdoms of the world on the face of the earth. Her merchandise and her wages will be dedicated to the LORD; her profits will not be stored or hoarded, but her merchandise will supply abundant food and fine clothing for those who live in the presence of the LORD. (Her commerce and profits, doing anything for gain will be judged, and then used for God.)

The next four chapters (24-27) called Isaiah's little Apocalypse, appear to give us a symbolic description of the end of the world. Chapter 24:1 says, Now the LORD is about to lay waste to the earth and make it desolate, and he will twist its surface and scatter its inhabitants. Verses 3-6 say, The earth will utterly be laid waste and utterly despoiled; for the LORD has spoken this word. The earth dries up and withers, the world languishes and withers; the heavens languish together with the earth. The earth lies polluted under its inhabitants, for they have transgressed laws, violated the statutes, broken the everlasting covenant. Therefore a curse devours the earth, and its inhabitants suffer for their guilt; therefore the inhabitants of the earth dwindled, and few people are left. Verses 10-13 say, The city of chaos is broken down, every house is shut up so that no one can enter. Desolation is left in the city, the gates are battered into ruins. For thus it shall be on the earth and among the nations, as when an olive tree is beaten as at the gleaning when the grape harvested is ended.

Verses 17-21 say, Terror, and the pit, and the snare are upon you, O inhabitant of the earth! Whoever flees at the sound of the terror shall fall into the pit; and whoever climbs out of the pit shall be caught in the snare. For the windows of heaven are opened, and the foundations of the earth tremble. The earth is utterly broken, the earth is torn asunder, the earth is violently shaken. The earth staggers like a drunkard, it sways like a hut; its transgressions lie heavily upon it, and it falls, and will not rise again. On that day the LORD will punish the host of heaven in heaven, and on earth the kings of the earth.

Chapter 25:1-2 begins with Isaiah's psalm of thanksgiving. He says, O LORD, you are my God; I will exalt you, I will praise your name; for you have done wonderful things, plans formed of old, faithful and sure. For you have made the city a heap, the fortified city a ruin; the palace of aliens is a city no more, it will never be rebuilt. Verse 6 says, On this mountain the LORD of hosts will make for all peoples a feast of rich food, a feast of well-aged wines, of rich foods filled with marrow, of well-aged wines strained clear. (Hope is again given.) In verses 8-9 he says, he will swallow up death forever. Then the Lord GOD will wipe away the tears from all faces, and the disgrace of his people he will take away from all the earth, for the LORD has spoken. It will be said on that day, Lo, this is our God; we have waited for him so that he might save us.

Chapter 26 is the song of victory. Verse 12 says, O LORD, you will ordain peace for us, for indeed, all that we have done, you have done for us. (This verse expresses the idea that the good we do is actually done by God working in us and through us.) In (19) Isaiah says, Your dead shall live; their corpses shall rise. But (20-21) say, hide yourself for a little while until the wrath is past. For the LORD comes out from his place to punish the inhabitants of the earth for their iniquity; the earth will disclose the blood shed on it, and will no longer cover its slain. (Apparently, this verse disagrees with those scholars who say there was no belief in the resurrection of the dead in the OT.)

Chapter 27:1 says, On that day the LORD with his cruel and great sword will punish Leviathan the fleeing serpent, Leviathan the twisting serpent, and will kill the dragon that is in the sea. (Leviathan, the symbol of evil, parallels with the dragon, the symbol of chaos.) Verse 6 says, In days to come Jacob will take root; Israel shall blossom and put forth shoots, and fill the whole world with fruit. Verses 12-13 say, On that day the LORD will thresh from the channel of the Euphrates to the Wadi of Egypt, and you will be gathered one by one, O people of Israel. And on that day a great trumpet will be blown, and those who were lost in the land of Assyria and those who were driven out to the land of Egypt will come and worship the LORD on the holy mountain at Jerusalem.

It is possible that these three chapters (25-27) are symbolic to express that after God judges Israel, Judah, and the nations, he will bring his people, the remnant, out from exile in Babylon to inhabit the land. It is then later used by Christians as a double fulfillment of prophecy to have reference to the end of time and eternal life. (This writer warns the reader to be careful of those who always seem to know exactly what all the prophecies mean and how they are applied in the future.)

Chapter 28:1-4 says, Ah, the proud garland of the drunkards of Ephraim (the ten tribes of the north) . . . Trampled under foot will be the proud garland of the drunkards of Ephraim . . . bloated with rich food, . . . Verses 7-10 in reference to the remnant of his people say, These also reel with wine and stagger with strong drink; the priest and the prophet reel with strong drink, they are confused with wine, they stagger with strong drink; they err in vision, they stumble in giving judgment. All tables are covered with filthy vomit; no place is clean. "Whom will he teach knowledge, and to whom will he explain the message? Those who are weaned from milk, those taken from the breast? For it is precept upon precept, precept upon precept, line upon line, line upon line, here a little, there a little."

In verse 14 he says, Hear the word of the LORD, you scoffers who rule this people in Jerusalem, and verses 16-18 say, I am laying in Zion a foundation stone, a tested stone, a precious cornerstone, a sure foundation: "One who trusts will not panic." And I will make justice the line and righteousness the plummet (measuring stick); . . . Then your covenant with death will be annulled, . . . (Some Jews say this is the Torah/ Talmud; some say it is the Messiah to come; Christians say this is the Messiah who came.) Verse 22 says, do not scoff, or your bonds will be made stronger; for I have heard a decree of destruction from the Lord GOD of hosts upon the whole land.

Chapter 29:10 says, For the LORD has poured out upon you a spirit of deep sleep; he has closed your eyes, you prophets, and covered your heads, you seers. (This biblical language was also used with Pharaoh in Egypt to show that God is in charge. If one chooses to go against him, he allows it.) In verses 13-14 the LORD said, Because these people draw near with their mouths and honor me with their lips, while their hearts are far from me, and their worship of me is a human commandment learned by rote; so I will again do amazing things with this people, shocking and amazing. The wisdom of their wise shall perish, and the discernment of the discerning shall be hidden.

But there will be a day when Israel's suffering will be completed. Verses 18-24 say, On that day the deaf shall hear . . . the blind shall see. The meek shall obtain fresh joy in the LORD, and the neediest people shall exult in the holy one of Israel. For the tyrant shall be no more, and the scoffers cease to be; all those alert to do evil shall be cut off—those who cause a person to lose a lawsuit, who set a trap for the arbiter in the gate, and without grounds deny justice to the one in the right . . . they will sanctify my name; they will sanctify the Holy One of Jacob, and will stand in awe of the God of Israel. And those who err in spirit will come to understanding, and those who grumble will accept instruction.

Chapter 30:1 says, Oh, rebellious children, says the LORD, who carry out a plan, but not mine; who make an alliance, but against my will, adding sin to sin; . . . Verses 9-11 say, For they are rebellious people, faithless children, children who will not hear instruction from the LORD; who say to the seers, "Do not see"; and to the prophets, "Do not prophesy to us what is right; speak to us smooth things, prophesy illusions, leave the way, turn aside from the path, let us hear no more about the Holy One of Israel."

This sounds like the thinking of many today which is do not show us the negative Scriptures, only the positive ones that make us feel good. People tend to want only positive things, and then block out the meaning of anything that is negative. This thinking is very prevalent in American society today. The people were saying we do not want to hear any more about the Holy One of Israel being against us or punishing us.

In verses 12-14 the Holy One of Israel says, Because you reject this word and put your trust in oppression and deceit, and rely on them; therefore this iniquity shall become for you like a break in a high wall, bulging out, and about to collapse, whose crash comes suddenly, in an instant; its breaking is like that of a potter's vessel that is smashed so ruthlessly . . . (Sounds like a message people of today need to hear.)

In verses 15-18 we learn that instead of demonstrating faith and trust, Judah sought hope in military devices and allies like Egypt to protect them. But hope is given to the afflicted. Verse 18 says, Therefore the LORD waits to be gracious to you; therefore he will rise up to show mercy to you. For the LORD is a God of justice; blessed are all those who wait for him. The prophets always hold out a positive hope for a remnant.

In chapter 32 the hope for a messianic king is stated. Verse 1 says, See, a king will reign in righteousness, and princes will rule with justice. Verses 5-8 say, A fool will no longer be called noble, nor a villain said to be honorable. For fools speak folly, and their minds plot iniquity: to practice ungodliness, to utter error concerning the LORD, to leave the craving of the hungry unsatisfied, and to deprive the thirsty of drink. The villainies of villains are evil; they devise wicked devices to ruin the poor with lying words, even when the plea of the needy is right. But those who are noble plan noble things, and by noble things they stand.

Verses 14-16 tell us that the palace and city will be forsaken until a spirit from on high is poured out, then justice, righteousness, peace, and trust will dwell. Verse 17 says, The effect of righteousness will be peace, and the result of righteousness, quietness and trust forever.

In chapter 33 Isaiah looks out and sees the destroyer coming. Verse 14 says, The sinners in Zion are afraid; trembling has seized the godless: "Who among us can live with the devouring fire? Who among us can live with everlasting flames?" Isaiah in (15-16) answers, Those who walk righteously and speak uprightly, who despise the gain of oppression, who wave away a bribe instead of accepting it, who stop their ears from hearing of bloodshed, and shut their eyes from looking on evil . . . Verse 17 says, Your eyes will see the king in his beauty, and verse 22 says, For the LORD is our judge, the LORD is our ruler, the LORD is our king; he will save us.

In chapter 34 the nations are judged illustrating the fate of all of God's enemies. Verse 2 says, the LORD is enraged against all the nations; and furious against all their hoards; he has doomed them, he has given them over for slaughter. But in (8) he says, the LORD has a day of vengeance, a year of vindication by Zion's cause.

Chapter 35:1-7 holds out hope saying, The wilderness and the dry land shall be glad; the desert shall rejoice and blossom; . . . They shall see the glory of the LORD, the majesty of our God . . . Say to those of a fearful heart, "Be strong, do not fear! Here is your God. He will come with vengeance, with terrible recompense. He will come and save you." Then the eyes of the blind shall be opened, and ears of the deaf unstopped; then the lame shall leap like a deer, and the tongue of the speechless sing for joy. For waters shall break forth in the wilderness, and streams in the desert; the burning sand shall become a pool, and the thirsty ground springs of water; the haunt of jackals shall become a swamp, the grass shall become reeds and rushes.

Verses 8-9 say, A highway shall be there, and it shall be called the Holy Way; the unclean shall not travel on it, but it shall be for God's people; no traveler, not even fools, shall go astray. No lion shall be there, nor shall any ravenous beast come up upon it; they shall not be found there, but the redeemed shall walk there. (Assurance is given that God's punishment will end, and the people will return to the promised land.)

Chapters 36-39:8 describe three special tests of King Hezekiah. This is an attached historical appendix. Chapter 36 begins by stating that in the fourteenth year of King Hezekiah, King Sennacherib of Assyria captured all the fortified cities of Judah and was on his way to Jerusalem. In great fear they sent for Isaiah who encourages in chapter 37:5-7 not to fear but trust God. When the servants of King Hezekiah came to Isaiah, Isaiah said to them, "Say to your master 'Thus says the LORD: Do not be afraid because of the words that you have heard with which the servants of the king of Assyria have reviled me. I myself will put a spirit in him, so that he shall hear a rumor, and return to his land; I will cause him to fall by the sword in his own land.' " In verses 15-21 Hezekiah prays to the LORD expressing his trust.

Verses 36-38 say, Then the angel of the LORD set out and struck down one hundred eighty-five thousand in the camp of the Assyrians; when morning dawned, they were all dead bodies. Then King Sennacherib of Assyria left, went home and lived in Nineveh. As he was worshiping in the house of his god Nisroch, his sons Adrammelech and Sharezer killed him . . . His son Esar-haddon succeeded him. (It is thought that God allowed a disease like the bubonic plague to fall upon them. Even so, the numbers seem to be a bit high, see 2 Kings 18-19.)

In chapter 38:1-3 Hezekiah becomes sick and is at the point of death. The prophet Isaiah son of Amoz came to him and said to him, "Thus says the LORD: Set your house in order, for you shall die; you shall not recover." Then Hezekiah turned his face to the wall, and prayed to the LORD: "Remember now, O LORD, I implore you, how I have walked before you in faithfulness with a whole heart, and have done what is good in your sight." And Hezekiah wept bitterly.

Verses 4-8 say, Then the word of the LORD comes to Isaiah: "Go and say to Hezekiah, Thus says the LORD, the God of your ancestor David: I have heard your prayer, I have seen your tears; I will add fifteen years to your life. I will deliver you and this city out of the hand of the king of Assyria, and defend this city. This is the sign to you from the LORD, that the LORD will do this thing that he has promised: See I will make the shadow cast by the declining sun on the (sun) dial of Ahaz turn back ten steps." So the sun turned back on the dial the ten steps by which it had declined. In (20-21) Hezekiah sings, the LORD will save me, and we will sing to stringed instruments all the days of our lives, at the house of the LORD. Now Isaiah had said, "Let them take a lump of figs, and apply it to the boil, so that he may recover."

In chapter 39 Hezekiah makes a big mistake. The king of Babylon hears that he is sick and sends envoys with letters and a present. Hezekiah welcomes them and shows them his storehouse of treasures. When Isaiah finds out, he is upset. In verses 5-8 Isaiah addresses Hezekiah saying, "Hear the word of the LORD of hosts: Days are coming when all that is in your house, and that which your ancestors have stored up until this day, shall be carried to Babylon; nothing shall be left, says the LORD. Some of your own sons who are born to you shall be taken away; they shall be eunuchs in the palace of the king of Babylon."

Hezekiah said to Isaiah, "The word of the LORD that you have spoken is good." For he thought, "There will be peace and security in my days." (Does this not sound typical of the politician who is only concerned with himself and his time in office with no real concern with what happens when he is out of office?)

Chapters 40-45 begin what is called Second Isaiah (Deutero-Isaiah). It was probably put together by a disciple of Isaiah. These chapters are filled with the good news of redemption. This section is sometimes called the Book of Consolation.

In 40:1-5 God says, Comfort, O comfort my people, says your God. Speak tenderly to Jerusalem and cry to her that she has served her term, that her penalty is paid, that she has received from the LORD's hand double for her sins. A voice cries out: "In the wilderness prepare the way of the LORD, make straight in the desert a highway for our God. Every valley shall be lifted up, and every mountain hill be made low; the uneven ground shall become level, and the rough places a plain. Then the glory of the LORD shall be revealed, and all people shall see it together, for the mouth of the LORD has spoken."

This figurative language describes the return of the exiles to Jerusalem, but the Gospels also see it as a prophecy of John the Baptist and his preparation for the coming of Christ as a double fulfillment of prophecy.

Then the prophet in verses 8-11 says, The grass withers, the flower fades; but the word of our God will stand forever . . . The Lord GOD comes with might, and his arm rules for him; his reward is with him, and his recompense before him. He will feed his flock like a shepherd; he will gather the lambs in his arms, and carry them in his bosom, and gently lead the mother sheep. Verses 28-31 say, The LORD is the everlasting God, the Creator of the ends of the earth . . . those who wait for the LORD shall renew their strength; they shall mount up with wings like eagles. They shall run and not be weary, they shall run and not faint.

In chapter 41:8-9 God says, Israel, my servant, Jacob, whom I have chosen, the offspring of Abraham, my friend; . . . "You are my servant, I have chosen you and not cast you off"; do not fear, for I am with you, do not be afraid, for I am your God; I will strengthen you; I will help you, I will uphold you with my victorious right hand. And (14) says, your redeemer is the Holy One of Israel.

Chapter 42 is the first of the suffering servant songs. Who is the suffering servant? Some say Israel. Some say Isaiah. The NT writers say Jesus. As a multiple fulfillment of prophecy it may be all of them. Verses 1-4 say, Here is my servant, whom I uphold, my chosen, in whom my soul delights; I have put my spirit upon him; he will bring forth justice to the nations. He will not cry or uplift his voice, or make it heard in the street; a bruised reed he will not break, and a dimly burning wick he will not quench; he will faithfully bring forth justice. He will not grow faint or be crushed until he has established justice in the earth; and the coastlands wait for his teaching.

Verse 6 says, I am the LORD, I have called you in righteousness. I have taken you by the hand and kept you; I have given you as a covenant to the people, a light to the nations, to open the eyes that are blind, to bring out the prisoners from the dungeon, from the prison those who sit in darkness. Verse 16 says, I will lead the blind by a road they do not know, by paths they have not known I will guide them. I will turn their darkness before them into light, the rough places into level ground. These are the things I will do, and I will not forsake them.

Chapter 43:1 says, But now thus says the LORD, he who created you, O Jacob, he who formed you, O Israel: Do not fear, for I have redeemed you; I have called you by name, you are mine. Verses 6-9 say, I will say to the north, "Give them up," and to the south, "Do not withhold; bring my sons from far away and my daughters from the end of the earth--everyone who is called by my name, whom I created for my glory, whom I formed and made." Bring forth the people who are blind yet have eyes, who are deaf yet have ears! Let all the nations gather together, and let the people assemble.

Verses 10-11 say, You are my witness, says the LORD, and my servant whom I have chosen, so that you may know and believe me and understand that I am he. Before me no god was formed, nor shall there be any after me. I, I am the LORD and besides me there is no savior. (The servant Israel is God's witness.)

Verse 18 says, Do not remember the former things, or consider the things of old. I am about to do a new thing; now it springs forth do you not perceive it? I will make a way in the wilderness and rivers in the desert. Verse 25 says, I, I am He who blots out your transgressions for my own sake, and I will not remember your sins. In chapter 44:3 the LORD said to Jacob (Israel), I will pour my spirit upon your descendants, and my blessing on your offspring. Verses 6-8 say, Thus says the LORD, the King of Israel, and his Redeemer, the LORD of Hosts: I am the first and I am the last; besides me there is no God.

In verses 21-22 he says, Remember these things, O Jacob, and Israel, for you are my servant; I formed you, for you are my servant; O Israel, you will not be forgotten by me. I have swept away your transgressions like a cloud, and your sins like a mist; return to me, for I have redeemed you. (It is interesting to note that God first redeems his people then challenges them to return to him.)

In verse 28 a promise is made to Israel that his people will return to their land. The Persian ruler, Cyrus will be God's instrument for Israel. Verse 28 says, "He is my shepherd, and he shall carry out all my purpose"; and who says of Jerusalem, "It shall be rebuilt," and of the temple, "Your foundation shall be laid."

Chapter 45:1-4 says, Thus says the LORD to his anointed (messiah), to Cyrus . . . God says, For the sake of my servant Jacob, and Israel my chosen, I call you by your name. I surname you, though you do not know me. Verses 5-7 say, I am the LORD, and there is no other; besides me there is no god . . . I form light and create darkness, I make weal and create woe; I the LORD do all these things.

This is the only OT passage in which "messiah" refers to a non Israelite. Cyrus is the king of the Persians who defeats the Babylonians and sets the exiles free to return to Jerusalem to rebuild the city and the temple. These verses also reaffirm the sovereign power of the one God and state that the all-powerful God is the God of all nations.

In chapter 46 God affirms that he will save Israel. In verses 10-11 he says, "My purpose shall stand, and I will fulfill my intention," calling a bird of prey from the east, the man for my purpose from a far country. I have spoken and will bring it to pass; I have planned, and will do it.

In chapter 47:1-9 Isaiah speaks to the Babylonians and warns them that judgment is coming to them because of their many sins such as worshiping pagan gods, being lovers of pleasure, being involved in sorcery, wickedness, and many injustices. In verses 10-11 he says, You felt secure in your wickedness; you said, "No one sees me." Your wisdom and your knowledge led you astray, and you said in your heart, "I am, and there is no one besides me." But evil shall come upon you, which you can not charm away; disaster shall fall upon you, which you will not be able to ward off; and ruin shall come on you suddenly, of which you know nothing.

In chapter 48 the prophecy of being set free from captivity is fulfilled. The people will be set free. Verse 20 says, Go out from Babylon, flee from Chaldea, declare this with a shout of joy, proclaim it, send it forth to the end of the earth; say, "The LORD has redeemed his servant Jacob!"

Chapter 49:1-6 is the second suffering servant song. Verse 1 says, The LORD called me before I was born, while I was in my mother's womb he named me . . .And he said to me, "You are my servant, Israel, in whom I will be glorified." But I said, "I have labored in vain, I have spent my strength for nothing and vanity; yet surely my cause is with the LORD, and my reward with my God." And now the LORD says, who formed me in the womb to be his servant, to bring Jacob back to him, and that Israel might be gathered to him, for I am honored in the sight of the LORD, and my God has become my strength—he says, "It is too light a thing that you should be my servant to raise up the tribes of Jacob and to restore the survivors of Israel; I will give you as a light to the nations, that my salvation may reach to the ends of the earth."

Verse 13 says, the LORD has comforted his people, and will have compassion on his suffering ones. Verses 22-23 say, Thus says the Lord GOD: I will soon lift up my hands to the nations, . . . With their faces to the ground they shall bow down to you, and lick the dust of your feet. Then you shall know that I am the LORD; those who wait for me shall not be put to shame.

In chapter 50:4-9 we have the third servant song. The Lord GOD has given me the tongue of a teacher, that I may know how to sustain the weary with a word. Morning by morning he wakens me—wakens my ear to listen to those who are taught. The Lord GOD has opened my ear, and I was not rebellious, I did not turn backward. I gave my back to those who struck me, and my cheeks to those who pulled out my beard. I did not hide my face from insult and spitting. The Lord GOD helps me; therefore I have not been disgraced; therefore I have set my face like flint, and I know I shall not be put to shame; he who vindicates me is near . . . It is the Lord GOD who helps me; who will declare me guilty? All of them will wear out like a garment; the moth will eat them up. (The suffering servant is now a person from the nation of Israel.)

Chapter 51: 4-7 says, Listen to me, my people, and give heed to me, my nation; for a teaching will go out from me, and my justice for a light to the peoples. I will bring near my deliverance swiftly, my salvation has gone out and my arms will rule the peoples; the coastlands wait for me, and for my arm they hope. Lift up your eyes to the heavens, and look to the earth beneath; for the heavens will vanish like smoke, and the earth will wear out like a garment, and those who live in it will die like gnats, but my salvation will be forever, and my deliverance will never be ended.

Verse 7 says, Listen to me, you who know righteousness, you people who have my teaching in your heart; do not fear the reproach of others, and do not be dismayed when they revile you. Verses 12-13 say, I, I am he who comforts you; why then are you afraid of a mere mortal who must die, a human being who fades like grass? You have forgotten the LORD your Maker, who stretched out the heavens and laid the foundations of the earth.

Chapter 52:1-3 says, Awake, awake, put on your strength, O Zion! . . . the unclean shall enter you no more . . . you shall be redeemed without money. Verse 6 says, Therefore my people shall know my name; therefore in that day they shall know it is I who speak; here I am. Then verses 7-10 say, How beautiful upon the mountains are the feet of the messenger who announces peace, who brings good news, who announces salvation, who says to Zion, "Your God reigns." Listen! Your sentinels lift up their voices, together they sing for joy; for in plain sight they see the return of the

LORD to Zion . . . all the ends of the earth shall see the salvation of our God.

Verses 13-15 begin the fourth servant song which goes from 52:13-53:12. It begins by saying, See, my servant shall prosper; he shall be exalted and lifted up, and shall be very high. Just as there were many who were astonished at him--so marred was his appearance, beyond human semblance, and his form beyond that of mortals--so he shall startle many nations; kings shall shut their mouths because of him; for that which they had not heard they shall see, and that which they had not heard they shall contemplate.

Chapter 53:1-5 says, Who has believed what we have heard? And to whom has the arm of the LORD been revealed? For he grew up before him like a young plant, and like a root out of dry ground; he had no form or majesty that we should look at him, nothing in his appearance that we should desire him. He was despised and rejected by others; a man of suffering and acquainted with infirmity; and as one from whom others hide their faces he was despised, and we held him of no account. Surely he has borne our infirmities and carried our diseases; yet we accounted him stricken, struck down by God, and afflicted. But he was wounded for our transgressions, crushed for our iniquities; upon him was the punishment that made us whole, and by his bruises we are healed.

Verses 6-9 say, All we like sheep have gone astray; we have all turned to our own way, and the LORD has laid on him the iniquity of us all. He was oppressed, and he was afflicted, yet he did not open his mouth; like a lamb that is led to the slaughter, and like a sheep that before its shearers is silent, so he did not open his mouth. By a perversion of justice, he was taken away. Who could have imagined his future? For he was cut off from the land of the living, stricken for the transgression of my people. They made his grave with the wicked and his tomb with the rich, although he had done no violence, and there was no deceit in his mouth.

Verses 10-12 say, Yet it was the will of the LORD to crush him with pain. When you make his life an offering for sin, he shall see his offspring, and prolong his days; through him the will of the LORD shall prosper. Out of his anguish he shall see light; he shall find satisfaction through his knowledge. The righteous one, my servant, shall make many righteous, and he shall bear their iniquities. Therefore, I shall allow him a portion with the great, and he shall divide the spoil with the strong; because he poured out himself to death, and was numbered with the transgressors; yet he bore the sin of many, and made intercession for the transgressors.

The Jews say the previous Scriptures describe the purpose of God's people, Israel, or even Isaiah himself, while the gospel writers apply all this to the person of Christ who comes from the nation of Israel. Since this was written hundreds of years before the first coming of Christ, this could be once again a double fulfillment of prophecy.

Chapter 54 is a song of assurance to Israel. Verse 5 says, For your Maker is your husband, the LORD of hosts is his name; the Holy One of Israel is your Redeemer, the God of the whole earth he is called. Verses 7-10 say, For a brief moment I abandoned you, but with great compassion I will gather you. In overflowing wrath for a moment I hid my face from you, but with everlasting love I will have compassion on you, says the LORD, your Redeemer. This is like the days of Noah to me; Just as I swore the waters of Noah would never again go over the earth, so I have sworn I will not be angry with you and will not rebuke you. For the mountains may depart, and the hills be removed, but my steadfast love shall not depart from you, and my covenant of peace shall not be removed, says the LORD who has compassion on you.

Verses 13-14 say, All your children shall be taught by the LORD, and great shall be the prosperity of your children. In righteousness you shall be established; you shall be far from oppression, for you shall not fear; and from terror, for it shall not come near you. Verse 17 says, No weapon that is fashioned against you shall prosper, and you shall confute every tongue that rises against you in judgment. This is the heritage of the servants of the LORD and their vindication from me, says the LORD.

Chapter 55:1-3 says, Ho, everyone who thirsts come to the waters; and you who have no money, come, buy and eat. Come, buy wine and milk without money and without price. Why do you spend your money for that which is not bread, and your labor for that which does not satisfy? Listen carefully to me, and eat what is good, and delight yourself in rich food. Incline your ear, and come to me; listen, so that you may live. I will make with you an everlasting covenant, my steadfast, sure love for David.

Verses 6-11 say, Seek the LORD while he may be found; call upon him while he is near; let the wicked forsake their way, and the unrighteous their thoughts; let them return to the LORD, that he may have mercy on them, and to our God, for he will abundantly pardon. For my thoughts are not your thoughts, nor are your ways my ways, says the LORD. For as the heavens are higher than the earth, so are my ways higher than your ways and my thoughts than your thoughts. For as the rain and snow come down from heaven, and do not return there until they have watered the earth, making it bring forth and sprout, giving seed to the sower and bread to the eater, so shall my word be that goes out from my mouth; it shall not return to me empty, but it shall accomplish that which I purpose and succeed in the thing for which I sent it.

Chapter 56 to the end of the book is called Tritero Isaiah (3 Isaiah) by some scholars. Unlike Second Isaiah with its elevated poetry and long descriptions of the coming salvation of Yahweh and practically no condemnation for sin, these chapters are a mixture of poetry and prose and hope and despair at the same time with much condemnation for sin. One also finds much stress on inner faithfulness as opposed to external sacrifices.

Chapter 56:1 says, Thus says the LORD: Maintain justice, and do what is right, for soon my salvation will come, and my deliverance be revealed. In (2-7) foreigners and eunuchs previously excluded from worship will now be welcomed to join the covenant and keep the sabbaths. Verse 7 says, my house shall be called a house of prayer for all peoples. Then in reference to the leaders in (10) he says, Israel's sentinels are blind, they are without knowledge; . . . Verse 11 says, The shepherds also have no understanding; they have all turned to their own way, to their own gain, one and all. "Come," they say, "let us get wine; let us fill ourselves with strong drink. And tomorrow will be like today, great beyond measure."

Chapter 57 is a description of their godless society. In verse 1 he says, The righteous perish, and no one takes it to heart; the devout are taken away, while no one understands. Then in (3) he calls them children of sorcerers, adulterers, whores, idol worshipers, offspring of the deceitful and those who covet. Then in (21) he says, There is no peace, says my God, for the wicked.

In 58:3 God says, Look, you serve your own interests on your fast day, and oppress all your workers. In verses 6-10 God says, Is not the fast that I choose: to loose the bonds of injustice, to undo the thongs of the yoke, to let the oppressed go free, and to break every yoke? Is it not to share your bread with the hungry, and bring the homeless poor into your house; when you see the naked, to cover them, and not hide yourself from your own kin? Then your light shall break forth like the dawn, and your healing shall spring up quickly; your vindicator shall go before you, the glory of the LORD shall be your rear guard. Then you shall call, and the LORD will answer; you shall cry for help, and he will say, Here I am. If you remove the yoke from among you, the pointing of the finger, the speaking of evil, if you offer your food to the hungry and satisfy the needs of the afflicted, then your light shall rise in the darkness and your gloom be like the noonday.

Chapter 59:1-7 says, See the LORD's hand is not too short to save, nor his ear too dull to hear. Rather, your iniquities have been barriers between you and your God, and your sins have hidden his face from you so that he does not hear. For your hands are defiled with blood, and your fingers with iniquity; your lips have spoken lies; your tongue mutters wickedness. No one brings suit justly, no one goes to law honestly; they rely on empty pleas, they speak lies, conceiving mischief and begetting iniquity . . . deeds of violence are in their hands. Their feet run to evil, and they rush to shed innocent blood; their thoughts are thoughts of iniquity, desolation and destruction are in their highways.

Verses 8-9 say, The way of peace they do not know, and there is no justice in their paths. Their roads they have made crooked; no one who walks in them knows peace. Therefore, justice is far from us, and righteousness does not reach us; we wait for light, and lo! there is darkness; and for brightness, but we walk in gloom. We grope like the blind along a wall, groping like those who have no eyes . . .

Verses 12-14 say, For our transgressions before you are many, and our sins testify against us. Our transgressions indeed are with us, and we know our iniquities: transgressing and denying the LORD, and turning away from following our God, talking oppression and revolt, conceiving lying words and uttering them from the heart. Justice is turned back, and righteousness stands at a distance; for truth stumbles in the public square and uprightness cannot enter.

Verses 15-18 say, Truth is lacking, and whoever turns from evil is despoiled. The LORD saw it, and it displeased him that there was no justice. He saw that there was no one, and was appalled that there was no one to intervene; so his own arm brought him victory, and his righteousness upheld him. He put on righteousness like a breastplate, and a helmet of salvation on his head; . . . and in (18) he says, According to their deeds so will he repay; but in verse 20 he says, he will come to Zion as redeemer, to those in Jacob who turn from transgression, says the LORD.

Chapter 60:1-3 says, Arise shine; for your light has come, and the glory of the LORD has risen upon you. For darkness shall cover the earth, and thick darkness the peoples; but the LORD will arise upon you, and his glory will appear over you. Nations shall come to your light, and kings to the brightness of your dawn. Verses 5-6 say, the wealth of the nations shall come to you. A multitude of camels . . . shall bring gold and frankincense, and shall proclaim the praise of the LORD. (The gospel writer will use this in his nativity account, see Mt 2:11.)

Verse 12 says, For the nation and kingdom that will not serve you shall perish; those nations shall utterly be laid waste, and (18-21) say, Violence shall no more be heard in your land . . . you shall call your walls, Salvation, and your gates, Praise . . . the LORD will be your everlasting light, . . . and your days of mourning shall be ended. Your people shall all be righteous; they shall possess the land forever. Verse 22 says, I am the LORD; in its time I will accomplish it quickly.

In chapter 61 the gospel writer (Luke 4:18-19) uses the first three verses for Jesus inaugurating his ministry. Verses 1-4 say, The spirit of the Lord GOD is upon me, because the LORD has anointed me; he has sent me to bring good news to the oppressed, to bind up the brokenhearted, to proclaim liberty to the captives, and release to the prisoners; to proclaim the year of the LORD's favor, and the day of vengeance of our God; to comfort all who mourn; to provide for those who mourn in Zion—too give them a garland instead of ashes, the oil of gladness instead of mourning, . . . they shall repair the ruined cities, the devastations of many generations.

Verse 6 says, you shall be called priests of the LORD; you shall be named ministers of our God; you shall enjoy the wealth of the nations, and in their riches you shall glory. (This becomes known as the priesthood of all believers.) Verse 8 says, for I the LORD love justice, I hate robbery and wrongdoing, I will faithfully give them their recompense, and I will make an everlasting covenant with them. Verse 11 says, For as the earth brings forth its shoots, and as a garden causes what is sowed in it to spring up, so the LORD will cause righteousness and praise to spring up before all the nations.

In chapter 62:2 Isaiah says, you shall be called by a new name that the mouth of the LORD will give, and (12) says, They shall be called "The Holy People, the Redeemed of the LORD." In chapters 63 and 64 Israel is repentant and appeals for God's mercy. In 64:6-9 they say, We have all become like one who is unclean, and all our righteous deeds are like a filthy cloth. We all fade like a leaf, and our iniquities, like the wind, take us away. There is no one who calls on your name, . . . Yet, O LORD, you are our father; we are the clay, and you are our potter; we are all the work of your hand. Do not be exceedingly angry, O LORD, and do not remember iniquity forever. Now consider, we are all your people. Verse 12 says, After all this, will you restrain yourself, O LORD? Will you keep silent, and punish us so severely?

In chapter 65 judgment is again emphasized, but verses 8-9 tell us that God will not destroy them all. (It is always only a remnant that will be saved never the majority.) In (17-19) the LORD says, I am about to create new heavens and a new earth; the former things shall not be remembered or come to mind. Be glad and rejoice forever in what I am creating; for I am about to create Jerusalem as a joy, and its people as a delight. I will rejoice in Jerusalem, and delight in my people; No more shall the sound of weeping be heard in it or the cry of distress. Verse 25 says, The wolf and the lamb shall feed together, the lion shall eat straw like the ox; but the serpent—its food shall be dust! They shall not hurt or destroy on all my holy mountain, says the LORD.

Chapter 66 is the last chapter of Isaiah. Verses 1-4 say, Thus says the LORD: Heaven is my throne, and the earth is my footstool; what is the house that you would build for me, and what is my resting place? . . . I will look to the humble and contrite in spirit, who trembles at my word . . . These have chosen their ways and in their abominations they take delight; I also will choose to mock them, and bring upon them what they fear; because when I called, no one answered, when I spoke, they did not listen; but they did what was evil in my sight, and chose what did not please me.

Verses 15 and 16 say, the LORD will come in fire, and his chariots like the whirlwind, to pay back his anger in fury, and his rebuke in flames of fire. For by fire will the LORD execute judgment, . . . Verse 18 says, I know their works and their thoughts, and I am coming to gather all nations and tongues; and they shall come and see my glory, and I will set a sign among them. From them I will send survivors to the nations . . . They shall bring all your kindred from all the nations, and they shall declare my glory among the nations as an offering to the LORD . . . And I will take some of them as priests and as Levites, says the LORD.

Verses 22-24 say, For as the new heavens and the new earth, which I will make, shall remain before me, says the LORD; so shall your descendants and your name remain . . . all flesh shall come to worship before me, says the LORD. And they shall go out and look at the dead bodies of the people who have rebelled against me; for their worm shall not die, their fire will not be quenched, and they shall be an abhorrence to all flesh. (This ending of the book of Isaiah may be the earliest symbolic reference to Hell and eternal punishment.)

Covenant-Judgment-Redemption is a major theme in all the prophets, first highlighted in Isaiah. God makes a covenant with his people that he will be their God, and they will be his people. They confirmed the covenant by worshiping him and obeying his teachings. Too often they ignore the covenant thus breaking their relationship with God.

God being a just and holy God can not be such and let their ignoring him pass. Therefore, he judges his people, but always offering hope (redemption) if they change their ways. When they do, he forgives them and redeems them, but it is always only a remnant, a minority, who repent and change their ways.

Another theme is hope expressed in a return from exile and the coming Davidic king which leads to a Messiah and a coming messianic age. It also leads to the centrality of the holy mountain which is Zion. There is a yearning for a universal peace that involves both Israel and the nations. It is also interesting to note that of all the prophets Isaiah is the most quoted in the NT.

As one reads Isaiah and the prophets, one needs to honestly look at society today, especially our society in America, and compare it with what you are reading. God's word is not just an ancient dead book. As the NT book of Hebrews 4:12 teaches, the word of God is living and active sharper than any two edged sword, piercing until it divides soul from spirit, joints from marrow; it is able to judge the thoughts and intentions of the heart. Before him no creature is hidden, but all are naked and laid bare to the eyes of the one to whom we must render an account. As we read the Scriptures we learn that not only individuals will give an account but also nations and their institutions as expressed in the example of Israel.

JEREMIAH

Jeremiah prophesies from about 627 to the fall of Jerusalem in 586-87 B.C. when the people are carried off to Babylon and the temple destroyed. God punishes his people in order to heal them to bring them to repentance and a change of heart. Jeremiah's oracles are about the religious, political and social situations of his time.

Jeremiah prophesied about one hundred years after Isaiah. His forty five years will be a record for biblical prophetic activity. More than any other prophet he reveals his strong emotional feelings.

Through Judah's last five kings, Jeremiah warns of coming disaster. Among his contemporaries are Habakkuk, Zephaniah, Ezekiel in Babylon and possibly Daniel. Jeremiah stands out as a lonely person, often imprisoned and in danger for his life. Jeremiah was a priest, a descendant of Abiathar, one of the two chief priests of David.

He is a priest also called to be a prophet. He is called by God to confront kings, false prophets, and hypocritical priests. In 9:1 he is called the *weeping prophet,* for he weeps when he watches his prophecies of doom being fulfilled. Jeremiah is a master of imagery who creates word pictures to give his message. He proclaims a new covenant that will eventually be written on hearts and will be a fulfillment and completion of the old Mosaic covenant (31:31-34). According to Christians this will find its fulfillment in Christ whom Christians call the righteous Branch (33:14-18).

With most of the prophets he condemns people of wealth and power when they cheat workers on their wages and benefit themselves at the expense of the poor and defenseless (5:27-31, 6:13-16). He has the boldness to question God on how he treats humankind as he attempts to deal with his feeling of being abandoned by God. These parts of Scripture are called his confessions (12:1-5, 15:10-21, 17:12-18, 18:18-23, 20:7-18).

Jeremiah prefigures Jesus in many aspects of his life such as his call to prophetic celibacy (16:1-4); his rejection by his home town (11:21-23); his prophecy of the destruction of the temple and Jerusalem (7:1-15); his trial over preaching about the destruction of the temple (26:1-9); his suffering, such as the suffering servant passages Isaiah used that Christians apply to Christ (chapters 36-38). He constantly calls both priests and prophets godless (23:9-17). Some interesting verses are the following. (1:6-10, 5:12-14, 8:21-22, 11:21-23, 20:1-18, 22:13-17, 23:9-40, 26:7-19)

The importance of Jeremiah for us can be seen if we read it like Isaiah and see what he says in relation to us in America today, and to the world, and not only to Judah in those times. Those who are able to read the Bible, as Karl Barth said with a newspaper in one hand and the Bible in another, will gain much wisdom by reading Jeremiah. Actually, the same can be said for most of the prophets.

Like Isaiah it is sometimes difficult to construct a chronological order. The book has both poetry and prose. It has original oracles of Jeremiah, and biographical accounts handed down and edited which makes the book a collection about Jeremiah as well as an anthology of his own sayings. Let us look at this fascinating book, which has much to say to those of us living today.

Chapter 1:1-3 says, The words of Jeremiah son of Hilkiah, of the priests who were in Anathoth in the land of Benjamin, to whom the word of the LORD came in the days of King Josiah son of Amon of Judah, in the thirteenth year of the reign. It came also in the days of King Jehoiakim son of Josiah of Judah, and until the end of the eleventh year of King Zedekiah son of Josiah of Judah, until the captivity of Jerusalem in the fifth month.

In verses (4-5) Jeremiah says, the word of the LORD came to me saying, "Before I formed you in the womb I knew you, and before you were born I consecrated you; I appointed you a prophet to the nations."

This passage is used by those who oppose abortion teaching to say it is plain that life begins at conception. Those who oppose using the passage this way point out the passage is poetry, and it is not good interpretive methodology to take poetry literally. Also, they say, even if taken literally that does not mean God, who put into motion all creation, has an extra special calling like Jeremiah's for all people. Again, this writer will refer the reader to his/her church for further information and insight. Neither side accepts the other side's argument.

Jeremiah in response to God in (6-10) says, Ah, Lord GOD! Truly I do not know how to speak, for I am only a boy." But the LORD said to me, "Do not say, 'I am only a boy'; for you shall go to all to whom I send you, and you shall speak whatever I command you. Do not be afraid of them, for I am with you to deliver you, says the LORD." Then, the LORD put out his hand and touched my mouth; and the LORD said to me, "Now I have put my words in your mouth. See today I appoint you over nations and over kingdoms, to pluck up and pull down, to destroy and to overthrow, to build and to plant." (As is so often the case, the person God chooses is not one looking to be called. In fact like Moses and others, at first, they reject God's call.)

Verses 11-13 say, The word of the LORD came to me saying, "Jeremiah what do you see?" And I said, "I see a branch of an almond tree." Then the LORD said to me, "You have seen well, for I am watching over my word to perform it." The word of the LORD came to me a second time, saying, "What do you see?" And I said, "I see a boiling pot tilted away from the north."

This is interpreted in verses 14-19 which say, Out of the north disaster shall break out on all the inhabitants of the land. For now I am calling all the tribes of the kingdoms of the north, says the LORD; and they shall come and all of them shall set their thrones at the entrance of the gates of Jerusalem, against all its surrounding walls and against all the cities of Judah. And I will utter my judgments against them, for all their wickedness in forsaking me; they have made offerings to other gods, and worshiped the works of their own hands. But you, gird up your loins; stand up and tell them everything that I command you. Do not break down before them, or I will break you before them . . . They will fight against you; but they shall not prevail against you, for I am with you, says the LORD, to deliver you.

In chapter 2 Jerusalem, Judah, and Israel are to be judged for breaking the covenant. Verses 5-9 say, Thus says the LORD, What wrong did your ancestors find in me that they went far from me, and went after worthless things, and became worthless themselves? They did not say, "Where is the LORD who brought us up from the land of Egypt . . ." I brought you into a plentiful land to eat its fruits and its good things. But when you entered you defiled my land, and made my heritage an abomination. The priests did not say, "Where is the LORD?" Those who handle the law did not know me; the rulers transgressed against me; the prophets prophesied by Baal, and went after things that do not profit. Therefore once more I accuse you, says the LORD, and I accuse your children's children.

Verse 13 says, my people have committed two evils: they have forsaken me, the fountain of living water, and dug out cisterns for themselves, cracked cisterns that can hold no water. Verse 19 says, Your wickedness will punish you, and your apostasies will convict you. Know and see that it is evil and bitter for you to forsake the LORD your God; the fear of me is not in you, says the Lord GOD of hosts. Verse 27 says, For they have turned their backs to me, and not their faces. But in the time of their trouble they say, "Come and save us!" Verses 34-35 say, Also on your skirts is found the lifeblood of the innocent poor . . . Now I am bringing you to judgment for saying, "I have not sinned." (Throughout the prophets God compares his people to an adulterer because they are always running to other gods.)

Chapter 3 consists of exhortations to repent. Verse 1 says, If a man divorces his wife and she goes from him and becomes another man's wife, will he return to her? Would not such a land be greatly polluted? You have played the whore with many lovers; and would you return to me? says the LORD. Verse 2 says, You have polluted the land with your whoring and wickedness.

In verses 14-15 the LORD says, Return, O faithless children, says the LORD, for I am your master; . . . I will give you shepherds after my own heart, who will feed you with knowledge and understanding. Verses 22-23 say, Return, O faithless children, I will heal your faithlessness. "Here we come to you; for you are the LORD our God. Truly the hills are a delusion, the orgies on the mountains. Truly in the LORD our God is the salvation of Israel . . . we have sinned against the LORD our God, we and our ancestors, from our youth even to this day; and we have not obeyed the voice of the LORD our God."

In chapter 4 of Jeremiah disaster is foretold. Verses-3-4 say, For thus says the LORD to the people of Judah and the inhabitants of Jerusalem: Break up your fallow ground, and do not sow among the thorns. Circumcise yourselves to the LORD, remove the foreskin of your hearts, O people of Judah and inhabitants of Jerusalem, or else my wrath will go forth like fire, and burn with no one to quench it, because of the evil of your doings. Verse 6 says, for I am bringing evil from the north, and a great destruction.

Verse 14 says, O Jerusalem, wash your heart clean of wickedness so that you may be saved. How long shall your evil schemes lodge within you? God in (22) says, "For my people are foolish, they do not know me; they are stupid children, they have no understanding. They are skilled in doing evil, but do not know how to do good."

Verses 23-27 say, I looked on the earth, and lo, it was waste and void; and to the heavens, and they had no light. I looked on the mountains, and lo, they were quaking, and all the hills moved to and fro. I looked, and lo, and there was no one at all, and all the birds of the air had fled. I looked and lo, the fruitful land was a desert, and all its cities were laid in ruins before the LORD, before his fierce anger. For thus says the LORD: The whole land shall be a desolation; yet I will not make a full end.

Chapter 5:1-3 says, Run to and fro through the streets of Jerusalem, look around and take note! Search its squares and see if you can find one person who acts justly and seeks truth—that I may pardon Jerusalem. Although they say, "As the LORD lives," yet they swear falsely . . . You have struck them, but they felt no anguish; you have consumed them, but they refused to take correction. They have made their faces harder than rock; they have refused to turn back.

Verses 7-9 say, How can I pardon you? Your children have forsaken me, and have sworn by those who are no gods. When I fed them to the full, they committed adultery and trooped to the houses of prostitutes. They were well fed lusty stallions, each neighing for his neighbor's wife. Shall I not punish them for these things? says the LORD; and shall I not bring retribution on a nation such as this?

Verses 12-13 say, They (the prophets) have spoken falsely of the LORD, and have said, "He will do nothing. No evil will come upon us, and we shall not see sword or famine." The prophets are nothing but wind, for the word is not in them. Thus shall it be done to them! Verses 21-23 say, Hear this, O foolish and senseless people, who have eyes, but do not see, who have ears, but do not hear. Do you not fear me? says the LORD; Do you not tremble before me? . . . But this people has a stubborn and rebellious heart; they have turned aside and gone away.

Verses 27-29 say, Like a cage full of birds, their houses are full of treachery; therefore they have become great and rich, they have grown fat and sleek. They know no limits in deeds of wickedness; they do not judge with justice the cause of the orphan, to make them prosper, and they do not defend the rights of the needy. Shall I not punish them for these things, says the LORD, and shall I not bring retribution on a nation such as this? Verses 30- 31 say, An appalling and horrible thing has happened in the land: the prophets prophesy falsely, and the priests rule as the prophets direct; my people love to have it so, but what will you do when the end comes?

Chapter 6:6-8 says, For thus says the LORD of hosts: Cut down her trees; cast up a siege ramp against Jerusalem. This is the city that must be punished; there is nothing but oppression within her . . . violence and destruction are heard within her . . . Take warning, O Jerusalem, or I shall turn from you in disgust, and make you a desolation, an uninhabited land.

Verses 10-11 say, See, their ears are closed, they cannot listen. The word of the LORD is to them an object of scorn; they take no pleasure in it. But I am full of the wrath of the LORD; I am weary of holding it in. Verses 13-14 say, For from the least to the greatest of them, everyone is greedy for unjust gain; and from prophet to priest, everyone deals falsely. They have treated the wound of my people carelessly, saying, "Peace, peace, when there is no peace." (They promised material and spiritual well-being when there was none to be had.)

Verses 15-16 say, They acted shamefully, they committed abomination; yet they were not ashamed, they did not know how to blush. Therefore they shall fall . . . Thus says the LORD: Stand at the crossroads, and look, and ask for the ancient paths, where the good way lies; and walk in it, and find rest for your souls. But they said, "We will not walk in it." Also I raised up sentinels for you: "Give heed to the sound of the trumpet!" But they said, "We will not give heed."

Verse 18-19 say, Therefore hear, O nations, and know, O congregation, what will happen to them. Hear, O earth; I am going to bring disaster on this people, the fruit of their schemes, because they have not given heed to my words; and as for my teaching, they have rejected it. Verses 28-30 say, They are all stubbornly rebellious, going about with slanders; they are bronze and iron, all of them act corruptly.

Chapter 7:1 says, The word that came to Jeremiah from the LORD. (This is the famous temple sermon.) Verses 2-4 say, Stand in the gate of the LORD's house, and proclaim there this word, and say, Hear the word of the LORD, all you people of Judah, you that enter these gates to worship the LORD. Thus says the LORD of hosts, the God of Israel: Amend your ways and your doings, and let me dwell with you in this place. Do not trust in these deceptive words: "This is the temple of the LORD, the temple of the LORD, the temple of the LORD."

Verses 5-7 say, For if you truly amend your ways and your doings, if you truly act justly one with another, if you do not oppress the alien (immigrants), the orphan, and the widow (the poor who have no power and wealth), or shed innocent blood in this place, and if you do not go after other gods to your own hurt, then I will dwell with you in this place, in the land that I gave of old to your ancestors forever and ever.

Verses 8-12 say, Here you are, trusting in deceptive words to no avail. Will you steal, murder, commit adultery, swear falsely, make offerings to Baal, and go after other gods that you have not known, and then come and stand before me in this house, which is called by my name, and say, We are safe!—only to go on doing all these abominations? Has this house which is called by my name, become a den of robbers in your sight? You know, I too am watching, says the LORD.

In verses 14-15 the LORD says, therefore I will do to the house that is called by my name, in which you trust, and to the place that I gave to you and to your ancestors, just what I did to Shiloh. And I will cast you out of my sight, just as I cast out all your kinsfolk, all the offspring of Ephraim. Then in (16) he told Jeremiah, do not pray for this people, do not raise a cry or prayer on their behalf, do not intercede with me, for I will not hear you. In verses 25-26 the LORD says, I have persistently sent all my servants the prophets to them, day after day; yet they did not listen to me, or pay attention, but they stiffened their necks. They did worse than their ancestors did. Verse 30 says, For the people of Judah have done evil in my sight, says the LORD; they have set their abominations in the house that is called by my name, defiling it.

In chapter 8 God through Jeremiah continues his warnings to the people about the destruction that will follow because they refused to hear his word. In (10-12) Jeremiah says, everyone is greedy for unjust gain; from prophet to priest everyone deals falsely. They have treated the wound of my people carelessly, saying, Peace, peace when there is no peace. They acted shamefully, they committed abomination; yet they were not at all ashamed, they did not know how to blush.

In (18) Jeremiah says, My joy is gone, grief is upon me, my heart is sick. Verses 20-22 say, "The harvest is past, the summer is ended, and we are not saved." For the hurt of my poor people I am hurt, I mourn, and dismay has taken hold of me. Is there no balm (healing medicine) in Gilead? Is there no physician there? Why then has the health of my poor people not been restored?

Chapter 9:2-9 says, they are all adulterers, a band of traitors. They bend their tongues like bows; they have grown strong for falsehood, and not for truth; for they proceed from evil to evil, and they do not know me, says the LORD. Beware of your neighbors, and put no trust in any of your kin, for all your kin are supplanters, and every neighbor goes around like a slanderer. They all deceive their neighbors, and no one speaks the truth; they have taught their tongues to speak lies; they commit iniquity and are too weary to repent. Oppression upon oppression, deceit upon deceit! They refuse to know me, says the LORD . . . Their tongue is a deadly arrow; it speaks deceit through the mouth. They all speak friendly words to their neighbors, but inwardly are planning to lay an ambush. Shall I not punish them for these things? says the LORD; and shall I not bring retribution on a nation such as this?

Verse 23 says, Thus says the LORD: Do not let the wise boast in their wisdom, do not let the mighty boast in might, do not let the wealthy boast in their wealth; but let those who boast boast in this, that they understand and know me, that I am the LORD; I act with steadfast love, justice, and righteousness in the earth, for in these things I delight, says the LORD.

Chapter 10:1-5 says, Hear the word that the LORD speaks to you, O house of Israel. Thus says the LORD: Do not learn the way of the nations, . . . For the customs of the peoples are false: . . . Their idols are like scarecrows in a cucumber field, and they can not speak; they have to be carried, for they cannot walk. Do not be afraid of them, for they cannot do evil, nor is it in them to do good. Verse 8 says, They are both stupid and foolish; the instruction given by idols is no better than wood! Verses 14-15 say, Everyone is stupid and without knowledge; . . . their images are false, and there is no breath in them. They are worthless, a work of delusion; at the time of their punishment they shall perish.

In verse 18 the LORD says, I am going to sling out the inhabitants of the land at this time, and I will bring distress on them, so that they shall feel it. Again the people are warned, and (21-22) say, the shepherds (leaders) are stupid, and do not inquire of the LORD; therefore they have not prospered, and all their flock is scattered. Hear a noise! Listen, it is coming—a great commotion from the land of the north to make the cities of Judah a desolation, a lair of jackals.

Chapter 11:1-4 says, The word that came to Jeremiah from the LORD: Hear the words of this covenant, and speak to the people of Judah and the inhabitants of Jerusalem. You shall say to them, Cursed be anyone who does not heed the words of this covenant, which I commanded your ancestors when I brought them out of the land of Egypt, from the iron smelter, saying, Listen to my voice, and do all that I command you.

Verse 8 says, Yet they did not obey or incline their ear, but everyone walked in the stubbornness of an evil will. So I brought upon them all the words of this covenant, which I commanded them to do, but they did not. In (10-11) God said to Jeremiah, They have turned back to the iniquities of their ancestors . . . I am going to bring disaster on them that they can not escape; though they cry out to me, I will not listen to them.

In chapters 11:16-12:6 is Jeremiah's first personal lament. Verses 18-19 say, It was the LORD who made it known to me, and I knew; then you showed me their evil deeds. But I was like a gentle lamb being led to the slaughter. And I did not know it was against me that they devised schemes, saying, "Let us destroy the tree with its fruit, let us cut him from the land of the living, so that his name will no longer be remembered."

In chapter 12:1 Jeremiah complains to God. He says, Why does the way of the guilty prosper? Why do all the treacherous thrive? But Jeremiah learns Judah's neighbors will be punished also. Verse 17 says, if any nation will not listen, then I will completely uproot it and destroy it, says the LORD. (It is plain that there will be consequences for both people and structures such as nations and institutions when they ignore and reject the God's teachings.)

Chapter 13:1-10 has an object lesson with a loin cloth. Jeremiah is told to take a loin cloth to the Euphrates and hide it in the cleft of a rock. Later he is told to get it, and when he does, he sees it is ruined. God in verse 10 says, This evil people, who refuse to hear my words, who stubbornly follow their own will and have gone after other gods and worship and serve them, shall be like this loin cloth, which is good for nothing.

In verse 24 the LORD says, I will scatter you like chaff driven by the wind from the desert. This is your lot, the portion I have measured out to you, says the LORD, because you have forgotten me and trusted in lies. I myself will lift up your skirts over your face, and your shame will be seen.

In chapter 14:11 the LORD said to Jeremiah, Do not pray for the welfare of the people. And in (14) the LORD said to me: The prophets are prophesying lies in my name; I did not send them, nor did I command them or speak to them. They are prophesying to you a lying vision, worthless divination, and the deceit of their own minds, and (16) says, I will pour out their wickedness upon them.

In chapter 15 Jeremiah, after constantly being persecuted for speaking God's word, finally succumbs to depression. His second personal lament goes from (10-21). In (10) he says, Woe is me, my mother, that you ever bore me, a man of strife and contention to the whole land! I have not lent, nor have I borrowed, yet all of them curse me. In verse 15 Jeremiah says, O LORD, you know; remember me and visit me, and bring down retribution for me on my persecutors . . . On your account I suffer insult. Your words were found, and I ate them, and your words became to me a joy and the delight of my heart; for I am called by your name, O LORD, God of hosts. Verse 18 says, Why is my pain unceasing, my wound incurable, refusing to be healed?

Verses 19-21 say, Therefore thus says the LORD: If you turn back, I will take you back, and you shall stand before me. If you utter what is precious, and not what is worthless, you shall serve as my mouth. It is they who will turn to you, not you who will turn to them. And I will make you to this people a fortified wall of bronze; they will fight against you, but they shall not prevail over you, for I am with you to save you and deliver you, says the LORD. I will deliver you out of the hand of the wicked, and redeem you from the grasp of the ruthless.

Chapter 16:1-2 says, The word of the LORD came to me: You shall not take a wife, nor shall you have sons and daughters in this place. Verse 4 gives the reason: they would die of deadly diseases, and perish by the sword and famine. They would not be buried, and they would become food for the birds and animals.

In verses 10-12 Jeremiah is told, And when you tell this people all these words, and they say to you, "Why has the LORD pronounced all this great evil against us? What is our iniquity? What is the sin that we have committed against the LORD our God?" then you shall say to them: It is because your ancestors have forsaken me, says the LORD, and have gone after other gods and have served and worshiped them, and have forsaken me and have not kept my law; and because you have behaved worse than your ancestors, for here you are, every one of you, following your stubborn evil will, refusing to listen to me.

In reference to the nations (19-21) says, to you shall the nations come from the ends of the earth and say: Our ancestors have inherited nothing but lies, worthless things in which there is no profit. Can mortals make for themselves gods? Such are no gods! In verse 21 the LORD says, " Therefore I am surely going to teach them, this time I am going to teach them my power and my might, and they shall know that my name is the LORD."

Chapter 17: 5-6 begins by saying, Thus says the LORD: Cursed are those who trust in mere mortals and make mere flesh their strength, whose hearts turn away from the LORD. They shall be like a shrub in a desert, and shall not see when relief comes. They shall live in the parched places of the wilderness, in an uninhabited salt land.

Verses 7-11 say, Blessed are those who trust in the LORD, whose trust is in the LORD. They shall be like a tree planted by water, sending out its roots by the stream. It shall not fear when heat comes, and its leaves shall stay green; in the year of drought it is not anxious, and it does not cease to bear fruit.

Verses 9-11 say, The heart is devious above all else; it is perverse--who can understand it? I the LORD test the mind and search the heart, to give to all according to their ways, according to the fruit of their doings. Like the partridge hatching what it did not lay, so are all who amass wealth unjustly; in mid-life it will leave them, and at their end they will prove to be fools.

In verses 14-18 is Jeremiah's third personal lament. He says, heal me, O LORD, and I shall be healed; save me, and I shall be saved; for you are my praise. See how they say to me, Where is the word of the LORD? Let it come! But I have not run away by being a shepherd in your service, nor have I desired the fatal day. You know what came from my lips; it was before your face. Do not become a terror to me; you are my refuge in the day of disaster. Let my persecutors be shamed, but do not let me be shamed; let them be dismayed, but do not let me be dismayed; bring on them the day of disaster; destroy them with double destruction!

Verses 19-23 say, Thus the LORD said to me: Go and stand in the People's Gate, by which the kings of Judah enter and by which they go out, and in the gates of Jerusalem, and say to them: Hear the word of the LORD, you kings of Judah and all Judah, and all the inhabitants of Jerusalem, who enter by these gates. Thus says the LORD: For the sake of your lives, take care that you do not bear a burden on the sabbath day or bring it in by the gates of Jerusalem. And do not carry a burden out of your houses on the sabbath or do any work, but keep the sabbath day holy, as I commanded your ancestors. Yet they did not listen or incline their ear; they stiffened their necks and would not hear or receive instruction.

Chapter 18:1-6 says, The word came to Jeremiah from the LORD: "Come, go down to the potter's house, and there I will let you hear my words." So I went down to the potter's house, and there he was working at his wheel. The vessel he was making of clay was spoiled in the potter's hand, and he reworked it into another vessel as seemed good to him. Then the word of the LORD came to me: Can I not do with you, O house of Israel, just as the potter has done? says the LORD. Just like the clay in the potter's hand, so are you in my hand, O house of Israel.

Verses 11-12 say, Thus says the LORD: Look, I am a potter shaping evil against you and devising a plan against you. Turn now, all of you from your evil way, and amend your ways and your doings. But they say, "It is no use! We will follow our own plans, and each of us will act according to the stubbornness of our evil will."

Chapter 18:18 begins Jeremiah's fourth personal lament. The people said, "Come let us make plots against Jeremiah—for instruction shall not perish from the priest, nor counsel from the wise, nor the word from the prophet. Come, let us bring charges against him, and let us not heed any of his words." In (23) Jeremiah said, Yet you, O LORD, know all their plotting to kill me. Do not forgive their iniquity, do not blot out their sin from your sight. Let them be tripped up before you; deal with them while you are angry.

Chapter 19:1 says, Thus says the LORD, Go and buy a potter's earthenware jug. In (4-6) he says to Jeremiah, Because the people have forsaken me, and have profaned this place by making offerings in it to other gods . . . and because they have filled the place with the blood of the innocent, and gone on building the high places of Baal to burn their children in the fire as burnt offerings to Baal . . . therefore the days are surely coming, says the LORD, when this place shall no more be called Topheth, or the valley of the son of Hinnom, but the valley of Slaughter.

In verse 10 the LORD said, Then you shall break the jug in the sight of those who go with you, and shall say to them: Thus says the LORD of hosts: So will I break this people and this city, as one breaks a potter's vessel, so that it can never be mended. Verse 15 says, I am now bringing upon this city and upon all its towns all the disaster that I have pronounced against it because they have stiffened their necks, refusing to hear my words.

Chapter 20:1-4 says, Now the priest Pashur son of Immer, who was chief officer in the house of the LORD, heard Jeremiah prophesying these things. Then Pashur struck the prophet Jeremiah and put him in the stocks . . . The next morning when Pashur released Jeremiah from the stocks, Jeremiah said to him, The LORD has named you not Pashur but "Terror-all-around." For thus says the LORD: I am making you a terror to yourself and to all your friends; and they shall fall by the sword of their enemies while you look on. And I will give all Judah into the hand of the king of Babylon, and he shall carry them captive to Babylon, and shall kill them with the sword. In verses 5-6 we are informed that all the wealth of the city and treasures of the kings as well as Pashur and his friends will be carried to Babylon, and they die there.

Jeremiah's fifth personal lament in (7-9) says, O LORD, you have enticed me, and I was enticed; you have overpowered me, and you have prevailed. I have become a laughing stock all day long; everyone mocks me. For whenever I speak, I must cry out, I must shout, Violence and destruction! For the word of the LORD has become for me a reproach and derision all day long. If I say, "I will not mention him, or speak any more in his name," then within me there is something like a burning fire shut up in my bones; I am weary with holding it in, and I cannot. Verse 12 says, for to you I have committed my cause.

Then in his sixth personal lament in (14-18) he says, Cursed be the day on which I was born! The day when my mother bore me, let it not be blessed! Cursed be the man who brought the news to my father, saying, "A child is born to you, a son," making him very glad. Verse 18 says, Why did I come forth from the womb to see toil and sorrow, and spend my days in shame?

Chapter 21:1-2 says, This is the word of the LORD that came to Jeremiah from the LORD, when King Zedekiah sent to him Pashur son of Malchiah and the priest Zephaniah son of Maaseiah, saying, "Please inquire of the LORD on our behalf, for King Nebuchadnezzar of Babylon is making war against us; perhaps the LORD will perform a wonderful deed for us, as he has often done, and will make him withdraw from us."

In verses 3-5 Jeremiah said to them: Thus you shall say to Zedekiah: Thus says the LORD, the God of Israel: I am going to turn back the weapons of war that are in your hands . . . I myself will fight against you with outstretched hand and mighty arm, in anger, in fury, and in great wrath. He told them in verse 7 that he would give them into the hands of King Nebuchadnezzar of Babylon, and (14) says, I will punish you according to the fruit of your doings, says the LORD; I will kindle a fire in its forest, and it shall devour all that is around it.

Chapter 22:1-3 says, Thus says the LORD: Go down to the house of the king of Judah, and speak there this word, and say: Hear the word of the LORD, O king of Judah sitting on the throne of David—you, and your servants, and your people who enter these gates. Thus says the LORD: Act with justice and righteousness, and deliver from the hand of the oppressor anyone who has been robbed. And do no wrong or violence to the alien, the orphan, and the widow, or shed innocent blood in this place.

Verses 13-17 say, Woe to him who builds his house by unrighteousness, and his upper rooms by injustice; who makes his neighbors work for nothing, and does not give them their wages; who says, "I will build myself a spacious house with large upper rooms," and who cuts out windows for it, paneling it with cedar, and painting it with vermillion. Are you a king because you compete in cedar? Did not your father (Josiah) eat and drink and do justice and righteousness? Then it was well with him. He judged the cause of the poor and needy; then it was well. Is this not to know me? says the LORD. But your eyes and heart are only on your dishonest gain, for shedding innocent blood, and for practicing oppression and violence.

In verses 21-22 he says, I spoke to you in your prosperity, but you said, "I will not listen." This has been your way from your youth, for you have not obeyed my voice . . . you will be ashamed and dismayed because of all your wickedness. (This writer believes this is a warning to all nations throughout time, for Scripture's purpose is not to become a dead history but to be alive to all generations.)

Chapter 23:1-2 says, Woe to the shepherds who destroy and scatter the sheep of my pasture! Says the LORD . . . It is you who have scattered my flock, and have driven them away, and you have not attended them. So I will attend to you for your evil doings, says the LORD. (This writer believes this a warning to all clergy throughout the ages.)

Verses 3-6 say, Then I myself will gather the remnant of my flock out of all the lands where I have driven them, I will bring them back to their fold, and they shall be fruitful and multiply. I will raise up shepherds over them who will shepherd them, and they shall not fear any longer, or be dismayed, nor shall any be missing, says the LORD. The days are surely coming, says the LORD, when I will raise up for David a righteous Branch (a Messianic title), and he shall reign as king and deal wisely, and shall execute justice and righteous in the land. In his days Judah will be saved and Israel will live in safety. And this is the name by which he will be called: "The LORD is our righteousness."

Verses 11-12 say, Both prophets and priests are ungodly; even in my house I have found their wickedness, says the LORD . . . I will bring disaster upon them in the year of their punishment, says the LORD. In (14-15) he says, in the prophets of Jerusalem I have seen a more shocking thing: they commit adultery and walk in lies; they strengthen the hands of evil doers, so that no one turns from wickedness, . . . "I am going to make them eat wormwood, and give them poisoned water to drink; for from the prophets of Jerusalem ungodliness has spread throughout the land."

Verses 16-17 say, Thus says the LORD of hosts: Do not listen to the words of the prophets who prophesy to you; they are deluding you. They speak visions of their own minds, not from the mouth of the LORD. They keep saying to those who despise the word of the LORD, "It shall be well with you"; and to all who stubbornly follow their own stubborn hearts, they say, "No calamity shall come upon you." In (36) these false prophets are told, you pervert the words of the living God, the LORD of hosts, our God.

In chapter 24:1-2 God shows Jeremiah two baskets of figs, one good and one bad. Verses 4-7 say, Then the word of the LORD came to me: Thus says the LORD, the God of Israel: Like these good figs, so I will regard as good the exiles from Judah, whom I have sent away from this place to the land of the Chaldeans (Babylonians). I will set my eyes upon them for good, and I will bring them back to this land. I will build them up, and not tear them down; I will plant them and not pluck them up. I will give them a heart to know that I am the LORD; and they shall be my people, and I will be their God, for they shall return to me with their whole heart. (Hope is always extended but only a remnant ever responds.)

Verses 8-9 say, But thus says the LORD: Like the bad figs that are so bad they can not be eaten, so will I treat King Zedekiah of Judah, his officials, the remnant of Jerusalem who remain in this land, and those who live in the land of Egypt. I will make them a horror, an evil thing, to all the kingdoms of the earth—a disgrace, a byword, a taunt, and a curse in all the places where I shall drive them. And I will send sword, famine, and pestilence upon them, until they are utterly destroyed from the land that I gave to them and their ancestors.

In chapter 25:11-12 God tells them Judah will be in exile for seventy years, and then after seventy years are completed, the king of Babylon and the Babylonians would be punished for their iniquity for making that land an everlasting waste. Verse 15 says, For thus says the LORD, the God of Israel, said to me: Take from my hand this cup of the wine of wrath, and make all the nations to whom I send you drink it.

Verse 31 says, The clamor will resound to the ends of the earth, for the LORD has an indictment against the nations; he is entering into judgment with all flesh, and the guilty he will put to the sword, says the LORD. In (34-36) Jeremiah tells them that the problem everywhere is poor leadership, and judgment will come to the shepherds that ignore God, his teachings, and his ways. Wail you shepherds, and cry out, roll in ashes you lords of the flock, for the days of your slaughter have come—and your dispersions, and you shall fall like a choice vessel. Flight shall fail the shepherds, and there shall be no escape for the lords of the flock. (Is this also a message for today's clergy in the synagogues, churches, and mosques?)

Chapter 26:1-3 says, At the beginning of the reign of King Jehoiakim son of Josiah of Judah, this word came from the LORD: Thus says the LORD: Stand in the court of the LORD's house, and speak to all the cities of Judah that come to worship in the house of the LORD; speak to them all the words I command you; do not hold back a word. It may be that they will listen, all of them, and will turn from their evil way, that I may change my mind about the disaster I intend to bring on them because of their evil doings. (The God of love always extends hope through repentance.) But in verses 7-9 when the prophets, priests, and people heard his message, they decide Jeremiah deserves to die.

They do not want to hear anything that calls them to repent and change their ways. Things do not seem much different in these modern times. Our nation and its people do not want to be called to repentance, and clergy do not want to be harassed, so the message in many cases has become a soothing one.

In verses 12-15 Jeremiah speaks to all the officials and all the people saying, "It is the LORD who sent me to prophesy against this house and this city all the words you have heard. Now therefore amend your ways and your doings, and obey the voice of the LORD your God, and the LORD will change his mind about the disaster that he has pronounced against you. But as for me, here I am in your hands. Do with me as seems good and right to you. Only know for certain that if you put me to death, you will be bringing innocent blood upon yourselves and upon this city and its inhabitants, for in truth the LORD sent me to speak all these words in your ears."

In verse 16 the officials and all the people said to the priests and prophets, "This man does not deserve the sentence of death, for he has spoken in the name of the LORD our God." And some of elders in the land arose and in (18-19) they reminded the people of Micah who prophesied the same thing during the days of King Hezekiah, and the people feared the LORD, and the people and city were spared. (But as we shall see the elders are ignored.)

Uriah is another man, in (20-24) who is prophesying in the name of the LORD. He escapes to Egypt, but King Jehoiakim sends his warriors to get Uriah, and they kill him. Jeremiah escapes because Ahikam, son of Shaphan shelters him.

Chapter 27:1-2 says, In the beginning of the reign of King Zedekiah son of Josiah of Judah the word of the LORD came to Jeremiah from the LORD. Thus the LORD said to me: Make yourself a yoke of straps and bars and put them on your neck. In (8) he tells all nations to put their neck under the yoke of Babylon and live or else they will be destroyed.

Verse 9 says, You, therefore, must not listen to your prophets, your diviners, your dreamers, your soothsayers, or your sorcerers, who are saying to you, "You shall not serve the king of Babylon." For they are prophesying a lie to you, with the result that they will be removed far from your land; I will drive you out, and you will perish. (But these prophets are the ones the people listened to because they spoke the soothing message that the people wanted to hear.)

In chapter 28 Hananiah the prophet in (10-11) took the yoke from the neck of the prophet Jeremiah, and broke it. And Hananiah spoke . . . "Thus says the LORD, This is how I will break the yoke of King Nebuchadnezzar of Babylon from the neck of all the nations within two years." At this the prophet Jeremiah went his way. But in (12-13) the word of the LORD came to Jeremiah: Go tell Hananiah, Thus says the LORD: You have broken wooden bars only to forge iron bars in place of them! (This means God's former word to Jeremiah stands.) In (16-17) he is also to tell Hananiah that he will be dead within the year. In that same year Hananiah died.

Chapter 29:4-7 says, Thus says the LORD of hosts, the God of Israel, to all the exiles whom I have sent into exile from Jerusalem to Babylon: Build houses and live in them, plant gardens and eat what they produce. Take wives, and have sons and daughters . . . multiply there, and do not decrease. But seek the welfare of the city where I have sent you into exile, and pray to the LORD on its behalf, for in its welfare you will find your welfare. (This verse has been a guiding light to Jews everywhere they have been located throughout the ages.)

Verses 10-14 say, For thus says the LORD: Only when Babylon's seventy years are completed will I visit you, and I will fulfill to you my promise and bring you back to this place. For surely I know the plans I have for you, says the LORD, plans for your welfare and not for harm, to give you a future with hope. Then when you call upon me and come and pray to me, I will hear you. When you search for me, you will find me; if you seek me with all your heart. I will let you find me, says the LORD, and I will restore your fortunes and gather you from all the nations and all the places where I have driven you, says the LORD, and I will bring you back to the place from which I sent you into exile.

The rest of the chapter from (21-32) mentions the false prophets Ahab, Zedekiah, and Shemaiah. The LORD in (23) tells them that they have spoken lies in his name and committed adultery with their neighbors' wives. The first two will be roasted in the fire of the king of Babylon, and the last will have no living descendants to see the good I will do to my people says the LORD.

Chapter 30:2-3 says, The word that came to Jeremiah from the LORD: Thus says the LORD, the God of Israel: Write in a book all the words I have spoken to you. For the days are surely coming, says the LORD, when I will restore the fortunes of my people, Israel and Judah, says the LORD, and I will bring them back to the land that I gave to their ancestors and they shall take possession of it.

Verses 8-9 say, On that day, says the LORD of hosts, I will break the yoke from off his neck, and I will burst his bonds, and strangers shall no more make a servant of him. But they shall serve the LORD their God and David their king, whom I will raise up for them. (This is another messianic prophecy.) Verse 18 says, Thus says the LORD: I am going to restore the fortunes of the tents of Jacob, and have compassion on his dwellings; the city shall be rebuilt upon its mound, and the citadel set on its rightful site. Verse 22 says, And you shall be my people, and I will be your God.

In chapter 31:3-4 the LORD says, I have loved you with an everlasting love; therefore I have continued my faithfulness to you. Again I will build you, and you shall be built, O virgin Israel! Verses 8-9 say, See, I am going to bring them from the land of the north, and gather them from the farthest parts of the earth, among them the blind and the lame, those with child and those in labor, together; a great company, they shall return here. With weeping they shall come, and with consolations I will lead them back . . . for I have become a father to Israel, and Ephraim is my first born.

Verses 31-34 say, The days are surely coming, says the LORD, when I will make a new covenant with the house of Israel and the house of Judah. It will not be like the covenant that I made with their ancestors, a covenant that they broke . . . But this is the covenant I will make with the house of Israel after those days, says the LORD: I will put my law within them, and I will write it on their hearts; and I will be their God, and they shall be my people. No longer shall they teach one another, or say to each other, "Know the LORD," for they shall all know me from the least of them to the greatest, says the LORD; for I will forgive their iniquity, and remember their sins no more.

For Christians this covenant begins with Christ and finds its completion in the final kingdom. For Jews it means when they return from exile they will focus on proper interpretation and inculcation among all the people as never before.

Chapter 32:1-3 says, The word that came to Jeremiah from the LORD in the tenth year of King Zedekiah of Judah, which was the eighteenth year of King Nebuchadnezzar. At that time the army of the king of Babylon was besieging Jerusalem, and the prophet Jeremiah was confined in the court of the guard that was in the palace of the king of Judah, where King Zedekiah of Judah had confined him. (Zedekiah wants to know why Jeremiah is prophesying against him. But Jeremiah does not respond.)

Verse 6 says, Jeremiah said, the Word of the LORD came to me. Hanamel son of your uncle Shallum is going to come to you and say, "Buy my field that is at Anathoth for the right of redemption by purchase is yours." Verse 9 says, I bought the field at Anathoth from my cousin Hanamel, and weighed out the money to him, seventeen shekels of silver.

Verses 16-17 say, After I had given the deed of purchase to Baruch son of Neriah,

I prayed to the LORD saying, Ah Lord GOD! It is you that made the heavens and the earth by your great power and by your outstretched arm! Nothing is too hard for you. (This is telling the people of Judah that God has a future for the land. This buying of property is the most detailed account of a business transaction in the Bible.)

Chapter 33:1 says, The word of the LORD came to Jeremiah a second time, while he was still confined in the court of the guard. In (7-9) God says, I will restore the fortunes of Judah and the fortunes of Israel and rebuild them as they were at first. I will cleanse them from the guilt of their sin against me . . . And this city shall be to me a name of joy, a praise and a glory before all the nations of the earth who shall hear of all the good that I do for them; they shall fear and tremble because of all the good and all the prosperity I provide for it.

Verses 14-17 say, The days are surely coming, says the LORD, when I will fulfill the promise I made to the house of Israel and the house of Judah. In those days and at that time I will cause a righteous Branch to spring up for David; and he shall execute justice and righteousness in the land. In those days Judah will be saved, and Jerusalem shall live in safety. And this is the name by which it will be called: "The LORD is our righteousness." (The righteous branch is always messianic.)

In chapter 34:14-17 God states another reason he is unhappy with them. The wealthy are to set their slaves free every seven years. He said, they promised to do so in a covenant made in the temple. But (16-17) says, you turned around and profaned my name when each of you took back your male and female slaves, whom you had set free according to their desire, and you brought them again into subjection to be your slaves. Therefore, thus says the LORD: You have not obeyed me . . . I will make you a horror to all the kingdoms of the earth.

Chapter 35 illustrates the Rechabites as a good example. They are a religious sect named in honor of their founder Jonadab, the son of Rechab, during the reign of Jehu (842-815 B.C.). They abstain from wine and are nomads living in tents. The loyalty to their covenant is contrasted with the disloyalty of God's people with the covenant they had with God. Verse 16 says, The descendants of Jonadab son of Rechab have carried out the command that their ancestor gave them, but this people has not obeyed me.

Chapter 36:1-3 says, In the fourth year of King Jehoiakim son of Josiah of Judah this word came to Jeremiah from the LORD: Take a scroll and write on it all the words I have spoken to you against Israel and Judah and all the nations, from the day I spoke to you, from the days of Josiah until today. It may be that when the house of Judah hears of all the disasters that I intend to do to them, all of them may turn from their evil ways, so that I may forgive their iniquity and their sin.

Verse 4 says, Jeremiah called Baruch son of Neriah, his secretary, and Baruch wrote on a scroll at Jeremiah's dictation all the words of the LORD that he had spoken to him. Verses 9-10 say, in the fifth year of King Jehoiakim son of Josiah of Judah, in the ninth month, all the people . . . proclaimed a fast before the LORD. Then in the hearing of all the people, Baruch read the words of Jeremiah from the scroll in the house of the LORD . . . In (20-23) the king is informed and sends Jehudi to get the scroll and read it to him. As the scroll is being read to him, the king cuts it up and throws it into the fire.

The king then commands Jeremiah and Baruch to be arrested, but as (26) says, the LORD hid them. Verses 27-28 say, Now, after the king had burned the scroll with the words that Baruch wrote at Jeremiah's dictation, the word of the LORD came to Jeremiah: Take another scroll and write on it all the former words that were in the first scroll, which King Jehoikim of Judah has burned. Verses 30-32 say, thus says the LORD concerning King Jehoiakim of Judah: He shall have no one to sit upon the throne of David, and his dead body shall be cast out to the heat of the day and the frost of night. And I will punish him and his offspring and his servants for their iniquity; . . . Then Jeremiah took another scroll and gave it to the secretary Baruch son of Neriah, who wrote on it at Jeremiah's dictation all the words of the scroll that King Jehoiakim of Judah had burned in the fire; and many similar words were added to them.

Chapter 37 tells us that while Zedekiah was king, neither he nor his servants nor the people of the land listened to the words of God that he spoke through the prophet Jeremiah. In fact (15-16) say, The officials were enraged at Jeremiah, and they beat him and imprisoned him in the house of the secretary Jonathan, for it had been made a prison. Thus Jeremiah was put in the cistern house, in the cells, and remained there many days.

In 38:4-5 the king's officials tell him that Jeremiah should be put to death for subverting the war effort. "This man ought to be put to death, because he is discouraging the soldiers who are left in this city, and all the people, by speaking such words to them. For this man is not seeking the welfare of this people, but their harm." (Sounds like something from a news broadcast during the war in Iraq.) Verse 6 says, So they took Jeremiah and threw him into the cistern of Malchiah, the king's son, which was in the court of the guard, letting Jeremiah down by ropes. Now there was no water in the cistern, but only mud, and Jeremiah sank in the mud. (The public officials did this because Jeremiah spoke against a war God did not approve, but the officials approved.)

In verse 7 Ebed-melech, the Ethiopian, a eunuch in the king's house, goes to the king and in (9-10) says, My lord king, these men have acted wickedly in all they did to the prophet Jeremiah by throwing him into the cistern to die there of hunger, for there is no bread left in the city. Then the king commanded Ebed-melech the Ethiopian, "Take three men with you from here, and pull the prophet Jeremiah up from the cistern before he dies." Verse 13 says, they drew Jeremiah up by the ropes and pulled him out of the cistern. And Jeremiah remained in the court of the guard.

The rest of Chapter 38 beginning in verses 14-23 is an encounter between Zedekiah who summoned Jeremiah to a private meeting. Justifiably suspicious Jeremiah makes Zedekiah give his word that he will be safe. Then in secret King Zedekiah tells Jeremiah he has something to ask of him. Jeremiah says to Zedekiah in (15), "If I tell you, you will put me to death, will you not? And if I give you advice, you will not listen to me."

Zedekiah swears an oath to Jeremiah, and Jeremiah in (17-18) says, "Thus says the LORD the God of hosts the God of Israel, if you will only surrender to the officials of the king of Babylon, then your life shall be spared, and the city will not be burned with fire, and you and your house shall live. But if you do not surrender to the officials of the king of Babylon, then this city will be handed over to the Chaldeans (Babylonians), and they shall burn it with fire, and you yourself shall not escape from their hand." In verses 24-26 Zedekiah said to Jeremiah, "Do not let anyone know of this conversation, or you will die." Verse 28 says, Jeremiah remained in the court of the guard until the day that Jerusalem was taken.

Chapter 39 informs us that in the ninth year of King Zedekiah in the tenth month of King Nebuchadnezzar of Babylon, the siege of Jerusalem begins. In the eleventh year and fourth month the city begins to fall. King Zedekiah and the soldiers in (4-8) try to run away at night, but the army overtakes them in the plains of Jericho. The king of Babylon slaughters the sons of Zedekiah before his eyes, then puts out the eyes of Zedekiah, and binds him in fetters and takes him to Babylon. The city and the temple are burned.

Verse 10 says, Nebuzaradan the captain of the guard left in the land of Judah some of the poor people who owned nothing, and gave them vineyards and fields at the same time. Nebuchadnezzar in verse 14 then sets Jeremiah free entrusting him to Gedeliah.

In chapter 40:4-5 Nebuzaradan says to Jeremiah, If you wish to come with me to Babylon, come, and I will take good care of you, but if you do not wish to come with me to Babylon you need not come . . . If you remain, then return to Gedeliah . . . whom the king of Babylon appointed governor of the towns of Judah and stay with him among the people; or go wherever you think it right to go. Verse 6 says that Jeremiah went to Gedeliah son of Ahikam at Mizpah and stayed with him among the people who were left in the land.

In chapter 41:2 Ishmael, loyal to King Zedekiah and one of his chief officers, strikes down Gedeliah at Mizpah because the king of Babylon appointed him governor. Many others are also struck down. In (11) Johanan and those with him go to fight against Ishmael, and after the fight Ishmael escapes.

In chapter 42:2-3 Johanan goes to Jeremiah and says, "Be good enough to listen to our plea and pray . . . Let the LORD your God show us where we should go and what we should do." Verses 7-17 inform us that at the end of ten days the word of the LORD comes to Jeremiah who tells Johanan and all the people in (10) If you will only remain in this land, then I will build you up and not pull you down; I will plant you and not pluck you up, for I am sorry for the disaster I brought upon you. They are then told not to be afraid of the king of Babylon, and he will grant them mercy if they stay in the land, but in verses 16-17 he tells them that if they are determined to settle in Egypt then they will die there by the sword, famine, and pestilence.

In chapter 43:2 Johanan and his men said to Jeremiah, "You are telling a lie. The LORD our God did not send you to say, 'Do not to go to Egypt to settle there'; but Baruch son of Neriah is inciting you against us, to hand us over to the Chaldeans, in order that they may kill us or take us into exile in Babylon." Verse 7 says, And they came into the land of Egypt, for they did not obey the voice of the LORD.

Apparently they force Jeremiah to go with them, for verses 8-11 say, Then the word of the LORD came to Jeremiah in Tahpanhes: Take some large stones in your hands, and bury them in the clay pavement that is at the entrance to Pharaoh's palace in Tahpanhes. Let the Judeans see you do it, and say to them, Thus says the LORD of hosts, the God of Israel: I am going to send and take my servant King Nebuchadnezzar of Babylon, and he will set his throne above these stones that I have buried, and he will spread his royal canopy over them. He shall come and ravage the land of Egypt, giving those who are destined for pestilence, to pestilence, and those who are destined to captivity, to captivity, and those who are destined for the sword, to the sword.

In chapter 44 God through Jeremiah tells the exiles in Egypt why they will be destroyed in Egypt. Not only did they disobey his command, but in (7-8) the LORD says, Why are you doing such great harm to yourselves . . . Why do you provoke me to anger with the works of your hands, making offerings to other gods in the land of Egypt where you have come to settle?

They rejected the one God and his teachings and are worshiping the different gods of Egypt including the queen of heaven, which was Ishtar the Babylonian-Assyrian goddess of the star Venus. Verse 11 says, thus says the LORD of hosts, the God of Israel; I am determined to bring disaster on you, to bring all Judah to an end. But in (16-19) they say to Jeremiah, "As for the word you have spoken to us in the name of the LORD, we are not going to listen to you . . ."

Chapter 45:1-3 says, The word that the prophet Jeremiah spoke to Baruch son of Neriah, when he wrote the words in a scroll at the dictation of Jeremiah, in the fourth year of King Jehoiakim son of Josiah of Judah: Thus says the LORD, the God of Israel, to you, O Baruch: You said, "Woe is me! The LORD has added sorrow to my pain; I am weary with my groaning, and I find no rest."

Verse 4-5 say, Thus you shall say to him, Thus says the LORD: "I am going to break down what I have built, and pluck up what I have planted—that is the whole land. And you, do you seek great things for yourself? Do not seek them; for I am going to bring disaster on all flesh, says the LORD; but I will give you your life as a prize of war in every place to which you may go."

The rest of the chapters (46-52) consist of prophecies of judgment against the nations. The word of the LORD came to the prophet Jeremiah concerning the nations. Jeremiah is a prophet to the nations as well as to Judah. The nations are used by God at different times to bring Israel and Judah to repentance. But these nations are also unjust with the same type of sins as Israel and Judah. Therefore they will be judged also. (This writer believes this is also a message for all nations even today.)

In chapter 46 Egypt will be judged. In chapter 47 the Philistines will be judged. In chapter 48 Moab will be judged. In chapter 49 the Ammonites, Edom, Damascus, and Elam will be judged. Jeremiah devotes two chapters 50 and 51 to Babylon because they burned down Jerusalem and destroyed the temple.

Chapters 50-51 seem to be part poem and hymn. In chapter 50:39-40 says, wild animals shall live with hyenas in Babylon, and ostriches shall inhabit her; she shall never again be peopled, or inhabited for all generations. As when God overthrew Sodom and Gomorrah and their neighbors, says the LORD, so no one shall live there, nor shall anyone settle there.

Chapter 51:37 adds, Babylon shall become a heap of ruins, a den of jackals, and an object of hissing without inhabitant. In verses 61-64 Jeremiah sends a scroll to Seraiah, brother of Baruch, foretelling Babylon's destruction. He says, "When you come to Babylon, see that you read all these words . . . When you finish reading this scroll, tie a stone to it, and throw it into the middle of the Euphrates, and say, 'Thus shall Babylon sink, to rise no more, because of the disasters I am bringing on her.' " (This is an obvious poetic hyperbole, for even though God had Babylon destroyed these verses were not literally fulfilled.)

Chapter 52 is the last chapter of Jeremiah. It parallels II Kings 24-26 and Jeremiah 39 and 40. It is an historical appendix. The content goes over key events in the conquering and destruction of Jerusalem and the exile of the people into Babylon. God did what he said he would do, and for the reasons he said. Tradition says Jeremiah was stoned to death in Egypt.

This ends the book of Jeremiah. After reading the book this writer would be curious to know if the reader believes the people of the United States and the people of the world act any differently than the way Israel, Judah, and the nations acted during the time of Jeremiah? One may even need to add many Christian churches, Jewish synagogues, and Islamic mosques to that list. This writer also wonders what percentage of today's clergy ignore the word of God, or adjust the word of God, or conform the word of God to their particular ideology in order to give people what they want to hear, as opposed to those who apply God's word to the happenings of the nation and the world even when it is biting to the ears. How do you think God analyzes our actions in our world in these times?

One final note. We must not use the words of Scripture to analyze other individuals or other nations before we first use it to analyze ourselves and our own nation. Jesus said it this way, first take the log out of your own eye (see Matt 7:4).

LAMENTATIONS

The book of Lamentations is usually put with Jeremiah to show that his prophecies came true. Jerusalem and the temple are destroyed and the people are in agony as they raise a sorrowful heart to God. The setting is one standing in the ruins recognizing the prophetic truth that there is a direct connection between the sin of the people's disobedience to God and the destruction of Jerusalem and exile. Even so, God still loves his people and calls them to return to him.

The first four chapters are alphabetic acrostics with a stanza for each of the twenty-two letters of the Hebrew alphabet. The fifth chapter has the same number of verses as the alphabet. All are composed or adapted for public recitation on days of fasting and mourning. Some interesting verses are the following: Chapter 1, 2:20-21, 3:25, 5:1-3, 19-22.

Lamentations is one of the Megilloth used as the five festival scrolls. The Megilloth consists of five major biblical books each one assigned to and read during the different major Jewish religious feasts. Lamentations is used for the fast of the ninth of Ab in the month of August. This is a day to remember the destruction of Jerusalem and its temple. It is also a day for remembering the Holocaust.

The literary style is poetry, the method many writers use to express their deepest emotions. Lamentations is a lament following the destruction of Jerusalem and the temple in 586 B.C. The theme stresses the agony of the people and the apparent desertion by God. It is also about the hope that God will restore a humble repentant remnant.

Jerusalem is not only the capitol of the nation, it is Zion, the symbol of God's presence. It is the center around which all revolves indicating that all creation revolves around God. There are few works in all literature that picture more vividly the hatreds and horrors that war and destruction bring.

Chapter 1:1 says, How lonely sits the city that was once full of people! How like a widow she has become, she that was great among the nations! Verse 5 says, because the LORD has made her suffer for the multitude of her transgressions; her children have gone away, captives before the foe. Verse 18 says, The LORD is in the right, for I have rebelled against his word; but hear, all you peoples, and behold my suffering; my young women and young men have gone into captivity.

Chapter 2:2 says, The LORD has destroyed without mercy all the dwellings of Jacob; in his wrath he has broken down the strongholds of daughter Judah; he has brought down to the ground in dishonor the kingdom and its rulers. The writer in (11) says, My eyes are spent with weeping; my stomach churns; my bile is poured out on the ground because of the destruction of my people.

Verse 14 says, Your prophets have seen for you false and deceptive visions; they have not exposed your iniquity to restore your fortunes, but have seen oracles for you that are false and misleading, and verses 17-19 say, The LORD has done what he purposed, as he ordained long ago, he has demolished without pity; he has made the enemy rejoice over you, and exalted the might of your foes. Cry aloud to the LORD! O wall of daughter Zion! Let tears stream down like a torrent day and night! Give yourself no rest, your eyes no respite! Arise, cry out in the night, at the beginning of the watches! Pour out your heart like water before the presence of the LORD! Lift your hands to him for the lives of your children, who faint for hunger at the head of every street.

Verses 20-21 say, Look O LORD and consider! To whom have you done this? Should women eat their offspring, the children they have born? Should priest and prophet be killed in the sanctuary of the LORD? The young and the old are lying on the ground in the streets; my young women and my young men have fallen by the sword; in the day of your anger you have killed them, slaughtering without mercy.

In chapter 3:4-6 the writer says, He has made my flesh and my skin waste away, and broken my bones; he has besieged and enveloped me with bitterness and tribulation; he has made me sit in darkness like the dead of long ago. Verses 15-17 say, He has filled me with bitterness, he has sated me with wormwood. He has made my teeth grind on gravel, and made me cower in ashes; my soul is bereft of peace; I have forgotten what happiness is; so I say, "Gone is the glory, and all that I had hoped for from the LORD."

But the writer in (21) says, I have hope: and (24-26) say, "The LORD is my portion," says my soul, "therefore I will hope in him." The LORD is good to those who wait for him, to the soul that seeks him. It is good that one should wait quietly for the salvation of the LORD. In (31-33) he says, the LORD will not reject forever. Although he causes grief, he will have compassion according to the abundance of his steadfast love; for he does not willingly afflict or grieve anyone. Chapter 3:40 says, Let us test and examine our ways and return to the LORD.

Chapter 4 describes the effects of the siege. Verse 1 says, The sacred stones lie scattered at the head of every street. Verse 4 says, The tongue of the infant sticks to the roof of its mouth for thirst; the children beg for food, but no one gives them anything, and verses 9-10 say, Happier were those pierced by the sword than those pierced by hunger, whose life drains away, deprived of the produce of the field. The hands of compassionate women have boiled their own children; they became their food in the destruction of my people.

Verses 13-14 say, It was for the sins of her prophets and the iniquities of her priests, who shed the blood of the righteous in the midst of her. Blindly they wandered through the streets, so defiled with blood that no one could touch their garments. Hope is offered in (22) when the writer says, The punishment of your iniquity, O daughter Zion, is accomplished, he will keep you in exile no longer; but your iniquity, O daughter Edom, he will punish, he will uncover your sins. (The leaders, priests and prophets, let the people down by not honoring God and his word.)

Chapter 5:1-3 says, Remember, O LORD, what has befallen us; look, and see our disgrace! Our inheritance has been turned over to strangers, our homes to aliens. We have become orphans, fatherless; our mothers are like widows. Verses 8-12 say, Slaves rule over us; there is no one to deliver us from their hand. We get our bread at the peril of our lives, because of the sword in the wilderness. Our skin is black as an oven from the scorching heat of famine. Women are raped in Zion, virgins in the towns of Judah. Princes are hung up by their hands; no respect is shown to the elders.

Verses 14-16 say, The old men have left the city gate, the young men their music.

The joy of our hearts has ceased; our dancing has turned into mourning. The crown has fallen from our head; woe to us, for we have sinned! Verse 21 says, Restore us to yourself, O LORD, that we may be restored; renew our days of old--unless you have utterly rejected us, and are angry with us beyond measure.

God was true to his word. For those who believe Scripture is God's inspired word, the message is as contemporary for people today as it was for people in those times.

EZEKIEL

Ezekiel is active between the years of 593-571 B.C. when Jerusalem is in the process of being conquered by the Babylonians. He is a prophet-priest deeply concerned about the temple and its worship. His revelation is more visual and mystical than most of the other prophets. He describes God's throne as a moving chariot no longer tied to the temple. A major theme is the need for inner conversion and worship from an inner spirit.

In chapter 1 Ezekiel has a lofty notion of God's transcendence and glory as he has a mystical vision. Ezekiel uses symbolism more than most prophets to get his point across. For example dry bones in chapter 37 shows that the dead (Judah) will rise.

He writes in chapter 3 and in chapter 33 that prophets are called to be a *sentinel* (watchman), to warn the people, and if the prophets do not, they will be called to account. Ezekiel is a visionary. He uses the term, *mortal* (son of man) a term Jesus constantly used about himself. Ezekiel uses this term ninety-three times.

His use of names influences the book of Revelation. For example, many fanciful theories will come from Gog and Magog in chapters 38-39. These chapters are a special type of literature called *Apocalyptic.* Isaiah 24-27, the book of Daniel, as well as parts of Zechariah are other examples of apocalyptic in the OT; the book of Revelation is an example of apocalyptic in the NT. Many of the books called *pseudepigrapha* written in the era before Christ are apocalyptic. Pseudepigrapha are books not considered canonical by anyone even as they attempt to appear as Scripture. Some of the Qur'an is written in the apocalyptic style. There will be more on the subject of apocalyptic later.

In chapters 40-48 he uses hyperbole to describe a magnificent perfected temple to be built. Some think it was fulfilled by the temple Herod builds, and then as far as Christians are concerned by Jesus, who said he is the temple of God. Others think it will literally be in the future. The perfection Ezekiel attempts to describe may also represent the time all God's people will be gathered with him. Some interesting verses are as follows: 3:1-8, 17-21, 13:1-23, 18:5-9, 22:6-12, 34:11-23.

Ezekiel, Jeremiah's younger contemporary, is transported to Babylon in 596 B.C. during the first exile when Jehoiakim surrenders Jerusalem and is taken into exile. With him go approximately ten thousand statesmen, soldiers, and skilled workers, but it will not be until 586 B.C. that Jerusalem is totally destroyed. In the meantime puppet kings are appointed to rule Jerusalem by the king of Babylon (see 2 Kings, 2 Chronicles, and Jeremiah).

While in exile, Ezekiel's job is to declare God's message to the exiles. Meanwhile, Jeremiah is preaching in Jerusalem. One of Ezekiel's key themes stresses individual responsibility before God. Ezekiel is a priest, who is a mystical visionary, and thus he appreciates and understands ritual. The book is basically written in the first person. His prophecies are similar to Isaiah, Jeremiah, and Daniel but different in that they are more ordered and dated. The phrase, they shall know that I am God, occurs sixty three times in this book.

The NT book of Revelation will borrow many of Ezekiel's symbols. The key to understanding the prophets is not trying to figure out what God is going to do in the far distant future, for that is not their purpose. The key to understanding the prophets is: what is God pointing out about how those people at that time were following his teachings individually, religiously, socially, and politically.

The challenge we moderns face is to transfer to our times the message and the themes expressed and the lessons learned. Let us look in more detail at this mystical book that has produced many different interpretations. In chapter 1 we immediately get a sense of Ezekiel's mystical visions and symbolism. God gives Ezekiel an overwhelming vision of his glory expressing the awesome holiness of God. Do not expect to rationally make much sense of it, for it is a mystical vision.

EZEKIEL

Chapter 1:1-3 says, In the thirtieth year, in the fourth month, on the fifth day of the month, as I was among the exiles by the river Chebar, the heavens were opened, and I saw visions of God. On the fifth day of the month (the fifth year of the exile of King Jehoiachin), the word of the LORD came to the priest Ezekiel son of Buzi, in the land of the Chaldeans by the river Chebar; and the hand of the LORD was on him there.

Ezekiel in chapter 1 describes his mystical experience in the following way. In verses 4-7 he said, As I looked, a stormy wind came out of the north: a great cloud with brightness around it and fire flashing continually, and in the middle of the fire, something like gleaming amber. In the middle of it was something like four living creatures. This was their appearance: They were of human form. Each had four faces, and each of them had four wings. Their legs were straight, and the soles of their feet were like the sole of a calf's foot; and they sparkled like burnished bronze.

Verses 8-11 say, Under their wings on their four sides they had human hands, and the four had their faces and their wings thus: their wings touched one other; each of them moved straight ahead, without turning as they moved. As for the appearance of their faces: the four had the face of a human being, the face of a lion on the right side, the face of an ox on the left side, and the face of an eagle; such were their faces. Their wings were spread out above; each creature had two wings, each of which touched the wing of another, while two covered their bodies.

Verses 12-14 say, Each moved straight ahead; wherever their spirit would go, they went, without turning as they went. In the middle of the living creatures there was something that looked like burning coals of fire, like torches moving to and fro among the living creatures; the fire was bright, and lightning issued from the fire. The living creatures darted to and fro like a flash of lightning.

Verses 15-18 say, As I looked at the living creatures I saw a wheel on the earth beside the living creatures, one for each of the four of them. As for the appearance of the wheels and their construction: their appearance was like the gleaming of beryl; and the four had the same form; their construction being something like a wheel within a wheel. When they moved, they moved in any of the four directions without veering as they moved. Their rims were tall and awesome, for the rims of all four were full of eyes all around. When the living creature moved, the wheels moved beside them; and when the living creatures moved from the earth, the wheels rose.

Verses 19-21 say, Wherever the spirit would go, they went, and the wheels rose along with them; for the spirit of the living creatures was in the wheels. When they moved the others moved; when they stomped the others stomped; and when they rose from the earth, the wheels rose along with them; for the spirit of the living creature was in the wheels.(All of this is symbolic language as Ezekiel attempts to put into language the mystery he experienced.)

Verses 22-25 say, Over the heads of the living creatures, there was something like a dome, shining like crystal, spread out above their heads. Under the dome their wings were stretched out straight, one toward another; and each of the creatures had two wings covering its body. When they moved, I heard the sound of their wings like the sound of mighty waters, like the thunder of the almighty, a sound of tumult like the sound of an army; when they stopped, they let down their wings. And there came a voice from above the dome over their heads; when they stopped, they let down their wings.

Verses 26-28 say, And above the dome over their heads, there was something like a throne, in appearance like sapphire; and seated above the likeness of a throne was something that seemed like a human form. Upward from what appeared like the loins, I saw something like gleaming amber, something that looked like fire enclosed all around; and downward from what looked like the loins I saw something that looked like fire, and there was a splendor all around. Like the bow on a cloud on a rainy day, such was the appearance of the splendor all around. This was the appearance of the likeness of the glory of the LORD. When I saw it, I fell on my face, and I heard the voice of someone speaking. (All this description is an attempt by Ezekiel to describe what in reality can not be described as he experiences God enthroned above his creatures.)

Chapter 2:1-3 says, He said to me: O mortal (also translated literally by others as son of man), stand up on your feet, and I will speak with you. And when he spoke to me, a spirit entered into me and set me on my feet; and I heard him speaking to me. He said to me, Mortal, I am sending you to the people of Israel, to a nation of rebels who have rebelled against me; they and their ancestors have transgressed against me to this very day.

Verses 6-10 say, O mortal, do not be afraid of them, and do not be afraid or their words, . . . do not be dismayed with their looks, for they are a rebellious house. You shall speak my words to them, whether they hear or refuse to hear; for they are a rebellious house. But you, mortal, hear what I say to you; do not be rebellious like that rebellious house; open your mouth and eat what I give you. I looked, and a hand was stretched out to me, and a written scroll was in it . . . and written on it were words of lamentation and mourning and woe.

Chapter 3:1-4 says, He said to me, O mortal, eat what is offered to you; eat this scroll and go, speak to the house of Israel. So I opened my mouth, and he gave me the scroll to eat. He said to me, Mortal, eat this scroll that I give you and fill your stomach with it; then I ate it and my mouth was sweet as honey. He said to me: Mortal, go to the house of Israel and speak my very words to them. But in (7) he was told, the house of Israel will not listen to you, for they are not willing to listen to me; because all the house of Israel have a hard forehead and a stubborn heart.

Ezekiel in (12-13) says, Then the spirit lifted me up, and as *the glory of the LORD rose* from its place, I heard behind me the sound of loud rumbling; it was the sound of the wings of the living creatures brushing against one another, and the sound of the wheels beside them, that sounded like a loud rumbling.

Kugel (2007) says, the Hebrew translation for, the glory of the LORD rose, is: Blessed be the glory of the LORD, or Blessed be the LORD's glory from his place. This coupled with Isa 6:3 Holy, Holy, Holy is the LORD of hosts is part of the daily Jewish prayer, the Kedushah.

Verses 14-15 say, The spirit lifted me up and bore me away; I went in bitterness in the heat of my spirit, the hand of the LORD being strong upon me. I came to the exiles at Tel-abib, who lived by the River Chebar. And I sat there among them, stunned, for seven days. (It has been said that modern Tel Aviv was named after this location.)

Verses 16-19 At the end of seven days the word of the LORD came to me: Mortal I have made you a sentinel (watchman) for the house of Israel; whenever you hear a word from my mouth, you shall give them warning from me. If I say to the wicked, "You shall surely die," and you give them no warning, or speak to warn the wicked from their wicked way, in order to save their life, those wicked persons shall die for their iniquity; but their blood I will require at your hand. But if you warn the wicked, and they do not turn from their wickedness, or from their wicked way, they shall die for their iniquity, but you will have saved your life. (Typical of Hebrew style he repeats this again in this chapter and in later chapters.)

Chapter 4:1-3 says, And you, O mortal, take a brick and set it before you. On it portray a city, Jerusalem; and put siege works against it, and build a siege wall against it, and cast up a ramp against it; set camps also against it, and plant battering rams against it all around. Then take an iron plate and place it as an iron wall between you and the city; set your face toward it, and let it be in a state of siege, and press the siege against it. This is the sign for the house of Israel.

Verses 4-8 say, Then lie on your left side, and place the punishment of the house of Israel against it; you shall bear their punishment for the number of days you lie there. For I assign to you a number of days, three hundred ninety days, equal to the number of the years of their punishment; and so you shall bear the punishment of the house of Israel.

When you have completed these, you shall lie down a second time, but on your right side, and bear the punishment of the house of Judah; forty days I assign you, one day for each year. You shall set your face toward the siege of Jerusalem, and with your arm bared you shall prophesy against it. See, I am putting cords on you so that you can not turn from one side to the other until you have completed the days of your siege.

Was he to lie there continuously? The last verse seems to indicate he did. Possibly he was to lie there part of each day instead of all the time every day, but never being loosed would certainly get the point across. The Septuagint, the Greek version of the Hebrew Bible, contains entirely different numbers. The Septuagint was used by the NT writers. This is an example of the literary style called an object lesson portraying what will happen to Israel and Judah. The rest of the chapter portrays the difficulty of surviving when that time comes.

Chapter 5:1-4 says, O mortal, take a sharp sword; use it as a barber's razor and run it over your head and beard; then take balances for weighing, and divide the hair. One third of the hair you shall burn in the fire inside the city, when the days of the siege are completed; one third you shall take and strike with the sword all around the city; and one third you shall scatter to the wind, and I will unsheathe the sword after them. Then you shall take from these a small number, and bind them in the skirts of your robe. From these, again, you shall take some, throw them into the fire and burn them up; from there a fire will come out against all the house of Israel.

The hair is the symbol of the fate awaiting the people of Jerusalem. The sword is used as the razor to express the idea of military defeat, and putting everything into thirds is how it will happen as shown in the following verses.

Verses 8-10 say, Thus says the Lord GOD, I, I myself, am coming against you; I will execute judgments among you in the sight of the nations. And because of all your abominations, I will do to you what I have never yet done and the like of which I will never do again. Surely, parents shall eat their children in your midst, and children shall eat their parents; I will execute judgment on you, and any of you who survive I will scatter to every wind. Verse 12 says, one third of you shall die of pestilence or be consumed by famine among you; one third shall fall by the sword around you; and one third I will scatter to every wind and will unsheathe the sword after them. (This will happen soon and again after the death of Jesus in AD 70.)

Verses 15-17 say, You shall be a mockery and a taunt, a warning and a horror, to the nations around you, when I execute judgments on you in anger and fury, and with furious punishments—I, the LORD, have spoken—when I loose against you my deadly arrows of famine, arrows for destruction, which I will loose to destroy you, and when I bring more and more famine upon you, and break your staff of bread. I will send famine and wild animals against you, and they will rob you of your children; pestilence and bloodshed shall pass through you; and I will bring the sword upon you. I the LORD have spoken.

In chapter 6 The LORD through Ezekiel prophesies against the mountains representing the high places where the people worshiped the pagan gods. Ezekiel in (3) says, You mountains of Israel, hear the word of the Lord GOD! . . . I myself shall bring a sword upon you, and I will destroy your high places. Verses 6-7 say, Wherever you live, your towns shall be waste and your high places ruined, so that your altars be waste and ruined, your idols broken and destroyed, your incense stands cut down, and your works wiped out. The slain shall fall in your midst; then you shall know that I am the LORD.

Chapter 7:2-4 says, The end has come upon the four corners of the land. Now the end is upon you, I will let loose my anger upon you; I will judge you according to your ways, I will punish you for all your abominations . . . Then you shall know I am the LORD. Verses 7-8 say, Your doom has come to you, O inhabitants of the land. The time has come, the day is near—of tumult, not of reveling on the mountains. Soon I will pour out my wrath upon you; I will spend my anger against you. I will judge you according to your ways, and punish you for all your abominations. Verse 19 says, Their silver and gold can not save them on the day of the wrath of the LORD. They shall not satisfy their hunger or fill their stomachs with it. For it was the stumbling block of their iniquity.

Verses 24-25 say, I will bring the worst of the nations to take possession of their houses. I will put an end to the arrogance of the strong, and their holy places shall be profaned. When anguish comes, they will seek peace, but there shall be none. Verse 27 says, According to their way I will deal with them; according to their own judgments I will judge them. And they shall know that I am the LORD.

Chapter 8:1-4 presents another mystical experience for Ezekiel. Ezekiel says, I sat in my house, with the elders of Judah sitting before me, the hand of the Lord GOD fell upon me there. I looked and there was a figure that looked like a human being; below what appeared to be its loins it was fire, and above the loins it was like the appearance of brightness, like gleaming amber. It stretched out the form of a hand and took me by the lock of my head; and the spirit lifted me up between earth and heaven, and brought me in visions of God to Jerusalem, to the entrance of the gateway of the inner court that faces north, to the seat of the image of jealousy, which provokes to jealousy. And the glory of the God of Israel was there, like the vision I had seen in the valley.

Ezekiel was brought visions of God at the gateway of the inner court in Jerusalem. In (7-12) Ezekiel was shown the people of Judah still worshiping pagan gods in the temple. They thought God could not see what they were doing. In (17) God said, "Have you seen this, O mortal? Is it not bad enough that the house of Judah commits the abominations done here? Must they fill the land with violence and still provoke my anger still further? . . . Therefore I will act in wrath; my eyes will not spare, nor will I have pity; and though they cry in my hearing with a loud voice, I will not listen to them."

In chapter 9:1-2 Ezekiel saw a vision of the executioners of the city. There was a man in linen with a writing case at his side. (Linen represents a priest.) Verses 3-4 say, The LORD called to the man clothed in linen, who had the writing case at his side; and said to him, "Go through the city, through Jerusalem, and put a mark on the foreheads of those who sigh and groan over all the abominations that are committed in it." To the others in (5) he said in my hearing, "Pass through the city after him, and kill; your eye shall not spare, and you shall show no pity . . . but touch no one who has the mark. And begin at my sanctuary." Verse 7 says, So they went out and killed in the city.

In verses 8-11 Ezekiel fell prostrate and cried out, "Ah Lord GOD! will you destroy all who remain of Israel as you pour out your wrath upon Jerusalem?" He said to me, "The guilt of the house of Israel and Judah is exceedingly great; the land is full of bloodshed and the city full of perversity; for they say, 'The LORD has forsaken the land, and the LORD does not see.' As for me, my eye will not spare, nor will I have pity, but I will bring down their deeds upon their heads." Then the man clothed in linen, with the writing case at his side, brought back word saying, "I have done as you commanded me."

In chapters 10-11 Ezekiel experiences mystery again as he sees a vision of the living creatures, the glory, and the whirling wheels he saw in chapter 1. Ezekiel sees the glory of God above the main processional entrance to the temple. Verse 18 says, Then the glory of the LORD went out from the threshold of the house and stopped over the cherubim.

In chapter 11:1-12 the spirit transports Ezekiel to see the rulers who are advocating resistance to Babylon despite the insistence of God's prophets that this would prove fatal. The spirit lifts him up and brings him to the east gate of the temple for him to see who they were. Ezekiel sees they will be punished.

God gives hope through Ezekiel when in (17-21) he says, I will gather you from the peoples, and assemble you out of the countries where you have been scattered, and I will give you the land of Israel. When they come here, they will remove from it all its detestable things and all its abominations. I will give them one heart, and put a new spirit within them; I will remove the heart of stone from their flesh and give them a heart of flesh, so that they may follow my statutes and keep my ordinances and obey them. Then they shall be my people and I will be their God. But as for those whose heart goes after their detestable things and their abominations, I will bring their deeds upon their own heads, says the Lord GOD.

Then verses 22-24 say, Then the cherubim lifted up their wings, with the wheels beside them; and the glory of the God of Israel was above them. And the glory of the LORD ascended from the middle of the city, and stopped on the mountain east of the city. The spirit lifted me up and brought me in a vision by the spirit of God into

Chaldea (Babylon), to the exiles. Then, the vision that I had seen left me. And I told the exiles all the things that the LORD had shown me. (Ezekiel is learning that God is not confined to the temple or even to a nation as many in the nation thought.)

In chapter 12:1-3 Ezekiel says, the word of the LORD came to me: Mortal, you are living in the midst of a rebellious house, who have eyes to see but do not see, who have ears to hear but do not hear; for they are a rebellious house. Then the LORD tells Ezekiel to act out the exile. He is told to take his baggage and dig through a wall in their sight. When they ask what you are doing, verse 10 says, Say to them, "Thus says the Lord GOD: This oracle concerns the prince in Jerusalem and the house of Israel in it." Say, "I am a sign for you; . . . they shall all go into exile, into captivity."

Chapter 13:1-4 says, The word of the LORD came to me: Mortal, prophesy against the prophets of Israel who are prophesying; say to those who prophesy out of their own imagination: "Hear the word of the LORD!" Thus says the Lord GOD, Alas for the senseless prophets who follow their own spirit, and have seen nothing! Your prophets have been like jackals among ruins, O Israel. Verse 6 says, They have envisioned falsehood and lying divination, they say, "Says the LORD," when the LORD has not sent them, and yet they wait for the fulfillment of their word!

Verse 10 says, they have misled the people saying, "Peace," when there is no peace; and because, when the people build a wall, these prophets smear whitewash on it (tell them smooth things). Verse 15 says, Thus I will spend my wrath upon the wall, and upon those who have smeared it with whitewash . . . the prophets of Israel who prophesied concerning Jerusalem and saw visions of peace for it, when there was no peace, says the Lord GOD.

In verses 22-23 the LORD said to Ezekiel, tell them, Because you have disheartened the righteous falsely, although I have not disheartened them, and you have encouraged the wicked not to turn from their wicked way and save their lives; therefore you shall no longer see false visions or practice divinations; I will save my people from your hand. Then you will know that I am the LORD. (This indicates that they were able to see visions, but they were false visions, and that God can stop the visions. There is a battle going on between good and evil in the spirit world also.)

Chapter 14:6 says, Therefore say to the house of Israel, Thus says the Lord GOD: Repent and turn away from your idols; and turn away your faces from all your abominations. Verse 9 says, If a prophet is deceived and speaks a word, I, the LORD, have deceived that prophet, and I will stretch out my hand against him, and will destroy him from the midst of my people Israel.

Apparently, according to the writer, God is sovereign and allows the false prophet to receive false visions. So what God allows, he can also take away. This does not take away the initial responsibility of the false prophet who initially chose to reject God's teachings. This is similar to Pharaoh and his hardened heart as discussed in Exodus.

Chapter 15 is an allegory of the vine which was a popular symbol for Israel. An allegory is a form of extended comparison in which familiar objects or persons stand for ideals, concepts, or other ideas that can not be seen or touched, such as love, faith, or righteousness. Verse 6 says, Therefore thus says the Lord GOD: Like the wood of the vine among the trees of the forest, which I have given to the fire for fuel, so I will give up the inhabitants of Jerusalem. Chapter 16:1 says, The word of the LORD came to me: Mortal, make known to Jerusalem her abominations . . . God then tells them he made them prosperous, but in their prosperity and comfort they thought only of themselves.

Israel is then pictured in symbolic imagery as a prostitute, an adulterer. Along with the sexual imagery in (6-14), God in (15) says, you trusted in your beauty, and played the whore because of your fame, and lavished your whorings on any passer-by. Verse 22 says, And in all your abominations and your whorings you did not remember the days of your youth, when you were naked and bare, flailing about in your blood. He then compares them with the fallen kingdom of the north and Sodom.

In verses 47-48 God says, You not only followed their ways (the kingdom of the north and Sodom) and acted according to their abominations; within a very little time you were more corrupt than they in all your ways . . . your sister Sodom and her daughters have not done as you and your daughters have done. Verses 49-52 say, This was the guilt of your sister Sodom: she and her daughters had pride, excess of food, and prosperous ease, but did not aid the poor and needy. They were haughty and did abominable things before me; therefore, I removed them when I saw it.

Samaria has not committed half your sins . . . So be ashamed, you also, and bear your disgrace, for you have made your sisters appear righteous.

Verses 59-60 say, Yes, Thus says the Lord GOD: I will deal with you as you have done, you who have despised the oath, breaking the covenant; yet I will remember my covenant with you in the days of your youth, and I will establish with you an everlasting covenant.

Chapter 17 is the allegory of the eagles and the cedar which explained what happened to Judah. Nebuchadnezzar, king of Babylon is the first eagle who took King Jehoiachin of Judah into captivity. The seed or king he plants or puts in charge of Judah is Zedekiah. But Zedekiah eventually goes against Babylon and the prophet's advice. He goes to Egypt for help. Egypt is the second eagle. This action will then bring back the Babylonians who destroy Jerusalem.

This prediction of Ezekiel comes true. But included in the prophecy are verses 22-24. Thus says the Lord GOD: I myself will take a sprig from the lofty top of a cedar; I will set it out. I will break off a tender one from the topmost of its young twigs; I myself will plant it on a high and lofty mountain. On the mountain height of Israel I will plant it, in order that it may produce boughs and bear fruit and become a noble cedar. Under it every kind of bird will live; in the shade of its branches will nest winged creatures of every kind. All the trees of the field shall know that I am the LORD . . . I the LORD have spoken; I will accomplish it. (This sprig of cedar is considered by many to be a messianic prophecy. Some Jews say this is a renewed Israel.)

In chapter 18 the exiles blame their ancestors for their misfortunes, but Ezekiel points out the blame rests on themselves. In verse 4 God says, Know that all lives are mine; the life of the parent as well as the life of the child is mine: it is only the person who sins that shall die. (This is reference to the person who lives in sin and refuses to repent.)

Verses 5-9 say, If a man is righteous and does what is lawful and right—if he does not eat upon the mountains or lift up his eyes to the idols of the house of Israel, does not defile his neighbor's wife, or approach a woman during her menstrual period, does not oppress anyone, but restores to the debtor his pledge, commits no robbery, gives his bread to the hungry, and covers the naked with a garment, does not take advanced or accrued interest, withholds his hand from iniquity, executes true justice between contending parties, follows my statutes and is careful to observe my ordinances, acting faithfully—such a one is righteous; he shall surely live, says the Lord GOD. (Here is a good definition of righteousness.)

In verses 10-13 the opposite of the above actions is mentioned, and then the writer says, he shall surely die; his blood shall be upon himself. Verses 20-22 say, The person who sins shall die. A child shall not suffer for the iniquity of the parent, nor a parent suffer for the iniquity of a child; the righteousness of the righteous shall be his own, and the wickedness of the wicked shall be his own. But if the wicked turn away from all their sins that they have committed and keep all my statutes and do what is lawful and right, they shall surely live; they shall not die. None of the transgressions that they committed shall be remembered against them; for the righteousness that they have done they shall live.

Verses 23-28 say, Have I any pleasure in the death of the wicked, says the Lord GOD, and not rather that they should turn from their ways and live? But when the righteous turn away from their righteousness and commit iniquity and do the same abominable things that the wicked do, shall they live? None of the righteous deeds that they have done shall be remembered; for the treachery of which they are guilty and the sin they have committed, they shall die.

Yet you say, "The way of the LORD is unfair." Hear now, O house of Israel: Is my way unfair? Is it not your ways that are unfair? When the righteous turn away from their righteousness and commit iniquity, they shall die for it; for the iniquity that they have committed they shall die. Again, when the wicked turn from the wickedness they have committed and do what is lawful and right, they shall save their life. Because they considered and turned away from all their transgressions that they had committed, they shall surely live; they shall not die.

Yet the house of Israel in verses 29-32 say, "The way of the LORD is unfair." O house of Israel, are my ways unfair? Is it not your ways that are unfair? Therefore, I will judge you, O house of Israel, all of you according to your ways says, the Lord GOD. Repent and turn from all your transgressions; otherwise iniquity will be your ruin. Cast away from you all the transgressions that you have committed against me, and get yourself a new heart and a new spirit! Why will you die, O house of Israel? For I have no pleasure in the death of anyone, says the Lord GOD. Turn, then, and live.

Up to this point the nation emphasized institutional sin and how the consequences of individual sin affected the nation of God's people or an individual family, but now Ezekiel also begins to stress the responsibility and consequences of individual sin on the individual and how it comes from the heart. Both institutional and individual sin are judged by God. This needs emphasized in the world including America.

Chapter 19 is a poem of lament over the demise of Jerusalem; verses 13-14 say, Now it is transplanted into the wilderness, into a dry and thirsty land. And fire has gone out from its stem, and has consumed its branches and fruit, so that there remains in it no strong stem, no scepter for ruling.

Chapter 20 is a history of the nation's rebellion which has been a history of rebellion against God's moral teachings as well as the worship of idols. As this writer has said numerous times the OT can be viewed basically as a history of God trying to maintain the one God concept. Many times throughout their history it seemed to be on the verge of slipping away. If it had not been always for a small remnant, the one God idea would have disappeared from God's good earth. Thankfully, he was not going to allow that to happen even though it looked as though at times the one God concept might be lost to the world.

Chapter 20:1-2 says, In the seventh year, in the fifth month, on the tenth day of the month, certain elders came to consult the LORD, and sat down before me. And the word of the LORD came to me: Mortal speak to the elders of Israel, and say to them: Thus says the Lord GOD: Why are you coming to me? To consult me? As I live says the Lord GOD, I will not be consulted by you. What follows is a history of Israel ignoring the teachings of the one God as Ezekiel assesses Israel's past and future.

Verses 45-49 say, The word of the LORD came to me: Mortal set your face toward the south, preach against the south, and prophesy against the forest land in the Negeb; say to the forest of the Negeb, (This is southern Judah where spies were sent into Canaan. Today it is a desert.) Hear the word of the LORD: Thus says the Lord GOD, I will kindle a fire in you, and it shall devour every green tree in you and every dry tree; the blazing flame shall not be quenched, and all faces from the south to north shall be scorched by it. All flesh shall see that I the LORD have kindled it; it shall not be quenched. Then I said, "Ah Lord GOD! they are saying of me, 'Is he not a maker of allegories?' "

Chapter 21:1-3 says, The word of the LORD came to me: Mortal set your face toward Jerusalem and preach against the sanctuaries; prophesy against the land of Israel and say to the land of Israel, Thus says the LORD: I am coming against you and will draw my sword out of its sheath, and will cut off from you both righteous and wicked. (The sword is the king of Babylon who will destroy both capital cities of Jerusalem and Ammon of the Ammonites.)

In chapter 22:6-11 all the abominable deeds of the land are declared. The princes of Israel in you, every one according to his power has been bent on shedding blood. Father and mother are treated with contempt in you; the alien residing within you suffers extortion; the orphan and widow are wronged in you. You have despised my holy things and profaned my sabbaths. In you are those who slander to shed blood, those in you who eat upon the mountains, who commit lewdness in your midst. In you they uncover their father's nakedness; in you they violate women in their menstrual periods. One commits abomination with his neighbor's wife; another lewdly defiles his daughter-in-law; another defiles his sister, his father's daughter.

Verses 12-15 say, In you they take bribes to shed blood. You take both advance interest and accrued interest, and make gain of your neighbors by extortion; and You have forgotten me, says the Lord GOD. See I strike my hands together at the dishonest gain you have made, and at the blood that has been shed within you . . . I will scatter you among the nations . . . I will purge your filthiness out of you. And I am profaned through you in the sight of the nations; and you shall know that I am the LORD.

The word of God continues in (23-27). You are a land that is not cleansed . . . Its princes within it are like a roaring lion tearing prey; they have devoured human lives; they have taken treasure and precious things; they have made many widows with it. Its priests have done violence to my teaching and have profaned my holy things; they have made no distinction between the holy and the common . . . they have disregarded my sabbaths, so that I am profaned among them. Its officials within it are like wolves tearing prey, shedding blood, destroying lives to get dishonest gain.

Verses 28-31 say, The prophets have smeared whitewash on their behalf, seeing false visions and divining lies for them saying, "Thus says the Lord GOD," when the LORD has not spoken. The people of the land have practiced extortion and committed robbery; they have oppressed the poor and needy, and have extorted from the alien without redress. Verse 31 says, Therefore I have poured out my indignation upon them; I have consumed them with the fire of my wrath; I have returned their conduct upon their heads, says the Lord GOD. (It must be noted that both individual and institutional sin is judged. The institutions of government, religion, and business are held responsible and judged just as individuals are held responsible and judged.)

Chapter 23:1-49 is the allegory of the sisters, Oholah and Oholibah. Oholah represents Samaria, the capital of the northern kingdom, Israel. Oholibah represents Jerusalem of Judah. Both sisters behaved like common whores. Their appetites for their lovers, the pagan gods, is without end. The chapter describes the apostasy to the gods of both kingdoms in vivid sexual language through the whole chapter. It is called adultery.

Verse 3 says, they played the whore in their youth; their breasts were caressed there, and their virgin bosoms were fondled. Throughout the chapter the writer mentions how the kingdom of the north lusted for the Assyrians, then the kingdom of the south lusted for the Babylonians playing the whore, meaning they adopted the pagan culture of Assyria and Babylon.

Verses 37-39 say, they have committed adultery and blood is on their hands; with their idols they have committed adultery; and they have even offered up to them for food the children whom they had borne to me. Moreover they have done to me: they have defiled my sanctuary on the same day and profaned my sabbaths. For when they had slaughtered their children for their idols, on the same day they came into my sanctuary to profane it. This is what they did in my house.

Verses 43-45 say, Then I said, Ah, she is worn out with adulteries, but they carry on their sexual acts with her. For they have gone into her, as one has gone into a whore. Thus they went into Oholah and to Oholibah, wanton women. But righteous judges will declare them guilty of adultery and bloodshed; because they are adulteresses and blood is on their hands. Verse 49 says, They shall repay you for your lewdness, and you shall bear the penalty for your sinful idolatry. In this way you shall know that I am the LORD God.

Chapter 24:1-2 says, In the ninth year, in the tenth month, on the tenth day of the month, the word of the LORD came to me: Mortal, write down the name of this day, this very day. The king of Babylon has laid siege to Jerusalem this very day. The chapter begins with an allegory of the pot (3-5). Verse 6 introduces the theme of corrosion referring to Jerusalem's bloody past by saying, Woe to the bloody city, the pot whose rust is in it, whose rust has not gone out of it! (The writer is saying Jerusalem is like a rusty cooking pot that is set on fire to burn.)

In verses 9-14 Ezekiel calls for the cleansing of Jerusalem by fire for its rust is too great. On the same day of the siege Ezekiel's wife dies. In (15-24) he is told not to mourn for her as a sign to the people that the loss of cherished persons and things will bring an inexpressible grief. Verse 16 says, Mortal, with one blow I am about to take away from you the delight of your eyes; yet you shall not mourn or weep, nor shall your tears run down. (His wife will represent Jerusalem.)

In chapters 25-32 God makes judgment on the nations. There is no nation beyond God's judgment. This includes nations throughout time. When nations do the same thing Israel and Judah did, which is in opposition to God's teachings, they will be judged also. In chapter 25 Ammon, Moab, Edom, and Philistia, all who found joy in Israel's downfall will be judged. In chapters 26-28 Tyre and Sidon will be judged. (They were seaports containing considerable wealth. Both would be located in modern day Lebanon.)

Chapter 28:1-2 says, Mortal, say to the prince of Tyre, Thus says the Lord GOD: Because your heart is proud, and you have said, I am a god; I sit in the seat of the gods, in the heart of the seas, yet you are but a mortal, and no god, though you compare your mind with the mind of a god. Verses 5-7 say, By your great wisdom in trade you have increased your wealth, and your heart has become proud in your wealth. Therefore, I will bring strangers against you, the most terrible of the nations; then they shall draw their swords against the beauty of your wisdom and defile your splendor. Verses 15-16 say, You were blameless in your ways from the day you were created, until iniquity was found in you. In the abundance of your trade you were filled with violence, and you sinned; . . . Verse 18 says, By the multitude of your iniquities, in the unrighteousness of your trade, you profaned your sanctuaries.

Chapter 29-32 concerns the punishment of Egypt. Chapter 29:6 says, Then all the inhabitants of Egypt shall know that I am the LORD . . . Verse 19 says, I will give the land of Egypt to King Nebuchadnezzar of Babylon; and he shall carry off its wealth and despoil it and plunder it, and it shall be the wages for his army.

Chapters 33-48 are oracles and visions of restoration. In chapter 33:7-9 God said to Ezekiel, So you mortal, I have made a sentinel for the house of Israel; whenever you hear a word from my mouth, you shall give them warning from me. If I say to the wicked, "O wicked ones, you shall surely die," and you do not speak to warn the wicked to turn from their ways, the wicked shall die in their iniquity, but their blood I shall require at your hand. But if you warn the wicked to turn from their ways, and they do not turn from their ways, the wicked shall die in their iniquity, but you will have saved your life.

Verses 10-11 say, Now, you mortal, say to the house of Israel, Thus you have said: "Our transgressions and our sins weigh upon us, and we waste away because of them; how then can we live?" Say to them, As I live, says the Lord GOD, I have no pleasure in the death of the wicked, but that the wicked turn from their ways and live; turn back, turn back from your evil ways; for why will you die, O house of Israel?

Verses 12-13 say, And you Mortal, say to your people, The righteousness of the righteous shall not save them when they transgress; and as for the wickedness of the wicked, it shall not make them stumble when they turn from their wickedness; and the righteous shall not be able to live by their righteousness when they sin. Though I say to the righteous that they shall surely live, yet if they trust in their righteousness and commit iniquity, none of their righteous deeds shall be remembered; but in the iniquity they have committed they shall die.

Verses 17-20 say, Yet your people say, "The way of the LORD is not just," when it is their own way that is not just. When the righteous turn from their righteousness and commit iniquity, they shall die for it. And when the wicked turn from their wickedness, and do what is lawful and right, they shall live by it. Yet you say, "The way of the LORD is not just." O house of Israel I will judge all of you according to your ways! Verse 21 says, In the twelfth year of our exile in the tenth month, on the fifth day of the month, someone who escaped from Jerusalem came to me and said, "The city has fallen." (It is plain that nations will be eventually judged in this world for their greed and unjust actions.)

Verses 28-31 say, I will make the land a desolation and a waste, and its proud might shall come to an end; and the mountains of Israel shall be so desolate that no one will pass through. Then they shall know that I am the LORD, when I have made the land a desolation and a waste because of all their abominations that they have committed. The people in (30) will say, "Come and hear what the word is that comes from the LORD," but (31) says they hear your words, but they will not obey them. For flattery is on their lips, but their heart is set on their gain.

In chapter 34:1-6 Ezekiel said, The word of the LORD came to me: Mortal, prophesy against the shepherds of Israel (religious leaders): prophesy, and say to them—to the shepherds: Thus says the Lord GOD: Ah, you shepherds of Israel who have been feeding yourselves! Should not shepherds feed the sheep? You eat the fat, you clothe yourselves with wool, you slaughter the fatlings; but do not feed the sheep. You have not strengthened the weak, you have not healed the sick, you have not bound up the injured, you have not brought back the strayed, you have not sought the lost, but with force and harshness you have ruled them. So they were scattered because there was no shepherd; and scattered, they became food for all the wild animals. My sheep were scattered, they wandered over all the mountains and on every high hill; my sheep were scattered over all the face of the earth, with no one to search or seek for them.

Verse 10 says, Thus says the Lord GOD, I am against the shepherds; and I will demand my sheep at their hand, and put a stop to feeding the sheep; no longer shall the shepherds feed themselves. I will rescue my sheep from their mouths, so that they may not be food for them. (This is a serious warning to all clergy and political leaders who are to feed and take care of the people they are to lead.)

In verses 11-16 he says, I myself will search for my sheep and will seek them out . . . I will rescue them from all the places to which they have been scattered on a day of clouds and thick darkness. I will bring them out from the peoples and gather them from the countries and will bring them into their own land; and I will feed them on the mountains of Israel, by the water courses, and in all the inhabited parts of the land. Verses 15-16 say, I myself will be the shepherd of my sheep, and I will make them lie down, says the Lord GOD. I will seek the lost, and I will bring back the strayed, and I will bind up the injured, and I will strengthen the weak, but the fat and the strong I will destroy. I will feed them with justice. (This is a warning to the rich and powerful who are concerned for their own interests and not God's interests.)

Verses 22-24 say, I will save my flock, and they shall no longer be ravaged; I will judge between sheep and sheep. I will set up over them one shepherd, my servant David, and he shall feed them: he shall feed them and be their shepherd. And I, the LORD, will be their God, and my servant David shall be prince among them; I the LORD have spoken. (This is a Messianic prophecy that Christians apply to Christ.)

Verses 25-26 say, I will make with them a covenant of peace and banish wild animals from the land, so that they may live in the wild and sleep in the woods securely. I will make them and the region around my hill a blessing; and I will send down the showers in their season; they shall be showers of blessings. Verses 30-31 say, They shall know that I, the LORD, their God am with them, and that they, the house of Israel, are my people, says the Lord GOD. You are my sheep; the sheep of my pasture, and I am your God, says the Lord GOD. You are my sheep; the sheep of my pasture, and I am your God, says the LORD God.

In chapter 35 Edom is going to be judged because of her unsympathetic reaction to Israel's downfall and attempt to grab some of Israel's land. In chapter 36 Israel's oppressors will be judged, and Israel will be restored for the sake of God's name.

Verses 22-26 say, Therefore say to the house of Israel, Thus says the Lord GOD: It is not for your sake, O house of Israel, that I am about to act, but for the sake of my holy name, which you have profaned among the nations to which you came. I will sanctify my great name, which has been profaned among the nations, and which you have profaned among them; and the nations shall know that I am the LORD, says the Lord GOD, when through you I display my holiness before their eyes. I will take you from the nations, and gather you from all the countries, and bring you into your own land. I will sprinkle clean water upon you, and you shall be clean from all your uncleanness, and from all your idols I will cleanse you. A new heart I will give you, and a new spirit I will put within you; and I will remove from your body the heart of stone and give you a heart of flesh.

Verses 27-30 say, I will put my spirit within you and make you follow my statutes and be careful to observe my ordinances. Then you shall live in the land I gave to your ancestors, and you shall be my people, and I will be your God. I will save you from all your uncleanness, and I will summon the grain and make it abundant and lay no famine upon you. I will make the fruit of the trees and the produce of the field abundant, so that you may never again suffer the disgrace of famine among the nations. (Always remember the first fulfillment of any prophecy is in the context of their times.)

In chapter 37 the LORD brought Ezekiel out and set him down in a valley full of dry bones. God said to Ezekiel in (3-6), "Mortal, can these bones live?" I answered, "O Lord GOD, you know." Then he said to me, "Prophesy to these bones, and say to them: O dry bones, hear the word of the LORD. Thus says the Lord GOD to these bones: I will cause breath to enter you, and you shall live. I will lay sinews on you, and will cause flesh to come upon you, and cover you with skin, and put breath in you, and you shall live; and you shall know that I am the LORD." (The following explains this prophecy.)

In verses 11-14 God said to Ezekiel, "Mortal, these bones are the whole house of Israel. They say, 'Our bones are dried up, and our hope is lost; we are cut off completely.' Therefore prophesy, and say to them, I am going to open your graves, and bring you up from your graves, O my people; and I will bring you back to the land of Israel. And you shall know that I am the LORD, when I open your graves, and bring you up from your graves, O my people. I will put my spirit within you, and you shall live, and I will place you on your own soil; then you shall know that I, the LORD, have spoken and will act, says the LORD."

Verses 24-28 say, My servant David shall be king over them; and they shall all have one shepherd. They shall follow my ordinances and be careful to observe my statutes. They shall live in the land that I gave to my servant Jacob, in which your ancestors lived; they and their children and their children's children shall live there forever; and my servant David shall be their prince forever. I will make a covenant of peace with them; it shall be an everlasting covenant with them; and I will bless them and multiply them, and will set my sanctuary among them forevermore. My dwelling place shall be with them; and I will be their God, and they shall be my people. Then the nations shall know that I the LORD sanctify Israel, when my sanctuary is among them forevermore.

This is about the reestablishment of Israel and Judah into one kingdom with a Davidic king. The people will return from exile, but there will not be a Davidic king until the Messiah who Christians call Jesus. The kingdom of God (which is the name Christians give to God's people who are of or from the house of Judah and Israel) will break into the world at that time, not in its fullest sense, but it breaks in for all who God adds to Israel and Judah and are called the people of God.

In the Gospels Jesus preaches about the kingdom of God. Later his disciples preach Jesus is the king of the kingdom that has broken into the world (Colossians 1-4, Ephesians 1-3). Then the fullest sense of this Scripture is realized at the end time when the kingdom of God breaks in eternally. Jews reject this interpretation and do not believe that Jesus is the Messiah.

Chapters 38-39 are the Gog and Magog oracles which describe in apocalyptic language the coming of the foe from the north. Apocalyptic literature lends itself to many different and strange interpretations by religious groups who like to focus on the end times. These chapters do describe a cataclysmic battle after which God will defeat the aggressor forces, and all nations will recognize God as the victor. In Ezekiel this has reference to the defeat of Babylon. Some think it may have symbolic reference to a double fulfillment pertaining to the end times indicating God will prevail in the end over all enemies. John in Rev 20:8 has Gog and Magog representing all who oppose God in the last battle as they are led by Satan.

Those who attempt to make these two chapters explain in detail what will happen exactly in the end times and assign the names in the chapter to modern day countries have no support from Jewish, Roman Catholic, Eastern Orthodox, or mainline Protestant scholars. As the centuries have gone by, the names of the different countries are always changed by those wanting to show that the Scriptures apply to the current times.

The names in these chapters such as Magog, Meshech, Tubal, and Gomer are the sons of Japheth (a son of Noah). They are Indo-European peoples living in the Black Sea area, which is north of Palestine. Ezekiel pictures an invasion of these peoples from the north led by Gog who personifies the forces of evil. They will have as allies countries who oppose Israel and Judah.

Chapter 38:23 says, I will display my greatness and my holiness and make myself known in the eyes of many nations. Then they shall know that I am the LORD. Chapter 39:11 says, on that day I will give to Gog a place for burial in Israel, the Valley of the Travelers east of the sea; it shall block the path of the travelers, for there Gog and all his horde will be buried; it shall be called the Valley of Hamon-gog. Verses 21-22 say, I will display my glory among the nations; and all nations shall see my judgment that I have executed, and my hand that I have laid upon them. The house of Israel shall know that I am the LORD their God from that day forward. (All God's people are part of the house of Israel.)

Verse 23-25 say, And the nations shall know that the house of Israel went into captivity for their iniquity, because they dealt treacherously with me … I dealt with them according to their uncleanness and their transgressions, and hid my face from them. Therefore thus says the Lord GOD: Now I will restore the fortunes of Jacob, and have mercy on the whole house of Israel; and I will be jealous for my holy name. Verse 28 says, Then they shall know that I am the LORD their God because I sent them into exile among the nations, and then gathered them into their own land. I will leave none of them behind; and I will never again hide my face from them, when I pour out my spirit upon the house of Israel, says the Lord GOD.

Chapters 40-48 end with Ezekiel having a vision of God returning to a new temple where God is again in the midst of his people. Everything is described in earthly terms and in perfection. The ideal is envisioned in the earthly terms the writer and his readers could envision. Beginning with chapter 40 there are chapters of perfect measurements and symbolism for the new temple. These chapters are not easy to interpret, and they have resulted in some very strange interpretations. The key is not to read too much into what is written. On this side of heaven this writer suspects we will not know all we would like to know about what the writer of Ezekiel had in mind.

Chapter 44:9-10 says, Thus says the Lord GOD: No foreigner, uncircumcised in heart and flesh, of all the foreigners who are among the people of Israel, shall enter my sanctuary. But the Levites who went far from me, going astray from me after their idols when Israel went astray, shall bear their punishment. We learn in (11-14) that they will be servants but no longer priests. In (15) the descendants of Zadok will be the priests.

Chapter 47:1 says, Then he (God) brought me (Ezekiel) back to the entrance of the temple; there, water was flowing from below the threshold of the temple toward the east (for the temple faced toward the east); and the water was flowing down from below the south end of the threshold of the temple, south of the altar. Verse 9 says, Wherever the river goes, every living creature that swarms will live, and there will be many fish, once these waters reach there. It will become fresh; and everything will live where the river goes.

Verse 12 says, On the banks, on both sides of the rivers, there will grow all kinds of trees for food. Their leaves will not wither nor their fruit fail . . . Their fruit will be for food and their leaves for healing. (The book of Revelation chapter 22 will talk about the river of the water of life.) In chapter 48:30-35 the new Jerusalem is described. There are three gates on each of the city's four sides with each gate named after a tribe. The name of the city from that time on shall be, The LORD is There. In this way the intriguing book of Ezekiel ends.

It is in the book of Revelation that the influence of Ezekiel particularly shows up: the four living creatures (Ezek 1, Rev 4:6-9); a voice like the sound of many waters (Ezek 1:24, Rev 1:15); Gog from the land of Magog (Ezek 38-39, Rev 20:8); the seer is carried to a high mountain (Ezek 40:2, Rev 21:10). The book of Revelation to some extent tends to simplify the bizarre features of Ezekiel's discourses.

In chapters 40-48 the perfect temple is described. Its symbolism easily lends itself to be understood as prophecy applied to the returned exiles and a new temple, to Jesus and his body as the new temple, and to the setting up of the eternal temple. What is the correct answer? Who knows, maybe all of them as multiple fulfillments of prophecy.

DANIEL

Daniel and his three Jewish companions, while in exile in Babylon, are chosen for service in the household of the king of Babylon. Their refusal to give up their food laws causes them to become stronger than their pagan associates. Because of their devotion, they are thrown into a fiery furnace and survive. This causes the king to praise Daniel's God.

The book is more an inspired story about faith rather than an exact history. The Hebrew canon does not list this book under the Prophets but under the Writings. That does not necessarily mean one should rule out real historical characters upon whom the story is based. One of the main purposes of the story is to show that it is possible for a good Jew to live in a foreign land and be both successful and faithful.

Later Daniel interprets a dream of the king that comes true. In chapter 5 we get the term "writing on the wall." A lone hand writes on a wall that the Babylonian king's days are numbered. This is the meaning of Mene, Mene, Tekel, and Parsin which is the writing on the wall. Persia then will defeat the Babylonians and free the Jews to return to Jerusalem and rebuild. The saying "feet of clay" also comes from chapter 2.

Chapters 7-12 recount the visions of Daniel. These visions are classified as apocalyptic. This form of literature uses symbols and bizarre figures of imagination in order to explain the unfolding of God's plan for the world.

In 7:13-14 Daniel saw one like a human being (some translate as son of man) coming on the clouds of heaven. When he reaches the Ancient One (others translate as the Ancient of Days) and is presented before him, he receives dominion and glory and kingship. Nations and peoples of every language will serve him. His dominion is an everlasting dominion that shall not be taken away; his kingship shall not be destroyed. Hundreds of years later Jesus will use the term *Son of Man* to describe himself. Finally, in Dan chapter 12:1-3 we will have the first real mention of a bodily resurrection.

While the apocalyptic prophecies have puzzled both Christians and Jews, both have been inspired by the book's stories of faith and courage. When freed from fanciful interpretations, the book of Daniel brings a message of steadfast faith and hope, especially to those who pray, "thy kingdom come." The book should be read not to discover the exact details of history; it is to be read for the purpose it was written: to inspire heroic resistance to the temptation of evil and the promise of a good future. God and his kingdom will triumph.

The book of Daniel can be divided in half. The first half, chapters 1-6, contain stories about Daniel. Exiled to Babylon he and his friends repeatedly risk their lives rather than conform to Babylonian paganism. The second half of the book, chapters 7-12, describe the development of the vision of successive kingdoms described in chapter 2. Let the reader be reminded that the three political kingdoms mentioned in this book are still in operation today. Babylonia is modern day Iraq; Persia is modern day Iran, and Judah is Israel. Some interesting verses are 5:25, 7:1-8, 9:21-27, 12:1-2.

Chapter 1:1-4 says, In the third year of the reign of King Jehoiakim of Judah, King Nebuchadnezzar of Babylon came to Jerusalem and besieged it. The LORD let King Jehoiakim of Judah fall into his power, as well as some of the vessels of the house of God. These he brought to the land of Shinar, and placed the vessels in the treasury of his gods. Then the king commanded his palace master Ashpenez to bring some of the Israelites of the royal family and of nobility, young men without physical defect and handsome, versed in every branch of wisdom, endowed with knowledge and insight, and competent to serve the king's palace; they were to be taught the language and literature of the Chaldeans.

Verses 5-7 say, The king assigned them a daily portion of the daily rations of food and wine. They were to be educated for three years, so that at the end of that time they can be stationed in the king's court. Among them were Daniel, Hananiah, Mishael, and Azariah, from the tribe of Judah. The palace master gave them other names: Daniel he called Belteshazzer, Hananiah he called Shadrach, Mishael he called Meshach, and Azariah he called Abednego.

Verse 8 says, Daniel resolved that he would not defile himself with the royal rations of food and wine; so he asked the palace master to allow him not to defile himself. In (11-16) an experiment is then organized where Daniel and his three friends eat only vegetables and water, for they do not want to violate any of the Hebrew food laws. The others are to eat from the king's table.

Verse 15 says, At the end of ten days it was observed that they appeared better and fatter than all the young men who had been eating the royal rations. Verse 17 says, To these four young men God gave knowledge and skill in every aspect of literature and wisdom; Daniel also had insight into all visions and dreams, and verses 20-21 say, In every matter of wisdom and understanding concerning which the king inquired of them, he found them ten times better than all the magicians and enchanters in his whole kingdom. And Daniel continued there until the first year of king Cyrus (539 B.C.).

Chapter 2:1-2 says, In the second year of Nebuchadnezzar's reign, Nebuchadnezzar dreamed such dreams that his spirit was troubled and his sleep left him. So the king commanded that the magicians, the enchanters, the sorcerers, and the Chaldeans (wise men) be summoned to tell the king his dreams. From (2:4) until the end of the seventh chapter (7:28) the text changes from Hebrew to the Aramaic language.

In chapter 2:9-11 the king wants them to tell him the dream. In that way he will be able to know that they can give him the true interpretation. The Chaldeans answered the king, "There is no one on earth who can reveal what the king demands! . . ." Daniel requests in (16-18) that the king give him time, and he would tell the king the interpretation. Then Daniel goes back and tells his three friends to seek mercy from God concerning this mystery.

Verse 19 says, the mystery was revealed to Daniel in a vision of the night, and Daniel in 20-23 blessed the God of heaven. In (25-28) Daniel (named Belteshazzer) is brought before the king, and in (28) Daniel says, "there is a God in heaven who reveals mysteries, and he has disclosed to King Nebuchadnezzar what will happen at the end of days . . ." (As we shall see the term end of days does not necessarily mean end of the world.)

In verses 31-35 Daniel proceeds to describe the king's dream. "You were looking,

O king, and lo! there was a huge statue . . . The head of that statue was of fine gold, its chest and arms of silver, its middle and thighs of bronze, its legs of iron, its feet partly of iron and partly of clay. (This is where the saying, "feet of clay" came from.) As you looked on, a stone was cut out, not by human hands, and it struck the statue on its feet of iron and clay and broke them in pieces. Then the iron, the clay, the bronze, the silver, and the gold, were all broken in pieces and became like the chaff of the summer threshing floors; and the wind carried them away, so that not a trace of them could be found. But the stone that struck the statue became a great mountain and filled the whole earth.

Verses 36-43 continue, "This was the dream, now we will tell the king its interpretation. You O king, the king of kings—to whom the God of heaven has given the kingdom, the power, the might, and the glory . . . you are the head of gold. After you shall rise another kingdom inferior to yours, and yet a third kingdom of bronze, which shall rule over the whole earth. And there shall be a fourth kingdom, strong as iron; just as iron crushes and smashes everything, it shall crush and shatter these . . . it shall be a divided kingdom; but some of the strength of iron shall be in it, as you saw the iron mixed with clay. As the toes of the feet were part iron and part clay, so the kingdom will be partly strong and partly brittle . . . but they will not hold together just as iron does not mix with clay.

Verses 44-45 continue, And in the days of those kings, the God of heaven will set up a kingdom that shall never be destroyed; nor shall this king be left to another people. It shall crush all these kingdoms and bring them to an end, and it shall stand forever; just as you saw that a stone was cut from the mountain not by hands, and that it crushed the iron, the bronze, the clay, the silver, and the gold. The great God has informed the king what shall be hereafter. The dream is certain, and its interpretation trustworthy."

Verses 46-47 say, King Nebuchadnezzar fell on his face, worshiped Daniel, . . . The king said to Daniel, "Truly, your God is God of gods and LORD of kings and a revealer of mysteries, for you have been able to reveal this mystery!" Then the king promoted Daniel, gave him many great gifts, and made him ruler over the province of Babylon and chief prefect over all the wise men of Babylon. In (49) Daniel made a request of the king, and he appointed Shadrach, Meshach, and Abednego over the affairs of the province of Babylon. But Daniel remained at the king's court.

In chapter 3 Nebuchadnezzar sets up a golden statue that is to be worshiped. In (6) he says, "Whoever does not fall down and worship shall immediately be thrown into a furnace of blazing fire." Later the Chaldeans in (12) point out to the king that the certain Jews appointed over the affairs of the province of Babylon: Shadrach, Meshach, and Abednego are not serving the gods and are not worshiping the golden statute. In a furious rage Nebuchadnezzar calls them and gives them another chance to worship the statue, but tells them if they do not worship, they will immediately be thrown into a furnace of blazing fire.

They tell him they will not bow down to the statue. So Nebuchadnezzar in (19-20) fires the furnace seven times more than normal and orders his strongest guards to bind them and throw them in the furnace. (In Roman Catholic Bibles inserted between 3:23 and 3:24 is the prayer of Azariah. A summary of this prayer is mentioned at the end of Daniel.) Verses 22-28 tell us that the raging flames kill the guards who threw them in. As the king and his counselors look in, the king in (25) said, " But I see four men unbound, walking in the middle of the fire, and they are not hurt; and the fourth has the appearance of a god." Then Nebuchadnezzar calls them to come out, and notices they are not even singed.

In verses 28-29 Nebuchadnezzar said, "Blessed be the God of Shadrach, Meshach, and Abednego, who has sent his angel and delivered his servants who trusted in him. They disobeyed the king's command and yielded up their bodies rather than serve and worship any god except their own God. Therefore I make a decree: Any people, nation, or language that utters blasphemy against the God of Shadrach, Meshach, and Abednego shall be torn limb from limb, and their houses laid in ruins; for there is no other god who is able to deliver in this way."

In chapter 4:1-3 Nebuchadnezzar makes a witness to the one God. He says, to all peoples, nations, and languages that live throughout the earth: May you have abundant prosperity! . . . How great are his signs, how mighty his wonders! His kingdom is an everlasting kingdom, and his sovereignty is from generation to generation.

The rest of the chapter involves Daniel interpreting another one of the king's dreams. In 4:10-11 he dreams of a tree in the center of the earth. The tree grows to where its top reaches heaven and it is visible to the ends of the earth. Verses 13-17 say, " I continued looking, in the visions of my head as I lay in bed, and there was a holy watcher (a celestial being) coming down from heaven. He cried aloud and said: 'Cut down the tree and chop off its branches, strip off its foliage and scatter its fruit. Let the animals flee from beneath it and the birds from its branches. But leave its stump and roots in the ground, . . . Let him be bathed with the dew of heaven, and let his lot be with the animals of the field in the grass of the earth. Let his mind be changed from that of a human, and let the mind of an animal be given to him . . . the decision is given by order of the holy ones, in order that all who live may know that the Most High is sovereign over the kingdom of mortals; he gives it to whom he will and sets over it the lowliest of human beings.' This is the dream that I King Nebuchadnezzar saw. Now you, Belteshazzar, declare the interpretation . . . for you are endowed with the spirit of the holy gods."

Verse 19 says, Then Daniel, who was called Beltesshazzar, was severely distressed for awhile. His thoughts terrified him. The king said, "Belteshazzar, do not let the dream or the interpretation terrify you." Belteshazzar answered, "My lord may the dream be for those who hate you, and its interpretation be for your enemies! Verses 24-27 continue, this is the interpretation, O king, and it is the decree of the Most High that has come upon my lord the king: You shall be driven away from human society, and your dwelling shall be with the wild animals. You shall be made to eat grass like oxen . . . As it was commanded to leave the stump and roots of the tree, your kingdom shall be re-established for you from the time that you learn that heaven is sovereign. Therefore, O king, may my counsel be acceptable to you: atone for your sins with righteousness, and your iniquities with mercy to the oppressed, so that your prosperity may be prolonged."

Verse 28 says, All this came upon Nebuchadnezzar. The dream is fulfilled in verses 28-33. Verse 34 says, When that period was over, I, Nebuchadnezzar, lifted my eyes to heaven, and my reason returned to me. I blessed the Most High and praised and honored the one who lives forever. For his sovereignty is an everlasting sovereignty, and his kingdom endures from generation to generation. Verses 36-37 say, At that time my reason returned to me; and my majesty and splendor were restored to me for the glory of my kingdom . . . I was re-established over my kingdom, and still more greatness was added to me. Now I, Nebuchadnezzar, praise and extol and honor the King of heaven, for all his works are truth, and his ways are justice; and he is able to bring low those who walk in pride.

In chapter 5 after many years the son of Nebuchadnezzar, Belshazzar, is king. A party is held where the people are drinking from the sacred vessels from the temple in Jerusalem while making libations to the gods. (This is sacrilege.) All of a sudden a hand and nothing else is seen writing on a wall.

Verses 24-28 say, "So from his presence the hand was sent and this writing was inscribed. And this is the writing that was inscribed: MENE, MENE, TEKEL, and PARSIN. This is the interpretation of the matter: MENE, God has numbered the days of your kingdom and brought it to an end; TEKEL, you have been weighed on the scales and found wanting; PERES, your kingdom is divided and given to the Medes and Persians." (This is where the saying, "the writing is on the wall" came from.) Verse 30 says, That very night Belshazzar, the Chaldean king, was killed. And Darius the Mede received the kingdom, being about sixty-two years old.

In chapter 6 King Darius is going to appoint Daniel over the whole kingdom, but the other leaders of the regions conspire against Daniel. They convince the king to pass an ordinance that individuals who pray to anyone other than the king in a thirty day period will be thrown into a lion's den. Daniel refuses to pray to the king, and he continues to pray to his God. The leaders of the region report this to the king, and even though the king wants to protect Daniel, the law will not permit the king to change his decree, thus in (16) Daniel is thrown into the lion's den.

Verses 19-24 say, Then, at break of day, the king got up and hurried to the den of lions . . . he cried out anxiously to Daniel, "O Daniel, servant of the living God, has your God whom you faithfully serve been able to deliver you from the lions?" Daniel then said to the king, "O king live forever! My God sent his angel to shut the lions' mouths so that they would not hurt me, because I was found blameless before him; and also before you, O king, I have done no wrong." Then the king was exceedingly glad, and commanded that Daniel be taken out of the den. So Daniel was taken up out of the den and no kind of harm was found on him, because he had trusted in God. In verse 24 the king gave a command, and those who had accused Daniel were brought and thrown into the den of the lions—they their children and their wives. Before they reached the bottom of the den the lions overpowered them and broke all their bones in pieces.

Verses 25-27 say, Then King Darius wrote to all peoples and nations of every language throughout the whole world: "May you have abundant prosperity! I make a decree, that in all my royal dominion people should tremble and fear before the

God of Daniel: For he is the living God, enduring forever. His kingdom shall never be destroyed, and his dominion has no end. He delivers and rescues, he works signs and wonders in heaven and on earth; for he has saved Daniel from the power of the lions." Verse 28 adds, Daniel prospered during the reign of Darius and the reign of Cyrus the Persian.

The second half of the book is a further development of the vision of successive kingdoms that was described in chapter 2. This time it is Daniel that has the dream. The four empires are now symbolized as beasts.

Chapter 7:1-6 says, In the first year of king Belshazzar of Babylon Daniel had a dream and visions of his head as he lay in bed. Then he wrote down the dream. I Daniel, saw in my vision by night the four winds of heaven stirring up the great sea, and four great beasts came up out of the sea, different from one another. The first one was like a lion and had eagles' wings. Then as I watched, its wings were plucked off, and it was lifted up from the ground and made to stand on two feet like a human being, and a human mind was given to it.

Another beast appeared, a second one, that looked like a bear. It was raised up on one side, had three tusks in its mouth among its teeth and was told, "Arise, devour many bodies!" After this, as I watched, another appeared, like a leopard. The beast had four wings of a bird on its back and four heads; and dominion was given to it.

Verses 7-8 say, After this I saw in the visions by night a fourth beast, terrifying and dreadful and exceedingly strong. It had great iron teeth and was devouring, breaking in pieces, and stamping what was left with its feet. It was different from all the beasts that preceded it, and it had ten horns. I was considering the horns, when another horn appeared, a little one coming up among them; to make room for it, three of the earlier horns were plucked up by the roots. There were eyes like human eyes in this horn, and a mouth speaking arrogantly.

Interpreting who these kingdoms are has been somewhat controversial. Most scholars believe the lion represents Babylon; the bear represents the Medes; the four headed leopard represents the Persians; the beast with ten horns represents Alexander the Great and the Greeks, and the ten horns represent the Seleucid rulers who succeeded Alexander. The little horn represents Antiochus Epiphanes who we will learn about later.

A minority group believes that the lion is Babylon, but the bear is the Medo-

Persian kingdom because they were basically together, while the leopard with four heads represents Greece and its later division into four empires. The terrible beast represents the Roman empire from which the everlasting kingdom of verse 27 comes. (In the NT book of Revelation the beast is Rome.)

Verses 9-12 say, As I (Daniel) watched, thrones were set in place, and an Ancient One (the Ancient of Days) took his throne, his clothing was white as snow, and the hair of his head like pure wool; his throne was fiery flames, and its wheels were burning fire. A stream of fire issued and flowed out from his presence. A thousand thousands served him and ten thousand times ten thousand stood attending him. The court stood in judgment and the books were opened. I watched then because of the noise of the arrogant words that the horn was speaking. And as I watched the beast was put to death, and its body destroyed and given over to be burned with fire. As for the rest of the beasts, their dominion was taken away, but their lives were prolonged for a season and a time.

Verses 13-14 say, As I watched in the night visions, I saw one like a human being (also translated son of man) coming with the clouds of heaven. And he came to the Ancient One (also translated Ancient of Days) and was presented before him. To him was given dominion and glory and kingship, that all peoples, nations, and languages should serve him. His dominion is an everlasting dominion that shall not pass away, and his kingship is one that shall never be destroyed.

This passage has been traditionally interpreted as messianic. In the Gospels Jesus will refer to himself as the Son of Man who came with the everlasting kingdom. Many Jews still see this as a reference to faithful Jews, or the archangel Michael, or the Messiah who will come.

Daniel was told in verses 17-18 "As for these four great beasts, four kings shall arise out of the earth. But the holy ones of the Most High shall receive the kingdom and possess the kingdom forever—forever and ever." (It is from this chapter that the NT book of Revelation, especially chapter 13, draws its imagery.)

Verses 21-28 say, As I looked, this horn (the little arrogant one) made war with the holy ones and was prevailing over them, until the Ancient One came; then judgment was given for the holy ones of the Most High, and the time arrived when the holy ones gained possession of the kingdom. This is what he said: "As for the fourth beast, there shall be a fourth kingdom on earth that shall be different from all the other kingdoms; it shall devour the whole earth, and trample it down and break it into pieces. As for the ten horns, out of this kingdom ten kings shall arise, and another shall rise after them . . . He shall speak words against the most high . . . Then the court shall sit in judgment, and his dominion shall be taken away to be consumed and totally destroyed. The kingship and dominion and the greatness of the kingdoms under the whole heaven shall be given to the people of the holy ones of the Most High; their kingdom shall be an everlasting kingdom, and all dominions shall serve and obey them."

Verse 28 says, Here the account ends. As for me, Daniel, my thoughts greatly terrified me, and my face turned pale; but I kept the matter in my mind. (Most Christians apply this everlasting kingdom to the kingdom Christ established. Many Jews believe this was in reference to the overthrow of Antiochus of Epiphanes (discussed in the book of Maccabees) where the Jews once again gain sovereignty over their land. Muslims would understand this as a reference to the Umrah, the Muslim community.)

In chapter 8 the text reverts from Aramaic to Hebrew. The Aramaic went from 2:4b-7:28. It is now two years later. In verses 1-14 Daniel gets a vision in the third year of the reign of King Belshazzar of a ram with two horns and a male goat while Daniel is in Susa, the winter capital of Persia. The male goat with a horn between his eyes came from the west. The male goat trampled the ram and grew great, but at the height of its power, the great horn was broken, and in its place four prominent horns came up. Out of one of them came another horn which grew great toward the south.

Verses 15-16 inform us that Daniel could not understand the vision, so Gabriel is called to help him understand it. In verse 16 Gabriel, the angel who will make an announcement to Zechariah, the father of John the Baptist, as well as to Mary, the mother of Jesus, is for the first time presented in scripture. (Muslims believe that it is Gabriel who gave Muhammad the Qur'an.)

In verses 18-22 Daniel says, As he was speaking to me, I fell into a trance, face to the ground; then he touched me and set me on my feet. He said, "Listen, and I will tell you what will take place later in the period of wrath; for it refers to the appointed time of the end. As for the ram that you saw with the two horns, these are the kings of Medo-Persia. The male goat is the king of Greece, and the great horn between its eyes is the first king (Alexander the Great). As for the horn that was broken, in the place of which four others arose, four kingdoms shall rise from his nation, but not with his power.

The four horns are the kingdoms into which his empire is divided representing Alexander's four main generals (Casander, Lysimachus, Seleucus, and Ptolemy). The little horn is Antiochus Epiphanes who came from the Seleucids. The terrible violence of his reign upon Jerusalem and the temple, and the Maccabean revolt will be discussed later in the book of Maccabees.

Verses 23-25 describe a power that will rise up at the end of their rule who will destroy the powerful and the people of the holy ones. Verse 25 says, Without warning he shall destroy many and shall even rise up against the Prince of princes. But he shall be broken, and not by human hands. (The idea is that eventually divine power will intervene and break this power that rose up.) Daniel in (26) is told, seal up the vision, for it refers to many days from now." (Verses 19-26 were a continuous quote.)

In verse 27 Daniel says, I was overcome and lay sick for some days; then I arose and went about the king's business. But I was dismayed by the vision and did not understand it. (The readers should not be surprised if they also do not understand.)

In chapter 9 the date is 538 B.C. Babylon has controlled Judah since its defeat of Egypt at Carchemish in 605 B.C. In verse 2 we are informed that the seventy years of captivity are almost fulfilled, so Daniel prays to God to send the people back to their homeland. Verses 18-19 say, Incline your ear, O my God, and hear. Open your eyes and look at our desolation and the city that bears your name. We do not present our supplication before you on the ground of our righteousness, but on the ground of your great mercies. O LORD, hear: O LORD forgive; O LORD, listen and act and do not delay! For your own sake, O my God, because your city and your people bear your name.

In verse 21 Gabriel comes to him again, and in (22-27) he prophecies. These verses are very difficult and have many interpretations. Basically, after a few comments, this writer will refer you to the scholarly works of your choice. In these verses God has ordained a period of seventy weeks of years (70 times 7 equals 490 years) in which the salvation of his people will be completed.

Verses 24-25 say, "Seventy weeks are decreed for your people and your holy city: to finish the transgression, to put an end to sin, and to atone for iniquity, to bring everlasting righteousness, to seal both vision and prophet, and to anoint a most holy place. Know therefore and understand: from the time that the word went out to restore and rebuild Jerusalem until the time of an anointed prince, there shall be seven weeks; and for sixty-two weeks it shall be built again with streets and moat, but in troubled time.

For the Jews seven symbolizes perfection, so it may be best to take the numbers symbolically. Some Christians think it is interesting to note that in verse 25 the 7 plus 62 weeks that equals 483 comes close to standing for the number of years it will be until the building and restoring of the temple and Jesus ministry begins. Of course, the problem is that there is more than one possible starting point as well as more than one possible ending date.

Verses 26-27 seem to point to the death and resurrection of Christ, then the end of the temple in AD 70. "After the sixty two weeks, an anointed one will be cut off and shall have nothing, and the troops of the prince who is to come shall destroy the city and the sanctuary. Its end shall come with a flood and to the end there shall be war. Desolations are decreed. He shall make a strong covenant with many for one week, and for half of the week he shall make sacrifice and offering cease; and in their place shall be an abomination that desolates, until the decreed end is poured out upon the desolater."

Those who do not apply this to Christ apply all this to the time of Antiochus Epiphanes and the Maccabees. It is to the latter that the majority of scholarship leans. Let the writer end this by stating there is no agreed interpretation of these verses, and it may be possible to have again a double fulfillment.

Chapter 10 begins in the third year of King Cyrus of Persia. Daniel is standing on the bank of the Tigris River when an angel appears. In (8) Daniel has a vision where his strength leaves him, and he falls into a trance. The angel in (12-14) said, "Do not fear, Daniel, for from the first day you set your mind to gain understanding and to humble yourself before your God, your words have been heard, and I have come because of your words. But the prince of the kingdom of Persia opposed me twenty-one days. So Michael one of the chief princes, came to help me, and I left him there with the prince of the kingdom of Persia, and have come to help you understand what is to happen to your people at the end of days. For there is a further vision for those days."

This writer must add that the term *end of days* has various interpretations, one of them being an end of an era. Daniel is given insight into the continual battle raging in the spiritual realm between those protecting God's people and those wanting to destroy them. We learn that Michael is the guarding angel of the Jewish people. The princes in the chapter are the angels of the various nations.

In verses 15-17 Daniel continues, While he was speaking these words to me, I turned my face toward the ground and was speechless. Then one in human form touched my lips, and I opened my mouth to speak, and said to the one who stood before me, " My lord, because of the vision such pains have come upon me that I retain no strength . . . no strength remains in me, and no breath is left in me." The angel told him in (18) not to fear and to be strong and courageous.

In chapter 11 the angel proceeds to unfold history. The chapter provides a detailed account of the struggle that occurred in the Persian and Greek periods. Most scholars believe this chapter was written after the events took place; therefore, it is not prophecy but history, even though the predictions of (40-45) are never fulfilled as far as we know. This writer refers the readers to their church teachings.

But most scholars believe (21-45) refers to Antiochus Epiphanes who sacked Jerusalem and plundered the temple in 167 B.C. He set up the Abomination of Desolation in the temple which was to slaughter a pig on the altar and set up a pagan god while refusing to allow the Jews to practice their religion.

Chapter 12:1-4 says, "At that time Michael the great prince, the protector of your people, shall rise. There shall be a time of anguish, such as has never occurred since nations first came into existence. But at that time your people shall be delivered, everyone who is found written in the book. Many of those who sleep in the dust of the earth shall awake, some to everlasting life, and some to shame and everlasting contempt. Those who are wise shall shine like the brightness of the sky, and those who lead many to righteousness, like the stars forever and ever. But you, Daniel, keep the words secret and the book sealed until the time of the end. Many shall be running back and forth, and evil shall increase."

Verse 6 asks, "How long shall it be until the end of these wonders?" In (7) The man clothed in linen, who was upstream, raised his right hand toward heaven. And I heard him swear by the one who lives forever that it would be for a time, two times, and half a time, and that when the shattering of the power of the holy people comes to an end, all these things would be accomplished.

This time is usually interpreted as three and a half years or a symbolization meaning a short time, whatever that means. We do know that in the NT 2 Peter 3:8 says, with the Lord one day is like a thousand years. Whether that has any bearing on it or not, who knows?

When Daniel asks the outcome of these things, Michael in (9-13) said to Daniel, "Go your way, Daniel, for the words are to remain secret and sealed until the time of the end. Many shall be purified, cleansed, and refined, but the wicked shall continue to act wickedly. None of the wicked shall understand, but those who are wise shall understand. From the time that the regular burnt offering is taken away and the abomination that desolates is set up, there shall be one thousand two hundred ninety days. Happy are those who persevere and attain the thousand three hundred thirty five days. But you go your way, and rest; you shall rise for your reward at the end of days."

Before we leave the book, let us look at a few of the characteristics of Apocalyptic Literature in the OT. Usually the revealing is secret and must be kept secret until the events come to pass. The language is symbolic and can only be understood by the elect, and as Daniel states sometimes it is not meant to be understood even by the elect at the present time.

Visions are given, and the prophet's predictions give authority to the revelation received. Old prophecies are being fulfilled. It is pessimistic about the world as it is, as well as the ability of human beings to change the world. The forces of evil are always battling the forces of good, and a final battle between those forces is near.

Confidence is expressed in divine intervention on behalf of the suffering and powerless. Hope in the resurrection of the dead and victory of the just is expressed. There is always the hope of a new and glorious kingdom or a new heaven and earth where no longer are there any tears. God will reign forever and the wicked will perish.

Intermediaries such as angels and demons or spiritual beings are usually experienced. There is much symbolism expressed in animals, numbers, and colors. The Day of the Lord is usually mentioned which is a day of judgment, change, and renewal. These are just some of the characteristics of apocalyptic literature. To interpret it properly one must understand the nature of metaphors and symbolism. Most of all one needs to be careful that one does not portray that the answers to what it means is plainly understood.

Another concept that needs to be considered is that most modern scholars think this book was written somewhere between 150 B.C.-200 B.C., and the purpose of the visions is to predict the end of the kingdom of Antiochus Epiphanes and his persecution of the Jews.

Most scholars believe this writing is a type of prediction after the events took place in order to give meaning to present events. The idea is that God has permitted everything that has happened, but he is planning to act soon, or he has already acted and, once again, liberated his people. Whatever position one takes, it has nothing to do with the inspiration of the writing.

DEUTEROCANONICAL/ APOCRYPHA DANIEL

The Deuterocanonical/Apocrypha adds three additional sections to this book of Daniel which basically consists of short stories and the prayer of Azariah and the Song of the Three Jews. They are written in Greek and are included in the Septuagint, a Greek translation of the Hebrew Scriptures. Roman Catholics and the Orthodox accept the Greek writings as Scripture, but Protestants and Jews do not, although they consider them worth reading. The following is a summary of these writings.

Inserted in Roman Catholic Bibles in chapter three is the prayer of Azariah. As they walked around in the midst of the flames, Azariah stood in the fire and prayed. The prayer goes from verses 3-22. The prayer is one of deliverance for the nation of Israel.

The song of praise goes from verses 29-68. The song is in two parts. The first is a song of thanksgiving for deliverance. The second is a litany exhorting all creation to praise God in the manner of Pss 136 and 138.

Chapter 13 says Susanna, a God fearing women, lives in Babylon. She is very beautiful and married to Joakim, a rich man who has a garden. Joakim is very respected by the Jews. Two elders who are judges frequent the house of Joakim. When the people would leave at noon, Susanna would enter the garden for a walk. When the old men see her every day, they begin to lust for her. They suppress their conscience and do not tell each other of their lust, even though they are enamored by her. Finally, they admit to each other their lust for Susanna.

One day while they are waiting for the right moment, they hide in the bushes as she is bathing. When they see her maids leave, the two old men hurry to her, and say give in to our desire and lie with us. If you refuse, we will testify that you dismissed your maids because a young man was here with you.

Susanna decides not to give in, so she yells, and people from the house run to them. At the accusations of the old men, the servants feel ashamed, for nothing like this was ever said about Susanna. The next day Susanna is brought before her husband and the elders. All her relatives and onlookers are weeping.

The old men relate their lie while Susanna prays to God who hears her prayer and stirs up the holy spirit of a young man named Daniel. As she is being led to execution, Daniel says that he will have no part in the death of the woman. He asks how one can condemn her without evidence? Then, all the people return to the court in haste.

Daniel begins to examine them, but he separates them and examines them individually. Daniel asks what tree they saw Susanna and the boy under? One said it was under a mastic tree while the other said it was under the oak tree. Then instead of Susanna being convicted the two old men are convicted, and thus innocent blood is spared. From that day on Daniel is greatly esteemed by the people. Two major points of this story are to show the wisdom of Daniel, and that God helps those who remain true to him, if they pray.

In one respect the story of Susanna has the same viewpoint as the rest of the book of Daniel. When she is trapped, she says, it is better for me to fall into your power without guilt than to sin before God. This is the same lesson that we learned from the three young men and Daniel in the lion's den and the fiery furnace.

Chapter 14 begins with Cyrus being the king of Persia. Daniel is the king's favorite; he is held in higher esteem than the friends of the king. The Babylonians have an idol called Bel to whom food is provided each day. The king adores and worships Bel every day, but Daniel adores only his God.

When the king asks Daniel why he will not adore Bel, he replies he only worships the living God who made heaven and earth. The king said Bel is a living god; can you not see how Bel eats every day? Daniel laughs and says to the king, do not be deceived, he is only clay and bronze. The king is enraged and calls his priests. He says, unless you tell me who consumes this food you shall die, but if you show that Bel consumes it, Daniel shall die. The priests are not perturbed, for under the table they have a secret door where they come to get the food, so they encourage the king to set up an experiment.

After the priests depart, the king sets out the food while Daniel orders his servants to bring ashes. Then he scatters the ashes throughout the whole temple, and then they leave sealing the door with the king's seal so no one else can enter. The next morning the king and Daniel unseal the door and look in. The king is excited when he sees the food is gone. Daniel laughs and says to the king, look at the footprints, for these have come through the secret door. The angry king arrests the priests, their wives and children, and has them put to death. The king then hands Bel over to Daniel who destroys it and the temple.

Another story in this chapter is about a great dragon which the Babylonians worship. The king tells Daniel that he can not deny that this is a living god, so he is told he must worship it. Daniel replies that he can only worship the living God. Daniel asks the king for permission to kill the dragon without a sword to show it is not the living God. He is given permission. Daniel prepares a concoction and gives it to the dragon to eat, and the dragon dies. When the Babylonians hear this they say the king has become a Jew. He has destroyed Bel, killed the dragon, and put the priests to death.

A group of people threaten the king with death if he does not turn Daniel over to them, so he gives Daniel up to them. They throw Daniel into a lion's den where he remains six days. In the den there are seven lions that have not been fed.

We are then told that in Judea there is a prophet named Habakkuk. An angel of God appears to him and tells him to take lunch to Daniel in the lion's den. Habakkuk says he does not know the den, so the angel picks him up by the hair and with the speed of the air, takes him to the den. Daniel said you have remembered me, O God; you have not forsaken those who love you.

On the seventh day the king comes to mourn Daniel, but he looks in and sees Daniel sitting there untouched by the lions. The king cries out aloud, you are great, O LORD, the God of Daniel, and there is no other beside you. (The king is obviously a slow learner.) The king has Daniel taken out of the den, and he throws into the den those who tried to destroy him. They are devoured before his eyes in a moment. Again Daniel's wisdom is expressed: God helps those who pray to him, are obedient to him, and do not believe in the gods of humankind's creation.

THE MINOR PROPHETS

The Minor Prophets are called such only because the books of these prophets are shorter than the Major Prophets. Major and minor have absolutely nothing to do with their importance. There are twelve minor prophets according to the Christian canon.

According to Jewish usage the twenty-four books of the Hebrew Scriptures fall into three divisions: the Law (Torah), the Prophets (Nevi'im), and the Writings (Kethuvim). Together they are called the Tanakh or the Bible. The Prophets are divided into the Former Prophets and the Latter Prophets.

In the OT Joshua, Judges, Samuel and the book of Kings are called the Former Prophets by the Jews, while Christians call them the Historical books. Former and latter have nothing to do with dates, only with their placement in the Bible. The latter prophets begin with Isaiah, Jeremiah, Ezekiel and Daniel for Christians. The Jews do not consider Daniel a prophet, but he is included in their Writings. The twelve minor prophets are considered one book called the Book of the Twelve by the Jews. The first minor prophet is Hosea followed by Joel, Amos, Obadiah, Jonah, Micah, Nahum, Habakkuk, Zephaniah, Haggai, Zechariah, and Malachi.

Again it must be stated that in the OT Scriptures a prophet basically is one who speaks for God. Prophets are more forth tellers than they are foretellers, and contrary to popular Christian fundamentalism, they do not tell us everything we want to know about the end times. God calls the prophets primarily to speak to their current religious, political, economic, social, and cultural situation, and most of their foretelling is to the near future in the times in which they lived. The basic message to God's people is, if they do not repent and change their ways as a nation, God will punish the nation in order to bring it back to him. It is also important to understand that when the prophets use the word justice, it is primarily in reference to what we moderns call social justice.

HOSEA

Hosea, a prophet of the northern kingdom (Israel), is a contemporary of Amos who also prophesied in the north. He is also a contemporary of Isaiah and Micah who prophesied in the southern kingdom (Judah). The century of their work is approximately 800-700 B.C.

It is a time when Assyria, from the area of northern Babylonia (Iraq), comes upon the stage as the world's power. They are among the most aggressive, brutal and violent nations in ancient history. This is a time when the powerful reign of Jeroboam II in Israel is ending as is the powerful reign of Uzziah (Azariah) in Judah. Decay and decadence in both the northern and the southern kingdom are prevalent. Hosea speaks to the north that is suffering from war with Assyria and is in virtual anarchy. Four Israelite kings are assassinated within fourteen years after the death of Jeroboam II.

Hosea's actual years of prophesy are from 745-730 B.C. The theme of the book is the love and fidelity of God for his people. This love is exemplified in Hosea's marital situation and problems with his wife Gomer. Gomer is unfaithful to her husband Hosea. He separates from her, but later takes her back. Hosea sees his relationship with Gomer as a metaphor of God's dealing with his people, Israel, as well as God dealing with each of us. Israel is unfaithful to God because of its crimes and oppression against the poor, for idolatry, and for injustice. Adultery is what Scripture calls these idolatrous actions.

The key to understanding Hosea is the story of his marriage to Gomer and her unfaithfulness that the Bible calls adultery. Finally, because of Hosea's great love, they reconcile. Her adultery and desertion of Hosea symbolize the violation of the people of Israel in their covenant with God. They will be disciplined and punished for their actions. This will take place when the northern kingdom (Israel) is conquered by Assyria, and the people are carried off into captivity in 721-22 B.C. But God still loves his people and wants to be reconciled with them. Hosea expresses God's compassion and his deep love for his people.

What God expects of his people is steadfast love, the type he has for his people. In 6:6 God says, I desire steadfast love and not sacrifice, the knowledge of God, rather than burnt offerings. It is not that God does not want their sacrifice and burnt offerings; the issue is: without steadfast love and knowledge of God, they are of no value. Hosea's message is that God will take them back upon repentance. Some interesting verses are the following: (4:1-13, 17-18, 9:1, 10:13-17, 12:8, 14:1-5).

Chapter 1:1 says, The word of the LORD came to Hosea son of Beeri in the days of Kings Uzziah, Jotham, Ahaz, and Hezekiah of Judah, and in the days of King Jeroboam, son of Joash of Israel. (Hosea lived in the last days of the northern kingdom (Israel) between 750-721 B.C.) In verses 2-3 the LORD said to Hosea, "Go take for yourself a wife of whoredom and have children of whoredom, for the land commits great whoredom by forsaking the LORD." So he went and took Gomer daughter of Diblaim, and she conceived and bore him a son.

Verse 4 says, And the LORD said to him, "Name him Jezreel (means God sows); for in a little while I will punish the house of Jehu for the blood of Jezreel, and I will put an end to the kingdom of the house of Israel . . ." (Jeroboam II belonged to the Jehu dynasty.) Verses 6-7 say, She conceived again and bore a daughter. Then the LORD said to him, "Name her Lo-ruhamah (means not pitied), for I will no longer have pity on the house of Israel or forgive them. But I will have pity on the house of Judah, and I will save them by the LORD their God; I will not save them by bow, or by sword, or by war, or by horses, or by horseman."

Verses 8-9 say, When she had weaned Lo-ruhamah, she conceived and bore a son. Then the LORD said, "Name him Lo-ammi (means not my people), for you are not my people, and I am not your God." But Hosea gives the people hope, for verse 11 says, The people of Judah and the people of Israel shall be gathered together, and they shall appoint for themselves one head; and they shall take possession of the land, for great shall be the day of Jezreel.

In chapter 2 Gomer is shown to symbolize Israel, for she will suffer public shame because Israel has adulterated the worship of the LORD with Canaanite Baalism. The scene moves from Hosea's actions to God's speech where God assumes the role of husband and Israel his wife. In verses 1-2 Hosea says to his children, Say to your brother, Ammi, and to your sister, Ruhamah. Plead with your mother, plead--for she is not my wife, and I am not her husband—that she put away her whoring from her face and her adultery from between her breasts, or I will strip her naked and expose her as in the day she was born, and make her like a wilderness, and turn her into a parched land, and kill her with thirst.

Verses 4-5 say, Upon her children also I will have no pity, because they are children of whoredom. For her mother has played the whore; she who conceived them has acted shamefully. (Through this prophet God assumes the role of husband and pictures Israel as his wife who committed adultery by whoring after the pagan gods. Gomer represents Israel as a nation while Gomer's children represent the people of Israel.)

In verses 13-16 God says, I will punish her for the festival days of the Baals, when she offered incense to them . . . and forgot me, says the LORD. Therefore I will now allure her and bring her into the wilderness, and speak tenderly to her. From there I will give her vineyards, and make the Valley of Achor a door of hope. There she shall respond as in the days of her youth, as at the time when she came out of the land of Egypt. On that day, says the LORD, you will call me, "My husband," and no longer will you call me, "My Baal."

The rest of the chapter promises the removal of the Baals, the establishment of a universal covenant, the abolition of war, and betrothal to the one God in steadfast love and faithfulness. Verses 19-20 say, I will take you for my wife forever; I will take you for my wife in righteousness and in justice, in steadfast love, and in mercy. I will take you for my wife in faithfulness; and you shall know the LORD. Verse 23 says, And I will have pity on Lo-ruhamah, and I will say to Lo-ammi, "You are my people," and he shall say, "You are my God." (God is always expressing his love for his people waiting for them to return to him.)

Chapter 3:1 says, The LORD said to me again, "Go love a woman who has a lover and is an adulteress, just as the LORD loves the people of Israel, though they turn to other gods and love raisin cakes." (Raisin cakes are used in pagan festivals as an aphrodisiac.) In (2) Hosea buys back Gomer. This is to be God's sign to his people that he loves them and will seek them and accept or buy them back.

In chapter 4:1-3 Hosea says, Hear the word of the LORD, O people of Israel; for the LORD has an indictment against the inhabitants of the land. There is no faithfulness or loyalty, and no knowledge of God in the land. Swearing, lying, and murder, and stealing and adultery break out; bloodshed follows bloodshed. Therefore the land mourns, and all who live in it languish; . . .

Verses 4-8 say, with you is my contention, O priest. You shall stumble by day; the prophet also shall stumble with you by night, and I will destroy your mother. My people are destroyed for lack of knowledge; because you have rejected knowledge, I reject you from being a priest to me. And since you have forgotten the law of your God, I also will forget your children.

The more they increased, the more they sinned against me; they changed their glory into shame. They feed on the sin of my people; they are greedy for their iniquity. Verse 13 says, They sacrifice on the tops of the mountains . . . Therefore your daughters play the whore, and your daughters-in-law commit adultery. Verses 17-18 say, Ephraim (a name for the northern kingdom) is joined to idols—let him alone. When their drinking is ended, they indulge in sexual orgies; they love lewdness more than their glory. Chapter 5 continues the chastisement of Israel's leaders both prophets, priests, and kings.

Chapter 5 :1 says, Hear this, O priests! Give heed, O house of Israel! Listen O house of the king! For the judgment pertains to you; for you have been a snare at Mizpah, and a net spread upon Tabor, and a pit dug on Shittim; but I will punish all of them. Verse 11 says, Ephraim is oppressed, crushed in judgment, because he was determined to go after vanity.

Chapter 6:1-3 says, "Come let us return to the LORD; for it is he who has torn, and he will heal us; . . . After two days he will revive us; and on the third day raise us up, that we may live before him. (Christians note that Jesus was raised from the dead on the third day.) Let us know, let us press on to know the LORD; his appearing is as sure as the dawn; he will come to us like the showers, like the spring rains that water the earth."

In verse 6 the LORD says, I desire steadfast love and not sacrifice (worship), the knowledge of God rather than burnt offerings (worship). (God is not saying he does not desire their worship, but he is saying without steadfast love and knowledge of him, worship is useless.) In verses 7-9 he says that like Adam they transgressed the covenant and dealt faithlessly with me. Gilead is a city of evil doers tracked with blood. As robbers lie in wait for someone, so the priests are banded together; they murder on the road to Shechem, they commit a monstrous crime.

Chapter 7:1-3 mentions wicked deeds, corruption, dealing falsely, and treachery of the northern kingdom which is also called Ephraim or Samaria. Verse 7 says, All their kings have fallen; none of them calls upon me, and verse 10 says, Israel's pride testifies against him; yet they do not return to the LORD their God, or seek him, for all this. Verse 13 adds, Woe to them, for they have strayed from me!

Chapter 8:1 says, Set the trumpets to your lips! One like a vulture is over the house of the LORD, because they have broken my covenant, and transgressed my law. Verse 4 says, With their silver and gold they made idols for their own destruction, and (14) says, Israel has forgotten his Maker, and built palaces; and Judah has multiplied fortified cities; but I will send a fire among his cities, and it shall devour his strongholds.

In chapter 9:7-9 Hosea says, The days of punishment have come, the days of recompense have come; Israel cries, "The prophet is a fool; the man of the spirit is mad!" Because of your great iniquity, your hostility is great. The prophet is a sentinel for my God over Ephraim . . . They have deeply corrupted themselves as in the days of Gibeah; he will remember their iniquity, he will punish their sins.

Chapter 10:13-15 says, You have plowed wickedness, you have reaped injustice, you have eaten the fruit of lies. Because you have trusted in your power and in the multitude of your warriors; therefore, the tumult of war shall rise against your people, and all your fortresses shall be destroyed, as Shalman destroyed Beth-arbel on the day of battle when mothers were dashed in pieces with their children. Thus it shall be done to you, O Bethel, because of your great wickedness. At dawn the king of Israel shall be utterly cut off. (Here is a warning to not trust in the nation's war machine.)

Chapter 11:1-2 says, When Israel was a child, I loved him, and out of Egypt I called my son. (The gospel writer uses this in reference to Jesus, see Matt 2:15.) The more I called them, the more they went from me; they kept sacrificing to the Baals, and offering incense to idols. (They trusted in the things that were not of God.)

The rest of the chapter shows how God is torn between love and justice. He loves his people with great compassion, but their sin is serious. God's love is not superficial and he is not a sloppy sentimentalist. God's love is costly and transforming. Christians see this displayed at its ultimate with Christ on the cross.

From chapters 12 through 14 the message is about rebellion and restoration. Chapter 12:7-8 says, A trader, in whose hands are false balances, he loves to oppress. Ephraim has said, "Ah I am rich, I have gained wealth all for myself; in all my gain no offense has been found in me that would be sin." (Does this not sound like some individuals, as well as nations, and many corporations who end up paying fines in the millions but admit no sin or guilt?) Verse 14 says, Ephraim has given bitter offense, so his LORD will bring his crimes down on him and pay him back for his insults.

Chapter 13 again stresses how the people violated the first commandment of having no other gods as they flocked to worship Baal. Chapter 14, the last chapter, is full of love, compassion, and pleading. Israel still has the opportunity to return to God, for he is full of mercy. The war machine, foreign alliances, and idols are futile. Because God loves freely, Israel will be healed and brought back to a fruitful life.

Verse 4 says, I will heal their disloyalty; I will love them freely, for my anger has turned from them. Verse 9 says, Those who are wise understand these things; those who are discerning know them. For the ways of the LORD are right, and the upright walk in them, but transgressors stumble in them. (No matter how much the people have sinned, God still has his arms open waiting for his people to return to him.)

Hosea's message of divine love and the need for loyalty to God is relevant to the modern world. The sins committed by individuals and nations are the same now as then. The world is still in chaos because individuals and nations continue in ways that displease God. Hosea like all the great prophets is a realist. He recognizes the nation will be destroyed if it does not accept God's offer of repentance. Do you think things are any different today? Do we have any prophets today? Or is it that we moderns no longer need any prophets?

JOEL

The dominant theme in Joel is the coming Day of the LORD. The Day of the LORD can be applied in three different senses (1) God will intervene for his people in those times (2) God will intervene at a later time in history (3) God will intervene in the end times to end the world as we know it and transform it. In the process God will destroy all human pride as he makes his judgments on the wicked and the just.

Joel sees a locust plague as a symbol of both the Assyrians conquering Israel and the foreshadowing of the eschatological, final intervention at the end of the world. In 2:28, as far as Christians are concerned, he foretells the Christian Day of Pentecost which is the beginning of the age of the church (see Acts 2:17-21).

Later Paul quotes Joel 2:32 when he says, " Then everyone who calls on the name of the LORD shall be saved." About Joel himself, nothing is known. From his book it appears he lives in Judah during the Persian period of Jewish history. He is well acquainted with the temple and the priesthood. There are only three chapters in Joel.

In chapter 1 the locust plague is described, and verse 4 says, What the cutting locust left, the swarming locust has eaten. What the swarming locust left the hopping locust has eaten, and what the hopping locust left the destroying locust has eaten. Verses 5-6 say, Wake up you drunkards, and weep; and wail all you wine-drinkers, over the sweet wine, for it is cut off from your mouth. For a nation has invaded my land, powerful and innumerable; its teeth are lion's teeth, and it has the fangs of a lioness. (This is a reference to Assyria.)

Joel in (14-15) says, Sanctify a fast, call a solemn assembly. Gather the elders and all the inhabitants of the land to the house of the LORD your God, and cry out to the LORD. Alas for the day! For the day of the LORD is near, and as destruction from the Almighty it comes. Verse 19 says, To you, O LORD, I cry. For fire has devoured the pastures of the wilderness, and flames have burned all the trees of the field.

In chapter 2:1-6 Joel says, Blow the trumpet in Zion; sound the alarm on my holy mountain! Let all the inhabitants of the land tremble, for the day of the LORD is coming. It is near--a day of darkness and gloom, a day of clouds and thick darkness! . . . Fire devours in front of them, and behind them a flame burns . . . nothing escapes them. They have the appearance of horses, and like war horses they charge. As with the rumbling of chariots, they leap on the tops of mountains, like the crackling of a flame of fire devouring the stubble, like a powerful army drawn up for battle. Before them peoples are in anguish, all faces grow pale.

Verses 10-11 say, The earth quakes before them, the heavens tremble. The sun and the moon are darkened, and the stars withdraw their shining. (This apocalyptic language, which is also used in the NT, is symbolic for a great change.) Verse 11 says, The LORD utters his voice at the head of his army; how vast is the host! Numberless are those who obey his command. Truly the day of the LORD is great; terrible indeed--who can endure it?

The darkening of sun and moon is a way of expressing that there will be a time of great tumult and confusion. The world order as we know it will be turned upside down. The magnitude of the upheaval is expressed through the imagery of the physical universe. This kind of imagery is very common in apocalyptic literature.

Verses 12-13 say, Yet even now, says the LORD, return to me with all your heart, with fasting, with weeping, and with mourning; rend your hearts and not your clothing. Return to the LORD, your God, for he is gracious and merciful, slow to anger, and abounding in steadfast love, and relents from punishing.

Verses 17-18 say, let the priests and ministers of the LORD weep. Let them say, "Spare your people, O LORD, and do not make your heritage a mockery, a byword among the nations. Why should it be said among the people, 'Where is their God?' " Then the LORD became jealous for his land, and had pity on his people. In (20) he says I will remove the northern army far from you, . . . He tells them in (21-27) that he will take care of them and give them plenty.

In verses 28-32 God says, Then afterward I will pour out my spirit on all flesh; your sons and daughters shall prophesy, your old men shall dream dreams, and your young men shall see visions. Even on the male and female slaves, in those days, I will pour out my spirit. I will show portents in the heavens and on earth, blood and fire, and columns of smoke. The sun shall be turned to darkness, and the moon to blood, before the great and terrible day of the LORD comes. Then everyone who calls on the name of the LORD shall be saved; for in Mount Zion and in Jerusalem there shall be those who escape, as the LORD has said, and among the survivors shall be those whom the LORD calls.

Joel is applying this imagery to the Jews in those times, but the Apostle Peter in the NT uses it as a double fulfillment of prophecy in Acts chapter 2. Peter uses it in his first sermon on the Day of Pentecost marking the first day of Christ's church where all nations and all people are called to call upon the name of the LORD. Then instead of God's call to a nation, God calls all nations to Christ's church.

Chapter 3:1-2 says, in those days and at that time, when I restore the fortunes of Judah and Jerusalem, I will gather all the nations and bring them down to the valley of Jehoshaphat, and I will enter into judgment with them there, on account of my people and my heritage Israel, because they have scattered them among the nations.

God in verses 9-11 says, Proclaim this among the nations: Prepare war, stir up the warriors. Let all the soldiers draw near, let them come up. Beat your plowshares into swords, and your pruning hooks into spears; let the weakling say, "I am a warrior." Come quickly, all you nations around, gather yourselves there. Bring down your warriors, O LORD.

Verses 12-14 say, Let the nations rouse themselves and come up to the valley of Jehoshaphat; for there I will sit to judge all the neighboring nations. Put in the sickle, for the harvest is ripe. Go in, tread, for the winepress is full. The vats overflow, for their wickedness is great. Multitudes, multitudes, in the valley of decision! For the day of the LORD is near in the valley of decision! The sun and the moon are darkened, and the stars withdraw their shining. (All this language is apocalyptic symbolism for great upheaval and change.)

Verses 18-21 say, In that day the mountain shall drip sweet wine, the hills shall flow with milk, . . . Egypt shall become a desolation and Edom a desolate wilderness, because of the violence done to the people of Judah, in whose land they have shed innocent blood. But Judah shall be inhabited forever, and Jerusalem to all generations. I will avenge their blood, and I will not clear the guilty, for the LORD dwells in Zion.

Joel helped to mark a notable change in OT prophecy. Taking the characteristic forms of classical prophecy, he expands their apocalyptic, poetic, and liturgical dimensions. We must remember that most of the prophets' writings are some form of poetry. Therefore one must be careful how much of it is interpreted literally. We do know that Joel is saying there will be a time of judgment for individuals and nations.

One last thing: There are two aspects of Joel's hope for a transformation of the earth. First, is the universal hope for freedom from hunger. This is a natural reaction to the locust plague. In a time of scarcity Joel promises that they will eat and be filled. Predictions that always give hope to the poor are very common among the prophets.

Second, God will make things right. God will bring vengeance on all oppressors who take advantage. We comfortable Americans have a difficult time understanding this, for most of us can not understand the mentality of those who see themselves oppressed and desire to see the tables turned on those who have power and wealth. Maybe some of us are so busy excusing our actions and the actions of our nation that we fail to see how individual and political actions of nations affect others.

Much of the world sees us as greedy oppressors, and most Americans do not understand why. What does the reader think? Are we Americans greedy oppressors? Are there reasons to support that thinking, or is it just being made up by those who hate America? Can the reader think of any reasons why another country could hate the United States of America? What is the thinking of other countries? What is the reader's thinking? How open minded do you think you are in your thinking? Is the reader able to gain thoughts from another perspective when it differs from your own thinking?

AMOS

The prophecies of Amos are delivered at Bethel to the northern kingdom (Israel) during the time of Jeroboam II (786-746 B.C.). Amos is a shepherd and cared for sycamore (fig) trees. He is from Tekoa a small town in Judea. Amos lived during a time of prosperity, but beneath the comfort and prosperity is a nation in the process of rotting.

In strong poetic language he stresses social justice. He condemns external religious ceremonies and practices used to cover up their injustices and social corruption. He says the people will be conquered and carried off to Assyria because of their social corruption.

He describes five symbolic visions (locusts, fire, a plumb line, a basket of ripe fruit, and sanctuary). These visions are given to him by God, which signal the coming destruction of Israel mainly because of social injustices, but God will preserve a remnant.

Some of the following verses are key for Amos. 2:6-7, 3:10-4:1, 5:10-15, 5:21-24, 8:4-7, 8:11-12. In 5:24 he says, let justice roll down like waters, and righteousness like an ever flowing stream. All OT prophets are concerned about social justice, but Amos is among the greatest in reference to such teachings. Amos is a shepherd and dresser of fig (sycamore) trees, a simple man, the type God uses to carry his message. Amos and Hosea prophesy about the same time. As they are finishing their prophesying in Israel, Isaiah and Micah are beginning theirs in Judah.

Chapter 1:1 says, The words of Amos, who was among the shepherds of Tekoa, which he saw concerning Israel in the days of King Uzziah of Judah and in the days of King Jeroboam, son of Joash of Israel, two years before the earthquake. The rest of chapter 1 over to 2:4 has Amos applying the same demanding standards to Israel's neighbors that he applies to Israel. The message is that God's word applies to all. The following will be judged as Israel will be judged: Damascus, Philistia, Tyre, Edom, Ammon, Moab, and Judah.

Chapter 2:6 begins with why Israel will be judged. Verses 6-8 say, I will not revoke the punishment; because they sell the righteous for silver, and the needy for a pair of sandals--they who trample the head of the poor into the dust of the earth, and push the afflicted out of the way; father and son go into the same girl, so that my holy name is profaned; they lay themselves down before every altar on garments taken in pledge; and in the house of their God they drink wine bought with fines they imposed.

Chapter 3:1-2 says, Hear this word that the LORD has spoken against you, O people of Israel . . . You only have I known of all the families of the earth; therefore I will punish you for all your iniquities. Verse 10 says, They do not know how to do right, says the LORD, those who store up violence and robbery in their strongholds. Verse 15 says, I will tear down the winter house as well as the summer house; and the houses of ivory shall perish, and the great houses shall come to an end, says the LORD.

Amos in chapter 4:1-2 says, Hear this word, you cows of Bashan who are on Mount Samaria, who oppress the poor, who crush the needy, who say to their husbands, "Bring something to drink!" The Lord GOD has sworn by his holiness: The time is surely coming upon you, when they shall take you away by hooks, even the last of you with fish hooks. Verse 12 says, Therefore thus I will do to you, O Israel; because I will do this to you, prepare to meet your God, O Israel!

Chapter 5:6-7 says, Seek the LORD and live, . . . you that turn justice into wormwood and bring righteousness to the ground! Verse 10 says, They hate the one who reproves in the gate (court), and they abhor those who speak the truth. In verse 11 he tells them because they trample on the poor, they will not live in their newly built houses or drink the wine of their vineyards.

Verses 12-15 say, I know how many are your transgressions, and how great are your sins--you who afflict the righteous, who take a bribe, and push aside the needy in the gate (court). Therefore the prudent will keep silent in such a time; for it is an evil time. Seek good and not evil, that you may live . . . Hate evil and love good, and establish justice in the gate; it may be that the LORD, the God of hosts, will be gracious to the remnant of Joseph. (The city gate is where the elders met to determine justice and do business transactions.)

Verses 21-24 say, I hate, I despise your religious festivals, and I take no delight in your solemn assemblies . . . I will not accept them; and the offerings of well-being of your fatted animals I will not look upon them. Take away from me the noise of your songs; I will not listen to the melody of your harps. But let justice roll down like waters, and righteousness like an ever-flowing stream.

It is not that God does not want their worship; the issue is: without practicing justice, their worship is of no value. He is simply telling them that morality, both personal and social, must go together with their worship.

Chapter 6:1 says, Alas for those who are at ease in Zion, and for those who feel secure on Mount Samaria, the notables of the first of the nations, to whom the house of Israel resorts! (Samaria was the capital city of Israel, the kingdom of the north.) Verses 4-8 say, Alas for those who live on beds of ivory, and lounge on their couches, and eat lambs from the flock, and calves from the stall; who sing idle songs to the sound of the harp, and like David, improvise on instruments of music, who drink wine from bowls, and anoint themselves with the finest oils, but are not grieved over the ruin of Joseph! Therefore they shall now be the first to go into exile, and the revelry of the loungers shall pass away. The Lord GOD has sworn by himself (says the LORD the God of hosts): I abhor the pride of Jacob and hate his strongholds; and I will deliver up the city and all that is in it.

In verses 12-14 he says, you have turned justice into poison and the fruit of righteousness into wormwood--you who rejoice in Lo-debar, who say, "Have we not by our own strength taken Karnaim by ourselves?" Indeed I am raising up against you a nation, . . . and they shall oppress you from Lebo-hamath to the Wadi Arabah.

In chapter 7:7-9 Amos says, This is what he (God) showed me: the Lord was standing beside a wall built with a plumb line, with a plumb line in his hand. And the LORD said to me, "Amos, what do you see?" And I said, "A plumb line." Then the Lord said, "See I am setting a plumb line in the midst of my people, Israel; I will never again pass them by; the high places of Isaac (pagan worship places) shall be made desolate, and the sanctuaries of Israel shall be laid waste, and I will rise against the house of Jeroboam with the sword."

The plumb line is a measuring stick that measures the people and their actions; the one God finds the people are not measuring up to his standards. Let us keep in mind the plumb line will be applied to all nations, including the nations of this modern world.

Amaziah, the priest of Bethel in (10-11) sends to King Jeroboam saying, "Amos has conspired against you in the very center of the house of Israel; the land is not able to bear all his words. For thus Amos has said, 'Jeroboam shall die by the sword, and Israel must go into exile away from his land.' "

In verses 12-13 Azariah told Amos to get out of Israel and go back to Judah to earn his bread, but Amos in (14-17) said, "I am no prophet, nor a prophet's son; but I am a herdsman, and a dresser of Sycamore trees, and the LORD took me from following the flock, and the LORD said to me, 'Go, prophesy to my people Israel.' Now therefore hear the word of the LORD. You say, 'Do not prophesy against Israel, and do not preach against the house of Isaac.' Therefore thus says the LORD: 'Your wife shall become a prostitute in the city, and your sons and your daughters shall fall by the sword, and your land shall be parceled out by line; you yourself shall die in an unclean land, and Israel shall surely go into exile away from its land.' "

In chapter 8:1-3 Amos says, This is what the Lord GOD has showed me--a basket of summer fruit. He said, "Amos what do you see?" And I said, "A basket of summer fruit." Then the LORD said to me, "The end has come upon my people Israel; I will never again pass them by. The songs in the temple will become wailings in that day," says the Lord GOD; "the dead bodies shall be many, cast out in every place. Be silent." (The ripe summer fruit symbolizes the sinful kingdom is ripe for ruin.)

Verses 4-6 say, Hear this, you that trample on the needy, and bring to ruin the poor of the land, saying, "When will the new moon (religious days) be over so that we may sell grain; and the sabbath, so that we may offer wheat for sale? We will make the ephah small and the shekel great, and practice deceit with false balances, buying the poor for silver and the needy for a pair of sandals, and selling the sweepings of the wheat." (They are charging higher prices for inferior products). Verse 7 says, The LORD has sworn by the pride of Jacob: Surely I will never forget any of their deeds.

Verse 9 says, On that day, says the Lord GOD, I will make the sun go down at noon, and darken the earth in broad daylight. (It is interesting that this word usage is also used on the day of Christ's crucifixion.) Verses 10-12 say, I will turn your feasts into mourning and all your songs into lamentation . . . The time is surely coming, says the Lord GOD, when I will send a famine on the land; not a famine of bread, or a thirst for water, but of hearing the words of the LORD. They shall wander from sea to sea, from north to east; they shall run to and fro, seeking the word of the LORD, but they shall not find it.

In chapter 9 Amos has his fifth vision. Verses 1-4 show devastation, and there is no way to hide from God. Verses 8-10 say, The eyes of the Lord GOD are upon the sinful kingdom, and I will destroy it from the face of the earth—except that I will not utterly destroy the house of Jacob, says the LORD. For lo, I will command, and shake the house of Israel among all nations as one shakes with a sieve, but no pebble shall fall to the ground. All the sinners of my people shall die by the sword, who say, "Evil shall not overtake or meet us."

But in verses 11-15 hope is given. On that day I will raise up the booth of David that is fallen, and repair its breaches, and raise up its ruins and rebuild it as in the days of old; in order that they may possess the remnant of Edom and all the nations who are called by my name, says the LORD who does this . . . I will restore the fortunes of my people Israel, and they shall rebuild the ruined cities and inhabit them; they shall plant vineyards and drink their wine, and they shall make gardens and eat their fruit. I will plant them upon their land, and they shall never again be plucked up out of the land that I gave them, says the LORD your God.

Those who are students of history know that this prophecy does not hold true. The Israelites are brought back to their land, but they will lose it to the Ptolemies, then to the Selucids, and then to Rome in A.D. 70 when the city of Jerusalem and the temple are destroyed, and then again in A.D. 135 when Rome demolishes Jerusalem. Later Muslims will control the land until 1948 A.D. when the Israelites will return to part of their land. That brings us to today where Muslims and Jews still battle over the land.

Amos in his era had a very difficult time. Israel had been in a time of great prosperity. God calls him to preach harsh words in a time of prosperity. He denounces the people for relying on military might, for injustice in social dealings, for their crass immorality, and shallow meaningless piety. His forceful, uncompromising preaching brings him into conflict with the rich and powerful, who are the political and religious authorities of the day, and they do not appreciate his preaching.

No prophet is more easily related to the modern world than Amos. The social inequities he denounces are still very much with us. Institutional government has a moral function of protecting its people's human rights and working for fairness and the common good of all. In the ancient world it was the role of the prophet to be the conscience of the nation, to speak truth to the powerful, and to speak for the powerless. It is they who rarely have anyone to speak for them.

A major lesson to be learned from Amos is that social justice is a major facet of religion. The test of religion is what happens in daily life and in the market place. This is as important as what happens in the church, the synagogue, and the mosque on the day of worship. God repeats numerous times that he will not accept the worship of those who practice or promote social injustices.

Another lesson is that there is a connection between the social justice of a society and its long term prosperity. The God who allows prosperity will also take it away when greed, exploitation of the powerless, and the individualism of the powerful get out of control and trump the common good. Is this a lesson even for modern day America?

OBADIAH

Obadiah means servant of God, but we know nothing about him. His prophecy concerns the downfall of Edom, who Scripture indicates came from Esau. Edom occupies the mountainous region southeast of the Dead Sea. The capital Sela (now Petra) is located high on a plateau above a sheer rock cliff. It is from here that Edom launches raids on Israel and attacks them on the day the Babylonians defeat Jerusalem and destroy the temple in 586-87 B.C. Obadiah is the shortest book in the OT consisting of one chapter.

Chapter 1:1-4 says, the vision of Obadiah. Thus says the Lord GOD concerning Edom: Verses 2-4 say, I will surely make you least among the nations; you shall be utterly despised. Your proud heart has deceived you, you that live in the clefts of the rock, whose dwelling is in the heights. You say in your heart, "Who will bring me down to the ground?" Though you soar aloft like the eagle, though your nest is set among the stars, from there I will bring you down, says the LORD. (The Edomites lived on top of this high cliff.)

Verses 10-12 say, For the slaughter and violence done to your brother Jacob (Israel), shame shall cover you, and you shall be cut off forever. On the day that you stood aside, on the day that strangers carried off his wealth, and foreigners entered his gates and cast lots for Jerusalem, you too were like one of them. But you should not have gloated over your brother on the day of his misfortune; you should not have rejoiced over the people of Judah on the day of their ruin; you should not have boasted on the day of distress. (Jacob who is now Israel, and Esau who is now Edom were brothers.)

Verse 15 says, the day of the LORD is near against all the nations. As you have done, it shall be done to you; Your deeds shall return on your own head. Verses 17-18 say, But on Mt Zion there shall be those that escape, and it shall be holy; and the house of Jacob shall take possession of those who dispossessed them. Verse 21 says, Those who have been saved shall go up to Mount Zion to rule Mount Esau; and the kingdom shall be the LORD's.

Christians believe Obadiah is saying that those who survive this Day of the LORD will eventually come to God's kingdom. This is the kingdom Jesus established with its roots in Zion. In this way Israel will rule over Edom. Jews and Muslims disagree over defining God's kingdom. Overall this oracle is really a testimony to the hope of a people who have been reduced to poverty and insignificance, and are at the mercy of their neighbors. A remnant will be saved on Mt Zion.

JONAH

Jonah is an Israelite called to present the good news of repentance to the hated enemy, Assyria. He tries to escape this responsibility that God gave to him because he hates the enemy Assyrians. In trying to escape he winds up in a giant fish, who after three days, spits him out. He goes on to Nineveh, the capital city. The people along with the king repent. Jonah is depressed. The theme is: God calls everyone, even the worst, even our enemies, to repentance and reconciliation.

Jonah represents the narrowness found among many Jews at that time. They think God can only love and show mercy to the Jews. They forget that God's love and salvation are for all, even though it comes through Israel the first chosen to be God's light to the world. The book is a protest against the extremes of nationalism.

The book is considered by most scholars to be a short story. It is a type of a comic art form to portray a prophet who thinks he knows better than God. Everyone in the story is more devout than this self righteous prophet.

The book is an example of God inspired biblical poetry designed by God to get a certain point across. To try to interpret poetry as literal history distorts the Scriptures. The purpose of the literature is not to focus on whether the fish is real or not. The focus must always be on the meaning and purpose of this inspired story. It is interesting that the 1941 Princeton Theological Review mentions a man who was chasing a whale near the Falkland Islands and was swallowed by it. After three days the whale was caught and killed. When they opened up the whale the man was alive but unconscious. They revived him and he lived.

Chapter 1:1-3 says, Now the word of the LORD came to Jonah, son of Amittai saying, "Go at once to Nineveh, that great city (in Assyria), and cry out against it; for their wickedness has come up before me." But Jonah sets out to flee to Tarshish (probably Spain) from the presence of the LORD. He went down to Joppa and found a ship going to Tarshish; . . . away from the presence of the LORD. (Today the ancient city of Nineveh is under the Kurdish city of Mosul in Iraq.)

But verses 4-7 say, the LORD hurled a great wind upon the sea, and a mighty storm came upon the sea that the ship threatened to break up. Then the mariners were afraid, and each cried out to his god. They threw the cargo that was in the ship into the sea to lighten it for them. Jonah meanwhile . . . was fast asleep. The captain came and said to him : "What are you doing sound asleep? Get up and call on your god. Perhaps the god will spare us a thought so that we do not perish." The sailors said to one another, "Come let us cast lots so that we may know on whose account this calamity has come upon us." So they cast lots, and the lot fell on Jonah. Then in (10) the men knew that he was fleeing from the presence of the LORD, because he confessed.

In verse 12 Jonah said, "Pick me up and throw me into the sea in order to quiet down the storm for you." After much reluctance in (15-16) they proceed to do so, and the sea ceases from its raging. Then the men fear the LORD even more, and they offer a sacrifice to the LORD and make vows. (The theology of this section is that storms may fall upon us when we flee from God's presence.)

As Jonah is thrown into the sea in (17) the LORD provides a large fish to swallow up Jonah; and Jonah is in the belly of the fish for three days and three nights. (Notice it is not a whale but a big fish, even though it is possible that a whale could be considered a big fish.)

Chapter 2:1 says, Jonah prayed to the LORD his God from the belly of the fish saying, "I called to the LORD out of my distress, and he answered me; out of the belly of Sheol I cried, and you heard my voice . . ." What follows in (2-9) is a psalm-prayer of Jonah in poetic form. Verse 10 says, Then the LORD spoke to the fish, and it spewed Jonah out on dry land. (Christians will point out that Christ will come out of the earth, rising from the grave, also after three days.)

In chapter 3:1 The word of the LORD came to Jonah a second time, saying, "Get up, go to Nineveh, that great city, and proclaim to it the message that I tell you."

Jonah set out and went to Nineveh, and in (4-6) Jonah cries out for repentance, and the people believe God, and they repent of their sin. Even the king repents, and (10) tells us that when God sees their repentance, he changes his mind about the calamity he said he would bring upon them.

Chapter 4:1-5 says, this was very displeasing to Jonah, and he became angry. He prayed to the LORD and said, "O LORD! Is this not what I said while I was still in my own country? That is why I fled to Tarshish in the beginning; for I knew you were a gracious God and merciful, slow to anger, and abounding in steadfast love, and ready to relent from punishing. And now, O LORD, please take my life from me, for it is better for me to die than live." And the LORD said, "Is it right for you to be angry?" Then Jonah went out of the city and sat down east of the city, and made a booth for himself there. He sat under it in the shade, waiting to see what would become of the city.

Verses 6-9 say, The LORD God appointed a bush, and made it come up over Jonah, to give shade over his head, to save him from his discomfort; so Jonah was very happy about the bush. But when dawn came up the next day, God appointed a worm that attacked the bush, so that it withered . . . the sun beat down on the head of Jonah so that he was faint and asked that he might die. He said, "It is better for me to die than live." But God said to Jonah, "Is it right for you to be angry about the bush?" And he said, "Yes, angry enough to die."

Then in 10-11 the LORD said, "You are concerned about the bush, for which you did not labor and which you did not grow; it came into being in a night and perished in a night. And should I not be concerned about Nineveh, that great city, in which there are more than a hundred and twenty thousand persons who do not know their right hand from their left, and also many animals?" (At that point the book ends.)

Jonah symbolizes Israel who hated foreigners, people who were not like them, people who had a different god than they had, and people who spoke a different language than they spoke. Israel was to be God's light to the nations, but they did not want others to come into God's fold. Jonah represents Israel who wants it their way instead of God's way. Isaiah summed it up when he said in 55:8-9, my thoughts are not your thoughts, nor are your ways my ways. For as the heavens are higher than the earth, so are my ways higher than your ways, and my thoughts higher than your thoughts.

With skill and great style the book of Jonah calls Israel, through the prophet Jonah, to repentance and to remind them of its mission to take the message of God's grace, mercy, and forgiveness to all the world. Israel was not performing this responsibility. In fact they had basically rejected it. Jonah's message is to remind the Jews of this call from God and to teach tolerance and forgiveness to those who are different from them. God forgives all of his created beings when they repent, and this makes us part of the one family of God.

MICAH

Micah is a contemporary of Isaiah so he prophesies approximately from 740-701 B.C. He is younger than Isaiah, but he says much of what the other prophets say. Unlike Isaiah he is not of noble descent nor is he from Jerusalem. Micah is from the common people.

Three things to remember are: first, he prophesies that eventually a new David will come out of the faithful remnant. Second, this new David will restore the nation in a way that surpasses its former glory (5:1-3). Matthew will quote these verses to show that Jesus is the Messiah because the prophet has predicted he will be born in Bethlehem. Third, in 6:8 he says that God's requirement for his people is to do justice, and to love kindness, and to walk humbly with your God. This summarizes three prophets. Do justice (Amos). Love mercy (Hosea). Walk humbly with God (Isaiah).

Chapter 1:1-2 begins by saying, The word of the LORD that came to Micah of Moresheth in the days of Kings Jotham, Ahaz, and Hezekiah of Judah, which he saw concerning Samaria and Jerusalem. Hear, you peoples, all of you; listen, O earth, all that is in it; and let the Lord GOD be a witness against you, the LORD from his holy temple.

Verses 3-5 say, For lo, the LORD is coming out of his place, and will come down and tread upon the high places (worship centers of syncretism) of the earth. Then the mountains will melt under him and the valleys will burst open, like wax near the fire, like waters poured down a steep place. All this is for the transgressions of Jacob and for the sins of the house of Israel. What is the transgression of Jacob? Is it not Samaria? And what is the high place of Judah? Is it not Jerusalem?

In verses 6-7 the end of Samaria and her idols is foretold. Verse 8 says, For this I will lament and wail; I will go barefoot and naked; I will make lamentation like the jackals, and mourning like the ostriches. For her wound is incurable.

Chapter 2:1-2 says, Alas for those who devise wickedness and evil deeds on their beds! When the morning dawns, they perform it, because it is in their power. They covet fields, and seize them; houses, and take them away; they oppress householder and house, people and their inheritance.

Verses 7- 9 say, Is the LORD's patience exhausted? Are these his doings? Do not my words do good to one who walks uprightly? But you rise up against my people as an enemy; you strip the robe from the peaceful, from those who pass by trustingly with no thought of war. The women of my people you drive out from their pleasant houses; from their young children you take away my glory forever.

In chapter 3:1-4 Micah says, Listen, you heads of Jacob and rulers of the house of Israel! Should you not know justice?--you hate the good and love the evil, who tear the skin off my people, and the flesh off their bones; who eat the flesh of my people, flay their skin off them, break their bones in pieces, and chop them up like meat in a kettle, like flesh in a caldron. Then they will call to the LORD, but he will not answer them; he will hide his face from them at that time, because they have acted wickedly.

Verses 5-7 say, Thus says the LORD concerning the prophets who lead my people astray, who cry "Peace" when they have something to eat, but declare war against those who put nothing into their mouths. Therefore it shall be night to you, without vision, and darkness to you, without revelation. The sun shall go down upon the prophets, and the day shall be black over them; the seers shall be disgraced, the diviners put to shame; they shall all cover their lips, for there is no answer from God.

In verses 8-11 Micah says, But as for me, I am filled with power, with the spirit of the LORD, and with justice and might, to declare to Jacob his transgression and to Israel his sin. Hear this, you rulers of the house of Jacob and chiefs of the house of Israel, who abhor justice and pervert all equity, who build Zion with blood and Jerusalem with wrong! Its rulers give judgment for a bribe, its priests teach for a price, its prophets give oracles for money; yet they lean upon the LORD and say, "Surely the LORD is with us! No harm shall come upon us." (Does that sound familiar in today's culture?)

In chapter 4 there are prophecies of Israel's glorious future and the restoration of the Davidic kingdom. Verses 1-2 say, In the days to come the mountain of the LORD's house shall be established as the highest of mountains, and shall be raised up above the hills. Peoples shall stream to it, and many nations shall come and say: "Come, let us go up to the mountain of the LORD, to the house of the God of Jacob; that he may teach us his ways and that we may walk in his paths." For out of Zion will go forth instruction, and the word of the LORD from Jerusalem.

Verses 3-5 say, He shall judge between many peoples, and shall arbitrate between strong nations far away; they shall beat their swords into plowshares, and their spears into pruning hooks; nation shall not lift up sword against nation, neither shall they learn war anymore; but they shall all sit under their own vines and under their own fig trees, and no one shall make them afraid; for the mouth of the LORD has spoken. For all the peoples walk, each in the name of its god, but we will walk in the name of the LORD our God forever and ever. (Here a picture of future peace is given because all people will have their needs met.)

Verses 6-7 say, In that day, says the LORD, I will assemble the lame and gather those who have been driven away, and those whom I have afflicted. The lame I will make the remnant, and those who were cast off, a strong nation; and the LORD will reign over them in Mt Zion now and forever more.

In chapter 5 the shepherd king, who is to be ruler of Israel, will be born in Bethlehem as David was born. Verse 2 says, But you, O Bethlehem of Ephrathah, who are one of the little clans of Judah, from you shall come forth for me one who is to rule in Israel, whose origin is from old, from ancient days. Verses 4-5 say, And he shall stand and feed his flock in the strength of the LORD, in the majesty of the name of the LORD his God. And they shall live secure, for now he shall be great to the ends of the earth; and he shall be the one of peace. (In the gospels Matthew (2:4-6) and John (7:42) use these verses in reference to Jesus.)

Verses 10-15 say, In that day says the LORD, I will cut off your horses from among you and will destroy your chariots; and I will cut off the cities of your land and throw down all your strongholds; and I will cut off sorceries from your hand, and you shall have no more soothsayers; and I will cut off your images, and your pillars (gods) from you, and you shall bow down no more to the work of your hands; and I will uproot your sacred poles (gods) from among you and destroy your towns.

And in anger and wrath I will execute vengeance on the nations that did not obey. (This message is not only for ancient times; it is also for those in modern times who worship the false gods of money, wealth, sex, pleasure or whatever it is that one puts in place over the God of Scripture.)

Chapter 6:2 says, the LORD has a controversy with his people, and he will contend with Israel. (The people have forgotten the saving acts of old and what it means to walk humbly with God even though they go through the motions of external worship.) So in verse 6 they ask, "With what shall I come before the LORD and bow myself before God on high? . . ."

Verse 8 then sums up the legal, ethical, and covenantal requirements by saying, He has told you, O mortal, what is good; and what does the LORD require of you but to do justice, and to love kindness, and to walk humbly with your God? Verses 10-13 say, Can I forget the treasures of wickedness in the house of the wicked, and the scant measures that is accursed? Can I tolerate wicked scales and a bag of dishonest weights? Your wealthy are full of violence; your inhabitants speak lies, with tongues of deceit in their mouths. Therefore I have begun to strike you down, making you desolate because of your sins.

Chapter 7:1-4 says, Woe is me! For I have become like one who, after the summer fruit has been gathered, after the vintage has been gleaned, find no cluster to eat; there is no first-ripe fig for which I hunger. The faithful have disappeared from the land, and there is no one left who is upright; they all lie in wait for blood, and they hunt each other with nets. Their hands are skilled to do evil; the official and the judge ask for a bribe, and the powerful dictate what they desire; thus they pervert justice. The best of them are like a brier, the most upright of them a thorn hedge. The day of their sentinels, of their punishment, has come; now their confusion is at hand. (Sounds like modern times.)

Micah in verse 7 says, But as for me, I will look to the LORD, I will wait for the God of my salvation; my God will hear me. He gives hope in verses 18-20 when it says, Who is like you, pardoning iniquity and passing over the transgression of the remnant of your possession? He does not retain his anger forever, because he delights in showing clemency. He will again have compassion upon us; he will tread our iniquities under foot. You will cast all our sins into the depths of the sea. You will show faithfulness to Jacob and unswerving loyalty to Abraham, as you have sworn to our ancestors from the days of old.

Micah stands solidly with Amos, Hosea, and Isaiah as a strong champion of the pure worship of the one God and social justice for the powerless. They all spoke a word from God against his people who are in comfort worshiping both Yahweh and the gods of their own making while they practice injustice.

NAHUM

Nahum's purpose is to pronounce judgment on Assyria. They are the Nazis of the ancient world. God uses Assyria to punish God's people for their disobedience to God just as Moses foretold in the book of Deuteronomy when he gave the people his speeches on blessings and curse.

Assyrians are extremely cruel, and they practically eliminate the 10 tribes located in the north called Israel. They will deport all the quality people and send their own people into the land to marry the few Israelites left. Eventually those people will become known as the Samaritans of the NT. But Assyria will not escape God's judgment.

They too are a sinful nation filled with self pride. God always will bring judgment on evil and those who oppress others. Assyria will later be conquered by Babylon. Assyria and Babylon are from the territory now known as Iraq.

Two prophets, Jonah and Nahum, deal specifically with Nineveh and Assyria. Jonah's context is probably around 785 B.C., and Nahum is around 630 B.C. which are about one hundred fifty years apart. Jonah's is a message of mercy to those who repent; Nahum's is a message of doom for those who do not repent. Together they illustrate God's method of dealing with both nations and individuals. There is grace and mercy for those who are his and follow his ways, but God is also an avenger of cruelty, immorality, social injustice, and wrong doing. With the nations it is this writer's opinion that judgment comes eventually in this present world, but for individuals, the final judgment is after this world.

Chapter 1:1 begins by saying, An oracle concerning Nineveh (the capitol of the great colonial power, Assyria). The book of the vision of Nahum of Elkosh. Verses 2-3 say, A jealous and avenging God is the LORD, the LORD is avenging and wrathful; the LORD takes vengeance on his adversaries and rages against his enemies. The LORD is slow to anger but great in power, the LORD will by no means clear the guilty.

In verse 6 Nahum says, Who can stand before his indignation? Who can endure the heat of his anger? His wrath pours out like fire, and by him the rocks are broken in pieces. But in (7) he says, The LORD is good, a stronghold in a day of trouble; he protects those who take refuge in him, even in a rushing flood. So in (9) he asks, Why do you plot against the LORD? He will make an end; no adversary will rise up twice.

Chapter 2 is mostly poetry describing the destruction and end of Assyria. God calls Nineveh a prostitute. The arrogant Assyrian empire will pass away because of her treacherous and deceitful dealing with other nations including God's people. Verse 13 says, See, I am against you, says the LORD of hosts, and I will burn your chariots in smoke, and the sword shall devour your young lions; I will cut off your prey from the earth, and the voice of your messengers shall be heard no more.

Chapter 3:1 says, Ah, city of bloodshed, utterly deceitful, full of booty--no end to the plunder! Verses 4-6 say, Because of the countless debaucheries of the prostitute, gracefully alluring, mistress of sorcery, who enslaves nations through her debaucheries, and peoples through her sorcery, I am against you, says the LORD of hosts . . . I will throw filth at you and treat you with contempt, and make you a spectacle.

Verse 7 says, Then all who see you will shrink from you and say, "Nineveh is devastated; who will bemoan her?" Where shall I seek comforters for you? Verses 18-19 say, Your shepherds are asleep, O king of Assyria; your nobles slumber. Your people are scattered on the mountains with no one to gather them. There is no assuaging your hurt; your wound is mortal. All who hear the news about you clap their hands over you. For who has ever escaped your endless cruelty?

The judgment against Assyria and its capitol Nineveh represents the fact that all nations will be judged for their behavior that goes against the ways of Yahweh, the one God. While Judah was freed from one oppressor, it would soon be subjected to another. Fifteen years after Nahum proclaimed security, Jerusalem would soon be under siege by another tyrant. The lesson to be learned is that the world never has a shortage of tyrants. One seems to follow another.

God's people must make sure that their nation does not become a tyrant, and if the tendency develops, it is the role of God's people, the church, to expose it. Unfortunately the real religion of most nations is civil religion where the nation's goals are the real religion. In the meantime too often a superficial worship of God continues while the real lords too often are the goals of the nation.

HABAKKUK

Habakkuk calls God to account for the way he is governing the world. Habakkuk is upset that God will use unbelieving Babylonians to defeat and conquer God's chosen. Jerusalem will be destroyed along with the temple. God replies that he is using the pagans to discipline his people and that the just Israelite will not perish in the disaster, for a remnant will be saved. St Paul in Galatians 3:11 will later quote Habakkuk 2:4 saying, the one who is righteous lives by faith.

Nothing is known about the prophet Habukkuk other than what we read in this book of three chapters. His prophecy is a complaint to God about his own nation being destroyed because of its wickedness by a nation that is more wicked than they are. Habakkuk could not understand that form of justice.

Chapter 1:1 says, the oracle that the prophet Habakkuk saw. Verses 2-4 say, O LORD, how long shall I cry for help, and you will not listen? Or cry to you, "Violence!" And you will not save? Why do you make me see wrong doing and look at trouble? Destruction and violence are before me; strife and contention arise. So the law becomes slack, and justice never prevails. The wicked surround the righteous--therefore, judgment comes forth perverted.

In verses 12-13 Habakkuk asks God, O LORD, you have marked them for judgment (Israel); and you O Rock, have established them for punishment. Your eyes are too pure to behold evil, and you cannot look on wrong doing; why do you look on the treacherous and are silent when the wicked swallow those more righteous than they?

In chapter 2:1-4 Habakkuk says, I will stand at my watchpost, and station myself on the rampart; I will keep watch to see what he will say to me, and what he will answer concerning my complaint. Then the LORD answered me and said, Write the vision; make it plain on tablets, so that a runner may read it. For there is still a vision for the appointed time; it speaks of the end, and it does not lie. In verse 4 God says, Look at the proud! Their spirit is not right in them, but the righteous live by their faith.

The idea is that the righteous live by their humble acceptance of faith in God and his ways, and God's work in them and not by faith in themselves, their ways, their creativity, and their works or actions as too many of the people are now doing. God has his ways that we do not always understand, and even though God's people may be less evil than others, God also sometimes disciplines his people to make them be what he calls them to be.

In verse 5 he says, Moreover wealth is treacherous; the arrogant do not endure. They open their throats wide as Sheol; like Death they never have enough. They gather all nations for themselves and collect all people as their own.

Five woes are now expressed against a nation that plunders people. Verses 6-9 say, How long will you load yourselves with goods taken in pledge? Will not your own creditors rise, and those who make you tremble wake up? Then you will be booty for them. Because you have plundered many nations, all that survive of the peoples shall plunder you—because of human bloodshed, and violence to the earth, to cities and all who live in them. "Alas for you who get evil gain for your houses, setting your nest on high to be safe from the reach of harm." Verse 12 says, "Alas for you who build a town by bloodshed, and found a city on iniquity!"

This is a lesson for both individuals and nations. Habakkuk is saying God will punish humanity's arrogant pride and those who greedily grab what belongs to others, who for selfish ends justify the cruelest means, and who give their lives to everything but the one God. This is in reference to a nation that plunders other nations, obtains gains by violence, builds towns with blood, shamelessly degrades its neighbors, and as verses 17-19 indicate for violence and the worship of idols, or the worship of things that are not of God. Then in (20) he says, But the LORD is in his holy temple; let the earth keep silence before him. (The theology is that God is present and aware of what is happening.)

Chapter 3 consists of a prayer by Habakkuk which is a psalm. The focus is on God. He sees the fury of God's judgment. Even though there is great loss, God is to be trusted. The prophet will wait for the time God will deal with the invader, the Babylonians. Verse 16 says, I hear, and I tremble within; my lips quiver at the sound. Rottenness enters my bones, and my steps tremble beneath me. I wait quietly for the day of calamity to come upon the people who attack us.

Habakkuk confronts honestly the disturbing problem of why a just God is silent when the wicked take advantage and hurt those who are more righteous than they, especially when those hurt are God's people. The prophet receives an answer that is forever valid for those who call themselves God's people. The righteous shall live by faith. The righteous are to live in relationship to God and be faithful. They are to be faithful to their calling. Meanwhile, God is sovereign, and in God's own way, and at the right time God will deal with all the wicked.

ZEPHANIAH

Zephaniah prophesies during the time of Manasseh who ruled for 55 years. There are only two outstanding kings according to the Deuteronomic editors. They are Hezekiah and Josiah. Manasseh rules between them, and he is Hezekiah's son. His rule is among the most evil, for paganism is rampant with idolatry and the time is filled with great injustices to the people.

Two themes stand out in Zephaniah's prophecy (1) a remnant in Judah will survive because of their faith, repentance, and submission to God 3:8-20, (2) the Day of the LORD is coming soon. Remember the Day of the LORD is a time of great change brought about by God's intervention. It is the end of things as they are, and the beginning of new things.

Thus the Day of the LORD is applied to numerous situations in Scripture not just to the end of the world. Zephaniah uses it 19 times. His writing will contribute significantly to apocalyptic thought. Some interesting verses are 1:2-6, 2:1-3, 3:8-9.

Chapter1:1 says, The word of the LORD that came to Zephaniah son of Cushi son of Gedeliah son of Amariah son of Hezekiah, in the days of King Josiah son of Amon of Judah. (He is of royal blood related to King Hezekiah which makes him related to Manasseh. Apparently, he prophesies toward the end of Manasseh's reign and the beginning of good King Josiah's reign.)

Verses 2-6 say, I will utterly sweep away everything from the face of the earth, says the LORD. I will sweep away humans and animals; I will sweep away the birds of the air and the fish of the sea. I will make the wicked stumble. I will cut off humanity from the face of the earth, says the LORD. I will stretch my hand against Judah, and against all the inhabitants of Jerusalem; and I will cut off from this place every remnant of Baal and the name of the idolatrous priests; those who bow down on the roofs to the host of the heavens; those who bow down and swear to the LORD, but also swear by Milcom; those who have turned back from following the LORD, who have not sought the LORD or inquired of him.

The problem is religious syncretism where the one God as well as the pagan gods are all worshiped in name while the people follow their own ways, and the ways of the gods. This is not contrary to modern times when we worship God while we follow the ways of money, wealth, sex, job, family, business, or whatever.

Verse 7 says, Be silent before the Lord GOD! For the day of the LORD is at hand; the LORD has prepared a sacrifice, he has consecrated his guests. In verses 12-13 God says, I will punish the people who rest complacently on their dregs, those who say in their hearts, "The LORD will not do good, nor will he do harm." Their wealth will be plundered, and their houses laid waste. Though they build houses, they shall not inhabit them; though they plant vineyards, they shall not drink wine from them.

Verses 14-18 say, The great day of the LORD is near, near and hastening fast; the sound of the day of the LORD is bitter, the warrior cries aloud there. That day will be a day of wrath, a day of distress and anguish, a day of ruin and devastation, a day of darkness and gloom, a day of clouds and thick darkness, a day of trumpet blast and battle cry against the fortified cities and against the lofty battlements. I will bring such distress on people that they shall walk like the blind; because they have sinned against the LORD, their blood shall be poured out like dust, and their flesh like dung. Neither their silver nor their gold will be able to save them on the day of the LORD's wrath; in the fire of his passion the whole earth shall be consumed; for a full, a terrible end he will make of all the inhabitants of the earth.

Zephaniah says in chapter 2:1-3, Gather together, gather, O shameless nation, before you are driven away like the drifting chaff, before there comes upon you the fierce anger of the LORD, before there comes upon you the day of the LORD's wrath. Seek the LORD all you humble of the land, who do his commands; seek righteousness, seek humility; perhaps you may be hidden on the day of the LORD's wrath. Then in (4-15) he lists Israel's enemies, the nations who will experience God's wrath.

In chapter 3:1-5 in reference to Jerusalem, he says, Ah, soiled, defiled, oppressing city! It has listened to no voice; it has accepted no correction. It has not trusted in the LORD; it has not drawn near to its God. The officials within it are roaring lions; its judges are evening wolves that leave nothing until the morning. Its prophets are reckless, faithless persons; its priests have profaned what is sacred, they have done violence to the law . . . the unjust know no shame.

Verses 6-7 say, I have cut off nations their battlements are in ruins; I have laid waste their streets so that no one walks in them; their cities have been made desolate, without people, without inhabitants. I said, "Surely the city will fear me, it will accept correction; it will not lose sight of all that I have brought upon it." But they were the more eager to make all their deeds corrupt.

Verses 8-9 say, Therefore wait for me, says the LORD, for the day when I arise as a witness. For my decision is to gather nations, to assemble kingdoms, to pour out upon them my indignation, all the heat of my anger; for in the fire of my passion all the earth shall be consumed. At that time I will change the speech of the peoples to a pure speech, that all of them may call upon the name of the LORD and serve him with one accord.

Verse 12 says, I will leave in the midst of you a people humble and lowly. They shall seek refuge in the name of the LORD--the remnant of Israel; they shall do no wrong and utter no lies, nor shall a deceitful tongue be found in their mouths. Verses 14-17 say, Sing aloud, O daughter Zion; shout, O Israel! Rejoice and exult with all your heart, O daughter Jerusalem! The LORD has taken away the judgments against you, he has turned away your enemies. The king of Israel, the LORD, is in your midst; you shall fear disaster no more.

Verses 19-20 say, I will deal with all your oppressors at that time. And I will save the lame and gather the outcast, and I will change their shame into praise and renown in all the earth. At that time I will bring you home, at the time when I gather you; for I will make you renowned and praised among all the peoples of the earth, when I restore your fortunes before your eyes, says the LORD.

Zephaniah proclaims doom, but he also promises comfort and consolation to those who wait patiently for God and serve him. Even after destruction there is hope. This is the style of most prophets.

HAGGAI

God's people are in exile in Babylon (Iraq) for 50-70 years. This is when God raises Cyrus the Persian (Iran) to be his anointed. Cyrus declares the Jews can return to Jerusalem and rebuild the city and the temple. A remnant returns, but because of opposition by the Samaritans, who under the Persians had been given control of both Samaria and Judah, the people give up building the city and the temple. Contributing to this stoppage of work is a lack of funds and personnel.

In 579 B.C. God raises up Haggai. He reminds the people of the prophet Nathan's promise to David in 2 Samuel 7 that from the descendents of David there will be a ruler in Judah and from him there will come an everlasting kingdom. Christians believe this was fulfilled in the Messiah, who they know as Jesus the Son of David.

Jews see a number of messiahs because the word means anointed but still wait for the final Messiah to set up the great kingdom of David's glory on earth. Some Muslims believe Jesus is the Messiah but view him differently than Christians. They see him as just a man who will return and set up an ideal kingdom based on the Qur'an. He will then die and be resurrected.

The book of Haggai ends on a very positive note. It ends with a promise to Zerubbabel, the current ruler and descendant of David. Haggai says that the messianic hope of Israel will be fulfilled through Zerubbabel, who is a type (typology) of the Messiah to come whom God will send in the future to restore and save all Israel in an everlasting kingdom. Some interesting verses are the following. (1:1-7, 2:20-23). The next three books Haggai, Zechariah, and Malachi take us to the time that the exiles returned to Judah. It will be the time of Ezra and Nehemiah.

Chapter 1:1-4 says, In the second year of King Darius, in the sixth month, on the first day of the month; the word of the LORD came by the prophet Haggai to Zerubbabel, son of Shealtiel, governor of Judah, and to Joshua son of Jehozadak, the high priest: Thus says the LORD of hosts: These people say the time has not yet come to rebuild the LORD's house. Then the word of the LORD came by the prophet Haggai, saying: Is it a time for you yourselves to live in your paneled houses, while this house lies in ruins?

In verses 5-8 he tells them if they wonder why they do not have enough to eat or do not have enough clothes to keep warm, or why they have sown much and harvested little while prices soar, it is because they have not been diligent about building God's house. In verses 7-8 they are told to notice that they have sown much, and harvested little because they have ignored God. Verse 9 says, My house lies in ruin while you run off to your own houses. (The people have their priorities wrong. They are wrapped up in their selfish concerns and neglect God's concerns.)

In verses 10-11 it is suggested that God has withheld the weather to keep their crops from growing. Verses 12-13 say, Then Zerubbabel son of Shealtiel, and Joshua son of Jehozadak, the high priest, with all the remnant of the people, obeyed the voice of the LORD their God, and the words of the prophet Haggai, as the LORD their God had sent him; and the people feared the LORD. Then Haggai, the messenger of the LORD, spoke to the people with the LORD's message, saying, I am with you, says, the LORD. Then in (14) God stirred up the spirit of all, and they worked on the house of the LORD.

Solomon's elaborate temple had been demolished seventy years before. Very few of them had seen it, but they heard about it from those who had. The new temple does not even begin to compare with the old one. But God suggests to them that this new temple will be just the beginning of what God has in store in the future for his people.

In chapter 2:4-5 the people are encouraged to work, for God says he will be with them because of the promise made when they came out of Egypt. God in (5) says, My spirit abides among you; do not fear.

Verses 6-9 say, Once again, in a little while, I will shake the heavens and the earth and the sea and the dry land; and I will shake all the nations, so that the treasure of all nations shall come, and I will fill this house with splendor, says the LORD of hosts. The silver is mine, and the gold is mine, says the LORD of hosts. The latter splendor of this house shall be greater than the former, says the LORD of hosts; and in this place I will give prosperity, says the LORD of hosts. (God is encouraging the people about the future for at this point the people are depressed because this temple can not compare to Solomon's temple.)

In verses 20-23 The word of the LORD came a second time to Haggai on the twenty-fourth day of the month: Speak to Zerubbabel, governor of Judah, saying, I am about to shake the heavens and the earth, and to overthrow the throne of kingdoms; I am about to destroy the strength of the kingdoms of the nations, and overthrow the chariots and their riders; and the horses and their riders shall fall, every one by the sword of a comrade. On that day, says the LORD of hosts, I will take you, O Zerubabbel, my servant, son of Sheatiel, says the LORD, and make you like a signet ring; for I have chosen you, says the LORD of hosts.

This reawakens the messianic hope and is a reference to the Messiah, and the kingdom that will come from him, and the promise made to David. Christians believe Haggai is saying that through Zerubbabel, a descendant of David will come, the one who will be the Messiah. Zerubbabel is the governor and not king, for at this point, the Persians would not be willing to accept a king.

This book has a positive lesson to offer on the value of religious symbols and ritual as a means of bringing the community together. It is largely through the efforts of Haggai that the temple is rebuilt. While the temple may not have satisfied immediate expectations, its contribution to Jewish life over the next five hundred years was enormous.

ZECHARIAH

Zechariah is a contemporary of Haggai. He shares Haggai's zeal for a rebuilt temple. He is a visionary on the order of Daniel and Ezekiel. The word of God comes to him in a series of eight night visions in chapter 1-6:15.

The first vision is one of divine horseman patrolling the earth. The second vision consists of four horns and four smiths. The third vision is a man going to measure Jerusalem. The fourth vision is one of Joshua and Satan. The fifth vision is of a golden lampstand and two olive trees. The sixth vision is of a flying scroll. The seventh vision is a woman in a basket, and the eighth vision is of four chariots.

In chapter 6 a messianic leader is crowned, and in chapter 8 God returns to Zion to do good for Judah and Jerusalem. From chapters 9-11:17 Israel is restored while chapters 12-14 involves the Day of the LORD, the final warfare and the final victory.

There is a sharp contrast between chapters 1-8 and 9-14. Most scholars do not believe Zechariah is the only author, so they call chapters 9-14 Deutero-Zechariah. Others even say chapters 12-14 could be Third Zechariah.

The NT Gospels quote Zechariah more than any other prophet in the narrative of Jesus' last days, especially in reflecting upon Jesus the Messiah. Zechariah refers to the necessity of moral conversion in preparation for the inauguration of the new era. The transcendence of God is stressed in that God does not speak directly to Zechariah but through angels and visions. The second part of Zechariah in addition to being heavily messianic is very apocalyptic.

There will be much symbolism: 4 horseman, 4 horns, 4 blacksmiths, lamp stand and olive trees, flying scrolls, 4 chariots, etc. The book of Revelation is influenced by this book. The NT writers will use numerous parts to apply to Jesus. In chapter 9:9-10, one is riding on a donkey proclaiming peace to the nations and having a world wide dominion. The NT writer will use these verses as Jesus rides into Jerusalem on Palm Sunday. Men and all nations will come to seek the Lord in Jerusalem (8:20-23). The writer of Acts has the Apostle Peter in Jerusalem giving the first sermon about Jesus the Lord to people of all nations.

In chapter 11 we have a good shepherd that is applied to Jesus by NT writers. In the same chapter thirty pieces of silver are mentioned and will be applied to Judas by the NT writer. Chapter 12:10 says, they shall look on me whom they have pierced suggesting it is God's own representative that they kill. The Gospel of John quotes from these passages applying them to Christ.

In chapter 13:7-9 the shepherd is stricken and the flock scattered which the NT will apply to Jesus and his followers at the crucifixion. The NT book of Revelation in chapters 14, 21-22 will use many of the details from Zechariah.

That is a basic summary of a book that is difficult to interpret. Apocalyptic literature is never easy to interpret. That is why there are usually many interpretations. Even so, Roman Catholic, Eastern Orthodox, and mainline Protestant scholars are usually very similar in their interpretation while the more fundamentalist churches are usually quite different, even bizarre from this writer's perspective. Jewish interpretation sees most of this book fulfilled in OT times.

Chapter 1:1-4 says, In the eighth month of the second year of Darius (The time is Oct. 520 B.C. during the time of Haggai.), the word of the LORD came to the prophet Zechariah son of Berechiah son of Iddo, saying: The LORD was very angry with your ancestors. Therefore say to them, Thus says the LORD of hosts: Return to me, says the LORD of hosts, and I will return to you, says the LORD of hosts. Do not be like your ancestors, to whom the former prophets proclaimed, "Thus says the LORD of hosts, return from your evil ways and your evil deeds." But they did not hear or heed me, says the LORD of hosts.

Zechariah's first vision begins in (8). He sees a man riding on a red horse. Behind him are three other horses colored red, white, and sorrel (brownish-red). Zechariah in (9-10) asks, "What are these, my Lord?" The angel who talked with me said to me

"I will show you what they are." So the man that was standing among the myrtle trees answered, "They are those whom the LORD has sent to patrol the earth." (The four horses are from the four corners of the earth.)

Verses 14-17 say, So the angel who talked with me said to me, Proclaim this message: Thus says the LORD of hosts; I am very jealous for Jerusalem and for Zion. And I am extremely angry with the nations who are at ease; for awhile I was only a little angry, they made the disaster worse. Therefore, thus says the LORD, I have returned to Jerusalem with compassion; my house shall be built in it, says the LORD of hosts, and the measuring line shall be stretched out over Jerusalem. Proclaim further: Thus says the LORD of hosts: My cities shall again overflow with prosperity; The LORD will again comfort Zion and again choose Jerusalem.

In the second vision verses 18-21 say, I looked up and saw four horns. I asked the angel who talked with me, "What are these?" And he answered me, "These are the horns that have scattered Judah, Israel, and Jerusalem." Then the LORD showed me four blacksmiths. And I asked, "What are they coming to do?" He answered, "These are the horns that scattered Judah, so that no head could be raised; but these have come to terrify them, to strike down the horns of the nations that lifted up their horns against the land of Judah to scatter the people." (The nations that defeated Judah will be defeated because they are morally as bad as Israel or worse and also because of their excess cruelty to God's people.)

The third vision in chapter 2:1-2 says, I (Zechariah) looked up and saw a man with a measuring line in his hand. Then I asked, "Where are you going?" He answered me, "To measure Jerusalem to see what is its width and what is its length." In (3-5) another angel came and said, "Run, say to that young man: Jerusalem shall be inhabited like villages without walls because of the multitude of people and animals in it. For I will be a wall of fire all around it, says the LORD, and I will be the glory within it."

Verses 10-11 say, Sing and rejoice, O daughter Zion! For lo, I will come and dwell in your midst, says the LORD. Many nations shall join themselves to the LORD on that day, and shall be my people; and I will dwell in your midst. And you shall know that the LORD of hosts has sent me to you. (Christians believe the NT book of Acts tells of the beginning and early advancement of this prophecy.)

In the fourth vision chapter 3:1-4 says, Then he showed me the high priest Joshua standing before the angel of the LORD, and Satan standing at his right hand to accuse him. And the LORD said to Satan, "The LORD rebuke you, O Satan! The LORD who has chosen Jerusalem rebuke you! Is not this man a brand plucked from the fire?" Now Joshua was dressed with filthy clothes as he stood before the angel. The angel said to those who were standing before him, "Take off his filthy clothes." And to him he said, "See I have taken your guilt away from you, and I will clothe you with festal apparel." (Joshua in these verses represents Judah. This is about ritual purity in preparation for the Messiah who will take away the sin and guilt of all people.)

Verses 6-9 say, Then the angel of the LORD assured Joshua saying: "Thus says the LORD of hosts; if you will walk in my ways and keep my requirements, then you shall rule in my house and have charge of my courts, and I will give you the right of access among those who are standing here . . . I am going to bring my servant the Branch . . . and I will remove the guilt of this land in a single day. (The Branch is the Davidic person who will usher in the Messianic age. For Christians this is a reference to Christ.) Verse 10 says, On that day, says the LORD of hosts, you shall invite each other to come under your vine and fig tree." (He is saying at that time the Jews shall invite all to come to God.)

In the fifth vision in chapter 4 the angel shows Zechariah a gold lampstand with a bowl on top of it. There are seven lamps on it with seven lips on each of the lamps. Zechariah asks what this is, and in (6) the angel said, "This is the word of the LORD to Zerubbabel: Not by might, nor by power, but by my spirit, says the LORD of hosts. What are you, O great mountain? Before Zerubbabel you shall become a plain; and he shall bring out the top stone amid shouts of 'Grace, grace to it!' " (In other words everything achieved will be the result of the spirit of God.)

Verse 9 says, The hands of Zerubbabel have laid the foundation of this house; his hands shall also complete it. Then you will know that the LORD of hosts has sent me to you. In (11-12) he then asks, "What are these two olive trees on the right and the left of the lampstand?" And a second time I said to him, "What are these two branches of the olive trees, which pour out the oil through the two golden pipes?" He said to me, "Do you not know what these are?" I said, "No, my lord." Then he said, "These are the two anointed ones who stand by the LORD of the whole earth."

This message seems to be saying that the role of priest and king are to go together. Christians say this is a reference to the Messiah who will be both priest and king who will pour out the oil or power of the Holy Spirit. Jews say that this simply means the priest and king are to work together.

The sixth vision in chapter 5:1-3 says, Again I looked up and saw a flying scroll. And he (the angel) said, "What do you see?" I answered, "I see a flying scroll; its length is twenty cubits, and its width ten cubits." Then he said to me, "This is the curse that goes out over the face of the whole land; for everyone who steals shall be cut off according to the writing on the one side, and everyone who swears falsely shall be cut off according to the writing on the other side . . ."

In verses 6-9 Zechariah looks up and sees a basket coming out, and the angel said, This is their iniquity in all the land. In the basket was a woman who represented their wickedness. Then I looked up and saw two women with wings like a stork who lifted up the basket between the earth and sky. In (10) I asked, "Where are they taking the basket?" He said to me, "To the land of Shinar, . . ." (The idea is that the sinful people of Judah will be carried off in exile to Babylon.)

In the eighth vision chapter 6:1-5 says, And again I looked up and saw four chariots coming out from between two mountains--mountains of bronze. The first chariot had red horses, the second chariot black horses, the third chariot white horses, and the fourth chariot dappled grey horses. Then I said to the angel who talked with me, "What are these, my lord?" The angel answered me, "These are the four winds of heaven going out, after presenting themselves before the LORD of all the earth . . . And he said, "Go patrol the earth." So they patrolled the earth. Verse 8 says, "Lo, those who go toward the north country have set my spirit at rest in the north country. (It is a time of peace.)

Verses 11-13 say, Take the silver and gold and make a crown, and set it on the head of the high priest Joshua son of Jehozadak, say to him: Thus says the LORD of hosts; Here is a man whose name is Branch: for he shall branch out in his place and he shall build the temple of the LORD. It is he that shall build the temple of the LORD; he shall bear royal honor, and shall sit upon his throne and rule. There shall be a priest by his throne, with peaceful understanding between the two of them. (In 3:8 the Branch is not Joshua but an individual presented to him. In 4:6-10 Zerubbabel, not Joshua, is commissioned as the temple builder.)

It seems as though this is saying that the king (the Branch) and the clergy work together in harmony. The religion of God will be united. And all will be ruled by God's morality. Christians will see a double fulfillment of this prophecy, for Christ will be prophet, priest, and king who will build the temple of God by becoming the temple of God (Jn 2:19-21).

In chapter 7:1-7 some men come to the temple to ask about keeping religious fasts. Zechariah tells them that it is the purpose or motive for fasting that is important. Their ancestors kept the external fast but it was not for the purpose of honoring God. Their lifestyle showed God that their religious observances meant nothing.

Verses 8-12 say, The word of the LORD came to Zechariah, saying: Thus says the LORD of hosts: Render true judgments, show kindness and mercy to one other; do not oppress the widow, the orphan, the alien, or the poor; and do not devise evil in your hearts against one another. But they refused to listen and turned a stubborn shoulder, and stopped their ears in order not to hear. They made their hearts adamant in order not to hear the law and the words that the LORD of hosts had sent by his Spirit through the former prophets.

Therefore, great wrath came from the LORD of hosts, and verses 13-14 say, Just as, when I called, they would not hear, so when they called I would not hear, says the LORD of hosts, and I scattered them with a whirlwind among all the nations that they had not known. Thus the land they left was desolate, so that no one went to and fro, and a pleasant land was made desolate.

Chapter 8:3 says, Thus says the LORD: I will return to Zion and dwell in the midst of Jerusalem; Jerusalem shall be called the faithful city, and the mountain of the LORD of hosts shall be called the holy mountain. Verse 7 says, I will save my people from the east country and from the west country; and I will bring them to live in Jerusalem. They shall be my people and I will be their God, in faithfulness and righteousness. (Jerusalem and Zion usually symbolize the realm of God's people.)

Verse 16 says, These are the things that you shall do: Speak the truth to one another, render in your gates judgments that are true and make for peace, do not devise evil in your hearts against one another, and love no false oath; for these are all things that I hate, says the LORD. Verse 19 says, love truth and peace.

Verses 22-23 say, Many peoples and strong nations shall come to seek the LORD of hosts in Jerusalem, and to entreat the favor of the LORD. Thus says the LORD of hosts: In those days ten men from nations of every language shall take hold of a Jew, grasping his garment and saying, "Let us go with you, for we have heard that God is with you." (Christians remind us that the Messiah, Jesus, was a Jew, and the first apostles and believers were Jews. Jews believe this will apply to them as a nation.)

Numerous scholars believe that chapters 9-14 were written by another writer who wrote in the spirit and tradition of Zechariah. Even so, the themes of the first part remain the same as the latter part. In 9:1-8 the shattering of Israel's enemies foreshadows the Messianic era. Then in (9) the writer says, Rejoice greatly, O daughter of Zion. Shout aloud, O daughter Jerusalem! Lo, your king comes to you; triumphant and victorious is he, humble and riding on a donkey, on a colt, the foal of a donkey.

He comes not on a war horse but on an animal that the common man used for work, and an animal meant to represent peace (see Pss 46:8-10, 72:8, Isa 11:6-9, 57:19, Hos 2:18, Mic 4:1-4, Mt 21:5, Jn 12:14-15).

Verse 10 says, He will cut off the chariot from Ephraim and the war horse from Jerusalem; and the battle bow shall be cut off, and he shall command peace to the nations; his dominion shall be from sea to sea, and from the River to the ends of the earth.

Verses 14-16 say, Then the LORD will appear over them, and his arrow go forth like lightning; the Lord GOD will sound the trumpet and march forth in the whirlwinds of the south. Verse 16 says, On that day the LORD their God will save them for they are the flock of his people; for like the jewels of a crown they shall shine on his land. (Christians see this as the Christ who came.)

Chapter 10:1 shows that God alone controls nature, and God alone controls history. It is God who gives rain and vegetation. Verses 2-3 say, For the teraphim utter nonsense, and the diviners see lies; the dreamers tell false dreams, and give empty consolation. Therefore the people wander like sheep; they suffer for lack of a shepherd. My anger is hot against the shepherds, and I will punish the leaders; for the LORD of hosts cares for his flock, the house of Judah, and will make them like his proud war-horse.

In verse 4 the writer says, Out of them shall come the cornerstone, . . . Verse 8 says, I will signal for them and gather them in, for I have redeemed them, and they shall be as numerous as they were before. In verses 9-12 a new exodus is described where God will gather his people from the nations. Verse 12 says, I will make them strong in the LORD, and they shall walk in his name, says the LORD.

In chapter 11 Because of their sins, God allows the Israelites to be abused by their rulers and breaks the covenant with them. The prophet portrays a good shepherd rejected by his sheep. Verse 6 says, I will no longer have pity on the inhabitants of the earth, says the LORD. I will cause them, every one, to fall each into the hands of a neighbor, and each into the hand of the king; and they shall devastate the earth, and I will deliver no one from their hand.

Verses 7-11 say, So, on behalf of the sheep merchants (Judah's leaders buying and selling the people), I became the shepherd of the flock doomed to slaughter. I took two staffs; one I named Favor (grace), the other I named Unity (the goals of the good shepherd for his sheep), and I tended the sheep. In one month I disposed of the three shepherds (false prophets or leaders), for I had become impatient with them, and they also detested me. So I said, "I will not be your shepherd. What is to die, let it die; what is to be destroyed, let it be destroyed; and let those that are left devour the flesh of one another!" I took my staff Favor and broke it, annulling the covenant that I had made with all the peoples. So it was annulled on that day, and the sheep merchants, who were watching me, knew that it was the word of the LORD.

In verses 12-14 I then said to them, "If it seems right to you, give me my wages; but if not, keep them." So they weighed out as my wages thirty shekels of silver. Then the LORD said to me, "Throw it into the treasury"--this lordly price at which I was valued by them. So I took the thirty shekels of silver and threw them into the treasury in the house of the LORD. Then I broke my second staff Unity, annulling the family ties between Judah and Israel. (Perhaps this a reference to the abandoned hope between Judah and Israel.)

Verses 15-17 say, Then the LORD said to me: Take once more the implements of a worthless shepherd. For I am now raising up in the land a shepherd who does not care for the perishing, or seek the wandering, or heal the maimed, or nourish the healthy, but devours the flesh of the fat ones, tearing off even their hoofs. Oh, my worthless shepherd, who deserts the flock! May the sword strike his arm and his right eye! Let his arm be completely withered and his right eye utterly blinded! (The prophet is portraying a worthless shepherd (religious leader) that exploits the sheep.)

In chapter 12:2-5 The word of the LORD said, See, I am about to make Jerusalem a cup of reeling for all the surrounding peoples; it will be against Judah also in the siege against Jerusalem. On that day I will make Jerusalem a heavy stone for all the peoples; all who lift it shall grievously hurt themselves. And all the nations of the earth shall come together against it. On that day says the LORD, I will strike every horse with panic, and its riders with madness. But on the house of Judah I will keep a watchful eye, when I strike every horse of the peoples with blindness. Then the clans of Judah shall say to themselves, "The inhabitants of Jerusalem have strength through the LORD of hosts, their God."

Verses 6-8 say, On that day I will make the clans of Judah like a blazing pot on a pile of wood, like a flaming torch among sheaves; and they shall devour to the right and to the left all the surrounding peoples, while Jerusalem again shall be inhabited in its place, in Jerusalem. The LORD will give victory to the tents of Judah first, that the glory of the house of David and the glory of the inhabitants of Jerusalem may not be exalted over that of Judah. On that day the LORD will shield the inhabitants of Jerusalem so that the feeblest among them on that day will be like David, and the house of David shall be like God, like the angel of the LORD, at their head. (The Davidic dynasty will be revived. Jews look forward to that, but some say it was fulfilled after the exile, while Christians say it was fulfilled in Christ.)

Verses 9-10 say, And on that day I will seek to destroy all the nations that come against Jerusalem. And I will pour out a spirit of compassion and supplication on the house of David and the inhabitants of Jerusalem, so that when they look on the one whom they have pierced, they shall mourn for him, as one mourns for an only child, and weep bitterly over him, as one weeps over a firstborn. (The Gospels of Matthew and John will use this in reference to Christ, see Mt 23:37, Jn 19:34-37, Isa 52:13-53.)

Chapter 13:1-2 says, On that day a fountain shall be opened for the house of David and the inhabitants of Jerusalem, to cleanse them from sin and impurity. On that day, says the LORD of hosts, I will cut off the names of the idols from the land, so that they shall be remembered no more; and also I will remove from the land the prophets and the unclean spirit. Verse 4 says, On that day the prophets will be ashamed, every one, of their visions when they prophesy; they will not put on a hairy mantle in order to deceive, but each of them will say, "I am no prophet, ..."

In verses 7-9 God's shepherd is smitten for the sheep. Verse seven says, "Awake, O sword, against my shepherd, against the man who is my associate," says the LORD of hosts. Strike the shepherd that the sheep may be scattered; I will turn my hands against the little ones. (Matthew 26:31 Jesus quotes this about himself.) In the whole land, says the LORD, two-thirds shall be cut off and perish, and one-third will be left alive. And I will put this third into the fire, refine them as one refines silver, and test them as gold is tested. They will call on my name, and I will answer them. I will say, "They are my people"; and they will say, "The LORD is our God."

Chapter 14 is the final warfare and the final victory. Verses 1-3 say, See, a day is coming for the LORD, when the plunder taken from you will be divided in your midst. For I will gather all the nations against Jerusalem to battle, and the city shall be taken and the houses looted and the women raped; half the people shall go into exile, but the rest of the people shall not be cut off from the city. Then the LORD will go forth and fight against those nations as when he fights on a day of battle.

Verses 4-7 say, On that day his feet shall stand on the Mount of Olives, which lies before Jerusalem on the east; and the Mount of Olives shall be split in two from east to west by a very wide valley, so that one half of the Mount shall withdraw northward, and the other half southward. And you shall flee by the valley of the LORD's mountain, . . . and you shall flee as you fled from the earthquake in the days of King Uzziah of Judah. Then the LORD my God will come, and all the holy ones with him. On that day there shall not be either cold or frost. And there shall be continuous day (it is known to the LORD), not day and not night, for at evening time there shall be light. Verses 8-9 say, On that day living waters will flow out from Jerusalem, . . . And the LORD will become king over all the earth; on that day the LORD will be one and his name one.

Verses 12-16 say, This shall be the plague with which the LORD will strike all the peoples that wage war against Jerusalem: their flesh shall rot while they are still on their feet; their eyes shall rot in their sockets, and their tongues shall rot in their mouths. On that day a great panic from the LORD shall fall upon them, so that each will seize the hand of a neighbor, and the hand of the one will be raised against the hand of the other; even Judah will fight against Jerusalem. And the wealth of all the surrounding nations shall be collected—gold, silver, and garments in great abundance. And a plague like this plague shall fall on the horses, the mules, the camels, the donkeys, and whatever animals that may be in those camps. Then all who survive of the nations that have come against Jerusalem shall go up year after year to worship the King, the LORD of hosts, and to keep the festival of booths (tabernacles).

Verses 17-19 declare that those who do not come to worship will be visited with a plague. Verse 21 says, there shall no longer be traders in the house of the LORD of hosts on that day. (Either no traders will be needed because everything is holy, or nothing will be permitted that defiles pure worship. This may be a reference to Jesus cleansing the temple in John's gospel.)

ZECHARIAH

Much of the writing in this book is apocalyptic poetry, and the interpretation of these events are many; there is little agreement. Jews are not in agreement with other Jews, and Christians are not in agreement with other Christians. In general, Jews apply these events to themselves after the exile. Christians see in this the era of Christ.

The NT book of Revelation chapters 21 and 22 echo many of these details. Zechariah shared Haggai's zeal for a rebuilt temple, purified community, and the coming of a messianic age. The portrait of a messianic prince of peace and the good shepherd smitten for the flock is used in the NT to describe the Christ.

MALACHI

Malachi prophesies around 450 B.C. The temple has been restored and 50-60 years have gone by. Once again the people drift back into spiritual complacency and lack of zeal for God. The priests and Levites have been unfaithful, are not teaching the law, and are neglecting the standards for the worship and sacrifices. He reminds them that another Day of the Lord will come.

He charges them with robbing God in their tithes and offerings (3:8-10). The prophet condemns social evils, especially divorce. In 2:16 the LORD the God of Israel says, I hate divorce, and covering one's garment with violence. In 4:5 (3:24 in NAB) he says, I will send you the prophet Elijah before the great and terrible Day of the LORD comes. The Gospel of Lk 1:17 applies this to the foretelling of John the Baptist who comes to prepare the way of the Lord. Jesus will say John is the Elijah to come (Matt 17:12-13).

Nothing is known about Malachi's personal life. One central theme dominates his thought: fidelity to the Lord's covenant and its teachings. From this standpoint he condemns the priests for corrupting worship and misleading the people.

Chapter 1:1-2 says, The word of the LORD to Israel by Malachi. I have loved you, says the LORD. But you say, "How have you loved us?" Is not Esau Jacob's brother? says the LORD. Yet I have loved Jacob but I have hated Esau. (Love and hatred here designate preference, for the Hebrew language does not express degrees of better and best very well; it designates preference, not emotional outburst.)

Verses 6-7 say, A son honors his father, and servants their master. If then I am a father, where is the honor due me? And if I am a master, where is the respect due me? says the LORD of hosts to you, O priests, who despise my name. The rest of the chapter shows that priests have denied him the proper worship due him by offering polluted worship. (They did this by making improper worship and giving improper instruction.)

Chapter 2:1-2 says, And now, O priests, this command is for you. If you will not listen, if you will not lay it to your heart to give glory to my name, says the LORD of hosts, then I will send the curse on you and I will curse your blessings; indeed I have already cursed them, because you do not lay it to heart. In verses 8-9 he says, you have turned aside from the way; you have caused many to stumble by your instruction; you have corrupted the covenant of Levi, says the LORD of hosts, and so I make you despised and abased before all the people, inasmuch as you have not kept my ways but have shown partiality in your instruction.

Verse 11 says, Judah has been faithless, . . . Judah has profaned the sanctuary of the LORD, which he loves, and has married the daughter of a foreign god. (By marrying women who worship other gods, the men are breaking their promise to not engage in pagan practices.) Then they ask why God does not hear them.

Verses14-15 say, Because the LORD was a witness between you and the wife of your youth to whom you have been faithless, though she is your companion and your wife by covenant. Did not one God make her? Both flesh and spirit are his. And what does the one God desire? Godly offspring. So, look to yourselves, and do not let anyone be faithless to the wife of his youth. Verse 16 says, For I hate divorce, says the LORD, the God of Israel, and covering one's garment with violence, says the LORD God of hosts. So take heed to yourselves and not be faithless.

Chapter 3:1-4 says, I am sending my messenger to prepare the way before me, and the LORD whom you seek will suddenly come to his temple. The messenger of the covenant in whom you delight—indeed, he is coming, says the LORD of hosts. But who can endure the day of his coming, and who can stand when he appears? For he is like a refiner's fire and like fullers' soap; he will sit as a refiner and purifier of silver, and he will purify the descendants of Levi and refine them like gold and silver, until they present offerings to the LORD in righteousness. Then the offerings of Judah and Jerusalem will be pleasing to the LORD as in the days of old and as in former years.

In verses 5-6 God says, I will draw near to you for judgment; I will be swift to bear witness against the sorcerers, against the adulterers, against those who swear falsely, against those who oppress the hired workers in their wages, the widow and the orphan, against those who thrust aside the alien (immigrants), and do not fear me, says the LORD of hosts. For I the LORD do not change; therefore you, O children of Jacob, have not perished.

Verses 7-10 say, Ever since the days of your ancestors, you have turned aside from my statutes and have not kept them. Return to me, and I will return to you, says the LORD of hosts. But you say, "How shall we return?" Will anyone rob God? Yet you are robbing me! But you say, "How are we robbing you?" In your tithes and offerings! You are cursed with a curse, for you are robbing me—the whole nation of you! Bring the full tithe into the storehouse, so that there may be food in my house, and thus put me to the test, says the LORD of hosts; see if I will not open the windows of heaven for you and pour down for you an overflowing blessing. (Notice he is talking also to the nation.)

Verses 14-15 say, You have said, "It is vain to serve God. What do we profit by keeping his command or by going about as mourners before the LORD of hosts? Now we count the arrogant happy; evildoers not only prosper, but when they put God to the test, they escape."

Verses 16-18 say, Then those who revered the LORD spoke with one other. The LORD took note and listened, and a book of remembrances was written before him of those who revered the LORD and thought on his name. They shall be mine says the LORD of hosts, my special possession on the day when I act, and I will spare them as parents spare their children who serve them. Then once more you shall see the difference between the righteous and the wicked, between one who serves God and one who does not serve him.

Chapter 4:1-3 says, See, the day is coming, burning like an oven, when all the arrogant and all evildoers will be stubble; the day that comes shall burn them up, says the LORD of hosts, so that it will leave them neither root nor branch. But for you who revere my name the sun of righteousness shall rise, with healing in its wings. You shall go out leaping like calves from the stall. And you shall tread down the wicked, for they will be ashes under the soles of your feet, on the day when I act, says the LORD of hosts.

Verses 4-6 are considered as an appendix. Remember the teachings of my servant Moses, the statutes and ordinances that I commanded him at Horeb for all Israel. Lo, I will send you the prophet Elijah before the great and terrible day of the LORD comes. He will turn the hearts of parents to their children and the hearts of the children to their parents, so that I will not come and strike the land with a curse. (Some scholars think that with Malachi the voice of the OT prophets falls silent.)

The value of all the prophets in our times is immense. For many of the principles stressed are as relevant for our time as it was in their time. This writer believes that if believers can not see the message to the United States and all the nations of the world, then those who call themselves Jews, Christians, or Muslims are not looking for it. They are as blind as the people for whom the prophets wrote.

One central theme dominates Malachi's thought which is fidelity to the covenant and its teachings on destruction. The figure of an appointed forerunner the messenger who prepares the way will be connected to John the Baptist by NT writers. As stated previously, the Jewish Bible organizes the same basic books differently and Malachi is not the last book in their canon; the last book in the Jewish canon is reserved for Chronicles.

Naturally, Christians, Jews, and Muslims will have different interpretations of the OT. One reason is because of Christ who Christians believe was the Messiah for whom everyone was waiting and their interpretation of the OT through the NT, while the Jews interpret the OT through the Talmud, and the Muslims through the Qur'an. But for all three the OT is a foundation book. They begin with the same basic history and stories but then branch in different directions.

In the Gospel of Luke 24:27 Jesus says, beginning with Moses and all the prophets, he interpreted to them all the things about himself in all the Scriptures. The book of Hebrews 1:1-2 says, Long ago God spoke to our ancestors in many and various ways by the prophets, but in these last days he has spoken to us by a Son whom he appointed heir of all things. This is the difference in the way Christians interpret the OT.

Therefore, Christians look at the Hebrew Scriptures (OT) through the eyes of Christ, through his words and actions, for he is the head to which the Hebrew Scriptures point. Christians believe that reading the Scriptures from the perspective of Christ leads one from the letter of the law to the spirit of the law, and from the written words of God to the living word of God.

Jews and Muslims see Jesus simply as one prophet among many. Jews do not believe he was the Messiah, for they still are looking for the Messiah, nor do they believe that Jesus rose from the dead, nor do they believe that God needs a mediator like Jesus to forgive sin.

Muslims do not believe Jesus was crucified nor do they believe he forgives sin, for only God can forgive sin. But they do believe he was born of a virgin, was resurrected, and will come again to set up a glorious age on earth but not heaven. They do not believe Jesus was the greatest of prophets, for that is reserved for Mohammad, the seal of all the prophets.

Even though all three religions interpret the OT in different ways, all three have as the foundation of their religion the OT.

DEUTEROCANONICALS/APOCRYPHA/ INTERTESTAMENTAL LITERATURE

This writer will not do a detailed description of these books as in the previous books. Eventually, a more detailed description is planned for another book. What will follow is a brief understanding and description of these books.

The Roman Catholics call these books the Deuterocanonicals meaning second canon. For them they are still considered Scripture. Protestants call these books the Apocrypha because for them it is not Scripture, but most of them do say these books are worthy to be read.

Some of the more popular books are as follows.

Tobit

Judith

Esther additions

Wisdom of Solomon

Ecclesiasticus (Wisdom of Jesus son of Sirach)

Baruch

Daniel additions

I and II Maccabees

Prayer of Manasseh (considered Deuterocanonical by the Eastern Orthodox only)

I and II Esdras (considered Deuterocanonical only by the Greek and Russian churches)

None of these books is included in the Hebrew canon of Scripture. All of them with the exception of II Esdras are present in the Greek version of the OT known as the Septuagint. The Old Latin translations of the OT made from the Septuagint include them along with II Esdras. As a consequence, many of the early church fathers quoted most of these books as authoritative Scripture.

When the NT writers quote Scripture, they quote the Septuagint, the Greek version of the OT. The Roman Catholic Church will eventually use as Scripture the books in the Septuagint. Because these books are not in the Hebrew (Jewish) Scriptures, Judaism and the Protestant Church will not accept them as Scripture. The Eastern Orthodox Church recognizes the Deuterocanonical/Apocryphal books, I Esdras, Psalm 151, the Prayer of Manasseh, and 3 Maccabees while 4 Maccabees is in an appendix. Slavonic Bibles approved by the Russian Orthodox Church contain the Duterocanonicals, 1 and 2 Esdras which they call 2 and 3 Esdras, Psalm 151, and 3 Maccabees.

Many other books written from 200 B.C.-200 A.D. have survived. Some of these books are called the Pseudepigrapha meaning falsely ascribed. Famous names are given to the books in order for them to be considered important. These books are not considered Scripture or Deuterocanonical by anyone. The books are called Pseudepigrapha by Protestants and called Apocrypha by Catholics. For Protestants the Apocrypha are the so-called Deuterocanonical works of the OT.

The names of some of these books are as follows: Book of Jubilees, Testament of the Twelve Patriarchs, Psalms of Solomon, Letter of Aristeas, 3 and 4 Maccabees, Dead Sea Scrolls, The Book of Enoch, 2 Baruch, 4 Ezra, the Assumption of Moses, and The Sibylline Oracles.

The following will be a brief summary of the Deuterocanonicals/Apocrypha though not in any particular order. These books are considered Deuterocanonical by Catholics and Apocrypha by Protestants. They are inspired Scripture for Catholics but not for most Protestants.

TOBIT - Tobit is a romantic short story with maybe some basis in history. The idea behind Tobit is that God's providence is always with us helping those who observe God's teachings. His guiding hand is upon us. The author wishes to show how God can manage the circumstances of people's lives in order to bring God's plan to fulfillment.

Tobit is a pious Jew deported from Israel to Assyria after the fall of Samaria in 722 B.C. There he is persecuted for practicing his religion. As he sleeps outside, bird droppings land in his eyes and blind him. His son Tobias meets a devil as well as the angel, Raphael, and with the help of Raphael his father is eventually cured of his blindness. The story is important because this is the first time the devil is mentioned and an angel is named. Also, it is here that the golden rule seems to develop.

Tobit becomes blind while burying the dead and in a depressed state he prays for death. His relative, Sarah, far off in Ecbatana, prays for death also because a demon has killed each of her respective husbands on their wedding nights. But God enables the son of Tobit, Tobiah, to cure Tobit's blindness and break the power of the demon that was killing Sarah's husbands. Tobiah is able to accomplish this with the help of the angel Raphael and a fish supplied by God. The idea is that God answers prayer in unexpected ways. We learn that angels and demons have an important role to play in the drama between God and humans. Angels are God's messengers who also mediate prayers to God. Meanwhile demons are hostile powers.

The book also shows the importance of the book of Deuteronomy. The book says the exile happened because of Israel's infidelity, but the exile will not be the final judgment on Israel, for there is hope of mercy. Tobit believes the temple in Jerusalem is the only legitimate place for worship. Tobit also teaches the duty to marry.

The author wishes to confirm the importance of the community of God's people, for one's commitment to community is the measure of one's commitment to God. It is important to support the poor, bury the dead, honor one's parents, and marry within the community. Another purpose of the book is to move people from despair to prayer.

JUDITH - In Judith we have the confrontation of true faith with the powers of the world. She becomes a hero because she cuts off the head of General Holofenes, the Babylonian general, who is on his way to destroy the Jerusalem temple in an attempt to end the Jewish religion. Judith is a short story with probably some historic basis.

The point of the book is that Yahweh is the true God, and he protects those who worship him. Because of Judith's faith, prayer, and obedience to God, evil power is defeated. Judith prayed then acted, while the men just prayed. The message is that God's deliverance comes through both prayer and action. The story demonstrates how God uses the weak of the world to overcome the mighty. This will be a theme of the Apostle Paul. Judith is a female model for Judaism as Mary is for Christianity.

The book offers a dissent from the assumptions of culture about the role and status of women, for God uses a woman for his purpose. God chose a woman to be the instrument of salvation and deliverance. In this story the men are the failures in the face of threats while the woman rises to the occasion. It is interesting that Judah is saved not by using military might but by a woman using her charm and beauty. A big part of the story is whose god is the God.

The author portrays Judith as a widow who lives in a state of mourning and fasting. She prays daily in the temple. She observes the Jewish dietary laws. She purifies herself by bathing in running water at the appropriate time, and she criticizes those who violate the law of first fruits and tithes.

1 MACCABEES - To understand these books it is necessary to understand the history and the political situation. The book is an historical narrative. The books are set in the time span of 175 and 134 B.C. in Palestine. It is after the time of Alexander the Great who has conquered the Persians making a Greek empire that rules the world. Through Alexander's efforts the Greek culture known as Hellenism is so advanced into the world that the known world becomes described as Hellenistic, and the language of the educated and business people of the known world becomes Greek.

At Alexander's death in 321 B.C. his empire is divided into four sections. The two most important will be the Ptolemies in Egypt, who will rule the Jews a long time, then the Seleucids in Syria. In 175 B.C., a new Seleucid king Antiochus IV Epiphanes begins a campaign to eliminate Judaism and to persecute all practicing Jews. He even butchers a pig on the temple altar, then sets upon it an idol. This is known as the Abomination of Desolation. A family of devout Jews led by Mattathias and his three sons resolve to fight a guerilla war against the Greek Seleucids. Mattathias is killed in battle but is followed by his sons, Judas, Jonathan, and Simon. The family is called the Maccabees, which means "hammer." They fought for purity in the temple and a strict observance of the law.

They are successful in defeating the pagan Greeks and eventually capturing Jerusalem and the temple which they purify and rededicate to Yahweh, the one God of Israel. From this liberation of the temple develops Hanukkah (Feast of Dedication). It is also called the Feast of Lights, for it involves a miraculous rekindling of the temple's menorah, a lampstand with seven candles. It becomes a symbol of liberation and freedom.

The period from 175-134 B.C. is a time of turmoil and war. The dynasty lasts until around 70 B.C. and is called the Hasmonean dynasty. They are the descendents of the Maccabees who became the priests and control the temple, the central governing institution. Eventually, they become more Hellenizing than the Hellenists. From this group will come the NT Sadducees.

Because of their Hellenizing, a group will break from them that will become the Pharisees. The NT Pharisees come from this group. They seem to be instrumental in developing synagogues to teach the law. This short period of time is the first time the Jews have had independence since 586 B.C., and it will be the last time until 1948 A.D.

2 MACCABEES - The story begins with two letters from Jerusalem to the Jews in Alexandria, Egypt which becomes the intellectual center for Greek speaking Jews. The letters are urging them to celebrate the rededication of the temple in Jerusalem. As stated previously this feast or holy day is called Hanukkah, or the Feast of Lights. The book summarizes the great military exploits of Judas Maccabee who is the one mainly responsible for Jewish success against the Selucids.

The book is very theological and spiritual where soldiers pray and fast before going into battle, and when victorious, they offer prayers of praise and thanksgiving attributing the victories to God's intervention for them. The book emphasizes the high value of suffering and martyrdom for the faith. The motivation for this is the belief in the resurrection of the body and that God will reward his faithful people in the next life. In the suffering of a Jewish mother and her seven sons the author says suffering can have a positive value. One of the strongest affirmations of the bodily resurrection is found in these passages (chapters 7 and 14). God will deliver the faithful despite their death at the hands of evil, and these wicked will suffer divine judgment.

Also, included in this book is the belief that the living can help the dead with their prayers and sacrifices which leads to the idea of purgatory (12:38-46), the creation of the world by God out of nothing (7:28), and the efficacy of intercessory prayer on the part of the saints in heaven (15:13-16). The belief in the resurrection of the body is taken up by the Pharisees and helps prepare the minds of the people for the bodily resurrection of Jesus as well as ours to eternal life.

BARUCH - He is Jeremiah's secretary. The purpose of this book is to call his people to repentance, conversion, and faith. The Deuteronomic theology is prevalent: sin, punishment, repentance, prayer, and restoration to God's favor. There is a lengthy prayer of confession of national guilt (1:13-3:8). The final section contains Jeremiah's letter addressed to the exiles in Babylon ridiculing idol worship and paganism (6:1-72).

Baruch, like Tobit and Wisdom, is a book for people who are separated from their normal environment. They learn it is possible to find God in a foreign land. After an introduction which recalls the Feast of Tabernacles and the renewal of the covenant, a humble confession of sin is made to God. A response of consolation is received. Included is a reflection on the way to conversion and renewed loyalty to God's law. Baruch stresses one God; the gods are totally rejected. God is the creator of all; he is the supreme source of wisdom and is just and merciful. Israel's problem is sin, and the nation needs to repent. With repentance comes hope. Without repentance there is no hope.

WISDOM (OF SOLOMON) - The book states many of the previous ideas from OT books pertaining to wisdom. The author appears to be concerned that the faithful not be led astray by those who have become enthralled with Hellenistic (Greek) culture. He is concerned that worldliness is creeping in even with the religious leaders. It is a summons to their religious traditions as opposed to philosophy.

For the first time the reader is introduced to the Greek concept of *psyche* (soul).

The Greeks held that human nature is a combination of an impermanent material body and an eternal spiritual soul which is dissolved at death. God made humans to be incorruptible. But the writer suggests that incorruptibility is based upon fidelity to wisdom.

A major section of the book acclaims the glories of wisdom. Wisdom is personified. Wisdom itself is called a spirit. Wisdom is a merging of intelligence and power. It is in this book that wisdom is referred to as the spirit of the Lord. Some of the major topics are as follows: the reward of justice which is the key to life, the wicked reject immortality and justice, the hidden counsels of God, the final judgment of the wicked, exhortation to seek wisdom, Solomon's praise of wisdom, and five examples of God's providence during the Exodus. The writer is committed to proving the enduring value of Israel's religion, but he did it using the ideas, language, and the literary style of Greek culture.

SIRACH (ECCLESIASTICUS) - It is similar to proverbs but develops the same ideas to a greater degree. The book is a collection of proverbs organized to resemble short essays. The book was greatly used for moral instruction in the early Church. Written in Hebrew the text was translated into Greek by the author's grandson. The author was Jesus Ben Sira (Greek is Sirach).

Some of the topics are as follows: Praise of wisdom, duties toward God, duties toward parents, humility, alms for the poor, sincerity, true friendship, conduct in public life, prudence in dealing with men, advice concerning women, sin of pride, moderation, care in choosing friends, caution regarding associates, the use of wealth, man's free will, divine wisdom seen in creation, the proper use of speech, wicked and virtuous women, dangers to integrity and friendship, the proper training of children, health of soul and body, proper attitude toward riches, table etiquette, providence of God, trust in the Lord not in dreams, true worship of God, sickness and death, a father's care for his daughter, the work of God in nature, and finally praise of the great holy ancestors of the faith.

The additions to Esther are at the end of the section on Esther.

The additions to Daniel are at the end of the section on Daniel.

Psalm 151 is at the end of the Book of Psalms.

Officially, the Protestant Bible has sixty-six books. The Roman Catholic Bible has seventy-three books. The Orthodox has seventy-six books. Every group has the same NT; the difference is the OT.

The Roman Catholics have all the Protestant books plus Tobit, Judith 1 and 2 Maccabees, Wisdom of Solomon, Sirach also called Ecclesiasticus, Baruch which includes the Letter of Jeremiah, and both Daniel and Esther add some Greek chapters.

The Orthodox are identical to the Roman Catholic except The letter of Jeremiah is a separate book. In the Roman Catholic Bible this letter is included in Baruch. The following are included by various Orthodox communities; 1 Esdras (a work combining parts of 2 Chronicles and Nehemiah, all of Ezra) is added after 2 Chronicles. The prayer of Manasseh is included at the end of 2 Chronicles. Psalm 151 is included at the end of Psalms.

The Jewish Bible is called the Tanakh which includes Torah (Pentateuch), Nevi'im (Prophets), Ketuvim (Writings). The Jewish Bible has twenty-four books which is basically the same as the Protestant OT but organized differently. The Jewish Bible ends with Chronicles. Jews and Protestants eliminate all the Greek books from their canon. The Talmud rooted in the Tanak relates Judaism to today's Jew.

The Islam religion uses many of the books and characters of the OT especially the Pentateuch (Torah), Psalms, and a few prophets but they revise some of it based upon the Qur'an. If something does not agree with what the Qur'an says, Muslims believe the Jews or Christians changed what took place to benefit their own teachings. They do not really read the OT, but read what the Qur'an and the Hadith (sayings of Mohammad) say about the OT. The insistence that biblical materials be evaluated on the basis of conformity to the Qur'an and explanations of the prophet Muhammad has continued. The OT and NT accounts are true only if confirmed by Muhammad and the Qur'an. There is another category in reference to the OT that is neither accepted or rejected as true or false; it is just stated without comment.

The Dogmatic Constitution on Divine Revelation in Vatican Council II (DV no. 16) affirms St Augustine's saying in reference to the OT where he said, The new is in the old concealed, and the old is in the new revealed. St Gregory said, What the OT promised is brought to light in the new; what was proclaimed in a hidden manner in the past is proclaimed openly in the present. The OT announces the NT, and the NT is the best commentary on the OT. Most Christians accept those statements.

Judaism and Islam do not see things in that manner, but all agree that the OT is to be understood as an indispensable stage in the development of their faith.

Without the OT Christian faith would have a deep void. God first made a covenant with Abraham and the nation of Israel, and then through Christ, according to Christians, he makes a new covenant and establishes the Church. This Church is established on the Day of Pentecost, and all the nations of the world and their people are invited to be reconciled to God and each other and be part of God's family. The last word in OT theology, one that never comes easily and is never separated from accountability and judgment, is hope for all. Being in covenant is life under promise and hope.

Finally, for those who take religion seriously, the OT needs to be read with a correct blending of the historical-literary sense and the theological-spiritual sense, and then for Christians, ultimately understood through the words and actions of Christ. He is the hope and goal to whom the Scriptures point. He is the center, the lens through which all texts of Scripture are ultimately interpreted and understood. This acknowledges both the value of the OT for Christians and the bond between the two testaments. As Colossians 1:15-16 says, he is the image of the invisible God, the firstborn of all creation, for in him all things in heaven and earth were created.

This writer is planning a second and third volume dealing with reading and understanding the New Testament; it will tell that story. The second volume will be *Reading and Understanding the Four Gospels: Jesus the Christ and the Beginning of Christianity.*

The third volume will be *Reading and Understanding Acts and the New Testament Letters: Peter, Paul, and John and the Development of the Church.*

BIBLIOGRAPHY OF SOURCES

As mentioned in the Introduction this book is based upon historical-literary exegesis, but it goes beyond this analysis to arrive at a theological and canonical interpretation of the Biblical texts to give beginning readers a basic understanding of the content of Scripture and to give them a way to understand it. The purpose was not to enter into the historical-critical debates. Once there is a basic understanding of the content, then those debates are possible.

The following bibliography is far from complete. Since my purpose is to keep the citation of footnotes to a bare minimum to enable beginning readers an easier reading format, the following are the sources that have most formed my thinking and writing.

Ackroyd, Peter. *Exile and Restoration: A Study of Hebrew Thought of the Sixth Century B. C.* Philadelphia: Westminster Press, 1968.

Adang, Camilla. *Muslim Writers on Judaism and the Hebrew Bible.* Leiden: E.J. Brill, 1996.

Agouridis, Savas. *The Bible in the Greek Orthodox Church.* Athens: University of Athens, 1976.

Albright, William F. *Yahweh and the Gods of Canaan.* New York: Doubleday, 1968.

Allis, Oswald T. *God Spake by Moses: An Exposition of the Pentateuch.* Nutley, NJ: The Presbyterian and Reformed Publishing Company, 1958.

Alter R. and F. Kermode, eds. *The Literary Guide to the Bible.* Cambridge: Harvard University Press, 1987.

Alter, Robert. *Five Books of Moses.* New York: W.W. Norton & Co., 2004.

------. *The Art of Biblical Narrative.* New York: Basic Books, 1981.

Anchor Yale Bible Series. New Haven, Conn: Yale University Press, 2007.

Anderson, Bernard W. *Understanding the Old Testament.* 4th ed. Englewood Cliffs, NJ: Prentice Hall, 1986.

Baley, Dennis. *The Geography of the Bible.* New York: Harper and Row, 1974.

Barbour, Ian G. *Religion and Science.* San Francisco: Harper Collins, 1997.

Barr, James. *Holy Scripture: Canon, Authority, Criticism.* Philadelphia: Westminster Press, 1987.

Barton, John. *Reading the Old Testament: Method in Biblical Study.* Louisville, KY: Westminster John Knox, 1996.

Bethany Parallel Commentary on the Old Testament: From the Condensed Editions of Matthew Henry, Jamieson/Fausset/Brown, Adam Clarke. Minneapolis: Bethany House Publishers, 1985.

Birch, Bruce C., Walter Brueggemann, Terence E. Fretheim, and David L. Petersen. *A Theological Introduction to the Old Testament.* Nashville: Abingdon Press, 1999.

Blenkinsopp, Joseph. *The Pentateuch: An Introduction to the First Five Books of the Bible.* New York: Doubleday, 1992.

------. *A History of Prophecy in Israel From the Settlement in the Land to the Hellenistic Period.* Philadelphia: Westminster Press, 1983.

Borg, Marcus. *Reading the Bible Again for the First Time: Taking the Bible Seriously but Not Literally.* San Francisco: HarperCollins, 2002.

Boadt, Lawrence. *Reading the Old Testament: An Introduction.* Mahwah, NJ: Paulist Press, 1984.

Bowley James E., ed. *Scripture in Jewish, Christian, and Muslim Practice.* St.Louis: Chalice Press, 1999.

Brettler, Marc Zvi. *How To Read The Jewish Bible.* New York: Oxford University Press, 2007.

Brown, Brian Arthur. *Noah's Other Son: Bridging the Gap Between the Bible and the Qur'an.* New York: Continuum International Publishing, 2007.

Brown, Raymond, Joseph A. Fitzmyer, and Roland E. Murphy, eds. *The New Jerome Biblical Commentary.* Englewood Cliffs, NJ: Prentice Hall, 1999.

Brown, Raymond, S.S. *The Critical Meaning of the Bible.* Ramsey, NJ: Paulist Press, 1981.

------. *Responses to 101 Questions of the Bible. NY: Paulist Press,* 1990.

Bright, John. *A History of Israel.* Philadelphia: Westminster Press, 1981.

Bruce, F.F. *The Canon of Scripture.* Downers Grove, Ill.: Inter varsity Press, 1998.

Brueggemann, Walter. *An Introduction to the Old Testament: The Canon and Christian Imagination.* Louisville: Westminster John Knox Press, 2003.

Brueggemann, Walter., and Hans W. Wolff. *The Vitality of Old Testament Traditions.* Atlanta: John Knox Press, 1975.

Bucaille, Maurice. *The Bible, The Qur'an and Science.* Paris: Islamic Books. 1999.

Burgess, John P. *Why Scripture Matters: Reading the Bible in a Time of Church Conflict.* Louisville: John Knox Press, 1998.

Catholic Study Bible: New American Bible. New York: Oxford University Press, 1990.

Charlesworth, James., ed. *The Old Testament Pseudepigrapha; Apocaltptic Literature and Testaments.* 2 Vols. New York: Doubleday, 1983, 85.

Charpentier, Etienne. *How to Read the Bible*: The Old and New Testaments. NY: Gramercy Publishing, 1991.

Childs, Brevard S. Biblical *Theology of the Old and New Testaments: Theological Reflections on the Christian Bible.* Minneapolis: Fortress Press, 1992.

------. *Introduction to the Old Testament as Scripture.* Philadelphia: Fortress Press, 1979.

Cleary, Thomas. *The Essential Koran.* New York: Harper Collins, 1993.

Cohen, Abraham. *Everyman's Talmud.* New York: E.P. Dutton & Co., 1949.

Collegeville Bible Commentary. Collegeville, MN: Liturgical Press, 1989.

Collins, Adela Yarbro. *The Apocalypse.* Wilmington: Michael Glazier, 1979.

Collins, John J. *The Apocalyptic Imagination: An Introduction to Jewish Apocalyptic Literature.* Grand Rapids: William B. Eerdmans,1998.

Countryman, L. William. *Biblical Authority or Biblical Tyranny.* Harrisburg, PA: Trinty Press International, 1994.

Crenshaw, James L. *Old Testament Wisdom: An Introduction.* Atlanta: John Knox, 1981.

------. Prophets, Sages, and Poets. St Louis: Christian Board of Publication, 2006.

Dardess, George. *Do We Worship the Same God? Comparing the Bible and the Qur'an.* Cincinnati: St Anthony Messenger Press, 2007.

Dawood N. J., trans. with notes. *The Koran.* New York: Penguin Books, 1990.

Dogmatic Constitution on Divine Revelation in Vatican Council 11: The Conciliar and Post Conciliar Documents, vol.1. Edited by Austin Flannery. Collegeville, MN: Liturgical Press, 1991.

Dulles, Avery. *Models of Revelation.* New York: Doubleday and Co., 1983.

Espoto, John L. *Islam: The Straight Path.* New York: Oxford University Press, 1988.

Fackre, Gabriel. *Ecumenical Faith in Evangelical Perspective, vol.1.* Grand Rapids: William B.Erdmans Publishing Co.,1993.

------. *The Christian Story. A Pastoral Systematics: Authority of Scripture in the Church for the World.* vol. 2. Grand Rapids: Willian B. Eerdmans Publishing Co., 1987.

Fee, Gordon D., and Douglas Stuart. *How to Read the Bible for All Its Worth.* Grand Rapids, MI: Zondervan, 2003.

Fishbane, Michael. *Biblical Interpretation in Ancient Israel.* Oxford: Clarendon, 1985.

Fitzmyer, Joseph A. Scripture, *The Soul of Theology.* Mahweh, NJ: Paulist Press, 1994.

Florovsky, George. *Bible, Church, Tradition: An Eastern Orthodox View.* Belmont, Mass.: Norland Press, 1972.

Frank, Harry T. *Atlas of the Bible Lands.* Maplewood NJ: Hammond Inc., 1990.

Fretheim, Terence E. *The Suffering of God: An Old Testament Prespective.* Philadelphia: Fortress, 1984.

Friedman, Richard E. *Commentary on the Torah.* San Francisco: One Harper, 2001.

Goldman, David. *Islam and the Bible: When Two Faiths Collide.* Chicago: Moody Publishers, 2004.

Gowan, Donald E. *From Eden to Babel: A Commentary on the Book of Genesis 1-11.* Grand Rapids: William B. Eerdmans Publishing, 1988.

Greenberg, Moshe. *Studies in the Bible and Jewish Thought.* New York: Jewish Publication Society, 1995.

HarperCollins Study Bible: New Revised Standard Version With the Apocryphal/Deuterocanonical Books. Edited by Wayne A. Meeks. New York: HarperCollins Publishers, 1993.

Hauer, Christian E., and William A. Young. *An Introduction to the Bible: A Journey Into Three Worlds.* Englewood Cliffs, NJ: Prentice Hall, 1994.

Hauerwas, Stanley. *Unleashing the Scripture; Freeing the Bible from Captivity to America.* Nashville: Abingdon Press, 1993.

Hertz, J. H., ed. *The Pentateuch and the Haftorahs.* 2nd ed. London: Socino Press, 1968.

Hertzberg, Arthur. *Judaism: An Anthology of the Key Spiritual writings of the Jewish Tradition.* New York: Simon & Schuster, 1991.

Heschel, Abraham. *Prophets.* New York: Perennial, 2001.

Henry, Matthew. *Commentary On The Whole Bible.* Grand Rapids: Zondervan Publishing House, 1966.

Jamieson, Robert, A.R. Fausset, and David Brown. *Commentary on the Whole Bible.* Grand Rapids: Zondervan Publishing House, 2002.

Jewish Study Bible. New York: Oxford University Press, 2004.

Jomier, Jacques, O.P., *The Bible and the Qur'an*. San Francisco: Ignatius Press, 2002.

Kelsey, David H. *The Uses of Scripture in Recent Theology*. Philadelphia: Fortress Press, 1995.

Kraus, Hans-Joachim. *Worship in Israel*. Atlanta: John Knox Press, 1966.

Kugel, James. *The Bible as it Was*. Cambridge, MA: Belknap Press, 1997.

------. *How to Read the Bible: A Guide to Scripture, Then and Now*. New York: Free Press, 2007.

The Cambridge History of the Bible. ThreeVolumes. Edited by G. W. Lampe Cambridge: Cambridge University Press, 1970.

Lysik, David., ed. *The Bible Documents: A Parish Resource*. Chicago, IL: Liturgy Training Publications, 2001.

Marsden, George M. *Fundamentalism and American Culture*. NY: Oxford University Press, 2006.

Marty, Martin E., and R. Scott Appleby. *The Glory and the Power: The Fundamentalist Challenge to the Modern World*. Boston: Beacon Press, 1992.

------. eds. *Fundamentalisms Comprehended*. Chicago: University Chicago Press, 1993.

Milgrom, Jacob. *Leviticus: A Book of Ritual and Ethics*. Minneapolis: Augsburg Fortress, 2004.

Neusner, Jacob. *The Talmud*.. Minneapolis, MN: Augsburg Fortress, 1991.

------. *From Testament to Torah: An Introduction to Judaism in its Formative Stage*. Englewood Cliffs, NJ: Prentice Hall, 1988.

Newsom, Carol L., and S. H. Ringe. *The Women's Bible Commentary*. Louisville: Westminster/John Knox Press, 1992.

New American Bible: The Catholic Study Bible. New York: Oxford University Press, 1990.

New Interpreters Bible: A Commentary in Twelve Volumes. Nashville: Abingdon Press, 1994.

New Oxford Annotated Bible: New Revised Standard Version With the Apocryphal/ Deuterocanonical Books. Edited by Bruce M. Metzger and

Roland E. Murphy. New York: Oxford University Press, 1991.

New *Interpreter's Dictionary of the Bible*. Nashville: Abingdon Press, 2008.

New World Dictionary-Concordance to the New American Bible. Iowa Falls IA: World Publishing, 1990.

NRSV Exhaustive Concordance: Includes the Apocryphal and Deuterocannonical Books. Nashville: Thomas Nelson Publishers, 1991.

Old Testament Message: A Biblical-Theological Commentary. Wilmington Del.: Michael Glazier, 1984.

Oxford Study Bible. Nashville: Thomas Nelson Press, 2008.

Pilch, John J. *Cultural Tools for Interpreting the Good News.* Collegeville, MN: The Liturgical Press, 2002.

Plotz, David. *Good Book.* New York: Harper Collins, 2009.

Presbyterian Understanding and use of Holy Scripture. Louisville: The Office of the General Assembly, 1983.

Pontifical Biblical Commission. *The Interpretation of the Bible in the Church.* Vatican City: Libreria Editrice Vaticana, 1993. Reprinted by United Stated Catholic Conference, Washington, DC, 1994.

Rad, Gerhad von. *Old Testament Theology.* 2 vols. New Your: Harper and Row, 1962, 1965.

Rahman, Fazlur. *Islam. Chicago: The University of Chicago Press, 1979.*

Ramsay, William M. *The Westminster Guide To The Books Of The Bible.* Louisville: Westminster John Know Press, 1994.

Rogers, Jack B., Donald K. McKim. *The Authority and Interpretation of the Bible: An Historical Approach.* San Francisco: Harper & Row, 1979.

Sanders, E. P. *Paul and Palestinian Judaism: A Comparison of Patterns of Religion.* Philadelphia: Fortress Press, 1977.

Sanders, James. *From Sacred Story to Sacred Text.* Philadelphia: Fortress Press, 1987.

Sandmel, Samuel. *The Hebrew Scriptures.* New York: Oxford University Press, 1978.

Scott, R.B.Y. *The Way of Wisdom in the Old Testament.* New York: Macmillan, 1971.

Smith, Huston. *The Illustrated World's Religion: A Guide to our Wisdom Traditions.* San Francisco: Harper Collins, 1994.

Shea, John. *Stories of God.* Allen, Texas: Thomas Moore Press, 1978.

Spohn, William C. *What They Are Saying About Scripture and Ethics.* NY: Paulist Press, 1995.

Stack, H. L., and G. Stemberger. *Introduction to the Talmud and Mishna.* Minneapolis: Fortress press, 1992.

Steussy, Marti J., ed. *Chalice Introduction to the Old Testament.* St Louis: Christian Board of Publication, 2003.

Stravinskas, Peter M.J. *The Catholic Church and the Bible.* Huntingdon, IN: Our Sunday Visitor, Inc.,1987.

Stuhlmueller, Carroll, *Psalms 1, Psalms 2.* Wilmington, Del.: Michael Glazier, 1983.

Vanderkam, James C. *The Dead Sea Scrolls Today.* Grand Rapids: William B. Eerdmans, 1994.

Vaux, Roland de. *Ancient Israel.* New York: McGraw-Hill, 1961.

Vawter, Bruce. *On Genesis: A New Reading.* New York: Doubleday, 1977.

Vehey, Allen. *Remembering Jesus: Christian, Community, Scripture, and the Moral Life.* Grand Rapids, MI: Willian B. Eerdmans, 2002.

Vermes, Geza. *The Complete Dead Sea Scrolls*: Harmondsworth, UK: Penguin, 1997.

Vine W.E. *Vines Expository Dictionary of Old and New Testament Words.* Nashville: Thomas Nelson Publications, 1996.

Ware, Timothy. The *The Orthodox Church.* New York: Penguin Books 1997.

Zondervan Handbook of the Bible. 3rd ed. Oxford: Lion Publishing, Mayfield House, 1991.

ABOUT THE AUTHOR

The author's teaching of the Bible, Religious Studies, and Theology over a forty year period has been in a public university, two Roman Catholic colleges and in the United Church of Christ, the Christian Church (Disciples of Christ), and the Roman Catholic Church.

If we understand the Scriptures, there is room in Christ's church for all who believe and attempt to relate their imperfect life to him. Life is a struggle to understand the Word and Spirit that comes from God and continues to work in the world, and there is no group who perfectly understands. 1 Cor 13;12-13 says, For now we see in a mirror, dimly, but then we will see face to face. Now I know in part; then I will know fully, even as I have been fully known. May God's mercy and grace bless all of us who struggle in our understanding and spiritual growth along life's journey.

My prayer is the prayer of Jesus in John 17:17-23. Sanctify them in the truth; your word is truth. As you have sent me into the world, so I have sent them into the world. And for their sakes I sanctify myself, so that they also may be sanctified in the truth. I ask not only on behalf of these, but also on behalf of those who will believe in me through their word, that they all may be one. As you, Father, are in me and I am in you, may they also be in us, so that the world may believe that you have sent me. The glory that you have given me I have given them, so that they may be one, as we are one, I in them and you in me, that they may be completely one, so that the world may know that you have sent me and have loved them even as you have loved me.

MORE ABOUT THE AUTHOR

EDUCATION

DMin, Pittsburgh Theological Seminary: Reformed Theology with an Emphasis in Comparative Christian Theology.

Dissertation: Protestantism, Roman Catholicism, and the Orthodox: A Comparison of Christian Theology. Dissertation Directors: Dr. Charles Partee and Dr. John Mehl.

PhD, Clayton University: Religious Studies/Counseling Psychology. Dissertation: Using Programmed Instruction in Teaching Religion and Counseling. Dissertation Directors: Dr. Harry Cargas, Roman Catholic author of 31 books and 2000 published articles, Dr. Barbara Finn, and Dr. Richard Foster. (Clayton University associated with the Menninger Foundation closed it doors in 1989. Until that time it was listed in the United States Department of Education Handbook of Accredited Colleges and Universities.)

MAT, Harding University: Biblical Studies.

MEd, University of NorthFlorida: Counseling.

BSEd, Lock Haven University: Social Studies and English.

Post Graduate Studies in Religion and Counseling Psychology at the University of Texas-El Paso, David Lipscomb University, Penn State University, and Indiana University (PA).

EMPLOYMENT

Instructor of Religious Studies, and Chaplain in the Campus

Ministry Program at Penn State University (Altoona Campus), teaching the following courses: Old and New Testaments, Comparative Christian Religions, World Religions, and Religion in America.

Adjunct Professor of Scripture and Theology at Mt Aloysius College.

Adjunct Professor of Scripture and Theology at St. Francis University (PA).

Catholic High School Teacher, Counselor, teaching the following courses: Biblical

Studies, Psychology, World History & Cultures, American History, Government, Economics, and English. Head basketball coach for the 1970 Bishop Guilfoyle high school (PA) state champions.

Public High School Teacher, Counselor, Basketball and Baseball Coach Teaching the following courses: Biblical Studies, World History & Cultures, American History, and English.

Peace Corps in Senegal, French West Africa. Helped train their Olympic basketball team for the 1964 Olympics in Japan.

Played professional baseball in the Cleveland and Minnesota minor league systems.

On the Altoona (PA) National Amateur Baseball Federation national championship team, getting the team's only hit in the tenth inning. The team was inducted into the Blair County (PA) Hall of Fame.

Certified Psychologist, Teacher, and Counselor by the state of PA.

Certified Counselor by the National Board of Certified Counselors.

Over 40 years of Ministry with the Roman Catholic Church, United Church of Christ, and the Christian Church (Disciples of Christ).

LaVergne, TN USA
12 January 2011
212197LV00003B/125/P